Books by the same author

Hugh Kingsmill
Lytton Strachey
Unreceived Opinions
Augustus John
Bernard Shaw 'The Search for Love'

Edited by the same author

The Best of Hugh Kingsmill
Lytton Strachey by Himself
The Art of Augustus John
(with Malcolm Easton)
The Genius of Shaw
The Shorter Strachey (with Paul Levy)
William Gerhardie's *God's Fifth Column*
(with Robert Skidelsky)

Endpapers

Front: The Cart and Trumpet.
Shaw on the hustings in
the early 1900s.

Back: The Individual and the Crowd.
Shaw speaking at a protest
meeting against a visit from
the Czar, about 1910.

Bernard Shaw

MICHAEL HOLROYD

======

Volume II · 1898–1918
The Pursuit of Power

======

Chatto & Windus

LONDON

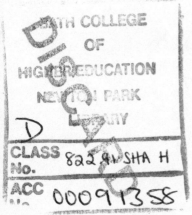
Published in 1989 by
Chatto & Windus Ltd
30 Bedford Square
London WC1B 3SG

A CIP catalogue record for this book
is available from
the British Library.

ISBN 0 7011 3350 3

Typeset by Opus, Oxford
from author's discs
prepared by Richard Bates, London
Printed in Great Britain by
Redwood Burn Limited, Trowbridge, Wiltshire

Designed by Ron Costley
Index by Vicki Robinson

CONTENTS

ILLUSTRATIONS

BERNARD SHAW

1898–1918

The unconscious self is the true genius.

'Maxims for Revolutionists'
Man and Superman

CHAPTER I

[1]

Every busy man should go to bed for a year when he is forty. (1918)

We are having such a honeymoon as never was. (1898)

The adventure began between Haslemere and Hindhead. After reconnoitring several places in Surrey, Charlotte had taken Pitfold, a rather 'small, stuffy house' (she later decided) on the south slope of Hindhead. 'I came down on crutches,' Shaw told Beatrice Webb. 'The air was so fine that our troubles seemed to be over; but they had only just begun.' Charlotte and Shaw had different ideas about air. It was medicinal: a convalescent substance, soporific, sympathetic, supportive – that was Charlotte's opinion. But on Shaw it appeared to act as an intoxicant. Air went to his head. The inflammation of energy it caused had to be soothed by paperwork. He had emerged from the London smoke into the ventilation of the country on 10 June 1898 and, despite his invalidism, set fiercely to work on *The Perfect Wagnerite*. The doctor remonstrated, Charlotte agonized; and Shaw went on with his dictation. Then, on the morning of 17 June, attempting to hurry downstairs on his crutches, he fell into the hall, breaking his left arm and making 'a hopeless mess of the Wagner book'. Charlotte rushed forward with some butter pats, fastened them into splints and called the doctor. For half an hour Shaw lay in the hall 'with all the strain gone, perfectly relieved and happy', and for the next few weeks was provided with a nurse to 'wash and dress and all but feed me'.

'I have a wheeled chair, which I cannot wheel, since when worked with one hand only, it simply spins round & round. Heaven knows what will happen to Charlotte when the anxiety about me is over . . . I no longer feel any confidence in my ultimate recovery: it seems certain to me that I shall presently break all my other limbs as well.'

As he predicted, this was the first of several accidents over the next eighteen months that were to keep Charlotte's anxieties well exercised and Shaw himself largely convalescent. His fall, aggravated by an abscess, a sty and a tormenting nettle rash, plunged him back to the abnormal condition following his operation the previous May. 'I am now slowly pulling round,'

3

he reported to Karl Pearson on 4 July; 'but the foot has to be kept open for the bit of bad bone to exfoliate & come away; so I am crippled hand & foot.' On 27 July an illustrious bone specialist named Bowlby, attended by three doctors, came down to perform a double operation. He dug out most of the bad bone from the instep, charged Shaw sixty guineas and instructed him he would be healed in three weeks. Then he went away: but – *he had forgot the arm*. 'I am so unspeakably tickled by this triumph over the profession that I cannot resist the temptation to impart it to you,' Shaw wrote the next day to his vegetarian friend Henry Salt. But Charlotte added a postscript: 'He is doing very well – but must be kept absolutely quiet . . .'

Shaw was discovering that his wife had a genius for worrying. She played the constant sentinel over him, registering his coughs and sneezes as a barometer registers the weather. Her mind ran largely on sickness and travel, diagnosing one, prescribing the other. Later that summer she carried him off to Freshwater Bay on the Isle of Wight where his improvement grew so rapid that, on his return to Pitfold, he threw away his crutches and bicycled – but the brute tossed him and he sprained his ankle; 'which in point of anguish has beaten all the rest of the calamities'.

In several letters dictated to Charlotte, Shaw represents these smashes as being of enormous benefit to his wife whom they keep 'in a state of exhausting devotion which would have killed any but a very strong man . . . My wife, more devoted than ever, is the happiest of women & is not even jealous of the nurse'. Shaw's prolonged disablement seemed to emphasize certain elements in their marriage. He felt 'as helpless as a baby'; she acted the attentive matron. Sex was postponed until its absence became part of the structure of their lives. Their giving and withholding were strangely mixed. 'Wincing at every accent of freedom' in his voice, Charlotte lovingly guarded him; he outwardly respected, though sometimes inwardly resented, her guardianship, knowing that he had the power to unsettle her by flirtations with women or by associating with some of the people he had known before their marriage. Having scarcely possessed him sexually, Charlotte felt peculiarly insecure. She had been sensitive over Ellen Terry; she did not feel altogether safe with Janet Achurch. 'Marriage creates a situation that cannot be rushed as I used to rush all personal situations,' Shaw informed Janet's husband, Charles Charrington. ' . . . my instinct warns me to avoid any appearance of being unable to exist without seeing Janet.' Being a reserved person, Charlotte dreaded having to *act* an effusive friendship with his theatrical friends. She felt it necessary to assert her predominance over his past. After a visit in the spring of 1900, Beatrice Webb noted that 'Charlotte Shaw did not want to have us.

4

Perhaps this is a morbid impression. But it is clear that now that she is happily married we must not presume on her impulsive hospitality and kindly acquiescence in our proposals. All this made me glad to get to work again – to enjoy the mental peace of research, unhampered by human relationships, except by the one ideal relationship of marriage.'

Work was another subject about which Shaw and Charlotte could not agree. She took dictation, prepared copy for his typist (Ethel Dickens, a granddaughter of the novelist), surrounded him with common sense and cushions. But, as she later admitted to Nancy Astor, 'I don't really like work.' G.B.S. liked nothing better – especially the sort of 'creative work', Charlotte complained, 'that pulls him to pieces'. She was in a difficult position, wanting to be of use to him, though not in the ways he wanted. 'I try to keep him from working as much as I can,' she confided to Beatrice Webb, 'but it is the only occupation he really cares for.'

Shaw's illnesses gave Charlotte an occupation that seemed to unite his needs with her wishes. He did not underrate what she had done: she 'brought me back to life', he told the actress Beatrice Mansfield. 'It was hard work.' But had it been worth the struggle, this lifting him from the Valley of the Shadow of Death on to the Hill of Difficulty? Charlotte did not question such things. But it was dismaying for her to see how tenuously her husband was attached to life. 'She has an instinctive sense that there is a certain way in which I do not care for myself,' Shaw wrote to Sidney Webb, 'and that it follows that I do not care, *in* that way, for anybody else either; and she is quite right.' He was going through a change of life, he believed, a little death. Whether it actually killed him, or helped to fortify him for another forty or fifty years' paperwork, 'I do not greatly care', he told Sidney Webb; 'I am satisfied that, on the whole, I have used myself economically and fired my whole broadside.'

'I would not trust a chicken's neck to save the rest of my life, even if I were convinced that chicken broth would save it, which I am not. But the inconvenience of being married is that one's wife sets up an interest in one's life. As for me, I have always been a patient, obstinate beast; and the more they threaten me with death (which they all consider it their Christian duty to do at every turn) the more they clear my mind as to the worthlessness of living in obedience to such threats & terrors. But Charlotte has none of my convictions.'

Charlotte always knew where he was, but not what he was thinking. The independence he had fixed upon before marriage had been shattered by his accidents. His income during the first year of marriage came to only £473 and by 1902 it had shrunk to £90. He lived almost entirely from

Charlotte's money. To safeguard himself from going 'soft with domesticity and luxury', he began to separate his work from the experience of his life. These early years of his marriage were illuminated by a burst of creativity. 'I no longer sleep: I dream, dream, dream,' he told Charrington. Once he had confided to Ellen Terry that his childhood had been 'rich only in dreams, frightful and loveless in realities'. Now he began to manufacture from his dreams another world locked deep in himself and fortified against the encircling love and invalidism of his marriage. In this place of fantasy he could 'make better people than real people to commune with'. This was another reason for Charlotte's opposition to his work: it gave him a legitimate escape from her loving custody into a solitary enjoyment that came only 'when I am worked to desperation'. As his existence grew more comfortable, his work became more oddly anarchical. 'He still writes,' Beatrice Webb noted after a visit to Hindhead, 'but his work seems to be getting unreal: he leads a hothouse life, he cannot walk or get among his equals.'

'He is as witty and as cheery as of old. But now and then a flush of fatigue or a sign of brain irritation passes over him. Charlotte, under pressure of anxiety for the man she loves, has broadened out into a motherly woman and lost her anarchic determination to live according to her momentary desires. There are some compensations for the sadness of the sudden cutting off of his activity.'

But between Haslemere and Hindhead Shaw was getting swallowed up in activity almost as if he were in London. He became an athletic photographer with his Kodak and experimented with meteorology, recording sunshine and wind velocity in the garden; he played to himself on a piano they had lodged in a barn, wrote on cottage libraries in the *Surrey Times*, and reviewed local concerts for the *Farnham, Haslemere and Hindhead Herald*; he sent letters to *The Times* about the duty of juries and commented on blasphemy in the *Daily Chronicle*; he joined a play-reading society formed by his neighbours, agitated in Hindhead Hall for a Disarmament Conference, and became a well-recognized figure swinging along on his crutches for three-mile walks that were 'equal to 10 off them'.

Much of this exasperated Charlotte. After six months, Shaw's foot was no better – indeed it seemed to Charlotte decidedly worse. 'G.B.S. has been most foolish,' she complained to Beatrice Webb, 'constantly walking on it . . . '

'I long for a little advice & help from someone whose judgment & good sense I really feel I can depend upon. I do feel rather isolated for, though everyone makes all sorts of preposterous suggestions, no one really gives me any feeling of confidence – the feeling I know I should have about you & Sidney if you were here.'

At the beginning of November, they went up to London to consult Bowlby, the specialist who that previous summer had predicted a three-weeks' cure. He examined the foot, observed that it was unchanged and recommended a further period of disuse – about three weeks. Shaw's patience had almost given out. Here was rest 'brought to the verge of killing the patient with inaction'. To Charlotte's horror, he suddenly decided that he would prefer to have his toe amputated than to endure a longer spell of inactivity. At the end of the month he returned to Bowlby and demanded an immediate removal of the whole bone and toe. To his surprise, Bowlby observed that if it were his toe, he would stick to it. 'He declares that my health is improving visibly; that I am pulling up from a breakdown . . . So I am waiting.'

While Shaw waited and worked, Charlotte acted, moving them both from Pitfold to Blen-Cathra, a larger house with 'lofty, airy rooms', she told Beatrice Webb, 'besides being in a better situation' on the main Portsmouth-London road between Hindhead and Haslemere. 'This place beats Pitfold all to fits,' Shaw told Henry Arthur Jones. 'I am a new man since I came here: the air would make a dramatist of – whom shall we say?' A week later, on 9 December, he completed *Caesar and Cleopatra*.

In spite of periodic relapses Shaw's health improved throughout 1899. By 23 March he reported himself in a doubly accurate phrase as being 'fed up' to eleven stone, a gain of five pounds. On 12 April he announced that 'the vegetables have triumphed over their traducers', an X-ray having shown a 'perfectly mended solid bone'. This was a more remarkable tribute to vegetarian power since a few days earlier he had 'surpassed all my previous achievements by alighting from a high framed bicycle on the bad foot with a crash that made it collapse like a leg of mutton which had been stabbed with an area railing'. It was 'astonishing how a physical accident of this kind relieves one's nerves & raises one's spirits'. His spirits were raised to the point of beginning in May and completing in July *Captain Brassbound's Conversion* – after which Charlotte insisted on an unmitigated holiday. 'It is proposed to go to some hole in Cornwall named Cadgwith, to sea-bathe my weak ankle,' Shaw wrote unenthusiastically to Ellen Terry. He was reconciled to this by the fact that all their servants, visitors and nurses had fallen ill. 'It is a blasted, poisonous year: *everybody* is ill,' he complained to his fellow writer Grant Allen. Perhaps, after all, Charlotte and he had miscalculated the air. 'Our patients' nurses report that there is a scarcity of disinfected sisters: they have to rush from one case to another. My own belief is that there is a specific venom in the air of

Hindhead. However our withdrawal will raise the average quota of health available for the rest of the community.'

In the middle of August they arrived at their rented house in Ruan Minor. 'I am down here, wallowing in the sea twice a day,' Shaw wrote, 'swimming being the only exercise I ever take for its own sake.' Not liking him to float off too far, Charlotte allowed Shaw to teach her to swim 'with nothing between her and death but a firm grip of my neck'. His publisher Grant Richards came down and Shaw, with his recently broken arm and sprained ankle, swam him out to sea and brought him back in terror of drowning. Altogether it was a happy month, even with the death on dry land of his seafaring uncle Walter Gurly who left a heavily-mortgaged Carlow estate to descend 'on me like an avalanche'. To meet such misfortunes 'I am putting up muscle & rather straightening myself up,' he reported.

So beneficial was the sea air that Charlotte felt justified in having ordered a six weeks' recuperative cruise round the Mediterranean in an Orient steamer, the SS *Lusitania*. 'Our cruise seems a success,' she wrote to Grant Richards, while poised off the coast of Syracuse. But Shaw felt differently. 'I am now practically well again, or was until I was dragged on the conventional voyage to restore me completely,' he told Mrs Mansfield. 'Anything better calculated to destroy me, body & soul, than a Mediterranean cruise on a pleasure steamer in October & Sept (the sirocco months) it would be hard to devise . . . Never before had I felt so keenly the force of the saying that life would be tolerable but for its pleasures.' Like Lady Cicely in *Captain Brassbound's Conversion*, Charlotte was in her element coping with these pleasures. She tackled the rigorous sightseeing, subdued blowy seas, digested the rich food, brushed aside their missed connections and charmed the waiters, paying their bills and calculating their gratuities in complicated currencies. Trapped on this 'floating pleasure machine' as it moved through a sickly blue sea, the band striking up perpetual polkas and skirt dances, Shaw came to feel that every moral and physical condition of a healthy life was violated 'except fresh air' – and even that was made poisonous with steam and cigar smoke. He was at the plutocratic centre of capitalism and unable to work. 'It is a guzzling, lounging, gambling, dog's life,' he cried. There were cholera and typhoid aboard. Passing through the Greek archipelago he was violently sick; in the overwhelming damp heat between Crete and Malta he sat at sunset in his overcoat, shivering, with the mercury as high as seventy-five Fahrenheit; at Constantinople even Charlotte felt ill and could only manage a couple of hours at a mosque. 'I wake up in the morning like one in prison,' Shaw wrote, 'realizing where I am with a pang.'

They arrived back at the end of October and went straight to London. At the time of their marriage they had agreed to retain their separate addresses in town, and Shaw openly speculated as to whether he would 'revert to my old state of mind & my bachelor existence'. Now, at the beginning of November 1899, he moved some of his belongings at 29 Fitzroy Square into Charlotte's double-decker apartment at the south corner of Adelphi Terrace. 'I am always to be found at my wife's address,' he wrote; 'but she is never to be found at mine.' It seemed a pleasant place to live, overlooking the river and Embankment Gardens and, except for the occasional hooting of the boats, undisturbed. Shaw slept in a converted box-room off Charlotte's bedroom. 'The dining-room and large drawing-room were on the second floor, with the bedrooms, a study for G.B.S., and the kitchen on the third floor. There was no bathroom; the maids took cans of hot water into the bedrooms and filled a hip bath.' On the staircase Shaw installed a huge wicker gate with a bell-push on the gatepost, marking the Shavian frontier and reinforced by a hedge of pointed steel spikes attached to the balustrade, making the place, he claimed, look like a private madhouse. He worked in a small plain oblong room, above the river, his desk planted near the window which, summer and winter, remained chillingly open. It was wonderfully neat: Dürer prints on the walls, Charlotte out of sight but within call. Much of the furniture in the flat was of the cottage type; there was a little Bechstein piano; an etching by Whistler, drawings by Sargent and Rothenstein, stuck like stamps on the flowered Morris paper which covered the ceiling as well as the walls, giving the impression of an inside-out box. The drawing-room mantelpiece had been designed by the Adam brothers: over the fireplace an old Scottish inscription was cut – *Thay say. Quhat say thay? Lat Thame say* – the morality of which Shaw reckoned to be 'very questionable'. He was to live here thirty-one years 'before I realised how uncomfortable I was'. Having left Fitzroy Street, he leased for one hundred and fifty pounds a year the whole house for his mother who was joined there by her half-sister Arabella Gillmore and her half-niece Georgina ('Judy') Gillmore.

Shaw and Charlotte went regularly to the country, like swimmers under water coming up for air. 'I spend my week ends down in Surrey only coming up for Wednesdays, Thursdays & Fridays when I have Fabian & Vestry committees & the like on all three afternoons,' Shaw was soon explaining to Will Rothenstein. Over Christmas and the New Year, they stayed at the Queen's Hotel in Aberystwyth where Shaw lectured on 'Socialism and the Universities'. His foot was now completely mended following treatment of the sinus by pipe water in place of idoform gauze;

he felt in rosy health and was 'diabolically busy'. The new century seemed full of promise and activity. He had two new plays on his hands, a preface to write and text to revise for his second collection; he was beginning to involve himself with the newly formed Stage Society which had chosen *You Never Can Tell* for its opening performance. The Boer War had started, forcing the Fabian Society 'to a new birth pang with a foreign policy', and Shaw to act as midwife with a manifesto, speeches and letters. The 'roaring honeymoon' was over: yet it was difficult to spot much difference. 'I spent eighteen months on crutches, unable to put my foot to the ground,' he summed up. Within that period he had produced *The Perfect Wagnerite*, *Caesar and Cleopatra* and *Captain Brassbound's Conversion*: and, though he had not married for happiness, 'I cannot remember that I was in the least less happy than at other times.'

[2]

Charlotte and Shaw have settled down into the most devoted married couple, she gentle and refined with happiness added thereto, and he showing no sign of breaking loose from her dominion. What the intellectual product of the marriage will be, I do not feel so sure: at any rate he will not become a dilettante, the habit of work is too deeply ingrained. It is interesting to watch his fitful struggles out of the social complacency natural to an environment of charm and plenty.
Beatrice Webb (1899)

Into Shaw's 'intellectual product' during these first eighteen months of marriage may be read his fitful struggles to break loose from Charlotte's dominion. First he uses Wagner's *Ring* to disparage the panacea of love between the sexes; then he improves on Siegfried with his own prototype of the superman, Julius Caesar, the teacher not the lover of Cleopatra; finally, in *Captain Brassbound's Conversion*, he invents an 'adventure' for his pre-marital grandmotherly love, Ellen Terry.

But looked into closely all three works tend to support rather than subvert his marriage. By describing 'vehement sexual passion' in *The Perfect Wagnerite* as 'an experience which it is much better, like the vast majority of us, never to have passed through, than to allow it to play more than a recreative holiday part in our lives', Shaw is upholding the *mariage blanc*, the 'sentiment of affectionate benevolence which has nothing to do with sexual passion' that he and Charlotte enjoyed. When he makes Caesar, busied with statecraft, prepare to leave Egypt without remembering to bid goodbye to

Cleopatra, he is by implication turning his back on the one woman who was to threaten his marriage, Mrs Patrick Campbell; and in Lady Cicely Waynflete, the heroine of *Captain Brassbound's Conversion*, there emerges the ideal version not of the theatrical lady whom he had wanted to dominate Henry Irving, but of the Irish lady who had dominion over him.

*

When William Archer first noticed Shaw in the Reading Room of the British Museum, he had observed how the young Dubliner was balancing Deville's French translation of *Das Kapital* against the orchestral score of *Tristan und Isolde*. Shavianizing Marx had been a matter of pulling politics off the barricades and into the tract. To key his second teacher to the Shavian temperament, Shaw needed to pull Wagner out of his antiquated heavens and place him in the contemporary socialist scene. Using Ashton Ellis's translation of Wagner's *Prose Works*, he attempted to transpose the sultry eroticism into concentrated intellectual music. By writing the poem as well as the music of the *Ring*, Wagner had added thought to feeling, and created a series of music dramas or, as he called them, 'stage festival plays'. Shaw throws the emphasis in his criticism on to what he supposed to be 'at the back of Wagner's mind', translating these thoughts and experiences into the vocabulary of his own mind, 'creatively melting them down', as Thomas Mann described the process, 'into something totally new and personal'. It is an extraordinarily lucid exposition, subtle and sustained, that uses Wagner as he had previously used Ibsen to work out his own philosophical position.

During the seven years that separated *The Quintessence of Ibsenism* from *The Perfect Wagnerite*, Shaw had begun to revise his political philosophy. In the earlier work he had divided human beings into three classes: philistines, idealists and those realists on whom progress depended. In the sequel he again makes a threefold division, representing the Wagnerian dwarfs, giants and gods as 'dramatizations of the three main orders of men: to wit, the instinctive, predatory, lustful, greedy people; the patient, toiling, stupid, respectful, money-worshipping people; and the intellectual, moral, talented people who devize and administer States and Churches'.

This change (subdividing the philistines into dwarfs and giants) reflects a shift towards a deeper pessimism in Shaw arising from his greater experience of national and local politics. Being more precisely concerned with capitalism, it is also a move in a more distinctly Marxist direction. Among the three categories he describes in *The Perfect Wagnerite*, the gods now being the idealists, there is no realistic deliverer of man. He had begun to feel that progress in prosaic instalments simply through the permeation tactics of the Fabians was no longer inevitable. A more romantic figure than that of the civil servant and political researcher was needed to seize the imagination of the philistine. Realists must call up their own brand of idealism. The quietist should dress himself in a loud coat – a magical garment, its pockets rattling with the fool's gold of those idealistic illusions Shaw had previously derided in *The Quintessence of Ibsenism*. For most people had to be paid in such coin. Appearance, providing it was a successful imposture, was an important feature of human politics. Change the appearance of things and you were a long way to changing the reality. Acknowledging this, Shaw appears to accommodate a fourth class of human being into his philosophy: 'History shews us,' he writes, 'only one order higher than the highest of these: namely, the order of Heros.'

In fact Shaw's heroes are his realists from the *Quintessence* in disguise; they are Wagner's blond warriors, raised out of recognition into a higher organization of man ready to do their work in the twentieth century. Wagner's cycle of music dramas had told a story of love lost and regained; Shaw's commentary is a retelling of the story as love lost and replaced by something else. His 'frightful & loveless' childhood, followed by his years of poverty and social unacceptability in London, made him immediately sympathetic to Wagner's view of human history. He followed it breathlessly, finding not only an allegory of contemporary political dilemmas, but also an image of the life he had himself been campaigning through. His sense of lovelessness makes him feel at one with all mankind in its expulsion from Eden. There is no mistaking his personal involvement. Man, he writes, 'may be an ugly, ungracious, unamiable person, whose affections may seem merely ludicrous and despicable to you'.

'In that case you may repulse him, and most bitterly humiliate and disappoint him. What is left to him then but to curse the love he can never win, and turn remorselessly to the gold?

' . . . It is just as if some poor, rough, vulgar, coarse fellow were to offer to take his part in aristocratic society, and be snubbed into the knowledge that only as a millionaire could he ever hope to bring that society to his feet and buy himself a beautiful and refined wife. His choice is forced on him. He forswears love as thousands of us forswear it every day; and in a moment the gold is in his grasp . . .'

From Shaw's reading of the *Ring* we see man forswearing love only when it was denied to him and made the instrument for murdering his self-respect. In his loveless desperation he either succumbs to (the giant philistines) or exploits (the dwarf philistines) the malign forces of loveless greed – those corrupt millions of the Rhinegold – on which our own capitalist systems are built. These systems displace the need for human love with a love for the machinery of power. They establish their dominion over the world through the idealistic gods who enshrine them with the majesty and superstition of the Church and guard them with the terrifying powers of the law. Only one quality can explode this tyranny of religion and law, and establish in its place the unfettered action of Humanity: and that is the quality of fearlessness. The redemption of mankind therefore depends upon the appearance in the world of a hero or the spirit of heroism.

Shaw agrees with Wagner on the inspiration of raising up the example of exceptional force of character and intrepidity; a person elevated to perfect confidence in his own impulses by an intense and joyous vitality which is above fear; someone who no longer bows to circumstance, environment, necessity, but takes his destiny in his own hands to shape it for himself. Wagner's Siegfried is a symbol of love, the original deprivation of which had been the genesis of man's tragic story. For Shaw, love was not a romantic nostrum for our evils or the solvent of all social difficulties because it could have little place in the down-to-earth conflict between humanity and its gods and governments. Love belonged to heaven where Wagner transported us once the *Ring* changed with *Götterdämmerung* from music drama into opera – which Shaw regarded as a decline, almost a betrayal. The Wagnerian concept of the supreme good of love, he argues, 'is that it so completely satisfies the desire for life that after it the Will to Live ceases to trouble us, and we are at last content to achieve the highest happiness of death'. Shaw does not seek to lead us from earth to heaven, but to conduct a marriage of heaven and earth, religion and politics. He was to supplant Siegfried as a dramatic symbol with a succession of eccentrically common-sense figures from Julius Caesar to St Joan and to experiment with ways of substituting eugenics for eroticism, the Shavian life force for Wagnerian resurrection. 'The only faith which any reasonable disciple can gain from The Ring is not in love,' he wrote,

'but in life itself as a tireless power which is continually driving onward and upward . . . growing from within, by its own inexplicable energy, into ever higher and higher forms of organization, the strengths and the needs of which are continually superseding the institutions which were made to fit our former requirements . . . we must, like Prometheus, set to work to make new men.'

From this faith emerged the creed of Creative Evolution Shaw was to explore in the dream sequence of *Man and Superman*. It is a moral commitment to progress through the Will, answering the need for optimism in someone whose observation of the world was growing more pessimistic. Concurrently with *The Perfect Wagnerite* he had been creating his own puritan hero, a man without the 'administrative childishness and romantic conceit of the heros of the revolutionary generation'. His Caesar was more directly descended from Parsifal than Siegfried, a protagonist conventionally seen less as a hero than a fool, 'with a spear which he held only on condition that he did not use it: one who, instead of exulting in the slaughter of a dragon, was ashamed of having shot a swan. The change in the conception of the Deliverer could hardly be more complete'.

*

'If I thought great men were like your Caesar, I should like them better,' a critic wrote to Shaw.

Shaw's Caesar was born from his longing that such men should exist and be thought great; and that in our better liking of them might lie a seed for the eventual advancement of man. The inspiration of the play therefore sprang from his concept of a naturally great man: it was, he told Mrs Mansfield, 'the first & only dramatization of the greatest man that ever lived ... the projection on the stage of the hero in the big sense of the word'. In the anecdotal sense, as he admitted, 'there is no drama in it': the drama resides in the contrast between Caesar's character and the immature personality of Cleopatra embodying *in excelsis* the conventional human being.

Caesar is a man of words – an author, great talker, rather given to preaching – a politician, financier and administrator who, in middle age, has turned his hand to the glories of war ('this tedious, brutal life of action') not for the sake of those glories (he fights to win rather than to accumulate military honours) but because public expectation has made it necessary. His battles are like Christ's miracles: 'advertisements for an eminence that would never have become popular without them'. At fifty-four he is not romantic-looking – 'old and rather thin and stringy' is how Cleopatra first sees him. Though he is greater off the battlefield than on it, his victories (particularly his paradoxical knack of turning defeats into victory) have given a sheen of heroic idealism to his pragmatic nature. By conventional people he is considered to be a dreamer, perhaps a little mad. He is plainly dressed, drinks barley water, is light-hearted and informal, works hard ('I always work') and is celebrated for clemency which he exercises more on the grounds of its expediency than its goodness. But though he rules 'without punishment. Without revenge. Without judgment', having a horror of 'judicial academic murder and

cruelty', he allows the removal of human obstacles by the sword if the slaying is instinctive and unmalicious. He is a man without vulgar lusts: even his ambition is no more than the instinct for exploration. He has the frank curiosity of a child and since his greatness resides in his humanity, he is not without human failings. He is rather vain and wears an oak wreath to conceal his baldness. He is also 'easily deceived by women', he confesses. 'Their eyes dazzle him; and he sees them not as they are, but as he wishes them to appear to him.' Yet he tends to make them his councillors for he 'loves no one . . . has no hatred in him . . . makes friends with everyone as he does with dogs and children'. This indiscriminate kindness is part of his avuncular superiority – what Shaw called his 'immense social talents and moral gifts'. Such was the man whom Shaw believed might be an initiator of evolutionary progress for mankind. From where had he come?

He had come initially from Mommsen's *History of Rome*, from the fifth volume of which in particular Shaw made extensive notes. *Caesar and Cleopatra*, he told Hesketh Pearson, was 'a chronicle play; and I took the chronicle without alteration from Mommsen . . . I found that Mommsen had conceived Caesar as I wished to present him'. The Mommsenite view of Caesar is of a democrat and republican whose impulse towards social reform opened up overseas possessions and remodelled the political structure of Rome so that it provided a material foundation for modern civilization. In Mommsen's hagiographic vision of 'the entire and perfect man' Shaw found what he wanted for his own conception of the hero. 'I stuck nearly as closely to him,' he wrote, 'as Shakespeare did to Plutarch or Holinshed.'

Shakespeare was also a contributory influence in the shaping of Shaw's play. A year before Shaw began to write it, he had speculated to Charrington about 'seriously pursuing my idea of entering the lists with Shakespeare & writing "Caesar & Cleopatra" (a girl Cleopatra)'. Shakespeare had 'made a mess of Caesar under the influence of Plutarch, and made Brutus his hero'. In his appraisal of *Julius Caesar* for the *Saturday Review* Shaw had expressed his 'revulsion of indignant contempt at this travestying of a great man as a silly braggart'. Lifting Caesar from Plutarch, Shakespeare had then added the qualities of vacillation and conceit from his general knowledge of dictators and his particular observation of Queen Elizabeth. Shaw replaced this Elizabethan stage tyrant by adding to Mommsen's Caesar something of Christ – a paraphrase, for example, at the climax of the play of the Sermon on the Mount and a prophecy that if 'one 'one man in all the world' can be found to accept Caesar's principles 'that man will have either to conquer the world as I have, or be crucified by it'.

Shaw also had someone in mind to represent Caesar. Reviewing *Hamlet* in the autumn of 1897 he had described Johnston Forbes Robertson as 'essentially a classical actor . . . What I mean by classical is he can present a dramatic hero as a man whose passions are those which have produced the philosophy, the poetry, the art, and the statecraft of the world, and not merely those which have produced its weddings, coroners' inquests, and executions'. Here was the man to give verisimilitude to his Caesar. The play, Shaw later explained, was composed for Forbes Robertson, 'the only actor on the English stage capable of playing a classical part in the grand manner without losing the charm and lightness of heart of an accomplished comedian'.

Caesar and Cleopatra would probably not have been written without Forbes Robertson. His attitude to the theatre was utterly unlike Henry Irving's: he would rather have been an artist than an actor and hated the publicity of the stage. His aristocratic features, engaging manner, and natural elegance of speech however all contributed to making him the most natural actor of his age. During the rehearsals of *Caesar and Cleopatra* a hammer fell from the grid, missing him by inches. He paused a moment, looked up and said quietly, 'Please don't do that again,' then went on with the rehearsals. A personality so unruffled exactly fitted Shaw's concept of an Olympian Caesar.

What he looked for, and eventually received from Forbes Robertson, Shaw was to set out in an article written at the time of the play's first presentation in London. *Caesar and Cleopatra*, he explained, was 'an attempt of mine to pay an instalment on the debt that all dramatists owe to the art of heroic acting'.

' . . . We want credible heroes. The old demand for the incredible, the impossible, the superhuman, which was supplied by bombast, inflation, and the piling of crimes on catastrophes and factitious raptures on artificial agonies, has fallen off; and the demand now is for heroes in whom we can recognise our own humanity, and who, instead of walking, talking, eating, drinking, sleeping, making love and fighting single combats in a monotonous ecstasy of continuous heroism, are heroic in the true human fashion: that is, touching the summits only at rare moments, and finding the proper level on all occasions.'

At another level Shaw was engaging the best Shakespearian actor of the time to help him make obsolete Shakespeare's *Julius Caesar* and undermine *Antony and Cleopatra*. His Caesar is a hero for the realists: Shakespeare's Antony is the idealistic hero created for the philistines. Their differing attitudes towards Cleopatra help to define the two categories of heroism. Most of the characters in Shaw's plays are likened to animals: Rufio is a dog; Ftatateeta a tiger and then a crocodile; Theodotus a viper; Achillas a poodle; and Cleopatra herself a kitten and a serpent. But Caesar is a man: and an example of biological advancement. 'You are a bad hand at a bargain, mistress,' Rufio tells Cleopatra at the end of the play, 'if you will swop Caesar for Antony.' Caesar's leave-taking, for which we have been prepared by a number of echoes from Shakespeare's play, reduces *Antony and Cleopatra* to a sequel to *Caesar and Cleopatra* and provides a method of rebuking Antony's genius by Caesar's – as, it is said, Macbeth's was by Octavius. Caesar is dazzled but not possessed by women; Antony struggles vainly for this self-possession:

> I must from this enchanting queen break off
> Or lose myself in dotage

Between the attractions of love and power Antony seems perpetually divided, prizing most wherever he has forfeited most, until this conflict of illusions is stopped by death. Caesar is subject to no such struggle: his priorities are clear. He is in earnest only about work. But Shaw rather sidestepped the issue. He had misread Mommsen (who mentions Cleopatra as being sixteen a few pages before he comes to Caesar's visit to Egypt) and held to this early age instead of twenty-one as most authorities agree she was at this time. By reducing her age these five years and following Mommsen in ignoring Caesarion, the legendary child of Caesar and Cleopatra, he is able to write off more easily the threat of sex. 'It is extremely important that Cleopatra's charm should be that of a beautiful child, *not of sex*,' he wrote years later. 'The whole play would be disgusting if Caesar were an old man seducing a child.' Shakespeare's Cleopatra was a physically mature woman drawn from life, a dramatic portrait of the 'black' mistress of the Sonnets from whom he created a role so consummate, Shaw judged, 'that the part reduced the best actress to absurdity'. Shaw's Cleopatra is an idea based on his observation of 'an actress of extraordinary witchery', Mrs Patrick Campbell, then in her thirties. It is a part conceived from the stalls, yet with a sense of seductive power and perhaps some faint foreknowledge of their emotional involvement to come. That involvement, which was to impair the Shavian Will in his mid-fifties, offers an ironic comment on Caesar's untroubled control of his sexual susceptibility.

For Caesar is a self-inspired creation. Whatever was taken from Mommsen, anticipated as Christ, or dressed up as Johnston Forbes Robertson, Caesar is Shaw: Shaw made heroic, a figure to promote his way of life and dramatize his philosophy. Caesar is as fearless in life as

Shaw was on the page, and becomes a fantasy image of Shaw himself upon the Fabian stage and in the theatre of politics.

Caesar also embodies Shaw's belief in the Will. It had been the Will that lifted Shaw out of neglect in Ireland into literary achievement in England and dramatic success in America. It was the Will that now protected him against those storms of sexual jealousy and rejection that buffeted Shakespeare's Antony and Wagner's Siegfried. 'We must learn to die, and to die in the fullest sense of the word,' Wagner had written. 'The fear of the end is the source of all lovelessness: and this fear is generated only when love begins to wane.' Caesar is an expression of Shaw's conviction that love may be replaced by a beneficent Will that overcomes fear of death by being used up with work-fulfilment in life. In a cancelled passage of the play, anticipating *Man and Superman*, Caesar says: 'As for me, Cleopatra, my passion is for life, ever fuller and higher life; and that is what makes me different from other men.' Other men had conducted human affairs in such a way that, 'to the end of history, murder shall breed murder, always in the name of right and honor and peace, until the gods are tired of blood and create a race that can understand'. In *The Perfect Wagnerite* Shaw had already imagined such a race. It was, he wrote, 'quite clear . . . that if the next generation of Englishmen consisted wholly of Julius Caesars, all our political, ecclesiastical, and moral institutions would vanish . . . as inexplicable relics of a bygone social order'. By rising above such contrivances and transferring his energy from love-and-death into marriage with a future he would not personally experience, Caesar stands as a prototype of the 'race that can understand'.

Behind this dawn of Shavian optimism hovers a deepening gloom over things as they are. 'He who has never hoped,' Shaw makes Caesar say, 'can never despair' – a statement he later damned as the 'worst' he had ever written in 'that cheap line' of 'philosophic despair of humanity'. He had clutched at philosophic salvation through the Will in much the same way as Wagner had: through Schopenhauer. On reading Schopenhauer, Wagner had come to believe that his *Ring* cycle contained an artistic demonstration of the philosopher's famous treatise. Shaw read Schopenhauer and disputed Wagner's contention. Like Shaw's Life Force, Schopenhauer's Will is all impulse (whether organic and psychic or mechanical and physical) in the world. This impulse, though it brings expanded self-awareness, leads to increased frustration and new forms of suffering through its conflict with more dedicated selfish wills. To Schopenhauer, Shaw wrote, 'the Will is the universal tormentor of man, the author of that great evil, Life; whilst reason is the divine gift that is finally to overcome this life-creating will and lead, through its abnegation to cessation and peace, annihilation and Nirvana. This is the doctrine of Pessimism'. Shaw took Schopenhauer's philosophy of Will and turned it into a doctrine of optimism by subduing the individual to the universal Will, the Will of Nature.

In his 'Notes to Caesar and Cleopatra' Shaw writes that '67 generations of promiscuous marriage' gave 'no reason to suppose that any Progress has taken place'. That is why, for example, he makes the ancient Briton, Britannus, so exactly like a modern Englishman. Shaw never wrote costume drama for its own sake: his plays were always addressed to the present. The figure of Britannus keeps the audience imaginatively half in the present – which was one of the ways Shaw became a model for Brecht. Since there had been no progress through sexual reproduction we are left with example and with schoolmastering as methods of improvement. Caesar's example, though attractively 'heroic', is not followed by anyone in the play and will lead, we know, to 'his assassination by a conspiracy of moralists' in the name of 'right and honor and peace'. His schoolmastering of Cleopatra, which provides the action of the play, is easily defeated by her egocentricity ('But me! me!! me!!! what is to become of me?'). At the beginning she is a child full of fear ('*She moans with fear . . . shivering with dread . . . white . . . she utters a cry . . . almost beside herself with apprehension*'). 'You must feel no fear,' Caesar instructs her. But when he leaves her at the end she is, he acknowledges, 'as much a child as ever'. She has learned only to dissemble. 'Oh, if I were not ashamed to let him see that I am as cruel at heart as my father,' she threatens Iras, 'I would make you repent that speech!' All she has added to herself is the trick of imitating Caesar and this trick (unlike a similar trick learned by Eliza Doolittle) has not altered her. She merely play-acts the role of queen, inflicts fear in place of feeling it – 'the advantage of this change seeming open to question', as Shaw comments in his stage directions. She has taken on the values not of Caesar, but of her nurse, Ftatateeta, who, Shaw wrote, 'must be the sexual attraction' of the play, and whose mature and savage femininity he allows to be neutered by a 'natural slaying' at which Caesar feels 'no horror'.

So having converted no one, Caesar is as alone at the end as when, at the beginning of Act I, he confronted the Sphinx: 'I have wandered in many lands, seeking the lost regions from which my birth into this world exiled me, and the company of creatures such as myself. I have found . . . no other Caesar, no air native to me, no man kindred to me, none who can do my day's deed, and think my night's thought . . . Sphinx, you and I, strangers to the race of men, are no strangers to one another.'

This is Shaw's own isolation. Caesar's address to the Sphinx anticipates a passage from the Preface to *Immaturity*, written over twenty years later, in which Shaw tells of a 'strangeness which has made me all my life a sojourner on this planet rather than a native of it'. That strangeness had not dissolved, but rather seemed intensified by his domestic life with Charlotte. For, as his next play would continue to protest, he was unfitted for the institution of marriage.

*

'Half a dozen such women would make an end of law in England in six months.' Lady Cicely Waynflete is the female equivalent in Shaw's world of Caesar, sharing with him Siegfried's quality of fearlessness. 'If you can frighten Lady Cicely,' her brother-in-law Sir Howard Hallam tells Captain Brassbound, 'you will confer a great obligation on her family. If she had any sense of danger, perhaps she would keep out of it.' But the contest between Captain Brassbound and Lady Cicely is (to use Shaw's word) 'unequal' since it 'soon becomes clear that a tranquil woman can go on sewing longer than an angry man can go on fuming'.

Lady Cicely is unorthodox and pragmatic. She has walked across Africa with nothing but a little dog and put up with six cannibal chiefs who everyone insisted would kill her – or worse. In fact: 'The kings always wanted to marry me.' Her power lies partly in the authority of a mother over her children: 'all men', she insists, 'are children in the nursery.' Her far-sightedness and tact being so much more effective than their conventional logic, she constantly runs rings round these men of law, religion and warfare. 'Strong people are always so gentle,' she announces, but her own air of gentleness is an obvious imposture. She unscrupulously forces gentleness on everyone else. She has the 'steadfast candor peculiar to liars who read novels' and is content to accept from men the chivalrous attribution of 'good nature and sweet disposition' if it assists her in imposing civilized standards on them. Like Caesar she is surrounded by harmless bullies, brought up to believe in the justice and morality of vengeance, cruelty and punishment, whom she must constantly outwit. She re-educates them by a mixture of shrewdness, will-power and an attraction that does not depend on the erotic use of sex. She is Shaw's ideal of womanhood: 'tall, very good looking, sympathetic, intelligent, tender and humorous, dressed with cunning simplicity . . . A woman of great vitality and humanity, who begins a casual acquaintance at the point usually attained by English people after thirty years' acquaintance when they are capable of reaching it at all . . . '

Captain Brassbound's Conversion, which Shaw called 'an excellent Christian tract and treatise on good manners', is a type of musical comedy without music, the interest of which focuses upon the character and performance of Lady Cicely. She is the only woman in the play and not merely 'the maternal managing woman who likes everybody and loves nobody', as Shaw wrote to one correspondent. 'She is also the adventurous fearless woman, seeking new countries and new people to play with. That combination is not common. Have you ever noticed that the highest type of conqueror is an incorrigible explorer?' Here is another attribute that Lady Cicely shares with Caesar and it gives Shaw the opportunity of making a statement about the policy of British Imperialism that was increasingly occupying the Fabian Society at this time. Captain Brassbound had served under General Gordon before he was killed by the Mahdi. Britain had then re-annexed the Sudan from the Mahdi and was about to annex the two Boer Republics. It was for such contemporary political reasons that Shaw set his play in Morocco, 'the very place where Imperialism is most believed to be necessary', he wrote, 'on the border line where the European meets the fanatical African, with judge on the one hand, and indomitable adventurer-filibuster on the other ... pushing forward "civilization" in the shape of rifles & pistols in the hands of Hooligans, aristocratic *mauvais sujets* and stupid drifters'.

Shaw wanted to contrast travellers with conquerors, to show Europe's *mission civilisatrice* carried forward by the 'jolly, fearless, good tempered, sympathetic woman' who rules by natural authority and a sort of divine right against 'little troops of physically strong, violent, dangerous, domineering armed men' who shoot and bully in the name of Imperialism. In a letter to Ellen Terry, he spelled out this opposition between the male and female principles in all human nature, telling her to read two books: H. M. Stanley's *In Darkest Africa* and Mary Kingsley's *Travels in West Africa*. 'Compare the brave woman, with her common-sense and good will, with the wild-beast man, with his elephant rifle, and his atmosphere of dread and murder, breaking his way by mad selfish assassination out of the difficulties created by his own cowardice,' he wrote.

'Think of all that has been rising up under your eyes in Europe for years past, Bismarck worship, Stanley worship, Dr Jim [Jameson] worship, and now at last Kitchener worship with dead enemies dug up and mutilated. Think also on the law – the gallows, penal servitude, hysterical clamoring for the lash, mere cowardice masquerading as "resolute government", "law and order" and the like ... I try to shew these men gaining a sense of courage and resolution from continual contact with & defiance of their own fears. I try to shew you [Lady Cicely] fearing nobody and managing them all as Daniel managed the lions, not by cunning – above all not by even a momentary appeal to Cleopatra's stand-by, their passions, but by simple moral superiority ... Here is a part which dominates a play because the character it represents dominates the world ... '

The character that Lady Cicely represents was an amalgam of various people. Her historical model was Mary Kingsley; her literary model Shelley's 'The Witch of Atlas' which provided Shaw with a working title for the play; her actress model was Ellen Terry; and her model from life was Charlotte whose passion for tourism had persuaded Shaw, while convalescent, to read a number of travel books and to pick up, after completing *Captain Brassbound's Conversion*, his only first-hand knowledge of Morocco: 'a morning's walk through Tangier, and a cursory observation of the coast through a binocular from the deck of an Orient steamer'.

When Lady Cicely learns how close to the Atlas Mountains she is at the missionary's cottage above Mogador, she determines to go there: 'The Atlas Mountains! Where Shelley's witch lived! We'll make an excursion to them tomorrow ... ' By setting the action of his adventure in the place where Shelley's platonic vision of a white goddess quenched

> ... the earth-consuming rage
> of gold and blood – 'till men should live and move
> Harmonious as the stars above

Shaw was emphasizing the asexuality of his heroine's power. In all his other plays he had 'prostituted the actress more or less by making the interest in her partly a sexual interest ... In Lady Cicely I have done without this, and gained a greater fascination by it', he informed Ellen Terry.

It was to Ellen, he let it be known, that the play owed its existence. In several accounts Shaw gave as its point of origin a remark made by Ellen on the birth of Gordon Craig's eldest daughter, that now she was a grandmother nobody would ever write a play for her. 'I immediately wrote Brassbound for her,' Shaw added, ' "out of a natural desire to contradict" as she said.' It is a pretty story, but it does not seem to fit the fact that Rosemary Craig had been born in April 1894, over five years before Shaw began writing *Captain Brassbound's Conversion*. 'Several of my characters are portraits,' he was to write, 'but not of actors and actresses. The original of the portrait is often very unlike the artist for whom the part is written.' Lady Cicely is not a portrait of Ellen Terry but a vehicle that incorporates something of her manner and magnifies it hugely. This is how he wanted her to be; this is how he believed she might become if she grew into the part. For the motive behind *Captain Brassbound's Conversion* was similar to that behind *The Man of Destiny*: to make one last effort to infiltrate the Lyceum with Shavian drama or, in failing, to detach Ellen Terry from

Henry Irving and rescue her from the massive floundering of his theatrical career.

Shaw had stepped back to Ellen and Irving after his lack of success in getting *Caesar and Cleopatra* staged with Forbes Robertson and Mrs Patrick Campbell. The Lyceum, over which Irving crouched as emperor, had in 1898 been turned into a limited liability company. It was a step that, though designed to ease the actor-manager's financial burdens, precipitated the end by making it more difficult for him to obtain credit. Early in 1899 Shaw approached Max Hecht, the principal investor in the new 'Lyceum Ltd' ('which I understand to be a benevolent society for the relief of distressed authors & actors') and made the 'entirely interested suggestion' that the newly-managed theatre should put on his 'magnificent, recklessly expensive play' *Caesar and Cleopatra*, with Forbes Robertson and Mrs Patrick Campbell in the title roles. 'On the whole, Forbes Robertson & Mrs Pat look more like the heir & heiress apparent to Irving & Ellen Terry than any other pair,' he wrote. 'When Irving goes to America, it would be much better to keep up the special character of the theatre by producing another spectacular historical play of the best literary class, with an actor of Shakespearean reputation in it, than to drop into pantomime . . .'

The copyright performance of *Caesar and Cleopatra* had taken place at 11 p.m. on 15 March 1899 at the Theatre Royal in Newcastle with Mrs Pat reading Cleopatra. But she 'was not attracted by her part', 'made fun of the play' and did not accept Shaw's invitation to 'bring Caesar down to lunch' at Hindhead. Forbes Robertson, without money or a theatre, could not risk such an expensive production and Shaw's scheme for entering the Lyceum by the back door while Irving was abroad stuck. It was at this moment, and not on the birth of Ellen's first grandchild, that he started 'Ellen's play'.

For years Ellen had supported Irving's romantic one-man dramas; now Shaw was presenting her with a non-romantic drama for one woman – 'a shocking leading lady business', he promised her, ' . . . but then, *such* a leading lady! All the other characters are the merest doormats for her. The wretched leading man has nothing in the last act but ignominious dumbness & ridicule until the final scene, in which he gets a consolation prize'.

But Shaw's prospectus did not entice Ellen. 'I dont think that Play of yours will do for me at all!' she answered. 'You suggest it is a *one part Play*! I loathe that sort of thing.' Yet it was that sort of thing she had consistently been helping Irving to produce. There was, in her abasement to him, a curious sense of superiority. She felt that he depended on her far more

23

than he could acknowledge; and she had come to rely on his dependence. She found difficulty in admitting that in some ways he actually depended on her less. She was not young enough now to act the heroines he needed; and she had become so much a part of his life at the Lyceum that he could no longer find in her company an escape from his worries and from himself. After she had complicated their relationship by introducing Shaw with his Napoleon play showing how a real Man of Destiny rises above jealousy, Irving had begun to turn for diversion to Mrs Aria. He said nothing to Ellen. 'But who is Mrs A?' she had asked Shaw.

Eliza Aria (whom Shaw described as 'a good sort') was a social journalist and *salonnière* who had contrived to make herself into a perfect companion. She was a shrewder, more ambitious woman than the title of her memoirs, *My Sentimental Self*, suggests. Attractive in appearance, generous with her praise and displaying an attitude when listening that signalled acute intelligence, she was able to give Irving an encouraging reflection of himself. In comparison with such sophisticated arts, Ellen felt herself a child. She could see how, stimulated and relaxed, Irving was renewed by Mrs Aria – and she determined to feel pleased for him. She did feel pleased: but she also felt betrayed. For she had the power to help him more than anyone, if only he would let her. 'Poor old King H. is at his downest,' she noted in her diary at the beginning of 1899, 'and I'm amazed at the few in number of his useful friends.' But Irving was almost impossible to help – a presence, rather than an intelligence, that cocooned itself in silence. 'Is it shyness?' she wondered. 'Indifference? Anger? *What? I* rather think self-consciousness by indifference out of conceit! ... I wonder how his other friends and lovers feel to him. I have contempt and affection and admiration. What a mixture!' He was curiously tortured: 'a silly Ass' Ellen called him. Sometimes she was frankly impertinent like this: at other times in awe. He still had the power to wound her. Appearing 'stouter, very grey, sly-looking, and more cautious than ever', he had informed her early in 1899 that he was ruined: but that he intended to mend his fortunes by touring the provinces with a small company. As for Ellen she could 'for the present' do as she liked. Perhaps he was responding to Mrs Aria's advice. Ellen was furious. But then he suddenly changed his mind and elected to do Sardou's *Robespierre* at the Lyceum, another one-man drama with only 'a wretched part' in it for her. After his previous production – an appalling romantic comedy in five acts, called *The Medicine Man* – she had contemplated leaving him: 'I simply must do something else.' Now, with *Robespierre*, she again felt like leaving: and again she did not leave. 'If H. were not in the dumps just now,' she wrote to Shaw, 'I'd "see him further" before I'd do it!'

This was why she wanted something special from Shaw, something of course to show her independence, but even more to demonstrate her value to Irving – something to revive Irving's fortunes and bring back the glorious days of the old Lyceum. She had first wanted *Caesar and Cleopatra*: Irving, she was convinced, 'could have done *wonders* with that Play'. But Shaw had not wanted her for his Cleopatra: 'She is an animal – a bad lot. Yours is a beneficent personality.' And Irving, to whom she had nevertheless given it, made it clear that he would never produce a play by Shaw – in which case, Shaw retaliated, the only feasible alternative would be to produce his next play at the Lyceum when Irving was not there.

He sent Ellen *Captain Brassbound's Conversion* at the end of July 1899 and she read it with dismay. It was a play for a little theatre, not the Lyceum, and therefore not for her. 'I couldnt do this one,' she told Shaw, 'and I believe it would never do for the stage . . . Mrs Pat for Lady C! . . . it is surely for Mrs Pat.'

Shaw was dismayed. *Captain Brassbound's Conversion* had been conjured out of the last four years of their letter-writing-love-affair: and she had not recognized it. 'Alas! dear Ellen, is it really so?' he wrote back. 'Then I can do nothing for you.'

'I honestly thought that Lady Cicely would fit you like a glove – that I had sacrificed everything to make the play go effectively from second to second . . . And now you tell me that it is a play for the closet, and that Lady Cicely would suit Mrs P. C. All of which proves that either I am mad, or you are mad, or else there is an impassable gulf between my drama and your drama.

'I wont suggest it to Mrs Pat, because I am now quite convinced that she would consider herself born to play it, just as you want to play Cleopatra . . .

'And so farewell our project – all fancy, like most projects.'

It was almost the end of a love affair, a divorce between her acting and his playwriting skills, dreams and reality. But he would not let them separate without a protest, without anger. 'Of course you never *really* meant Lady Cicely for me,' she had written to him. 'Oh you lie, Ellen,' he answered, 'you lie':

'never was there a part so deeply written for a woman as this for you, silly, self-unconscious, will o' the wisp beglamored child actress as you still are . . .

'Lyceum advantages! Haven't you had enough of them yet? You talk to me, ME, *ME*, of this ogre's den into which your talent has been thrown and eaten. Go then, wretch, and get . . . some nice new part with a name like the latest hairwash, and be as romantic and picturesque as you please, and bury what reality there is in Ellen under ten tons more of tomfoolery.

'Listen to me, woman with no religion . . . Have you had any sympathy with the punishments of the judge? Have you found in your own life and your own small affairs no better way, no more instructive heart wisdom, no warrant for trusting to the good side of people instead of terrorizing the bad side of them. I – poor idiot! – thought the distinction of Ellen Terry was that she had this heart wisdom, and managed her own little world as Tolstoy would have our Chamberlains & Balfours & German Emperors & Kitcheners & Lord Chief Justices and other slaves of false ideas and imaginery fears manage Europe . . . Here then is your portrait painted on a map of the world – and you . . . want to get back to Cleopatra! . . . do you think I regard you as a person needing to be arranged with sphinxes & limelights to be relished by a luxurious public? Oh Ellen, Ellen, Ellen, Ellen, Ellen. This is the end of everything.'

How much of this impassioned letter could Ellen afford to understand? In her autobiography she was to write of Shaw as a 'good, kind, gentle creature whose "brain-storms" are just due to the Irishman's love of a fight'. She was to advise her readers that 'it doesn't answer to take Bernard Shaw seriously. He is not a man of convictions.' She was to recommend his plays for the 'charms' that sprang from this agile lack of conviction. Here certainly were the methods of Lady Cicely Waynflete, but used for the opposite ends: to keep out the truth. Yet the intensity of Shaw's letter pierced through this self-protective niceness and unsettled her as the play had never done. She *did* know what he meant: 'the horridness of it all is, that all the time I think exactly as you do!' But to convert his words into her actions and make them come true would mean emerging from the womb of the Lyceum and becoming independent – and it was too late. 'Of course I know it's *me* all the while . . . What is the good of words to me?' But words were all Shaw had to give her: the power of words to change our lives. And she could not change. All Shaw had done was to force her to recognize this fact. They were useless to each other. She felt ill, retreated into tears, and wrote to tell him so.

She who has never despaired can never hope. Though Ellen could not change, perhaps, she thought, Henry might; perhaps too the play would act well after all – it was enjoyable to read; her maid had read it two or three times. Catching a peculiar expression in her face, Ellen had questioned her and the girl, inflated with laughter, replied, 'Oh, I'm very sorry. Excuse me, but Lady Cicely is *so* like you! . . . she gets her way in *everything – just like you!* 'I cant understand it,' Ellen protested to Shaw. Despairing of herself but filled with vicarious hope, she had decided to show it to Henry. 'I will read with pleasure the Play you speak of,' Irving intoned – and hearing those stilted words she knew how hopeless it was. She had read it again herself and liked it more and more – 'the freshness, the picturesqueness, the delicious fun and sweetness . . . The last bit grows tragic-er and tragic-er as I see it before me.' But Irving did not think it fresh or delicious or tragic. He suspected that Shaw had 'planned the comic effect of introducing the hero suddenly in the last act in an exquisite suit of modern fashionable clothes to get him laughed at. And,' Shaw added, 'he was quite right.'

So *Captain Brassbound's Conversion* went back on the shelf and did not receive its first public presentation in London for another seven years. As a consolation, Irving allowed Ellen to go through the copyright ceremony with the Lyceum company at the Court Theatre in Liverpool before they sailed for America in the autumn of 1899. 'I've studied Lady C. now, and am *transported*,' she wrote to Shaw. 'The tragic end I go over and over again and just – *see* it. A triumph for us both. I love the whole thing and am certain I could do it.' But the copyright performance was not such a triumph and left Ellen feeling less certain. Brassbound was read by Henry's son, Laurence Irving; but Henry himself 'never came near the place!' Ellen reported. 'Horrid of him.' And nobody liked Lady Cicely, thinking her a detestable humbug. 'It's because I read it wrong,' Ellen reasoned, taking as usual the blame upon herself. But her daughter Edy, sitting out in front, remarked that she couldn't have read the lines differently, and that it seemed Shaw had thought his Lady Cicely one sort of woman but had written another. It was the same ambiguity that had marked Candida and was to become habitual with Shaw's heroines.

The other woman was Charlotte: the only person, apparently, who had got the better of him in the days of his philandering campaigns. This conventional matronly lady now controlled his domestic life. When she commanded him to go travelling, he went as obediently and unwillingly as Sir Howard Hallam and Captain Brassbound and his crew followed Lady Cicely into the Atlas Mountains. The routine of life beat time to Charlotte's customs and fixed ways: but Shaw's intellectual independence had hardened. 'My contempt for the status quo grows from year to year,' he told his Fabian friend Graham Wallas, 'and I do not despair of expressing it yet in a mind-changing manner.' *Captain Brassbound's Conversion* represents an advance in optimism on *Caesar and Cleopatra* in the sense that whereas Caesar changes no one's mind in Egypt, Lady Cicely Waynflete does convert Brassbound in Morocco – 'the conversion assisting in his renunciation of a terrible scheme of revenge which he has foolishly cherished all his life', Shaw explained to Mrs Mansfield.

In his coda to the play, when Brassbound and Lady Cicely are alone on the stage, the humour dissolves into a mood of tenderness and pathos. 'In spite of philosophical precautions of great antiseptic severity,' commented the critic Desmond MacCarthy, 'germs of romance will, occasionally, get into his work and play havoc with it, to the astonishment and exhilaration of beholders.' Robbed of his Old Testament religion of revenge for what he imagined had been done to his mother, the idealistic Brassbound is left without dignity, without aim or coherence in his life. He proposes to fill this emptiness with love. 'I want to take service under you,' he tells Lady Cicely. 'And theres no way in which that can be done except marrying you. Will you let me do it?' But love is rejected as the solution as it had been earlier by Caesar and by Shaw himself in *The Perfect Wagnerite*. It would have made him only second-in-command and been a misalliance for her – who was 'made for something better'. Lady Cicely hesitates ('Oh, you are dangerous!'), realizing that marriage might lead to something she has never experienced: real love for one man. But that sort of romantic indulgence would alter her indiscriminate attitude of sweetness to all men. It is not Ellen Terry or Charlotte or any other woman who gives Lady Cicely's answer to Brassbound: 'I have never been in love with any real person; and I never shall. How could I manage people if I had that mad little bit of self left in me? Thats my secret.' By forestalling their marriage with warning gunfire ('Rescue for you – safety, freedom!'), Shaw is asserting his own 'mad little bit of self', his intellectual isolation from Charlotte.

Several other components from Shaw's life were absorbed into Brassbound's last-minute laconic conversion. Before writing the play, he had read Cunninghame Graham's volume of philosophic travel and adventure, *Mogreb-el-Acksa*, and been so delighted by it, he told the author, that 'I find myself unable to resist stealing the *mise-en-scène*'. In so far as Brassbound contained aspects of Shaw's character, to that degree was Shaw himself converted from the fastidious Fabian who had *skedaddled* back to tea on Bloody Sunday in Trafalgar Square to the hero who had held his ground and been arrested with a red flag in his hand.

In Brassbound's saturnine and joyless features, grimly set mouth, dark eyebrows, his wordless but significant presence, we may also see something of Henry Irving – and the conversion of Irving to Shavianism. But this conversion never actually took place. Ellen had pretty well decided to leave Irving – but not quite. What would she do? Where would she go? She was frightened of poverty – and then Henry could always weaken her resolve when she was most determined to go by appealing for her help. 'I appear to be of strange *use* to H, and I have always thought to be *useful, really* useful to any one person *is* rather fine and satisfactory.' It may have been this nice perversion of Shaw's own doctrine of usefulness that persuaded him to give up the struggle. 'Very well, dear Ellen: we cry off Brassbound,' he conceded early in 1900. 'I have always foreseen, and foretold to you, that when it came to the point, you would find it practically impossible to detach yourself from the Lyceum.'

'And apart from the business reason, the breaking up of an old partnership like yours and H. I.'s is not a thing to be done except on extreme occasion . . . obviously if he really wants you to stay, stay you must. Consequently I am in no way disappointed or surprised: destiny has fulfilled itself exactly as I foresaw it would if affairs took their normal course.

'. . . So now for one of my celebrated *volte-faces*. I hold on pretty hard until the stars declare themselves against me, and then I always give up and try something else . . . now I recognize that you and I can never be associated as author and player – that you will remain Olivia, and that Lady Cicely is some young creature in short skirts at a High School at this moment. I have pitched so many dreams out of the window that one more or less makes little difference – in fact, by this time I take a certain Satanic delight in doing it and noting how little it hurts me. So out of the window you go, my dear Ellen; and off goes my play to my agents as in the market for the highest bidder.'

This letter reveals in what depth of disappointment Shaw lit his candle of optimism and how he converted its spectral shadows into a world of solid reality. In retrospect, despite building 'a Heaven in Hell's despair', it seemed to Shaw that he had aimed the play at strengthening Ellen's hold on Irving to 'make it doubly certain that he would not let you go for want of asking you to stay'. It was easier to adapt the past to such satanic optimism than to make the future conform to it. In the open market only Charrington's Stage Society ('a sort of Sunday night Independent Theatre started by an energetic Fabian') was interested in presenting his play – with (the final shuddering irony) Ellen's role given to Janet Achurch!

Now that Shaw and his play seemed no longer to be threatening him, Irving retreated into his private prison, 'so icy, indifferent, and almost contemptuous'. Ellen had had to choose: and she had chosen Henry. Was it loyalty or lack of courage? 'Ah, I feel so certain Henry just hates me!' she wrote to Shaw. 'I can only *guess* at it, for he is exactly the same sweet-mannered person he was when "I felt so certain" Henry loved me!'

'We have not met for years now, except before other people, where my conduct exactly matches his of course. All my own fault. It is *I* am changed, not he. The last four or five years, grain by grain, my respect for him has filtered out, & now I can only *care* for him, & think not highly at all for him. It's all right, but it has squeezed me up dreadfully.

'. . . But who for Brassbound? Oh dear, oh dear! I and H. would have been *perfect* in it. He riles me so (but nowadays I've learned from him and never show I'm riled) when he says "Brassbound is like *a Comic Opera!*" '

Here was Shaw's consolation. From *The Man of Destiny* to *Captain Brassbound's Conversion*, he had provoked Irving to act so ungenerously as to forfeit Ellen's good opinion. Into Shaw's love for Ellen had been poured a poisonous hatred of Irving. Like two stage monsters, Dracula and Svengali, they had fought with all their magical powers over the leading lady, both claiming victory at the final curtain. 'Of course he hates you when you talk to him about me,' Shaw burst out. 'Talk to him about himself: then he will love you – to your great alarm.'

Captain Brassbound's Conversion was first presented by the Stage Society at the Strand Theatre on 16 December 1900. 'What exciting news!' Ellen exclaimed. 'Brassbound on the 16th and I *shall* be able to see it.' She came, and after the performance, on her way to the dressing-room of Laurence Irving (who played Brassbound), passing under the stage, she spoke to Shaw for the first time. They had been corresponding with each other for more than five years – hundreds of letters. They had feared, with intervals of regret, that a meeting would rub the bloom off their letter-writing romance. And now, having met briefly and parted, they apparently did not send each other a loving letter for almost a year and a half. 'They say you could not bear me, when we met, that one time, under the stage,' Ellen went on to explain in December 1902. *Thay say. Quhat say thay? Lat Thame say.* Ellen was not confident enough to accept this doctrine. Her self-esteem, undermined and exploited (with her own co-operation) by Irving, had to be fed by an atmosphere of niceness and the persistent reassurance of her usefulness. 'But you cant abide me!' she questioned Shaw. 'And no wonder! Can I ever abide myself!' What Shaw had said that could have reached her in this form and who carried such words to her is unknown. But it is difficult not to suspect that her daughter Edy was involved: Edy who had watched their long-running romance while two of her own had been ended by Ellen; Edy whose jealous gossip (Ellen went on to warn Shaw that same December) needed a 'little salt'.

It was at the end of this silent period that Ellen began to separate from Irving. Hearing that he had engaged another actress to play some of the parts for which she was now too old, she nerved herself to ask him whether she might act in Beerbohm Tree's production of *The Merry Wives of Windsor* at Her Majesty's, and Irving conditionally assented. For two years intermittently Henry and she had discussed the break-up of their partnership: and now it was actually breaking up. After waiting so long Shaw was to step forward and award himself the credit. Their Lyceum partnership had 'enraged me', he wrote.

' . . . Then her position became unbearable; and she broke loose from the Ogre's castle, as I called it, only to find that she had waited too long for his sake, and that her withdrawal was rather a last service to him than a first to herself.'

Ellen's last service to Shaw was to play Lady Cicely at the Royal Court Theatre in 1906, eighteen months after Irving's death and a controversial obituary of him by Shaw. 'Sooner or later I know I'll play Lady C.,' she had promised him almost six years earlier. Often, in this interval, he had teased her about this play, dangled it before other actresses, even whispered to Ada Rehan that *she* was 'in the authors mind when he wrote' it. Then he had come back to Ellen. 'Mr Bernard Shaw, with a last flash of a trampled out love . . . has been actuated . . . by an angry desire to seize Miss Ellen Terry by the hair and make her play Lady Cicely.' To which she had replied: 'Dont break her heart along with the rest but let her have the play.' And so he did. It had been a torture, a flirtation, a regret, a distant intimacy, a hope: and finally it was a fact. 'It was written for you; and unless you do it at least once, posterity will never forgive you', he told her. ' . . . I will gravely offer this impossible quintessence of Ellen as a real woman; and everybody will be delighted.' He had interpreted her niceness as the ingenious force of self-assertion rather than a more conventional self-protection. But she needed protection as she went through the rehearsals. She was fifty-eight, could not remember her lines, felt easily demoralized. Shaw made certain that the producer treated her with tact and gentleness and to Ellen herself he wrote: 'Behave as if you were more precious than many plays, which is the truth . . . The only other point of importance is that you look 25; and I love you.'

When the play opened on 20 March, *The Times* drama critic noted that 'Miss Terry is, as always, a little slow, the victim of a treacherous memory'; and Desmond MacCarthy in *The Speaker* observed that 'there was a hesitation in her acting sometimes, which robbed it of effect'. She recognized this herself: 'GENTLE SHEPHERD – You are a faithful heroic DEAR!' she wrote to Shaw. 'You try to keep up your illusions about me, about my acting, altho' you know all the while – ' But Shaw refused to know. He had no time for what friends called this 'saintly humility', her guilt. The marriage of her acting with his playwriting had at last taken place and its beauty was preserved for him by an hallucination: 'She is immense, though she is 58, and cant remember half my words,' he wrote to a friend. ' . . . now that she has at last actually *become* Lady C, and *lives* the part, saying just what comes into her head without bothering about my lines, she is very successful . . . '

The following year Ellen took *Captain Brassbound's Conversion* on her farewell tour of America. She had promised Shaw that 'I am going to "try, try again" at Lady Cicely'. But on 22 March, in Pittsburg 'of all places in the world' she married James Carew, the American actor who played Captain Kearney in the play. 'I am furiously jealous of Carew, with whom you fell in love at first sight,' Shaw had protested. Though Dame Ellen would never become Lady Cicely, Cicely had become Ellen, the impossible quintessence reduced to the actual woman: 'You are Lady Cicely,' Shaw insisted, but added, 'her history has become your history.' To this extent had life undercut the Shavian drama. 'This habit of getting married is the ruin of theatrical art,' Shaw complained. ' . . . Why could you not have been content with my adoration?' But most people preferred conventional romance to Shavian adoration and would attempt to infiltrate it into his plays. When in 1912 Gertrude Kingston acted the role of Lady Cicely, she replaced in rehearsal Shaw's final line – 'How glorious! And what an escape!' – with her own: 'How glorious! How glorious! And what a disappointment!' But the disappointment, brilliantly concealed, was Shaw's. By the time Gertrude Kingston was playing Lady Cicely, he was growing involved (as Caesar never had) with his model for Cleopatra, Mrs Patrick Campbell, and raising in Charlotte tides of jealousy unknown to Lady Cicely. 'Lady Cecilys [*sic*] no longer exist,' he conceded in a letter to Gertrude Kingston, ' – if they ever did.'

*

Shaw was developing into an ingenious 'Ladies' Tailor'. Out of his fantasies he had made two excellent roles. He had magnified Ellen Terry from a Lyceum nanny into a ruler of men, and reduced the sexual power of Mrs Patrick Campbell to a fragment, a cold morsel moved by the Shavian Caesar to the edge of his plate. But neither of these fantasies was to invade life and neither play came into the normal traffic of the stage until 1906 and 1907. *Caesar and Cleopatra* was rejected even by Richard Mansfield, a peculiar humiliation for Shaw who promised the American actor in its place a twopenny melodrama 'suited to your capacity, as soon as I can think of something'.

What was the use of becoming a ladies' tailor if no lady would wear your clothes? The late Victorian theatre was so different from any living world outside, certainly from any world which Shaw inhabited, that he could see 'no real women in the plays except heavily caricatured low comedy ones', he later wrote to Edy Craig; 'and what the leading actresses had to do was to provide an embodiment of romantic charm and keep it up with an air of being human and soulful without having a single touch of nature in the lines and gestures dictated by the author's script ... unless they could smuggle in something of their own between the lines the play could not succeed.'

Shaw had been at this smuggling game now for ten plays and was almost always caught, either by the Lord Chamberlain's office, or by the male actor-manager's régime of the West End. Together, they policed a theatre-going public that was not yet ready for the New Drama as a vehicle for the New Woman. The Shavian emancipation of women was, in any case, a complicated self-protective manoeuvre that turned her either into a piece of biological machinery for the production of children superior to their parents, or else an isolated freak – a man in petticoats wedded to work – who stood as a feminine counterpart to the Shavian writing-machine. These huntresses and persons 'exactly like myself' peopled the army Shaw had called up to invade the *fin de siècle* theatre, topple the womanly women from their stage pedestals, then march down from the boards into the stalls and out into the world. But finding the doors of the theatre too heavily barricaded, Shaw's regiment veered off instead to the offices of Grant Richards. Shaw-the-dramatist became Shaw-the-author ready to risk infuriating theatre managers and drama critics with the production of another unorthodox volume of his stage sermons: *Three Plays for Puritans*.

'I love the sordid side of business: the play of economic motive fascinates me,' he wrote to Ellen Terry. One day he would produce his own plays and publish his own books. 'And now, what about *Three Plays for Puritans?*' he warned Grant Richards. 'It is going to involve a lot of composition ... ' Richards for the time being still held on as his publisher, putting up with the copious revisions, deletions and additions on every page. On top of 'a thousand other things, I am working like mad sixteen hours a day', Shaw exulted. 'Such is life – *my* life.'

Once again, as with the two volumes of *Plays Pleasant and Unpleasant*, he expanded the stage directions into narrative, inserted descriptions, eliminated all 'repulsive stage technicalities' and added, by way of postscript, a Preface that was part advertisement, part short story. He had failed as a novelist and, it seemed, also as a dramatist: but from these two failures he proposed to manufacture success with a new literary genre composed of essay, play and novel. The technique, he explained, was to

'write nothing in a play that you would not write in a novel; and remember that everything that the actor or the scene-painter *shows* to the audience must be described – not technically specified, but imaginatively, vividly, humorously, in a word, artistically described – to the reader by the author. In describing the scene, take just as much trouble to transport your reader there in imagination as you would in a narrative.'

By November 1900 *Three Plays for Puritans* had been passed for the press and in January 1901, in the same green cloth crown octavo format, an edition of two thousand five hundred copies was finally published. 'The effort has almost slain me,' Shaw told Golding Bright. ' . . . A play costs two or three times as much real work as a novel, which involves nothing but inkslinging. Yet I give an ungrateful public *three* plays in a volume, besides prefaces, notes & sermons without end. When I say *give* I mean give; for the book will not yield me dock laborer's wages for the mere manual toil it costs.'

He had not done it for money; he had not worked sixteen hours a day with Charlotte's approval; and he had gone directly against the advice of William Archer who predicted popularity for at least one of these plays leading to an inevitable Shaw boom if he would give it 'a chance, by waiting at least two years for somebody to produce it before publishing it'. Why then had he done this? The answer runs between the lines of Shaw's Preface and was unconsciously picked up by Archer in his review of the book. Shaw, he objected, was under a misapprehension 'monstrously and fantastically wide of the truth' that the drama sought to live by stimulating the erotic instincts.

Sleeping spasmodically in the stalls, Archer had passed even more time in the theatre than Shaw, and had not detected a single serious contemporary play that 'owed its success to any sort of "voluptuous" appeal, to any titillation of sensuality in any sane spectator'. Shaw was nevertheless more acutely aware than Archer of the continuous current of sex in the Victorian theatre because, like the sex in his own life, it was suppressed. His attack in the Preface to *Three Plays for Puritans* on the 'ordinary sensuous ritual of the stage' which had become 'as frankly pornographic as good manners allowed' was conducted on two levels. He argued that the heartwearying conventionality of Victorian stage sex was pornographic in that it was not frank. This lack of frankness, he added, had been what 'finally disgusted me'. With such passages – and there are many of them in this Preface – he disclaims being a thin-skinned moral prude and identifies himself as a proponent of the realistic treatment of sex in contemporary drama, indignant at the 'reverence for gentility which governs our theatres today' and which ensured that no plays ever 'had the courage of their vices'. But for Shaw realistic sex meant less sex. 'We long ago gave up imposing celibacy on our priests,' he wrote, 'but we still impose it on our art, with the very undesirable and unexpected result that no editor, publisher, or manager, will now accept a story or produce a play without "love interest" in it.' It is towards this obsession with sex – which Shaw paradoxically labels celibacy because the sexual intercourse inevitably takes place offstage or between the acts – that his Preface is pointed. His target is the 'systematic idolatry of sensuousness' which so persistently misled audiences that they had 'finally accepted and acted upon' this misrepresentation. Such a 'substitution of sensuous ecstasy for intellectual activity and honesty' prevented the late Victorian theatre turning 'from the drama of romance and sensuality to the drama of edification': prevented, in short, the staging of Shaw's own plays.

Throughout the first half of this Preface the argument, presented with great force, is continually being displaced: the objective and subjective facets never exactly fit, and the thought is fractured from the emotion from which it derives. 'What epithet is contemptuous enough for the people who produce the would-be popular plays?' Shaw asks. The effect upon him of such productions, he tells us, had been disastrous. 'The principle of appealing exclusively to the instinct of self-gratification in people without power of attention, without interests, without sympathy: in short, without brains or heart. That is how they were conducted whilst I was writing about them; and that is how they nearly killed me.' The anger is real: but the placing of it in the stalls is oblique. For it is not chiefly from his boredom as a critic (a job he had given up over two years before writing this Preface) but from his failure as a playwright (particularly of his last two Puritan plays) that his anger arises. It is the frustrated dramatist who injects virulence into this writing. His criticisms of the theatre are trenchant, but Shaw passes almost unnoticeably from demolishing the genteel assumptions of the sex instinct as shown on the stage, to a demolition of the sex instinct itself. The power of these pages comes from his having joined his renunciation of sex after marriage with his inability to get his anti-romantic plays performed.

Before marriage, in his three-cornered affairs with women, Shaw's part had been an impersonation of George Vandeleur Lee, the interloper in his parents' marriage. In marriage he had taken on a double role, that of George Carr Shaw and George Vandeleur Lee together. He was legitimately married but it was a *mariage blanc*. The dominant role was that of Lee whose 'potency' arose from his public life – as did Shaw's. Casting off the ambiguous skin of 'George', Shaw had literally 'made a name for himself' as a writer, the magnificently impersonal G.B.S. (his equivalent of Lee's 'Vandeleur'). His ordinary frustration at not getting the work of G.B.S. performed – particularly the recent plays for Mrs Patrick Campbell and Ellen Terry – manifested itself as an impotence. From this impotence came his impatience – his inability to take Archer's advice to wait – and his confusing paradoxes in the Preface between celibacy and pornography. He had already waited too long. His only channel for reaching the public was the book world. But this outlet was unsatisfactory since he could not put his potent words into the mouths of the actresses or dress and direct them on a stage, could not witness them or his audiences, could only, with the aid of his written narrative, transport them into his imagination. There was more of masturbation in this than consummation, and it gave him only temporary relief.

'No: it is clear that I have nothing to do with the theatre of today,' he had written to Ellen Terry: 'I must educate a new generation with my pen from childhood up – audience, actors & all, and leave them my plays to murder after I am cremated.' To create this family of plays, unpopular plays, for future generations, was still Shaw's ultimate aim. In the short term, however, there was another theatre where he could perform: the theatre of politics. 'It is time to do something more in Shaw-philosophy, in politics & sociology. Your author, dear Ellen, must be more than a common dramatist.'

[3]

If I were not a politician I would be a Fabian.
R. B. Haldane to Bernard Shaw
(15 October 1900)

Shaw was with Charlotte on board the 'floating pleasure machine' SS *Lusitania* when on 11 October 1899 the war in the Transvaal broke out. The news alarmed him, for he saw at once its danger to the Fabians. 'Dont let us, after all these years, split the society by declaring ourselves on a non-socialist point of policy,' he wrote from the ship to the Fabian secretary Edward Pease. 'To wreck ourselves on the Transvaal after weathering Home Rule would be too silly.'

When he arrived back in England he found the country in a state of civil war over South Africa. The prosperity of the Empire, the longevity of the widowed Queen herself, seemed to have sunk Britain in the doldrums of world peace and the public was more than ready to take off for some foreign adventuring. The novels of Trollope, with their solid domestic themes, were beginning to lose popularity and were being replaced in the public imagination by Kipling's Indian stories, the adventures of R. L.

Stevenson and the historical romances of Conan Doyle. Doyle, who was to spend four and a half months in South Africa attached to a hospital unit, had been a neighbour of Shaw's at Hindhead and converted by him (Shaw liked to claim) 'from Christmas-card Pacifism to rampant Jingoism'. Early in 1899 they had shared the platform at a disarmament conference at Hindhead Hall, and Shaw wrote to Doyle proposing 'a combination of the leading powers to police the world and put down international war just as private war is put down'. Though the two men's instincts were widely separated, Shaw's concept of a militant League of Nations using warfare to arrest war gave intellectual pigment to the attitude Doyle shared with thousands of 'men in the street' throughout Britain – an attitude that converted warfare into sport. 'If ever England gets into a hole,' Doyle had declared, 'you may depend on it that her sporting men will pull her out of it' – and that was what he and others considered they were doing in South Africa. Doyle, who was knighted shortly after the publication of his patriotic pamphlet *The Cause and Conduct of the War in South Africa*, enjoyed praising the sportsmanlike qualities of his Boer opponents and looked forward to the 'splendid *entente*' they would be able to achieve once they wearied of fighting. This changing-room spirit of camaraderie had something of the same retrospective optimism that, in its more cerebral manner, Shaw forced himself to adopt on behalf of the Fabians.

He had wanted at first to have nothing to do with it. But the eruption of hostilities was of such violence, shifting the landscape of British politics, that non-involvement became impossible. The atmosphere in Britain of conflicting imperialist and pro-Boer passions, gathering up the vague discontents of years, was considerably less sportsmanlike than on the smoke-filled battlefields of South Africa. John Burns, 'the Man with the Red Flag' who ten years ago had led the Dock Strike, was obliged to take up his cricket bat one night to defend his Liberal pacifist principles against a crowd attempting to break into his home. In the House of Commons Joseph Chamberlain accused his old Liberal colleague Henry Labouchère of 'moral treason'; and Labouchère, calling himself pro-Englander rather than pro-Boer, accused Chamberlain of making Britain the most hated country in the world. 'I prefer my country to my party,' he added.

Shaw was right in viewing Irish Home Rule as a precedent in party political terms for the Boer War. The Conservative Party, united by the romantic bellicosity in which most of the country was bathing, saw Englishmen riding 'the white steed of destiny' all over South Africa. On the other side, despite the chauvinist confusion of Hyndman and the old-soldier loyalty of Robert Blatchford, most socialists balanced their militarist tactics at home with a policy of pacifism abroad and joined together in aggressive opposition to the war – Keir Hardie, for example, picturing the Boers as pure-living, God-fearing farmers grazing peacefully under the Christ-like guardianship of President Kruger. Between the romanticism of the right and the sentimentality of the left floundered the Liberal Party with its cautious new leader Campbell-Bannerman. It was the middle ground of British politics that was torn apart by the South African war; and since the Fabian Society, with its policy of permeation, had been cultivating this middle ground, it now found itself at the centre of a crisis.

One of the Fabians had immediately proposed that a resolution expressing sympathy for the Boers and 'deep indignation' at the 'wanton and unjustifiable war' be moved as 'urgent business' at the Fabian meeting on 13 October. The Fabian executive, by a majority of seven votes to five, decided to oppose this motion, and the members, by twenty-six votes to nineteen, supported them. But the closeness of this voting showed how deeply the Fabians were divided, and the prominence of some of the Fabian anti-imperialists ensured that the matter could not be ended so easily. Sydney Olivier (whose daughter burned an effigy of Chamberlain on Guy Fawkes Night) argued that 'you can't get ahead of a real elementary force except by going better in elementary force yourself . . . that is what Socialism came to the front with and formed, *inter alia*, the Fabian Society'. If the Fabians now refused to oppose the war they would begin to suffer from dry rot. Olivier therefore proposed that the Society issue a leaflet condemning the war. But the executive refused this proposal too – though only by one vote, and passed on to its Publications Committee a notice to report on the advisability of a tract on Imperialism.

The departure of Olivier for Jamaica to take up his post there as colonial secretary, and Shaw's return from the Mediterranean greatly strengthened Sidney Webb's puppet-string control over the Society. The Webbs' attitude to South Africa was simple. They saw it as an embarrassing incursion on parish-pump socialism and exercised their full capacity for ignoring it. Beatrice, who described the war as an 'underbred business', felt that Chamberlain had been as 'vulgar and tricky' in his dealings with the Boers as he had previously been 'coarse-grained' and indifferent to herself. The whole business stirred within her an awkward 'combination of bias and counter-bias', and she was determined that the Fabians should be 'so far removed from political influence that it is not necessary for Sidney to express any opinion'.

It was Sidney's adamant lack of interest in foreign politics – despite his years at the Colonial Office – that had up to now dictated the Fabian silence over Imperialism and was to set in motion an elaborate policy of

38

avoidance over the next two years. In sentiment Sidney was pro-Boer. He loathed the war but, believing the annexation of the Transvaal to be inevitable, could not think out what his attitude should be. 'It suits him infinitely better to keep out of the whole affair,' Beatrice decided. ' . . . he feels uncertain as to his own opinions, having carefully avoided reading anything on the subject. "It is not my show," he has often said when I have suggested he should read blue-books.'

Early defeats in South Africa had inflamed both imperialist and pro-Boer passions and bitterly divided public opinion in Britain. Since it was impossible much longer to smother everything in silence, Webb handed over the 'show' to the Fabian literary expert. Shaw's brief was complicated. He had to find some device for welding together a split that might otherwise capsize the society; he had to discover some honourable method by which, while the war issue dominated British politics, the Fabians could legitimately continue to produce tracts on municipal bakeries, fire insurance, pawnshops, slaughterhouses, steamboats and the milk supply. By favouring neither side, Sidney had aroused antagonism from both. Shaw's job was to make Sidney's neutrality bilaterally popular and explain, in the context of South Africa, the importance of his uninterrupted labours on the London School of Economics and the reform of public education, the Fabian concern over garden cities and the nationalization of Irish railways.

He made his first move on 24 November after a speech (changed at the last minute from 'England in the Mediterranean' to 'England and South Africa') by Frederick Whelan. In the discussion Shaw advanced Webb's point of view: the war might have been avoided by better management, he suggested, but since its progress was now inevitable the Fabians should, as a matter of urgency, do nothing until it was over. This was merely a skirmish for the real contest at a special meeting on 8 December. A long resolution stating that, since the war sprang from the character of the British governing classes, it was essential 'for the furtherance of its own special aims' that the Society dissociate itself from 'the Imperialism of Capitalism and vainglorious Nationalism', was put by S. G. Hobson. To this motion Shaw replied with an amendment, overlooking the war, and focusing on the need to nationalize the South African coal mines and introduce legal protection for the mine workers during the *entente* that would inevitably follow. This diversion, which aimed at getting unanimity, succeeded in uniting most of the membership against it. Shaw's amendment was quickly thrown out and, following a painstaking debate, the discussion adjourned. This demonstration by the intelligentsia of the country of not knowing what to think was picked up with great joviality by the press and persuaded the executive to give reluctant agreement to a proposal from Ramsay MacDonald that the 'sense' of the membership be taken by a postal ballot.

It was the first referendum held by the Society. The question, dispatched to the membership in February 1900, was: 'Are you in favour of an official pronouncement being made now by the Fabian Society on Imperialism in relation to the War?' Those in favour argued that the Society should attach itself to international socialism which was opposed to aggressive capitalism and to the militaristic use of funds needed for social reform. Those against – including Webb, Shaw and Hubert Bland – claimed that an unresearched official pronouncement came within the 'prohibited degrees' of Tract No. 70 (the 1896 *Report on Fabian Policy* by Shaw), would have no effect on the war, but might seriously damage the solidarity of the Society. Of the total membership of 800, 217 Fabians voted for a pronouncement, and 259 supported Webb, Shaw and Bland. Eighteen members then resigned. It was a small number but included such prominent names as Ramsay Mac-Donald, Emmeline Pankhurst, Walter Crane, Henry Salt and two future Labour Members of Parliament, George Barnes and Pete Curran.

And still the battle went on. During the April election of the Executive Committee, S. G. Hobson attempted to run an anti-imperialist ticket and Webb responded with a counter-ticket. The result, which closely followed the noncommittal postal ballot, returned all but one of Webb's list but included four of Hobson's, at the head of which was placed the actor-manager Charles Charrington. The following month, at the Annual General Meeting, this new executive requested Shaw to draft a manifesto on imperialism.

Shaw's attitude had begun to change over this year until, with the publication of *Fabianism and the Empire*, it seemed completely to invert the traditional socialist standpoint – supporting pacifist permeation tactics at home while tolerating a good deal of bloodshed overseas. From the start he urged all Fabians to stick together. No party or society could entirely discharge the soul's message of every member; and no member, he added, 'can find a Society 800 strong which is an extension of his own self – even the society of 2 called marriage is a failure from that point of view . . . '

Shaw tried to suffocate the moral issue of the war by spreading over it his theory of pragmatism. In its most negative phase Shaw's pragmatism meant that socialism should not touch any problem that it did not have a reasonable chance of solving; more positively it meant in this case waiting for the inevitable annexation of the Transvaal, and then introducing there the higher social organization on which the Fabians had been experimenting. In a letter to Ramsay MacDonald he explained, 'Radicalism we found to be sentiment without administration; and we opposed to it administration without sentiment.'

'Now, if you can draft a resolution that will combine the two, let us have it by all means. I have done my best to avert the fight for which the democratic spirit and the large grasp of human ideas is always spoiling, and for which the jingo spirit is no doubt equally ready. If you wont take my way, and wont find a better way, then punch one another's heads and be damned.'

Shaw's way was a synthesis between radicalism and unsentimental administration which he called International Collectivism. This principle of collectivism, he argued, should unite the Fabians by virtue of it being the only practical socialist policy available to them. Of what use, he asked, were ethics that were taken out of the cupboard from time to time and that led to conclusions no one could act on? 'I am a revolutionist in ethics as much as in economics,' he told Walter Crane;

'and the moment you demand virtuous indignation from me, I give you up . . . I have done my best to keep the peace . . . the Fabian ought to be warproof; and yet Capitalism has only to fire a gun, and split a great shaving off us.'

In fact Shaw was extraordinarily successful in keeping the peace, encouraging all members to support the best candidates regardless of their attitude to South Africa. By the time the Treaty of Vereeniging was signed in 1902 (leaving the enfranchisement of the native population to be settled in due course) 22,000 British soldiers had been killed and £223,000,000 spent – but no great shaving had been split off the Fabian Society. In steering them out of war-range, Shaw had removed the Fabians from the rest of the socialist fleet, taken them, it seemed, out of politics and stranded them on the high ground of political philosophy. He had also plucked from politics the 'heroic' quality he had so recently inserted into his plays. Apropos *Caesar and Cleopatra*, he wrote in the summer of 1902 to Gilbert Murray that 'literature is no longer the game of style it was to Cicero's pals'. But the political speeches and writings by which he dexterously avoided a staging, with all its casualties, of the Boer War in the Fabian debating halls, was a triumph of the Shavian style and the game of words over divisive action.

The war in South Africa forced Shaw to re-examine his earlier political thinking and extend its perspective. 'We have never thrashed this matter out,' he wrote to Walter Crane, 'because we were too lazy, or had other things to occupy us (other aspects of the movement, I mean) or, alas!

found the ethics too handy a stick to beat "the capitalist" with to be conveniently disowned.'

'We have been morally rotten from the beginning with this hypocrisy of trying to put the blame of our civilization on some villain in the human melodrama at whose expense we could shew off our own virtue. And now, having been virtuous all these years at the expense of our political opponents, we feel bound to be virtuous at the expense of one another.'

In this reaction to South Africa, which was a rehearsal for the policy he would adopt during the First World War, may be seen the origin of his inter-war attitude towards Hitler and Mussolini. Shaw hated war; he hated the human beings who were roused and attracted by war; and he felt that every human being, whatever his moral stance, was hideously implicated. We were all as bloodguilty as one another. His revulsion to the Boer War, and the policy he formed based on this revulsion, is most succinctly expressed in a letter to a fellow Fabian, George Samuel. 'The Boer and the Britisher are both fighting animals, like all animals who live in a chronic panic of death and defeat,' he wrote. 'They are also carnivorous animals and alcohol-drinking animals . . . '

'Do you expect me solemnly to inform a listening nation that the solution of the South African problem is that the lion shall lie down with highly-armed lamb in mutual raptures of quakerism, vegetarianism, and teetotalism? . . . Let us face the facts. Two hordes of predatory animals are fighting, after their manner, for the possession of South Africa, where neither of them has, or ever had, any business to be from the abstractly-moral, virtuously indignant Radical, or (probably) the native point of view . . .

' . . . the moral position of the Boers and the British is precisely identical in every respect; that is, it does not exist. Two dogs are fighting for a bone thrown before them by Mrs Nature, an old-established butcher with a branch establishment in South Africa. The Socialist has only to consider which dog to back; that is, which dog will do most for Socialism if it wins.'

The only Fabian who reasoned on this level was Sydney Olivier. In a memorandum sent to Shaw, he had argued that the power of the British Empire to assimilate and govern South Africa was an illusion, and that South Africa would do better without British interference – from which it followed that the Fabians should give their support to the Boers and add their voice to those who were calling for the expulsion of imperialism from South Africa. 'I am by no means sure that this may not be the Way of

Destiny,' Shaw had confided to Hubert Bland at the end of 1899. His case for what Olivier had called 'corned beef' imperialism depended on the analogy of a trust annexing a small shopkeeper – a capitalistic transaction, he owned, 'but one making, like all advanced capitalism, for Socialism'. It was along these lines, and in general terms, that he propounded an alternative Way of Destiny in *Fabianism and the Empire*: 'a Great Power, consciously or unconsciously, must govern in the interests of civilization as a whole,' he wrote, 'and it is not to those interests that such mighty forces as gold-fields, and the formidable armaments that can be built upon them, should be wielded irresponsibly by small communities of frontiersmen.'

'Theoretically, they should be internationalized, not British-Imperialized; but until the Federation of the world becomes an accomplished fact, we must accept the most responsible Imperial federations available as a substitute for it.'

This historical hypothesis, enabling him to look through what was actual and present to an imagined future, became the focus of Shaw's morality and the device by which he converted spontaneous pessimism into a distant attitude of optimism. His feelings about war were clear. 'I regard war as wasteful, demoralizing, unnecessary, and ludicrously and sordidly inglorious in its reality,' he wrote in that summer of 1900. 'This is my unconditional opinion.'

'I *dont* mean war in a bad cause, or war against liberty, or war with any other qualification whatever: I mean war. I recognize no right of the good man to kill the bad man or to govern the bad man.'

This unconditional opinion receded to a blurred background when he looked at warfare through the lens of politics. Shaw's human response is conditioned by the need to be hopeful – the luxury of which became his equivalent to other people's 'virtuous indignation'. His genuine emotional horror is diverted into an intellectual joy at the contemplation of mass suicide by such a loveless species as human beings. 'As for me, I delight in the war more and more,' he told Henry Salt.

'It has waked the country up out of its filthy wallowing in money (blood is a far superior bath); and it has put fourpence on the Income Tax which will never come off if the Fabian can help it; so that Old Age Pensions will be within reach at the end of the ten years repayment period, if not sooner. And it has put a stop to the Chartered company game ... Kruger as Joshua will also be exploded; and British military prestige of the schoolboy kind has been handsomely "reversed".'

Conceived as a penny tract arising from the South African war, *Fabianism and the Empire* was eventually produced as a Fabian foreign policy document, one hundred pages long, published at one shilling by Grant Richards and directed at the 'Khaki' election in the autumn of 1900. The first draft, which took Shaw three months to complete, was sent to every member of the Fabian Society, 134 of whom returned comments which, with extraordinary ingenuity, he attempted to stitch into his text. 'The business of examining over a hundred marked proofs of a document of 20,000 words, every line of which was more or less controversial, was an immense one,' commented Pease. But the final version was such a 'masterpiece' of literary craft that no more than fourteen Fabians voted against its publication. 'By this time the controversy over the war had reached an intensity which those who cannot recollect it will find difficult to believe,' Pease remembered, 'and nobody but the author could have written an effective document on the war so skilfully as to satisfy the great majority of the supporters of both parties in the Society.'

'Bernard Shaw has accomplished many difficult feats, but none of them, in my opinion, excels that of drafting for the Society and carrying through the manifesto called "Fabianism and the Empire".'

Very little of *Fabianism and the Empire* deals with South Africa which, though topical, is seen as part of an historical pattern. The design of socialism in this pattern is to turn Empires into true Commonwealths. Shaw's manifesto imagines a Fabianizing of the Empire in the cause of efficiency – a cause that Webb himself was to put his signature to the following year with Tract No. 108, *A Policy of National Efficiency*. Foreign policy, being merely an extension of domestic policy, pursues similar objectives. Shaw recommends reforms for the army, the Consular Service and the administration and social justice of Imperialism. He grafts socialism on to Colonialism with such statesmanlike prose and sweeping vision as to reduce the differences of the Fabians to family bickering.

'The Manifesto has passed: all is well save its shattered author,' Shaw wrote to Grant Richards. He had drafted what Beatrice Webb called 'the most prescient and permanently instructive public document of its date'. But on the General Election, the Treaty of Vereeniging and the subsequent social conditions in South Africa, *Fabianism and the Empire* had no influence at all. It was favourably reviewed, quickly forgotten. Unlike Conan Doyle's pamphlet, it did not become popular and 1,500 copies were remaindered the following year.

In the new Parliament the Tories had won 402 seats, the Liberals 186 and the Nationalists 82. Keir Hardie was the only independent Labour politician to survive the election – but it was not through him that the Fabians sought to operate. *Fabianism and the Empire* had aimed at exporting Fabianism: its effect was to import a foreign policy. For dinner-party politics, Beatrice noted, 'a Conservative Government is as good for us as a Liberal Government'. The Fabians were ascending in society, becoming friendly with Bishops and Tory Cabinet Ministers, while among the Liberals, they chose Lord Rosebery as their man – partly on account of his admiration for Shaw's manifesto. '*Our* policy is clearly to back him for all we are worth,' Shaw urged Beatrice who noted in her diary: 'We have succumbed to his flattery.' A few weeks later, in the autumn of 1901, Sidney published 'Lord Rosebery's Escape from Houndsditch' – an invitation for him to lead the progressive Liberals (including Asquith, Grey and Haldane) in their campaign to raise each department of national life to its maximum capability.

CHAPTER II

[1]

I stand just now at a point where a failure would put me quite out of court, and a success would 'chair me ever'. (26 March 1902)

In his middle forties Shaw had reached a position between politics and literature, work and life, that by 1903 had forced into the language a new word: Shavian. Politically he was committed for ever to socialism, yet he had refused to enter politics as a Parliamentary candidate during the socialist boom of the late nineteenth century. In the imperialist phase that spread from the Victorian age into the early twentieth century, most of his energies had been piped into municipal work, though after 'six years' Borough Councilling', he concluded in 1903, ' . . . I am convinced that the Borough Councils must be abolished'.

Shaw's method of quitting local politics was characteristically perverse. In the spring of 1904 he stood as a Progressive candidate for one of the two London County Council seats in South St Pancras. Sidney Webb rushed in to help him: packing off to the twenty-one clergymen in the district an appeal to 'go hard for Shaw' accompanied by a complimentary copy of his own *London Education*; squeezing a distant blessing out of the Bishop of Stepney; flaunting Shaw's virtues in the *Daily Mail*; fitting his own secretaries in the local committee rooms and calling up the full forces of the Fabian Society to march behind G.B.S. as he wandered his eccentric way 'slashing to the right and the left among his own nominal supporters'.

'The Shaws have been good friends to us,' Beatrice wrote in her diary, 'and we would not like them to have a humiliating defeat.' The party organizers however had long ago given up the seat as lost and even Beatrice admitted 'he is not likely to get in'. But this was not good enough for G.B.S. He needed, while campaigning with tremendous gusto and geniality, to make *absolutely certain* of not getting in. Every day of the campaign he showed himself as 'hopelessly intractable' – except to his enemies, to whom he was 'the most accommodating candidate that was ever known'. He 'refused to adopt any orthodox devices as to address and polling cards, inventing brilliant ones of his own . . . Insisted that he was an atheist; that, though a teetotaller, he would force every citizen to imbibe a quartern of rum to cure any tendency to intoxication; laughed at the

46

Nonconformist conscience; chaffed the Catholics about transubstantiation; abused the Liberals, and contemptuously patronized the Conservatives – until every section was equally disgruntled'. As a result, he was triumphantly beaten into third place. And so, with honour high, his unfurled Shavianisms making terrible comedy of the degrading election joust, Shaw paraded out of party politics. 'I have been defeated – wiped out – annihilated at the polls, mostly through the stupidity of my own side. Consequently I am perfectly furious,' he pretended. Beatrice, who really was furious, also pretended. 'We are not wholly grieved. G.B.S., with a small majority might have been useful; with an overwhelming one, would simply have been compromising . . . '

'His bad side is very prominent at an election – vanity and lack of reverence for knowledge or respect for other people's prejudices; even his good qualities – quixotic chivalry to his opponents and cold drawn truth, ruthlessly administered, to possible supporters, are magnificent but not war.'

Beatrice knew that politics was war, and that Shaw's magnificent string of gestures and devices was not good military tactics. His erratic genius, she now concluded, would have been unsettling for Sidney. It was a pity. She had looked forward to him becoming 'the *enfant terrible* of the Progressive Party' whose verbal antics would make Sidney 'look wisely conventional'. After all, in the Fabian Society they had 'managed to supplement each other in a curiously effective way . . . '

One thing was certain: 'He will never be selected again by any constituency that any wire-puller thinks can be won.' And since the Fabians, with their perpetual transit from camp to camp, were now recognized principally as political wire-pullers, this result was conclusive. 'I havent the faintest intention of standing again in South St Pancras in any capacity whatever,' Shaw confirmed.

*

Shaw's election defeat was probably more disappointing to Charlotte than to the Webbs. It had been Charlotte who had asked Sidney to find G.B.S. a seat. Her attitude seemed oddly ambiguous, almost (in its fashion) Shavian. She thought of her husband as a 'Genius' and of herself as the helpmeet of a great man. Yet she wanted to prevent him working on 'things dramatic' and to find him a respectable career in politics. By themselves the Fabians were too much like clever schoolboys to impress Charlotte as being real politicians. As a pacifist, she had actually disagreed with G.B.S.'s pamphlet on the Boer War. Then, while she did not really like the theatrical world that was part of her husband's past, she did believe in his wonderful gifts as a playwright. Yet she could not blink at the facts. In the summer of 1903, Shaw published *Man and Superman*: it was his twelfth play, he was in his forty-eighth year and still almost wholly unknown to British audiences. From these various facts and her conflicting reactions to them, Charlotte hit on a curious programme of redirecting G.B.S.'s career. She attempted to nudge him into professional politics at home while furthering his reputation as a dramatist abroad.

Her opportunity to help Shaw's plays on to the European stage came with a visit to London of a young Austrian writer, Siegfried Trebitsch. Trebitsch had been introduced to Shaw's writings by William Archer who had also given him the warm letter of introduction with which he arrived at Adelphi Terrace early in 1902. 'First of all I was received by Mrs Shaw, a lady who made an uncommonly likeable impression at the very first glance,' Trebitsch remembered, 'and whose understanding gaze revealed the intense vigour of her mind.' With Irish cunning, Trebitsch concluded, Charlotte 'chatted with me about matters of no importance'. From this he became aware that her conversation was a pretext 'to observe the visitor without his being aware of it'. Meanwhile, in another room, G.B.S. had been reading Archer's letter. He then 'made an impatient appearance in the doorway and held out his hand to me'. Trebitsch looked round, but Charlotte had skilfully 'vanished'.

Trebitsch was an extreme Quixote, a sentimentalist of wonderful persistence, of the sort Shaw, in theory, had been sent into the world to quell but who, in practice, so often got the better of him. His generosity was alarming. 'I held forth for quite a while about his plays,' he wrote. They had 'set me afire'. He believed *Candida* to be supreme among them: an 'infinitely beautiful poetic' masterpiece; while Shaw himself was 'one of the most original and greatest dramatic poets and thinkers of our days'.

'What do you mean to do with me?' Shaw interrupted.

Trebitsch knew the answer to this. He meant to become Shaw's 'interpreter and apostle in Central Europe'. He had set himself 'the aim of conquering the German stage for him'. In short he allowed himself to 'speake straight forward' and give his 'dear adored Shaw' what he called 'a peace of my mind'. The result, which may have bewildered him, was that Shaw jumped up and ran out of the room, crying that Archer had played a terrible practical joke on him and appealing to Charlotte to 'come and try to calm' this 'young lunatic'.

Obediently, if with some embarrassment, Charlotte re-materialized and Trebitsch 'expounded my intentions to her'. The grandeur of these intentions, contrasted with the inadequacy of the language in which they were expressed, did not strike Charlotte as funny. 'She nodded in smiling agreement, apologised for her impatient husband, and spoke words of encouragement to me,' Trebitsch recalled. Then she summoned her husband back into the room and acted as interpreter between them. Why should the author of *The Admirable Bashville*, Shaw's latest play, not be given the same honour in the German theatre as the poet Shakespeare? The next session was 'business-like'. Shaw spoke forbiddingly about the 'extremely important matter of copyright' of which Trebitsch knew nothing; Trebitsch produced the galley-proofs of a French translation of his own first novel; and Charlotte nodded and smiled. Trebitsch left soon afterwards and a few days later received a letter from Charlotte inviting him to lunch. It became clear to him during this meal that, though she took no part in the conversation, Charlotte approved of him and that this approval had been responsible for a change in her husband's manner. At the end of their lunch, she withdrew, leaving an atmosphere of sympathy in which the two men could debate. 'I did what I could to dissuade him from what seemed a desperate undertaking,' Shaw wrote, 'but his faith in my destiny was invincible.' Trebitsch noticed that Shaw listened 'to my resolution, which I kept on emphasising, with a smile'. There was a 'thin crust of embitterment that covered the real character of this under-estimated writer, who though in the prime of life was not yet recognised'. In that listening smile Trebitsch saw 'the faint mistrust that a lonely man feels for the approval and admiration that he prefers to consider a misunderstanding until he knows the source from which they come'. As their conversation grew friendlier this mistrust evaporated. 'I recognised,' Trebitsch wrote, 'that this was a kindly man, a tower of strength for all who trusted him and would entrust themselves to him.'

One reason why Shaw had tried to dodge Trebitsch ('by asking my wife to see him') may have been a presentiment of what taking on a translator would entail – he had previously refused Count A. Guilbert de Voisins permission to make a translation into French of *Arms and the Man*. For Trebitsch to translate his plays into German involved Shaw in mastering the German language – or at least buying 'a devil of a big dictionary, also a grammar'. But 'every German book seems to have a new vocabulary of its own. None of Trebitsch's words are in the dictionary'. He teased and tutored Trebitsch terrifically. His translation of *Caesar and Cleopatra* was so stuffed with misunderstandings as 'to make it necessary that I should go through every sentence carefully'; *Arms and the Man* was 'full of hideous and devastating errors'; *Candida*, Trebitsch's favourite, was worst of all. 'You didnt understand the play: you only wallowed in it,' Shaw told him. ' . . . I tore out large handfuls of my hair and uttered screams of rage . . . I

49

plucked up my beard by the roots and threw it after my hair ... I sometimes wish "Candida" were at the bottom of the sea.'

From such comments, over several years, Trebitsch began to sense that something could be wrong. It was difficult sometimes to catch what Shaw was driving towards. 'I have just met the most beautiful Shavian I have ever seen,' Trebitsch deciphered at the end of one of Shaw's letters to him. 'She is the wife of one of our diplomatic staff, who is joining the British Embassy in Vienna very soon. I think I will ask her to correct your translations: you can make mistakes on purpose.' What could this mean? 'You must learn to laugh,' Shaw suggested. Was it all some joke? Probably not, since Shaw had also advised him: 'I have no objection to being taken seriously. What ruins me in England is that people think I am always joking ... I want the Germans to know me as a philosopher, as an English (or Irish) Nietzsche (only ten times cleverer) ... '

Through his correspondence with Trebitsch Shaw began to rewrite the story of his life. 'Write me a catechism & I will answer all your questions,' he invited. He was soon burying Trebitsch under a ton of information and adding to his other areas of expertise the art of translation. 'What is a Looking Glass?' he demanded.

'A thing that reflects what is before it with exquisite fidelity, but that has ... neither memory nor hope, neither reason nor conscience. And that is what you are as a translator. You translate a sentence beautifully, but you do not remember the last sentence, do not foresee the next sentence, and when you finish the play it goes out of your head just as your head vanishes from your mirror when you have finished shaving ... You must never dramatize anything until you get above it ... Correct it by all means; but dont *polish* it: why perfume the sea air? a little roughness is all the better.'

To be the perfect translator of Shaw's plays Trebitsch needed not only to become a Shavian but to be resolved into a German edition of G.B.S. Shaw spelled out the prescription minutely. Trebitsch suffered from neuralgias and nerves. 'Is it overwork, or romantic attachments to women,' Shaw wanted to know. If it was romance then Trebitsch should know that everything romantic, 'or romantically artistic, is just what I have come into the world to trample on, laugh out of countenance, and finally slay'. If it was food then Trebitsch must read Alexander Haig's *Diet and Food Considered in Relation to Strength and Power of Endurance Training and Athletics* and eat from the same menu as Shaw himself. 'Never eat meat or drink tea, coffee, or wine again as long as you live,' he warned. 'If you are very bad, hire yourself out as a laborer and live on your wages for a month or so. If you are very very very bad, become religious, and go every day three times to the nearest Roman Catholic Church. Go round all the Stations of the Cross on your knees, and pray incessantly. When you begin to feel sceptical you will be getting well.'

After their discussion at lunch it had been agreed that Trebitsch should translate three of Shaw's plays and would hold exclusive rights in them for one year. If he was unsuccessful he would hand the rights back; if successful, he would obviously have earned the chance to become the translator of all Shaw's work into German. He chose *The Devil's Disciple*, *Candida* and *Arms and the Man*.

'Give up *wanting* to have the plays produced if you value your happiness as a man and your dignity as an artist.' This was curious advice for Trebitsch to read since if he was to have any success at all he had to give up all notions of dignity and relaxation. He kept the three plays 'ceaselessly circulating among publishers, theatrical people, producers', but met with 'great difficulty and all kinds of trouble'. The proprietor of the Entsch theatrical publishing firm in Berlin refused 'to have anything to do with this crazy Irishman' whom he described as 'a lost cause'. From other theatrical publishers and agents Trebitsch received refusals that were equally radical. He was advised to 'stop being so obstinate' or he would endanger his own career by meddling with 'foreign plays that have not the slightest chance of success now or at any other time'. 'I was somewhat desperate,' Trebitsch wrote. 'But I did not lose heart.' He continued working 'feverishly, usually the whole day, and often half the night as well, for, after all, I had a time limit'. He did succeed in publishing an article on Shaw in the *Neue Freie Presse*, but only because the editor was so delighted by what he took to be Trebitsch's inventiveness. This Irishman with the pious name was obviously a hoax: 'our readers won't believe in this devil of a chap of yours any more than I do or you yourself.'

But within the year Trebitsch began to accomplish what Shaw had been failing to achieve in Britain over more than a decade. He persuaded the director of the Raimund Theatre in Vienna to stage *The Devil's Disciple* in February 1903, and the Stuttgart publishers Cotta to bring out all three plays, *Drei Dramen*, in the same year. In 1904 the Deutsches Volkstheater produced *Candida* and *Arms and the Man*; and within the next three years there were productions by leading directors of *You Never Can Tell*, *Mrs Warren's Profession* and *Man and Superman*, all in Trebitsch's translations. Through his 'curiously unerring instinct', Germany had come to recognize Shaw's 'importance to the modern stage', Thomas Mann wrote, 'indeed to modern intellectual life as a whole, earlier than the English-speaking world'.

'His fame actually reached England only by way of Germany, just as Ibsen and Hamsun conquered Norway, and Strindberg Sweden, by the same roundabout route, for London's independent theatre fell short of doing for Shaw's reputation – soon to grow to world-wide dimensions – what men like Otto Brahm and Max Reinhardt . . . were able to accomplish, for the simple reason that at that time the German stage was ahead of its British counterpart.'

Trebitsch recorded that it 'made a very great impression on Shaw that I had kept my word and accomplished what I set out to do'. What Shaw felt for Trebitsch was naked gratitude – the emotion he usually denied and invariably distrusted. With a devotion that Shaw described as 'extraordinary', Trebitsch went on to introduce to the German-speaking public almost the entire body of Shavian literature. The enterprise seemed the more remarkable because it had been begun, almost against Shaw's own wishes, at a time when 'I was rated in the theatrical world of London as an absurd pamphleteer', Shaw later wrote.

' . . . Today I have only to lift up my finger to attract a hundred translators. When Trebitsch volunteered for the job, the hundred would have fled from my invitation as one man . . . my personal debt to him is incalculable.'

But Trebitsch also owed a debt to Shaw. The knowledge of this was not altogether pleasing to him. 'The Shaw business means sometime a lot of trouble for me,' he explained to an American Shavian, 'not to speak of my own novels and plays I often have to leave behind to fight for my friend's sake.' In fact, as their correspondence shows, Shaw was scrupulous about Trebitsch's own work. 'Keep writing,' he tells him: 'that is your business – your own stories first, and the translations when you are tired of original invention.'

In the conflict of gratitude between Shaw and Trebitsch, a rather contradictory picture of what happened emerges. Trebitsch in his autobiography presents a chronicle of unchecked success. The first night of *The Devil's Disciple* 'was one of the most remarkable I have ever experienced', he writes. 'One could feel a breath of something alien in the air; one could feel the impact of a new atmosphere; . . . Shaw had got a foothold on German-speaking territory even then, on that memorable evening. The audience was not grudging with its applause . . . ' *Arms and the Man*, Trebitsch continues, 'did its part in making Shaw's name widely known'. *Mrs Warren's Profession* 'was the greatest success of the season'. The production of *Candida* 'turned out to be a sensation' and so on. The stream of Shaw's letters along this triumphant passage form a curious undercurrent. Over a period of two and a half years, he writes:

'Give up all anxiety about those plays . . . let this experience cure you of your excessive sensitiveness to reviews . . . If I bothered about such things I should go mad three times a week, and die on the alternate dates . . . you must not lie awake and get neuralgia: you must correct the mistakes and disarm the enemy . . . As to the play being ruined for all German stages, do not trouble about that. When you have been ruined as often as I have, you will find your reputation growing with every successive catastrophe. Never ruin yourself less than twice a year, or the public will forget about you . . . Dismiss it from your mind now: there is no use bothering about a commercial failure . . . All this is excellent so far as it gives the failure the air of being like the failure of Tannhäuser in the forties at Dresden: we can say that it is the public that failed . . . let us laugh and try again . . . A failure is half a success when it leaves a controversy behind . . . nothing succeeds like failure . . . You are perfectly mad – mad as a hatter . . . get back to something of your own . . . We shall be hissed into celebrity if this goes on . . . This is horrible news. I was hoping that your confounded play would fail. *Now* you must go on writing plays, and stop translating . . . '

Shaw wanted to succeed: but he protected himself against disappointment by avoiding any expectation of success. 'What was hard on Trebitsch was my lack of desire to have my plays performed – almost a reluctance. But I always did my best for his sake, though I of course would not let him, in his boyish anxiety, make fatal and unnecessary concessions when they tried to bluff him.' He developed a paternal tenderness for Trebitsch and created for them a dual identity. Trebitsch was never the artist in translation that G.B.S. publicly proclaimed. His dialogue was so stiff and sometimes so awkwardly put into German that the actors and producers often changed his words in rehearsal in order to get their tongues round them. For many years he was violently attacked in Germany for knowing neither German nor English – and, despite a massive opportunity, he never learned what Shaw called 'the grand style of fighting', falling upon your opponent and clubbing him dead with the weapons of generosity and politeness. In spite of Shaw's exacting work with the dictionary, many misunderstandings persisted, the most notorious being Trebitsch's interpretation of the Waiter's remark in *You Never Can Tell*: 'I really must draw the line at sitting down' – after which, following Trebitsch's stage directions, he goes to the window and, before taking his seat, draws the curtains. Shaw knew all about these howlers but was impervious to criticisms of his friend which he represented as the pedantic schoolmastering of disappointed rivals. Had he not been attacked like this himself in his own language by grammarians? Were not Archer's translations of Ibsen invariably so attacked? It was traditional for reviewers to shoot the translator. 'Never join in attacks on translators,' he advised one of his biographers, 'they are always made. Trebitsch only suffered as all the rest suffered.' His loyalty to Trebitsch took the form of claiming for these 'so-called translations' the status of 'excellent original plays'. Had they been the least like his own, he explained, they could never have succeeded so well.

Over their relationship floated the friendly spirit of Charlotte. 'My wife sends you always some kind messages,' G.B.S. assured Trebitsch, 'but I generally forget to give them to you.' So Charlotte began a separate correspondence, more ordinary in tone, a sort of *criticus apparatus* that helped Trebitsch to reach a better understanding of Shaw.

Shaw's experiences with Trebitsch gave a pattern for his arrangements with other translators. 'Remember,' he instructed Trebitsch, 'a book must be translated within *ten* years of publication to secure copyright; and the years are running out. I wish I had caught you younger.' His success in Germany made Shaw alive to the danger of losing the copyright in his plays abroad and, when commercial arrangements were not practicable within the ten-year period, he would protect it by underwriting the costs of publication himself. 'My European reputation was engineered systematically on a heroic scale,' he advised the playwright Henry Arthur Jones in 1908.

' . . . I calculated that the only way to make the job really worth doing was to catch some man in each country who would undertake *all* my work, and thus get something like an income out of half the fees. At last I succeeded everywhere except in Portugal. Sometimes the men came of their own accord as devoted disciples. Sometimes I picked a man who had never dreamt of the job and hypnotised and subsidised him into it. Whenever possible, I got a man with an English or American wife . . . The results have been very varied . . . Printing operations to save lapse of copyright have been costly, and, on the whole, I have perhaps consulted my own peace of mind in not making out the total profit and loss account. The trouble, including occasional lawsuits, is sometimes so devilish that I curse the day when international copyright was invented, and wish the whole world were like Holland and Russia, out of the Berne Convention. Still, when I get the pirates thoroughly intimidated by reckless litigation and my men trained, there will be much less bother.'

This bother was part of Shaw's complicated 'peace of mind' which depended upon 'losing himself' in a vast quantity of mechanical work. He chose his translators eccentrically – because they charmed him, touched his sense of humour or presented impeccable political credentials. That one man wished to combine the translation of his plays with the profession of dental surgeon; that another had the part of Marchbanks played by a woman; that 'the Bernard Shaw of Spain' was reputed to be a Belgian at home only in his native tongue – all this tickled him. His most extreme translators were Augustin and Henriette Hamon. He was a socialist and an anarchist of 'terrific intellectual integrity ... whose main means of subsistence has always been borrowing money'; she knew some English, which was helpful. Hamon had actually sent Shaw a young Frenchman, then studying in London, recommending him as a translator of *Man and Superman*. Shaw's response was to invite Hamon himself to become his French translator. Stupefied, Hamon did what he could to wriggle away. He did not have English, was not a literary man, had never written a play and knew little of the theatre. It was true that he had published a number of works on hygiene and sociology and also the *Psychologie militaire professionelle*. It was also true that he was the radical editor of *L'Humanité Nouvelle*, a periodical frequently visited by the police. His literary experience was, in Shaw's own summing-up, 'that of a desperado – an editor of impossible reviews and the author of such desperate pamphlets as these reviews live on'. Yet Shaw seemed determined to prove Hamon 'a born homme de théâtre'. Hamon was 'as obstinate as twenty thousand devils', but he did not have the obstinacy of G.B.S. He offered, in his place as French translator, a Russian Jew with an alliterative double-barrelled name – but Shaw was hardly tempted. Hamon's contemporaries used to say of him with surprise what had been said of Robespierre: 'He believes everything he says.' It was a more difficult job to believe what Shaw said of him: that he had the literary dexterity of Sardou. Nevertheless, despite his protests, he had found himself before the end of 1903 appointed Shaw's authorized translator into French: 'He had about as much notion of becoming a translator of plays,' Shaw remembered, 'as of becoming a banker ... I beguiled him into it.' Shaw's reasons for beguiling Hamon were peculiar. That Hamon was an individual bicyclist and a walking revolutionary with exemplary collectivist principles obviously pleased him. 'I knew very well what I was about,' he wrote. As evidence of his good choice, he pointed to the 'dramatic liveliness' of Hamon's reports on various socialist congresses. By this he meant that Hamon would understand the modern social organism that was at the centre of his plays, which was far more essential than the knowledge of dramatic devices that would in any case take care of themselves. 'My plays are studies in the natural history of mankind,' he told Hamon.

55

' . . . To make life intelligible & interesting, you have to select typical incidents & typical people, & shew how they act and re-act upon one another by clearing away all the accidents and irrelevances which in actual life obscure their relations, . . . arranging the incidents to shew their true economic, social and emotional relations to one another . . . This, according to me, is the whole function of the dramatist.'

So Shaw bought a Larousse dictionary and set about becoming a co-translator of his plays into the French language. Soon he was pouring out plans for the sets and prescriptions against his women characters speaking like bishops; to the typescript of *On ne peut jamais dire* (which suggested a speech impediment) he added the picture of a butterfly being broken on a wheel. He enjoyed firing off letters in a French that was so 'extremely Brittannic' that it 'must be positively painful' to any man of literary sensibility to read them. ' "Hard as nails" – "dure comme un clou" – is an expression which ought', he judged, 'to enrich the French language.' The Hamons were able, he discovered, to concentrate into ten amazing lines of their translated text 'all the errors which I spend my life in combating'. Hamon was additionally a man without humour. He had no notion that he might be translating comedies, and once rushed from the theatre when the audience began to laugh, crying to his wife, *'Mon Dieu! On rit. Tout est perdu.'*

All Shaw's schooling could not make these bad translations good. They were caustically attacked in France as forming a permanent barrier to the acceptance of Shaw's plays by the French public, though G.B.S. claimed that Hamon had made enemies by being 'too faithful to me instead of turning my works into Parisian articles'. Shaw's private letters to Hamon reveal, however, that he clearly saw their limitations. Hamon never fathomed 'the utter illiteracy of the playgoing public', to prepare for which, Shaw reminded him, Molière used to read his plays aloud to his cook. The great failing of the Frenchman, Shaw maintained, was his academicism. 'Every Frenchman is a born pedant,' he advised Hamon. 'He thinks it a crime to repeat a word – the crime of tautology.'

'He wants to have in every sentence a subject, a predicate, a noun, a verb, a complete grammatical structure. Now on the stage, where the word is spoken, and so much depends on the way it is spoken, grammatical completeness does not matter at all. If a string of interjections or broken phrases will give the meaning, so much the better. So far from it being a crime to repeat words and phrases, it is the worst of crimes to vary them, since the effect is often lost by doing so. Ne cherchez pas le style: cherchez toujours la vie.'

To protect his copyright, Shaw paid for the publication of the first seven of his plays in the Hamons' translations, in editions of one hundred copies each, in 1908. 'These copies will someday be scarce & sell at high prices,' Shaw warned Hamon who, despite the pleas of many eminent translators (including André Antoine, founder of the Théâtre Libre), went on to translate almost all Shaw's plays. Only seven or eight of these plays were eventually produced in Paris, not at the commercial *théâtres du boulevard* but the small *coterie* theatres. 'I have given up all hope of getting into touch with France,' Shaw conceded in the 1920s, shortly before the success of *Saint Joan*. 'Every attempt I have made has been baffled on the ground that it would offend French susceptibilities; and as my journalistic tactics are nothing but attacks on susceptibilities – whether English, Irish, or American, makes no difference – to insist on my respecting French susceptibilities is to silence me completely.'

'This is all the more annoying as I do not believe for a moment that the French reading public is less accessible to my methods than any other public . . . as a matter of business I wrote France off my books as a dud country years ago . . . But I still believe that if only I could have secured a pulpit in France, I could have amused the inhabitants quite as effectively as the Germans.'

Between Hamon and Shaw, as between Trebitsch and Shaw, a current of gratitude had been switched on. In the words of Vicomte Robert d'Humières, Shaw became attached to his translator 'like a criminal is attached to the rope which hanged him'. It was 'a defiant and heroic act', intensely Shavian, that would end in 'suicide on the threshold of our admiration'. To a perpetual gunfire of criticism Hamon dug in for the rest of his life with the work he had never wanted to do, lecturing with deep solemnity on Shaw at universities, and placing many articles about his work in scholarly journals. With three daughters, he and his wife remained desperately poor. 'Dont you recognize it', Shaw asked him, 'as a frightful defect in yourself that you are indifferent to money and care for nothing but abstractions?' Feeling perhaps his own part in the Hamons' poverty, he purchased their house in Brittany for them and in the 1930s bought 'an annuity for his own and his wife's life, of £12 a month', Shaw revealed to Trebitsch. 'And this enables him to live comfortably according to his standard of comfort.'

Trebitsch and Hamon were two principal members of Shaw's family of translators over whom he exercised great power and generosity. The antagonism which their amateur status and exclusive rights brought them in their own countries intensified their loyalty. They became part of a special Shavian clan, their intimacy seldom tested by an actual meeting, through which Shaw aimed to work his will. He worked to his heart's content at reviving himself through these chosen men and women. Like pollen in the wind, his words were spread by such agents of the Life Force operating in conspiracy with the Shavian Will.

'I am before all things a believer in the power of Will (Volonté),' Shaw instructed Hamon. 'I believe that all evolution has been produced by Will, and that the reason you are Hamon the Anarchist, instead of being a blob of protoplasmic slime in a ditch, is that there was at work in the Universe a Will which required brains & hands to do its work & therefore evolved your brains & your hands.'

[2]

Nothing is worse than giving your whole attention to things that do not really interest you at all. (1904)

A true dramatist should be interested in everything. (1903)

Charlotte treated her husband partly as an employer, partly as her child. It was the employer whose correspondence she dealt with, whose manuscripts she revised and took to the typist. She also arranged lunches with people he should meet and protected him from other people who would worry him needlessly. It was on behalf of this employer, too, that she still sat on committees at the London School of Economics and the School of Medicine for Women, and had joined the play-reading committee of the Stage Society.

But it was the child who exercised her talent for anxiety. Some of his young hobbies – photography or the pianola – were harmless and even rather fun. She didn't mind him taking her picture in the least (though she hated others doing so) and she grew to like his playing to her in the evening. Bicycles were dangerous: he was always toppling off them; and he often did other very naughty things – writing to the newspapers, for example, after the Queen died to denounce the rapturous lying-in-state as 'insanitary' and to recommend, as socially invaluable, her quick cremation or shallow burial in a perishable coffin.

A lot of these high spirits were probably symptoms of his genius – as were his teetotalism and vegetarianism. She had given instructions to the servants to vary his diet as much as possible, and from time to time felt half-persuaded of its efficacy herself. Whenever she was unwell she would pick at something of his vegetarian food, more or less, washed down with a glass of whisky. 'My wife has at last become a convinced vegetarian,' Shaw ironically reported to Henry Salt in the summer of 1903, ' . . . and she now eats nothing but birds & fish, which are not "butcher's meat".'

'She is also converted to simplicity of life, and now, although we have both a town & country residence, we keep no horses and spend hardly £3,000 a year on our housekeeping. I have great hopes of reducing this ultimately to £2,500, especially as Charlotte is never happy except when we are staying in some grubby public house out of reach of the servants & the two residences.'

It was not surprising perhaps, though still distressing, that someone who caricatured things as recklessly as he did should himself become the subject of public caricature. Included in Max Beerbohm's first one-man show at the Carfax Gallery towards the end of 1901 were a couple of Beerbohm drawings. One, a 'frontispiece' to *Three Plays for Puritans*, showed G.B.S. in Salvation Army uniform with a periodical, 'The Shaw Cry', sticking out of his pocket. One of his hands points to heaven; the other rests on the shoulder of a prostitute who is asking him, ''Ow should I earn my livin'?' The second cartoon depicted G.B.S., the erstwhile champion of the oppressed, as a fat plutocrat above the caption 'Popular Notion of Bernard Shaw since Marriage'. When Shaw looked in at the gallery, he found Charlotte on the point of buying this second drawing 'with the object of concealing or destroying it as a libel on her husband's charms' – and he dashed off a note to tell Beerbohm the story.

Charlotte regarded G.B.S.'s lust for publicity as part of the odder equipment of his genius. There was no other respectable way of explaining it. In the case of Max Beerbohm, for example, he had literally *asked* for what he got, arriving at the Beerbohms' house on his bicycle and requesting the cartoonist to do a drawing of him. 'Max was less gratified by this than might have been expected,' Lord David Cecil wrote. 'He realized that he was as yet an amateur in his art and suspected that Shaw was actuated less by admiration than by a desire for the publicity the cartoon might bring him.'

'Max also found Shaw's appearance unappetizing; his pallid pitted skin and red hair like seaweed. And he was repelled by the back of his neck. "The back of his neck was especially bleak; very long, untenanted, and dead white," he explained.'

Max seemed inspired by his dislike of Shaw's appearance and opinions. He did over forty caricatures of G.B.S.'s 'temperance beverage face' and, as dramatic critic, reviewed more than twenty of his plays. 'My admiration for his genius has during fifty years and more been marred for me by dissent from almost any view that he holds about anything,' Max was to acknowledge in a letter written for Shaw's ninetieth birthday. And G.B.S. endorsed this: 'Max's blessings are all of them thinly disguised curses.'

Shaw knew that Max was activated not so much by malevolence as genuine antipathy. Shaw, he seems to have felt, was a good man who had come under the bad influence of himself. 'I am afraid he is afraid of me,' Max decided; and though he may have extended his pinpricks into rapier thrusts, there is no doubt that he unsettled Shaw. 'I saw ... the waxen effigy of G.B.S. when I was in London,' he wrote to his friend Reggie Turner. 'I thought it might form a good basis for a caricature.'

'Some days later I was lunching at his place, and I mentioned the effigy to him; at which he flushed slightly, and waved his hands, and said he had *had* to give Tussaud a sitting as "it would have seemed so *snobbish* to refuse". Considering that it had been the proudest day in his life, I was rather touched by this account of the matter.'

One of the reasons why Max discomforted G.B.S. was that he reinforced the disgust Shaw himself felt at the Shavian publicity phenomenon. After a couple of highly successful speeches in Glasgow during the first week of October 1903 – an overture for his 'succulent' pamphlet, *The Commonsense of Municipal Trading*, which was published the following February, he wrote to Trebitsch: 'I have hardly yet quite recovered from the self-loathing which such triumphs produce ... '

'I always suffer torments of remorse when the degrading exhibition is over. However, the thing had to be done; and there was no doing it by halves ... I am not at all ashamed of what I said: it was excellent sense; but the way I said it – ugh! All that assumption of stupendous earnestness – merely to drive a little common sense into a crowd, like nails into a very tough board – leaves one empty, exhausted, disgusted.'

Max and Charlotte, when they sat next to each other at dinner several years later, found themselves in agreement over G.B.S. He was never an artist, they chimed, but a reformer. 'That is what I always tell him,' insisted Charlotte. But in their married life it was she who attempted to reform him. She tried to introduce him to leisure, admit him to a little privacy. Since it was only on holiday that, as he put it, 'I prefer to leave my public character behind me and to be treated as far as possible as a quite private and unknown individual', she tried to lead him on a succession of long holidays. During April and May 1901 she had him touring through

France with her; and in July and August she planted him in Studland Rectory at Corfe Castle in Dorset. 'This is a very enchanting place – to look at,' Shaw informed Beatrice Webb. 'It also has the curious property of reviving every malady, every cramp, every pain, every bone fracture even, from which one has ever suffered. And I have neatly slit my big toe into two symmetrical halves by stepping on a sharp flint whilst bathing.'

Next year Charlotte packed them both off to a safe hotel on the Norfolk coast for the summer. 'The only way to rest and get plenty of work done at the same time is to go to sea,' Shaw later concluded. Left to himself, he travelled only for work. 'I am off tomorrow morning to Bruges to see the collection of Flemish art there,' he told Ensor Walters in September 1902: 'it is a sort of thing I must see as a matter of business as the chance may never occur again during my lifetime as a critic.' This was not what Charlotte had in mind. She wanted to take him away from all his business and papers and interviews and occupations. She wanted to banish the employer and make him wholly, for a time, her child. His obsession with work exasperated her: if it was good for him why was he attacked so regularly by headaches? 'G.B.S. is not at all well,' she was to instruct Trebitsch. 'I wish I could persuade him to go with you to Egypt: I know that is what he wants – sun and rest! However he will not move for anyone, and he works all day . . . '

She did her best. In the spring of 1903 she rushed him through Parma, Perugia, Assisi, Orvieto, Siena, Genoa and Milan. 'I am getting old and demoralized,' he confessed to Janet Achurch, 'I have been in Italy for three weeks . . . ' Three months later she placed him in Scotland, and held him there for ten weeks. 'There is no railway, no town, no shops, no society, no music, no entertainments, no beautiful ladies, absolutely nothing but fresh air and eternal rain,' Shaw invited Trebitsch (who decided not to join them). 'Our house is primitive; our food is primitive; we do nothing but wander about, cycle against impossible winds, or pull a heavy fisherman's boat about the loch . . . '

Charlotte developed a vicarious ingenuity over their travelling. 'I *must*, it appears, clear out to give the servants a holiday & the spring cleaners a chance,' Shaw complained on one occasion. For most Christmases Charlotte would board him out with her at a bracing hotel or in one of the houses she had rented. In April 1902 they had given up Piccard's Cottage at Guildford and the following year took instead a country house, Maybury Knoll, in a favourite part of Surrey, near Woking, 'within an hour of Charing +'. Here they spent winter weekends and the whole of Christmas at the end of 1903, after which Charlotte was to rent a grander place which she liked better. The Old House was 'a 16th or at latest 17th century house – a gem', Shaw wrote to Ellen Terry. 'Welwyn is 2 miles off: we are at Harmer Green, on the other side of the line and only half a mile from the station. Also at the top of the hill.'

No sooner had Charlotte marched him up to the top of the hill than she marched him down again – and back to Italy. Her hyperbolical anticipation of the delights of each place they were about to visit was so quickly disappointed that she had to keep on the move: from Turin to Pisa, from Pisa to Rome and, on their way back, from Rome to Geneva. They had started out on 1 May 1904 and arrived back in London on 10 June. A week later Shaw began a new play, his thirteenth, to be called *John Bull's Other Island.* Charlotte shuttled him between Adelphi Terrace and Harmer Green, and then returned him, protesting, for the summer to Scotland. 'Our expedition has been so far a ruinous failure,' he calculated. 'The place is impossible – no place to write – no place to bathe – the inn a new tumor on an old public house in a village shed – the firth a sludgy morass except at high tide. The journey wrecked me; put me out of my stride; lost me four days work for nothing. Oh these holidays, these accursed holidays!'

Over all Charlotte's peripatetic interruptions Shaw was extraordinarily self-controlled. For fourteen years they were to campaign through every holiday side by side, despite his belief that married people 'should never travel together: they blame one another for everything that goes wrong'. It was particularly irritating for him to see how she preened herself on toning up his health while really driving him mad; it was exasperating for her to find, however exorbitant their journeys, he never failed to carry his work with him, everywhere. But still they manacled themselves, each for the sake of the other: it was the true *reductio ad absurdum* of marriage. 'I am overacting the part of a respectable married man,' Shaw admitted. 'But I am only rehearsing for my old age: my guiltiest passions are still glowing beneath the surface.'

[3]

I am not writing popular plays just now. (1901)

I never go to the theatre now. (1901)

'You know all about "The Admirable Bashville", or at least you would know if you ever read my books,' Trebitsch read in one of Shaw's letters. ' . . . It would be impossible to translate it, first, because it would be necessary to raise Tieck and Schlegel from the grave to write the blank verse, and second, because the hero is a prizefighter, and Germans know nothing about English prizefighting, and would not enjoy a burlesque of it.'

The Admirable Bashville or *Constancy Unrewarded* was itself a translation from Shaw's novel, *Cashel Byron's Profession*, into a three-act play in what Shaw called 'the primitive Elizabethan style'. This was his eleventh play and he had finished it in a week on 2 February 1901. He did everything to make 'my confounded foolishnesses' irresistibly absurd in order to ridicule the anomalies in copyright law at that time. He had heard rumours that there were several pirated stage versions of his novel in America. One had been produced at Herald Square Theatre in New York at the end of 1900, and when it was proposed to bring this production to Britain, Shaw 'took the opportunity to produce a masterpiece' in order to protect his copyright. He squeezed out of this exercise all the fun he could, using it as another squib against bardolatry and claiming that he had been forced to employ the rigmarole of Shakespearian verse (of which 'I am childishly fond'), occasionally patching in actual lines from Shakespeare and Marlowe, because he did not have the time to write it all in prose. Having plagiarized his own work and parodied Shakespeare's, he produced a caricature of his advertising methods. 'The best of everything is good enough for me,' he conceded at the play's first presentation: it was, he assured Trebitsch, 'my greatest play'. But this delight in what he told Hilaire Belloc was 'my only achievement in pure letters' began to recoil once other playwrights hit on the notion of agreeing with him. 'Henry Arthur [Jones] implores me to pursue this wonderful vein & recognize that my true genius lies in burlesque,' he told William Archer.

'Unfortunately, as I have to write the works in burlesque, I should have to spend the latter half of my life caricaturing the former half, which I am likely enough to do without any prompting & with the most serious intentions.'

A number of Shaw's 'serious intentions' are planted in the burlesque. He has some fun with phonetics; he airs his expertise on self-defence; he owns up to the loneliness of excellence and devotes some mighty lines to family and filial sentiment.

> . . . Oh, mothers, mothers,
> Would you but let your wretched sons alone
> Life were worth living! Had I any choice
> In this importunate relationship?
> None. And until that high auspicious day

When the millennium on an orphaned world
Shall dawn, and man upon his fellow look,
Reckless of consanguinity, my mother
And I within the self-same hemisphere
Conjointly may not dwell.

Also autobiographical are Cashel Byron's ill thoughts on political elections.

> . . . When your friends
> Contest elections, and at foot o' th' poll
> Rue their presumption, tis their wont to claim
> A moral victory. In a sort they are
> Nature's MPs.

And there is a surge of real feeling when Cashel contrasts the presumed barbarities of boxing with the concealed cruelties of polite life.

> . . . this hand
> That many a two days bruise hath ruthless given,
> Hath kept no dungeon locked for twenty years,
> Hath slain no sentient creature for my sport.
> I am too squeamish for your dainty world,
> That cowers behind the gallows and the lash,
> The world that robs the poor, and with their spoil
> Does what its tradesmen tell it. Oh, your ladies!
> Sealskinned and egret-feathered; all defiance
> To Nature; cowering if one say to them
> 'What will the servants think?' Your gentlemen!
> Your tailor-tyrannized visitors of whom
> Flutter of wing and singing in the wood
> Make chickenbutchers. And your medicine men!
> Groping for cures in the tormented entrails
> Of friendly dogs. Pray have you asked all these
> To change their occupations? Find you mine
> So grimly crueller? I cannot breathe
> An air so petty and so poisonous.

Shaw assisted Harley Granville Barker in directing the first professional presentation of the play, put on by the Stage Society on 7 and 8 June 1903 at the Imperial Theatre in London 'as a joke to wind up the last evening[s] of the season'. It was an early instance of the working association between the two men, and laid down the lines for their later collaborative work at the Court Theatre. Barker was (in the modern sense) stage-manager and

Shaw arrived fairly late in the preparation of his play, giving the effect of upsetting the work Barker had already done with the actors. He hunted enthusiastically for props (bird-whistles, some soft-nosed spears, a white beaver hat, a post-horn, one crimson and one enormous blue handkerchief with white spots, a moss-grown tree trunk, one throne: also 'We shall want a crowd'); and directed it in the Elizabethan stage manner with traverses, and two beefeaters with placards denoting the scenes. Despite a facetious programme note, Shaw insisted that it should not be called a burlesque, but announced simply as 'Bernard Shaw's celebrated drama in blank verse ... the only authorized dramatic version of the author's famous novel ... ' – with, possibly, an epigraph: '"If you have tears, prepare to shed them now." Shakespeare.'

As in his subsequent 'Interlude', *The Dark Lady of the Sonnets*, the humour is literary and depends upon the audience's familiarity with Shakespeare. Those with no Shakespearian knowledge would sit bewildered or else, in all earnestness, break into applause. Despite its awkward playing length, the Stage Society production 'went with a roar from beginning to end', he reported. The policeman (played by the cricketer C. Aubrey Smith, later to become famous as a Hollywood film actor) was made up as G.B.S. and satirized him so effectively that his aunt Georgina felt convinced he had played the part and his mother, sitting next to him, was deeply perplexed. 'I had a very good cast,' he told Trebitsch; 'and there was great laughter, and as many press notices as if it had been Caesar and Cleopatra at Drury Lane.' Max Beerbohm, who came to the first of the two nights, wrote of this 'strangely prolonged convulsion' in the *Saturday Review*: 'The right way to act it is to take it quite seriously, reproducing in all their beauty the sonorous elocution and dignified deportment of the traditional Shakespearean mimes. Pre-eminently ... this trick was performed.'

Also performed was the copyright trick of upstaging all American dramatizations of the novel including, in 1906, a popular one by Stanislas Strange (who was to write the libretto for *The Chocolate Soldier*) and starring, as Cashel Byron, former world heavyweight champion 'Gentleman Jim' Corbett.

The Admirable Bashville was published by Grant Richards in October 1901 as part of a new edition of *Cashel Byron's Profession* that also included Shaw's essay 'A Note on Modern Prizefighting'. As he had promised ten years earlier, every purchaser was to have 'a first class fight for his money'. The book was reviewed at length, and disconcertingly, by Max Beerbohm. 'Mr Shaw is fully himself in it, and throughout it. It tallies with all his recent work,' Beerbohm claimed.

'We hear the loud, rhythmic machinery of this brain at work. The book vibrates to it as does a steamer to the screw; and we, the passengers, rejoice in the sound of it, for we know that tremendous speed is being made. As a passage by steam is to a voyage by sail, so is Mr Shaw's fiction to true fiction . . . he wants to impress certain theories on us, to convert us to this or that view. The true creator wishes mainly to illude us with a sense of actual or imaginative reality. To achieve that aim, he must suppress himself and his theories: they kill illusion. He must accept life as it presents itself to his experience or imagination, not use his brain to twist it into the patterns of a purpose. Such self-sacrifice is beyond Mr Shaw.'

Here was the most coherent argument so far raised against the Shavian art. Shaw could not create: his characters were all victims of Shavian theses, all parts of himself differentiated only by quick changes and superficial idiosyncrasies. On another level, as a personality, Shaw was immortal. There was no one like him. Seriousness and frivolity, threaded in and out of each other, were the essence of Shavianism. 'He is not a serious man trying to be frivolous,' Beerbohm explained. 'He is a serious man who cannot help being frivolous, and in him height of spirits is combined with depth of conviction more illustriously than in any of his compatriots . . .'

'Even when he sets out to be funny for fun's sake, he must needs always pretend that there is a serious reason for the emprise; and he pretends so strenuously that he ends by convincing us almost as fully as he convinces himself. Thus the absurdity, whatever it be, comes off doubly well. Conversely, even when he is really engrossed in some process of serious argument, or moved to real eloquence by one of his social ideals, he emits involuntarily some wild jape which makes the whole thing ridiculous – as ridiculous to himself as to us; and straightaway he proceeds to caricature his own thesis till everything is topsy-turvy; and we, rolling with laughter, look up and find him no longer on his head, but on his heels, talking away quite gravely ; and this sets us off again.'

Shaw was a serious man incapacitated from maintaining true seriousness through his work: that was Beerbohm's depth-charge. It did not matter what he wrote. All his writing was filleted with Shavianism – that quality whose deep seriousness of tone served artistically to raise the humour. 'As a teacher, as a propagandist, Mr Shaw is no good at all,' Beerbohm joyfully concluded. It was as a comedian whose frivolity, vampire-like, sucked the seriousness from his work, that he was unique. So when he claimed apropos his next play, Man and Superman, that 'the matter isnt really in my hands. I have to say the things that seem to me to want saying', everyone sharing Beerbohm's view of G.B.S. drew in their breath and prepared to greet it with a rousing laugh.

[4]

My latest play is very unlike Candida. You must not translate it, as you would get six years in a fortress for the preface alone.
Shaw to Trebitsch (7 July 1902)

The characters had started talking inside Shaw's head over two years before. In May 1900 he began outlining a Parliament in Hell between Don Juan and the Devil – the third act of what he provisionally called *The Superman, or Don Juan's great grandson's grandson*. 'My next play will be a Don Juan,' he announced the following month, ' – an immense play, but not for the stage of this generation.' Around the Socratic debate he composed a three-act comedy, completing the scenario between 2 July and 8 October 1901. He worked between accidents and on journeys, in hotels and at home: he worked whenever Charlotte took her eye off him, 'pulling it straight', and adding 'prefaces and postfaces' until, in June 1902, this many-layered work, now called *Man and Superman. A Comedy and a Philosophy*, was finished – when the business of revision ('a longish job') immediately began. By January 1903 it had evolved far enough for Shaw to read it aloud to the Webbs, Graham Wallas and his wife and Charlotte at the Overstrand Hotel at Cromer in Norfolk. '[I]t has taken a whole week to get through [it],' he wrote, 'even with the preface omitted.' In fact the three friends and their wives were staying by the sea for a whole week and Shaw's reading lasted 'three delightful evenings', Beatrice recorded in her diary. 'To me it seems a great work; quite the biggest thing he has done,' she wrote. 'He has found his *form*: a play which is not a play; but only a combination of essay, treatise, interlude, lyric – all the different forms illustrating the same central idea.'

Shaw continued struggling through revision and towards publication that summer. Since it was 'useless as an acting play', he explained to Hamon, being 'as long as three Meyerbeer operas and no audience that had not already had a Shaw education could stand it', he had decided to publish *Man and Superman* as a book. 'I am printing it on my own account,' he told the photographer Frederick Evans, 'and will publish on commission, abandoning [Grant] Richards this time . . . Can you suggest anything?' Of the publishers he had already approached, John Murray had replied that in his old-fashioned view the book was *wicked*; and Methuen 'opened his mouth too wide as to terms'. Evans suggested Archibald Constable with whom Shaw came to terms as commission agent for his works in the early summer of 1903 – an agreement of a few lines on a sheet of writing paper that lasted the remaining forty-seven years of his life. 'You virtually shifted me to Constable, and changed my system,' Shaw congratulated Grant Richards; 'and it is now inevitable in the course of business that I should get all my books into my own hands & work the thing myself. I am growing old & avaricious & fond of handling capital instead of being dry nursed like the ordinary author-duffer.'

Shaw treated Constable as he treated other publishers. 'The first thing to grasp in this matter is that you are hopelessly and entirely in the wrong, and that I am absolutely and solidly in the right.' For the firm's two partners, Otto Kyllmann and William Maxse Meredith, he developed a degree of affection that enabled him to object, for aesthetic reasons, to the firm's Christian name which, he explained, 'does not fit my page at all. An alteration of Archibald to Osbaldiston would just do it.' In 1910 Constable jettisoned Archibald.

Man and Superman was published on 11 August 1903. The most interesting reviews – those by William Archer in the *Morning Leader*, G. K. Chesterton in the *Daily News* and Max Beerbohm in the *Saturday Review* – were remarkably similar in their admiration of the author mixed with criticism of his book. Archer compared Shaw's work, as dramatic art, unfavourably with that of Pinero; and in a letter went on to complain that in no sense was G.B.S. 'making the mark either upon literature or upon life, that you have it in you to make'.

'The years are slipping away . . . and you have done nothing really big, nothing original, solid, first-rate, enduring . . . You are a great force wasted . . .

'You say "*your* men are Wagner, Ibsen, Tolstoy, Schopenhauer, Nietzsche" – I should reverse it & say you are *their* man. Why should this be? Why should you always be flying somebody else's banner and shouting somebody else's war-cry, with only the addition of your own Irish accent?'

In the *Daily News* the paradoxing optimist confronted the paradoxical pessimist. The play was 'fascinating', 'delightful', 'bewilderingly interesting', Chesterton acknowledged. But it betrayed Shaw's central fallacy. 'He has always prided himself on seeing things and men as they are. He has never really done so: as one might have guessed from his not admiring them.'

'The truth is that he has all the time been silently comparing humanity with something that was not human, with a monster from Mars, with the Wise Man of the Stoics, with Julius Caesar, with Siegfried, with the Superman . . . And this is what Mr Shaw has always secretly done. When we really see men as they are, we do not criticise, but worship.'

Because Shaw found present conditions unbearable he had to invent, as symbols of future improvement, a series of characters who, Chesterton suggested, did artificially what most people did naturally.

Shaw used such criticisms as flames with which to temper the Shavian steel. Surely a man whose mornings, given to playwriting, were 'followed by afternoons and evenings spent in the committee rooms of a London Borough Council, fighting questions of drainage, paving, lighting, rates, clerks' salaries' knew more about 'things and men as they are' than those members of the Dramatists' Club who had made the theatre into 'that last sanctuary of unreality'. As to art, that depended not upon empty virtuosity but the depth of an author's opinions. Who then would say that G.B.S. was unopinionated? 'I cannot be a bellettrist,' he had written in his Preface.

'Effectiveness of assertion is the Alpha and Omega of style. He who has nothing to assert has no style and can have none: he who has something to assert will go as far in power of style as its momentousness and his conviction will carry him. Disprove his assertion after it is made, yet its style remains.'

Between style and art and power and reality Shaw crossed the lines of his argument with such dexterity as to bring almost everyone into confusion. Critics, still adhering to their weapons, were fixed in his net of words – though not the miniature critic Max Beerbohm. He seemed to slip between the meshes, sometimes using Shaw's own standards and finding Shaw lacking in them. In the Preface, for example, Shaw had pronounced his contempt on writers 'so in love with oratory' that they 'delight in repeating as much as they can understand of what others have said or written aforetime'. Max was to draw a caricature of Shaw bringing a bundle of clothes to the Dutch critic, Georg Brandes (who is represented as a pawnbroker) and asking for immortality in exchange for the lot. Brandes protests: 'Come, I've handled these goods before! Coat, Mr Schopenhauer's; waistcoat, Mr Ibsen's; Mr Nietzsche's trousers – .' To which Shaw answers: 'Ah, but look at the patches!' As for oratory, Max astutely judged the style and construction of his narrative, his Alpha and Omega, to be 'more akin to the art of oral debating than of literary exposition. That is because he trained himself to speak before he trained himself to write.'

For the same reason, Max conceded, Shaw excelled in writing words to be spoken by the human voice. 'In swiftness, tenseness and lucidity of dialogue no living writer can touch the hem of Mr Shaw's garment,' Max wrote. 'In *Man and Superman* every phrase rings and flashes. Here, though Mr Shaw will be angry with me, is perfect art.' For Shaw *used* art. He used it 'as a means of making people listen to him', and of appealing 'most quickly to the greatest number of people'.

'He is as eager to be a popular dramatist and . . . willing to demean himself in any way that may help him to the goal . . . I hope he will reach the goal. It is only the theatrical managers who stand between him and the off-chance of a real popular success.'

Man and Superman, Max concluded, was Shaw's masterpiece so far. This 'most complete expression of the most distinct personality in current literature' showed G.B.S. able to employ art without becoming an artist and excelling in dialogue without developing into a playwright. Max's instinctive response to the play-within-the-book, though similar to that of Archer and of Chesterton, was less easy for Shaw to wave aside. The letter he sent to Max after reading his review moves from outspokenness to rudeness and back. 'This wont do,' he told him. 'Your article in the Saturday is most laborious, most conscientious: the spasms of compliment almost draw tears; but the whole thing is wrong: the *gene* of offended academicism makes it almost unreadable.'

' . . . You idiot, do you suppose I dont know my own powers? . . . Quit the theatre & *draw* for a living. Shake the Playgoers' dust off your shoes. Abjure Academicism. Urgent. Important. Forward immediately.'

Max's response to Shaw's play had been similar to Shaw's response to Max's criticism of the play and he used the same words of dismissal with which Shaw had begun his letter. 'My specific objection to your John [Tanner] and Ann [Whitefield] is that neither he in his passiveness nor she in her activity draws any ordinary human breath,' Max wrote. 'Such life as they have comes by artificial respiration of your own wit and ratiocinativeness.'

'Ann doesn't throw herself at John's head. You throw her. John gets slight concussion of the brain. If either had a heart, it would be a diseased one, and your rough violence would be dangerous. But there is no rudiment of a heart in either of them . . . That is why Anne and John, as types, won't do.'

From this opinion Max somewhat recanted two years later when he saw *Man and Superman* (in its three-act version) performed on stage. It was not only the humanizing of Shaw's words by living actors that changed his mind. He also appears to have been swayed by Shaw's argument that, as a caricaturist, Max also did not 'see things and men as they are', but that his unnatural distortions, far from disqualifying him as an artist, were the essential style of his art. The artist creates his own reality and his own epoch: and Britain was about to enter a Shavian epoch. Max sensed this. Shaw was one of those for whom the visible world had largely ceased to exist and was being replaced by a world seen through his mind's eye. That it was a world disliked by Max was partly the reason why he had denied its creator artistic capacity. He had argued (as had Archer) that, but for the blindness of theatrical managers, Shaw might be a box office success with his plays-that-were-not-plays. The production of *John Bull's Other Island* in 1904 was to convince him that Shaw had 'an instinct for the theatre'. And so, when in 1905 he saw *Man and Superman* on stage, he 'climbed down' with much generosity and prophetic judgement, and prepared to make way for the coming Shavian revolution in the British theatre:

'Mr Shaw, it is insisted, cannot draw life: he can only distort it. He has no knowledge of human nature: he is but a theorist. All his characters are but so many incarnations of himself. Above all, he cannot write plays. He has no dramatic instinct, no theatrical technique . . .

'That theory might have held water in the days before Mr Shaw's plays were acted. Indeed, I was in the habit of propounding it myself . . . When *Man and Superman* was published, I called it "Mr Shaw's Dialogues", and said that (even without the philosophic scene in hell) it would be quite unsuited to any stage. When I saw it performed, I determined that I would not be caught tripping again. I found that as a piece of theatrical construction it was perfect . . . to deny that he is a dramatist merely because he chooses, for the most part, to get drama out of contrasted types of character and thought, without action, and without appeal to the emotions, seems to me both unjust and absurd. His technique is peculiar because his purpose is peculiar. But it is not the less technique.'

*

Twenty years before, after reading Henry George's *Progress and Poverty*, Shaw had accepted 'the importance of the economic basis'. Training himself as a public speaker, he had advanced experimentally into the world of politics, but found that political life left much of his talent unemployed. Following such incidents as Bloody Sunday in Trafalgar Square, he came to acknowledge his unfittedness for pell-mell politics. 'Think of me always as the hero of a thousand defeats,' he was to write; 'it is only on paper and in imagination that I do anything brave.'

Man and Superman is the first in a trilogy of plays. Shaw was to display the full plumage of his talent in an area of political philosophy he had previously marked as barren ground occupied only by the middle class. Ten years before he had reconciled communism with 'uncompromising Individualism'; in a wider sense he had come to believe that an uncompromising exercise of individual talent achieved the best co-operation with the collective will, or what he now called the Life Force.

By turning away from a Parliamentary career, Shaw was giving up nothing. He translated the facts of his life into a spiritual autobiography. His thesis and antithesis of fact and fantasy produced the synthesis of evolutionary progress – a formula for absorbing his own needs into a universal pattern. Creative evolution had the potential for replacing his lonely sense of being 'a sojourner on this planet rather than a native of it' with the feeling of being part of the corporate consciousness 'up to the chin in the life of his own time'. It gave his talent a use and his writing career a sense of purpose. The Life Force was not a rival scientific theory to Darwin's Natural Selection, but a fundamentally opposed philosophy implying a different outlook on life. By making external a division he felt to exist within himself Shaw was able to use an intellectual method – the Hegelian triad which he had picked up from the British socialist philosopher E. Belfort Bax – of reconciling opposites and bringing harmony to his life. Through an effort of will and a sustained act of faith he wished to create the new drama in which, as in a series of parables, he could rewrite history and set it on a new course.

The Hegelian structure became a model for his thought, working in terms of dramatic dialogue and as a metaphor for conception and birth. Reviewing a novel by Moncure Conway early in 1888, he had written of Hegelianism having entered German socialism, adding that 'its positive side had never been adapted and translated into practical English politics, and it remained, in the hands of Marx, chiefly effective as a scathing but quite negative criticism of industrial individualism'.

It was this positive Hegelianism, as a force for unification in place of the civil war of employers versus employees, that Shaw wanted to import into English politics. His 'old friend and fellow-heretic' Belfort Bax, 'a ruthless critic of current morality', had shown in *The Ethics of Socialism* and *A Handbook of the History of Philosophy* that such a thing might be done. By turning to the theatre Shaw hoped to send his ideas rather than himself into the House of Commons. This is made explicit in a letter he sent some fifteen years later to the Labour Member of Parliament Charles

Trevelyan. 'We shall never make any headway against the old order as long as it has a solid and settled mind, and we are an intellectual mob,' Shaw was to write. '. . . a Government . . . if it is really to govern and propagate its species . . . must have a common religion, which nowadays means a philosophy and a science, and it must have an economic policy founded on that religion.'

'Well, I contend that such a nexus exists. Out of the mere destruction and confusion and excitement about mere Bible smashing, and the emptying out of mind and soul and spirit along with Jehovah, which Darwin produced, there has come a quite sufficiently definite and inspiring religion of evolution. Its crystallization has been taking place everywhere: you will find it in Thomas Hardy's poems at one extreme of literature and in the blitherings of Christian Science at the other. But take two expositions that may be known to you: the third act of Man and Superman and Bergson's Creative Evolution. These are totally independent of one another: Bergson and I would have written as we did, word for word, each if the other had never been born. And yet one is a dramatization of the other. Our very catchwords, Life Force and Élan Vital, are translations of one another. The Irishman & the Frenchman find their thoughts in focus at the same point; and both of them had the way pointed out by that intensely English Englishman, Samuel Butler. I can now, when asked what my religion is, say I am a creative-evolutionist . . . Well, why not a creative-evolutionist party? . . .

'The economic policy of the party is clear enough. Everyone who can see the sun shining at noon can also see that there is only one main problem to be solved, and that is the redistribution of income. Also that it is not only an economic question, but a political and biological one. Here you have a body of doctrine on which a party could be built literally over a whole epoch.'

Towards this third Act of his play Shaw felt especially protective, describing it as 'a careful attempt to write a new Book of Genesis for the Bible of the Evolutionists'. Its long second scene is held in a chronological paradox 'Beyond Space, Beyond Time': a science fiction made from Shaw's retrospective longings. The focus of the debate is set in the future while the characters themselves are returned in Tanner's dream to their sixteenth-century equivalents: Tanner himself (the realist) appearing as Don Juan; the brigand leader Mendoza (the idealist) as the Devil; Roebuck Ramsden (the male philistine) as the Statue; and Ann Whitefield (the female philistine) as Doña Ana de Ulloa.

The Parliament in Hell is a contest between Shaw's own optimism for which the Tanner-surrogate Don Juan speaks, and his pessimism which is

73

represented by Mendoza's counterpart, the Devil. Agreeing on much, they are divided in their debate over the need and practicality of human progress. Both are contemptuous of the morality of pretence which filled the Victorian theatre and reflected the conventions of life outside. But what are the alternatives? The Devil says fantasy and play; Don Juan says the evolution of a higher type of man.

Marriage, 'the most licentious of human institutions', has been Nature's method in highly civilized societies for producing babies. Man is woman's instrument for fulfilling Nature's plan, and marriage her contrivance for trapping him into continuing to perform Nature's bidding. In Shaw's sex war, woman is always the pursuer and man the pursued. Woman's weapon has been romantic deceit, which is the subject of the three-act comedy of manners enveloping the dream, and it has worked tolerably well in the past. There are however, Juan points out, two objections. Mankind has an evolutionary appetite that is not satisfied by servicing the procreative urge, but expresses itself in imaginative, mental and heroic activity. The Life Force of the artist, thinker, man of action – 'men selected by Nature to carry on the work of building up an intellectual consciousness of her own instinctive purpose' – rejects the tyrannized role of breeder and domestic breadwinner. 'Here Woman meets a purpose as impersonal, as irresistible as her own; and the clash is sometimes tragic.' The sex war between the artist man and mother woman is a battle therefore between conflicting ways of serving the Life Force.

But, Don Juan predicts, there is another objection to the romantic tradition. Man will soon take woman at her word. He will say: 'Invent me a means by which I can have love, beauty, romance, emotion, passion, without their wretched penalties.' He will manufacture new forms of contraceptive sex which will lead to depopulation of the more advanced countries and a reduction in the educated classes. This seems like a prescient forecast. We have learnt, as the Devil wishes, to combine pleasure with sterility. But though Shaw understood the flight of man from woman, he was in this play apparently less sensitive (despite being married to Charlotte) to the flight of woman from motherhood. This was to be an element in *Saint Joan*; and neither Mrs Clandon in *You Never Can Tell* (despite her children) nor Vivie Warren in *Mrs Warren's Profession* have Ann Whitefield's mission. But the real threat to the Shavian socialist comes from the domestically-centred woman, the Victorian ideal of the hand that rocks the cradle – and which is part of the bourgeois quality of *Man and Superman*. Shaw's simple dramatic contrivance of making the man into the thinker and artist actually created a division for which there is no absolute requirement in life. Apart from a brief reference in his 'Epistle

Dedicatory' to George Sand as an example of the woman of genius who became a mother for the same reason as Shaw became Jenny Patterson's lover – 'to gain experience for the novelist and to develop her' – there is little sense in *Man and Superman* of the possibility of combining motherhood with creative work; no sense that the 'wretched penalties' of actual life could stimulate improvement in the quality of the father's creative work. For Shaw's own marriage was a masculine contrivance for the procreation of plays and prefaces. Its distancing of him from some of the human discomforts and interruptions of his previous life was to coat his thought with a layer of inhumanity that the Devil specifically warns us against: 'Beware of the pursuit of the Superhuman: it leads to an indiscriminate contempt for the human.'

Heaven and hell are not states of afterlife but metaphors for opposing temperaments, values and philosophies. Juan defines hell (with the Devil's concurrence) as 'the home of the unreal and of the seekers for happiness ... Here you escape this tyranny of the flesh; for here you are not an animal at all: you are ... in a word, bodiless ... here there are no hard facts to contradict you, no ironic contrast of your needs with your pretensions, no human comedy, nothing but a perpetual romance ... '

This aspect of Shaw's hell was to become a factor of his theology almost twenty years later in *Back to Methuselah* where the tyranny of the flesh disappears in a whirlpool of pure thought. Here was a three-hundred-year romance by an extremely fastidious man whose disgust with the physical condition of human beings compelled him to eliminate them from his philosophy. The three-meals-a-day, the cold and thirst, decay and disease that forces reality on the human imagination have now vanished. 'There are no social questions here, no political questions, no religious questions, best of all, perhaps, no sanitary questions.' Shaw's formula for hell in *Man and Superman* has enough in common with the bodiless Utopia of *Back to Methuselah* to suggest that the Devil may surreptitiously be going to win a good part of his case – though in the end the Devil is an Impossibilist, and all his utopias disintegrate.

Conventional morals, represented by Doña Ana and the Statue, will always succumb to the Devil's attractions. To resist his hell, Juan argues, we need evolutionary morals. If reality is worry, ugliness and age, sadness and tragedy and death, why not, asks the Devil, use your ingenuity to create a life of endless escape from it? For two reasons, answers Juan. Nature has given man a brain; he needs the power of self-awareness and understanding. The direct pursuit of happiness and beauty leads to misery – happiness may only be gained as a by-product of other endeavours. Secondly, life is not composed as the Devil would like us to believe. It is an illusion to think that we can solve our problems. From each problem solved springs some new challenge. So life must forever progress upwards: or end. Man's quest for knowledge and understanding has set him off on the great adventure of transforming his environment and mastering the universe. He may not stop the world and go off on a perpetual holiday.

Juan's belief in brains provokes the Devil into his first great counter-attack – the powerful 'force of Death' speech. 'Have you walked up and down upon the earth lately?' he enquires. What have human brains done but produce more awful weapons of destruction? It is when we become ambitious on behalf of the human race that we end up destroying ourselves. His monologue amounts to a conservative attack on the dangerous self-congratulatory illusions of progress and a recommendation of the aristocratic principle of cultivated living.

Shaw's evolutionary ethics, as voiced through Juan, have an urgency that shows him to be an instinctive believer in punctuated equilibrium. 'The survival of the fittest' was for him a tautology. He did not believe that steady progress to a higher consciousness was guaranteed by the facts and accidents of evolution, but that it operated irregularly and depended upon the urge to transcend past achievements. It was easily conceivable to him that the world would blow itself up, or western civilization peter out, unless this human urge was renewed. He was not a determinist and avoided the Marxist interpretation of history. Shaw's Life Force, blindly working through human will and brain, was similar to Belfort Bax's definition of 'the good' as 'essentially a process of eternal Becoming which is never complete'.

The Devil reiterates his vision of hell. He is no vulgar hedonist. 'I am also on the intellectual plane,' he says. It is the credulous strivers after perfection in the social organization, he insists, who slaughter millions. He, the Devil, stands for moral principles in that he treats people as ends, not means. It is a telling counter-thrust, but the argument between the two men seems futile, for it takes place in hell and is 'mere talk'.

The resolution to their debate comes through Doña Ana with her cry at the end of the scene: 'a father for the Superman!' And so, from the two ways of serving the Life Force, the biological and the intellectual, Shaw gives priority in time to the first – reflecting his own sense of impotence as a pragmatic thinker. Evolutionary progress, he suggests, depends on sexual instinct; on the coming together of opposites to produce through generations a better human combination of mind and body. In *Caesar and Cleopatra* it had been the realist, with heroism added, on whom the future depended. In *Man and Superman* the seeds of hope reside in the philistine. In Shaw's earlier books, *The Quintessence of Ibsenism* and *The Perfect*

Wagnerite, the battle had been fought between realist and idealist for the mind of the philistine; now the evolutionary need for greater intelligence lies in the sexual conquest of the realist by the philistine. So the three-act comedy, which dramatizes the pursuit and submission of the intellectual Tanner by the predatory Ann, is not a defeat for intelligence after all, but, from the perspective of this extra act, the birth of renewed possibilities for which Shaw gave the code-name 'Superman'.

From these beliefs, and Shaw's treatment of them, certain implications arise. Robert Loraine, who created the part of Don Juan when it was first publicly presented in 1907, recorded that the script 'twinkled with crotchets, crescendos and minims; with B clefs, F clefs and pianissimos'; and Granville Barker, the producer, reminded his cast that 'this is Italian opera you are performing'. Shaw had acknowledged that 'my method, my tradition, is founded upon music' and that Mozart had taught him how profound things could be said in a light way. It was from Mozart that he had learned to astonish 'mere literary barbarians' by his style in comedy, and from Beethoven that he had learned how to develop his themes. He was to advise Arnold Bennett when trying to turn him from a novelist into a dramatist, that he had nothing to learn from Scribe, 'and everything to learn from Beethoven'.

'A play should go like a symphony: its themes should be introduced emphatically at the beginning and then hit on the head again and again until they are red hot, the pace and intensity increasing to the end with every possible device of unexpected modulations and changes, and sudden pianissimos, as in the Preislied and the finale of Mozart's Figaro.'

Tanner's dream and disquisition with the Devil is Shaw's attempt, through operatic argument, to achieve the 'drama of thought' he had foretold in the Preface to *Mrs Warren's Profession*. But though Shaw's humorous self-doubt is lightly and wittily orchestrated through the Devil, Don Juan's earnest speeches grow too long and, behind their resolute optimism, reveal Shaw's panic.

There is no doubt that Shaw intended Don Juan to win the debate. Against the common belief in a God who looked at the world and saw that it was good, he postulated a God who looked and saw it could be bettered. 'I tell you that as long as I can conceive something better than myself I cannot be easy unless I am striving to bring it into existence or clearing the way for it,' says Juan. 'That is the law of my life. That is the working within me of Life's incessant aspiration to higher organization, wider, deeper, intenser self-consciousness, and clearer self-understanding.' That the supremacy of this purpose is Shaw's own is made clear by a parallel passage in the 'Epistle Dedicatory', where he writes: 'This is the true joy in life, the being used for a purpose recognized by yourself as a mighty one; the being thoroughly worn out before you are thrown on the scrap heap; the being a force of Nature instead of a feverish selfish little clod of ailments and grievances complaining that the world will not devote itself to making you happy.'

But the message of *Man and Superman* is that biological progress must precede intellectual development. Tanner wins all his word-battles. He is immeasurably superior to a set of characters who pay no attention to a word he says. Ann wins the actual battle between them, and since Tanner (who is as blind to the emotions as Bluntschli) can contribute more to evolutionary advancement through producing children than political handbooks, this is a happy ending. But it does not fit Shaw's own life. Critics have sometimes pointed to the irony, even cynicism, of his writing (from the man's point of view) an attack on the institution of marriage so recently after having himself been married. Such inappropriateness exists only when Acts I, II and IV are cut off from the rest of the work. In *The Revolutionists' Handbook,* which brings present and future, pessimism and optimism, the Devil and Juan together on to common ground, Shaw recommends the separation of marriage from childbearing. If we trust to the guidance of the sex instinct for 'that superiority in the unconscious self which will be the true characteristic of the Superman', he reasons, then we must perceive the importance of giving the widest possible sexual choice to everyone. The obstacles in Edwardian society to this thriving copulation were property and class. 'To cut humanity up into small cliques, and effectively limit the selection of the individual to his own clique, is to postpone the Superman for eons, if not for ever,' Shaw wrote in Tanner's *Revolutionists' Handbook.* ' . . . Equality is essential to good breeding; and equality, as all economists know, is incompatible with property.'

' . . . it is quite sufficiently probable that good results may be obtained from parents who would be extremely unsuitable companions and partners, to make it certain that the experiment of mating them will sooner or later be tried purposely almost as often as it is now tried accidentally. But mating couples must clearly not involve marrying them. In conjugation two complementary persons may supply one another's deficiencies: in the domestic partnership of marriage they only feel them and suffer from them.'

Therefore, Shaw concludes, the association of marriage with mating must be dissolved. Sexual intercourse is distinct from domesticity, and this connection between the two has fatally held back the breeding of man as a political animal. To some extent he attempted to side-step the implications of these views by letting it be understood that Tanner had been based on H. M. Hyndman, leader of the Social Democratic Federation (as he had previously claimed that Marchbanks was a version of Shelley or De Quincey). In fact the Tanner and Don Juan dual self-portrait is a more sophisticated version of the Trefusis and Smilash *alter ego* from *An Unsocial Socialist*. The philosophy of *Man and Superman*, when all its parts are joined, is logically coherent. But to translate it into life Shaw would either have had to marry Charlotte to produce children as Tanner is to do with Ann; or, representing the future, father children out of wedlock while remaining domestically married to Charlotte, as Tanner recommends in *The Revolutionists' Handbook*. To continue 'talking' on the page without your audience or readers taking any more sensible notice of what you say than Ann takes of Tanner is to live in hell. It was a hell, placed in the division between his own thought and action, that was increasingly to torment Shaw.

The Superman was his symbol for the synthesis between word and deed. But 'Superman' would later bring to mind an immature figure of power, and though this was not intended by Shaw, it suggests the replacement of sexual or parental love by a flirtation with dictators who, unlike himself, actually got things done. Shaw's hell was compounded of hesitation over embodying his own beliefs while urging others to act on them, and the renunciation, as a punishment for a sterile marriage, of sexual pleasure. As Brigid Brophy has noticed, it was curiously fatalistic that he chose (as an Anglicized version of Don Juan di Tenario) the name Tanner, which was also the maiden name of a woman whose sexual attraction was to overpower him: Mrs Patrick Campbell.

Though the four-act version of *Man and Superman* is more satisfactory as literature, it is significantly almost impossible to stage in its entirety, the effect being, Shaw said, that of 'grand opera in the middle of musical comedy'. He seemed to be in several minds, writing that the four-act version was 'never intended to be played', but was 'forced on the stage by the way the public rose to it'. At a meeting of the British Drama League, he declared: 'I tried to see it myself once and nearly died of it.' To Archer, on the other hand, he wrote that he knew that all four acts could not be played under existing conditions 'and therefore designed it in such a fashion that it could be played without the third act. But I fully intended every word of it to be given when my Bayreuth is founded'. And this was probably the truth since, as he wrote elsewhere: 'No man writes a play without reference to the possibility of performance.'

Almost two years after publication of the book the three-act play was first performed. Only the obtuseness of theatre managers, as Archer and

Beerbohm had said, was able to postpone Shaw's success as a playwright now: the younger generation of theatre audiences was waiting for him. This version, full of melancholic autobiographical undertones, has a precise theatrical unity. It is a romantic courtship comedy about the stock subjects of marriage (represented by Ann Whitefield) and money represented by Violet Robinson), and has all the farcical episodes of the love-chase. The Victorian and Edwardian theatregoer would easily recognize the situations and characters. Shaw's exploitation of popular dramatic conventions had seldom been more extreme. There is a love-pursuit through Europe, a capture by brigands and a rescue; there is a clandestine marriage, an emotional triangle (Octavius-Ann-Tanner), the reading of a will, a happy ending; the stage is peopled by standard figures – the romantic artist, the heavy father, the lover and the servant (in a long line from Leporello and Sancho Panza to Sam Weller and Jeeves) who is more practical than his master.

Yet nothing is what it seems to be and everywhere romantic expectation is confounded. Shaw replaces the woman-on-a-pedestal with the stereotype female huntress; the new woman with the new man. The play is crowded with paradoxical reversals. His brigands are vestrymen and Fabians, their leader a love-afflicted sentimentalist; the rich and difficult father turns out to be a social eccentric who wants a misalliance for his son and is reconciled to his marriage not by his daughter-in-law's purity and sweetness but her business acumen. A daughter dominates her mother; a servant rules his employer; and the governing action of the play is the woman's pursuit of her lover. No wonder hell is to be revealed as a sentimentalist's picture of heaven.

In this skill at inverting popular conventions and creating genre anti-types lay the special power of his 'heretical' plays. Shaw welcomed his audience into a world where everything was familiar to them, and then altered all its values. This was the chief ploy in what he was to call 'my persistent struggle to force the public to reconsider its morals'. And he added:

'I regard much current morality as too economic and sexual relations as disastrously wrong; and I regard certain doctrines of the Christian religion as understood in England to-day with abhorrence. I write plays with the deliberate object of converting the nation to my opinion in these matters. I have no other effectual incentive to write plays . . . '

*. . . The object of the play is to teach Irish people the value of an
Englishman as well as to shew the Englishman his own absurdities.*
'Author's Instructions to the Producer', *John Bull's Other Island*

Two years separated the completion of *Man and Superman* from the
composition of Shaw's next play. He was held back partly by the business
of turning his comedies into books but also by the familiar difficulty of
seeing them performed.

There was, admittedly, the topsy-turvy Shaw-Trebitsch boom in
Germany, four of the plays having been produced in Vienna, Leipzig,
Dresden and Frankfurt by the end of 1903. 'They have all failed so
violently, and been hounded from the stage with such furious execrations,'
Shaw told Johnston Forbes Robertson, 'that the advanced critics proclaim
me the choice and master spirit of the age; and no manager respects
himself until he has lost at least 200 marks by me. My plays . . . simply
cannot be kept off the stage'. In America *The Devil's Disciple* had ended a
successful tour and *Candida*, in the hands of the young actor-manager
Arnold Daly, had stirred up oceans of sentiment in New York. By 1904
the city was suffering from 'an outbreak of Candidamania', Shaw noted,
but the play 'is ancient history for me now'.

He took little interest, too, in an experimental season of uncommercial
drama, featuring six matinées of *Candida*, that had opened that spring at
the small Court Theatre in Sloane Square. London having failed him, he
was preparing to return in his imagination to Dublin. Yeats had already
urged him to go back and 'stir up' things. Shortly before the publication of
Man and Superman, Shaw confided to Yeats that he had it 'quite seriously
in my head to write an Irish play (frightfully modern – no banshees or
leprechauns)'; but he did nothing further until what seemed a fair chance
appeared.

It was Yeats who gave him this chance. Together with Lady Gregory
and Edward Martyn, he had founded the Irish Literary Theatre which
proposed to create in Dublin 'a Celtic and Irish school of dramatic
literature . . . [with] that freedom to experiment which is not found in
theatres of England'. They would produce no play 'which could not hope
to succeed as a book,' Yeats wrote, since they must 'escape the stupefying
memory of the theatre of commerce' which clung to London's West End.

There was much that was familiar in this to Shaw and much that
appealed to him. Lady Gregory was to his mind 'the greatest living

Irishwoman'; Edward Martyn, a vast owl-blinking misogynist, lover of wine and caviar, and first president of Sinn Fein, was an admirer and imitator of Ibsen; and Yeats manoeuvred his theatre colleagues with all the skill Shaw devoted to his Fabian gang. For example, Yeats had briefly plucked George Moore back from London, despite Moore's insistence that it was a forlorn thing this bringing literary plays to Dublin – 'Dublin of all cities in the world'. Then, recruiting a company from England, Yeats had given them a couple of seasons, one at the Antient Concert Rooms (once patronized by Vandeleur Lee), the second at the Gaiety Theatre (the place of entertainment where Sonny had grown familiar with *opéra bouffe*, extravaganza and the stage-Irish hero). In 1902 Yeats fell in with the Fay brothers, Frank and Willy, and their little band of Irish actors. From this association, the following year, the Irish National Theatre Society was born with Yeats himself as president, and a new set of colleagues, Maud Gonne, Douglas Hyde and the poet, theosophist and visionary painter George Russell (known as A. E.), its vice-presidents. In the spring of 1904, as the company's first appearance on the legitimate stage, the Society was invited to play at the Royalty Theatre in London, and Shaw went along to watch them. They played Synge's *In the Shadow of the Glen* and *Riders to the Sea*; Yeats's *The King's Threshold* and *A Pot of Broth*; and Padraic Colum's *Broken Soil*, all showing the influence of Gordon Craig's revolt against the elaborate productions of Irving and Beerbohm Tree. It was then that Shaw opened his eyes to a renaissance in the Irish theatre.

Yet it had been, until this year, a hole-and-corner rebirth not dissimilar, in its fashion, to the Stage Society. What changed matters was the midwifery of Annie Horniman who had promised, if her shares in the Hudson Bay Company 'do anything very exciting', to present the Irish National Theatre Society with 'a little theatre in Dublin'. Her investment rising spectacularly, she swiftly bought a ninety-nine year lease on a small music-hall theatre within the Mechanics Institute on the corner of Lower Abbey Street, and adjacent premises in Marlborough Street that 'had served as a bank, the home of a nationalist debating society, a recruiting centre for the Fenian movement, and the City Morgue'. Annie Horniman was a Fabian, antagonistic to the Fay brothers, and no friend to Irish Nationalism. But by financing Florence Farr's season in 1894 she had given Yeats and Shaw their débuts on the London stage. She now offered Yeats, as president of the Society, use of the new theatre cost-free. 'I can only afford to make a very little theatre and it must be quite simple,' she wrote. 'You all must do the rest to make a powerful and prosperous theatre with a high artistic ideal.'

The Abbey Theatre was to open its doors at the end of 1904, and it was for this opening, 'as a patriotic contribution to the repertory of the Irish

Literary Theatre', that Yeats invited Shaw to write his next play. The omens seemed good – particularly the patronage of Miss Horniman. 'I am greatly touched', Shaw told Yeats, 'by learning that history is repeating itself in the matter of our backer.'

'Not a word of the play yet on paper,' Shaw promised Lady Gregory on 20 June. In fact he had begun writing it, under the provisional title *Rule Britannia*, in a pocket notebook three days earlier while staying with Charlotte at Hindhead. It continued seething in his mind and filling his notebooks over much of the next ten weeks. 'I have finished the first act of my Irish play and am plunging through it at a great rate,' he reported on 13 July to Arnold Daly who was pressing him for a new one-act play for America. But *John Bull's Other Island*, as he was to call it, centred on Ireland. It was not, he informed Trebitsch, 'of much use for Germany'; and he discouraged the Court Theatre in London by describing it as 'a sort of political farce, of no use to anybody but cranks'.

He had finished the first draft on 23 August 1904, and began his revision and staging the next morning. He was working 'like ten galley slaves all the time' and, as he worked, keeping in communication with Yeats. For the change of scene – Rosscullen Hill to the Round Tower – in Act II he wanted to know what 'modern appliances' he could rely on at the Abbey. 'It seems to me,' he wrote to Yeats, 'that as you will deal in fairy plays you may have indulged yourself with hydraulic bridges.'

Hideous tempests and 'a long series of little contretemps' with Charlotte so interrupted his work that for four days he did 'nothing' – by which he meant polishing off 'a screaming curtain-raiser', *How He Lied to Her Husband*, for Arnold Daly, intended as a prescription against sentimental Candidamania.

On 7 September Shaw sent the completed play to Ethel Dickens with instructions to type it out and forward a copy to Yeats. He had been horrified to find that the autograph manuscript, scattered through four pocket notebooks (including twenty-five dictated pages in Charlotte's handwriting) contained about thirty-two thousand words. Henry Arthur Jones, he recollected, had put eighteen thousand as the correct length. 'To my great dismay it turns out to be much too long,' he told Yeats, 'but I am too exhausted to attempt to cut it: I must get a few days holiday or I shall collapse.'

Before the end of the month the typescript had reached Yeats. Shaw meanwhile fell back under Charlotte's care. 'I must rest or die,' he declared, 'for if I turn over in bed without great care my heart stops for half an hour. This comes of writing plays against time.'

*

In *John Bull's Other Island* Shaw continued his spiritual autobiography, using the years before marriage as his starting point: the twenty years of his upbringing in Dublin versus the twenty years of his career in London. At one level, which he later developed in his Preface, the play is about the contrasting political histories and national characteristics of the two countries. But Ireland and England are also metaphors for opposing philosophies of life: and Shaw's experiment at reconciling them is the theme of this sombre and self-revealing work.

The *ménage à trois* in which he had grown up may have made the Hegelian triad, as a dramatic vehicle for his thought, 'magical' to Shaw. In the dream scene of *Man and Superman* he used it to replace his feeling that it would have been better never to have been born with his rebirth into another world. In the next two plays of the trilogy he attempted to focus this optimism from his dreams upon waking life: first, in *John Bull's Other Island*, autobiographically; then, in *Major Barbara*, on the world he saw around him emerging into the twentieth century.

'Live in contact with dreams and you will get something of their charm: live in contact with facts and you will get something of their brutality. I wish I could find a country to live in where the facts were not brutal and the dreams not unreal.' This wish, voiced by Larry Doyle, the exiled Irishman working in England, was the motive-power behind these middle-period plays. Larry Doyle is the vertex of a triangle at one corner of which stands the successful English businessman Tom Broadbent, and at the other Peter Keegan, the disfrocked Irish priest.

In Broadbent Shaw created, for Irish audiences, the stage-Englishman, having in the first scene chased the stage-Irishman Tim Haffigan off as an impostor. Broadbent represents the world of facts, however brutal; Keegan the world of dreams, however unreal. Broadbent is the perfect philistine, a 'robust, full-blooded, energetic man in the prime of life'. His kingdom is the material world. He feels happily at home in what Keegan describes as 'very clearly a place of torment and penance'. On the contrary, Broadbent declares, it is 'quite good enough for me: rather a jolly place, in fact'.

The key to Broadbent's success is his narrowness of intelligence, imagination, sensitivity and humour. He is Shaw's Dr Pangloss, a man whose moral self-satisfaction shields him from all uncertainty. He reduces everything to the mundane and simplifies everything for profitable use. He speaks a different language from Keegan, recommending him to take phosphorus pills ('I'll give you the address in Oxford Street') to change his outlook on life. 'The only really simple thing is to go straight for what you want and grab it,' says another philistine, Ann Whitefield, in *Man and*

Superman. Broadbent is the acquisitive man. He combines obtuseness with a genius for action and will always succeed where Keegan fails. Within twenty-four hours of arriving at Rosscullen he has collared the Parliamentary seat, swallowed up Larry's sweetheart Nora Reilly and acquired the land for development. He brings to Ireland a terrible corruption of Shaw's belief in improvement, but he brings it cheerfully, expansively. Like the devil in *Man and Superman* he is sympathetic. In his 'Instructions to the Producer', Shaw makes clear that he is a big man with an imposing personality who 'must be thoroughly likeable and good-natured through all his absurdities . . . ' The stage directions picture him as 'always buoyant and irresistible', and Shaw's revisions to the first act make his unscrupulous self-interest largely unconscious.

Everything that is absent from Broadbent goes to make the character of Peter Keegan. Broadbent is beefy – he could be played by a Falstaffian performer – but Keegan 'must be incorporeal' and needed 'a poetic actor . . . a masterly speaker, able to put on the authority of a priest'. Broadbent is a land speculator interested in the modern technology of killer motor cars, neat golf links, hygienic new hotels. Keegan, who loves the land, speaks with grasshoppers and calls the donkey, the ass and the pig his brothers. His kingdom is not of this world, which has labelled him mad and 'silenced' him. In contrast to Father Dempsey, the parochial reality, Keegan is 'an ideal Catholic', the first and most convincing of Shaw's mystical sages, who retreats at the end of the play to the Round Tower and will reappear briefly as Androcles and later as the damaged Captain Shotover in *Heartbreak House*.

Into Keegan's mouth Shaw put his fastidious sense of horror, his spiritual revulsion, at Broadbent's world – a 'place where the fool flourishes and the good and wise are hated and persecuted, a place where men and women torture one another in the name of love; where children are scourged and enslaved in the name of parental duty and education; where the weak in body are poisoned and mutilated in the name of healing, and the weak in character are put to the horrible torture of imprisonment, not for hours but for years, in the name of justice. It is a place where the hardest toil is a welcome refuge from the horror and tedium of pleasure . . . ' This sepulchral litany is another version of Don Juan's speech and clearly identifies this earth as hell. Broadbent's schemes for the future ('this place may have an industrial future, or it may have a residential future') do not impress Keegan who replies that it 'may have no future at all'. For Keegan there are 'two conditions of men: salvation and damnation'; for Broadbent there are 'only two qualities in the world: efficiency and inefficiency', and he adds: 'The world belongs to the efficient.' But Keegan recognizes only damnation in this efficient service of Mammon and opposes it with his vision of a day 'when these islands shall live by the quality of their men rather than by the abundance of their minerals . . . '

Keegan's annihilating indictment of Broadbent's and Larry Doyle's practical business methods (which will ruin everyone but themselves) is a precisely accurate statement of what will happen. Shaw makes this clear with his stage directions. '*Broadbent and Larry look quickly at one another; for this, unless the priest is an old financial hand, must be inspiration.*' The stern prophecy, ending on a note that is '*low and bitter*' is unanswerable – and is answered by Broadbent (who, as Keegan has ironically congratulated him, has 'an answer for everything') with meaningless approval. Keegan's 'chaff' as Broadbent calls it (adding 'these things cannot be said too often') is of as little consequence in *John Bull's Other Island* as Tanner's 'talking' had been in *Man and Superman*.

Broadbent embodies action, Keegan speaks for the emotions and Larry Doyle represents the intellect. Throughout the play there is a bias in favour of action. Broadbent believes that 'something *must* be done'; Larry has had only two ideas: 'to learn to do something; and then to get out of Ireland and have a chance of doing it'; and Keegan too says that 'when we cease to do, we cease to live'. It is for this reason that he 'may even vote' for Broadbent who has 'some excuse for believing that if there be any future, it will be yours'. For, he adds, 'our faith seems dead, and our hearts cold and cowed'. From this dead faith, this coldness, Larry has been conceived. Ireland 'produces two kinds of men in strange perfection: saints and traitors', we are told. If Keegan is the saint, Larry Doyle is the traitor. He has repressed everything he shares with Keegan: he has rejected Ireland and has helped by his exile to turn it from a Land of Dreams into a Land of Derision. Shaw's stage directions throughout Larry's long speech on 'the dreaming! the torturing, heart-scalding, never satisfying dreaming, dreaming, dreaming, dreaming!' of Ireland underline the personal feeling he put into these pages: '*With sudden anguish . . . hastily . . . Going off into a passionate dream . . . Savagely . . . bitterly, at Broadbent . . . With fierce shivering self-contempt . . . Dropping his voice like a man making some shameful confidence . . .* '

Not sharing Keegan's solitary self-sufficiency, Larry must borrow his strength from Broadbent's self-confidence. Otherwise, he says, 'I should never have done anything'. It is Broadbent who sees clearly the price Larry has paid for the suffocation of his emotional life. 'He has absolutely no capacity for enjoyment,' Broadbent tells Nora: 'he couldn't make any woman happy. He's as clever as be-blowed; but life's too earthly for him: he doesn't really care for anything or anybody.'

1 Shaw in the late 1890s

2A Shaw and the pastel portrait of Charlotte by G. A. Sartorio, commissioned by her in 1895; B Charlotte at the time of her marriage in 1898

3 Mary Cholmondeley, Charlotte, Mrs Payne-Townshend and Hugh Cholmondeley

4 Famille-rose vase painted in sepia with a portrait of Shaw, c.1916

5 Max cartoon, c.1913. The caption reads: 'Mild surprise of one who, revisiting England after long absence, finds that the dear fellow has not moved.'

6 Poster for 1911 revival

7 Poster for 1907 revival

8 Ellen Terry

Keegan is the man Sonny might have grown into if he had been able to endure the anguish of living in the Land of Dreams; Larry Doyle is the man Shaw has become and who believes he belongs to 'the big world . . . solid English life in London, the very centre of the world'. Larry with his 'clever head', his 'suggestion of thinskinnedness and dissatisfaction' and determination to be ruthless, embodies what must have been some of Shaw's most awful nightmares. He is a displaced person who has escaped poverty and failure, but must put himself in double harness with the 'efficient devil' Broadbent to justify his decision with success. But the syndicate which they have formed (in which Larry owns a 'bit of the stock') is not the synthesis between dreams and facts for which Shaw was looking. It is a business partnership in which Larry's intellectual powers are used to serve Broadbent's philistine aims. As capitalism may be interpreted as a transitory stage in the development of communism, so Broadbent's values may eventually be superseded by Keegan's – that is the hope behind Larry's permeation of the big world.

The second partnership in the play, that between Broadbent and Nora, is not a marriage of body and spirit, but a devouring of the spirit by the body. She is a 'frail figure', 'almost sexless' and he, with his 'good broad chest', promises to 'plump out your muscles and make em elastic and set up your figure'. He tells Larry: 'I must feed up Nora. She's weak; and it makes her fanciful.' She is his ethereal 'ideal' and he will make her into the housewife of 'a solid four-square home'. There is no sense here, as in *Man and Superman*, of improvement through procreation. It is the response of the English genius to the Irish.

On the subject of politics, about which he still thinks independently, Larry (like Keegan) is labelled 'mad'. Larry is in principle an internationalist: 'my business and yours as civil engineers is to join countries,' he tells Broadbent, 'not to separate them.' But he cannot join Broadbent's present to Keegan's future. He has attached himself to a man whose ideas, he sees, are 'in watertight compartments, and all the compartments warranted impervious to anything it doesnt suit you to understand'. So everyone remains separated in the play and no one is converted. Broadbent takes charge of the world; Keegan retires alone to his tower; and the conflict within Larry is not reconciled. He has split life into dreams and facts, and chosen facts as being reality. It is only by working with Broadbent, he says, 'that I have learnt to live in a real world and not in an imaginary one. I owe more to you than to any Irishman'.

But was the world of facts real? Shaw's insistence that it was, that the State must look after its inhabitants as a mother should look after her children, and that for practical purposes money could replace the emotions, is continually interrupted by his subversive humour and a pessimism that undermines much of what he dedicated his career to establishing. 'Every dream is a prophecy: every jest is an earnest in the womb of Time,' says Keegan who explains to Nora that 'my way of joking is to tell the truth'. It is Keegan who sees reality in dreams and strikes an apocalyptic note over Shaw's own Fabian territory of statistics: 'For four wicked centuries the world has dreamed this foolish dream of efficiency; and the end is not yet. But the end will come.'

It is Keegan, too, who suggests at the end of the play the possibility of a different synthesis. This is the third empire from *Emperor and Galilean* of which Shaw had written briefly in *The Quintessence of Ibsenism*, 'the third empire, in which the twin-natured shall reign . . . the God of earth and the Emperor of the spirit in one'. Here Keegan finds his reality. When asked by Broadbent what heaven is like in his dreams, he replies:

'In my dreams it is a country where the State is the Church and the Church the people: three in one and one in three. It is a commonwealth in which work is play and play is life: three in one and one in three. It is a temple in which the priest is the worshipper and the worshipper the worshipped: three in one and one in three. It is a godhead in which all life is human and all humanity divine: three in one and one in three. It is, in short, the dream of a madman.'

These are Keegan's last words. By sending him away across the hill to the Round Tower, a solitary figure acknowledging that 'the gates of hell still prevail against me', Shaw was silencing a voice capable of finding the magical synthesis of his quest. Without this voice we are left with a makeshift syndicate that gives relief from thinskinned dissatisfaction in the ecstasy of work linked to the illusions of action. Keegan was buried alive in Shaw, but from time to time, prompted by the unconscious will, we hear his accents mocking the pragmatic programme of G.B.S.

*

The play was 'a wonderful piece of work' and 'full of good things', William Fay, the Abbey Theatre manager, reported to Yeats: but 'the difficulty of getting a cast for it would be considerable'. Synge, too, believed it would 'hold a Dublin audience, and at times move them if even tolerably played', though he recommended that Shaw eliminate the grasshopper at the beginning of Act III and some talk on Free Trade and tariffs. Yeats himself had been disappointed by the first act and a half. 'Then my interest began to awake,' he wrote to Shaw. ' . . . I thought in reading the first act that you had forgotten Ireland, but I found in the other acts that it is the only subject on which you are entirely serious.'

'... You have said things in this play which are entirely true about Ireland, things which nobody has ever said before, and these are the very things that are most part of the action. It astonishes me that you should have been so long in London and yet have remembered so much. To some extent this play is unlike anything you have done before. Hitherto you have taken your situations from melodrama, and called up logic to make them ridiculous. Your process here seems to be quite different, you are taking your situations more from life, you are for the first time trying to get the atmosphere of a place, you have for the first time a geographical conscience ... To my surprise I must say, I do not consider the play dangerous ... Here again you show your wonderful knowledge of the country. You have laughed at the things that are ripe for laughter, and not where the ear is still green ... we can play it, and survive to play something else.'

But the Abbey did not stage *John Bull's Other Island* for another twelve years. The company met to discuss the matter in the second week of October 1904 and rehearsed the difficulties: the difficulty of length; the difficulty of getting a cast, especially someone to play Broadbent; the difficulty of handling modern appliances such as grasshoppers and hydraulic bridges. These difficulties accumulated as they argued, silencing a more fundamental difficulty: that (to use Shaw's words in the Preface to the 1906 edition) 'it was uncongenial to the whole spirit of the neo-Gaelic movement, which is bent on creating a new Ireland after its own ideal, whereas my play is a very uncompromising presentment of the real old Ireland'. Yeats was to concede when he saw it performed in London that 'it acts very much better than one could have foreseen ... [and] certainly keeps everybody amused'. Like Max Beerbohm, he had underrated Shaw's instinct for the theatre partly because he disliked the play's structure. 'I don't really like it,' he wrote. 'It is fundamentally ugly and shapeless.'

The shape of the play, loosely constructed round a string of character-turns with the emphasis directed away from the action and focused on a parallel series of discussions that occur at rather unremarkable moments (the after-breakfast pause, the after-tea stroll), is a step towards the full-scale debate of ideas Shaw was to reach four years later in *Getting Married* where the conversation of the play becomes its action. In *John Bull's Other Island*, he uses some of the conventional props of Irish Romance to explode the Irish romantic ideal, but moves so far from the well-made conventions of nineteenth-century drama that William Archer, writing in *The World*, could think of 'no other play, English or foreign, with which it can properly be classed'.

Yeats instinctively felt opposed to the inclusiveness of what Archer called this inorganic 'philosophico-political prose extravaganza'. Yeats's writing was oblique and Shaw's was assertive; and Yeats wrote poetry where Shaw laughed. They shared the same enemies and Yeats (who almost alone in the Senate was to stand up for the right of divorce) became a fine representative of what Shaw, in his Preface to this play, declares that Protestantism should be. But Shaw had turned away from Yeats's vision of life early on. 'If I had gone to the hills nearby to look upon Dublin and to ponder upon myself, I too might have become a poet like Yeats, Synge and the rest of them,' Shaw stated. 'But I prided myself on thinking clearly, and therefore could not stay. Whenever I took a problem or a state of life of which my Irish contemporaries sang sad songs, I always pushed it to its logical conclusions, and then inevitably it resolved itself into comedy.'

Such a passage helps to explain Yeats's description of Shaw as a 'barbarian of the barricades'. When Shaw made Larry Doyle deride Keegan as sentimental, chastise the eternal dreaming in himself, and question the holy ground on which they both stood, he uprooted the Irish legends from which sprang Lady Gregory's and Yeats's plays; when he described Nora Reilly as 'an incarnation of everything in Ireland that drove him [Larry Doyle] out of it', he banished one of those idealized stage figures – the Irish heiress – into which Synge breathed new life and poetry. *John Bull's Other Island* seemed antagonistic to everything the Abbey Theatre was to achieve. So, after months of negotiation, Yeats released 'that queer elephant' so that it might perform with an English company in Ireland. 'We all admire it,' he wrote: and between them all a polite understanding was kept up that it had merely been too large and difficult a work for the Abbey to handle. Yet privately they believed, as Frank Fay wrote, that the play was 'not *alive*'.

Yeats could recognize the wonderful power of Shaw's pen – its logic, justice, audacity, drive of conviction; he was even moved by the 'gay heroic delight in the serviceable man' he sensed in *Caesar and Cleopatra*. But Shaw represented 'the spirit of the press, of hurry, of immediate interests' over what Yeats felt was the slow-burning spirit of literature. He was consuming his own talent with superficial theatricality, the unnerving tic of his wit, rambling vulgarity – anything that seemed to stiffen the purpose of the moment.

If Shaw felt resentment he did not reveal it – unless it may be seen reaching the surface over twenty years later in his response to the Abbey's rejection of another exiled Irish writer's play: Sean O'Casey's *The Silver Tassie*. Why had Yeats and Lady Gregory, he asked, treated O'Casey 'like a baby'? *The Silver Tassie* was 'literally a hell of a play', he told Lady

According to Annie Horniman, Barker had been an understudy in Florence Farr's season at the Avenue Theatre which performed *Arms and the Man*; and he had taken part in the copyright performance of *Caesar and Cleopatra* given by Mrs Patrick Campbell's company at Newcastle. At the sixth 'meeting' of the Stage Society, he played Marchbanks and was 'the success of the piece', Shaw confirmed to Archer. 'It was an astonishing piece of luck to hit on him.' This performance of *Candida* completed the Stage Society's first season which had begun with *You Never Can Tell*. Since Archer's New Century Theatre, planted so as to bloom into a National Theatre sometime in the twentieth century, had become lost to view in 1899, the struggling Stage Society was left as the principal rallying point for things modern in the theatre. Its success was measured at the first annual meeting on 16 July 1900 when the maximum membership was increased from three to five hundred (each paying a yearly subscription of two guineas) and a decision was taken to add to the private Sunday evening presentation a weekday matinée to which the press (though required to pay) would be admitted. No other publicity was allowed. Tickets were not transferable (though members could invite one guest to each play); performances were quietly described as 'meetings'; no scenery was employed and no salary offered to the actors who all received the same nominal sum – one guinea – for expenses. These rules, which had been drafted by the chairman, Frederick Whelan (a Fabian on the staff of the Bank of England), were meticulously within the law and enabled the Society legally to present new British plays as well as classical and contemporary foreign dramas (for some of which the Censor had refused a licence) to the audiences of eight or nine hundred members and guests.

Though he remained faithful to the Stage Society (which also produced *Captain Brassbound's Conversion*, *Man and Superman*, a courageous *Mrs Warren's Profession* and the rollicking performance of *The Admirable Bashville*), Shaw felt that such a small rough-and-tumble club, with its jealousies and intrigues, incomplete casts and inadequate rehearsals, was not (as he told Gilbert Murray) 'a very eligible opening for professional ambition'. In any event, it could no longer reach Shaw's own ambitions: you couldn't even fail at the Stage Society. He had turned his back on the amateur ways of that rogue elephant Charles Charrington and his impossible Janet. 'The next performance of Candida will probably take place at about the date of the final partition of China by the Powers,' he told Barker after refusing the Charringtons permission to transfer his play. Nevertheless, in its little coterie-theatre way, the Stage Society was catching on. At the end of 1900 Granville Barker played Captain Kearney in its presentation of *Captain Brassbound's Conversion*, though neither to his own nor to Shaw's satisfaction. 'Your divine gifts of youth, delicacy and distinction will be murdered; and so will the part,' Shaw had confidently told him. But, he added:

'My only misgiving with regard to you is as to whether the Stage, in its present miserable condition, is good enough for you: you are sure to take to authorship or something of the kind. Meanwhile, however, you give me the *quality* of work I want; and I hope to get some more of it out of you before you get tired of it.'

With ten years' acting experience on the stage and ambitions to be a dramatist, Barker had been working in the theatre with gathering distaste. The Stage Society's Sunday evening and Monday afternoon performances were however affording him some experience as a director as well as actor, particularly in the presentation of his own four act comedy, *The Marrying of Ann Leete* – 'by far the finest bit of literature', Shaw judged, since the appearance over fifteen years earlier of R. L. Stevenson's romance *Prince Otto*. 'How do you get on with Granville Barker?' he demanded of Henry Arthur Jones. 'Do you realise that he is a great poet and dramatist who feels towards us as we feel towards Sheridan Knowles? His *The Marrying of Anne Leete* is really an exquisite play. I truckle to G. B. in order to conciliate him when he is forty . . . '

Behind this half-frivolous tone was the feeling that he was no longer alone: at last he had a successor in the theatre, someone to share, inherit and modify the Shavian stage experiment. In his opinion, Barker was 'altogether the most distinguished and incomparably the most cultivated person whom circumstances had driven into the theatre at that time.'

Before *Ann Leete*, Barker had written other plays. Like Shaw's, they had seemed unplayable. But Shaw read them and 'found them fascinating'. He recommended Barker ('a very fine talent indeed') to Mrs Patrick Campbell as a possible translator of Rostand's *La Princesse Lointaine* and 'made him go on writing, which was difficult and slow work to him, as having been on the stage since he was 14, he had no apprenticeship as an author, only as an actor'. G.B.S. was in earnest about *Ann Leete*. At first he had doubted whether its 'delicacy of style' would travel across the footlights. But on seeing it performed under Barker's own stage management, 'I had to confess that he had succeeded', Shaw was to tell Trebitsch. 'His style is so difficult that most of his plays are unintelligible at the first reading or hearing; and Archer always describes Ann Leete as a play written down to his comprehension, as it is much more perspicuous than the others.'

'There is a sort of dainty strangeness about it that fits its eighteenth century period and costumes; and the curious way in which it begins in a garden at midnight takes it so effectually out of the Philistine key that its quaint fantastic conversation, consisting mostly of hints and innuendoes, seems to belong to it naturally.'

Here (and not, as some supposed, with flat blank verse of Stephen Phillips) lay the theatre of the future. Barker was 'fastidious and low toned whereas I was blatantly declamatory and melodramatic'. But Shaw felt a special tenderness towards the young man, as if his own blatant qualities, obliterating much that was sensitive in himself, had served to protect him. After all, it had been to bulldoze Irving and his execrable Lyceum mutilations off the stage that the phenomenon of G.B.S. had been partly manufactured. That Barker could afford to take no notice of Irving was partly due to G.B.S.; and partly, of course, a matter of age.

Shaw was twenty-one years older than Barker, 'old enough', he wrote, 'to be his father'. This was indeed the peculiar kinship he felt for him. Their backgrounds had much in common. Barker's father was 'spoken of' as an architect, but the family had been largely dependent on his mother, a well-known elocutionist, at whose literary recitals the boy precociously took part. All his life he kept in a silver locket a picture of her before her marriage. 'There is no record of his schooling,' the *Dictionary of National Biography* notes, 'but he grew up in an atmosphere of good speech and drama and at an early age had a thorough knowledge of Dickens and Shakespeare.' He scored his first stage success in 1899 playing Richard II for William Poel, but was to be no happier as a successful actor than Shaw was as a successful platform speaker. For all his 'peculiarly delicate talent', he struck people as remote, sterile, sometimes even cold-blooded. Beatrice Webb observed him to be 'a most attractive person – young and good looking – good looking in a charming refined fashion – with a subtle intellectual expression – faculties more analytic than artistic?'

'I think with self-control, industry, freedom from vulgar desires and common fears, with varied interests, good memory, a sharp observer of human nature and above all a delicate appreciation of music, poetry and art – a medley of talents of which I do not yet see a very definite whole. He has not yet emancipated himself from G.B.S.'s influence or found his own soul.'

Barker's incompleteness bewildered and fascinated people. What Beatrice thought of as the influence of G.B.S. was probably a similarity of temperament. 'I am an intellectual, but by no means a dramatic disciple of G.B.S.,' Barker declared. 'We have quite different ideas . . . ' And G.B.S. agreed. 'We were as different as Verdi from Debussy.' Yet their natures seemed to complement each other and there was a natural intimacy between them. Shaw felt no need to be diplomatic with Barker. His letters took on a naturally directive tone, scorning professional decisions that wandered away from the driving concentration on his own advancement. Perhaps the withholding of maternal praise had created in him the need to let go in this way. But though he used histrionic devices to remove the sting, some of this steamrollering assault must have bruised Barker. They talked much in quotations from Dickens and Shakespeare, using them as a private code excluding others. But they seldom discussed their own plays. 'We took them as they came, like facts of nature.' Shaw was able to watch and direct Barker in a number of his roles during the early stages of their friendship: he was Marchbanks, the poet Shaw had repressed in himself; he was Father Keegan, the best self Shaw had sealed up in the Round Tower; he played Jack Tanner made up with a beard to look like a younger G.B.S.; and in Shaw's next play *Major Barbara*, he was to play Adolphus Cusins, the foundling academic who is adopted as his heir by the Shavian father figure of Undershaft, also a foundling. From this succession of sympathetic roles a whisper arose that Barker was Shaw's natural son. 'At one of the earliest rehearsals ... a question of birthdays arose; and Granville Barker blighted me by remarking "Oh! youre exactly the same age as my father" (I had up to that moment regarded him as a contemporary),' Shaw later told Archer. 'When we became fashionable, Edith Nesbit (Mrs Bland) said to me one day, "Shaw: IS Granville Barker your natural son?"' The notion appealed to Shaw who observed that most people rejected the hypothesis 'on the ground that I am physically incapable of parentage'.

Barker fulfilled the imaginative role of son to Shaw's father and Charlotte's mother, replacing the natural child they never had. He seemed all things to all people – whatever they wanted most. Charlotte was one of several childless women in whom he prompted a maternal instinct. G.B.S. felt protective too. Barker was someone for him to scold and schoolmaster, encourage and idealize; he was the juvenile lead with whom G.B.S. shared the family companionship of work. 'He played up by becoming an intimate friend in my house and falling in love with my wife,' Shaw wrote. 'But he had none of the Marchbanks boyish De Quincey helplessness and inexperience. He was full of enterprise, self-sufficiency, and normal ability.'

In the summer of 1901 Barker and Shaw had joined the management committee of the Stage Society which had decided to put on *Mrs Warren's Profession* towards the end of that year. Because the play had not been granted a licence, however, thirteen theatres, three hotels, two music halls and the Royal Society of British Artists refused to lend their premises before, early in 1902, the tiny New Lyric Club agreed to accommodate the play's first presentation, with Shaw as producer and Barker playing Frank Gardner.

From these difficulties and delays Shaw and Barker drew differing lessons. Shaw's conclusion seemed to be endorsed by the events of 1903. The Stage Society was capable of putting on a 'tomfoolery' such as *The Admirable Bashville*; but a performance even of the first act of *Caesar and Cleopatra*, starring Johnston Forbes Robertson and Gertrude Elliott, was too large and difficult an enterprise and had to be abandoned: the Society could not scrape together 'the price of a sphinx & an old pantomime wardrobe for the Egyptian & Roman soldiers'. It was for this reason that he had turned to the Abbey Theatre.

For Barker, the cap-in-hand, door-to-door experiences over *Mrs Warren's Profession* had emphasized the need for a permanent theatre. His chance came early in 1904 when he was invited to produce *Two Gentlemen of Verona* at the Court Theatre in Sloane Square. The lease of this theatre had recently been bought by J. H. Leigh, a wealthy businessman and amateur actor, to stage a series of 'Shakespearean Representations' featuring his wife (and one-time ward) Thyrza Norman. The first two productions had been unsatisfactory and Leigh, coming to William Archer for help, was advised to employ Granville Barker for his next play. This plan appealing to his wife, Leigh struck up an arrangement with Barker that allowed him to give six matinées of *Candida* at the Court. Here was 'hideous folly' according to Shaw who was unaware that Charlotte had given a private guarantee against loss of £160 for the production. Once again Barker's acting of March-XKbanks 'was, humanly speaking, perfect'; the play itself was well-received by the critics; and this experiment in uncommercial drama actually made a profit – including thirty-one pounds and three xkshillings for the playwright.

Three weeks later Barker was producing Gilbert Murray's rhyming translation of Euripides' *Hippolytus* at the Lyric Theatre. 'In the harmony and equipoise of its parts,' wrote Archer, 'the play is constructed like a noble piece of architecture.' Murray's version was curiously well attuned to the times. With his dialogue assembled on the loose framework of William Morris and his choruses remodelled on the personal idiom of Swinburne, Euripides had been translated into a late-Victorian poet-dramatist. Barker's production aimed at making this archaic structure seem as natural as possible on the stage. His own last speech as the Messenger, with its lyrical description of the hero's death, was, according to Desmond MacCarthy, 'the most memorable feature' of the play. Certainly its impact was tremendous. Murray was extolled for 'illuminating antiquity and restoring beauty and deep poetic feeling' to the theatre. He spoke 'directly to the heart', remembered Ben Iden Payne, the theatre manager; and Wilfrid Scawen Blunt recorded in his diary that he had never seen tragedy like this. 'At the end of it we were all moved to tears, and I got up and did what I never did before in a theatre, shouted for the author, whether for Euripides or Gilbert Murray I hardly knew.' Arthur Bourchier wanted to get *Hippolytus* transferred to the Garrick Theatre; William Poel wanted the opportunity of putting it on almost anywhere. But Barker confided to Murray that 'J. H. Leigh has expressed himself bitten with the idea of doing Greek plays. Not a word – but let us talk anon.'

This talk between Barker, Leigh and the Court Theatre's manager J. E. Vedrenne 'led to the most important development in Barker's career', wrote his biographer C. B. Purdom. It was also, at long last, to provide a home for Shaw's plays. Barker believed that they were living at a time of theatrical renaissance in Britain. The starting of the new Abbey Theatre was one of many signs of fresh inspiration and creative experiment. 'The dramatists were turning away from old conventions and trying to formulate the experience of modern man,' Margery Morgan has written. 'The English theatre was once more open to the fructifying influence of a various European drama and was taking its place once more in the main stream of European tradition in the arts.'

Possibly because of the presence of the cautious Vedrenne, Barker's initial proposal was spectacularly modest. He had proved with Shaw's *Candida* and Murray's *Hippolytus* that there were actors who excelled at intellectual stage work; and he had shown that there was a cultivated public for such work – 'a big block of marble to chip, instead of putty as most plays are'. He therefore suggested giving regular matinées at the Court on those afternoons when the London West End theatres were closed. The management would then be able to engage first-class professional actors who would not be playing at those hours and, because they were interested in this new work, would be prepared to act for a nominal salary. To this proposal Leigh assented. Vedrenne took charge of the management and, with the backing of small sums of money from friends, they agreed to begin the experiment that autumn.

Barker believed that the ideal relation between stage and public was such as had existed in the Greek city-state. As the opening performance at the Court Theatre, he repeated the Murray-Euripides *Hippolytus*. The second Court play, after a good deal of negotiation, was *John Bull's Other Island*.

As a matter of policy Shaw continued to insist that the play could not do well in London. 'I dont mind its being announced as Vedrenne's Folly,' he allowed. It would, he promised, 'send the audience away howling'. At the same time he worked extraordinarily hard to make it succeed. 'The cutting bothers me fearfully,' he admitted to Barker. 'There is too much in the play.' With Barker's help he reduced it considerably – partly for the sake of the actors. As a drama critic he had kept an extensive file of actors of whom he thought highly and his knowledge of stage business and determination to get the players he wanted was to win him a reputation for excellent casts. Nominally it was Barker who produced *John Bull's Other Island*; in fact it was Shaw. Even the dullest theatrical matter seemed to engross him. 'You can imagine the state I am in with rehearsing,' he invited the actress Ada Rehan. 'It is great fun; and I have got them all to the point of believing that this is the turning point of their careers, and that something immense is happening . . . ' He had got himself to believe this too, and was anxious to arrange that the play did not open until Parliament reassembled. 'The political people will count for a great deal in the stalls,' he counselled Vedrenne, 'and they will not come back to town before the session opens.'

Shaw had strong opinions as to how all the parts should be played and scenes orchestrated. But these opinions were for the actors to interpret and adapt: 'Dont worry yourself by trying to carry out my suggestions exactly or hampering yourself in any way with them,' he advised J. L. Shine, who was playing Larry Doyle. 'Very likely when you study them over you will be able to improve on them.'

'That's all they're for. I think I am probably nearly right as to the best changes and stopping places on the journey; but as to the way of making them, follow your own feeling and make the most of your own skill: turn the whole thing inside out if you like – in fact you wont be able to help yourself when the spirit takes possession of you at full pressure – but dont hesitate on my account to make the part entirely your own: my idea of having my play acted is not to insist on everybody rattling my particular bag of tricks.'

He was full of advice, but also ready to learn; and his tirades, being comic performances themselves, did not shrivel the actors' self-confidence. 'I know very well that it is often the artists who give the author least trouble who get the least acknowledgement and have their virtues taken as a matter of course,' he wrote to Ellen O'Malley, who took the part of Nora. 'This is not so, I hope, with me: I am very sensible of how good you have been in every way, though I have had no opportunity of saying so.'

Being in part an actor himself, Shaw held a reasonable balance between the interests of playwright and player. He was respected for his understanding, vitality, expertise. By the opening performance, on 1 November 1904, he had filled everyone at the Court with a belief in the value of their work and a spirit of dedication to himself. 'You are a man *worth* working for,' J. L. Shine wrote to him just before the first matinée, 'and, if your brilliant play is not efficiently rendered, we alleged actors & actresses deserve extermination, for your Godlike patience and courteous consideration, combined with your skilful and workmanlike handling of detail, has been a revelation to me.'

The reviews, though sometimes niggardly, were good, and the best critics wrote most enthusiastically. Max Beerbohm's notice in the *Saturday Review* was headed 'Mr Shaw at his Best'. Desmond MacCarthy declared the play to be 'an absolute success'; and William Archer in *The World* wrote that Shaw 'has done nothing more original . . . There is no other country in the world, I believe, where its qualities would have been so grudgingly recognised'.

To the fifth matinée, on 10 November, Beatrice Webb brought the Conservative Prime Minister, Arthur Balfour. To her surprise he liked the play so much that he eventually saw it five times, bringing with him two leaders of the Liberal opposition, Campbell-Bannerman and Asquith. Most people in London saw it as a largely affectionate satire on the Liberal Party's attitude towards Ireland, and Balfour himself praised it for clearing away humbug at any cost. His interest and the good notices led to the play being revived three times the following year, and to a special evening performance being given, on 11 March 1905, for King Edward VII. Short of organizing a revolution, Shaw told Vedrenne and Barker, 'I have no remedy'. The King laughed so forcefully that he broke the special chair Vedrenne had hired for the evening and, in falling, flung Shaw's dramatic reputation high into the air. Except for a period during the First World War, Shaw never fully recovered his unpopularity. Here, a few months short of his fiftieth year, was success: yet he felt uneasy. What was it worth? What had been the cost? 'I am getting quite maddened by the business (mostly refusing it) that my recent boom has brought on me,' he wrote to Florence Farr. 'It is enough to make one curse the day I ever wrote a play. If I would consent, the whole 13 plays would be produced simultaneously about the middle of April.' The Prime Minister had told the King, and the King had told his countrymen, and now they were all telling the world that G.B.S. was the funniest of funny Irishmen. He began to react against the play. It had been received so well because it was '*not* profound' and did 'not involve the usual struggle with me as a moral revolutionist'. He refused to accept royalties for Edward VII's performance and gave his answer to his sovereign's heehawing by adding to the programme of a later production a 'personal appeal' to the audience not to demoralize the actors with shouts of laughter and noisy applause.

'Have you considered that in all good plays tears and laughter lie very close together, and that it must be very distressing to an actress who is trying to keep her imagination fixed on pathetic emotions to hear bursts of laughter breaking out at something she is supposed to be unconscious of? . . .

'Would you dream of stopping the performance of a piece of music to applaud every bar that happened to please you? and do you not know that an act of a play is intended, just like a piece of music, to be heard without interruption from beginning to end? . . .

'Have you noticed that people look very nice when they smile or look pleased, but look shockingly ugly when they roar with laughter or shout excitedly or sob loudly? Smiles make no noise.'

Success and failure also lie close together and Shaw's appeal seems to be questioning which he had achieved. He did not feel he had succeeded. Other people had agreed to rank him as successful: that was all. Eleven days after the royal command performance of *John Bull's Other Island*, he began a new play. In this, the last of his 'big three', he would open up again the public's struggle with him as a moral revolutionist. He would challenge his own popularity with something that was 'all religion and morals and Fabian debates'. 'The play is wildly impossible,' he told the actress Eleanor Robson. ' . . . It would run for a week. But what a week that would be!'

[7]

*It seems to me that what Barbara finds out is that the ancient Greek
(whoever he was) who said 'First make sure of an income and then
practise virtue' was rightly preaching natural morality.*
Shaw to Gilbert Murray (5 September 1941)

Father Keegan had been 'an immense success (I mean inside myself, though he did very well on stage); and now I want to see whether I can make a woman a saint too', Shaw wrote to Eleanor Robson. The previous autumn he had been 'bowled over' by her acting in the title role of Israel Zangwill's *Merely Mary Ann*. 'I have just seen Mary Ann,' he told her, 'and I am for ever yours devotedly. I have no interest in mere females; but I *love* all artists; they belong to me in the most sacred way and you are an artist . . . ' Since Charlotte too had been 'enchanted', they invited this good-looking young actress to lunch. There was a business reason for their invitation – that was why G.B.S. had differentiated so emphatically between females and artists; that was why Charlotte had remained enchanted. He wanted her for Gloria in *You Never Can Tell*. But Eleanor could not see her way to joining the Court crowd in what her business manager called 'freak plays'. They would not suit her at all. Shaw answered politely that he would write a new play for her – not a comedy: and four and a half months later reported that 'Fate has done its work'. Eleanor had gone to America, Shaw had been working for three weeks at *Major Barbara* and 'there you are in the middle of it', he wrote to her.

'I swear I never thought of you until you came up a trap in the middle of the stage & got into my heroine's empty clothes and said Thank you: "I" am the mother of that play. Though I am not sure that you are not its father; for you simply danced in here & captivated me & then deserted me & left me with my unborn play to bring into existence. I simply dare not count the number of months. Anyhow the heroine is so like you that I see nobody in the wide world who can play her except you.'

Charlotte was not happy with the way her husband sometimes corresponded with actresses. But she knew he had a cerebrum of good sense. He believed that Eleanor Robson was exceptional; he wanted her for the Court Theatre and thought she would be particularly striking in the piquant role of his Salvation Army officer. She was little more perhaps than a physical and professional model for the part: the intellectual and biographical model was Beatrice Webb. Like Barbara, Beatrice was a rich man's daughter and had gone East Ending with the gospel of social salvation. Her violent reaction to the play ('a dance of devils . . . hell tossed on the stage, with no hope of heaven . . . the triumph of the unmoral purpose') registered her involvement in the ruin of Barbara's salvationism.

Barbara, as a prototype of St Joan, is a woman apparently converted from religion to a creed of action. She moves from innocence to disillusionment and then takes a further step by accepting a reality beyond the moralist's dichotomy of 'good' and 'evil' and becoming capable of effective action as a practical idealist. But hers is not really a conversion: it is a growing-up. She is a chip off the old block, her father Undershaft owning (like St Joan) a genius for action that Barbara inherits. The man who stands between Barbara and Undershaft, Adolphus Cusins, is the real convert. Modelled on the classicist Gilbert Murray, Cusins represents Shaw's own position: that of the fastidious scholar trying to find his place in the political world. He is attracted to Undershaft as the only man who can make him effective through marrying his academicism to power. However the problem that confronted Shaw was how to reveal Cusins's conversion as something other than the simple triumph of Undershaft – and outright victory for the devil.

There are more false starts, deletions and drastic changes in the holograph manuscript of *Major Barbara* than in any of Shaw's previous plays. He was working under pressure, but essentially it was pressure 'inside myself' which he externalized and located in the surrounding circumstances. He was 'too busy rehearsing and producing' to do anything else. Between the beginning of March and the beginning of June 1905 there had been rehearsals and productions at the Court of *How He Lied to Her Husband*, *John Bull's Other Island*, *You Never Can Tell*, *Candida* and *Man and Superman*. There were plans too for Ellen Terry to appear in *Captain Brassbound's Conversion* and Johnston Forbes Robertson in *Caesar and Cleopatra*. In America this year Robert Loraine staged a hugely successful production of *Man and Superman*; and Arnold Daly put on, rather less successfully, *Candida*, *John Bull's Other Island* and a controversial production of *Mrs Warren's Profession*. 'I have been overwhelmed,' Shaw told Eleanor Robson.

In retaliation and 'mostly in Great Northern express trains', he polished off a 'new and original tragedy' early that summer. *Passion Poison and Petrification or The Fatal Gazogene* completed a trilogy of 'tomfooleries' done while still at work on his 'big three'. The invitation had come from Cyril Maud on behalf of the Actors' Orphanage which each year commissioned a playwright to compose a burlesque of old time melodrama to be performed in the Royal Botanical Gardens of Regent's Park during the Theatrical Garden Party. Shaw's idea came from a story he had once told the Archer children about his aunt, who liked making plaster of Paris figures, and her cat which one day mistook the liquid plaster of Paris for milk and, while asleep, turned into a ponderous mass of cement – to be used by the aunt as a doorstop. 'It may interest Mrs Archer to know that the Petrifaction alludes to a great human development of the tragedy of the plaster cat,' Shaw told Archer. This 'wildest nonsense' anticipates the Theatre of the Absurd. From the beginning when the cuckoo clock strikes sixteen (signifying eleven o'clock at night) to the moment when Lady Magnesia Fitztollemache's lover is obliged to eat part of the ceiling (containing lime) as an antidote to the jealous husband's poison, we are, in Irving Wardle's words, 'into Ionesco territory' which overlaps Shaw's fantastical landscape.

This 'brief tragedy for Barns and Booths' by the 'Chelsea Shakespeare' was performed 'for the first time in any tent' at intervals during the afternoon of 14 July. The author, who was absent, described it as a 'colossal success', and arranged for the royalties on all performances for the rest of its copyright life to be paid to the Actors' Orphanage Fund. 'Charities are remorseless,' he explained.

He returned to, but could not finish, *Major Barbara*. At the beginning of July Charlotte took charge. Their tenancy of the Old House at Harmer Green had just come to an end. She proposed removing G.B.S. from the horrors of this domestic earthquake and returning him to Ireland. It was twenty-nine years since he had packed his carpet bag and boarded the North Wall boat for London. Like Larry Doyle, he had 'an instinct against going back to Ireland: an instinct so strong that I'd rather go with you to the South Pole . . . ' Nevertheless, like Larry Doyle, he went. It was not of course on his own initiative. 'I went back to please my wife; and a curious reluctance to retrace my steps made me land in the south and enter Dublin through the backdoor from Meath rather than return as I came, through the front door on the sea.'

Shaw consented because he felt exhausted. He would rest and then he would finish his play. Charlotte was particularly excited. They were to stay at Derry, her father's house three miles out of Rosscarbery, a little market town in County Cork. Charlotte had wanted G.B.S. to see her childhood home. It was a solid grey stone structure built on rising ground with gardens that sloped down to a lake. She described it to him. From the terrace, facing south, they 'could look out on a great sweep of the bay, with a lighthouse rising like the stub of a pencil on the farthest point of land'. But could he work there? That was what Shaw needed to know. Did the house have a sitting-room well away from the drawing-room? This was vital since they were to be joined by Charlotte's sister, Mary Cholmondeley, and her husband who was a colonel. It was important to be out of earshot.

G.B.S. spent much of the next three months in that sitting-room getting on 'scrap by scrap' with his new play. It progressed very slowly – 'a speech a day or so', he informed Vedrenne. He also asked Eleanor Robson to let her manager know it would be announced as 'a Discussion in Three Long Acts', and be more freakish than anything he could have dreamed 'or dreaded'. And he promised Granville Barker that he intended to treat the public to a stiff dose of lecturing: 'if you want the higher Shaw drama you must take the higher chances.' But behind his screen of confidence, all this 'gambling with ideas and emotions' was causing Shaw anxiety. His words flew up but nothing was resolved. 'I have not yet finished the play,' he wrote to Eleanor Robson on 21 August; 'and my inspiration, as far as the heroine is concerned, is gone. I shall finish it with my brains alone; and it will not now go right up into heaven.' On 11 September he reported that it was 'just finished': but he had been left 'in a condition of sullen desperation concerning it'.

He had turned back from autobiography to politics – from his marriage and the country of his childhood to the economic questions that had first brought the Fabians together and provided the themes of his *Plays Unpleasant*. 'It is clear that *Widowers' Houses* and *Major Barbara*, being dramas of the cash nexus (in plot) could not have been written by a non-economist,' he declared. Over twenty years separated the beginning of *Widowers' Houses* from the completion of *Major Barbara*, and though the living standards of the middle class had risen in this period there were now almost a million people in the country receiving Poor Law relief. In London at the beginning of 1905 the number of paupers had risen to one hundred and fifty thousand, of whom fifteen hundred were 'casual paupers' sleeping in the streets or the casual wards of workhouses and living, according to William Booth, 'below the standard of the London cab-horse'. Booth had founded the Salvation Army in 1878 to make war on poverty. Though Britain was still at the summit of her imperial power, much of her population existed on the edge of destitution. It was this paradox that Shaw investigated in his play using, as a symbol of Imperialist prosperity, the armaments industry.

Why Are the Many Poor? the Fabians had asked in their first pamphlet twenty-one years before. The 'slum sisters' of the Salvation Army had given minor relief and the Fabians an academic answer, but the problem had deepened beyond reach of individualistic enterprise or debating-room tactics. What was needed, Shaw felt, was drastic collective action – a big bang to restart the world with its two nations of rich and poor fused into one.

'One never really makes portraits of people in fiction,' he wrote: 'what happens is that certain people inspire one to invent fictitious characters for them, which is quite another matter.' Beatrice Webb wondered whether her father might have inspired the character of Undershaft. In fact the millionaire munitions capitalist seems to have had a composite inspiration: there was the dramatist Charles McEvoy's father, a benign grey-haired gentleman who, after fighting on the side of the Confederacy in the American Civil War, settled down quietly to establish a torpedo factory; there was Hans Renold, a businessman belonging to the higher grades of culture who came to lecture the Fabian Society on the principles of 'service before self' in the manufacture of high explosives. Another prototype was Alfred Nobel, 'the gentle Bolshevik' who had patented dynamite in 1867 and in 1901 endowed the Nobel Peace Prize which, as the critic Louis Crompton commented, 'challenged the humanitarian liberals among his personal friends to solve the problems his discoveries had created'. Nobel was a deeply paradoxical man – a verse imitator of

Shelley and sardonic humanitarian who sold his patents to the highest bidder and liked to claim that 'my factories may end war sooner than your peace congresses'. He was immensely wealthy since 'my home is where my work is and my work is everywhere' – a motto that would perfectly suit Undershaft, whose practice was 'to give arms to all men who offer an honest price for them, without respect of persons or principles'. William Manchester has argued that Shaw's model was Friedrich Alfred Krupp, the Prussian 'Cannon King' whose paternalistic welfare arrangements for his workers in Essen may have suggested Undershaft's model town. Krupp had died in 1902 and was succeeded by his daughter Bertha. 'In 1906 – the year after the publication of *Major Barbara* – she married Dr Gustav von Bohlen und Halbach,' wrote Maurice Valency, 'who later assumed the name of Krupp, and took over the management of the Krupp combine, thus fulfilling in reality the role of Dr Cusins in Shaw's play.' Shaw himself wrote that Undershaft emerged into the world as Henry Ford. Other critics assumed that he derived from the legendary Basil Zaharoff, chief salesman of Vickers, who boasted: 'I was a Russian in Russia, a Greek in Greece, a Frenchman in Paris. I made wars so that I could sell arms to both sides.'

Such a multiplicity of candidates attests to the rise of arms traffic throughout the world at the turn of the century. Some, like Zaharoff, made no apology for their merchandise. Others, such as Britain's largest arms maker Sir William Armstrong, placed the responsibility for 'legitimate application' of weapons on the buyer and speculated that better armaments might well render war less barbarous. Others again, such as Nobel, argued for the deterrent effect of explosives. 'The day two army corps can destroy each other in one second, all civilized nations will recoil from war and disband their armies.'

Undershaft expresses all these attitudes. But when he challenges Cusins to 'make war on war' he is deliberately tempting him with the conventional paradox of those times which soon led to German, French and British soldiers being shot down with guns made by their fellow-countrymen in a 'war to end wars' that did not end wars.

Though Undershaft deceives others he is not self-deceived. He knows that 'the more destructive war becomes, the more fascinating we find it'. The demonic force of this mood gained on Shaw as he wrote the last half of *Major Barbara* at Derry. The first act of the play is a drawing-room comedy set in the library of Lady Britomart's house in Wilton Crescent which displays the wealth of capitalist society; the second act is a Dickensian melodrama showing capitalism's destitution at the West Ham Shelter of the Salvation Army. Shaw had got as far as Undershaft's arrival at West Ham when he took his manuscript to Ireland. From then on Undershaft begins to take control of the play and in the third act, a political fantasy set in Perivale St Andrews, a futuristic model town 'beautifully situated and beautiful in itself', he dominates the stage.

The day before Shaw left for Ireland, he had written to Eleanor Robson describing Barbara as 'a religious young person, who has been a wonderful success in the Salvation Army, making converts in all directions, and as to violent and brutal roughs who beat women on the stage in the most melodramatic manner, she stands them on their heads as if they were naughty children'. Cusins he described as a poet and a professor who has fallen in love with Barbara 'and joined the Army for her sake. She makes him play the drum because he has a fine ear for metrical quantities. But he is far too subtle for the Salvationist religion; and his one dread is that she will find out that he is in the Army to worship her and not god'. As for Undershaft, he has 'a most terribly wicked religion of his own, believing only in money and gun-powder' and he forces Barbara 'to recognize that her gift is not the result of any organized religion, but a magic of her own which sets her as far apart from the Salvation Army as from any other invention of Man . . . [and] is akin to something that makes the professor of Greek a poet'.

This was Shaw's plan. But he had not been in Ireland three weeks before he was writing to Louis Calvert, the actor who was to play Undershaft at the Court Theatre, that 'the part of the millionaire cannon founder is becoming more and more formidable. Broadbent and Keegan rolled into one, with Mephistopheles thrown in; that is what it is like . . . Undershaft is diabolically subtle, gentle, self-possessed, powerful, stupendous . . . '

On 8 September Shaw scribbled 'End of the Play' at the conclusion of the third act. But Undershaft's annihilation of everyone else had left him feeling dissatisfied. Why had it happened? 'As I write plays as they come to me, by inspiration and not by conscious logic, I am as likely as anyone else to be mistaken about their morals,' he later wrote to Gilbert Murray. He had told Eleanor Robson what, by conscious logic, he intended to do. But what he had actually done was to let his unconscious Will, with its fantasies of violence, speak through Undershaft. That name itself brings together the wishes of the unconscious and the underground kingdom of the Devil, and moves the debate to a contest between Shaw's conscious Fabian endeavours and the unconscious impulses that subvert them.

In London earlier that year he had blamed the pressure of business for his difficult progress on the play; at Derry he attributed his difficulties to the moisture of the Irish climate. His murderous instincts, however, are more likely to have been aroused by three months' niceness to 'Mrs Chumly', Charlotte's sister. In the six years since she had begged Charlotte to fortress her money from her firebrand husband, Mary Cholmondeley's determination never to see her brother-in-law had wavered. She had read and heard a good deal about him and, pricked by curiosity, allowed Charlotte to persuade her finally to meet him. She was still wary, however, and for the first week or two, perhaps feeling her disapproval, G.B.S. stayed working all day in the sitting-room at Derry. Charlotte joined him there in the mornings to do secretarial work; and in the afternoons she would visit friends in the neighbourhood with 'Sissy'. Soon G.B.S. was accompanying them on these walks, and the two women enjoyed themselves 'so extraordinarily that I got a sort of secondhand enjoyment – largely mixed with resignation – out of it', he confided to Beatrice Webb. ' . . . Mrs C and I, in view of our previously rather distant relations, laid ourselves out to conciliate one another, and rather more than succeeded.'

'I have the important advantage in such matters of not being nearly so disagreeable personally as one would suppose from my writings. I am now completely adopted on the usual lunatic privileged terms in the Cholmondeley household. I have taken several photographs of Mrs C and taught her to swim. The Colonel has presented me with a watch which tells the date and the phases of the moon. I play accompaniments to Mrs C's singing and the past is buried.'

From that past and behind this polite patina the sinister figure of Undershaft expanded. So favourable an impression meanwhile was G.B.S. making on the Cholmondeleys that they invited him to go with them on a round of Irish peers in their castles and only accepted his refusal ('the worm turned at last') on the understanding that he would rejoin them the following month at Edstaston, their home in Shropshire.

Shaw arrived back in London alone on 30 September and the next day went down to read his play at Gilbert Murray's house in Oxford. He was obviously worried but, having escaped the Irish weather, hoped to regain his tone. The ostensible reason for his visit was to ensure that those people on whom his characters were modelled would not be offended. When starting the play he had written to Murray saying that he intended calling it *Murray's Mother-in-Law* and asking whether Murray himself minded being represented as a foundling. Murray replied that the only thing that Shaw did at his peril was to fasten on him the Christian name Adolphus – a reference to the King of Sweden, Gustavus Adolphus, a brilliant linguist who subsequently mastered the art of war. In Shaw's first draft the professor had been called Dolly Tankerville. But Shaw changed this Wildean surname to Cusins (which Murray invariably misspelled 'Cusens'), suggesting the foundling's curious relationship (his own cousin) to himself. Names are carefully chosen in *Major Barbara*. Bodger, for example, the whisky distiller (who never appears on stage) is based on Dewar, replacing the 'doer' with the person who botches what he does. Lady Britomart sounds like a British martinet and is exactly right for the imperious personality of Lady Carlisle (Murray's mother-in-law) whose biographer used as epigraph a quotation from *Hamlet*: 'An eye like Mars, to threaten and command.' No one appears to have minded being Shavianized for the stage, partly because, as Murray acknowledged, 'you can manage to be so exceedingly personal without being in the faintest degree disagreeable or offensive' and partly because such portraits were only cursorily suggested by their originals. Shaw later admitted that he had got a false impression of Murray from a first meeting – though this was useful enough for self-camouflage.

His audience at Oxford that day included Murray and his wife, and Granville Barker who was shortly to play the part of Cusins. At the end of the second act they were, Murray remembered, 'thrilled with enthusiasm, especially at the Salvation Army scenes. Act 3, in which the idealists surrender to the armaments industries, was a terrible disap-pointment to us and, I think, unsatisfying to Shaw himself. He tried to justify his general line of solution, but muttered: "I don't know how to end the thing." '

Shaw returned to London and that night wrote to Murray confessing that he felt 'quite desperate about my last act: I think I must simply rewrite it. Merely cutting the cackle – and cackle is just what it is – will be of no use.'

To encourage himself he went next day to the Albert Hall where the Salvation Army was holding a festival to commemorate dead comrades. As a music critic, he had praised the liveliness and efficiency of Salvation Army Bands and now, as they confidently played

' "When the roll is called up yonder
I'LL BE THERE"

'I stood in the middle of the centre grand tier box, in the front row, and sang it as it has never been sung before,' he told Vedrenne. 'The Times will announce my conversion tomorrow.'

The following afternoon he joined Charlotte and the Cholmondeleys at Edstaston. He had received a letter from Gilbert Murray enclosing some ideas set down in dialogue for the third act. 'What I am driving at, is to get the real dénouement of the play, after Act ii,' Murray explained. 'And I think that something like what I suggest *is* the real dénouement.'

'It makes Cusens come out much stronger, but I think that rather an advantage. Otherwise you get a simple defeat of the Barbara principles by the Undershaft principles ... the Barbara principles should, after their first crushing defeat, turn upon the U principles and embrace them with a view of destroying or subduing them for the B. P.'s own ends. It is a gamble, and the issue uncertain.'

The rewriting of his last scene took Shaw eleven days. 'I want to get Cusins beyond the point of wanting power,' he replied to Murray. ' . . . his choice lies, not between going with Undershaft or not going with him, but between standing on the footplate at work, and merely sitting in a first class carriage reading Ruskin & explaining what a low dog the driver is and how steam is ruining the country.'

The Edstaston manuscript, which was completed on 15 October 1905, differs from the Derry manuscript in the way Gilbert Murray had outlined. The excisions have the effect of making Barbara and Cusins less facetious and more decisive. Barbara no longer tells Undershaft, as she does in the Derry manuscript, that if she owned the munitions factory she would 'give the people a weeks notice to get out of danger; and then give Cholly [Lomax] the high explosives shed for a smoking room'; Cusins no longer tells Undershaft that if he 'were to put all the Kingdoms of the earth along with your cannons and millions into one scale, and one of Barbara's hairpins into the other, the hairpin would be the heavier scale for me'. During the Faustian bargaining for Cusins's soul ('Does your soul belong to him now?' Barbara asks) the Edstaston manuscript shows Cusins accepting Undershaft's bid without consulting Barbara ('If I had thrown the burden of the choice on you,' he tells her, 'you would sooner or later have despised me for it'). In the Derry manuscript he had tried to throw this burden of choice on Barbara: 'Dont you understand that I am ready to do what you wish – that I would not take a thousand foundries or a thousand fortunes and lose you. It is you who must decide.'

This last scene is perhaps the most complex and ambiguous Shaw ever wrote. The debate between Undershaft, Barbara and Cusins takes place at many levels. Barbara, who represents evangelical Christianity, has lost her faith by the end of Act II, using Christ's words upon the cross: 'My God: why hast thou forsaken me?' Cusins represents scepticism, a purely negative force by itself; and Undershaft embodies Shaw's concept of the Life Force, a mindless, aimless power for good-or-evil depending (like all technology) on what human beings themselves decide to do with it.

Barbara's transfiguration must come through a resurrected faith that involves Cusins and Undershaft – her future husband and her father: three in one and one in three. While she occupies the position of the Son, Cusins is the Holy Ghost and Undershaft God the Father. But Undershaft is also the Devil – 'You may be a devil; but God speaks through you sometimes,' Barbara admits. In the religion of Creative Evolution the Old Man with a Beard sitting on a cloud is replaced by the anonymous concept of energy as a force without morality. So Barbara discovers that 'there is no wicked side [of life]: life is all one'. By the same token God and the Devil are one. Cusins recognizes in Undershaft the mysterious spirit of Dionysus, capable of creation and destruction. 'This spirit that I call Dionysus,' wrote Gilbert Murray, 'this magic of inspiration and joy, is it not as a matter of fact the great wrecker of men's lives?'

Human beings therefore 'create' God or the Devil according to the way in which they employ Divine Energy. On the psychological level Barbara is the superego, Cusins the ego and Undershaft the id: three in one and one in three. According to the system laid out in *The Quintessence of Ibsenism*, Barbara is the idealist, Cusins the realist and Undershaft the philistine. In this last scene Shaw attempts to unite all three: Cusins is to be Barbara's husband and, as the foundling inheritor of his father-in-law's munitions factory, will become Andrew Undershaft VIII. This represents a step up the evolutionary ladder since Cusins will be able to join his intelligence and imagination, and Barbara's spiritual passion, to his father-in-law's inheritance of money and material strength.

For all his pragmatism and lack of hypocrisy, Undershaft is a limited man. He writes up UNASHAMED as his motto and is contemptuous of democratic shams – the 'common mob of slaves and idolators', as he calls them, that piously fill in its ballot papers and imagine it is governing its masters. The 'ballot paper that really governs', he says, 'is the paper that has a bullet wrapped up in it'. Though he exults in his power he is also its prisoner. 'I can make cannons,' he says: 'I cannot make courage and conviction.' He can provide food and housing only for his employees; he cannot change society. His factory is the 'Works Department of Hell', but the garden city attached to it (like one Broadbent is to bring to Rosscullen) 'only needs a cathedral to be a heavenly city instead of a hellish one'. Armaments are the instruments of revolutionary change and also the means by which authoritarian governments repress change. The will to live must do battle with the tendency to self-destruction. Undershaft is trapped by his trade, the slave of a munition works that, as Cusins points out, is run by the 'most rascally part of society, the money hunters, the pleasure hunters, the military promotion hunters'.

The ambiguity of the play partly derives from the conflict of Undershaft's motives. By inviting Cusins to be his successor is he tempting him, as Mephistopheles tempted Faust, to his damnation? Or is he an instinctive agent for the Life Force seeking in Cusins a better use of the power he commands? In fact he is doing both: that is how life operates. 'You cannot have power for good without having power for evil, too.'

Cusins believes that he 'has more power' than Undershaft, that he will reject the armourer's faith and 'sell cannons to whom I please and refuse them to whom I please'. To this Undershaft replies: 'From the moment when you become Andrew Undershaft, you will never do as you please again.' This seems to be the percipient voice of the Devil having recruited a partner in his hellish trade. But elsewhere Undershaft appears to challenge Cusins and Barbara to use this power in a fundamentally different way: 'Society cannot be saved,' he says (paraphrasing Plato's *Republic*), 'until either the Professors of Greek take to making gunpowder, or else the makers of gunpowder become Professors of Greek.'

Cusins, however, sees beyond this pact between idealists and realists. It is upon the philistines that the betterment of society finally depends. In the Derry manuscript Undershaft had posed a conundrum for Cusins: 'Why is a government a government?' And Cusins answered: 'Because the people are fools.' In the Edstaston manuscript Cusins states his belief in the common man:

'As a teacher of Greek I gave the intellectual man weapons against the common man. I now want to give the common man weapons against the intellectual man. I love the common people. I want to arm them against the lawyer, doctor, the priest, the literary man, professor, the artist and the politician, who, once in authority, are the most dangerous, disastrous and tyrannical of all the fools, rascals and impostors. I want a democratic power strong enough to force the intellectual oligarchy to use its genius for the general good or else perish.'

Is Cusins the vehicle for a power 'simple enough for the common man to use' and 'strong enough to force the intellectual oligarchy to use its genius for the general good'? Or is he the literary man, a prig and a professor, who will prove disastrous in authority?

Cusins enshrines something of Gilbert Murray's political idealism – it is not surprising that Murray's later work for the League of Nations should be in line with Cusins's decision to 'make war on war'. Shaw and Barker felt the excitement of working in the theatre with this brilliant young Oxford professor – a world-changer with fierce strength of conviction who shared his ideas of true democracy with them. He was, Shaw told Pinero, a 'genuine artistic anarchic character'. Shaw obviously has Murray in mind when he describes Cusins as torn between a benevolent temperament and angry impatience. 'He is a most implacable, determined, tenacious, intolerant person who by mere force of character presents himself as – and indeed actually is – considerate, gentle, exploratory, even mild and apologetic, capable possibly of murder, but not of cruelty or coarseness.' Murray steered Shaw between historical misconceptions and pedantic caricature, urging him to stick to the development of his arguments instead of exploding them prematurely into jokes that unsettled Murray's prim resistance to ridicule. Shaw wanted to bring Murray's classical scholarship to bear on twentieth-century politics and he uses Undershaft to give muscle to a man D. H. Lawrence was to call 'all disembodied mind'. The passionate thinking Shaw put into *Major Barbara* was partly the result of this association with Murray; and their friendship became a bonus added to the successful breakthrough of Shaw's plays at the Court. Both these factors helped to make the positive ending to *Major Barbara* – an ending with the 'inconsequence of madness in it'.

This hard-won optimism had survived the initial effects of Shavian irony, but there are some signs of rejection to the graft. Shaw wanted to create in Cusins 'the reverse in every point of the theatrical strong man', he told Murray. 'I want him to go on his quality wholly, and not to make the smallest show of physical robustness or brute determination. His selection by Undershaft should be a puzzle to people who believe in the strong-silent-still-waters-run-deep hero of melodrama.' Cusins is to be a theatrical paradox and a philosophical synthesis between the spiritual passion of Barbara and her father's material power: between emotion and money. But he never convincingly realizes this idealized concept, perhaps because it does not exist in society and because Undershaft steals the show by becoming, as Shaw had revealingly written to Louis Calvert, 'Broadbent and Keegan rolled into one'.

Beatrice Webb records Shaw as arguing 'earnestly and cleverly, even persuasively, in favour of what he imagines to be his central theme – *the need for preliminary good physical environment before anything could be done to raise the intelligence and morality of the average sensual man*'. But Undershaft's general attitude towards life continued to trouble people. To one of them, Shaw wrote:

'Spiritual values do not and cannot exist for hungry, roofless and naked people. Any religion that puts spiritual values before physical necessities is what Marx meant by opium and Nietzsche called a slave morality. Barbara despairs only for the moment before she grasps this truth. She ends in very high spirits, having at last got the values in their proper places.'

Shaw's allusion here to *King Lear* points to his difficulty with *Major Barbara*. Shakespeare's storm rages within and around Lear: in *Major Barbara* the spiritual and physical elements, symbolic and literal meanings, are separated. 'Come, come, my young friends: let us live in the real world,' Undershaft says to Cusins and Barbara in the Derry manuscript. 'Your moral world is a vacuum: nothing is done there, though a good deal is eaten and drunk by the moralists at the expense of the real world. It is nice to live in the vacuum and repeat the fine phrases and edifying sentiments a few literary people have manufactured for you . . . ' Yet *Major Barbara* is a morality play whose last scene develops into a philosophical debate set in the white walled vacuum of Perivale St Andrews and powered by Shaw's rising sense of frustration. The armaments industry was a sign of that frustration as well as a good metaphor for capitalist society: it works less well on a simple level as a provider of food and the coin for optimism in a socialist co-operative movement of the future.

Of all the play's authoritative aphorisms and ideas echoing from Plato, Euripides, Nietzsche, the most significant derive from Shaw's reading of Blake's *Marriage of Heaven and Hell*. What Shaw believed to be the central theme of *Major Barbara* – that 'the way of life lies through the factory of death' – is similar to several proverbs of Blake, with whom Shaw shared a religious faith in Energy. He could expound this faith so well that even Beatrice Webb 'found it difficult to answer him'. Yet, she added, 'he did not convince me'.

' . . . the impression left is that Cusins and Barbara are neither of them convinced by Undershaft's argument, but that they are uttering words, like the silly son, to bridge over a betrayal of their own convictions.'

Shaw's genius went into the creation of Undershaft. The armaments manufacturer loves his enemies because they have kept him in business. Like Christ, he comes 'not to send peace but a sword'. Cusins ('an exceedingly curious and difficult part') he had constructed 'with my brains alone' – and with Gilbert Murray's. 'But you are driving me against my nature,' Cusins protests to Undershaft. 'I hate war.' Undershaft leads Cusins across the 'abyss of moral horror between me and your accursed aerial battleships'. Shaw, too, seems to be driven against his nature. He had wanted to move Cusins and Barbara 'beyond the point of wanting power'. But their final permeation of the Undershaft firm lacks conviction on stage. Shaw knew this. He continued tinkering with this last scene up to 1930 when the Standard Edition of the play was published, trying to make Barbara and Cusins 'more prominent' and giving them 'more commanding positions on stage and stronger movement'. But as he told Robert Morley ten years later during the making of the film version of the play: 'That's always been a terrible act. I don't think anyone could do anything with it.'

Shaw explained Undershaft's 'triumph' as being inevitable, since Barbara and Cusins 'are very young, very romantic, very academic, very ignorant of the world'. For these reasons it seems more likely that, in their passage from innocence to experience, they are moved not beyond but towards wanting power. The stage directions describe Barbara as being '*hypnotized*' when Undershaft, 'looking powerfully into her eyes', asks her to tell him 'what power really means'. Behind the theme of priorities lay Shaw's growing obsession with power. 'I am half tempted to take the play right up to the skies at the end,' he had written to Eleanor Robson. In the Edstaston manuscript this is what he does. Barbara 'has gone right up into the skies', says Cusins. It is not a happy image next to a high-explosives shed. Like Cusins being driven against his nature, Barbara tries to resist this raising of hell to heaven: 'Oh, if only I could get away from you,' she says to Cusins after his acceptance of Undershaft's proposal, 'and from father and from it all! if I could have the wings of a dove and fly away to heaven!' But Shaw could not allow this. Barbara must be what he wanted himself to be: part of a world will.

'You have learnt something,' Undershaft tells Barbara at a genuinely touching moment. 'That always feels at first as if you have lost something.' Shaw himself seems to have felt this sensation of loss. 'But oh! Eleanor between ourselves, the play, especially in the last act, is a mere ghost, at least so it seems to me . . . It was a fearful job . . . Brainwork comes natural to me; but this time I knew I was working – and now nobody understands.'

This lack of understanding proceeds from the complexity of what Shaw was questioning. Is socialism at odds with human nature? Are the self-destructive impulses of human beings ineradicable? Are there ways of disarming oppressive power that do not betray the cause that uses them? Is Shaw himself merely an idealist? Though the affirmation comes out strongly, getting through to it had been the hardest work the playwright had done. And the chance that he is wrong remains; the adversaries still flourish and may win. No play can alter the nature of reality. The shifting conflict of ideas which Shaw was trying to resolve in *Major Barbara* shows us the intransigence of the world in which Shavian realists have to work.

Barbara's ecstasy of mysticism looks like 'a mere ghost' when compared to her instinctive attraction to her father's weapons factory. 'After all, my dear old mother has more sense than any of you. I felt like her when I saw this place – felt that I must have it – that never, never, never could I let it go.' This is the voice of power with its ability to devour other feelings. In Barbara it is the spiritualist equivalent of Lady Britomart's acquisitiveness

– and a psychological need to pull her back from despair. But the Devil's Force of Death speech in *Man and Superman*, with its more efficient engines of destruction ('of sword and gun and poison gas') leads straight to Undershaft's weapons factory with its 'aerial battleships' that eventually will fly over Captain Shotover's villa in Sussex, at the climax of *Heartbreak House*, threatening with its '*terrific explosion*' the end of humankind.

Shaw's optimism was a perilous act of faith focused, as in *Man and Superman*, on the future. He had looked in *John Bull's Other Island* for a country where the 'facts were not brutal and the dreams not unreal'. In Perivale St Andrews nothing is achieved 'by words and dreams', by preaching and reasoning: killing is 'the final test of conviction'. It is the nightmare of a man with 'honour and humanity on my side, wit in my head, skill in my hand, and a higher life for my aim', who has a vision of world war to come. In the aftermath of which, through the fantasy of *Back to Methuselah*, he will refashion humankind in the image of his heart's desire.

*

The Salvation Army lent uniforms for the production at the Court Theatre. 'I have strained the resources of the stage to breaking point,' Shaw claimed. He continued altering the text in the prompt book during rehearsals which Barker (who had cultivated a remarkable resemblance to Gilbert Murray) persistently interrupted with his drum (having, Shaw complained, 'no proper sense of the degradation of playing it'). *Major Barbara* needed 'a quite exceptionally strong company'. Some of the actors, in particular Louis Calvert, had difficulty in learning their lines: there were so many. 'Once or twice at the early rehearsals I felt I ought to kill you,' Shaw wrote to Eleanor Robson in America. Barbara was her baby – and she had left the actress Annie Russell to nurse it. To Annie Russell herself, Shaw was characteristically helpful. He sent link after link in a chain of advice, but warned her not to lock herself up in it. 'You have already shewn me more about the part than I could possibly have shewn you,' he wrote. 'If I make suggestions or offer criticism freely it is only on the understanding that you need not give them a second thought if they do not chime in with your own feeling . . . You have much greater resources in the direction of gentleness than I have; and I assure you you will go wrong every time you try to do what *I* like instead of letting yourself do what *you* like.'

Rumours about the new play had been fanned by Shaw through London. In an interview with himself in the *Daily Mail*, he had ('as an act of public charity') warned all romantic playgoers to 'keep away'; and in another

CHAPTER III

[1]

What a transformation scene from those first years I knew him: the
scathing bitter opponent of wealth and leisure, and now! the adored
one of the smartest and most cynical set of English Society. Some
might say that we too had travelled in that direction: our good sense
preserve us!
Beatrice Webb (1905)

The early years of the twentieth century were confusing for the Fabians.
'Politics are very topsy-turvy just now,' Beatrice Webb wrote at the end of
December 1903, 'and one never knows who may be one's bedfellow!'
Many of the middle-class Fabians were growing suspicious of the social
glamour with which the Webbs surrounded themselves. Sidney himself
warned Beatrice that they should not be 'seen in the houses of great
people'. But though Beatrice tore up a number of important invitation
cards and put away her new party dress, the Fabian policy of permeation
made it obligatory for them to enter the drawing-rooms of Edwardian
political society. Curbing her 'lower desires', she decided to confine her
salon politics to small dinner parties. 'The more cliques you have access to
the broader the foundations of your power to get things done.'

This infiltration of political and social cliques was taking the Webbs
further away from the evolution of the Labour Party. As far back as 1899
the Fabian executive had been asked to send delegates to a conference of
socialist and trade union representatives to discuss the formation of a
working-class political party. There had been plenty of such conferences
before, and by now none of the Old Gang seemed much interested. Shaw,
who was actually nominated, did not attend. Only Edward Pease, the
invincibly dry Fabian secretary, turned up and, as if by accident, found
himself the token Fabian of a new organization run by Ramsay
MacDonald and called the Labour Representation Committee. For more
than six years Pease obscurely sat there, an unspectacular figure,
burrowing on subcommittees, coming up with occasional resolutions,
holding a watching brief and reporting back to the Fabian executive.

But the Fabian executive took little notice of these attempts to bring
socialism and the trade unions together as a Labour Party in Parliament.

They were wary of too great a co-operation with larger socialist groups because, as Shaw warned Pease, 'any sort of amalgamation means, for us, extinction'. Power, they believed, still resided with the traditional parties in Parliament and access to power must still lie through persuading them.

Among the Liberals, they had chosen Lord Rosebery, an enigmatic figure who had left the leadership of the party in 1896 and placed himself at the head of the Imperialist section of the Liberals. 'I must plough my furrow alone,' he declared in the summer of 1901. 'That is my fate, agreeable or the reverse; but before I get to the end of that furrow it is possible that I may find myself not alone.' This was not the speech of someone eager to re-enter a Cabinet that, in his own words, was run 'on prize-fighting principles'. Rosebery preferred his fighting to take place far off in South Africa or on the literary pages where he had examined the battles of Napoleon. He also enjoyed a good fighting speech, as he did a good horse race. The speech he made in Chesterfield at the end of 1901 owed much to 'Lord Rosebery's Escape from Houndsditch', the article that Sidney Webb had written, and Shaw toned up, the previous September. Using this as his brief, Rosebery attacked the record of party politics and called for a 'clean slate' on which to draft a programme of national efficiency.

At the top of this clean slate, the Webbs hoped to chalk up housing and education. But what did Rosebery himself intend? The ex-Premier's speech was less a signal that he meant to resume the Liberal Party leadership than a gesture aimed at discomforting those professional politicians who were consolidating their leadership: Campbell-Bannerman (whom Beatrice dismissed as a 'weak, vain man'), Lloyd George (who described Rosebery as 'a one-eyed fellow in blinkers') and his enemy the ex-Liberal Joseph Chamberlain. Unlike Chamberlain, Rosebery did not have the nerve to break away or the will to create a new party. He was grateful to Sidney Webb for, as it were, giving him something to say before he left and gratified to have pinned Imperialism onto such an unlikely political limb as the Fabian Society. But he was ready to depart. He had taken off his 'Gladstonian old clothes' and, instead of putting on the new collectivist garments that Sidney Webb handed him, he simply put himself to bed and switched out the light. 'Why are we in this galley?' Beatrice wondered. And Shaw himself was driven to concede the emptiness of their Rosebery campaign, adding that if he were seriously involved in politics he 'would not waste another five minutes on permeation'.

But the Fabian policy of permeation did seem to work with the Conservatives. 'We have in fact no party ties,' wrote Beatrice. 'It is open to us to use either or both parties.' Their Tory bedfellow was Arthur Balfour who succeeded his uncle Lord Salisbury as Prime Minister in the summer of 1902 and 'will I think', Beatrice predicted, 'make no ripple of change'. There was much in Balfour to appeal to the Webbs and much to appal them. By temperament he was an intellectual, quietly scintillating at the dinner table, well-spoken and precise-sounding in the House of Commons, and as a political thinker elegantly indecisive. Like Beatrice, he sometimes felt he would have preferred a contemplative to a public life – in fact it struck Beatrice as 'the oddest fact' that he should be 'mixed up . . . with democratic politics'. Really he had gone into politics to please his mother and then developed the knack of pleasing all sorts of people. He was one of nature's diplomats, at home on the golf course, in the concert hall and among the 'gallants and graces' of the fashionable world; popular too with the finer minds of the universities, the pick of the clergy, the flower of the bench: and also with the Webbs. 'A man of extraordinary grace of mind and body – delighting in all that is beautiful and distinguished – music, literature, philosophy, religious feeling and moral disinterestedness – aloof from all the greed and grime of common human nature,' decided Beatrice in her diary. 'But a strange paradox as Prime Minister of a great Empire!'

From the drudgery of political thought the Webbs hoped to exonerate Balfour. It seemed to them incredible that a Prime Minister in his mid-fifties should have preserved an open mind on so many political questions. His opinions shifted uneasily between the need for action and the futility of taking it. Unlike Rosebery he was not to be persuaded by what might be dramatically popular or unpopular, but by whether he was bored or not. He was easily bored – so much politics was without refinement of thought or sensibility. It was here that the Webbs saw their opportunity. Between 1902 and 1905 they 'slipped into' friendship with him. 'He comes in to dinner whenever we ask him, and talks most agreeably,' Beatrice noted, ' – perhaps our vanity is flattered by his evident interest in our historical and philosophical paradoxes and enjoyment of our conversation.' It was difficult to tell who was the manipulator: the Webbs with their permeation or Balfour with his opportunism. He responded to these Fabians as a connoisseur might respond to an unusual wine. He was curious about human character and the processes of reasoning, and believed Shaw to be 'the finest man of letters of to-day' – though he would not read his Plays Unpleasant because 'I never read unpleasant things'. He counted on the Fabians painlessly fitting such unpleasant things into the perfect equilibrium of his life, and the Webbs endeavoured to oblige. 'I set myself to amuse and interest him,' Beatrice wrote. And he was so responsive intellectually, so courteous, that 'we found ourselves in accord on most questions'. Sidney's academicism and Beatrice's social grace gave Balfour the knowledge he lacked without the tedium that often prevented him from acquiring it.

But Beatrice distrusted her attraction to Balfour. She had with difficulty walked away from the social world to which her family belonged and dedicated herself to disinterested public service – and now found that this service was leading her back into the milieu she had abandoned. For Balfour belonged to 'the Souls', that exquisite group of intellectuals with artistic and aristocratic tastes who, during the twenty years before the Great War, spun for themselves a fashionable paradise between the Athenaeum in London and various grand country houses at weekends, and were to find an obituary in *Heartbreak House*. In her contact with Balfour, Beatrice experienced the charm of these souls and spirits so seductively that she had to remind herself frequently how objectionable it was to have the affairs of the country conducted in an atmosphere of cliquey conversations between 'Arthur' and 'Alfred' and 'Bob' and 'George' – sometimes unintelligible in their intimate allusions even to the outer circle of the Cabinet.

Her immersion in party-giving-and-going seemed justified by what the Fabians, especially Sidney, achieved over the Education Acts of 1902 and 1903. His Fabian Tract No. 106, *The Education Muddle and the Way Out*, had been published in January 1901 after twenty months of detailed wrangling. It recommended the abolition of School Boards and the passing of control for education to the local government bodies which would in future fund all schools, including the denominational schools run by the Church, from the rates. Balfour's Conservative Government, which was sympathetic to the Church, used Sidney's Tract to support this reform. The Education Act of 1902 (which did not apply to London) 'followed almost precisely the lines laid down in our tract', wrote Edward Pease. 'Our support of the Conservative Government in their education policy caused much surprise.'

It caused more than surprise. Among some Fabians, led by Graham Wallas and Stewart Headlam, it caused misgivings over the invasion of party politics into education. Among Rosebery and the Liberals, who supported the School Boards that had been established by Gladstone, it provoked enmity. And from other socialist organizations and individuals, in particular Ramsay MacDonald and the Labour Representation Committee, the proposal to give assistance out of public funds to reactionary Church schools fermented outright opposition. Webb argued that it was impractical to destroy Anglican and Catholic schools, and undesirable for dogma's sake to relinquish more than half the children of the nation to institutions that were understaffed, ill-equipped and inefficient. It was better to have efficient standards and a variety of methods and atmospheres he said, even if this involved for the time being subsidizing religious teaching. But it was far from being the 'clean slate' other socialists wanted.

Over the Education Act of 1903, which transferred the School Boards' powers to the London County Council, Webb experienced still greater difficulties since he had to persuade the Conservatives to drop an alternative plan and, for sectarian reasons, was met with bitter hostility by the progressives on the London County Council itself – including once again Ramsay MacDonald (who helped to spread a rumour that Sidney was collaborating with Balfour in order to get a Government post).

The architect of these reforms, which brought elementary and secondary education within a coherent structure, was Robert Morant, Permanent Secretary to the Board of Education. He is not mentioned in Pease's *History of the Fabian Society* which leaves it to be inferred that Webb was their only begetter. In fact it was by assisting Morant that Webb brought off the Fabians' most influential campaign of political lobbying. It showed, Shaw remarked to A. B. Walkley, that the Cabinet always eventually agreed with the Fabian Society.

But their success had been achieved at a dismaying price. There was, as Beatrice put it, 'a slump in Webbs' on the political market. After the local elections of 1904 Sidney was voted off the Progressive Party Committee and denied all positions of authority on the London County Council. He had hoped to be brought back into communication with the trade union world through his appointment by Balfour to a new Royal Commission on trade union law. But this became what Sidney called a 'fiasco' when the trade unions boycotted the commission. Suddenly the Fabians seemed isolated. Through their educational reforms they had lost much of the interest they had spent years nurturing among the Liberals; and by their pronouncements on tariff reform they were to assist in the downfall of their one political ally, Balfour.

*

Webb had conducted the Fabian policy on education; it was Shaw who stage-managed their fiscal policy. After a visit to South Africa in the winter of 1902-3, Chamberlain had returned declaring his faith in the doctrine of an imperial preferential tariff. Until then the establishment of free imports had seemed as 'stable and final', wrote Shaw, 'as the disestablishment of the Irish Church, of Purchase in the Army, of duelling, and of the property qualification for the franchise'. Balfour hardly knew what to think. This was one of the questions on which he held an open mind. Eventually he gave forth a compromising pamphlet, *Economic Notes on Insular Free Trade*, in which, for the sake of holding the Conservative and Unionist Party together, consolidating the Empire and protecting the British producer, he rejected the proposed taxes on food but accepted the use of tariffs as a means of securing reciprocal concessions. As a result Chamberlain resigned as Secretary of State for the Colonies and embarked on his own campaign for tariff reform.

This campaign, and Balfour's concession to it, rallied the Liberals in opposition. To them the revival of the tariff seemed equivalent to putting the clock back to the Corn Laws of the 1840s. Among socialist groups, too, though it was not seen as a solution to the country's social ills, the rightfulness of Free Trade had been taken for granted. At the 1904 conferences of the Independent Labour Party and Labour Representation Committee, resolutions supporting Free Trade against tariff manipulation were decisively carried, and a single LRC amendment asking for an inquiry into the tariff system was overwhelmingly rejected.

This was not the Fabian position. As with the Boer War, Sidney Webb would have preferred to take no part in the debate. Nothing good seemed to come out of South Africa. But following Chamberlain's tariff speech in May 1903 'Free Trade versus Fair Trade' was obviously to become an important electioneering issue. 'I think we are clearly called upon to oraculate on the present crisis,' Shaw wrote to Pease: and Webb reluctantly agreed. At a Fabian meeting in June 1903 he had given a tentative analysis of the situation, on balance against tariffs, but in effect recommending more Fabian research into the subject.

Shaw's attitude was more dramatic. Following instinct rather than research, he had come out as 'a Protectionist right down to my boots', at one with Ruskin and Carlyle in his belief that 'Free Trade is heart-breaking nonsense'. He begged Beatrice to 'anaesthetize' Sidney while he extracted the last stump of classical Liberalism from him. 'I do not think we can intervene in a sudden crisis of this kind without risking a mistake or two which a couple of years investigation might avert; but we can at all events make our position as sure as we can; and then take our chance, as all great commanders do.'

Over the last six months of 1903, amid a good deal of agitated debate, Fabian opinion had come to lodge halfway between tariff and Free Trade. To give commanding expression to such mixed opinion needed unusual dexterity, and the job of formulating the collective opinion of the Fabians was therefore handed over to their literary wizard. Shaw was convinced that the Fabian Society 'must say something that nobody else is saying'. He had wanted to demonstrate that sensible tariff reform involved, as a preliminary step, the introduction of socialism. He proposed an agreement between the workers and the new administration where, in exchange for their support of Chamberlain's protectionist scheme, the workers were guaranteed a minimum wage (a legal revision that would involve the revision of rent and other contracts). He also proposed that Chamberlain be invited to give a pledge that any extra revenue arising from tariffs would be applied to 'public purposes' and not 'to still further reduce the existing shamefully inadequate taxation of unearned incomes'. To this he wanted to attach, for the benefit of the incoming Government, a short lesson for the future: 'the history of the world is not going to be the history of the British or any other Empire, but of Federated Commonwealths, whose predominance as Great Powers will depend, not on their command of guff and bugaboo, but on their power of high organization and wise administration.'

Sidney Webb, who was unwilling to align himself with Chamberlain, feared that Shaw might sweep the Fabian Society into the Protectionist camp and alienate half the membership. Shaw argued that, in principle, there was no objection to State control from a socialist point of view. 'The Fabian Society in particular has demanded extensive and energetic State interference with trade, both to suppress sweating at home and to guide and assist our exporters abroad.' Socialists were therefore necessarily anti-Free Trade as they were anti-Laissez-faire, both systems being historical counterparts of each other and idealizing the natural working of market forces. Against this, and by way of putting off the threatened tariff, Webb recommended a bounty system (which did not raise prices) on colonial imports acting as a compromise between the British consumer, the British manufacturer and the colonial producer. From all over the country Fabians sent Shaw their thoughts, often so illegible they appeared to have been written on horseback, and he attempted to knead them into a single narrative.

At a Fabian meeting on 22 January 1904 this draft of Shaw's Tract No. 116, *Fabianism and the Fiscal Question*, was fought over page by page. At the end of the battle Graham Wallas and Aylmer Maude (who supported Free Trade) moved that the tract as amended be left unpublished. They were defeated and Wallas resigned. 'I have found time once or twice to wonder, now that I am fifty years old, whether I have been entirely "futile",' he wrote to Shaw. 'I am blessed if I know.'

Fabianism and the Fiscal Question came out on 31 March. 'Though I am the pen man of this Tract, its authorship is genuinely collective,' Shaw explained in a Preface. It was as adept a performance as *Fabianism and the Empire*. The latter had assumed the worthiness of Free Trade but, as Shaw explained to Beatrice Webb: 'I switch off the old current & switch on the new with treacherous & disconcerting suddenness.' Both tracts submerge immediate election questions and extreme Fabian differences in the creed of international collectivism and a lucid exposition of the practical benefits of domestic socialism that might be wrung out of an imperial policy.

'*Fabianism and the Fiscal Question*, considered as a publication designed to bridge the deep divisions amongst the Fabians themselves, is a masterpiece,' wrote A. M. McBriar in his *Fabian Socialism & English Politics*. But Pease described it as 'perhaps the least successful of the many pronouncements written by Bernard Shaw on behalf of the Society'. Shaw had used two methods of keeping the Fabian craft afloat. In the first he moved from an analogy of 'free trade' in human labour to recommend as the Fabian 'alternative policy' various schemes for social reconstruction that were supported by one or other faction within the Society. He plucked from *Fabianism and the Empire* the reorganization of the Consular Service in the interests of the export trade; from Webb he took the system of bounties, adding improved facilities for technical education and research investigations into Britain's resources. He proposed free ocean transit within the Empire and, as a corollary, the nationalization of the railways to provide cheaper transport rates. But this programme of action was, Pease wrote, 'too futurist'. Not for more than a quarter of a century would the Labour movement in Britain begin to reconsider its position on Protection along the lines Shaw had seen. Meanwhile his tract, stringing together a selection of proposals all ahead of their time, failed to give Fabian voters a clear-cut policy on tariff for the election.

Shaw's second method of preserving Fabian unity was to make a scarifying attack on that 'plague of pantaloons in politics' who were not Fabians. The Conservatives are described as 'Nincompoops' who had effectually cleared themselves of 'all suspicion of Conservatism, perhaps in despair of competing with the Opposition on that point . . . '

'The imagination will not bear the strain of conceiving these gentlemen struggling with the huge and ruthless commercial interests which will . . . lobby the tariff to suit their own balance-sheets without the smallest reference to the common weal.'

The Liberal Party ('with one leader [Campbell-Bannerman] whom nobody will follow, and another [Rosebery] who in theory dreams of the Individualism of William Pitt') is seen as having spent its reputation in 'negative Obstinacy'.

'There is no more gratitude for them to abuse, no more confidence to betray, no more hope to defer . . . it is impossible not to rejoice in the fact that so comparatively progressive an institution as the House of Lords retains a veto on their powers of reaction.'

More conservative than the Tories and reactionary than the Liberals were the working classes, who responded with 'intense hostility' to almost any scheme for social improvement, even cheap food. The Labour Party 'still bolts into the Liberal camp at every alarm and will continue to do so until it accepts Socialism as the basis of its policy'. If it 'were really in earnest', Shaw added, 'it would redouble its efforts to capture seats enough to enable it to enforce its own requirements'.

Shaw did not believe that the Labour Party would win seats at the next election. He expected Chamberlain to become Prime Minister – though he was careful not to credit Chamberlain with much political capacity or economic knowledge. 'If the next Cabinet be the usual Conservative Cabinet with Mr Chamberlain at the head of it, then it is hard to say whether Mr Chamberlain or the nation will be the more to be pitied.' But if Chamberlain could be persuaded to bring sense to his tariff infatuation by accepting a minimum wage for workers, 'well, then we shall see what we shall see'.

What Shaw and the Fabians saw was something else. In 1905 Lord Rosebery's horse had again won the Derby. He made as if to re-enter politics but, after declining Campbell-Bannerman's Liberal programme and repudiating Chamberlain's fiscal policy, contented himself with leading his horse off the field. In the electioneering following Balfour's resignation on 4 December, Shaw's fiscal tract lay forgotten under thousands of posters illustrating, with pictures of the Big and the Little Loaf, the appeal of cheap food to the British worker.

The Liberals with 377 seats (supported by 83 Irish) won an unprecedented majority. Their leader, Sir Henry Campbell-Bannerman, that 'weak, vain man' whom 'nobody will follow', became Prime Minister and various Liberal friends of the Webbs (Asquith, Grey and Haldane), making their peace, accepted office under him. The Conservative Party was reduced to 132 seats (with 25 Liberal Unionist allies). Balfour was never again to lead the party in office; and Joseph Chamberlain (who suffered a stroke not long afterwards) never again held political office.

There was one other surprise at the election: fifty-three seats were captured by Labour men. Of these, twenty-four were trade unionists (mostly textile and mining men) who owed their primary allegiance not to Ramsay MacDonald and Keir Hardie, but to the Liberal Party which had pledged to restore protection of union funds from liability for loss caused through industrial disputes. But the other twenty-nine Labour members were socialists, run by the Labour Representation Committee, whom MacDonald, using Fabian tactics, had placed (with the approval of the Liberal Chief Whip) in constituencies where they would be opposed only by Conservative candidates.

The complexion of British politics was changing. A successful pact had been made between socialism and trade unionism that gave the Labour movement a parliamentary base in national politics. Among the large number of Liberal members were men 'so small in fortune as to be objects of contempt to the governing families', wrote Margaret Cole, 'and in the Cabinet itself was Lloyd George, the pro-Boer, the demagogue, the son of an elementary teacher brought up by a village cobbler'.

Towards both this 'New Liberalism' and the Labour group, the depleted Fabian Old Gang preserved its scepticism. In the *National Review* Webb drafted an article, 'The Liberal Cabinet: an Intercepted Letter', that pretended to be a circular sent by Campbell-Bannerman to his newly appointed ministers listing the socialist reforms he wished them to enact. In *The Clarion* Shaw laid down some 'Fabian Notes' on the election. The Labour members had provided nothing more than 'a nominally independent Trade Unionist and Radical group', he wrote. ' . . . I apologise to the Universe for my connection with such a party.'

[2]

We have always been misunderstood, mistrusted, and from time to time roundly denounced and vilified not only by the other Socialist Societies but even by a minority of the Fabian Society. Fortunately, it has always been a small minority, which has never been recruited faster than we could convert it. The great bulk of the Society has always rallied to us when a change of policy has been demanded. From William Morris in 1890 to H. G. Wells in 1906, all the able, energetic and impatient spirits have begun by demanding an abandonment of the Fabian policy, and have ended by perceiving that is the only possible policy under the circumstances. (1907)

The unease felt by growing numbers of Fabians swelled after the General Election of January 1906 into a tumour of discontent. Sydney Olivier had been absent too long; Wallas had resigned; Webb had wasted time parleying with reactionaries; Shaw's reputation was pulling him into places beyond the circumference of the Society; and Bland, the only member of the executive Old Gang to have advocated setting up a new and separate Socialist Party from the start, had constantly been out-manoeuvred by Shaw and Webb. The Fabians were in disarray. In retrospect their policy of permeation looked like a series of little interferences and minor activities that had wasted resources and produced dubious results. The more dissident Fabians began to ask questions. What was the point of Sidney Webb ingratiating himself with Tories and Liberals at the dinner table while Shaw drastically insulted both parties in his tracts? Where were their political discipline and seasoned statesmanship? How was the Fabian policy of permeation being co-ordinated? 'I quite understand that you can so define permeation as to cover all forms of Socialist activity,' S. G. Hobson wrote to Shaw. 'But that won't help us.'

Despite its great prestige, Hobson and others felt that the Fabian Society was in danger of counting for very little in politics. During its first twelve valiant years, it had done great things and lined up' what was potentially a great following in the country. Then, as Sydney Olivier admitted, it had 'ossified'. The last ten years seemed to be a history of lost opportunities. Their hearts had failed: they had been supplanted by Ramsay MacDonald and Keir Hardie, by the Independent Labour Party and the Labour Representation Committee. Between 1899 and 1904 the membership had subsided to 730; the number of branches too had fallen and several that survived appeared moribund. At the 1906 General Election they had done nothing but disperse themselves among Labour and Liberal candidates – perhaps even among Chamberlain's and Balfour's Tories.

The new century arrived and, like Fabius, the Fabians had waited. But when the time came they had not struck hard – they had gone on waiting. Rising numbers of the Fabians however were insisting that they should now take a more distinctive line in politics. The waiting game must end. 'The Socialist movement is now large enough to justify the Society in sloughing off all exterior connections and definitely working inside and through Socialist organisations,' Hobson urged Shaw. 'Webb has repeatedly told me that he does not believe in the possibility of a Socialist Party. On the contrary, I think that an organised Socialist Party which shall include the LRC and the ILP is quite feasible and in every sense desirable.'

Shaw was not unsympathetic to this argument – he was not unsympathetic to anything that might happen. He wanted paternity of the future. The General Election had undermined his confidence at political prediction. Therefore it was necessary to sound bold while remaining cautious: to back, with all his available capital, every horse in the party political race. The only difference that the last general election had made for the Fabians was that 'there is now one more parliamentary party to be permeated'. The Fabian tracts gave the new Labour Party a programme for a decade of electioneering. But while remaining 'friendly' to the Labour Party, Shaw argued that the Fabian Society must continue with the old policy of placing its work unreservedly at the disposal of 'anybody and everybody, including the established capitalist governments, who can and will carry out any instalment of it'.

Concurrently with this work, as S. G. Hobson had suggested, the Fabians might have to deal with the formation of a real socialist party in Parliament. Recently Shaw had begun to feel that suspended socialism could at last precipitate itself into a political party – and if that happened the Fabian Society must back it for all it was worth. There would be trouble with the trade-unionist Labour Party – but that did not deeply worry him: it was a young party and naturally petulant. Shaw's reservations about the Labour Party came from the fact that he was not at its conception: it belonged to Keir Hardie and Ramsay MacDonald. He tried to overcome this antagonism by pretending that the Fabian Society had actually helped to form the ILP and indirectly to create the Labour Party: but it was difficult to establish such wholesale fathering. He needed to do this, nevertheless, in case its egalitarianism proved sufficiently strong to change it into a truly socialist body. But if, as Shaw expected, trade unionism and traditional anti-bureaucratic radicalism prevailed, then the next job for the Fabians would be to detach socialists from the Labour Party and 'form a Socialist party in parliament independent of all other parties, but leading the advanced elements in all of them by its ideas and its political science'.

He envisaged the bulk of this new party coming from the middle-class proletariat, and substituting middle-class methods of business and conceptions of democracy for trade union methods – representative government in place of bodies of delegates. Fabian socialism was the very thing for the middle-class proletariat. Their socialism (what Shaw would later call communism) would work to reverse the policy of capitalism by discarding the institution of private property and transferring it into common wealth. But could such a revolutionary programme be carried out by instalments of public regulation and administration enacted through Parliament, the municipalities and parish councils? Some of Shaw's speeches following the election seemed to be testing the method and the moment for converting Britain to socialism.

'Do not let us delude ourselves with any dreams of a peaceful evolution of Capitalism into Socialism, of automatic Liberal Progress . . . The man who is not a Socialist is quite prepared to fight for his private property . . .

'We must clear our minds from cant and cowardice on this subject. It is true that the old barricade revolutionists were childishly and romantically wrong in their methods; and the Fabians were right in making an end of them and formulating constitutional Socialism. But nothing is so constitutional as fighting.'

Once a true red socialist party was born in Britain, Shaw warned Pease, the old Fabian Society 'would shrink into a little academic body'. Shaw had been on the Fabian executive now for twenty years. He felt loyalty; he felt weariness. He wanted freedom as well as ownership – his child must grow up, become independent and powerful: *his child*. 'We cannot sit there any longer making a mere habit of the thing,' he advised Webb, 'knowing all the time that we shall have to drop it within, at the utmost, 5 years from now, & that it will then perish miserably & abortively unless we make the end of it the beginning of something else.'

That 'something else' must be a Fabian party in Parliament – a consummation of the Fabian section of their lives. For what was socialism but Fabianism? If the thing caught on it would prove the 'right climax of the whole Fabian adventure' – and if it failed what was there to lose? 'This is the psychological moment,' Shaw told Webb late in 1906. He had been convinced of this, not by the mood of the country nor in Parliament, but by a new leader that the insurgent spirit of the Fabians had thrown up – a brilliant intellectual prospector on whom he might unload his political burden, as he hoped one day to hand over the theatrical future to Harley Granville Barker.

*

H. G. Wells was ten years younger than Shaw. As a student at the Normal School of Science in South Kensington during the mid-1880s, he had seen the aggressive Dubliner with his 'thin flame-coloured beard beneath his white illumined face', addressing socialists on Sunday evenings in the conservatory of Kelmscott House. Like other students, Wells had been converted to socialism under the aesthetic influence of Blake, Carlyle and Ruskin. The galaxy of picturesque and perplexing leaders at Kelmscott – anarchists, poets and painters – represented for him in an intensely exciting way the world's imaginative expansion. Late at night, walking back from Hammersmith through the gas-lit streets, or travelling by the sulphurous underground railway, their red ties giving zest to frayed and shabby costumes, Wells and his fellow-students would chatter enthusiastically of Morris and Shaw – how fierce they were in spirit, how sage in method. A revolution was breaking out, swiftly and irresistibly, around them. 'Let us have a new world,' men and women were saying: and they called it socialism.

But by the time Wells and Shaw met almost a decade later, this revolution seemed to have been reduced to its minimum terms. The revolutionaries were scattering and leaving the political field to littérateurs and civil servants. Wells himself, at the beginning of 1895, had suddenly been given the post of theatre critic for the *Pall Mall Gazette*. On 5 January he turned up at the St James's Theatre to see *Guy Domville*, 'an extremely weak drama' by Henry James. There were two audiences in the theatre that night. When the curtain came down 'jeers, hisses, catcalls were followed by great waves of applause . . . The two audiences declared war. The intellectual and artistic élite answered the howls of derision; the howls grew strong in defiance.'

Wells, in his new evening clothes, had noticed Shaw in the audience – 'he broke the ranks of the boiled shirts and black and white ties in the stalls, with a modest brown jacket suit, a very white face and very red whiskers'. The new drama critic of the *Pall Mall Gazette* accosted the new drama critic of the *Saturday Review* as a colleague and, as Wells had to pass Fitzroy Square to reach his home near Euston, the two writers walked back together, a lean spring-heeled marcher and a valiant sparrow hopping beside him.

'Fires and civil commotions loosen tongues,' commented Wells, who described Shaw as talking 'like an elder brother to me in that agreeable Dublin English of his'. He spoke about 'the uproar we had left behind us and the place of the fashionable three-act play amid the eternal verities'. Henry James belonged to a different camp. They were both part of the cyclone of social change, Shaw believed. 'But there is in the centre of that cyclone a certain calm spot where cultivated ladies and gentlemen live on independent incomes or by pleasant artistic occupations. It is there that Mr James's art touches life, selecting whatever is graceful, exquisite or dignified in its serenity.' Wells remembered how Shaw had responded to the music of James's language. 'Line after line comes with such a delicate turn and fall . . . I am speaking of the delicate inflexions of feeling conveyed by the cadences of the line.' It was like listening to Mozart after Verdi.

Shaw's conversation was a 'contribution to my education', Wells recalled. By the time he sat down to write his review, 'I already knew something of the business I had in hand'. But Wells also knew he did not understand the theatre. He felt out of place there. He felt impatient. What was the gist of all that complex unreality? For G.B.S., who aimed to make it his kingdom, the theatre offered 'great opportunities to the human mind'. At Kelmscott he had preached only to confederates of like opinion; the open air meetings round the country were miscellaneous outpourings of words crackling round a single topical event, floating and drifting away. But the theatre was the world in essence, a place of art, education and activity. That brawling and pandemonium at the St James's, likened by Henry James to a set of savages pouncing on a gold watch, had been a warning of what might have to happen in Britain if peaceful Fabian tactics failed.

Wells continued to see G.B.S. intermittently, but after four months on the *Pall Mall Gazette* he decided to throw over theatre reviewing. During the next half-dozen years, with an extraordinary surge of productivity, he created a new genre of scientific fairy tale with his vivid fantasies, allegories, fables and adventures – *The Time Machine, The Island of Dr Moreau, The War of the Worlds, The First Men in the Moon* . . . He wrote one book, then another, and then half a dozen more. They came like magic. 'It did not take us long to recognise that here was Genius,' wrote Ford Madox Ford. ' . . . And all great London lay prostrate at his feet.'

Shaw too had been impressed. In a letter to Beatrice Webb, he was to describe Wells as 'a giant among the pigmies'. He liked the fact that Wells was not tethered to an enclosed literary establishment and had walked away from a conventional career in the sciences. A natural story-teller, with a wonderfully fertile imagination, he spoke directly to the people and was 'our nearest to a twentieth century Dickens'. Wells's romances of time and space stimulated Shaw's romantic optimism. Dickens's world 'becomes a world of great expectations cruelly disappointed', he wrote. 'The Wells world is a world of greater and greater expectations continually being fulfilled.'

What appealed to Shaw was the enquiring unorthodoxy of Wells's mind. Here was the modern man who accepted nothing of the past and questioned everything in the future. In the summer of 1901 Shaw is recommending the autobiographical novel *Love and Mr Lewisham* to Archer on the grounds that it 'blows the gaff on the system of proving theories to students by shewing them faked experiments'. Wells felt so impatient he could hardly wait to experiment with the future. He wanted to write history before it happened. It was after his next book, a 'prospectus' called *Anticipations*, that Shaw asked Graham Wallas (whose sister-in-law was Wells's neighbour at Sandgate) formally to introduce them. 'He [Wells] interests me considerably.'

Wells had also begun to interest the Webbs with his attempt, in *Anticipations*, to forecast various technological and human developments and to make obsolete 'the monarch monogamy and respectability . . . all under the guise of a speculation about motor cars and electrical heating'. Beatrice Webb confided in her diary that *Anticipations* was the 'most remarkable book of the year: a powerful imagination furnished with the data and methods of physical science, working on social problems . . . his work is full of luminous hypotheses and worth careful study by those who are trying to look forward'. She gave the book to Sidney and he wrote to Wells ('as a friend of Graham Wallas and Bernard Shaw whom you know') an enthusiastic though characteristically uninviting letter. Wells had imagined a technocratic élite called 'the New Republicans' that could regenerate the nation. This fell in closely with the Webbs' ideal of national efficiency, but struck them as 'weak' and 'ignorant' in that his freemasonry of enlightened men and women did not number among its chemists, electricians and engineers, trained administrators like themselves. Though I 'find myself in sympathy with many of your feelings and criticisms and suggestions,' Sidney wrote, 'I do not intend to refer to all these points of agreement'. He went on to introduce himself and Beatrice as experts in organizing men: 'all experience shows that men need organising as much as machines, or rather, much more; that the making of such arrangements, and constant readjustments, as will ensure order, general health and comfort, and maximum productivity, among human beings, is a professio-nal art in itself.' As sugar coating round this pill he enclosed, like giant boxes of candies, their two volumes of *Industrial Democracy* which he suggested Wells read backwards ('Begin with the last *three* chapters . . . ').

It was natural that Wells should feel flattered by the attention of this distinguished and formidable couple. The Webbs seemed to stand for the maturer, more disciplined, better-informed expression of all that he was eager to achieve. Their effect upon him was considerable. 'We discovered each other immensely; for a time it produced a tremendous sense of kindred and co-operation,' he wrote. This was the beginning of a pincer movement by the Webbs and the Shaws to recruit him to the Fabian Society. 'We have been seeing something lately of H. G. Wells and his wife,' Beatrice noted in her diary early in 1902. 'Wells is an interesting though somewhat unattractive personality . . . He is a good instrument for popularising ideas, and . . . it is refreshing to talk to a man who has shaken himself loose from so many of the current assumptions, and is looking at life as an explorer of a new world.'

Even in the first year of their friendship there were signs of antagonism. Sidney believed that Wells's reckless schoolboy intelligence was overrated; Beatrice felt him to be untrustworthy: and neither of them thought he had the patience and good manners of a natural Fabian. Yet he struck them as so extraordinarily quick in his apprehensions that the Fabian experience must gradually and inevitably educate him. Before the end of 1902 they had elected him as one of the founder members of the Co-Efficients – a dining-club of Twelve Wise Men with 'diverse temperaments and varied talents', all anxious to expound (over their eight hotel meals a year) how 'each department of national life can be raised to its highest possible efficiency'.

Wells was nervous of the Webbs. Sidney was so full of exasperating information, so excessively devoted to the public service; and the handsome figure of Beatrice alarmed him. But he liked the notion of meeting influential people – Members of Parliament such as Asquith, Haldane and Grey, philosophers such as Bertrand Russell, and Pember Reeves, soon to be made High Commissioner for New Zealand – at these political dinners. He was setting out to be a new kind of social scientist and needed to be taken seriously. The Fabians endorsed this need, offering him a platform, an audience and an atmosphere of power. After lecturing at the Royal Institution on 'The Discovery of the Future', he received a note from Shaw urgently inviting him to deliver his words to the Fabians – 'a live audience is better than a stuffed one'.

So in February 1903, sponsored by Shaw and Graham Wallas, Wells joined the Fabians – and Charlotte immediately sent him 'a humble petition' to lecture them 'about Administrative Areas'. The Society 'is always open to new ideas', she innocently encouraged him, '& to criticism of its past action & especially energetic about the propaganda of any "better dream" that comes along the moment it has assimilated it'. On this occasion Wells's better dream was of a World State that would be brought about by faster methods of communication. But the lecture laboured under a ponderous title – 'The Question of Scientific Administrative Areas in Relation to Municipal Undertakings' – and was unnervingly spoken by Wells 'addressing my tie through a cascade moustache that was no help at all, correcting myself as though I were a manuscript under treatment'. He was to place this lecture as an appendix to *Mankind in the Making*, a scolding essay in revivalism that was his sequel to *Anticipations*, and sent this piece of field preaching to Shaw. 'I have no patience with it,' G.B.S. replied: 'half of it is a righteous exposure of that impostor & quack, the schoolmaster, and the other half is a demand for more schoolmasters. Do you call this good sense? I much prefer your stories [*Twelve Stories and a Dream*], which I bought on Saturday – four & six laid on the altar of friendship.'

This friendship was a mix-up of resemblances and incompatibilities, emulation and antagonism, admiration and the perpetual struggle for ascendancy. 'Though we were not quite enough in the same field nor near enough in age to be rivals,' Wells wrote in his autobiography, ' . . . [this] did not prevent our carrying ourselves with a certain sustained defensiveness towards each other.'

Sidney Webb had listed Wells's *Anticipations* as one of his favourite books of 1901. Wells had chosen *Three Plays for Puritans*. 'You are, now that Wilde is dead, the one living playwright in my esteem,' he wrote to Shaw. Now that he had passed the phase of hero-worship there swam within his approbation a mass of minute criticisms. Yet in spite of these qualifications, 'I know of no other playwright quite like you'. He went to see *John Bull's Other Island* at the Court Theatre, pretended that the figure of Broadbent had been a 'disgusting caricature' of himself ('even my slight tendency to embonpoint was brought in'), and concluded: 'The play has some really gorgeous rhetoric, beautiful effects, much more serious Shaw than ever before & I'd rather see it again than see anyone else's new play.'

Each offered the other valuable contrasts while serving in the ranks of the same profession: that of giving (as Shaw phrased it) 'civilization a shove forward'. Shaw made many attempts to manoeuvre Wells onto his own ground. 'We must pull together,' he continued to urge, 'for we are both in the same boat.' He pondered several shared schemes – including the joint production of a comic Bible that would kill all the ridiculous legends and revive religion throughout Europe. He chided him for not taking the theatre seriously. 'I blush to recollect that I have written five novels. I refuse to treat you as my equal until you have written half a dozen good plays.' Ostensibly flattering, such teasing really arose, Wells suspected, from an impulse to opposition that was fundamental to Shaw's character. 'He got his excitement by rousing a fury of antagonism and then overcoming & defeating it,' he wrote. 'At that game, which covered a large part of his life, he was unsurpassable.'

Underlying Wells's admiration of Shaw boiled a vast irritation. In the mid-1890s he had been prepared to learn from the elder writer as from an elder brother: he was not content to do so ten years later – especially on subjects about which he was educated and G.B.S. was not. 'I was a biologist first and foremost, and Shaw had a physiological disgust at vital activities,' he was to write. 'He rebelled against them. He detected an element of cruelty, to which I am blind, in sexual matters.' As if it were an asset, Shaw boasted that he had learned nothing of biology since he was sixteen – and then went on to lecture Wells about it 'like a bright girl at a dinner'. And how wrongheaded he was! 'Why do you say such silly things about science?' Wells demanded. But it was impossible to catch someone who had perfected the nimble art of simultaneous assertion-and-denial. 'When I venture to say that a thing is so, it is so,' Shaw explained. 'But you have to get what I say exactly, and not substitute the nearest thing in your own stock, and reject that.' Wells was often made to appear a beginner at the subject in which he felt himself an expert. When, for example, he politely sent Shaw one of his scientific articles, he had it returned to him scored with corrections as if it were the work of a schoolboy. And really it was Shaw, with his 'flimsy intellectual acquisitive sort of mind', who was adrift and chattering in a flesh-and-blood world he did not understand. His phrase, 'the Life Force', embodied 'an almost encyclopaedic philosophical & biological ignorance'. Yet Wells could see that Shaw's string of disconnected half-truths impressed people and that he worked, with immense application, at being impressive. His main impulse towards other human beings was to establish a dominant relationship over them – something which Wells fiercely resisted. He regretted having fallen in with these Fabians.

A year after joining the Society, Wells took advantage of Graham Wallas's resignation over *Fabianism and the Fiscal Question* and attempted to follow him. 'I would do my poor best to establish my views . . . against the prevailing influences,' he told Pease, 'in spite of my distinguished ineptitude in debate.' But he was working so hard at his new books – *A Modern Utopia* and *Kipps* – he did not have time to attend the Fabian meetings. At once the prevailing influences of the Fabians, the Webbs and the Shaws, closed in on him again – the Webbs with several soothing invitations, and Shaw with a piece of prescient finger wagging. 'I dont believe you have any views on Free Trade or any other subject,' he scolded. 'I believe you are so spoiled by living in a world of your own invention, peopled by your own puppets, that you have become incapable of tolerating the activity or opinions or even the phrases of independent individuals.' And Wells, responding to this carrot and stick, grudgingly capitulated. It was absurd to quit over Tariff Reform. But 'I highly disapprove of the Fabian Society', he warned Pease.

He had wanted to leave and now felt trapped. For Wells was an escapologist. This need to escape lay at the centre of his politics, utopias and love affairs. The claustrophobia of marriage was to become endurable for him only after he had set up an alternative household with a mistress and could oscillate between two homes. He presented great obstacles to Shaw and the Webbs in their determination to organize and approve of him. 'He is a romancer spoilt by romancing,' Beatrice decided in her diary, ' – but in the present stage of sociology he is useful.'

Of the two romances he published in 1905, *Kipps* was an affectionate glance backwards at what had moved him in the past, and *A Modern Utopia* a blue book vision of the future disinfected of pain. His anxiety to escape from the present fitted perfectly with the mood of a country travelling from solid Victorian traditions into the complex territory of the twentieth century. He had quickly won a large audience and made converts to socialism by translating the Fabian creed of national efficiency into popular fiction. In *A Modern Utopia* he reinvented the 'New Republicans' as a benevolent dictatorship of voluntary noblemen called 'the Samurai', a league of sane and superior beings who rise above the laws of nature through self-denial and preside as social engineers over the ideal state. 'The chapters on the Samurai will pander to all your worst instincts,' he assured Beatrice Webb. But he had done what the Webbs had wanted. 'He is full of intellectual courage and initiative,' Beatrice observed.

A Modern Utopia made Wells a hero among the more radical Fabians. 'He is, we think, grown in self-confidence, if not conceit, as to his capacity to settle all social and economic questions in general,' Beatrice Webb was to write in her diary, 'and to run the Fabian Society in particular, with a corresponding contempt for us poor drudgers . . . ' Often and often Wells had dreamed of what he would do to the world if he were a great man of action. It was time to 'make things hum in a business-like way,' he told Haden Guest. Young Fabians like Guest were urging him to 'get our attack on the Fabian definitely into focus'; some older ones too encouraged him to defend the Society against 'the increasing insanity of our compatriots'; and even Shaw saw no harm in a 'stir up and stock-taking to make Fabianism interesting again'. Help came in from every side and so eagerly that the initiative was almost wrenched from Wells's hands. But he held on. He did not want to make Fabianism 'interesting' to a Shavian prescription – he would rather dismantle it altogether. 'I'm going to turn the Fabian Society inside out,' he promised Ford Madox Ford, 'and then throw it into the dustbin.'

*

Wells's campaign opened on 6 January 1906 with a Fabian lecture, 'This Misery of Boots', using the shoe trade to satirize the condition of England. This indictment of private enterprise was both an illustration of what he wanted from the new Fabian propaganda, and an indictment of Shaw and the Webbs, 'who will assure you that some odd little jobbing about municipal gas and water is Socialism, and backstairs intervention between Conservative and Liberal is the way to the millennium'.

He launched his main attack in a second lecture, which had been held back by the election (and was to gain in momentum from its result), a month later on 9 February. 'Faults of the Fabian' was Wells at his most comic-destructive. Where was the new world that socialism had promised? Almost everything in the sphere of thought had changed in the last twenty years – unless it was the Fabian Society. 'I am here to-night to ask it to change.'

What must it change from? What should it change to? Wells's imagination worked more powerfully when dealing with the paralysis of the Fabian tradition than when analysing its new career of usefulness. 'My experience burns within me,' he told his audience, and he forced into this small Fabian vessel all his recent experience, his sense of growing literary power and domestic frustration. He had come to the Society almost as he had come to marriage, anticipating romantic ideals, experiencing routine and drudgery. He chaffed against these confining forces. He needed to expand.

The Fabians had preened themselves on their permeation and it was here that Wells centred his attack. A great deal of work, 'with a certain lack of charm perhaps', had been invested in permeation. Some of it was gratuitous, some of it unfortunate; and almost all of it was removed from socialistic ideals. The vigorous working-class movements in the direction of socialism covered a world of activity that lay outside the Fabian sphere of influence. The tone of their indirect methods could be recognized by a senile conceit of cunning: 'something like a belief that the world may be manoeuvred into socialism without knowing it; that . . . we shall presently be able to confront the world with a delighted, "But you *are* socialists! We chalked it on your back when you weren't looking . . . "'

'The mouse decided to adopt indirect and inconspicuous methods, not to complicate its proceedings by too many associates, to win over and attract the cat by friendly advances rather than frighten her by a sudden attack. It is believed that in the end the mouse did succeed in permeating the cat, but the cat is still living – and the mouse can't be found.'

Wells's second criticism of the Society was its size. It was, in short, the wrong size. It was small – needlessly and ridiculously small. It had an air of arrested growth, as if by the effort of taking an office in a cellar in Clement's Inn, it had exhausted its energy. From this cellar, through the burrowings of one secretary and his assistant, the Fabian Society was to shift the industrial basis of civilization. Amid the jungle of politics it looked to Wells like 'a pot-bound plant'.

They were also poor, the Fabians. Their hands were tied by poverty; they were always in debt. 'You have it from Mr Bernard Shaw that poverty is a crime, and if so, then by the evidence of your balance-sheet ours is a criminal organization.'

Wells spoke on, adding enthusiastically to this catalogue of defects and accusations. The Fabians were not simply unsocialistic, he explained: they had evolved into a conservative society, fumbling bureaucratically over the admission of new members, parading a long inventory of lecturers who

137

never lectured, flattering themselves on being the only authoritative socialists in the country. Yet they were a collectivist society only by the definition of their collective inactivity. 'We don't advertise, thank you; it's not quite our style. We cry socialism as the reduced gentlewoman cried "oranges": "I do so hope nobody will hear me." '

After an hour and a half of speaking in a monotonous voice addressed to the corner of the hall, Wells had nearly concluded his Fabian indictment. He had just one more pettiness to nail. 'Our society is small; and in relation to its great mission small minded; it is poor; it is collectively, as a society, inactive; it is suspicious of help, and exclusive,' he summarized. And, he added: 'it is afflicted with a giggle'.

With his purge on this foolish forced laughter of the Fabians, Wells does to Shaw what Shaw had done to him. He treats him as immature. Of all the faults of the Fabians, he declared, this juvenile joking was probably the worst. No wonder, with such an offensive deterrent, they were never taken seriously by politicians. The giggling excitement that ran through their meetings 'flows over and obscures all sorts of grave issues, it chills and kills enthusiasm', he said. 'Its particular victim in this society is Mr Bernard Shaw.'

'It pursues him with unrelenting delight, simply because he is not like everybody else, as he rises, before he opens his mouth to speak it begins. Shaw has a habit of vivid statement, he has a habit, a brilliant habit, of seeking to arrest the attention by a startling, apparent irrelevance, and he has a natural inclination to paradox. Our accursed giggle lives on these things. Now Bernard Shaw is at bottom an intensely serious man, whatever momentary effect this instant dissolution of sober discussion into mirth may produce on him, he does in the long run, hate this pursuit of laughter . . .

' . . . you will not suppose that in attacking laughter I am assailing Bernard Shaw. But I do assail the strained attempts to play up to Shaw, the constant endeavour of members devoid of any natural wit or wildness to catch his manner, to ape his egotism, to fall in with an assumed pretence that this grave high business of Socialism, to which it would be a small offering for us to give all our lives, is an idiotic middle-class joke.'

By turning his animus against Shaw into an ingenious attack on the political insidiousness of Shavianism, and his temperamental differences with the Webbs into a humorous requiem over permeation, Wells was raising a platform on which he hoped the Fabians would enthrone him as their new leader. His timing was perfect and during the discussion afterwards, and in the weeks that followed, he was engulfed by enthusiastic support. 'We look up to such as you to convert the professional and middle classes to socialism,' the secretary of a Socialist League branch in a Yorkshire mill town wrote to him: 'People in the provinces think H. G. Wells is a great man, and I can assure you they pay great attention to anything you say. Your audience is assured already, let the prophet appear.'

The prophet's chariot took the form of a Special Committee – a squadron of Wells-picked men and women whose mission was to increase the 'scope, influence, income and activity of the Society'. Wells had wanted them to move fast, finishing their work before he left at the end of March for a lecture tour in America. But Shaw and the Webbs, word-perfect in gradualism, entangled him with their assistance. 'I advise you to make a Royal Commission of that committee of yours,' Shaw pressed him. ' . . . Appoint a secretary and ask for power to examine witnesses. Then you can call Pease & examine him. You can also examine me, Webb & Bland *separately*, and compare our stories & views. The discrepancies will provide all the levity you want in your report.'

Wells wanted speed rather than detail, revolution not levity. Above all, he refused to work under Shaw's instructions. He demanded the power to nominate the members of the Special Committee himself and to include among them some Fabians from the executive. Shaw explained to him that this was out of the question. 'Your position is that the executive is a stick-in-the-mud body and the secretary a duffer,' he wrote. 'Now you cant reasonably make an unrepresentative minority of the executive a party to an inquiry which has primarily to establish that fact.'

Wells would not accept Shaw's advice and it was in Shaw's interests to give him the best advice. Determinedly Wells went his own way and seconded to his Special Committee four members of the executive. These included Sydney Olivier (briefly returned from abroad) as its chairman, and (risking the charge of 'political adultery') Charlotte Shaw. Wells had won his point: but he had used up his time. Before leaving for America he could do no more than submit to the executive a revised *Basis* (the rules of joining and belonging to the Society). This was 'obviously much better than the existing Basis', Shaw allowed, and yet it was useless; since it did not aim (as Shaw's Imperialist and Tariff tracts had done) for cordial co-operation among all Fabians. 'You must study people's corns when you go clog dancing,' he advised – and then went dancing all over Wells's corns with pages of tuition on his committee's terms of reference and the executive's duties. 'During your absence I will write the report of your committee, probably, and get it adopted through

Charlotte,' he threatened. And Wells warned: 'You leave my committee alone while I'm in America.'

The Webbs believed that, lacking the capacity for co-operation, Wells would not have the skill and stamina to carry through his revisionist programme. Shaw was less certain. He wanted Wells to succeed – but only if, like an actor, he would allow himself to be stage-managed by G.B.S.

'The more I think of Mr Wells's Fabian Reforms the more do I welcome them & if only everyone will be sensible & broadminded I foresee a new era for Fabianism,' wrote Marjorie Pease. Shaw too believed Wells was vitally important to the future of Fabians. But below his admiration lay resentment, almost envy. He saw Wells as attractive where he was not, gifted with intimacy where he had none, and lovable while he was fated always to be unloved. Wells had succeeded at once and (so it seemed to Shaw) without effort, and he scoffed at the laborious practice by which G.B.S. had taught himself. Shaw knew the price he had paid for excellence: Wells had been granted excellence at birth. He was in consequence a spoilt child insisting on an adult life of unchecked promotion. 'He was born cleverer than anybody within hail of him,' Shaw wrote, using his own upbringing as an invisible comparison. 'You can see from his pleasant figure that he was never awkward or uncouth or clumsy-footed or heavy-handed . . . '

'He was probably stuffed with sweets and smothered with kisses . . . He won scholarships . . . The world that other men of genius had to struggle with, and which sometimes starved them dead, came to him and licked his boots. He did what he liked; and when he did not like what he had done, he threw it aside and tried something else.'

Shaw knew nothing of the illnesses and insecurities of Wells's early years. He simply saw, in contrast to himself, someone who had 'always been indulged as more or less of an infant prodigy'; someone who had 'never missed a meal, never wandered through the streets without a penny in his pocket, never had to wear seedy clothes, never was unemployed'. And here he was being pampered in the literary greenhouse, fussed over by the whole family of Fabians – well known to his readers as a 'nice, cheerful, friendly soul' and to his colleagues for his 'transports of vituperative fury in which he could not spare his most devoted friends'.

Wells arrived back from America even more eager to put 'woosh' into the Fabians. The contrast between the go-ahead Americans and recalcitrant Englishmen had stimulated his radical energies. Throughout most of the summer he prepared his devastating report. 'Keep your pecker up,' he encouraged Haden Guest. 'We'll have a big rush next September to make a good fight . . . '

The fight erupted first among his own committee. 'You have let me in [for it] in the most abominable manner, you treacherous man, over this business,' Charlotte wrote to him after receiving his explosive draft. ' . . . you assured me over & over again that the past work of the Society formed no part of our business: that we were to devise forms of activity for the future . . . '

'I explained to you then that if your Committee meant criticism & discussion of past work & methods of the Executive *I* could not be on it; as I was part of the Executive, & it reduced the matter to an absurdity that I should criticise myself. But in spite of this misunderstanding . . . the Committee has been nothing from its very first meeting but a Committee of Public Safety to try the Executive; with the foregone conclusion that we were to be condemned.'

In this way, with the spirit of G.B.S. hovering near, Wells's initial victory was turned to his disadvantage. 'You want everything better and everything just the same & it can't be done,' he grumbled to Charlotte. He felt let down. He felt impatient. He wrote another draft; and then another. 'I am immensely relieved that the whole thing is so modified,' Charlotte assured him on 7 October, '& I do really now feel we shall be able to achieve a modus vivendi, & do some real work. I am *so very* glad!'

The Special Committee's report that October was described as 'unanimous'. In the opinion of Edward Pease it was consequently 'a much less inspiring document than the irresponsible and entertaining "Faults of the Fabian" '. But traces of what Pease thought of as 'the megalomania of the original scheme' were still there.

Wells wanted to change permeation into propaganda: to make the Society into a far bigger, richer, simpler, less centralized organization. He wanted to obliterate Shaw's influence on the Society, to fade him out of its past by rewriting the Fabian tracts himself, and by realigning Fabian loyalties with the Labour Party and Keir Hardie who had fought the battle for socialism while Shaw had been making jokes elsewhere. He proposed changing the name of the Society to the British Socialist Party – but this was unanimously rejected by the executive which also rejected (by eight votes to three) a proposal to make the *Fabian News* into a weekly paper appealing to outside readers and (by six votes to five) a revision of the *Basis* so as to define the purpose of the Society as forwarding the progress of socialism 'by all available means'.

The matter then went to the full membership. The Special Committee's report was published in November together with a Counter Report and Resolutions on behalf of the executive which had been written by

Shaw. This was an accommodating yet dismissive response, long and confusing to the Fabians. To Wells it seemed 'the most irresponsible, irritating and mischievous piece of writing I have read for a long time,' destined, with its preposterous fables of Fabian foresight, to become 'a classic in the humorous literature of Socialism . . .' Reading it, Wells declared, he had the giddy feeling of participating in greatness again – he was completely carried away.

'The Fabian Society had planned and foreseen everything. We were the sole authors of all the remedial legislation of the past fifteen years . . . Every development in the Socialist thought in Europe had been due to Fabian Tracts . . . There seems to me a certain strain of baseness in this greedy claim to achievements . . .'

Most of the issues which divided these two teeming documents were matters of internal reorganization and not difficult to reconcile. Some of Wells's ammunition, too, had been stolen from him by the executive's decision to constitute a new class of Associates (as Wells had suggested) and allow the young Fabians to set up an informal group, nicknamed 'the Fabian nursery'. But beneath this administrative business lay what Wells's biographers, Norman and Jeanne MacKenzie, called 'a hidden agenda'. The Fabians were a family, with Wells their rebel son. They had prevented him leaving and he now turned murderously back on them. He wanted to kill off the parents and, in his own image, father a new breed of this family. His fantasy of omnipotence, with its current of sexual energy, attracted crowds of excited Fabians for his dramatic confrontation with G.B.S.

Their first crossing of swords took place on 7 December at Essex Hall. Shaw moved the Executive's resolution. His tone was friendly, his argument reasonable, his manner ominously disarming. He welcomed the criticisms (however unreasonable) by the Special Committee. Some of its recommendations (variously modified) would be adopted; others would have to remain 'pious aspirations' until there was enough money to implement them. The executive rejected, however, the breathless rush to join other radical organizations and help them run socialist candidates for Parliament. It was time for the Fabians to educate middle-class opinion for socialism as effectively as the ILP and Labour Party were representing working-class opinion in Parliament. One day perhaps these middle-class Fabians would form the new Socialist Party – and this would be the Society's achievement. He sat down.

It was the job of Sydney Olivier, as chairman, to present the Special Committee's report. But Wells rushed up in front of him and began to address the meeting. Until then it had seemed as if, like the magical hero in his story 'The Man Who Could Work Miracles', he might perform anything he wished. But he spoke badly, he spoke dreadfully, he spoke (as Shaw remarked) like a shop assistant addressing a customer. His proposals for reorganizing the Society degenerated into a list of accusations against Shaw and the Webbs. The Old Gang were on trial and Wells was pressing for a maximum sentence. He moved an amendment calling for the abolition of the executive and its replacement by a larger representative body that would endorse the 'spirit and purport' of his Special Committee's proposals. 'It is not a numerical change we propose, it is revolution,' he piped. 'It is the letting in of the Society to the control of its own affairs.'

There had been a swell in favour of his amendment at the start; by the time he ended it had sunk. Webb rose to make a short plea for loyalty; Olivier followed, insisting that the necessary reforms need not involve wholesale dismissals. They then arranged for a second-reading debate one week later.

Wells had badly punctured his case, but the battle was not over. He had recently published a romance describing an England wonderfully changed from disorder into peace by the gas of a comet. Some people believed that *In the Days of the Comet* was a parable of how Wells himself would transform the Fabian Society. But Shaw scoffed at this: 'You want to play the part of the Comet,' he had chided. ' . . . You cannot go on spinning comets out of your head for ever.'

During the interval between the two debates both parties prepared. Wells printed his speech. He had accused Shaw of ingenious misrepresentation amounting to a breach of faith, dismissed the Shavian mirage of a Fabian Socialist Party in Parliament as a stupendous feat of bluff, and described as 'shabby and unwise' the Fabian failure to co-operate with Keir Hardie. What he did not reveal was that he had written to Keir Hardie and been advised by him not to waste time bullying these steady-going Fabians 'who would continue to do their own useful work' into becoming semi-revolutionaries. It would provide friction and disappointment – besides it was 'not quite fair' to the Society. 'Why not leave it to pursue its own way by its own methods,' Keir Hardie suggested, 'and come in and take your part in the political side of the movement as represented by the ILP?'

The answer to this was that Wells wanted to capture the Fabian army from Shaw, lead it over to Keir Hardie, and then go off to do something else. His part in the political side of the movement was not represented by the ILP but by literature. So was Shaw's – and Keir Hardie had been critical of him too. Had his Executive report been 'more accurate historically and less bombastic', he wrote to G.B.S., 'the task of averting a menace to the movement wd have been easier.'

'That apart what I wd like to see passed wd be a declaration of loyalty to the Labour Party which wd be binding on the Society and on its officials [who] . . . shall not support the candidates of other political parties . . . in this respect members of the Fabian Society are sad sinners.'

This advice (which included a recommendation to campaign among non-socialist trade unions) cut diagonally across the Fabian lines of argument. Neither Wells nor Shaw mentioned their letters from Keir Hardie when Wells turned up at Adelphi Terrace the day after the Essex Hall encounter. He came with an apology and an offer of compromise. 'Why dont you see how entirely I am expressing you in all these things?' he had asked G.B.S. For months Shaw had been advocating compromise: now he rejected it, and Wells left accusing him of being an Irishman – 'meaning, as far as I could make out, that I was vindictive', Shaw confided to Hubert Bland.

Shaw had scented victory. He proposed taking on himself the weight of this second debate. It would be a peculiarly Shavian exercise – a 'moral game' played in 'an eye-opening manner' and leading to a 'terrific' verbal victory achieved without 'saying anything unkind'. He asked Bland and others who did not feel kindly towards Wells to keep silent and leave the job to him. 'I have all the points of detail noted,' he mildly predicted, 'and can smash him to atoms on every one of them.' He dispatched an 'urgent whip' appealing to Fabians to attend the adjourned meeting, then retreated into the country to gather his strength and superiority. 'All I dread is being in bad form,' he wrote; 'for I am overworked.'

The crowd was even larger for this second meeting. Not everything went as Shaw had hoped, but it was clear from the early speeches that Wells had lost much support, and that most of the audience would not vote for him if it meant the dismissal of the executive. At nine o'clock Shaw rose to speak, and at once focused the issue on two sets of resignations. If Wells's amendment were passed, he said, the executive would obey it 'by not offering themselves for re-election'. It would be dismissal with dishonour: they would be drummed out. But this amendment, he reminded the audience, had nothing to do with the two reports. Over the serious business of the proposals in these reports, the executive would never resign, even if defeated on every resolution, but would faithfully carry out the decisions of the Society. There would be no sulking, no hesitation to co-operate loyally with Wells. But the amendment, which they had met to discuss, was a flat instruction to the executive to stand down. He read it out carefully to show its meaning. There was already much heated dissent in the hall and above the uproar Wells was heard pledging himself not to resign. 'That is a great relief to my mind,' answered Shaw. 'I can now pitch into Mr Wells without fear of consequences.'

He then offered up Wells for Fabian entertainment. If the style of the executive report had been unpleasant the fault was his, admitted G.B.S., for he 'perhaps had not that conciliatory charm of manner which distinguished his friend Wells'. Besides he had had less time than Wells. 'During his Committee's deliberations he [Wells] produced a book on America,' Shaw told his audience. 'And a very good book too. But whilst I was drafting our reply I produced a play.' Shaw paused and there was silence. S. G. Hobson in the audience noticed his eyes vacantly glancing round the ceiling. 'It really seemed that he had lost his train of thought,' Hobson remembered. 'When we were all thoroughly uncomfortable, he resumed: "Ladies and gentlemen: I paused there to enable Mr Wells to say: 'And a very good play too!' " '

'. . . We laughed [continued Hobson], and went on laughing. Shaw always has been adept at the unexpected; never did he put his gift to such practical purpose. He stood on the platform waiting. Wells, also on the platform, smiled self-consciously; but the audience went on laughing.'

Wells had paid the penalty for having attacked the Shavian joke. For it was this joke which magically seemed to dissolve him and his faction into nothingness. The effect was so complete that after Shaw had finished his speech the chairman took it for granted that the amendment was withdrawn by consent: and Wells made no protest. The conflict was over and the Fabians trooped out for refreshments. 'Keats was snuffed out by an article,' commented Hobson; 'Wells was squelched by a joke.'

The Comet had passed leaving a debris of disorder. Wells, 'a very lively resentment' throbbing through him, felt he had been tricked by what Graham Wallas called Shaw's 'mixture of gerrymandering, bluffing, browbeating, quibbling, baiting and playing to the gallery.' He suspected that the Webbs had contrived it all. He did not know that Beatrice had responded to Shaw's victory as 'an altogether horrid business'. In her diary she calculated that if Wells had 'pushed his own fervid policy, or rather, enthusiasm for vague and big ideas, without making a personal attack on the Old Gang, he would have succeeded.'

But Wells's motives had been mixed. 'No part of my career rankles so acutely in my memory with the conviction of bad judgement, gusty impulse and real inexcusable vanity,' he afterwards admitted. But: 'I was fundamentally right.' He had reacted with imaginative enthusiasm to the future; and to the past with splenetic vengeance. The present, which he overlooked, had been turned into theatre, which he had never liked or understood. 'Now we shall see whether he will forgive G.B.S.,' commented Beatrice.

This was not how G.B.S. saw it. He had taken on this horrid job because he was confident that he could accomplish it to the satisfaction of Bland, Webb and others, but without making Wells into another Ramsay MacDonald. He had done it technically, like a surgeon. He had used the anaesthetic of laughter. He had arranged everything so that Wells could 'come up smiling' again among the Fabians. His purpose extended not a frown further. For, unlike Bland and Webb, he recognized that 'Wells is a great man'. His qualities made him a glamorously popular figure among the Fabians, particularly the young women of the new Fabian nursery. 'Tell the dear man that it is almost impossible to do anything without him,' Maud Reeves wrote to Wells's wife. Other Fabians, too, begged him not to desert them. To Shaw it seemed that the worse Wells behaved the more he was indulged. 'Any other man would have been hurled out of the society by bodily violence with heated objurgation,' he wrote. Wells was allowed to go on 'unhindered, unchecked, unpunished, apparently even undisliked'. Though it was Wells who had 'knocked himself out at every exchange', it was Shaw who was reproached. 'He had so much the worst of it in mere ringcraft,' Shaw told Pease, 'that I got my victory at the cost of losing all the sympathy of the tender hearted. People actually told me that it was a disgraceful exhibition; that I had played cat and mouse with him; that I ought to be ashamed of myself . . . I certainly was not proud of it and was very anxious that its aspect as a personal exploit should be forgotten.'

Wells was equally anxious that this should be remembered. While Shaw drafted an austere impersonal account of the debate for the *Fabian News*, Wells sent in a letter complaining of being the victim of an 'entirely personal attack'. In writing this he had the satisfaction of acting against the wishes of G.B.S. who had advised him to retrieve the situation by doing 'exactly what I tell you'. Wells's position was intolerable. He had given a public pledge not to resign, but could not co-operate by putting himself and his followers up for the executive without appearing to obey Shaw's dictates. 'I am reluctantly taking up a secondary position for a time,' he informed Pease. By March 1907, however, he agreed to stand. The poll in April was headed by Webb with 819 votes, Pease with 809, Shaw with 781 and Wells with 717. Nine of his supporters were elected to the new and enlarged executive of twenty-one, all representing '20th Century Socialism'.

No one knew what Wells would do next. The past still rankled: he felt a grievance. It seemed to him that Shaw's mind had been corrupted by public speaking and destroyed by the committee habit. This should not happen to him. Nevertheless he accepted positions on the General Purposes and Propaganda Subcommittee, and another special committee – and was extremely difficult, even with his admirers, on both of them. But he told Shaw: 'you are always sound hearted & I am always, through all our disputes & slanging matches, Yours most affectionately, H. G.' And Shaw agreed that, between his gusts of temper and occasional panics, Wells had played a 'great game' with 'immense vitality and fun'. They had so many public objects in common that there was no excuse for quarrelling – yet it seemed inevitable.

'I'm damnably sorry we're all made so,' wrote Wells.

'To complain of such things is to complain that the leaves are green and the sky blue,' wrote Shaw.

But what good came of it in the end? The issue had been shifted from a comparison of reports and policies to a gladiatorial contest of personalities. Wells's goring of the Old Gang threw into relief Shaw's patience and public good humour. To Wells's frankness, his raging desire to discover the truth, Shaw had opposed something polemically formidable and professionally correct – yet somehow dubious. Had the Fabians been brilliantly misdirected? Or could the mingling on the executive of old and new, Shaw and Wells, transform the relation of the Society to the political world? The next few years would decide. 'I incline to the prophecy that five years will see H. G. Wells out of the Society,' Beatrice Webb wrote. ' . . . It will be interesting to watch.'

[3]

As a matter of fact, I am overrated as an author: most great men are.

When the curtain came down on 28 November 1905, it was clear that *Major Barbara* was to be Shaw's most controversial success. The critics were impressively divided. Desmond MacCarthy told his readers: 'Mr Shaw has written the first play with religious passion for its theme and has made it real. That is a triumph no criticisms can lessen.' But the anonymous critic of the *Pall Mall Gazette* found that the play betrayed 'an utter want of the religious sense' and that its author was 'destitute of the religious emotion'. An unsigned notice in the *Morning Post* wondered at such a performance 'escaping the notice of the censorship . . . its offences against good taste and good feeling are of a kind not to be readily forgiven'. From *The Clarion* came the advice that 'critics who accuse Shaw of the remotest approach to blasphemy do not know what they are talking about'. In the *Sunday Times*, while acknowledging G.B.S. to be 'the most original English dramatist of the day', J. T. Grein recoiled from Bill Walker's punching of the down-and-out Rummy Mitchens and his assault on the young Salvation Army lass Jenny Hill; this 'double act of brutality literally moved the audience to shudders. It was beyond all bounds of realism in art. It was ugly and revolting'. From the same audience, Max Beerbohm saw this incident as neither an exaggeration of real life nor 'enacted realistically on the stage of the Court Theatre . . . the actor impersonating the ruffian aimed a noticeably gentle blow in the air, at a noticeably great distance from the face of the actress impersonating the lass. I happen to be particularly squeamish in the matter of physical violence on the stage . . . The mere symbolism at the Court Theatre gave me not the faintest qualm.' Critics who professed themselves outraged, Beerbohm concluded, 'must have been very hard up for a fair means of attack'.

These critics felt inconvenienced on several counts. The play's 'lack of straightforward intelligible purpose' (*Morning Post*) made it spectacularly difficult for them to decide how good or bad it was, or to calculate its effect on audiences. Collectively they offered the choice between 'an audacious propagandist drama' (*Clarion*), 'one of the most remarkable plays put upon the English stage' (*Speaker*), a work of 'deliberate perversity' (*Morning Post*) or of the 'keenest insight and sense of spiritual beauty' (*Saturday Review*). '*Major Barbara* is a play to be heard, to be seen, to be read,' exclaimed J. T. Grein. 'It will raise discussion and arguments galore.' But these arguments were making the popular critics look foolish. It was their business to decide whether G.B.S. was 'ephemeral' (John Galsworthy) or 'a high genius' (Oliver Lodge); whether he 'has heart' (*Sunday Times*) or was 'a writer whose absence of feeling makes him a very unsafe guide' (*Pall Mall Gazette*).

The war that had opened between the two audiences at Henry James's *Guy Domville* was now breaking out between critics and the public. Against all odds Shaw had become a fashionable craze. 'The old order is changing', calculated one of the *Clarion* writers. Shaw's message to society 'to cast all its obsolete creeds and moral codes to the scrap heap' matched the new order.

Yet Shaw's career was now being blessed by the guardians of a society he was working to destroy, by dynamite if necessary. After the reputation of this 'inveterate Republican' had bloomed with the royal command performance of *John Bull's Other Island* the previous spring, all London knew of G.B.S. On the first night of *Major Barbara* there were almost as many carriages and motor cars outside the Court 'as there are in the Mall on a Drawing-room day'. Shaw was box office at last because 'now the English middle class pays to see that which is seen by the English upper class, and (more especially) to see the English upper class', Max Beerbohm wrote in the *Saturday Review*. 'Whether either of these classes really rejoices in Mr Shaw as yet, is a point on which I am doubtful.' But there they all were, laughing and elated.

For the critics who had denigrated Shaw's playwriting over the past dozen years it was galling to find themselves suddenly at odds with public opinion. Shaw was voicing the opinion of the young. Rupert Brooke, after flying visits to the Court from Rugby and then Cambridge, described *John Bull's Other Island* as 'unspeakably delightful', *Candida* 'the best play in the world' and *Major Barbara* 'highly amusing & interesting, & very brutal'. G.B.S. had been voted 'one of our leaders in the revolutionary movement of our youth', wrote Leonard Woolf. Though Shaw's dramas did not have the grandeur of Ibsen's, they were played at the Court Theatre with relentless gusto, and experienced as a hurricane sweeping into the alley of Victorian morality and scattering the accumulated litter. Shaw, the champion of free speech and free thought, of paradoxical common sense and the ingenious use of reason, had 'a message of tremendous importance to us', Leonard Woolf recorded. Along with Wells and Arnold Bennett, he had become one of the idols of young intellectuals. 'We felt that, with them as our leaders, we were struggling against a religious and moral code of cant and hypocrisy which produced and condoned such social crimes and judicial murders as the condemnation of Dreyfus.'

Many of the young men and women who attended the Court Theatre were to join the Fabian nursery or other socialist groups. The Court was their place of extramural studies: they entered as *fin de siècle* Bohemians and emerged as twentieth-century radicals. 'My present pose is as a Socialist,' decided Rupert Brooke whose aesthetic pose faded after he turned to Fabianism. He would go regularly to see the work of the Court's playwright-in-residence: but he also went to see the Court at work. 'The average of acting all round at the Court is exactly four times as high as any other theatre in London,' he wrote. Even A. B. Walkley, the reactionary critic of *The Times*, was obliged to agree. 'There is no such all-round acting in London as is nowadays to be seen at the Court theatre,' he wrote. ' . . . Where all are excellent it is needless to single out names.'

The ensemble playing at the Court handed over the actor-manager's authority to the dramatist-producer. In part a reflection of Barker's lowly view of the acting profession and a response from Shaw to being humiliated by Henry Irving, this new theatrical spirit also expressed a more general reaction. For over two centuries, from Thomas Betterton to Beerbohm Tree, the history of the British theatre had been the history of great actors whose popularity with the public, often in emasculated Shakespearian roles, enabled them to conduct their establishments like discreet hotel managers catering for the tastes of fashionable patrons. When George Alexander, the most consistently successful of the actor-managers, introduced *Guy Domville* as a modest new dish on the menu at the St James's Theatre, the uproar had shown that the public apparently wanted more old-fashioned fare: more of what G.B.S., the drama critic, had been attempting to bulldoze off the stage to clear the way for the works of Bernard Shaw and his contemporaries.

The Court Theatre ignored the appetite of the public and set up a different standard of merit, bringing the acting and production of plays more in line with that of the contemporary Scandinavian and German stage. It changed the public's attitude towards the theatre. There was a story, illustrating this, that Barker used to tell. For a night or two he went down with influenza and could not play the part of Tanner in *Man and Superman*. A notice to this effect was pinned above the pay-box at the entrance to the pit, and a playgoer, descending the stairs, asked what it meant. 'It means,' explained an official, 'that Mr Barker will not be playing the part of Tanner this evening.' 'Who is Barker?' asked the playgoer. 'The actor who usually plays John Tanner,' he was told. 'But I suppose somebody will play it?' 'Yes it will be played.' 'Then,' said the gentleman, 'take my half-crown, young man, and don't make such a fuss.' This, added Barker, was the 'proper spirit in which to go to the theatre' and the spirit 'in which most of our audience came to the Court'. They went to see the play rather than an actor; and they had confidence in the all-round excellence of the cast.

Because the actors recognized Barker and Shaw as practical men of the theatre and respected their choice of plays, knowledge of stagecraft and skill at casting, they were willing to work as a team, accepting the smallest parts however successful they had earlier been in major roles. Acting at the Court was part of an orchestral theory of dramatic production. Barker believed in repertory as a method of sustaining this general theory. A variety of parts extended the actor's range, teaching him his business, which was that of an instrument and not of the composer.

Barker was a more literary and autocratic producer than Shaw. His directions, intended to stimulate the actors' imaginations, were sometimes alarming. He liked to question them over the past history of their

9 Shaw photographed at the rehearsals for *Pygmalion*, 1913

IOA Fabian Summer School at Harlech, Wales; B Beatrice and Sidney Webb

11A 'Mr George Bernard Shaw learns to drive a motorcar.' *Motor*, 5 November 1907;
B The well-practised driver, 12 years later

12 Shaw and Harley Granville-Barker, 1901

13 Lillah McCarthy, sculling, photographed by Shaw

14A The Rectory, Ayot St Lawrence; B Shaw sawing wood with Henry Higgs

15A & B Husband and wife: two photos by Shaw *c.* 1900 and 1905

16 Erica Cotterill

characters. 'You are not, I hope, going to tell me that the fellow drops from the skies, ready-made, at the moment you walk on the stage?' The biographies he provided became green-room legends. 'I want when you enter to give the impression of a man who is steeped in the poetry of Tennyson,' he was reputed to have told Dennis Eadie. For a scene in one of his own plays, he advised an actress that 'from the moment you come in you must make the audience understand that you live in a small town in the provinces and visit a great deal with the local clergy; you make slippers for the curate and go to dreary tea-parties'. Her one line in this scene was: 'How do you do?' Though a target for jokes, Barker was introducing a form of Stanislavsky's method of psychological realism which, he claimed, had been forced on actors by the bare dialogue of Ibsen with so much implicit in it.

Shaw was more matter-of-fact. If the producer, watching rehearsals, noted 'Show influence of Kierkegaard on Ibsen in this scene' or 'the Oedipus complex must be very apparent here. Discuss with the Queen', then 'the sooner he is packed out of the theatre the better'. If he noted 'Ears too red', 'Further up to make room for X', 'He, not Ee', 'This comes too suddenly', then, Shaw concluded, 'the producer knows his job and his place'.

Shaw would read his plays, first to friends, then to the company. One actor who worked for him recalled: 'His readings were extraordinarily vivid. He had an unerring dramatic sense; each character was carefully differentiated, and he could maintain the voice peculiar to each right up to the end of the play without the least suggestion of strain; he was never monotonous; he used no gestures, getting his effects solely by the tempo and modulation of his voice.' Before the first rehearsal, he worked out on a chessboard with chessmen and a boy's box of assorted bricks, every entry, movement, rising or sitting, disposal of tambourine and tennis racket.

The first rehearsals at the Court were always choreographic, the actors having their books in hand and the producer on the bare stage with them (the exits marked by a couple of chairs) teaching them their movements. Once these had been mastered, the words learned, and the actors comfortable with what was going on, the books were discarded and the producer would leave the stage to sit in the front of the house with a notebook and torch. 'From that moment, he should watch the stage as a cat watches a mouse,' Shaw advised, 'but never utter a word or interrupt a scene during its repetition no matter how completely the play goes to pieces, as it must at first when the players are trying to remember their parts and cues so desperately that they are incapable of acting.'

' . . . At the end of each act, the producer returns to the stage to explain or demonstrate such of his notes as may be judicious at the moment. But no fault should be mentioned or corrected unless and until its constant repetition shews that the player will not correct it in his or her own way as the play is gradually learnt. When all the players are letter-perfect their memorizing will be so mechanical that . . . they will catch one another's speech and tone, betraying to the audience that they are only gabbling off prearranged lists of words, each knowing what the other will say next and fielding their cues like cricketers. The producer must accordingly take care that every speech contrasts as strongly as possible with the one which provokes it, as if coming unexpected as a shock, surprise, stimulant, offence, amusement . . . '

The producer at the Court (whom we now call director) involved himself in reading plays, choosing casts, inventing the machinery, arranging the lighting, designing scenery and costume, adding incidental music, superintending the whole business of stage-management and co-ordinating everything except finance, which belonged to Vedrenne. Shaw liked to take a week over the stage movements, a fortnight for memorizing, and a final week for the dress rehearsals, when he would come on the stage again, going through passages that needed finishing, and interrupting now whenever he felt like it. Barker liked longer but in the crowded Court schedule such a stretch of time was seldom practicable.

The Court Theatre company was an orchestra with two conductors – both also being Court composers and one of them a principal player. Shaw had come to the theatre with the twin aspirations of giving the British public a political education and creating verbal opera; Barker's aim was to discover, through fractured syntax, crafted inarticulateness, oblique denouement, the naturalistic dialogue to express a new stage situation. From those different aims as composers of plays arose their different styles of conducting the players.

Barker produced all the plays at the Court except those of Shaw who was said to produce his own – though with a company trained by Barker, and sometimes leaving rehearsals to Barker. 'The combination works better than the single cylinder,' Shaw conceded, ' . . . a bit of training does them no harm, it will enable me to let them rip recklessly.' There was one oddity, a revival of *You Never Can Tell*, that appeared when Shaw was abroad. On his return he went to see it, discovered 'a degree of infamy which took away my breath' and enquired of Barker: 'What was the name of the author of that play?'

Barker had never witnessed the heroic acting of old-timers and knew little of the technique by which they made themselves appear superhuman.

His taste for low tones, which worked perfectly for his own plays and those of Galsworthy, did not seem to suit Shaw who entreated him to 'leave me the drunken, stagey, brassbowelled barnstormers my plays are written for'. Barker's restrained style 'makes me blush for the comparative blatancy of my own plays,' Shaw conceded. His own flamboyant productions were sometimes criticized for proceeding too slowly and exploiting the comic turns, whereas Barker's understated arrangements were criticized for reducing everything to miniature. Shaw, with his card-index of actors, was responsible for introducing typecasting into the Court. He complained that Barker was so clever a stage-manager that 'he has come to think that it does not matter who acts as long as he produces'. Shaw denounced this as 'a deadly mistake. Get your cast right . . . and stage management can be done without'.

As Shaw's principal actor, Barker knew Shaw's stage methods better than Shaw knew Barker's, and followed his technique of rehearsal so far as his different personality allowed. Shaw was patient and persistent, used a good deal of flattery, and took advice from some of the better actors. Barker was more persistent and less patient, parsimonious with praise, and inclined to make his cast perform their parts as he would have performed them himself. Like Shaw he took things quietly and talked matters over intimately; but like many actor-producers he could be hard. Shaw set a limit of three hours (preferably between breakfast and lunch) and ensured that actors with only a few lines to speak were not kept hanging around all day while the principals rehearsed. Barker was a perfectionist and sometimes refused to leave off rehearsing until, according to Shaw, 'the unfortunate company had lost their last trains and buses and he had tired himself beyond human powers of maintaining the intense vigilance & freshness' a good production demands. He also got terrifyingly annoyed. 'His curses are neither loud nor deep: they are atmospheric,' one actor remembered. 'It is what he doesn't say that paralyses one. He *looks*; and having looked, he turns his back to the stage – and you can still see him looking through the back of his head . . . '

'Sometimes he will execute a little dance, a quiet, solitary waltz with ghastly possibilities . . . The best thing to do is to hide yourself from him completely until he calls you back. By that time he will have recovered, and will be quite charming. Perhaps he will take you by the arm and call you his "dear friend". Later, you will ask someone what happened after you had gone away. You will be told that nothing happened – nothing whatever! That is the appalling thing about Barker. Nothing happens. But all sorts of things are *going* to happen. He is the supreme artist of Suggestion.'

Barker might be inconsiderate, but it was an exciting experience to work for him. If he did not spare his actors, he did not spare himself. They had the sense of being fellow-artists collaborating at the beginning of a revolution in British stage production. Though not always understanding his aims and methods – the action 'composed of layer upon layer of movement, speech, and silences held together in the completed form' – they were conscious of being made to give forth a quality that had previously been dormant and might vanish again in other theatres. The plays Barker presented had the appearance of being more natural, more lifelike, than anything else being performed in London and gave audiences a sensation of participating in the drama, rather than watching it from the auditorium.

Shaw's fatherly feelings for Barker spilled over on to the whole company at the Court. They were conscious of having been carefully picked and felt part of a family, working to restore the English theatre to its rightful place in national life. The most vivid illustration of this feeling was the career of Lillah McCarthy. 'It is an actress's profession to be extraordinary,' wrote Shaw; 'but Lillah was extraordinary even among actresses.' He had seen her first in 1895 as a sixteen-year-old Lady Macbeth – 'immature, unskilful, and entirely artificial'. From the professional standpoint the performance had been 'very bad', yet she had gone at it bravely, her instinct and courage helping where her skill failed, and produced an effect that was 'very nearly thrilling'. 'It is clear to me,' Shaw wrote in the *Saturday Review*, 'that unless she at once resolutely marries some rich gentleman who disapproves of the theatre in principle, she will not be able to keep herself off the stage . . . '

'she can hold an audience whilst she is doing everything wrongly . . . In short, I should like to see Miss Lillah McCarthy play again. I venture on the responsibility of saying that her Lady Macbeth was a highly promising performance, and that some years of hard work would make her a valuable recruit to the London stage.'

After ten years of heroic hard work she wrote and asked to see Shaw. He was at this time in despair of finding someone to play Ann Whitefield in *Man and Superman*. When she arrived at Adelphi Terrace ('a gorgeously good-looking young lady in a green dress and huge picture hat . . . in which she looked splendid, with the figure and gait of a Diana'), he gave her a broad smile of recognition: 'Why, here's Ann Whitefield.'

Beautiful, statuesque, saturated with declamatory poetry and rhetoric, Lillah seemed to have arrived straight from the Italian or eighteenth-century stage – a lovely instrument on which to play a repertoire of

Shavian tunes. As one of the principal players at the Court, she 'created the first generation of Shavian heroines with dazzling success'. Her technique, which combined the manner of 'the grand school with a natural impulse to murder the Victorian womanly woman', fell in perfectly with his stage needs. 'And with that young lady,' he wrote a quarter of a century later, 'I achieved performances of my plays which will probably never be surpassed.'

Part of Shaw's tribute derived from her acceptance of his authority. Though there were brief temperamental interruptions, Lillah was far more obedient to his will than Florence Farr or Janet Achurch. She seemed to find in him again the parent who had once loved and ruled her – a tall, eccentric Irishman, her teacher, and the man in whom she recognized the poetry of life. The prose was represented by her mother 'burdened with eight children, assorted relatives, housework, and a meagre income'. From that fate she looked to escape on the stage, and in her association with Shaw's plays 'a new life began for me; the new life of the Court Theatre and of the new women'.

Working at the Court was a revelation for Lillah. She seemed hypnotized by G.B.S. 'With complete unselfconsciousness he would show us how to draw the full value out of a line,' she wrote. ' . . . With his amazing hands he would illustrate the mood of a line. We used to watch his hands in wonder. I learned as much from his hands, almost, as from his little notes of correction.' During rehearsals they often lunched vegetarianly together at the Queen's Restaurant in Sloane Square – apples, cheese, macaroni and salads with chilly milk and soda. 'I ate it because everything he did seemed right to me,' she remembered. ' . . . I never knew what a vivid personality meant until I knew Shaw. He, of all men, is most alive; not only on grand occasions but all the time.'

Lillah worshipped Shaw: but she did not understand him or his play. Mrs Pankhurst was to tell her that Ann Whitefield had 'strengthened her purpose and fortified her courage' and many other women declared to her that Ann had 'brought them to life and that they remodelled themselves upon Ann's pattern'. Lillah played Ann Whitefield at the Court in May and June 1905, and again in October and November, and bore witness that 'she made a new woman of me'. But Shaw's new women express either the need for immediate economic independence or the biological imperative of a superior future. To neither of these aims, except through her professional career as an actress, did Lillah contribute. She thought the concluding love scene of *Man and Superman* especially beautiful.

'At the climax of the scene Tanner takes Ann in his arms and says: "I love you. The Life Force enchants me. I have the whole world in my arms when I clasp you . . . " And, as the play closes, Tanner sums up all things with words that sound like sighs, "Ann looks happy: but she is only triumphant, successful, victorious. That is not happiness, but the price for which the strong sell their happiness".'

If she had not played such scenes, Lillah proclaimed, 'I should never have developed as a woman'. She acted the part of Ann with earnest intensity. Barker, in the role of Tanner, was got up to resemble Shaw, and (as the critic of the *Daily News* commented) 'carried the thing through remarkably well'. But it was difficult to keep Lillah's feet on the ground, Shaw remarked. 'Her life was rich in wonderful experiences that had never happened, and in friendships with wonderful people (including myself) who never existed.' She did not really know what was happening on stage or how to separate these happenings from her life. She pursued Barker, a red-bearded Shavian phenomenon, with regal authority across the Court Theatre: and on 24 April 1906, at the West Strand Registry Office, she caught and married him.

Shaw had wanted his work to burst out from the theatre and influence what went on outside. He had thrown Barker and Lillah into each other's arms. Their marriage had the air of being a brilliant success. Profession-ally they were necessary to one another, as he was necessary to them both. They were never really in love, but for the moment they enjoyed good times together. 'She was an admirable hostess; and her enjoyment of the open air and of travelling made her a most healthy companion for him,' Shaw explained. The dignity of marriage, too, suited Barker, who was no Bohemian. 'The admirations and adorations the pair excited in the cultured sections of London society could be indulged and gratified in country houses where interesting and brilliant young married couples were welcome.' Barker, who enjoyed country house life, had every reason for finding this arrangement a convenient one. Why then was Shaw 'instinctively dismayed'? As his Court 'children', their marriage was that of brother and sister. They had no children, and were not well cast for what the other needed: a mother for him, a father for her. 'I knew that this was all wrong; that there were no two people on earth less suited to one another,' Shaw wrote. It was the marriage of actors and actresses, a stepping aside from reality, an escapade.

That summer after their marriage they went to stay with the Webbs. Barker was soon to be promoted in Shaw's other family, the Fabians, to the Executive; and Beatrice examined him and Lillah intently. It was as if they were playing at being an attractive married couple. It was difficult to distinguish what was real from artificial. 'I think what he [Barker] lacks is warmth of feeling – he is cold, with little active pity or admiration, or faithful devotion,' Beatrice wrote in her diary. 'A better acquaintance than a friend, a better friend than a husband. At least that is his pose . . . '

'She is a strikingly handsome lady, also hard-working and dutiful – a puritan, I think, by temperament . . . Otherwise, I fear she is . . . commonplace, and he has all the appearance of being bored by her after two months' marriage.'

By the end of October 1906, they were back on stage as Tanner and Ann Whitefield. Next month they stepped into a new play by Shaw at the Court: a tragedy where Barker was the husband, an artist dying of consumption, and Lillah his wife, 'the sort of woman I hate', Shaw notified her. ' . . . [It] will be a complete success for you, for me, for the Court and for the universe.'

[4]

Here am I, for instance, by class a respectable man, by common sense a hater of waste and disorder, by intellectual constitution legally minded to the verge of pedantry, and by temperament apprehensive and economically disposed to the limit of old-maidishness; yet I am, and have always been, and shall now always be, a revolutionary writer . . . I am an enemy of the existing order for good reasons.
Preface to *Major Barbara*

Over the early summer of 1906 Shaw wrote long prefaces to *John Bull's Other Island* and *Major Barbara*. The first, discursively favourable to Home Rule, contained an impassioned exercise in ridicule of nationalism and of the military and bureaucratic imagination that supported it. The second, in celebration of social equality, included some powerful invective against the malicious injury of judicial punishments and the evil of an inequitable distribution of money. These two prefaces were assaults on institutions of power, on those conspiracies of legal, political and plutocratic priesthoods that employed power without responsibility. Then over the late summer, he wrote *The Doctor's Dilemma*, a play aimed at another powerful trade union, the medical profession.

It was Barker who asked Shaw for a new play at the Court; and Charlotte who reminded her husband of a good dramatic subject he had come across earlier that year at St Mary's Hospital, Paddington. The Principal of the Institute of Pathology there was Almroth Wright who had recently created a scientific sensation by claiming to have found a method of measuring the protective substances in the human blood. Following what Shaw called one of the 'most suggestive biological romances', the principle of phagoctosis, Wright 'discovered that the white corpuscles or phagocytes which attack and devour disease germs for us do their work only when we butter the disease germs appetizingly for them with a natural sauce'. The chemical condiments, which Wright called 'opsonins' (from the Greek *opsono* – I prepare food for), ebbed and flowed like the tide. Wright believed he had invented a means of calculating the periodical climaxes by counting the number of bacteria taken up by phagocytes in a patient's serum. Vaccine therapy could now proceed, he announced, on a scientific basis.

Shaw's scepticism was aroused by Wright who, in the summer of 1905, had sent him his pamphlet on tuberculosis inoculation together with an invitation to visit his laboratory. In his reply, Shaw poked fun at Wright's pamphlet as 'one of the best attempts I have yet seen to make serumpathy fact-proof' and volunteered that his own sister, who had been inoculated against tuberculosis, found patent medicines safer and more effective. He urged Wright to persevere with his researches to the point of discovering that 'the safest way to deal with tuberculosis is not to get it', since every failure then becomes 'an exquisite confirmation of the most ingenious part of the theory'. He would, Shaw added, be enormously amused to visit Wright's laboratory. The debate, forming the narrative texture of *The Doctor's Dilemma*, had begun.

Shaw was keen to let the London drama critics know that the 'scientific side' of his play was 'correct and up to date'. Sir Colenso Ridgeon, the hero, 'is, serum pathologically, Sir Almroth Wright, knighted last birthday (May [1906]) for his opsonic discovery', he informed A. B. Walkley. His description of his discovery in the first act is accurate in every detail. St Anne's in the play is St Mary's, Paddington. In another letter, to William Archer, Shaw issued a Child's Guide to Medicine:

'The production of this dripping [opsonin] rises and falls in a series of actions & reactions called the positive & negative phases; & to inject a vaccine during the negative phase is deadly. Consequently the vaccine in the hands of a man who does not know Wright's discovery of phases is a most dangerous weapon. Grasp this & you will follow the scientific side of the play with ease. The dramatic side is as easy as Box & Cox.'

This dramatic side developed from a debate one night between Wright and Shaw at St Mary's. Wright's literary flair and glamorous experiments had helped to make his treatment of microbe infections highly fashionable. The small laboratory at St Mary's, besieged by patients from all over the world, was soon enlarged into a research institute where his assistants sat up late into the night preparing slides, staring through microscopes and counting the number of microbes engulfed by the patients' phagocytes. Towards midnight they would pause to make tea, and this was the moment for some of Sir Almroth's friends to drop in and, among the glass tubes, bottles, powders, plasters, discuss the medical sorcerer's newest theories of 'Vaccinotherapy'. Shaw was present at one of these late-night tea parties when a discussion arose among the physicians over admitting an extra tuberculosis patient who had arrived that day for treatment by a new experimental method. Wright's chief assistant objected: 'We've got too many cases on our hands already.' Shaw then asked: 'What would happen if more people applied to you for help than you could properly look after?' And Wright answered: 'We should have to consider which life was worth saving.' Shaw laid a finger to his nose and exclaimed: 'I smell drama! . . . I get a whiff of a play.'

This weighing of human worth on the scales of life and death is superficially the problem that floats at the centre of Shaw's problem play, the dilemma of the title. Whose life is of greater value to humankind: the unprincipled artist of genius or the sixpenny doctor, honest and decent? If there is an air of unreality about this choice it is because, as G. K. Chesterton pointed out, nobody at sea shouts 'Bad citizen overboard!' In real life, the doctor 'doesn't fool himself that the moral value of the characters comes into it', James Fenton was to write. 'He chooses the people he has the best chance of saving.' In the event-plot, the crisis and hypothesis are also false because Shaw's doctor could easily have saved both men. There is apparently enough serum: all that Sir Colenso Ridgeon needs to do in Act III is to explain to one of his colleagues (as he had begun to do in Act I) how to administer it.

The real dilemma in the play, and the pivot of Colenso Ridgeon's choice, involves the nature of our unconscious motives and the idealizing process of logic by which we justify them to ourselves and represent them to one another. Almroth Wright was a misogynist whose relaxation was the establishment of a technique of accurate thinking and grammar. His *Alethetropic Logic* is ostensibly a rationalist's scrutiny of the emotional basis of popular fallacies about religion, politics and sex. He took issue with Shaw's contention that 'there is not any specific . . . psycho-physiological difference between men and women,' having concluded in *The Unexpurgated Case Against Woman Suffrage* that the feminine mind, over-influenced by individual instances, 'accepts the congenial as true, and rejects the uncongenial as false: takes the imaginary which is desired for reality, and treats the undesired reality which is out of sight as non-existent, building

159

up for itself in this way, when biased by predilections and aversions, a very unreal picture of the external world.'

In *The Doctor's Dilemma*, Shaw takes Wright's view of the inferior and irrational feminine mind and applies it remorselessly to his gallery of scientific men. In particular he focuses on the unconscious sexual motives of Sir Colenso Ridgeon, the fashionable physician modelled on Wright who, listing his symptoms, innocently takes medical advice when he is about to fall in love.

Shaw liked Wright and disagreed with him about almost everything. Temperamentally they were akin: two teetotal, word-intoxicated polymaths. Wright had been educated at Trinity College, Dublin where he won a gold medal for English Literature. After collecting degrees in literature and medicine, he studied physiological chemistry in Germany, read law in London and took a clerkship at the Admiralty. He also occupied posts at innumerable universities – Leipzig, Sydney, Cambridge and so on – appeared in Calcutta as a member of the Indian Plague Commission and in Oxfordshire as professor of pathology at an Army medical school before arriving at St Mary's. Five years younger than G.B.S., he had already begun to assemble an extraordinary pile of medals, prizes, honours and university doctorates. His educational experience was therefore fundamentally different from Shaw's and their opposing disciplines fuelled the battle of debates that went on between them for nearly forty years. Lord Moran, who heard some of these contests at St Mary's, remembered feeling sorry for Wright once Shaw had finished speaking. 'I felt that he had been pulverized, but at the end of Wright's reply I blushed to think that Shaw, who was after all a guest, had been so mercilessly shown up. The devastating effect of such speech depends on the art of selection. Every single sentence was a direct hit; there was not a single word which did not contribute to the confusion of the enemy.' Many years later, Moran continues, the septuagenarian grammarian and his alphabetical octogenarian adversary were still duelling away.

Here is a source and echo of the medical crosstalk in *The Doctor's Dilemma*. Shaw's sense of vulnerability to the power of this medical élite, displacing his fear of death, gave his satire its edge; his fierce and friendly sparring matches with Wright also enabled him to parody his own habits of presenting himself as morally superior to human emotion and smash bang up to date with the latest scientific fashion on all subjects from photography to automobiles. For poets and dramatists, he conceded, 'might be as wrong as anyone else' at working out the rationale of their work, and 'might even repudiate the true explanation with indignant horror'.

Shaw's arguments with Wright were continued in their letters. 'Am I an educated man?' he demanded. Unlike Wright, he had never learned anything at school. 'I could not pass an examination and win a certificate in an elementary school to this day,' he challenged. 'But at the age at which my contemporaries were taking their degrees and diplomas, and even winning the Ireland Scholarship and gold medals, I knew Handel, Mozart, Beethoven, Italian opera from Rossini to Verdi, Michael Angelo, Raphael, Rembrandt, Shakespear, Bunyan, Swift, the Bible etc . . . '

'It was possible for a man to have 20 letters after his name, and a whole collection of doctorial hoods in his wardrobe, and yet be barbarously ignorant of all this.'

Shaw was an academic *manqué* and resented his early exclusion from university excellence – that nest of singing birds. Behind these years of correspondence and controversy with Wright, and the play that derived from their association, there lay a wish to take authority from the orthodoxly educated and give it to outsiders. Like the scholastic profession, the medical freemasonry was a closed circle of privileged people whose mesmeric power over other human beings angered Shaw. 'It is awful how these scientific men wallow in orthodoxy, when they get the chance,' he complained to Gilbert Murray. ' . . . Free thought really depends on the men of letters – and progressive thought, too.'

*

Almroth Wright had welcomed G.B.S. into his laboratory as another adornment for his career. The presence of this controversial man of letters made fine advertisement for a vaccine therapy that was to be used on diseases as various as acne, cystitis and pneumonia. On Shaw's side, living under what he called the 'superstition that a playwright cannot be a biologist', he needed this entrée to a medical research centre to steal some of their magical language and gain power for himself with the public. His holograph manuscript of *The Doctor's Dilemma* (the last but one of the plays to be written in longhand) shows the scientific matter to have been repeatedly revised and corrected, almost certainly under Wright's supervision. Though Shaw was to own that the play was 'conceived in Wright's laboratory' and written 'under careful medical instruction' he never revealed what Wright called 'my guilty collusion with you in the play' because Wright himself was nervous over other doctors' reactions. 'What about the Court Physicians – the whole pack of them', he predicted, 'will set upon me saying I got you to show them up and to puff my wares.'

St Mary's Hospital, where Alice Lockett had worked as a nurse, became Shaw's medical college. Apart from attending Wright's late-night seminars he actually lectured there, in Shavian style, on the 'modern craze' for immunizing inoculations. It was a marvellous opportunity for using his own experiences to challenge existing medical practice. He explained to his audience of physicians that after years of compulsory vaccination, there had been two of the worst smallpox epidemics on record. The conclusion must be that the reduction in the normal incidence of smallpox, on which the whole case for vaccination was founded, was actually delayed by vaccination and effected in spite of it by sanitation. QED.

Shaw's medical scepticism is voiced in *The Doctor's Dilemma* through the 'rather arid common sense' of Sir Patrick Cullen, which undermines every new experiment and discovery made by his younger colleagues. 'Most discoveries are made regularly every fifteen years,' he informs Ridgeon; 'and it's fully a hundred and fifty since yours was made last. Thats something to be proud of.' What is missing from the play is anyone to represent Shaw's positive views which, as the St Mary's lecture illustrates, were upheld with all the credulous self-deception of his medicine men.

At the end of this lecture, Wright had sprung up and exclaimed impatiently: 'I believe that the effect of sanitation is aesthetic.' Shaw pounced on this remark as an 'inspiration' – that is, a conclusion arrived at by a process of reasoning in which (like a baby's digestion) the several stages are integrated too rapidly for awareness. When Wright, responding to his friend's congratulations at having opened up a new epoch in biology, demanded to know what he meant by pretending that anything 'aesthetic' could have scientific significance, Shaw began to expound his concept of 'aesthetic science'. This was a method of finding a role for himself in the scientific revolution of the twentieth century. He wanted to blow up the iron curtain separating science from art, and hand over the reconstruction to socialist planning. 'I belong to a generation which, I think, began life by hoping more from Science than perhaps any generation ever hoped before, and possibly, will ever hope again . . . ' he was to tell the Medico-Legal Society a couple of years later. ' . . . Science will always be extraordinarily interesting and hopeful to me.' But in the public imagination, artists and scientists and politicians were completely dissociated. Shaw used Wright's statement to put art on speaking terms with science, and give art the advantage. 'As a matter of hard fact,' he was to tell Wright, 'the aesthetic factor in life is prodigiously vaster than the so-called scientific.' Human beings, he argued, lived on a borderland of anxious thinking between the long-passed reasonings which had established automatic habits, like breathing and blood circulation, and the immense horizon of the undiscovered and unreasoned towards which our evolutionary appetite was always propelling us. In that undiscovered future Shaw marked out a territory for his aesthetic science adjoining the socialism of William Morris. 'The evidence is that all the improvement in our vital statistics that has been credited to doctors' prescriptions, to leeches, drugs, antiseptics, and preventive operations, has been really produced by pleasant colors, pleasant smells, handsome buildings, furniture and utensils, fine clothes, noble pictures, music, and beauty everywhere.'

Only through the State organization of medicine could doctors promote the maximum of hygienic influence and contribute efficiently to this dream of progress. There being no such exhaustive State organization, *The Doctor's Dilemma* shows us a cabal of physicians driven into the position of private tradesmen with a pecuniary interest in what Ruskin called 'Illth'. We see them on stage engaging in the compulsory commercial competition of healing, abjectly dependent upon their patients' incomes and delusions. 'Blenkinsop recommends greengages as a panacea, Schutzmacher phosphates; the difference has nothing to do with the intrinsic merits of these remedies or with medical science at all, but is simply the difference between a bone-poor district and one where people are in slightly less desperate straits,' writes Louis Crompton. 'Both doctors believe in their prescriptions to the point of taking them themselves merely because self-respect leaves them no alternative.'

Beneath the invented drama of the play with its surface tension of ethics versus aesthetics, lies a theme that confronts the philosophies of science for science's sake with the social usefulness of art, balancing Wright's way of looking at the world against Shaw's. Though he cautiously did not go to the opening night of the play, Wright took his mother to see it later on. 'I promise myself much mirth from your portraiture,' he wrote. 'No man is any good who cannot laugh at himself.' But he was reported to have walked out of the performance, leaving his mother 'most indignant'. This was not surprising. Ridgeon's choice, which is intended to illustrate the subjective foundations of scientific reasoning, exposes him at the end of the play as having been so emotionally self-deluded as to have 'committed a purely disinterested murder!' In a later programme note Shaw rather gratuitously added that 'Sir Almroth Wright is in no way responsible' for this choice. But when preparing the play and its Preface for publication in 1910, he sent Wright the proofs. 'You must frankly give in to my political science as completely as I give in to your bacteriological science,' he instructed him.

The most effective sections of the play depended on Shaw's instinct rather than his research. He sensed that something was wrong with Wright's reputation. In 1906, shortly before Shaw started *The Doctor's Dilemma*, the War Office, wanting to use Wright's anti-typhoid injections, 'first had him knighted and then used his knighthood as evidence of the unassailability of his theories' – a similar looking-glass irony to that attending Ridgeon's knighthood in Act I of the play. One reason for the popularity of Wright's treatment – it remained fashionable until the Second World War – seems to have been the novelty of subcutaneous injection. In the scramble for a living no Harley Street specialist could afford to reject the use of vaccines and see his patient leave him for someone more 'up to date'. But looking back from 1970, W. D. Foster concluded in *A History of Medical Bacteriology*: 'It is doubtful if this form of treatment produced any good results and certainly in most instances, it was valueless to the point of fraudulence.'

Shaw said of Wright that it was 'useful to know a man who has discovered the philosopher's stone but does not know the value of gold.' It was a percipient statement. The concept of certain body cells reacting in a measurable way to an invasion by bacteria 'had great importance for the future development of bacteriology and immunology', wrote Dr Gregory Scott in *British Medicine*. But the significance of this discovery was taken up by Wright's junior at St Mary's, Alexander Fleming. While accidentally finding a drug that would take the place of vaccine therapy, Fleming was financed by money raised from the use of Wright's vaccine, and obliged to pay perpetual lip-service to the man who became nicknamed 'Sir Almost Wright'. The story was to end with letters to *The Times*, public insults, the renaming of St Mary's laboratory as the Wright-Fleming Institute and the development of the wonder-drug penicillin by Florey and Chain that temporarily obscured Fleming's original discovery.

All of this would fit perfectly on the stage of *The Doctor's Dilemma*. Shaw's instinct had alerted him to recurring patterns within the medical community – the more recent examples of which may be found in cancer and the claims for interferon; the choice of patients for kidney machines; and the star media rating of heart transplants. 'It is much more closely founded on fact than most of the critics realise,' Shaw wrote during the play's revival at the Court.

Most of the 'originals' on whom he had modelled his characters are long forgotten – Sir Robert Christison, for example, who gave him the notion of Sir Patrick Cullen and whose autobiography he had reviewed in the *Pall Mall Gazette* ('Even when modern scientists rediscovered old discoveries of his, and blew the trumpet over them a little, he was not stung with jealousy or provoked to self-assertion, although he did not deny himself the pleasure of referring the discoverers, with a quiet chuckle, to some forgotten paper of his in which he had anticipated them'); or the Newspaper Man who was a simple adaptation to the stage of a reporter who called on Mrs Patrick Campbell immediately the news of her husband's death had been wired from South Africa, to interview her 'on how it feels to be a widow'.

More memorable were the several models who unconsciously sat for Dubedat. Chief among them was Edward Aveling, the basilisk-eyed 'blackguard' whom Eleanor Marx had idolized. When Ridgeon assures Jennifer Dubedat that 'your hero must be preserved to you ... At all hazards ... the one chance of preserving the hero lies in Louis [Dubedat] being in the care of Sir Ralph', he is protecting Jennifer from Eleanor Marx's suicidal destiny by ensuring that her illusions survive her husband's death. 'The most tragic thing in the world is a man of genius who is not also a man of honor,' says Ridgeon. For his portrait of the amoral artist Shaw recycled some of his feelings for H. G. Wells and Charles Charrington, used the case histories of Beardsley and Rossetti and the public persona of Whistler, and cast a backward look at Vandeleur Lee. He also borrowed something that had happened a little earlier that year. On 15 March a story appeared in *Truth* exposing the unprofessional conduct of Sir Alfred Gilbert, sculptor of Eros in Piccadilly Circus, who had accepted (from widows among others) money for commissions he never completed. Shaw kept this cutting and a week later, in reply to one of Gilbert's friends who had solicited his support, suggested that, if the stories were true, the sculptor 'should be drowned in the fountain with which he disfigured Piccadilly Circus'.

'Pray do not suppose that I deny an artist's right to be judged by a different standard to other people. I grant that – in fact I insist on it – and as the artist's standard is more exacting and higher than the tradesman's standard I know that it not only binds the artist to accept obligations that are too severe for the tradesman, but also relieves him from obligations that the tradesman accepts. But Gilbert accepts neither the artist's obligations nor the tradesman's.'

In the play Dubedat becomes the figure through whom 'the Shavian devil is most active', writes Margery Morgan. 'For the debate reflects a division that ran deep in the author himself.' Critics have proposed that since Dubedat admits 'I'm a disciple of Bernard Shaw', he represents the supermaniac opinions of G.B.S. But Shaw threw in this aside as a token of the misinformation that rules all the characters, and a pleasing reversal of his relationship with Lee of whom he had been reminded while at work on the play by a letter from one of his old musical associates, Katie Samuels. This incident too he had taken more recently from life. A youth called Rankin, sentenced early that year to six months' imprisonment for attempting to blackmail his father, a schoolmaster, had pleaded guilty in court to being a disciple of Bernard Shaw as the explanation of his crime. In Wormwood Scrubs he refused the ministrations of the chaplain, and asked that G.B.S. be sent for. As Shaw was abroad, Stewart Headlam visited him in gaol. 'It was quite clear that he was under the impression that my teaching was simply an advocacy of reckless and shameless disregard of all social and moral obligations,' Shaw later reported, 'an error which he owes, I should say, not to reading my works unsophisti- catedly, but to reading the follies which the press utters about me, and then perhaps reading me in the false light of those follies. It was as a reductio-ad-absurdum of this error and partly as a warning against it that I made Dubedat in the play use Rankin's defence.'

The Doctor's Dilemma is a demonstration of what Swift meant by describing happiness as 'a perpetual possession of being well-deceived'. Shaw's comment on this was to subtitle his play 'A Tragedy'. To peddle self-delusion and advertise it as a happiness-drug was to manufacture human tragedy. Shaw recommended people instead to 'stop taking any opiates or palliatives if you can endure life without them'; and he used the medical profession as a metaphor for every conspiracy of self-deception that worked against the public interest. The doctors in his play are all amiable men. It is public fear that insists on their omniscience, public superstition that equips them with their hocus-pocus of charms and cures, public ignorance that obliges them to trade in hypochondria. They are the idealists of Shaw's philosophy, who are paid to give the philistines what they want and will be out of a job unless they do so. Observation and experience had taught him that disease was the product of 'ugliness, dirt, and stink offending every aesthetic instinct'; that 'dirt and ugliness and squalor are products of poverty'; and that 'though the Life Force is still an ultimate mystery, zymotic diseases can be abolished by abolishing poverty, the practical problem being one of economic distribution'. Shaw's belief in 'natural' or hygienically imposed good health indicates faith in an ultimate mystery that is beneficent. His fastidious optimism confined itself to matters that were specifically economic and political, and was fortified by his sense of being able to control them.

The question at the centre of the play is whether Dubedat is a 'realist' or merely a neurotic whose illness depresses the Life Force. Shaw believed that most progress depended on heretics but that most heretics were not vehicles for progress. In Dubedat we are shown the dishonoura-ble man of genius, which Shaw described as 'the most tragic of all themes to people who understand its importance'. The tragedy is of someone whose work has been perverted from an expression of the evolutionary appetite into a futile exercise in subversion. It is the story of a realist infected by poverty and the atmosphere of idealism. Ridgeon romantically idealizes Jennifer who romantically idealizes Dubedat who idealizes his work as the murderous doctors idealize theirs.

The embodiment of romanticism is Jennifer. 'I cannot very well call the lady Lillah,' Shaw wrote to Lillah McCarthy from Cornwall. 'Provisionally I have called her Andromeda; but Mrs Andromeda Dubedat is too long. Here in King Arthur's country the name Guinevere survives as Jennifer.' The names reveal Shaw's intention which was to parody the Greek and Arthurian myths of chivalry. Ridgeon, who claims to 'know when a woman is interested in me' and believes that Jennifer unconsciously is, sees himself as a Perseus rescuing his beautiful Andromeda by killing her monster-husband. By calling her Jennifer (which she explains is 'only what you call Guinevere') and preserving the connection with Arthurian legend, Shaw recalls his own 'Mystic Betrothal' to May Morris whose mother Jane had been painted as Guinevere by William Morris. The more recent case in this epidemic of Guineverism, Shaw implies, had been Lillah and Barker.

Shaw wrote his play, he said, in response to a challenge from Archer who that summer had published an article entitled 'Death and Mr Bernard Shaw'. Archer's view was that, being 'fatally at the mercy of his impish sense of humour', G.B.S. was unable to write a convincing death scene. 'It is not the glory but the limitation of Mr Shaw's theatre that it is peopled by immortals,' he wrote. In the death of Dubedat, which he told Mrs Patrick Campbell 'is a miracle of my lack of taste', Shaw attempted to 'get a chemical combination which made the spectator laugh with one side of his mouth and cry with the other'. In a letter to one of his biographers, he explained that he meant his dramatization of the medical profession as currently practised in England to be a 'tragic comedy, with death conducting the orchestra. Yet the play is funnier than most farces'.

'The tragedy of Dubedat is not his death but his life; nevertheless his death, a purely poetic one, would once have seemed wholly incompatible with laughter. It takes place in the presence of the newspaper reporter, who is almost as ludicrous and farcical as such people are in real life; and the perfectly genuine and moving distress of B[loomfield] B[onnington] is expressed by misquotations of Shakespear in the manner of Huckleberry Finn.'

To assist the critics, who had not yet heard of black comedy, Shaw issued a press release in which he prophesied 'it will probably be called a *farce macabre*'; and as aid for his audiences he added a quotation to the programme: 'Life does not cease to be funny when people die, any more than it ceases to be serious when people laugh.'

The death of Dubedat is usually more interesting to scholars than spectators. The serious artist in Dubedat is already dead and the tragedy over. What remains is an actor performing a death scene for his audience on stage. The 'fanciful poetry and pathos' which Shaw wanted to combine with irony and realism are theatrical properties placed in the correct dramatic position, but separate and sentimental. Shaw has distributed his genuine reactions to the King of Terrors among his medical cast who act as angels of death, with the newspaper man representing 'the world'.

The phrase 'purely poetic' which he used to describe Dubedat's death is in Shaw's vocabulary similar in meaning to the word 'aesthetic' in Almroth Wright's: signifying 'decorative' or 'unreal'. The long operatic farewell, with its comic chorus, has none of the sordidness of death from tuberculosis. It is simply 'an artistic spectacle'.

But Shaw was fond of his death scene. It 'is the most touching and beautiful one in all dramatic literature', he confessed to Mrs Patrick Campbell, 'because, Princess, it is *inspired*'. It is inspired by Shaw's reading rather than his experience: a death planned to match, with a degree of Brechtian alienation, the philosophical game of the dilemma. He described it as 'none the worse because its climax is "derived" (not to say stolen) from Wagner's End of a Musician in Paris', and wielded this reference to protect his abstract experiment in style and form against criticism. For a number of critics, responding perhaps to Shaw's representative of the press ('disabled for ordinary business pursuits by a congenital erroneousness which renders him incapable of describing accurately anything he sees, or understanding or reporting accurately anything he hears'), selected Dubedat's end as their ideal point of retaliation. 'Amateurs of the morbid will revel in this realistic death-scene,' wrote *The Times* critic. 'Other people will dislike its bad taste and cheap art . . . to secure an emotional thrill.' The *Daily Mail* described it as 'offensive', the *Daily Telegraph* as 'pathetic' and the *Standard* fulfilled all Shaw's expectations by misquoting the artist's creed and converting 'the most serious and touching passage in my play into a silly blasphemy'. But they had walked into a trap. The scholarship with which Shaw had wrapped death round becomes the weapon for a perfect riposte. 'I will now make the *Standard* the confident of a little secret,' he wrote.

' . . . The creed of the dying artist, which has been reprobated on all hands as a sally of which only the bad taste of Bernard Shaw could be capable, is openly borrowed with gratitude and admiration by me from one of the best known prose writings of the most famous man of the nineteenth century. In Richard Wagner's well known story, dated 1841, . . . the dying musician begins his creed with the words, "I believe in God, Mozart and Beethoven". It is a curious instance of the enormous Philistinism of English criticism that this passage should not only be unknown among us, but that a repetition of its thought and imagery 65 years later should still find us with a conception of creative force so narrow that the association of Art with Religion conveys nothing to us but a sense of far fetched impropriety.

I am, Sir, your obedient servant

G. Bernard Shaw.'

[5]

Touchstone: Wast ever at the Court, shepherd?
Corin: No, truly.
Touchstone: Then thou art damned.
Shakespeare, 'As You Like It'

The materials for his play had accumulated gradually: but the writing was fast. Shaw had begun it on 11 August 1906 at Mevagissey on the coast of Cornwall. 'I am taking what is called a holiday by the sea: that is, I am getting my work concentrated on me with an intensity impossible in London,' he wrote that day.' . . . I have begun a new play, and am already through the best part of the first act. This means a devouring and importunate job; but I think I see my way through quickly.' By 21 August, on Polstreath Beach, he finished the first act and felt confident enough to tell Barker that *The Doctor's Dilemma* might be announced for next season at the Court. A week later – and another act was completed. 'I am writing the new play at hurricane speed,' he told Trebitsch. 'It springs into existence impetuously with leaps & bounds: the only trouble is to get it inked.' He reached the end of the last three acts between 3 and 12 September, and predicted that 'it will be a lucky play'.

This speed was more extraordinary in view of the interruptions and Shaw's methods of avoiding them. He wrote everywhere. He ended the third act on St Austell's Station in Cornwall and started the fourth the same day after joining the train from Exeter to London. He came to the end of this act at the village of Moulsford in the Thames Valley, then started the last on the train from Reading to London. The first draft was completed at twenty minutes past six in the evening aboard a steamer on the Thames, as it docked at Cherry Garden Pier below Tower Bridge.

There were a great many interruptions: the pleasure of bathing in the sea; the comfort of the house; the care of the servants, and Charlotte's accidents and anxieties. There were also his headaches, their guests, and the world's correspondence. He wrote to G. K. Chesterton about Dickens; to H. G. Wells about Chesterton; and to Sidney Webb about Wells. He fired off letters to *The Tribune* about the political plight of the radical middle class in Britain and to the *New York Times* on the economics of reformed spelling. There were also a number of deputy Bernard Shaws round the world writing for instructions – an aspiring biographer in North Carolina and several European translators who had to beat the 1908 copyright deadline of the Berne Convention.

One postal interruption was absorbed into the play. That August some pictures had been left at Adelphi Terrace by an impoverished artist named Louis A. Sargent. They included 'a night pastel with buildings and equestrian statue' called 'The Statue of Karl Marx' and were accompanied by an invitation for Shaw to visit Sargent in Hampstead where there were 'other things in my studio you might like better'. In a letter of 18 August, Sargent delineated the peculiarly Shavian circumstances of his life. He had studied at the Camden School of Art and won two scholarships. 'Unfortunately, I never had any social connections,' he explained. ' . . . due to having been brought up on a diet of tea and white bread I have a very fickle digestion, and . . . my time has been spent, for the last 9 months, between more or less violent attacks of alternating appendicitis and pleurisy.' This well-researched letter continued with details of Sargent's average earnings over six years of seven shillings a week, his three-month bout of typhoid fever, a blighted exhibition, and prejudice against his socialism leading to expulsion from the Royal Academy Schools. 'I stop here to consider if I am piling it on thick,' he wrote candidly – then piled on the information that the Royal Academy had been 'highly indignant that I should refuse to eat meat, and thus undermine my health, and then come and throw myself on them for support. I was presented with a £10 cheque . . . and then told . . . that I should not be allowed to attend the Schools any more . . . evidently I was not the right class – artistically, intellectually, or economically'. The letter ended enlisting Shaw to help him with money and useful introductions. 'I am confronted with the extremely difficult task of convincing you that I am a genius,' Sargent admitted.

Shaw often gave money to those who appealed to him: there can have been few people secretly more generous. But the recipients were usually artisans, not artists. Sargent's letter was so skilful it must have prompted his suspicion. On 22 August he wrote to check the story with the Royal Academy which next day replied that following a charitable grant of £10 made to him in November 1903, 'nothing has been heard of Mr Sargent. He did not attend the Schools any more, and at the end of the first term of three years [January 1906] for which he had been admitted, as he did not send up the required work for the examination for the second term, he ceased, ipso facto, to be a Student'. Shaw notified Sargent of this reply and at the end of August received back a plausible and unabashed long letter renewing the plea for financial help. By which time Shaw had signalled Sargent's value to his play by giving Dubedat his Christian name, Louis.

*

Shaw's revisions ('a slower job than the writing was') persisted, through rehearsals, almost up to opening night on 20 November. A week before the opening there was a crisis when the *Daily Express* published a synopsis, quoting pieces of dialogue from the last act, in its 'Green-Room Gossip' column. Shaw wrote to complain, perhaps fearing among other things that a comparison of his play might be made with St John Hankin's *The Return of the Prodigal*, a tragi-comedy anticipating some of his observations on the medical profession that had lost money at the Court the previous autumn. But even under threat of legal action the *Daily Express* refused to reveal its informant and the Court was put under such close security over these last days that some of the actors had difficulty in making their entrances.

From the Carfax Gallery (in which Shaw owned shares) the Court leased pictures by Augustus John, William Orpen and Will Rothenstein – suggesting an extraordinary diversity of Dubedat's styles; and from Neville Lytton (who had painted Shaw's portrait earlier in the year) Barker borrowed an authentic smock. 'Will you lend me for the play, one that you have *dirtied* thoroughly?' he asked. All this was done in the pursuit of verisimilitude which Barker embraced so fiercely that 'people used to go out & faint & ask for brandy at the Court Theatre', Shaw claimed.

Again the critics were divided. Desmond MacCarthy summed up their position as best he could by stating that *The Doctor's Dilemma* 'must surely have a strong peculiar flavour to affect different palates so violently, making some critics grimace, some smile, and bringing tears to the eyes of others'. Max Beerbohm compared it in imaginative power somewhat unfavourably to Henry James's novel *Roderick Hudson*, while later commentators (notably James Bridie) have compared it in satirical realism also somewhat unfavourably to Molière's *L'Amour médecin* or *Doctor Cupid*. But Shaw himself noticed how many critics had begun to compare him somewhat unfavourably to himself. They seemed to him permanently out of step with his progress, raising each work of his to the skies, only to strike a blow with it at some emerging work struggling to find its feet. This critical celebration of his past, elevating each old play to the status of a *pièce de résistance* against which to disparage each new one, threatened to detract everlastingly from his present. 'In the future, instead of abusing the new play and praising the one before, let them abuse the one before and praise the new one,' he recommended.

'. . . That will satisfy their feelings just as much as the other plan, and will be really helpful to us. It is not the revivals that we want written up: the revivals can take care of themselves. Praise comes too late to help plays that have already helped themselves. If the press wishes to befriend us, let it befriend us in need, instead of throwing stones at us whilst we are struggling in the waves and pressing life-belts on us when we have swum to shore.'

The Doctor's Dilemma, which had 'set the teeth of the critics on edge', was successfully brought back at the end of the year for six weeks and ran altogether for fifty performances. Shaw was genuinely anxious for the press to act as a helpful patron to the Court. The 'atmosphere of good humour' which the newspapers could promote, he told Vedrenne, was 'next to an atmosphere of solid money' the most precious possession they could own. He felt a commitment to their enterprise not simply because it had given him an audience and made his name as a dramatist of performable plays, but because it represented a step towards establishing the theatre in England as a place of culture. The profit to the public, and to the theatre as an institution, had been considerable. 'It is a huge factory of sentiment, of character, of points of honour, of conceptions of conduct,' he wrote later when appealing for the building of a National Theatre, 'of everything that finally determines the destiny of a nation.'

*

Barker used these years at the Court to test some of the ideas he and Archer had proposed in their book, *A National Theatre: Scheme and Estimates*. This book, 'the blueprint and the bible for the National Theatre movement,' envisaged a grand enterprise appealing to the whole community by means of a large repertory of plays, both ancient and modern, foreign and English. The Court, being too small and removed from the centre of London to compete with the West End, was necessarily more avant-garde than anything that, for political reasons, they were modestly recommending to the general public. But its success was an excellent advertisement for the scheme. By discovering how nearly the National Theatre proposals could be implemented by a privately owned theatre, they had demonstrated that the scheme was practicable. Privately printed and circulated before the Court pilot project began in October 1904, their book was published shortly after the Vedrenne-Barker management left the Court in June 1907. In a new preface Barker reported to Archer how three years' experience of theatre management had affected his views. 'It hasn't really altered them at all,' he wrote. 'The need for a repertory theatre remains the same: no less, and it could not well be greater.'

Barker and Shaw had introduced repertory into the London theatre and achieved what the young Hesketh Pearson called 'the most famous epoch in theatrical management since the days of the Globe on Bankside'. But concealed behind this shining achievement were many difficulties and disappointments. Shaw had not been successful when urging a number of novelists, including Chesterton, Conrad, Kipling and Wells, to write plays for the Court. Besides Barker and Laurence Housman, none of the contemporary playwrights (who included Galsworthy, St John Hankin, John Masefield and W. B. Yeats) wrote work that was really popular. There was only one outstanding success and this was G.B.S. himself. Of the thirty-two plays by seventeen dramatists presented at the Court over almost three years, eleven were his; and of the 988 performances altogether, Shaw's plays made up 701 – the three most frequently performed being *Man and Superman*, *You Never Can Tell* and *John Bull's Other Island*. The artistic success of the Court experiment and its beneficial reaction on the theatre were to be generally admitted; yet all this could be explained away as having depended upon the triumph of one man. And even the profit from Shaw's work was something of a commercial windfall – the long-delayed dividend from twenty years' investment. To the four plays he wrote expressly for the Court he was able to add no less than eight other 'music hall entertainments' that were virtually new to the public. But after June 1907, when *Don Juan in Hell* and *The Man of Destiny* were presented in a double bill, his portfolio was pretty well exhausted. He also sensed that, the novelty being over, 'something like the anti-boom has arrived'. There was a feeling that the Court had been rather too successful and that Shaw himself was growing over-affluent. John Quinn, the American patron and collector, reported that the theatre was 'brimming over with Shaw and Shaw's plays at present. They appear to pay better than anything else. Yeats says he will soon become a public nuisance'. In the opinion of Arnold Bennett he already was a nuisance. Vedrenne, who 'seemed a decent sort of chap, more sincere than the run of them', had told Bennett that he was beginning to lose money and had paid Shaw (who struck Bennett as 'naturally self-conscious and egotistic') four thousand pounds a year between 1904 and 1908 – a sum that would have been hardly possible even if the theatre had performed Shaw's plays to full houses every day of these four years. Such inaccuracies were echoed in the newspapers. 'We must fight the press,' Shaw wrote to Vedrenne, 'and whilst defying them by playing all the pieces they slate as if they were aces of trumps, take great care that the said pieces are highly entertaining as variety shows . . . [We] can force the public to reverse the press verdict.'

Despite this turbulence, the reputation of the Court was a rock that owed its solidity not only to Shaw's plays and Barker's productions, but also to 'the prudent pessimism' of Vedrenne. 'Barker, aiming at a National Repertory Theatre, with a change of program every night, was determined to test our enterprise to destruction as motor tyres are tested, to find out its utmost possibilities,' Shaw wrote. 'I was equally reckless. Vedrenne, made prudent by a wife and family, was like a man trying to ride two runaway horses simultaneously.' In fact Vedrenne was a businessman who simply wanted to make money out of the theatre, unlike Barker, who simply wanted to create the higher drama. With their opposing temperaments they had 'created a Frankenstein's Monster (the firm of Vedrenne & Barker, with a Goodwill for a soul) that they cannot easily slay, however much they may loathe it', Shaw diagnosed. They listened reluctantly to his optimism. Vedrenne felt upset by Barker's ideological commitment to the short run, and would sit groaning in his office whenever one of Shaw's plays was taken off while still making money. Barker felt constantly baulked by Vedrenne's subtle economies such as reducing the salary list, hiring cheaper furniture and welcoming all fresh ideas with extravagant horror. Shaw appeared to have no choice but to represent their mutual dislike as a miraculous bonus. 'The partnership of V & B has every aspect of permanence: you are exactly on the terms which bind men to one another for ever & ever,' he promised Vedrenne, 'each with a strong grievance against the other to give interest & life to what would otherwise be a tedious & uneventful routine. And the business will not bear anyone else: that is the final economic fact that governs the situation.'

Nevertheless everyone pulled in different directions. There were schemes to oust Vedrenne and make a Shaw-Barker-Beerbohm Tree combination; schemes to oust Barker, schemes to oust Shaw, schemes to 'drive any reasonable man to destruction'. Their antipathy was enlivened by what Barker felt to be Vedrenne's 'vendetta' against Lillah McCarthy. 'My position between you is very fearful,' Shaw warned Lillah. 'I ask myself repeatedly Is Lillah the greatest liar known to history, or is Vedrenne?' And he cautioned Vedrenne: 'You will end by busting up Vedrenne & Barker.'

Shaw agreed with Barker that the short run system was the only way to stay solvent: but 'flesh and blood cant stand the racket of it'. Under this pressure they were all driven to abuse each other. 'What with Barker gradually losing all desire to act, and Vedrenne gradually losing all desire to do anything else but act, the position has become more & more impossible,' expostulated Shaw. 'If I could only get V on the stage & B off it, I should amaze the world.' While Vedrenne was performing better, more frequently, and without charging admission (except exorbitantly to the dramatist for each presentation of his play), Barker 'has for months past been fit only for a padded room', Shaw judged early in 1907. ' . . . Until he gets a holiday and recovers his sanity the safe rule is to do exactly the opposite of everything he recommends.'

What then was to be done? In Shaw's opinion, the job of producing plays was ruining Barker's acting: 'instead of thinking of his own part he watches the others all the time and ceases to be an actor.' But Shaw minimized Barker's distaste for the rough air of public performance. The imperfect conditions of the stage – its lack of money, lack of time and Caliban-like public – dispirited him. 'I do believe my present loathing for the theatre is loathing for the audience,' he was to write a decade later. 'I have never loved them.' He had taught them language, and (to judge by the press) they knew how to curse. He wished to retire and write for a more refined theatre – the National Theatre of his imagination. Shaw's advice to him seemed partly to assist the first step in this retreat. 'The next thing *you* have to do is to finish the play [*Waste*] & produce it,' he had urged in the summer of 1906; 'then publish it with Ann Leete & Voysey in a single volume.'

But Barker's writing, always exquisitely slow, was held up by his other jobs at the Court on which he was financially dependent. He needed money to write at his ease and produce his plays fastidiously. By 1907 two possibilities lay open to him.

*

'There is to be a new theatre in America financed by 23 millionaires; and I have been asked whether Barker will go over and manage it,' Shaw announced to Lillah. 'I think he and Vedrenne . . . had better take the

Court program right over to New York & shake the dust of London off their feet.' This Millionaire's Theatre, between 62nd and 63rd Streets on Central Park West (a proper distance from Broadway), was being built to run on the repertory principles described in Barker and Archer's blueprint, and it offered Barker an opportunity to cut free from Vedrenne and join a more intellectual partnership with Archer. 'America looks rather real at moments,' he wrote to Archer, 'and it would be a correct sequel to the blue book if we went together.'

But the New Theatre, in New York, was still under construction and other arrangements had to be made for the coming season of 1907-8. Barker, Shaw and Vedrenne were agreed that larger audiences must be brought to see the new drama; but they were not agreed on how to achieve this. Shaw believed that repertory meant playing in London for advertisement and then playing on tour for money. 'The Court system must be fortified by the provinces or it cannot hold out,' he insisted. 'It is from the number one towns that the big profits of John Bull and Major Barbara must come; for in Sloane Square there is only a bare living in them, with no margin for failures . . . ' Vedrenne believed that they must capitalize on their success at the Court by advancing straight into the West End of London. Perhaps because touring was such a helter-skelter business, Barker mainly supported Vedrenne and together they leased the Savoy Theatre in the Strand. 'I hope this foolish Savoy business will fall through,' Shaw had written to Barker. But once the lease had been taken, he ominously acknowledged its existence: 'The game is up at the Court: it has not yet begun at the Savoy.'

Their invasion of the West End seemed to intoxicate Vedrenne who had originally wanted to form a syndicate for the building of a new theatre and had even taken an option on a site in central London. He now proposed turning the Vedrenne and Barker management into a limited company but was dissuaded by Shaw's refusal to have anything to do with this. 'Limited liability does not really exist in companies which are only nominally companies, and are really family or personal concerns,' he explained to Vedrenne. 'Although we could not be forced into bankruptcy for the liabilities, we should practically have to pay them in full as long as we had a farthing left in the world to do it with. This would apply to you, Barker and me only . . . I think you will either go smash at the Savoy, or else be placed by it and by the tour in a position to find all the capital you want inside the partnership.' Nor did Shaw intend to join this partnership: 'I shall act simply as usurer,' he told them. To enable the Savoy season to open he put up two thousand pounds at five per cent interest – to which was added a thousand pounds each from Vedrenne and Barker who were both to draw salaries of a thousand pounds a year (with extra fees to be paid to Barker as actor and author). 'My own salary – another thousand – ' added Shaw, 'is to be taken out in moral superiority.'

The Savoy was twice the size of the Court and had become celebrated for its Gilbert and Sullivan productions. Shaw had no new play ready for their new theatre which, despite his belief that the boom in his work was over, traded in revivals of *You Never Can Tell* and *Arms and the Man*, and gave first West End presentations of *The Doctor's Dilemma* and *Caesar and Cleopatra*. They were treated by the press, he later said, 'as if they were the libretti of light opera, and no reference whatever was made to the one-time brilliance of the Court Theatre propagandist'.

With this memory of the past something of the spirit of their enterprise was also disappearing. The audiences from the Court never took to the Savoy which seemed an awkward place – the management actually played the National Anthem and made them stand up! It seemed too as if the clashes between Barker and Vedrenne were now affecting the quality of their productions. In his excitement Vedrenne appeared to Shaw to have thrown aside all his prudence. 'I believe that Vedrenne pawns the scenery and spends the proceeds in unbridled personal extravagance,' he wrote. 'There is no other way of accounting for the fact that however often I extricate the firm from debt, it is as insolvent as ever within a week.'

With his hopes focused on New York, Barker held aloof and would have been content with Restoration comedy. Shaw complained of his reluctance 'to tackle anything but easy plays and easy people – easy, that is, to his temperament'. He also objected to the many revivals of his own plays, which were losing their sparkle. 'The thing to aim at now,' he told Barker, 'is a season without a single Shaw evening bill. Every night of Shaw is now time lost: I am not going to sit down in the way I have cleared, and block it.' He wanted Galsworthy's new play *Joy* and Barker's *Waste* to take up the running. But Galsworthy's sentimental work was a disappointment; Barker's *Waste* was banned by the censor; and even the weakly-cast production of Gilbert Murray's version of the Euripides *Medea* appeared lustreless. The Savoy season, which closed on 14 March 1908, had turned out a failure.

Immediately afterwards Barker took off with Archer for New York. But the New Theatre which they inspected had no storage space for scenery and was far too large for their purposes, 'with an enormous, gaping, cavernous proscenium, fit only for old-fashioned, nineteenth century spectacle'. They returned to London, but the days of the Vedrenne-Barker management were drawing noisily to a close.

Before the end of 1907 Vedrenne had taken a second West End theatre, the newly built Queen's in Shaftesbury Avenue, to which he transferred *The Doctor's Dilemma*. In the spring of 1908 he leased yet another theatre, the Haymarket, to present (with Barker and Frederick Harrison) Shaw's new 'dramatic masterpiece' *Getting Married*. This was to be followed in the summer with *The Chinese Lantern* by Laurence Housman whose *Prunella* (in collaboration with Barker) had been one of the Court's non-Shavian successes, and a new play called *Nan* by John Masefield whose *Campden Wonder* Shaw felt had been seriously underrated at the Court.

'The Vedrenne and Barker enterprise then is as much alive as ever?' Shaw made a *Daily Telegraph* reporter ask him in May 1908 – to which he answered: 'More so, unfortunately, for Vedrenne and Barker and myself. We honestly did our best to bury it. But it seems to be immortal.' They longed, he added, for the peace of irretrievable ruin but seemed incapable of falling into it. In fact he was having to 'disgorge thousands [of pounds] to bolster up the drama here'. He reasserted his belief in what he was to call 'beating the provinces with the Old Court Repertory'. The education and propaganda value of a good touring company would sustain their reputation and 'help to build up a real public for us later on'. But the tour of *You Never Can Tell* and *Man and Superman* was undertaken more as an attempt to recoup the Vedrenne and Barker losses than create new audiences.

Barker and Vedrenne longed to be free of each other, but (being so heavily in debt to him) could not come to any arrangement without Shaw's consent. And Shaw was reluctant to announce their legal separation. 'A definite arrangement would have meant a winding-up,' he wrote to Vedrenne; 'and what I want is a hanging-up . . . ' He succeeded in hanging up their divorce until early in 1911. Barker had by then written *The Madras House*, directed a season of plays at the Duke of York's Theatre with the American producer Charles Frohman and begun a theatrical partnership with his wife; Vedrenne had first joined Lewis Waller and was now starting on a new partnership, 'Vedrenne and [Dennis] Eadie', at the Royalty Theatre. To reunite them was no longer possible or desirable. Shaw, who had advanced £5,250 to them over the years and arranged for Barker to be repaid his loans first, agreed to accept £484 3s. 10d. (plus some assets from the sale of scenery) as a final settlement.

The public good done had been 'worth the cost a hundred times over', he declared; 'but the cost fell on us, and the benefit went to the nation'. In 1909 he had joined the Organizing Committee of the Shakespeare Memorial National Theatre, and converted his Vedrenne & Barker loss into an investment in the campaign. What could be done without an endowment had been exhaustively tried at the Court, he argued, and it was on this proved commercial impossibility that the National Theatre project was founded. 'Messrs. Vedrenne & Barker were not rich men,' he wrote. 'They voluntarily forewent the opportunity of turning the enterprise into a lucrative commercial speculation and left themselves at the end with all their resources mortgaged. My own income falls very far short of the point at which the loss of sums of four figures becomes a matter of no importance. I have a good deal of public work to do outside the theatre; and when it came to endowing the theatre with months of work and half my income, I had to stop.'

CHAPTER IV

[1]

Do you know Shaw's writings? That's the man who has quite a good
way of coming to terms with life – of putting himself into harmony
with it (which is no small achievement). He is proud of his work, like
Wilde or Whistler but without their pretension, rather like a dog that
is proud of its master . . .
Rainer Maria Rilke (1906)

'We are in the agonies of househunting,' Shaw had appealed to Wells in April 1904. 'Now is the time to produce an eligible residence, if you have one handy.' Several times he and Charlotte went to visit Wells and his wife Jane, but could find nothing comparable to Spade House at Sandgate. It seemed as if they were committed for ever to the habit of floating around the country or abroad, then drifting back to their harbour at Adelphi Terrace. At the end of 1905 Charlotte had steered G.B.S. up to Edstaston again to stay with 'the Chumlys' for Christmas; and between early February and the middle of June 1906 she deposited him for most weekends in Harmer Green where she had once more rented a house. On the train between Hertfordshire and London Shaw's contribution to letters rushed unintermittently along.

Charlotte had grown vainly more ingenious at braking this flow of work. She was beginning dramatic writing herself, translating two plays by Eugène Brieux – one of which, *Maternité*, was produced by the Stage Society in the spring of 1906. This challenge, if such it were, failed to distract G.B.S. who assimilated the cause of Brieux into his body of campaigns and uttered a Preface, fifteen thousand words long, to *Three Plays by Brieux* claiming him to be the most important dramatist west of Russia since Ibsen and 'incomparably the greatest writer France has produced since Molière'.

To this shared conviction, which was also an expression of loyalty to his wife, Charlotte could not object. But her concern over his other work seldom abated. Early in 1906 she had conducted an experiment by encouraging G.B.S. to sit for his portrait by Neville Lytton. It was an extraordinary picture, owing much to a stray observation by Granville Barker that the Velázquez portrait of Pope Innocent X in the Doria Palace at Rome was uncannily similar to G.B.S. Working in imitation of Velázquez, and placing his subject in papal vestments and throne, Neville Lytton achieved what Shaw was to call a 'witty jibe at my poses'.

These poses multiplied over the last half of Shaw's career – as busts, statuettes, medallions, stamps, portraits in oils, watercolours, crayon and needlework; as wooden marionettes, caricatures on posters and in papers, on film, as photographs (poised either naked or eccentrically tailored) on land, in cars, under parasols, at sea; and as likenesses rendered in stained glass, from a simple stick of shaving soap, as a brass door-knocker or waxwork tricyclist and, most extreme of all perhaps, in grisaille with hands held to ears on a Chinese *famille rose* vase decorated with dense peony, chrysanthemum, lily and vine . . .

People were aghast at Shaw's Everest of vanity. But, admitting his addiction to public attention, he tried to employ it usefully. He provided artists with work and his commissioned portraits and busts may be seen as evidence of generous patronage. He was curious too about the public phenomenon he had manufactured to replace the unloved Sonny, and amused by these reflections of it.

But Charlotte was not amused. What evidence there is suggests that she did not enjoy seeing her husband paraded in the costume and attitude of Velázquez's Pope. Taking advantage of a visit to England by Rodin, and even before the Neville Lytton portrait had been completed, she invited the French sculptor to visit her at Adelphi Terrace at half-past three on the afternoon of Friday 1 March 1906. '*Il faut monter jusqu'au premier [étage] et vous trouvez là une petite grille sur l'escalier qui est notre porte,*' she instructed him. He came, they talked, and the consequence was that, as Shaw wrote to Trebitsch later that day, 'my wife insists on dragging me to Paris for twelve days at Easter so that Rodin may make a bust of me!!!!!'

They left for Paris on 15 April, stayed at the Hôtel Palais d'Orsay, and after meeting Rodin next day began the sittings at his private studio in Meudon. 'He had, I believe, a serious friendship for us,' Shaw was to write. He and Charlotte were at his house all day, most days, until they left France on 8 May. And Charlotte was delighted. She had lodged one thousand pounds in Rodin's bank at the beginning of April, explaining untruthfully that '*[mon homme] est, comme vous, travailleur acharné et vous êtes le seul artiste auquel il consente à poser*'. She had also made it clear that this money, which was to be treated as an endowment of Rodin's work in general, placed him under no obligation and was not returnable. Talking to Rodin as he was preparing to begin, Charlotte complained that other artists and photographers had automatically produced the sort of mephisthophelean figure they assumed her husband to be, without taking the trouble to look at him. Rodin, who had never read Shaw, replied that he knew nothing of his reputation: 'but what is there I will give you.'

The collaboration between these two extreme personalities was recorded by Rainer Maria Rilke, then Rodin's secretary. Shaw was determined to prove a champion sitter. He acted the artist's model rather than a fashionable client. Seldom has a likeness received such vibrant assistance from its subject. Shaw gave himself unconditionally into the sculptor's hands, putting immense vitality simply into standing still. 'The portrait makes tremendous strides, thanks to the energy with which Shaw stands,' wrote Rilke. 'He stands like a thing which has the will to stand, over and above its natural capacity for it . . . '

'Shaw as a model surpasses description. He . . . has the power of getting his whole self, even to his legs and all the rest of him, into his bust, which will have to represent the whole Shaw, as it were, that Rodin has before him something quite unusually concentrated, which he absorbs into himself and into his work (you can imagine with what zest).'

Rodin's studio seemed transformed into a theatre. Each day an audience assembled and sat in mesmerized silence as Shaw ('ce modèle extraordinaire') collected and concentrated himself and Rodin filled the place with 'his raging activity, his gigantic movements', and volleys of unintelligible sound. In the intervals Charlotte played about G.B.S. 'like a spring wind about a goat' and people approached to see how the bust 'vibrant de vie et de caractère' was taking shape under Rodin's hands. 'He plodded along exactly as if he were a river-god doing a job of wall-building in a garden for three or four francs a day,' Shaw remembered. Having taken the measurement from the parting of Shaw's hair to the end of his beard, Rodin gave this proportion to the lump of clay by adding more clay to it. Rilke, in a letter to his wife, sent a beautifully exact description of the work's development. Rodin 'took two further measurements: from the nose to the back of the head and from ear to ear round the back,' he wrote. 'After rapidly cutting out the eyebrows so that something like a nose appeared, and marking the position of the mouth by an incision such as children make in a snowman, he began to make first four, then eight, then sixteen profiles, letting the model, who was standing quite close to him, turn every three minutes or so . . . '

'In the third sitting, he placed Shaw in a low child's chair (all of which caused this ironical and mocking spirit, who is however by no means an unsympathetic personality, exquisite pleasure) and sliced the head off the bust with a wire – (Shaw, whom the bust already resembled very strikingly, watched this execution with indescribable delight.)'

What appealed to Shaw was Rodin's monumental matter-of-factness. He reminded him of Morris – a big man with a similar divinity of instinct and 'an astonishing gift of shaping things into intense life'. Though aware of Shaw's *'gloire d'écrivain'*, he never pretended to a knowledge of his plays, ('he knows absolutely nothing about books,' Shaw commented, ' – thinks they are things to be read'), his eyes never twinkled, his hands did not gesticulate: he worked – and 'like all great workmen who can express themselves in words, was very straight and simple'. Shaw's words, according to Rodin, were less straight but even more simple: *'M. Shaw ne parle pas très bien,'* he said; *'mais il s'exprime avec une telle violence qu'il s'impose.'* Nevertheless, they talked and talked using 'that lingua franca of philosophy and art which is common to all languages'.

These *séances* at Meudon became one of the features of Paris's spring season. Everyone seemed to be speaking of them. People as various as G. K. Chesterton and Gwen John were reported to have bulged or peeped in for a moment. William Rothenstein exclaimed in astonishment that 'Shaw should have the means to employ Rodin' – eleven years ago he had been one of the earliest sitters to Rothenstein who admired him for not waiting 'until he was famous to behave like a great man'. From Vienna came Trebitsch to marvel at these artistic performances and, in the intervals, absorb the 'lofty mind' of Charlotte in 'profound talk about God and the universe'.

To other acquaintances – including Sydney Cockerell who had been William Morris's secretary at the Kelmscott Press, and the young American Alvin Langdon Coburn ('on the whole, the best photographer in the world') – Shaw sent invitations for the unveiling of Rodin's sculpture 'Le Penseur'. Coburn had photographed Shaw two summers earlier, and at the beginning of 1906 Shaw had written, luxuriating in the technical vocabulary of printing processes, in a preface to the catalogue for an exhibition of Coburn's work in which he compared Coburn's photograph of Chesterton to Rodin's statue of Balzac. The inauguration of 'Le Penseur' outside the Panthéon took place on the afternoon of 21 April. Next morning Shaw surprised Coburn with the suggestion that 'after his bath I should photograph him nude in the pose of Le Penseur'. This photo of G.B.S. suspended in thought on the edge of his bath was a 'first step' Shaw explained, 'towards the realization of Carlyle's antidote to political idolatry: a naked parliament'. Coburn believed that Shaw was justifiably 'proud of his figure' but there was another impetus behind the picture. 'Though the body was my body,' Shaw wrote, 'the face was the face of my reputation.' By dividing reality from reputation and using these images to illustrate this separation, G.B.S. seems to have sought reassurance that his reputation was not damaging him. His generosity to Coburn was genuine, but with the parody of 'Le Penseur' he came close to sabotaging his purpose in going to Rodin for evidence of himself 'just as I am, without one plea'. Before Rodin's bust he wanted to feel cleansed of the revulsion that periodically rose up in him over his own notoriety. He wanted it to extinguish G.B.S. But this Shavian fame arose from so deep a need and had seeped back into him so centrally that he sentimentalized his humility towards Rodin when famously remarking: 'at least I was sure of a place in the biographical dictionaries a thousand years hence as: "Shaw, Bernard: subject of a bust by Rodin: otherwise unknown".'

Shaw gave a more private reaction to the bust in a letter to Jacob Epstein. Rodin had told Charlotte that he would give her 'what is there'. He should more accurately have offered her what he could see was there. 'I am a comedian as well as a philosopher; and Rodin had no sense of humor,' Shaw wrote. ' . . . Accordingly, the bust has no sense of humor; and Shaw without a sense of humor is not quite Shaw, except perhaps to himself.' Still Charlotte was delighted. Six years later she used a photograph of the bust as frontispiece to her anthology, *Selected Passages from the Works of Bernard Shaw*, which G.B.S. recommended as an excellent volume omitting all his humour.

Charlotte and Shaw had planned to visit the Hamons in the Côte du Nord, but Rodin being unwell the sittings were extended and they remained in Paris, going to concerts, to various plays including Ibsen's *Canard Sauvage* and to the Grand Guignol with Trebitsch. The more blood-curdling these plays, Trebitsch observed, the more of an effort Shaw had to make 'not to burst out laughing'. He particularly enjoyed the guillotine. Nothing, it seemed to Trebitsch, could frighten G.B.S., not even the evening newspaper predictions of a revolution in Paris on May Day which he dismissed as announcements of 'the next instalment of the horror-play we have just been seeing'. Shaw spent the afternoon of May Day ('like London on Sunday') with Charlotte on the Place de la République and afterwards sent a message to the *Labour Leader* commenting that the French Government wanted to win the General Election 'by suppressing a revolution. Unluckily there is no revolution to suppress. The Government therefore sends the police and the dragoons to shove and charge the lazy and law abiding Parisians until they are goaded into revolt. No use: the people simply WON'T revolt'.

'But several respectable persons have been shoved and galloped over and even sabred. Surely it ought to be within the resources of modern democracy to find a remedy for this sort of official amateur revolution making. It is a clear interference with our business as scientific revolutionists.'

Shaw believed that the press had the power, by its good or malign will, to effect what actually happened. His article in the *Labour Leader* was intended as a cheerful antidote to a number of sensational French newspaper reports. In a letter to Granville Barker he admitted there had been a little more activity, describing Charlotte as clinging to lamp posts in order to see over people's heads and growing 'so furious when she saw a real crowd charged by real soldiers that she wanted to throw stones'. Charlotte's biographer Janet Dunbar describes the crowd as noisy; after the police charge with batons, Charlotte 'was pushed roughly hither and thither' before being led back by Shaw ('by dignified strategy which did not at any time go to the length of absolutely running away') to their hotel 'bursting into fresh spasms of rage all the way'. They had quitted the field without wounds and Shaw insisted that Charlotte had 'rather enjoyed being part of a revolution and having to run out of danger from time to time'. 'We are still alive,' he notified Trebitsch. ' . . . We finished up in the evening with a very stirring performance of Beethoven's 9th symphony at the Opera; so the day was a pretty full one.'

On 8 May Shaw sat to Rodin for the last time, then he and Charlotte caught the four o'clock train back to London. She carried with her two pencil-and-wash sketches of herself inscribed by Rodin '*Homage à sympathique Madame Charlotte Shaw*'. From London she sent him chocolates and her photograph of him (none of Shaw's had come out) and in October the marble bust arrived at Adelphi Terrace; '*maintenant je suis immortel*' wrote Shaw in a letter to Rodin that was returned to him as insufficiently addressed. Twenty-five years later, when visiting the Musée Rodin, he was to discover that this had not been the end of the matter. Having completed the bust in terracotta and done the marble-and-water imitation, Rodin had then gone 'seriously to work on his recollections of me and produced a small bronze mask . . . and a sort of marble Christ with the head drooping to one side . . . for which I obviously served as the model: both being frankly exhibited as portraits of me . . . The contrast between the heads done from life and the others is very curious, the others being much better'.

Shaw had enjoyed his time in Paris. Within six weeks of returning to London he was turning his head to William Strang for a good tight portrait. The following year, 1907, began with a couple of quick sittings for a bust by Troubetzkoy and ended with a very preliminary one for Epstein. Shaw was to use these busts (and others by Sava Botzaris, Kathleen Bruce, Joseph Coplans, Jo Davidson, Sigismund de Strobl and

Clare Winsten) to pull faces at his 'reputation' and compound it with that of each sculptor. Prince Troubetzkoy, being paternally Russian, 'made me flatteringly like a Russian nobleman'; and in the hands of Jacob Epstein, an American expatriate, he later became 'a Brooklyn navvy ... my skin thickened, my hair coarsened, I put on five stone in weight, my physical strength trebled'. It followed that his plaster reputation lay in the imaginations of other people, not within himself. And while the artists recreated him in bronze, marble or terracotta, he recreated them in pen portraits and impressions.

'Troubetskoi once made a most fascinating Shavian bust of me. He did it in about five hours, in Sargent's studio [31 Tite Street]. It was a delightful and wonderful performance. He worked convulsively, giving birth to the thing in agonies, hurling lumps of clay about with groans, and making strange, dumb movements with his tongue, like a wordless prophet. He covered himself with plaster. He covered Sargent's carpets and curtains and pictures with plaster. He covered me with plaster. And, finally, he covered the block he was working on with plaster to such purpose that, at the end of the second sitting, lo! there stood Sargent's studio in ruins, buried like Pompeii under the scoviæ of a volcano, and in the midst a spirited bust of one of my reputations, a little idealized (quite the gentleman, in fact) but recognizable a mile off as the sardonic author of Man and Superman ... '

Charlotte accepted that the extraordinary multiplication of facsimiles might be part of the equipment of a man of genius, and she welcomed the respite from work these sittings and standings and posings obtained for him. But Epstein's ungentlemanly bust (completed in 1934) was 'like a blow in the face' and she told everyone who mentioned it to her that if this object 'came into our house she would walk out of it'. It was a troublesome business. When Epstein had come to London at the beginning of 1905 with a letter of recommendation from Rodin, Shaw had helped him with introductions to Will Rothenstein and the Carfax Gallery. He felt sympathetic, as one outsider in English artistic circles to another, admiring Epstein's primitivism and power in breaking up 'the brassy surfaces of his busts in his determination to make them flesh'. But Shaw's relationship with Charlotte was not of the flesh, and Epstein's attempt to reveal the atavistic passions underlying the witty and polite exterior of G.B.S. ('the aboriginal savage beneath the civilized sitter') revolted her. Shaw's first loyalty was to his wife, but he also felt a duty to Epstein, having arranged these sittings in the belief that the sculptor could 'benefit materially' from them. Here was an ideal position for the exercise of comic diplomacy.

Having banned the piece from their house, he explained to Epstein's wife that Charlotte had fallen in love with Strobl's bust (also a masterpiece depicting him as a dramatic poet and philosopher) and that she did not want to see him debunked by Epstein's biological theorizing, though this 'does not console me for the loss of it'. To Epstein himself he wrote that Charlotte's rage had been brought about by an unusual photograph. 'When the bust went to the Leicester Galleries, a workman, who was evidently a profound critic, completed the effect by putting his hat on it; and a press photographer snapped it in that condition.' And finally, in a single sentence, he simultaneously supported both Epstein and Charlotte. 'The bust is a masterpiece; but it is not a portrait.' As Rodin had not understood his humour so Epstein had overlooked his Shavian veneer: and 'without my veneer I am not Bernard Shaw'.

This veneer, he had sometimes argued, was his reputation. In these busts and portraits, Shaw often felt he recognized part of himself; but never, in a single image, could he find all parts combined. Perhaps there was no method, even in his own work, of allying the opposing patterns within himself. At the age of fifty he had proposed 'to furnish the world with an authentic portrait-bust of me before I had left the prime of life'; the search for perfect authenticity continued almost to the end of his life and well after he had had 'more than enough of being a sculptor's model'. He became so frequent a sitter to artists and photographers that it was impossible, H. G. Wells complained, to move around Europe without being outfaced by Shavian images. This gallery of replicas seemed at the same time to mock and celebrate his rising success.

In the summer of 1906, as if in sympathy with this success, Shaw ascended from Wandsworth Gas Works in a balloon (a happening he would later re-compose for his play *Misalliance*). He rose and floated and descended over two and a half hours, without Charlotte's knowledge yet in the company of her sister, with Granville Barker and the aviator-actor Robert Loraine. Loraine was a combination of artist and man-of-action Shaw particularly admired. His acting, full of vitality and earnestness, was wonderfully well suited to Shavian roles (his other triumphs were in *Cyrano de Bergerac* and Strindberg's *The Father*). Though he hated Lillah McCarthy, Shaw considered him as a possible successor to Barker. 'I was never free from the impression when Shaw was speaking to me,' Loraine had written in his diary (after playing Tanner in New York and Don Juan in London), 'that he might at any moment ascend to Heaven like Elisha on a chariot of fire.' They were guided in their balloon by an aeronaut Percival Spencer (who became the Shavian Joey Percival in *Misalliance*) to a height of nine thousand feet. After forty minutes' drifting 'very pleasant and seraphic with nothing happening, except that Shaw would peer through a hole in the boarding at his feet which made him feel rather sick, we discussed landing,' Loraine wrote. ' . . . I thought the people would be rather interested to receive visitors from the air, and especially flattered when they discovered Shaw's identity. "Don't be so certain," said Shaw. "They may think my works detestable."' In the event they bumped down in a field near Chobham and were met by a purple-faced landowner, unacquainted with Shaw's *oeuvre* but waving a shooting-stick: 'and the welcome he gave us was a curt direction as to the quickest way off his property'.

[2]

I was born to do odd jobs.
Shaw to Beatrice Webb
(9 December 1910)

Their agonies of house-hunting ended when they came across the Rectory at Ayot St Lawrence, not far from Wheathampstead in Hertfordshire. The Rector, who could not afford to keep up the grounds, had no need of such a large house himself, and Charlotte decided to rent it. She did not plan to stay there long.

Later on, when asked by people why he had come to Ayot St Lawrence, Shaw would take them to a tombstone in the churchyard inscribed in memory of Mary Ann South. She had lived in the village from 1825 to 1895 and the inscription read: 'Her Time Was Short'. If the biblical span of three score years and ten was reckoned short at Ayot, then here was an appropriate place, Shaw would explain, for the future author of *Back to Methuselah* to inhabit. They continued renting the place for fourteen years and shortly after the First World War bought it – following which it became known as 'Shaw's Corner'.

'People bother me,' he told his housekeeper near the end of his life. 'I came here to hide away from them.' The red-bearded revolutionary who promoted G.B.S. as a world-wide publicity phenomenon showed himself as a quietly-mannered gentleman in this remote twelfth-century village where 'the last thing of real importance that happened was, perhaps, the Flood'. Ayot had two churches, one shop, no omnibus or train service and, even by the 1930s, no gas or water supply, no delivery of newspapers and no electricity – the Rectory itself making use of a private generating plant. The agricultural community seemed to have withstood centuries of civilization and improvement: which was, Shaw said, 'a very wonderful thing'.

The Rectory, which had been built in 1902, was a plain dark-red suburban villa standing in a sloping two-acre plot with scraps of kitchen-garden, orchard, lawn and a belt of conifers. Besides the dining-room, study and a small drawing-room, there were eight bedrooms. Shaw and Charlotte moved in at the beginning of November 1906, with a married couple, Henry and Clara Higgs, to look after them. Higgs took over the garden, with an odd-job man to help him; and Charlotte engaged two maids to assist Mrs Higgs indoors. The Higgses, who had already been with them at Adelphi Terrace, were to remain in their service for about forty years. 'Mrs Shaw looked upon my wife almost as a daughter,' Higgs reckoned; 'they were like a father and mother to us.' Shaw treated them with invariable good manners, recognizing their value to him with an inscription in one of his books at the beginning of 1940: 'To Harry and Clara Higgs, who have had a very important part in my life's work, as without their friendly services I should not have had time to write my books and plays nor had any comfort in my daily life.'

The Rectory was a fairly comfortable, fairly dismal house. Charlotte filled it with furniture – stiff armchairs, bureaux, beds: lodging-house objects with hardly a good piece among them. She also took charge of the household accounts, and saw that every item, from the sticking on of a postage stamp to the buying of a beetroot, was noted. Shaw, authoritatively surveying far-ranging aspects of political economy from his study, could not be trusted to add up the milk bill ('he would make it a different total every time').

They had grown tired of house-hunting and the Rectory had been one of the few houses about which they were agreed: neither of them liked it. Every day at Ayot felt like a Sunday. But in Shavian terms this was an advantage. Their new home could interrupt neither Charlotte's passion for travel nor Shaw's obsession with work. Once they had settled in, they were free to move out and about.

*

They had kept their maisonette in Adelphi Terrace, went regularly between London and Hertfordshire, and erratically everywhere else. Shaw travelled in pursuit of work, Charlotte to avoid it. Between 20 October and the end of November, he delivered eleven lectures – three in London and others in Manchester, Birmingham and Reading. 'I am a distracted creature,' he wrote to Edith Bland, ' . . . and my hair is as white as the driven snow in consequence.' At the end of March 1907, Charlotte carried him off to France and they whirled through town after town – Yvetot – Caudebec – Laon – Rheims – Amiens for twelve days of hectic relaxation. 'I shall go to Beauvais probably tomorrow or next day,' Shaw wrote from Rouen, 'and shall either do the cathedral in ten minutes & hurry on Lord knows where, or stay there a day or two.' But, he owned, 'the cessation of writing & talking has done me a lot of good.' Never had the pressure of Shaw's writing and talking been so intense. 'I am quite desperate with nervous exhaustion,' he complained. ' . . . If I make even one more engagement I feel something will burst.'

To lighten the load of correspondence he had devised in 1906 a series of five stereotyped postcard messages. Over the next years the range of these cards was greatly expanded. He attempted to give them (in a proliferation of shades) a series of coloured codes, though eventually running out of colours. His views on capital punishment, on temperance, and the forty-letter British 'alfabet' were to be relayed in tones of green, orange-brown and blue. Neat piles of these coloured cards lay on his desk and, as he read through his mail each day he was able to cap many letters with an appropriate card. Snap! They were particularly potent for saying no. Politely and with force, they spelled out his reasons for being unable to read and report on unpublished manuscripts, discuss his published views in private correspondence, give spoken interviews, inscribe books that were not his personal gifts, or comply with requests from strangers for his signature (with or without a photograph); why he could not receive visitors, acknowledge gifts, encourage people to celebrate his birthdays, respond to appeals (particularly from schools, churches, and parents eager to give their children an expensive education) founded on the notion that he was a suitable multi-millionaire, take part in new movements, open bazaars, give lectures, eat or speak at public dinners, write articles, write prefaces, read or write letters. In short: why he could not do so many of the things he spent his life doing.

In a postscript to one of these cards he noted to a correspondent: 'You will see by my having to keep printed cards that demands for the above run into millions. The only way to avoid giving offence by refusing is to refuse everybody by rule.' But Shaw consistently disobeyed his rule – even his authoritative refusals to provide autographs were sometimes signed. The cards (like the 'alfabet' he would one day sponsor) were conceived as an economy: a method of saving time. He invested many hours in drafting variant texts. But always there was an ample margin that he could fill with extensive commentary, outwitting the economic purpose of a printed message.

In 1907, to spare Charlotte as well as himself, he engaged Georgina Gillmore, daughter of his mother's half-sister Arabella, as his secretary. Charlotte and Shaw were fond of 'Judy' as she was called, and were said to have treated her also 'like a daughter'. She was eighteen and lived with Lucinda Shaw in Fitzroy Square when she started work for G.B.S. He sent her to secretarial college and she became his first full-time secretary until her marriage in 1912.

Even with her help, Shaw complained that only brute self-preservation 'and the fear of my wife' were keeping him from a breakdown. During the summer of 1907 he revised *The Sanity of Art* for a new edition in German and English; published an analytical programme for *Don Juan in Hell*; saw *John Bull's Other Island* and *Major Barbara*, also *How He Lied to Her Husband* through the press, and began writing a new play, *Getting Married*. Throughout the year, more than fifty of his articles, statements, interviews and letters appeared in the newspapers on such wide-flung topics as financial aid following an earthquake in Jamaica, the imprisonment of Egyptians after the Danshawaii affair and the suppression of Richard Strauss's *Salome* by the Metropolitan Opera House in New York. There was Shaw on disarmament in the *Evening Standard*, on polygamy in *The Times* and on diet in the *Daily Mail*. His most common subjects were marriage, censorship, theology and women's suffrage. But readers of the *Daily Graphic* could pick up what he had to say on 'the imperfections of phrenologists'; and *Clarion* subscribers could learn about 'the Gentle Art of Unpleasantness', a social exercise in three parts. He wrote about old age pensions, women typists' salaries, corporal punishment and the railway strike. His fantastic short story 'Aerial Football', appearing in *Collier's Weekly*, won a prize of a thousand dollars which Shaw indignantly sent back. He fired off a piece on Delacroix to the *Saturday Review*; composed a famous essay on Belloc and Chesterton for the *New Age;* and published a review of A. R. Orage's book on Nietzsche in *Fabian News*. The variety seemed infinite, the quantity endless.

The mysterious figure of Orage absorbed a good deal of Shaw's interest. He was an ex-school teacher who divided his enthusiasms between Nietzsche and Guild Socialism and in May 1907 had become editor of the *New Age*. He did not, as Shaw put it, 'belong to the successful world, and was what I should call a desperado of genius, [who] kept the paper living on air for 15 years before he went to America'. He had received from Shaw five hundred pounds (and been given another five hundred from a banker) to keep the *New Age* from insolvency; and this was followed during the next twelve months by what Shaw calculated to have been a further thousand pounds' worth of free copy. 'It is still insolvent,'

Shaw reported wonderingly to Graham Wallas. But Orage had none of Frank Harris's vulgarity or the quarrelsomeness and cliquishness that blighted so much London journalism. Shaw responded to his inexhaustibly erratic interests. 'His plan was to keep the first three or four pages to himself as his pulpit and leave the rest to anyone who could and would write an article for nothing, no matter what his politics or fads were, provided only the ginger was hot in the mouth. Orage's success in getting copy on these terms was astonishing.' Shaw's own contributions numbering more than two dozen, persisted until 1921.

It was Charlotte's duty of course however to remove him from such abuses. From the middle of July to the middle of October 1907 she secreted him remotely in Merionethshire, while the Webbs moved, with three secretaries, into their house at Ayot. At a large house in Llanbedr, a village on the Welsh coast between Barmouth and Harlech, he also participated in the first Fabian Summer School. This innovation had been proposed at the start of the year by a Fabian dentist, F. Lawson Dodd, and conceived by a Fabian bluestocking Mabel Atkinson. It was supported by Shaw and underwritten by Charlotte who regarded it as a method of ventilating study and lecturing with fresh air and a holiday atmosphere.

The Fabian Summer Schools, which were attended by students and later came to be seen as a foundation of the intellectual wing of the Labour Party, were originally designed to get country members to meet metropolitan Fabians, and grey-haired socialists to mingle with the Fabian nursery. Occasional romances glimmered, but the exhilarations were generally those of a 'joyous monastery'. The day would begin with classes in Swedish Drill led by Mary Hankinson, a much-loved muscular games mistress and leading Fabian cricketer, who was to be the target of a lyric poem by the Shakespearian scholar J. Dover Wilson, and a prototype for Shaw's St Joan. Breakfast, an experimental meal, was followed by a venture into co-operative washing-up and a dose of voluntary housework. Cold baths were free (hot baths cost sixpence); rooms were set aside in which to practise silence, and no smoking was permitted (except, literally, in the smoking-room). There were courses of lectures available on Municipal Rates, Agricultural Reconstruction, on the National Debt and the Modern Novel. Additional fixtures included swimming and 'other excursions' such as climbs and tugs-of-war (Vegetarians versus Meat-eaters); and people were allowed to bring bicycles and eventually tennis balls – though never dogs or children. Conservatives were theoretically welcome. A vegetarian table was usually the rule. Highly organized games were discouraged, but there was always some tonic recreation – walking, music and convivial country dances with the aid of Cecil J. Sharp's *The*

Country Dance Book (3 vols.). Lights went out and doors were bolted at 11 p.m., and Fabians were requested 'to refrain from loud talk and noises' in the dormitories.

'The Fabian School is sleeping five in a room, and apparently enjoying it,' Shaw wrote to Granville Barker. 'Webb has been here in frightful weather. Charrington has promised.' Shaw himself was the chief attraction. He lectured on marriage, education and foreign politics; gave readings from his plays; and chatted informally with everyone. The place was 'beauteous' but the weather 'so damp that it is a mere form to put a roof on a house', he observed. Thirty-nine Fabians camped in the old schoolhouse down the road from the Shaws, who had been joined in their house by Charlotte's floating sister and Robert Loraine. More Fabians boarded nearby. Since everyone's spirits fell with the barometer, Shaw precipitated himself with gusto into the programme – which included open-air speeches under a red flag on Barmouth Sands and on Sunday evenings, for the benefit of villagers, socialist addresses in Welsh. A few times he overshot the mark and after one day's hike failed to return. Dressed in convenient drill-costumes and equipped with lanterns, a party of almost a hundred Fabians, reinforced by Henry Higgs, streamed across the mountains and valleys: and he was discovered asleep in a hotel.

More alarming was one of Shaw's exploits at sea. Each morning at half past ten he swam and one morning, after a storm, almost drowned. Robert Loraine, 'bathing with me & following me out, shared my fate', he wrote to H. G. Wells. Striking a sandbank, the two of them staggered ashore and lay gasping there until Shaw felt well enough to switch off 'with my usual inhuman suddenness', casually remarking that they had had a close shave. 'We kept up appearances to the last,' he assured Wells. Loraine, pressing him later as to what thoughts had jetted through his mind during what might have been his last few moments alive, was told that he had been almost completely preoccupied by the business inconveniences of his death. How would Charlotte understand the arrangements with his translators? How would she cope with his lateness for lunch? 'I thought of nothing but pressing practical things,' he told Loraine. ' . . . I wanted to tell you not to try to swim to shore, as it was no use and the effort would exhaust you.'

' . . . Then my foot struck a stone, and instead of saying "Thank God!" I said, "Damn!" . . . When I got on my legs you had vanished. It was my clear duty to dive after you and rescue you . . . then came the frightful humiliation of realizing that I was utterly incapable of swimming another stroke . . . it took the conceit out of me.'

It was against this terrible capacity of endangering himself, and his instinctive 'Damn!' rather than 'Thank God!' on reaching safety, that Charlotte had to be so fiercely on guard. Increasingly, as Arnold Bennett noticed, she looked 'like the mother of a large family'. For Christmas she tucked Shaw up again in her sister and brother-in-law's house, where it was pretty well impossible for him to get into scrapes. And she kept him under her supervision and out of the country for three summer months of 1908 while the drains at Ayot were being replaced. 'I am now going off into the wilds,' he reported despondently to Archer at the beginning of July, 'leaving no address . . . ' First they went, via Gothenburg, to Stockholm, 'a very jolly town to look at,' he judged, whose population was 'very superior within certain limits of high mediocrity'. To help preserve its exclusiveness, he promised to 'perpetrate the notion that Sweden is a frightful place, where bears wander through the streets and people live on cod liver oil'. He then descended, via Hamburg, to Bayreuth where he heard Richter conduct Wagner's *Ring* including 'the most perfectly managed performance [of *Parsifal*] I ever saw (and I had seen six before)'. Finally, Charlotte escorted him round the railway hotels of Ireland, from Galway to Dublin, where he was to present Hugh Lane as Director of the Municipal Art Gallery with one of his Rodin busts.

The visit marked a change from their previous tours of Ireland when they had stayed at the Big Houses of the county families and with the 'Brandons and Castletowns and Kingstons & other Irish peers in their castles'. These families from Charlotte's social milieu were hostile to G.B.S., whom they regarded as a jumped-up Dublin office boy and no gentleman. 'Charlotte seems perfectly happy and delighted with her cad,' reported Edith Somerville, 'for cad he is in spite of his talent.' For Charlotte's sake Shaw made himself 'very agreeable and quite affable', as Edith Somerville admitted – so much so that Lady Kingston confessed with surprise that 'he is always most pleasant to me' when staying at Mitchelstown Castle; and Nora Robertson, seeing him at Bantry House, wondered if such grand places and people were 'as uncongenial as his admirers might wish to imagine'. But this affability cost him a good deal in patience and energy, and after 1907 (when he declined to accompany Charlotte to Castle Haven) they stayed at hotels or with more recent friends such as Lady Gregory who found them both 'very easy to entertain' and G.B.S. 'extraordinarily light in hand, a sort of kindly joyousness about him'. Besides: 'they have their motor so are independent'.

Their motor tour of Europe had been an ambitious excursion, yet Shaw did not seem especially gratified. He amended the advertisement for one German hotel by completing the printed statement that it was 'opposite the railway station' with the words: 'and thus provided with a means of escape always within sight'. Among other attractions he listed:

'Melted ice creams at all hours ... Antique carpets – seven years old – uninjured by beating or sweeping. Relics of former visitors – scraps of paper, crumbs, twine. Waste paper baskets always full.

'The nose continually feasted. Largest assortment of smells in Europe.

'Two hip baths. One always ready when not in use by another guest. The second can be cleaned with petroleum & brought to bedroom at 40 minutes notice except when in use as percussion instrument by band in garden restaurant.'

'I was crushed, I am now exasperated,' Shaw cried out in a letter to Granville Barker, ' ... another day's motoring will murder me.' But the next day's motoring near Rothenburg had almost murdered Charlotte, the motor having 'backjumped', Shaw explained, '& sent Charlotte like a rocket to the roof of the car (a limousine, unluckily)'. Her symptoms (fever and a bad throat) made her uncertain whether or not her neck was broken. 'She leans to the belief that it is,' observed Shaw who had the advantage, while she recuperated, of remaining four days in the same place. Pathetically he signalled his friends for business letters, and confided to Granville Barker the seriousness of their situation. 'I am fed up with vagabondage, and with the cat and dog life I lead with poor Charlotte, who takes every unguarded expression of my loathing of travelling as a personal insult to herself. Another month of it would end in a divorce.'

A most curious holiday episode had been their encounter with Strindberg. The meeting was apparently proposed by Hugo Vallentin, a Swedish journalist and Shaw's translator, while they were in Stockholm. 'I thought it my duty to pay my respects to a great man whom I considered one of the great dramatists of Europe,' Shaw afterwards remembered. 'People told me it was not of the slightest use. He is absolutely mad, they said, he won't see anybody, he never takes walks except in the middle of the night when there is nobody about, he attacks all his friends with the greatest fury. You will only be wasting your time.' Nevertheless, 'I achieved the impossible', Shaw wrote to Archer. He had sent Strindberg a note and received in reply an enormous letter written 'in several languages – French, German and English – any language but Swedish' which seemed to say that Strindberg was suffering from a mortal disease, never saw anybody, and could not speak English. 'What is the use of a dumb man speaking to a dumb man?' This letter was closely followed by a note asking Shaw to come at once to his own Intimate Theatre. 'He was quite a pleasant looking person,' Shaw recalled, 'with the most beautiful sapphire blue eyes I have ever seen. He was beyond expression shy.' To unravel the knot of language Strindberg had prepared some conversational material in French, 'but took the wind out of his own sails by addressing me in German', Shaw reported. Their exchange developed by way of some embarrassed silences, a 'pale smile or two' from Strindberg, gushes of 'energetic eloquence' from Shaw in 'a fearful lingo', and an undercurrent of polite French from Charlotte.

Strindberg had hurriedly arranged for them to see that morning a special performance of *Miss Julie*, having summoned August Falck and Manda Björling back from their holiday in the archipelago to play the two protagonists. Despite their familiarity with the roles, something apparently went wrong. Falck believed that his own playing had been too tense. Probably the absence of an audience and the presence of Strindberg had been unsettling – this astonishingly being 'the first time Strindberg had accepted to see the play in the 20 years of its existence,' Anthony Swerling records, 'so much did he shy from the theatre'. Some people claimed to have seen him in tears after the performance; others that Shaw was in tears during it. In any event, though Strindberg had proudly shown the Shaws round his theatre beforehand, he came out if it in a maudlin mood. Shortly afterwards, in a celebrated spasm of gloom he consulted his watch and, noting it was almost half past one, remarked in German that at two o'clock he was going to be sick. 'On this strong hint the party broke up,' Shaw informed Granville Barker.

How much did they comprehend each other, the author of *Married*, that paean of passionate misogyny revealing what Strindberg called 'the reverse side of my fearful attraction towards the other sex'; and the author of *Getting Married*, a tentative 'conversation' with feminist implications dramatizing the economic relations of marriage? Shaw was to describe what he had seen at the Intimate Theatre as one of Strindberg's 'chamber plays', suggesting that he may not have been aware it was *Miss Julie*. With the emotional concentration of chamber music he had never felt easy. But generally he knew where Strindberg stood. 'I was born too soon to be greatly influenced by him as a playwright, but', he was to write 'he is among the greatest of the great.' In the Preface to *Three Plays for Puritans* he had described him as 'the only genuinely Shakespearean modern dramatist', a resolute tragi-comedian, logical and faithful, who gave us the choice either of dismissing as absurd his way of judging conduct or else, by accepting it, concluding that 'it is cowardly to continue living'. Strindberg's and Shaw's uneasiness with women operated at different levels and moved them in opposite directions. 'I have a technical objection to making sexual infatuation a tragic theme,' Shaw declared. 'Experience proves that it is only effective in the comic spirit.' Shaw's technical objection came from his conviction that Strindberg's way led through havoc and ended in pessimism. His own commitment to the 'effective' took the form of sociological comedy apparently about the alterable conditions of life – those public institutions, whose improved architecture casts transcendental shadows where Shaw's optimism darkly flowers.

The suffering men and women inflict on each other in the name of love never appears in Shaw's work as it does in Strindberg's. Greatness 'implies a degree of human tragedy, of suffering and sacrifice', wrote Thomas Mann. 'The knotted muscles of Tolstoy bearing up the full burden of morality. Atlas-like. Strindberg, who was in hell; the martyr's death Nietzsche died on the cross of thought; it is these that inspire us with the reverence of tragedy; but in Shaw there was nothing of all this. Was he beyond such things, or were they beyond him?'

Shaw's tragedy lay in the need to suppress such things; Strindberg's in the need so horrifically to enact them. That Shaw felt the force of that enactment, and acknowledged its indestructibility, is indicated by his subsequent actions. He tried to persuade Beerbohm Tree to put on *Lycho Pers Resa* at His Majesty's (the play closest to Ibsen's *Peer Gynt*, which he also wanted to see on the English stage), but without success. Almost none of Strindberg's plays had been translated into English before Shaw's sister Lucy, with Maurice Elvey, produced a version of *Miss Julie* that was first presented in London by the Adelphi Play Society in 1912. That year, the Swedish newspaper *Dagens Nyheter* circulated a letter eliciting opinions of Strindberg's role in European culture to be published in the event of his death from cancer. 'Strindberg is a very great dramatist: he and Ibsen have made Sweden and Norway the dramatic centre of the world,' Shaw replied. ' . . . Time may wear him out; but Death will not succeed in murdering him.' Strindberg died a fortnight later. Many years afterwards Shaw was able to give a new lease of life to his work by donating the money from the Nobel Prize to financing a society for making Swedish literature available in English – the Anglo-Swedish Literary Foundation – whose first volume was to be four plays by Strindberg.

[3]

*This multiplicity of motives is, I like to think, typical of our times.
And if others have done this before me, then I congratulate myself in
not being alone in my belief in these 'paradoxes' (the word always
used to describe new discoveries).*
Strindberg. Preface to *Miss Julie*

'On the question of technique, I have, by way of experiment, eliminated all intervals,' wrote Strindberg in his Preface to *Miss Julie*. For *Getting Married* Shaw used a similar experiment. 'There is a point of some technical interest to be noted in this play,' he wrote. 'The customary division into acts and scenes has been disused, and a return made to unity of time and place as observed in the ancient Greek drama.' He had been influenced, he said, by Gilbert Murray's translations of Euripides. But though *Getting Married* proceeds without divisions into acts, changes of scenery, or impossible lapses of time, it does contain shifts of mood and genre: beginning as farce that merges into sociological comedy and then attempts a leap into magic realism.

By directing critics to the play's Aristotelean rules, Shaw swept their attention past an embarrassing and far closer parallel. For years in the *Saturday Review* he had made fun of what he called 'Sardoodledom'. The plays of Victorien Sardou, full of a 'bewildering profusion of everything that has no business in a play', were cut out of bits of paper and stuck together, he wrote, by a safe old hand 'playing the safe old game according to the safe old rules'. They were 'feats of carpentry in constructing show-cases for some trumpery little situation.' Of his *Madame Sans-Gêne* Shaw wrote: 'Sardou's Napoleon is rather better than Madame Tussaud's, and that is all that can be said for it.' As for his *Delia Harding*, 'so stale, so obviously factitious, so barrenly inept', it was 'the worst play I ever saw'. Only *Divorçons*, which Sardou wrote with Emile de Nâjac, was different. That play, which he had read before reviewing a partially successful adaptation called *The Queen's Proctor*, surprised him. He had expected – almost wanted – to be put in the worst possible temper by it but acknowledged by the end that here, 'in all its witty liveliness,' was 'a real play'.

Getting Married is in places little short of an ingenious adaption of *Divorçons*. The parallels are 'not only in the overall fusion of Farce with a genuine discussion of marriage and divorce,' observed the critic Martin Meisel, 'but in particulars and details'. There is a connection too between

Shaw's apparently formless disquisitory technique and the Sardoodledom dramatic formula he had loved to ridicule. 'Sardou's plan of play-wrighting,' he had written, 'is first to invent the action of his piece, and then to carefully keep it off the stage and have it announced merely by letters and telegrams.' The Shavian play structure too moved the action off stage, and reversed the relationship between dialogue and incident. Predictably the critics were to complain that *Getting Married* was never a play, simply interminable talk with a minimum of interrupting events. This too had similarities with Shaw's own critical response to Sardou: 'I admire the ingenuity', he had written of *Madame Sans-Gêne*, 'with which Sardou carried out his principle of combining the maximum of expenditure and idle chatter with the minimum of drama.'

Shaw's play progresses by means of a series of conversations: duologues and trios that form and dissolve one into another. It is as if a conventional well-made play were being performed backstage, and we witness the performers discussing its event-plot during the intervals. As Shaw's own simplified summary makes clear, the incidents (though unobtrusive) are plentiful. 'It is the wedding day of the bishop's daughter,' he wrote. 'The situation is expounded in the old stage fashion by that old stage figure the comic greengrocer, hired for the occasion as butler.'

'The fun grows fast and furious as the guests arrive, invited and uninvited, with the most distracting malapropos ity. Two are missing: the bridegroom and the bride. They have each received anonymously a pamphlet entitled "*Do you know what you are going to do? By one who has Done It*," setting forth all the anomalies and injustices and dangers of marriage under the existing British law. They refuse to get up and dress until they have read this inopportune document to the last word. When at last they appear they flatly refuse to face the horrors of the marriage law. Thereupon the whole company plunges into a discussion of marriage, and presently sits as a committee to draw up a form of private contract, as in the later days of ancient Rome, to supersede the legal ceremony. They are utterly unable to agree on a single article of it.'

Though Shaw claimed a classical provenance for his play, it actually represented 'a new dramaturgy' as Eric Bentley wrote, 'and not, as its critics thought, a mere pamphlet in dialogue form'. He had already staged such a disquisitory scene in *Don Juan in Hell*, lodging his philosophy within a comedy of manners that ends in 'Universal Laughter'. *Getting Married* was Shaw's reaction to that dismissive laughter and his revenge on those idealist critics who gave it respectability. The play confers priority on talking over action, and restores potency to the word as the impulse for reform. The marriage itself is postponed and finally entered into with a different understanding as the result of two pamphlets which are shown as having the devastating educational power that all Fabians must have wished for their tracts.

Like *The Doctor's Dilemma*, this new play stages an institution. 'The play is about marriage as an institution and about nothing else.' His method of treating it was one that he had first attempted, and been persuaded to abandon, fifteen years before in the original last act of *The Philanderer*. It had been the celebrated divorcée Lady Colin Campbell who opened Shaw's eyes to 'the fact that I have started on quite a new trail and must reserve this act for the beginning of a new play'. With *Getting Married* Shaw finally started out on a trail that was to include *Misalliance* and lead to *Heartbreak House*. Called initially *Any Just Cause or Impediment?*, this 'conversation' employed all its variety of characters to reinforce a similar argument to that of *The Philanderer*'s rejected last act: the social need to humanize our marriage laws. But *The Philanderer* had been one of Shaw's most directly autobiographical plays; with *Getting Married* he had grown more skilfully oblique.

The origins of several characters and situations are discreetly conveyed. Bill Collins, the elderly greengrocer with the youthful waist, who has a similar role to the waiter in *You Never Can Tell*, gains vitality from Shaw's observations of the greengrocer who became mayor of St Pancras; and the scene in which the whole company sits as a committee ineffectually attempting to draft an English Partnership Deed superseding the legal ceremony of marriage reflects some of Shaw's experiences on the St Pancras Vestry merged with the contract Annie Besant once presented to him over their piano duets.

More complex are the characters of Mrs George Collins and St John Hotchkiss. Mrs George, as she is called, assimilates several people. She is a mayoress, a coal merchant's wife and also 'Incognita Appassionata', the mysterious writer of love letters to the Bishop of Chelsea: altogether 'a wonderful interesting' woman, her brother-in-law the greengrocer tells everyone. This seems to be Shaw's opinion of her too. She was, he later told Mrs Patrick Campbell, 'the most wonderful of all my serio-tragic woman's parts'; an extraordinary creation 'half all-but-low comedy and half mystically tragic: it requires an actress who can combine something like a genius for clowning with a power of touching the highest note of serious drama'. This figure, whom the others believe to be 'too good to be true' until her appearance, is described in Shaw's stage directions at the moment of her entrance as a 'triumphant, pampered, wilful, intensely alive woman . . . Her age, which is certainly 40, and might be 50, is carried off by her vitality, her resilient figure, and her confident carriage . . . But her beauty is wrecked, like an ageless landscape ravaged by long and fierce war. Her eyes are alive, arresting and haunting . . . The whole face is a battle-field of the passions, quite deplorable until she speaks, when an alert sense of fun rejuvenates her in a moment, and makes her company irresistible'.

She is irresistible to Shaw because she represents three women in one. Her age is approximately Charlotte's, and the span of ten years she is given covers the period Shaw had by now been married to Charlotte. Into this framework he then puts the qualities of two other women covered by Mrs Collins's other two names. As 'Incognita Appassionata' she embodies the sexual passion that had been excluded from his marriage. For more than two years Shaw had been receiving a series of extraordinary letters from a girl in her early twenties. Filled by the Shavian ejaculation of words at the Court Theatre, she first poured out her passions in a letter from 'Poste Restante, Godalming', signed 'Miss Charmer'. And Shaw could not resist replying. He replied telling her that such romantic notions were the 'greatest nonsense'; that love was an infinite mystery 'like everything else'; and that she had better 'marry and have children: then you will not ask from works of art what you can get only from life'. The result of this advice was that the girl, who revealed herself as Erica Cotterill, a cousin of Rupert Brooke's and daughter of a respectable Fabian schoolmaster, Charles Clement Cotterill, transferred her infatuation from the plays to the playwright whose unorthodox theories of sexual intercourse outside marriage for the procreation of babies she urgently wanted them to put into practice together. Her repeated letters, rhythmically ecstatic and ill-spelled, challenged Shaw to confront all he had turned his back on: which he obliquely attempts to do by transferring them to Mrs Collins's correspondence with the Bishop.

Then as 'Mrs George' Shaw summons up a third woman: the figure of his mother who appeared in his dreams as 'my wife as well as my mother'. These dreams elevated his affection for Charlotte and intensified his feelings for his mother since, Shaw explained to Gilbert Murray, there was 'the addition of the filial feeling and the redemption of the sexual feeling from "sin" and strain'.

From the strain that his marriage to Charlotte had begun to exert was conceived this magic trinity of Mrs George Collins who in her clairvoyant trance becomes 'the entire female sex crying to the ages from her lips'. In her non-transcendental operations she is either companion, lover or maternal figure: but never all three simultaneously, as her renewed relationship with St John Hotchkiss makes clear.

Shaw's practice of obscuring the self-portraits of his plays by giving the characters a superficial resemblance to other people – Marchbanks to De Quincey, Tanner to H. M. Hyndman, Professor Higgins to Henry Sweet – extends to St John Hotchkiss who is ostensibly modelled on his fellow playwright St John Hankin. But when the 'St John' falls away and he confesses to Mrs George that 'my own pet name in the bosom of my family is Sonny' the pretence becomes transparent. In Hotchkiss we may see something of the reaction that Shaw produced on his contemporaries: 'He talks about himself with energetic gaiety. He talks to other people with a sweet forbearance (implying a kindly consideration for their stupidity) which infuriates those whom he does not succeed in amusing.'

When Hotchkiss meets Mrs George on stage he recognizes her as the coal merchant's wife with whom ('when I was a young fool') he had fallen in love. 'I felt in her presence an extraordinary sensation of unrest, of emotion, of unsatisfied need,' he remembers. It is not fanciful to feel in this 'unsatisfied need' Shaw's own emotional response to his mother when in Dublin. What he depicts is not so much lust as worship: 'A hideous temptation to kiss the doorstep because her foot had pressed it . . . ' In *Getting Married* Shaw makes Hotchkiss run away abroad in place of his mother leaving for England. And now that they meet again, Hotchkiss again falls in love, becomes detached from the elderly Bridgenorth's young wife Leo (whom he persuades to return to her husband), and settles for a platonic union with Mrs George in her matrimonial home. The relationship is essentially that of an adopted son. 'I want to talk to him like a mother,' says Mrs George who tells Hotchkiss that 'Sonny is just the name I wanted for you.' And Hotchkiss exclaims: 'Oh, if only I didnt selfishly want to obey you!'

So Shaw provides another scenario for the Dublin *ménage à trois*, now that his mother, merged with the figure of Charlotte, has returned to him in his dreams. But there is a difference arising from his own experience of marriage. Charlotte had accepted a sexless marriage, and Shaw agreed. In *Getting Married* Mrs George also demands 'a friend', not a lover: and Hotchkiss assures her that she has 'nothing to fear' since sexual involvement with a married woman, like theft, would be contrary to his moral code. But Mrs George's reply is disconcerting. If she has nothing to fear, what has she to hope? 'Like most men, you think you know everything a woman wants, dont you?' she says. 'But the thing one wants most has nothing to do with marriage at all.'

Shaw's sense of the incompleteness of his marriage pervades this play. It was an incompleteness for which Charlotte was to compensate with mystical hoverings comparable to Mrs George's Blakean 'inspirations';

and from which Shaw escaped in work, dreams and plays. That need to escape in fantasy, and the impossibility of doing so in fact, is conveyed at the beginning of the play when, in answer to Mrs Bridgenorth's 'Did you ever feel inclined to run away, Collins?' the greengrocer replies:

'Oh yes maam, yes: very often. But when it came to the point I couldnt bear to hurt her feelings. She's a sensitive, affectionate, anxious soul; and she was never brought up to know what freedom is to some people. You see, family life is all she knows: she's like a bird born in a cage, that would die if you let it loose in the woods. When I thought how little it was to a man of my easy temper to put up with her, and how deep it would hurt her to think it was because I didnt care for her, I always put off running away til next time; and so in the end I never ran away at all. I daresay it was good for me to be took such care of; but it cut me off from all my old friends something dreadful, maam: especially the women, maam. She never gave them a chance . . . She never understood that married people should take holidays from one another if they are to keep at all fresh. Not that I ever got tired of her, maam; but my! how I used to get tired of home life sometimes. I used to catch myself envying my brother George.'

Shaw edges fact a little closer to fantasy by recommending, through the person of the Bishop, that we 'make divorce reasonable and decent'. It is the Bishop, too, whom we hear musing on 'who will begin the stand against marriage. It must come some day'. Shaw gives himself the Bishop's authority for beginning this stand and warning 'our Governments so earnestly that unless the law of marriage were first made human, it could never become divine'. Out of his own isolation, Shaw insists through the voice of the celibate chaplain, Oliver Cromwell Soames, the dryest most aloof character in the play, that 'We are members of one another'. From the abnormality of his own marriage he argues with the tolerant voice of Collins that 'theres almost as many different sorts of marriages as theres different sorts of people'.

The cast of characters has been assembled to illustrate this observation. At one level they are the stereotypes of the Victorian theatre: crusty old general, thundering priest, dashing philanderer and so on. But there is another level where they are shown, wearing their official costumes, as representatives of the Church, the Army, the Landed Gentry and the Municipality. Finally Shaw removes their masks as stage characters and sociological types, to reveal them as ourselves and the people we know. He wants to show us the varieties of human nature that must share the earth. The individual temperaments range from romantic and classical enemies of marriage (Hotchkiss and Soames) to the personification of domesticity

(Mrs Bridgenorth); from the woman who loves children but not men (Lesbia Grantham) to the woman who wants lovers but does not seem interested in babies (Leo). From the interweaving of all these public and private voices Shaw conducts his symposium: a surrealist seminar which arrives at the conclusion that marriage as a legal institution 'doesn't bear thinking about', but must be redeemed as part of the general transformation of our society.

*

'It will improve by keeping,' Shaw had told Granville Barker. But Vedrenne needed a new play and Shaw was persuaded to place the action of *Getting Married* on 12 May 1908, the day of its first performance at the Haymarket. He was not confident that the critics would grasp his purpose (it 'is really a sermon on Equality') or that his new disquisitory methods were valid. Five days before the opening he published in the *Daily Telegraph* the most extreme of his self-drafted interviews, attempting to neutralize criticism and appeal beyond the professional critics to the public. 'There will be nothing but talk, talk, talk, talk, talk – Shaw talk,' he promised. 'The characters will seem to the wretched critics to be simply a row of Shaws, all arguing with one another on totally uninteresting subjects.

'Shaw in a bishop's apron will argue with Shaw in a general's uniform. Shaw in an alderman's gown will argue with Shaw dressed as a beadle. Shaw dressed as a bridegroom will be wedded to Shaw in petticoats. The whole thing will be hideous, indescribable – an eternity of brain-racking dulness. And yet they will have to sit it out . . . they will suffer – suffer horribly, inhumanly . . . I am not a vindictive man . . . We shall not be altogether merciless. The curtains will be dropped casually from time to time to allow of first-aid to the really bad cases in the seats allotted to the Press.'

Getting Married was greeted with what Shaw called a 'torrent of denunciation'. H. Hamilton Fyfe on *The World* insisted that he had 'degenerated into dullness for the very simple reason that he is so tremendously in earnest'. Other more sympathetic critics were also nonplussed. Max Beerbohm believed that *Getting Married* 'has been over-rated by its maker', because Shaw had been too fearful of doing the very thing he proclaimed himself of being afraid of doing: 'that is, of boring us'.

'Usually, his fun and his seriousness are inextricable one from another: you cannot see where one begins and the other ends. In "Getting

Married" the fun does not seem integral: it seems to have been foisted in, for fear lest we should fidget.'

Desmond MacCarthy was also to question how we could take seriously characters who are presented to us merely as knockabout figures of farce: why should we be attentive to their opinions or moved by the absurdity of their passions? The 'scenes between Hotchkiss and Mrs George seem to me deplorable', MacCarthy was to write; 'too funny to be serious, and too serious to be funny'. Lord Alfred Douglas, under the heading 'For Shame, Mr Shaw' in *The Academy*, called for the censor to put a stop to such insidiously feminine work making 'serious inroads on the British home'. Shaw continued to bait and tease: challenging anyone to name a play that was not all talk, and enquiring whether they had expected ballet. 'I prophesied exactly what the critics would say,' he confirmed; 'and it is greatly to their credit under the circumstances that they were honest enough to say it instead of pretending to be cleverer than they really are.' Audiences, he testified, had grown genuinely involved in the dramatic argument – 'the audience simply hung on every word of the contract scene and were furious when it was interrupted by the beadle,' he reported to Vedrenne after seeing the play again ten days after its opening. 'The cast finds out more every time of what it is all about; and so, consequently, does the audience. It just wants to be made an hour longer and played every day for the next ten years, like Madame Tussaud's . . . to nurse it into a full grown institution.'

As this reference to Madame Tussaud's (which he had also used for Sardou's Napoleon play) may indicate, Shaw was fundamentally uncertain about *Getting Married*. Was it a dead thing? Or had he created, in the movements of his argument, a new category of stage music? The doubts expressed by some critics touched his own doubts. 'Poor people!' exclaims the Bishop. 'It's so hard to know the right place to laugh, isnt it?' Max Beerbohm and Desmond MacCarthy judged that he had orchestrated the laughter in the wrong place. And J. T. Grein believed that the play traded on Shaw's peculiar weakness: 'His loquacity is literally torrential,' Grein complained, ' . . . the hearer's mind is taxed to over-straining.' Shaw had bargained for this, yet in the play itself he makes Reginald Bridgenorth impatiently exclaim: 'It's no good talking all over the shop like this. We shall be here all day.' In a work aiming to preserve all the unities of time and place, this spasm of impatience articulated a genuine qualm which he was happy to submerge beneath the sound of battle with the critics. At the Haymarket, *Getting Married* was a success on a modest highbrow scale: and this 'has been a tremendous victory over the press'.

I am a slave of that car and of you too. I dream of the accursed thing
at night.
Man and Superman

'I shall take to motoring presently,' Shaw threatened in the summer of
1908. He had already studied at the National Motor Academy and
prepared himself with lessons from a professor of driving, H. E. M.
Studdy, from whom Charlotte was also able to take tuition. Additionally
they had made several chancey experiments on the Continent; while in
London Higgs received instruction at the Royal Automobile Club. By the
end of 1908 the household at Ayot St Lawrence stood ready to receive the
Shaws' first automobile, a 28-30 horsepower Lorraine-Dietrich. 'It is a
double cabriolet, with detachable hind part,' reported *The Autocar*.
' . . . The lines of the car are uncommon and graceful.' They became a
little more uncommon after the first day when Charlotte, attended by Mr
Studdy, crushed it mildly into a local obstruction, scattering the
splashboards and other impedimenta; and Mr Studdy, accompanied by
Charlotte, knocked off the paddle-box against the gate on their way back.

Charlotte's career as motorist was brief. Higgs, too, was much happier
with plants and vegetables. And Shaw himself was rather too fond of
reading in the car. So a trained chauffeur, Albert James Kilsby from
Notting Hill, was employed. As a technically qualified motor engineer,
Kilsby's expert opinion that the De Dietrich was 'a proper bugger' to start
was obviously of value. But the car was also, Shaw reckoned, awkward to
stop, the accelerator pedal being placed on the left with the brake to the
right of it. He kept this car for fifteen years and never lost the habit of
treading on the right pedal to arrest a vehicle.

Kilsby was the chauffeur and Shaw drove. Charlotte, who sat in the
back seat, campaigned for Kilsby and the two men, dividing the
fun-and-labour of it, would swap driver and passenger positions fairly
evenly. 'I'm not a pioneer motorist but I used to drive quite a lot,' Shaw
admitted to *The Motor* in an article entitled 'They Shouldn't Allow Me to
Drive'. Had he been a pioneer, the motorcar (like the airship) might have
been jettisoned. After three weeks, it was reported that he was seriously
disabled. 'Say I'm dead', he cabled the *Daily Mail*. He was extraordinarily
reckless – though always chivalrous to the injured and the alarmed,
especially when the fault was theirs. He was also shockingly Bohemian at
the wheel, sometimes (when Charlotte was not travelling) giving lifts to

tramps, and presenting them with money. He could credit these expeditions as research trips for scholarly contributions to the *Automobile Engineer*, *The Car* and the *Royal Automobile Club Journal*. The De Dietrich was a car for all seasons and subjects: a philosophical vehicle. He reported on its capacity to penetrate Swiss avalanches and its place in the future of Ireland; on its moral claims versus the road dog, its tax-generating properties, and the lessons it gave (such as 'How to Narrow a Road by Widening It') in Shavian engineering. Of the detachable wheels, movable hood and electric klaxon horn, its cork and brass, the invisible locks and variable speed dynamo, Shaw grew academically fond. For a man entering his mid-fifties this was a more appropriate contraption than the bicycle. Also: 'Since I have taken to motoring my loathing of railway journeys has become unbounded,' he told Beatrice Webb. He still used the train for long political journeys – electioneering for Keir Hardie in Merthyr Tydfil, lecturing on socialism at Edinburgh and Glasgow or attending the Labour Conference at Southsea. But for serious holiday-making its humorous potential made it an essential item of equipment.

They took it first to Algeria and Tunisia for five spring weeks: Kilsby and Shaw jostled up front; Charlotte and her sister Mrs Cholmondeley occupied the back. Among the luggage they had room for the Koran, but no spare parts. 'Now I come to think of it, it's a wonder we got anywhere,' Shaw remarked. ' . . . If we'd broken down in the desert we'd probably be there still.'

Charlotte and Shaw employed the car differently. Charlotte viewed it as a machine for pressing on from one hotel to the next; Shaw as an instrument to prevent himself succumbing to fits of fury at this frightful waste of working time. 'It is a demoralizing country,' he noticed in the depths of the Algerian desert. 'I am shockingly off any work but driving.' At Biskra he rode for two hours on a camel and 'my seat on this most difficult of mounts was admitted to be superb'. Next day however he was stiffly back in the driver's seat and, careering a hundred miles north into Constantine, achieved a dramatic change of climate (something inconceivable on a camel). 'At Biskra, exquisite soft heat and southern airs: here, a cold as of liquid air evaporating on the skin; rain in colossal blobs instead of drops; and a wind against which I had to hold the car straight by main force.' Kilsby's time was much filled with repairing burst tyres and then veering melodramatically away from wonderful seas with coasts and headland, from fresh meadows, trees, islands rising out of mirror waters and other mirages in which he could not bring himself to disbelieve.

Shaw suspected Charlotte. He suspected her of turning on a sore throat at any place she liked so as to justify a longer pause there. He would then use the motor for risky dashes into the desert, the clean emptiness of which calmed him after the crowded sanitary arrangements of some hotels. 'We are in a frightful place: I cannot bear to go to bed,' he cried out from La Calle. ' . . . Indescribable. I really cant go on . . . I slept, shuddering, in my motor coat & gloves, fully dressed, and rose at daybreak to bathe in the Mediterranean.' Occasionally they motored up to some pleasant experience – a deep stone tank of blazing water, for example, 'produced gratuitously by the internal fires of the globe', at Hamman-Meskontine in which Shaw floated at evening until the liquid turned into pure 'G. B. essence, and I came out a mere bone smelling powerfully of sulphur'; or at El Hanel, a cup of coffee with the Marahout who deeply regretted through his interpreter that the custodian with the key to his wives was away.

For the summers of 1909 and 1910 they escorted the car on holidays to Ireland, parking it at an extraordinary gabled and turreted hotel, the Great Southern, by the woods of Parknasilla on the Kerry coast. Shaw liked Parknasilla. It was a place of long sea views and intricate walks between ferns and fuchsias, rock and rhododendron, to burnt-out castles lost within the woods, and along the various fingers of land that pointed south-west into the warm Atlantic. Sometimes they would try out the Irish roads with an expedition to Lady Gregory at Coole (where Shaw collected a stupendous migraine) or, on Shaw's fifty-fourth birthday, an exploration of the Giant's Causeway where 'I sat under my umbrella in my aquascutum, like a putrid mushroom,' he told Barker, 'whilst a drenched mariner rowed me round the cliffs and told me lies about them'. Further out to sea – and leaving the car on the coast – he was rowed by ten men in an open boat for a couple of hours and landed on the legendary Skelligs: 'the most fantastic and impossible rock in the world,' he described it. ' . . . at the top amazing beehives of flat rubble stones, each overlapping the one below until the circles meet in a dome – cells, oratories, churches, and outside them cemeteries, wells, crosses, all clustering like shells on a prodigious rock pinnacle, with precipices sheer down on every hand, and, lodged on the projecting stones overhanging the deep, huge stone coffins made apparently by giants, and dropped there, God knows how. An incredible, impossible mad place . . . '

Upon this Gothic cathedral of the sea, so odd and isolated, the man who generally seemed a stranger on our planet felt at home. Standing in the graveyards at the Skellig summit, above the caverns and arches, spire and pinnacles, he recalled the summers of his early years when Sonny roamed over the rocks and goat-paths of Dalkey, and gazed across the blue waters to Howth Head; or had lain on the grassy top of the hill above the bay –

then raced down to the shore known as White Rock and plunged into the waves. Sonny had been a product of Dalkey's outlook: there was little place for him in the bustling world where G.B.S. moved. Exiled to a thin atmosphere of fantasy, he breathed again in the magic climate of this island, surrounded by its endless seas and skies. 'I tell you the thing does not belong to any world that you and I have ever lived and worked in,' Shaw wrote next day to Frederick Jackson, a political journalist and solicitor: 'it is part of our dream world'.

From his dreams they rowed him back in the dark, without a compass, the moon invisible in the mists: two and a half Atlantic hours. Then he drove to Parknasilla, to Charlotte, and the world he lived and worked in.

During April 1910, in more orthodox style, the car had taken them for a spin in France. It was an interesting test of men, women, roads, and the hotels on which Shaw had undertaken to give reports to the Royal Automobile Club. In the first five and a half days they whizzed along six hundred and sixty miles, going for all they were worth through snow and wind – and this despite Shaw's view that, owing to the lethally-cambered roads, it was unsafe to pass anything without first slowing to a halt. But he seemed determined to prove the optimist. 'I am already twice the man I was when I left,' he reported to Barker. Though accompanied by her sister, Charlotte felt less cheery. 'I am all right,' she told Barker, 'but G.B.S. does not allow us one moment of peace – we are *harried* from place to place!'

From their series of cards Barker could feel a tense struggle developing between Shaw's unyielding gaiety and Charlotte's protesting illnesses. 'I drive half the day,' Shaw exulted; 'lie deliciously awake half the night; and am visibly waning towards my grave.' At each shattering explosion of the exhaust, each driving snowstorm, and other upsets such as buffeting into big stones, his spirits soared. At lunch he actually seemed to egg Kilsby on to drink the *vin compris* so that their progress immediately afterwards would be more exciting. His plan appears to have been the desperate one of curing Charlotte for ever of their compulsory holiday-making. At Aix she decided to abandon the car, taking her sister by train to Toulouse, where Shaw and Kilsby caught breathlessly up with them. 'We are all exhausted and demoralized,' Shaw was able to tell Barker by the end of the month. 'Charlotte positively loathes me, and is, as usual pathetically unable to dissimulate.'

'Mrs Chumly keeps in good humor and even in good spirits, in spite of asthma, sore throat, and a bad cold in the head. Even Kilsby, sleeping in damp sheets every night, is off color. Every morning I feel as if I had had a drunken debauch the night before; but when I get up and out, my energy returns; and I drive off and dash into churches and round the towns as if I really had something at stake in them from the mere habit of energy. Another month of it and I should drop dead in the middle of some such burst of false activity.'

Back in England, Charlotte diverted some of her loathing from her husband to his car. Their next holiday abroad was to be, not yet apart, but separated from Kilsby and his roving machine. As for Shaw, he had concluded that, since motoring in France was rather like driving along the roof of St Pancras Station, 'there is something to be said for the Hertfordshire lanes after all'.

[5]

People like to back a winner ... However, nothing succeeds like failure ... Even nonsense is sometimes suggestive.

During these years before the Great War, Shaw became a familiar feature of the Hertfordshire lanes. 'The villagers all thought he was a rum one – a *very* rum one,' remembered his neighbour Mrs Reeves. Sitting bolt upright in his car, he would career very fast (over 20 miles per hour) through the village, leaving behind him a wake of grumbling. But Edith Reeves never heard of him knocking anyone down. Living so near, she had got to know the Shaws better than had the other villagers. They would put the mown grass from their extensive lawn over the wall as fodder for the Reeves's cows and livestock, and give them cabbages and other vegetables from the garden. In retaliation, Mr Reeves sold the Shaws raspberries and White Hart cherries. Though Shaw paid for these, he would never accept anything for the vegetables. 'I think his view was that fruit and vegetable growing was part of our business as farmers,' Mrs Reeves speculated, 'but only a hobby with him.'

Mr and Mrs Reeves named one of their sons Bernard. Shaw and Charlotte were obviously fond of children and took great interest in the small Reeveses. During Mrs Reeves's confinements, while Mr Reeves was out with his sandwiches working in the fields, they would send cooked meals in to her – not vegetarian spreads, but chicken or fish with fresh vegetables from their garden. Charlotte confided once that she would have liked children of her own: and Mrs Reeves was given to understand that it was on account of her asthma that she had none. Shaw 'didn't want her to have the hurt of it. Child-bearing was much more painful half a century ago ...'

His fondness for animals too was notorious. Mr and Mrs Reeves would feel quite uncomfortable loading their squealing pigs into the cart for market – though Shaw never said anything. He had a pigeon-cote and several hives of bees in the garden; and there was an erratic little white dog, Kim, which would streak in and out of the house, sometimes barking, sometimes rolling on its back, sometimes being fed tit-bits by Mrs Higgs who, to Shaw's dismay, encouraged it to beg at table. But Kim didn't 'belong' to Shaw who never bought a dog, though 'I always own a dog in the country'. He was glad there had been a dog in his home in Dublin since this put him on easy terms with what was often a pleasant extension of human society. 'I have no lies to tell about dogs,' he declared. Simply, he had a fellow feeling for them, as well as for cats: any species of animal in fact. He did not claim to like all dogs and cats any more than he liked all humans.

The Shaws were good neighbours but they minded their business; and, since they were often away, the villagers regarded them as 'characters' rather than native people. They attached little importance to Shaw's literary fame.

*

This fame, though it stopped short at Ayot, had been spreading round the world with the publication of several books about him. The first, appearing in 1905, had been by the American critic H. L. Mencken who aimed to bring all Shaw's commentators on to common ground. After this, the commentators began to multiply and the common ground grew thickly crowded. From America and Britain, Finland, France, Germany and Holland they made their entrance, eighteen of these critical and biographical volumes appearing before the war. The most brilliant of them was written by G. K. Chesterton; the most persistent of his biographers was Archibald Henderson.

Henderson was twenty-five and an Instructor in Mathematics at the University of North Carolina when, early in 1903, he had been 'electrified' by a performance of *You Never Can Tell* in Chicago. Between his mathematics and his marriage, he spent the next year studying Shaw's writings. He then sent Shaw a letter threatening to write his life: 'it never occurred to me,' he admitted, 'that perhaps I was wholly unfitted for the job.' Shaw stayed calm. He added Henderson's name to an extensive card index marked 'Disciples' and sent back a postcard commanding him to 'send me your photograph!' Henderson put himself to a good deal of bother over this, all of which amounted to placing himself in line for a kindly Shavian joke: 'You look like the man who can do the job.'

Having had his photograph ('my counterfeit presentment' as he called it) taken, Henderson noted, 'I began making notes'. And for the next fifty years he continued making notes that Shaw himself orchestrated into a semi-Shavian melody: the left hand turgid, the right hand fantastical. Henderson's first book on Shaw (*His Life and Works*) appeared in 1911. By 1932, in his blockbuster *Playboy and Prophet*, he reported having published 'the eighth book of mine devoted, in part or in whole, to interpretation of your life, character and significance'. Shaw had rashly remarked that his biography should be a posthumous work for them both. It almost was. Henderson reached his apotheosis six years after Shaw's death and seven years before his own in *Man of the Century*, when the century still had forty-four declining years to run. Of Henderson it may literally be said that no man could have done more. But the question remains: why had G.B.S. encouraged him to do so much?

Shaw had been amused by the notion of his biography being written innumerable times by an American mathematician. But within this joke there was a serious point. During a period of increasing specialization, he wanted discipline to speak unto discipline, and culture to culture. He also believed that he could manipulate his own egotism through Henderson to reasonably unegotistical ends. 'I want you to do something that will be useful to yourself and to the world,' he told him initially 'and that is, to make me a mere peg on which to hang a study of the last quarter of the XIX century.'

But Shaw also wanted to make use of his biographer to recreate the life of G.B.S., replacing the isolated person who had presided over the death of Sonny and felt out of touch with the world he wished to influence, by a representative figure 'who is up to the chin in the life of his own times'. His help to Henderson was invaluable and sincerely grounded in the belief that 'the best authority on Shaw is Shaw'. In his fashion G.B.S. was a truth-teller; but the fashion was complicated and far from literal. It needed ingenious interpretation and independent checking – and neither temperamentally nor geographically was Henderson positioned to supply these. He was a 'disciple' rather than a scholar, who manufactured what Shaw himself was to call 'a colossally expanded extract from Who's Who', and then went on manufacturing it. The surviving galley proofs of *Playboy and Prophet* reveal how large a part of this narrative was actually drafted in the third person by G.B.S. himself. He did not do this for facile self-aggrandizement, but to provide his ideas with the endorsement of biographical authority. If his childhood had been 'rich only in dreams, frightful & loveless in realities' this was because the social and economic conditions of those times were frightful. By leaving the twilight of Ireland,

Shaw believed he had turned his back on dreams and set out through the body of his literary and political work in England to make the realities of his times less frightful. And yet it might be possible for a biographer, by charting his thought as a fantastical development of those early dreams, in which economic argument now displaced emotional need, to question the moral and political legitimacy of his writings. Shaw feared that if his instincts, like a compass, were represented as having been eccentrically affected by his early experiences, then his thinking itself might be seen to be adrift. He used biography therefore as adjustments to the rudder, keeping his work in the mainstream. From these secret collaborations he learned how to ghost his own life through later biographers, from Frank Harris to Hesketh Pearson. So he became the very author of himself, though in a way that might ultimately not be in his best interests.

'You are threatened with more than one competitor,' Shaw had written to Henderson in 1907. The chief competitor seemed to be G. K. Chesterton whose book, Shaw promised, 'will not contain any facts; but it will be exceedingly interesting'. Shaw completed the comic circle by reviewing the book in the *Nation* and describing it as 'the best work of literary art I have yet provoked'. This compliment was not all it appeared to be. Shaw separated art from information rather as he divided feeling from thought. Henderson had the information; Chesterton was the literary artist: one book complemented the other – though neither book intensified its perception of truth through a fusion of form and content. But Shaw felt apprehensive of that. He was reasonably happy with Chesterton's *Shaw* because, despite its title and its being 'very fine indeed', it 'has little to do with me'. 'My last word must be,' Shaw concluded, 'that gifted as he is, he [Chesterton] needs a sane Irishman to look after him.' In other words, Chesterton needed Shaw to write the book for him. Reviewing it was the next best thing.

While encumbering another biographer, St John Ervine, with advice, Shaw was to write: 'I have found that if I invent all my facts on a basis of my knowledge of human nature I always come out right, whereas if I refer to documents and authorities they weary me and set me wrong. Trust to your genius rather than to your industry: it is the less fallible of the two.' This is precisely what Chesterton did – and what Shaw complained of his having done. He represented Chesterton's commentary as a flapping washing-line on which hung all manner of crucified shirts and dancing trousers. But take down these waving garments, measure them quietly against G.B.S., and you would find that none of them nearly fitted him. Indeed, some more nearly fitted G.K.C. For biographers, like portrait painters and sculptors, 'put something of themselves into their subjects and sitters when there is anything of themselves to put in', Shaw explained to T. E. Lawrence. There was so much of the corpulent beer-drinking G.K.C. to put into his short volume, he implied, as to leave little room for the slim teetotal G.B.S.

'The truth is I have a horror of biographers,' Shaw admitted to Frank Harris. He felt almost as apprehensive of Chesterton's inspiration as he would of St John Ervine's industry and Harris's inventions: of any factor that shed light on some independent truth not absorbed in the Shavian dream-reality. Chesterton had loaded his gun with guesses, but from time to time his aim was true. In his review, Shaw gave a wonderfully clownish performance, trying on all the conjectures that were 'madly wrong'. On others he turned his back, leaving them strung out along the line of Chesterton's impressions:

'quick-witted [and] . . . long-winded . . . the very forest of the man's thoughts chokes up his thoroughfare . . . if there is anything that Shaw is not, it is irresponsible. The responsibility in him rings like steel . . . a kind of intellectual chastity, and the fighting spirit . . . he is not rooted in the ancient sagacities of infancy . . . Shaw is like Swift . . . in combining extravagant fancy with a curious sort of coldness . . . benevolent bullying, a pity touched with contempt . . . sincere, unsympathetic, aggressive, alone . . . He never gives his opinions a holiday . . . he never said a thing that he was not prepared brilliantly to defend . . . There was in this thirst to be "progressive" a subtle sort of double-mindedness and falsity . . . Socialism is the noblest thing for Bernard Shaw; and it is the noblest thing in him . . . he cares more for the Public Thing than for any private thing . . . This is the greatest thing in Shaw, a serious optimism – even a tragic optimism . . . '

Shaw recognized in Chesterton, as he had in Wells, a quality absent in himself. Wells, who claimed to 'have got Great Britain Pregnant', had the power of sexual attraction; Chesterton, as champion of the common people against intellectuals and politicians, could magically elicit affection. People adored him for his wit and extravagance, his whacking style.

He was eighteen years younger than Shaw, had been an early member of the Fabian Society, but had resigned at the time of the Boer War. The Fabians were a society, he later said, with 'webbed feet', and incapable of the spontaneous activity in which he exulted. But he needed some external discipline to obliterate the cloud that enveloped his spirit with violent images. His creation of the jolly toby-jug Chesterton had similarities with Shaw's invention of the pantomime ostrich. These cheery images displaced for both what Chesterton called 'the morbid life of the lonely

17 Shaw, Hilaire Belloc and G. K. Chesterton after one of their public debates

18A Shaw and H. G. Wells; B Window ordered by Shaw in 1910. He is depicted remoulding the world, Wells thumbing his nose at his elders.

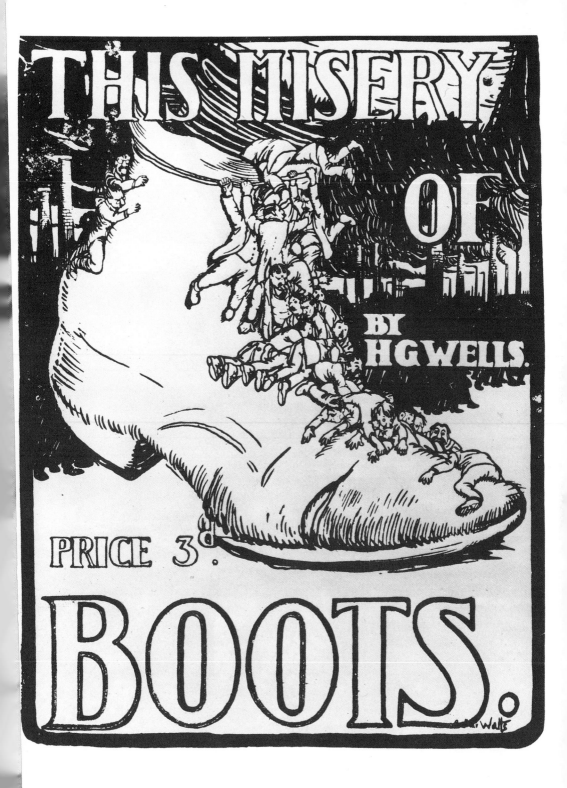

19 H. G. Wells's first pamphlet for the Fabian Society, 1905

24 *Major Barbara*, New York, 1915

mind'. For religious authority Chesterton had turned to the isolated institutionalism of Hilaire Belloc. Shaw schemed to lock up this fabulous Chesterbelloc in his own Shawchest, and release the energies of the Shavianized Chesterton for employment by the Life Force.

Conceiving it as his duty to help Chesterton do his appointed work, Shaw developed a proprietary interest in him. He wrote cautionary reviews of his work, sent him the scenario of a play he wanted him to write (offering financial arrangements to support it), and eventually squeezed him into 'A Glimpse of the Domesticity of Franklyn Barnabas', a discarded segment of *Back to Methuselah*. Here, Chesterton is caricatured as Immenso Champernoon, 'a man of colossal mould, with the head of a cherub on the body of a Falstaff ... friendly, a little shy, and jokes frequently enough to be almost always either still enjoying the last or already anticipating the next'. The Shavian woman, Mrs Etteen, speaks Shaw's mind when she accuses him of being the worst flirt in England. 'You flirt with religions, with traditions, with politics, with everything that is most sacred and important,' she tells him. 'You flirt with the Church, with the Middle Ages, with the marriage question, with the Jewish question, even with the hideous cult of gluttony and drunkenness ... you are not a bit in earnest ... '

Shaw thought of Chesterton as immature, the real Peter Pan of those days, and a marvellous boy who never grew up. He was a political innocent too – when asked what he would do if he were made Prime Minister, he replied: 'Resign at once.' To Shaw this was a gigantic waste. By a prodigious sort of journalism and sheer literary force, Chesterton had taken the position created in the eighteenth century by Dr Johnson. In short: he was 'the greatest publicist we possess'. For over a quarter of a century, in newspapers and on debating platforms, Shaw struggled to convert him to socialism and creative evolution.

Their debates began in 1911. On 29 May Shaw addressed the Heretics Society on 'The Religion of the Future'. The Victoria Assembly Rooms at Cambridge were packed with an excited crowd when Shaw appeared there 'gloriously irreverent, transparently sincere, divinely prophetic'. He told his audience that superstitious religion had died in the Middle Ages, though it was artificially kept in existence by the stimulants of idolatry and intimidation. The English, he declared, had no fundamental religion: they simply made idols of people who were capable of giving orders and resorted to the stage management of them. Such people were given crowns, or gold lace on their collars, a certain kind of hat, a different income and a particular kind of house to live in. Their sons and daughters could not marry common people: and we pretended to believe that they were agents of a loftier idol. But in our democratic age we were gradually getting rid of idols. There was now a need to replace them with religions that were practical systems. 'As for my own position, I am, and always have been, a mystic,' Shaw announced. 'I believe that the universe is being driven by a force that we might call the life-force. I see it as performing the miracle of creation, that it has got into the minds of men as what they call their will . . . '

'We are all experiments in the direction of making God. What God is doing is making himself, getting from being a mere powerless will or force. This force has implanted into our minds the ideal of God. We are not very successful attempts at God so far, but I believe that if we can drive into the heads of men the full consciousness of moral responsibility that comes to men with the knowledge that there never will be a God unless we make one – that we are the instruments through which that ideal is trying to make itself a reality – we can work towards that ideal . . . '

'The Religion of the Future' was one of a series of heterodox sermons Shaw had started to give after the writing of *Major Barbara*. He preached the gospel of Creative Evolution as a complement to his socialism. He spoke to the Progressive League, the Guild of St Matthew and the New Reform Club; to Ethical Institutes and literary groups, to Medico-Legal and Coal Smoke Abatement societies, to Quakers, Secularists, Christians: anyone who would come and listen to this 'Unofficial Bishop of Everywhere'. As one commentator observed, he sounded 'disarmingly orthodox and shockingly radical at the same time'. His new theology redefined the terms and vocabulary of Christianity. God was impersonally reshaped into the Life Force; the Trinity was interpreted as 'You are the father of your son and the son of your father'; and the Immaculate Conception made an everyday happening: 'I believe in the Immaculate Conception of Jesus's mother, and I believe in the Immaculate Conception of your mother.'

The effect of Shaw's addresses on the public was extraordinary. They sat appalled, in pain, squirming and twisting in their seats, 'fascinated by his quite terrifying earnestness and by the merciless vigour of his attack,' wrote a reporter on the *Christian Commonwealth*. ' . . . the sight of his tall, tense figure in the pulpit, electrical in its suggestion of vital energy completely under the control of his will . . . compelled a similar intensity of interest and attention from his hearers . . . Several times I looked round upon my fellow-auditors to mark the effect of his words. I saw consternated faces, hostile faces, faces which bore an expression of alarm and even horror . . . '

216

Many who heard him were convinced that here was the finest public speaker in England. In debate, when his voice was so fresh, so pleasant, so confiding, there seemed no one who could match him. His certainty was annihilating. During the question-and-answer session at Cambridge, he disclaimed any desire for immortality either for himself or for his wife whose presence in the audience, he added, called for restrained language on the topic. People laughed, but wondered at such perversity. He was admired, especially by the young; but he was not liked, he was not loved. And his intellectual authority on the platform provoked extreme reactions from the press. The *Daily Express* reported his Cambridge address under the headline 'Christ a Failure'; *The Fortnightly Review* objected to its 'unwarrantable assault upon some of the loftiest and noblest spirits of our time'; and *The Academy*, which described the lecture as a 'Detestable Outrage ... vile and blasphemous ravings', protested against this 'dissemination of poisonous theories amongst young persons' and regretted that Shaw had not been 'kicked out of the window, or ... thrown into the Cam'.

When they invited Chesterton to reply to 'The Religion of the Future' with a speech entitled 'Orthodoxy', the Heretics at last found a Christian champion capable of standing up to Shaw. Chesterton delivered his reply on 17 November at the Guildhall, Cambridge, and the first thing he did was to defend his adversary from newspaper attacks. *The Academy* report had been 'not merely written by an idiot but by an idiot who had no belief in the Christian religion', he pronounced. ' ... How could Mr Shaw blaspheme by saying that Christ or the Christian religion had failed in England when the remark is obviously true.'

'I happen to believe myself that Christianity is the true religion but I do not believe for one moment any more than Mr Shaw that England is a Christian country ... the majority of the governing classes believe in no religion. I have known many editors and newspaper proprietors but I have yet to meet one who believed in religion ... Mr Shaw is living in a comparatively Pagan world. He is something of a Pagan himself and like many other Pagans, he is a very fine man.'

These words were characteristic of the intellectual magnanimity existing between Chesterton and Shaw. Each attacked the other's opinions but neither wished to wound. 'I enjoyed him and admired him keenly,' Shaw was to write of Chesterton in the late 1930s; 'and nothing could have been more generous than his treatment of me.' And at about the same time Chesterton was saluting Shaw in his autobiography. 'It is not easy to dispute violently with a man for twenty years, about sex, about sin, about sacraments, about personal points of honour, about all the most sacred or delicate essentials of existence . . . I have never read a reply by Bernard Shaw that did not leave me in a better and not a worse temper or frame of mind; which did not seem to come out of inexhaustible fountains of fair-mindedness and intellectual geniality; which did not savour somehow of that native largeness which the philosopher attributed to the Magnanimous Man.'

Shaw needed this atmosphere of fair-mindedness and geniality to disperse the apprehensions of his audiences, and reduce the hostility of the press. He rejoiced in the tone of Chesterton's reply at Cambridge and having made an appointment to lunch with him shortly afterwards, arranged the first of their debates at the Memorial Hall in London on 30 November. It turned out to be a contest between Shaw's socialism and Chesterton's distributism, of equality of income against peasant proprietorship. Shaw defined socialism as 'that state of society in which the income of a country would be divided exactly equally amongst all the people of that country, without reference to age, sex or character'. Chesterton warned against the totalitarianism and nationalization within socialism. 'The existing system is proletarian. Large masses of men depend upon wages doled out to them by somebody else,' he said. 'The whole Socialist theory is proletarian. I do not care whether the man who deals out the money is called Lord So-and-so, and is the employer and head of the great soap works, or whether he is . . . called the Social Administrator in the name of the State of the same soap works.'

'You cannot draw the line across things and say, You shall have your garden hose, but not your garden; your ploughshare, but not your field; your fishing rod, but not your stream; because man is so made that his sense of property is actually stronger for such things as fields or gardens or water than for such comparatively unnecessary things as garden hose or rakes or fishing rods . . . if you want self-government apart from good government you must have generally distributed property. You must create the largest possible number of owners.'

Shaw had protected his socialism against the charges he knew Chesterton would bring. He had described collectivism as a necessary condition of socialism, but conceded that collectivism without socialism might indeed be a system of tyranny – the tyranny that was later to emerge as fascism. He suggested therefore that the difference between Chesterton and himself appeared to be that one wanted distribution of property and the other *equal* distribution of property. But Chesterton immediately questioned whether equality of income meant equality in the possession of property. 'This is not the normal definition of the term [socialism],' he concluded. 'That the State should be in possession of the means of production, distribution, and exchange was always called Socialism when I was a Socialist.'

It was a good and serious contest. Shaw had the better of the beginning, Chesterton of the end. And it was the first of a series of spectacular tournaments between puritan and cavalier. Their jousting over the years developed into an aesthetic performance, a perfect balance of contrasting styles, romantic and idealistic, with breathtaking displays of analogy and tricks of paradox in which the chivalric ideal was central. Chesterton's rolling good nature was obvious in his bulky swaying presence, the immense range of illustration he gave his simple ideas, his spirit of enjoyment and comic inventiveness. Shaw was less simple, more incisive, his emphatic eyebrows like two supplementary moustaches, an assured and wiry figure standing with arms folded who could speak with a force thrilling to all who heard it. They talked all over the shop. To Chesterton's eyes, Shaw's strengths were limited in their humanity. There was pity in his heart but no love. 'Shaw is like the Venus de Milo,' he declared: 'all that there is of him is admirable.'

But Chesterton's cordiality, especially over religious matters, worried Hilaire Belloc: 'he gets on too well with the enemy'. These exhibition spars were sometimes three star affairs with Belloc – a man who, according to Shaw, was 'wasting prodigious gifts' in the service of the Pope – chairing them. Chesterton's conversion to Catholicism in 1922 (a 'startling gesture' Shaw called it) showed how far he was from agreeing with Shaw. 'If I wandered away like Bergson or Bernard Shaw,' he wrote at the end of his life, 'and made up my own philosophy out of my own precious fragment of truth, merely because I had found it for myself, I should soon have found that truth distorting itself into a falsehood.' Chesterton's truth seemed to Shaw a blind alley up which he had been led by Belloc, 'with the odd result,' Shaw wrote to Wells, 'that he is now dreadfully in earnest about beliefs that are intellectually impossible.' It was not the job of twentieth-century men and women to rediscover other-worldly reasons for believing in mediaeval religion, but to seek a new position, spiritually nourishing and intellectually tenable, between the fatalism of Darwinism and the fatalism of Marxism, whose omissions of human character, passion, will and even consciousness as factors in social evolution Shaw experienced as life-denying.

These were fundamental issues: but as the debates went on, and the years went by, they seemed to become less fundamental. 'I wish I could persuade Mr Chesterton that I really am a serious man dealing

dealing with a serious question,' Shaw exclaimed during an event he had previously called 'this silly debate of ours'. For Chesterton, he believed, intellectual activity was always a lark; whereas Chesterton believed that even Shaw's larks were over-serious. 'Most people either say that they agree with Bernard Shaw or that they do not understand him,' Chesterton explained. 'I am the only person who understands him, and I do not agree with him.' Such parries and ripostes, with no blood drawn, increasingly delighted the spectators. For both duellists were responding to a change in public taste, and controlled by a public demand they had helped to create. Starting out on their pilgrimage as prophets, they had been re-equipped by their disciples and set dancing along as a couple of high-stepping knock-down comedians. The air of outrage puffed up following Shaw's speech at Cambridge had floated away, and the aftermath echoed with laughter and applause. The public loved to witness Chesterton and Shaw as Judge and Foreman of the Jury respectively, in a mock trial held at Covent Garden to solve *The Mystery of Edwin Drood*; or see them dressed as cowboys for a projected film by James Barrie. Their debates were welcomed in a similar spirit. The public did not go for instruction, but to be dazzled. It wanted what Shaw had called a 'clowns' cricket match'; and it was tickled by the notion that G.B.S. and G.K.C. were opposite manifestations of the same humorous and fantastic personality, each treating the other as Sherlock Holmes treated Dr Watson.

The two warriors met for their last public exchange at Kingsway Hall in the final week of October 1927. Tumultuous crowds struggled in the corridors, burst open the doors, flowed round the building like hot lava. Belloc again presided and the British Broadcasting Corporation relayed their words through the country. 'Do We Agree?' was the question they debated. Both spoke well. They spoke of socialism and distributism, income and property – of all they had spoken about sixteen years and one world war earlier in the Memorial Hall. And they said similar things. The change was in the audience, baying for good sport. 'This is not a real controversy or debate,' Chesterton admitted. What they said was what they could most effectively perform as actors. 'I suspect that you do not really care much what we debate about,' Shaw said, 'provided we entertain you by talking in our characteristic manners.' This they did. 'Obviously we are mad,' remarked Shaw, taking what seemed a good embarkation point for a voyage of agreement. But it was when Shaw drew on his reservoirs of optimism that Chesterton felt dispirited. Shaw insisted on agreement. 'I find that the people who fight me generally hold the very ideas I am trying to express.' He tried to wrap Chesterton up in a jacket of agreement: 'He has arrived by his own path at my own position.' And the agreement of two mad people (in the East they would be reverenced) was important;

'it matters very little on what points they differ: they have all kinds of aberrations which rise out of their personal circumstances, out of their training, out of their knowledge or ignorance. But if you listen to them carefully and find that at certain points they agree, then you have some reason for supposing that here the spirit of the age is coming through, and giving you an inspired message. Reject all the contradictory things they say and concentrate your attention on the things upon which they agree, and you may be listening to the voice of revelation.'

And did they agree? 'Ladies and gentlemen. The answer is in the negative.' Chesterton did not agree with Shaw and 'nor does Mr Shaw'. And the people watching and listening did not experience a voice of revelation. The spirit of the age had moved from the platform to themselves: it would be heard in their interruptions, their urging for disagreement to flourish, and their belief that none of it any longer mattered. The religious motive seemed to be slipping quietly out of the modern world. 'In a very few years from now,' Belloc continued, 'this debate will be antiquated.'

[6]

It is a mistake to meet authors, living or dead. All that is tolerable in them is their books.
Meeting the Immortals (1928)

Success in the theatre is very largely a matter of being able to flirt with the public. (1908)

Had Chesterton and Wells united with the Webbs and himself, what an unbeatable new band of musketeers the Fabians would have made. Shaw believed they could have brought public opinion to their side: and socialism might have swept forwards. For people found Chesterton's and Wells's excesses encouraging, where they reviled the Webbs as soulless instruments of social engineering, and were intimidated by Shaw's uppish efficiencies.

For years G.B.S. had been acquiring the impersonal habit of mind, which was the committee habit. He was patient, opinionated, good-humoured, hard-working and he treated every meeting as a matter of life and death. When his political committees began to diminish, he replaced them by working for organizations and institutions connected with the arts – the Academy of Dramatic Art, the London Shakespeare League and others. Of these the most generally important was the Society of Authors.

He had joined this society 'for the Prevention of Cruelty to Authors' in 1897 when deciding to publish his plays as books. Soon afterwards he started making his views and experiences known through the Society's paper, *The Author*. He paid *The Author* the compliment of treating it as a serious business paper. He wrote there of the ugliness of stage directions and the beauties of phonetic spelling and simplified punctuation; he warned parents and schoolmasters against inflicting literature compulsorily on their children, and appealed for the wonderful economies of a forty-two letter 'alfabet'; he described the pathos of British bookselling, calculating that 'the average man wears out over fifty pairs of boots whilst he is reading a single book'; he cautioned fellow-authors against the over-indulgent use of literary agents (his own American agent, he revealed, was as good as any agent could be and seldom got him less than two-thirds of what he could get for himself); and he concocted by a process of elimination the ideal publisher – 'I dont want a patron. I dont want an amateur collaborator. I dont want a novelist . . . Whenever a publisher gives me literary advice I take an instant and hideous revenge on him. I give him business advice . . . and I urge him to double his profits by adopting my methods.' Some of these contributions to *The Author* – such as his advice to novice playwrights on the submission of manuscripts – were printed as circulars and sent to correspondents demanding guidance on how to establish themselves as rival dramatists.

'I am one of the unhappy slaves who, on the two big committees of your Trade Union (the Society of Authors),' Shaw wrote to Chesterton, 'drudge at the heart-breaking work of defending our miserable profession against being devoured, body and soul, by the publishers – themselves a pitiful gang of literature-struck impostors who are crumpled by the booksellers . . . We get nothing but abuse and denigration . . . and spend our time like water for you.' Chesterton's lackadaisical attitude to money was characteristic, Shaw felt, of an innumerate and independent-minded profession. In most matters of negotiation, it seemed to him, authors presented themselves as a flock of sheep bleating, while it waited to be fleeced, that Barabbas was a publisher. This was why all authors, humble and exalted, needed the shepherding of their Society. 'Nothing will save the majority of authors from themselves,' he declared, 'except a ruthlessly tyrannical Professional Association.'

He had been elected to its committee of management in February 1905, and joined its dramatic subcommittee the following year. He took this work extremely seriously. 'The chief glory of every country arises from its authors,' pronounced Dr Johnson. Shaw interpreted this as meaning that the literature of a country created its mind since (whether or not it was aware of this) each country largely took its ideas from what it read. He saw this 'creation of mind' as the great function of authorship, giving it dignity, and its practitioners courage and self-respect. What he looked for within the Society was the creation of a corporate consciousness. His ideas of how the Society must evolve ran parallel to his beliefs in a God who was creating himself through human agency. 'Remember, there is no such thing as the Society of Authors really,' he wrote to Pinero. 'There is an office, and an office staff, and a capital fund, and an income and an agency for collecting debts & bullying dishonest publishers & managers, all of which we can use for our purposes as a professional organization . . . But that organization doesnt exist yet: we have got to make it . . . an organization capable of coping with the managerial combinations which are now being forced into existence by economic pressure.'

In Shaw's perfect world there would have been no law of copyright, no advances or retreats, no giving or receiving of royalties (the very word sounded dreadful to a republic-minded person such as himself). The prestige of literature would have been the business of the State, rather than allowed to bob about in the fumbling hands of competing publishers. All authors would be equal financially; and all other professions would be paid the same as authors. Pending this, authors were necessarily capitalists and literature a sweated trade. As an artistic and learned profession, it had to be defended relentlessly against the philistine presumption that its interests must give way to the most trivial political consideration. All authors owed the Society a share of their time, means and influence: and in that work they developed their social conscience – which Shaw defined as the 'instinctive habit of never acting or even thinking without reference to the opinions and welfare of millions of other men. This is the habit and that is the spirit,' he said at the Annual Dinner in the summer of 1906, 'which the Society of Authors is striving to foster and create in the relatively small circle of our profession.'

Authorship was a good Shavian example of a profession that was helpless without collective action. A writer who was poor, Shaw argued, had not time or means to defend himself; and when, suddenly, he became famous, his time was so valuable that it was not worth his while wasting it on bad debts. It was pitiable, he wrote, to see these 'professional men on whom the Copyrights Acts have conferred a monopoly of enormous value unable to do for themselves what is done by porters and colliers and trade-unionists generally with no monopoly at all at their backs'. Shaw believed that unionism was most practicable in trades where the members worked together in large bodies, lived in the same neighbourhoods and belonged to the same social class. Nevertheless, he thought the Society of Authors should be careful how it disclaimed the idea of being unionized. He looked on trade unions as conspiracies against the public interest that would become unnecessary in a socialist state, but that acted meanwhile as the debit side of the capitalist account. And he emphasized that 'trade union functions were a very great attraction at a time when authors were suffering so much at the hands of profiteers'.

Shaw discovered in his commitment to the Society of Authors, which developed into one of his most dedicated interests, some of the hopes other men look for and disenchantments they may find, in romance. His work on its committees was equivalent to their social lives. He was prepared to spend hours drafting and revising documents, and never lost his temper when sometimes they were whimsically put aside. It was admirable: but did he succeed?

On the whole, Shaw concluded, the ten years he spent as the most vital member of the Society's 'two big committees' might have been passed at the top of Everest. Over such matters as the model treaty with West End managers, on which he negotiated interminably, no progress was made. His frustration led him eventually to doubt the validity of unrefined democracy. For who, in their efforts to make improvements, had used the democratic equipment more thoroughly than himself? He had earned the right to a dissenting opinion. In the interests of getting things done much had been suppressed and little accomplished. His deepest disenchantment sounded from suppression itself: the censorship laws. What a heartbreaking business it had been. 'I had ten years of it; and I know.'

*

Shaw started his war against stage censorship in 1892 after the Lord Chamberlain's Examiner of Plays, E. F. Smyth Pigott, had refused to license *The Cenci*. 'I advocate the abolition of the censorship [because] . . . the effect of the Censor's interference is to make the stage worse instead of better than it would be without him,' he wrote that year, following a debate at the Players' Club. 'People are not prevented from appearing naked in Regent St by compelling everyone to obtain a licence from a censor before going out for a walk. If people abuse free institutions, prosecute them; but don't deny them freedom on the assumption that they will abuse it.'

He had formed this opinion in his early thirties when a Select Committee of both Houses of Parliament failed to recommend a reform of the Theatre Act; and it remained his opinion through many battles for the rest of his life. He was to write more than fifty articles against the censorship, reinforced with many speeches and letters to newspapers. As early as 1900 it was reported that 'Mr Bernard Shaw loses Patience' with the Lord Chamberlain. Almost fifty years later, his patience threadbare, he could still be heard objecting to the appointment of 'an ordinary official with a salary of a few hundreds a year to exercise powers which have proved too much for Popes and Presidents'.

Part of Shaw's tactics was to exploit censorship absurdities. When speaking to the police he pointed out that censorship prevented police prosecution of a play. All plays publicly performed in the country had been licensed by the Lord Chamberlain. Since the Lord Chamberlain was the chief officer of the King's household, prosecution by the police on grounds of blasphemy, sedition or obscenity was an act 'verging on high treason'. For total removal of the censorship, he sometimes felt, he might have to abolish the monarchy itself. 'Perhaps you would like to draft a Bill to do that first!' suggested Pinero.

In theory there was nothing wrong with the concept of a licensing system, Shaw believed, providing that the licensing authority was a person of infallible judgement and encyclopedic erudition, for whom time did not exist. In fact the Lord Chamberlain never read plays but delegated this job to a series of under-paid clerks. These officials fell back on making a list of controversial subjects (religion and sex) that must not be mentioned, and words that must not be used: they then worked to this list automatically. Professional pornographers soon learnt these inventories and how to get round them, with the result that the commercial theatre had become a prostitution market masquerading as theatre.

Shaw argued that the censorship was damned both by the pernicious trash its licence prevented the police from prosecuting, and by the good work it suppressed. Here he detected the real political motive hidden behind all the apparent principles. The censorship was an ingenious device made by idealists for use by the philistines. The object of the censorship was to suppress immorality: the objection to the censorship was that what it meant by immorality was deviation from custom. It was assumed that every Englishman knew the difference between wicked and virtuous conduct. But Shaw reasoned that what was wanted from dramatists, and all other writers, was a constant challenge to such accepted knowledge. The notion that everything uncustomary was wicked helped to keep many people in line with their neighbours and gave Government what appeared to be a moral basis for penalizing change. But without change there could be no development. Progress depended upon the toleration of unexpected behaviour, and heresy was essential to the welfare of a community. A nation that did not permit heresy was stagnant.

Shaw realized that he must not only discredit this function of the Lord Chamberlain's office, but also propose a wiser control of the stage by the community. He attempted to do this in 1907 in an article for *The Academy* called 'The Solution of the Censorship Problem'. The alternative was not anarchy, he wrote, but control by the municipality which would allow reasonable freedom in return for reasonable guarantees. 'The municipality will not read plays and forbid or sanction them,' he explained. 'It will give the manager both liberty and responsibility ... Let him manage how he pleases, knowing that if he produces utterly vile plays, he will find himself without a defender in council when the question comes up as to whether his licence shall be continued.' It was important, Shaw stressed, to license the management, not the theatre. A manager could then pursue his business as any other professional man, while the annual licensing system would ensure that he could be struck off like a solicitor. Shaw was therefore taking a moral line more democratic than the official guardians of morality by recommending a transference of the care of the nation's morals from a few paid clerks to the county councils and city corporations, with watch committees to warn them when managers were conducting their theatres as disorderly houses. As for the Examiner of Plays Shaw concluded, let his 'doom be a handsome pension, and leisure to write the perfectly moral plays he has failed to extract from the rest of us'.

It is difficult to fault Shaw's logic. The Achilles' heel of the argument was that it came from G.B.S., the celebrated joker, troublemaker and the author of an obscene play described by the *New York Sun* as 'a dramatized stench'. Shaw acknowledged this handicap. Though he was one of the over seventy writers to sign a letter to *The Times* on 29 October 1907 recording that the Prime Minister had consented to receive them and hear their complaints against the censorship, he did not in fact join the deputation for fear that his difficult reputation would irritate Campbell-Bannerman – or his deputy Herbert Gladstone who actually met the writers.

He was propelled, however, into the front line again when Granville Barker's new play *Waste* was refused a licence late that year, writing to the *Nation* to point out that the Censor's objection had not been founded on general ethical principles but 'was a matter solely of the observation of an absurd rule forbidding dramatists to mention the subject of obstetric surgery'.

This ban, and another in respect of Edward Garnett's *The Breaking Point*, led to a renewed attack by the playwrights. 'Stiffen your back,' Shaw exhorted Gilbert Murray. 'The oftener we try to get a move made,' he advised Garnett, 'the better.' And he told the actress Lena Ashwell that 'Pinero, Barrie and the rest of us are working like Trojans to get at the Censorship from above; and there is now no doubt that we shall obtain at least some concession.' Throughout 1908 this agitation was kept up with Shaw acting as one of the chief protagonists – 'another crushing straw added to the camel's load' he described it that summer to Archibald Henderson. Six months later he had lured the censorship into committing another blunder and made his own reputation still more mischievous.

*

For the past half-dozen years Beerbohm Tree had been prompting Shaw to write him a modern stage version of *Don Quixote*. 'I should like to show him as the idealist [i.e. Shavian realist] who is always right,' Tree mused, 'and always apparently wrong with the smaller and more practical people round him.' As a rather startling variation on this theme, and reverting to his method in *The Devil's Disciple*, Shaw dashed off *The Shewing-up of Blanco Posnet* between 16 February and 8 March 1909. This one-act 'Sermon in Crude Melodrama', as he subtitled it, was commissioned for a matinée performance at His Majesty's to benefit a children's charity. 'I am rather clever at fitting actors with parts,' he remarked. ' . . . I wrote a perfect triumph of this made-to-measure art for Tree in *Blanco Posnet*, and he was simply shocked by it, absolutely horrified.' Tree was then three months short of his knighthood. He spoke delicately. What worried him were Blanco's references to God as 'a sly one . . . a mean one', and his statement that the chief witness in the trial had had 'immoral relations with every man in this town', including the Sheriff. Surely it could not be wise for him to voice such words? He appealed to Shaw to 'cut that bit about God and that other bit about the prostitute'. But Shaw convinced him there was nothing to fear. If the Examiner of Plays passed the words, Tree would have obtained official blessing; and if he didn't the actor would never have to utter them. So Tree submitted the play to the Censor: and the Censor, on the grounds of blasphemy, refused to license it.

'I should say [it] will be played by Tree,' Shaw had innocently written to Archibald Henderson a week after completing *Blanco Posnet*, 'if it were not that my plays have such an extraordinary power of getting played by anybody in the world rather than by the people for whom they were originally intended.' There is no doubt that this play was intended less for Tree and His Majesty's than for Redford and the Lord Chamberlain's office. Set in a Town Hall 'in a Territory of the United States of America' sometime during the nineteenth century, it is pervaded with an air of unreality, its real inspiration being so far removed from this *mise-en-scène*. 'Let the imagination play,' Shaw later counselled Martin Harvey. 'There never was no such place and no such people.' His own imagination was literary and showed its derivations from Bret Harte, Dickens and Tolstoy's play *The Power of Darkness*: but the debt was more obvious than its value. What he wanted was a respectable provenance for a piece of moral propaganda that had as its point the protest of a horse-thief against his punishment for an admitted crime. From the consequence of this crime he would have escaped but for his yielding to the first good impulse of his life: the giving up his plunder to an unhappy woman in order to save her sick child. It 'is really a religious tract in dramatic form', Shaw explained. But by using some phrases from the Lord Chamberlain's proscribed list, he adapted this blameless drama of religious conversion into a ten-inch gun in the censorship war. 'I have taken advantage of the Blanco Posnet affair to write a tremendous series of letters to The Times,' he informed Trebitsch that summer; 'and the result has been that the Prime Minister has promised to appoint a Select Committee of both Houses of Parliament to enquire into the whole question of Censorship.'

Shaw's methods were to harass the enemy as a dramatist by all ingenious means: then hurry to their rescue as a responsible committee man. Almost the first thing he did was to give vent to a broadside: 'The decision whether a play is morally fit to be performed or not, rests with the King absolutely; and I am not in the King's confidence,' he wrote. 'To write a play too vile for public performance even at the very indulgent standard applied to our London theatres is as grave an offence as a man can commit, short of downright felony . . . but the disgrace will depend on the extent to which the public shares the King's faith in this matter . . . I shall allow the play to be performed in America and throughout Europe. I shall publish it . . . the other countries will have their Blanco Posnet.'

The opportunity of performing *Blanco Posnet* to the maximum embarrassment of the Censor came after a visit by Lady Gregory to Ayot. Shaw gave her the play, and she took it back to Coole where Yeats read it and agreed to put it on at the Abbey Theatre – Dublin being the one place in Britain beyond the Lord Chamberlain's jurisdiction. 'I think we could do it well,' Lady Gregory wrote to Shaw, 'and I don't think anything could show up the hypocrisy of the British Censor more than a performance in Dublin where the audience is known to be so sensitive.'

As soon as the Abbey production was announced, the Under-Secretary of the Lord Lieutenant of Ireland wrote from Dublin Castle threatening to revoke the Abbey Theatre's patent. Lady Gregory and Yeats were summoned to the Castle by the Viceroy Lord Aberdeen, and one of the

Castle lawyers warned their solicitors that if *Blanco Posnet* was performed, the authorities would use against the theatre all the legal powers at their command. But the decision remained theirs and it was a difficult one. Lady Gregory, while trying to produce Shaw's play herself, was continually being dragged away from her actors to her lawyers. Yeats too found himself forced into a position where he had either to abandon the principle of theatrical freedom or risk, by the closure of the Abbey, the livelihood of its players and the fruit of half a dozen years' work. Since this had been done not upon the Castle's own judgement, but upon the say-so of a discredited English official at the very time when that official's own employers had appointed a Commission to consider whether he should be dismissed, Lady Gregory and Yeats gladly seized the opportunity to further their campaign for artistic freedom. They decided to confront the Lord Lieutenant's precautionary notice with a provocative manifesto. 'If our patent is in danger it is because the English censorship is being extended to Ireland, or because the Lord Lieutenant is about to revive, on what we consider a frivolous pretext, a right not exercised for 150 years, to forbid at his pleasure any play produced in any Dublin Theatre, all those theatres holding their patent from him,' their statement warned. ' . . . we must not, by accepting the English Censor's ruling, give away anything of the liberty of the Irish theatre of the future . . . The Lord Lieutenant is definitely a political personage holding office from the party in power, and what would sooner or later grow into a political censorship cannot be lightly accepted.'

The issue had now been adroitly spread from blasphemy to cover almost the whole area of Anglo-Irish politics. Sinn Fein and the Gaelic League, neither of them friendly to Shaw, joined with their protests on his side. 'The officials made an appalling technical blunder in acting as agents of the Lord Chamberlain in Ireland,' Shaw wrote to Lady Gregory. She, having defied the Castle, tactfully offered the Lord Lieutenant a small face-saver in the way of two tiny omissions. It was essential, Shaw pointed out, that such concessions should be ridiculous. ' . . . to oblige the Lord Lieutenant, I have consented to withdraw the word "immoral" as applied to the relations between a woman of bad character and her accomplices,' he explained in a programme note. 'In doing so I wish it to be stated that I still regard these relations as not immoral but vicious; nevertheless . . . I am quite content to leave the relations to the unprompted judgement of the Irish people. Also, I have consented to withdraw the words "Dearly beloved brethren", as the Castle fears they may shock the nation.'

The Shewing-up of Blanco Posnet opened at the Abbey, with Lady Gregory's *The Workhouse Ward* and Yeats's *Cathleen Ni Houlihan*, on 25

August 1909. In a newspaper interview the day before, Yeats predicted that *'Blanco Posnet* will have a triumph. The audience will look at one another in amazement, asking what on earth did the English Censor discover objectionable. They will understand instantly.'

'The root of the whole difference between us and England in such matters is that though there might be some truth in the old charge that we are not truthful to one another here in Ireland, we are certainly always truthful to ourselves. In England they have learned from commerce to be truthful to one another, but they are great liars when alone. The English Censor exists to keep them from finding out the fact. He gives them incomplete arguments, sentimental half-truths, and above all he keeps dramatists from giving them anything in sudden phrases that would startle them into the perception of reality.'

It was Horse Show Week in Dublin, the peak of the summer season, which 'draws to the Irish capital a vari-coloured crowd, of many languages', wrote James Joyce. ' . . . For a few days the tired and cynical city is dressed like a newly-wed bride. Its gloomy streets swarm with a feverish life, and an unaccustomed uproar breaks its senile slumber. This year . . . all over town they are talking about the clash between Bernard Shaw and the Viceroy . . . between the representative of the King and the writer of comedy . . . while Dubliners, who care nothing for art but love an argument passionately, rubbed their hands with joy.' So great had been the publicity that many people now entering a theatre for the first time in their lives were offering guineas for standing-room in the wings. The little theatre, which had sold out seven times, was crammed to the roof. Foreign newspapers had sent their critics – James Joyce sent in a review to *Il Piccolo della Sera*. Charlotte was there with her sister but G.B.S. preferred to stay holed up in Parknasilla with its wasps and robins. The Castle had made no move: the responsibility for what was to happen was wholly the Abbey's. Lady Gregory's fear was that there might be a hostile demonstration, or complaints from the Church, that would give the Viceroy an excuse for taking legal action.

'A heavy crowd thronged about the Abbey Theatre that evening,' reported Joyce, 'and a cordon of giant guards maintained order.' The reception of the play must have disappointed many who had come looking for a disturbance. The audience took to *Blanco Posnet* enthusiastically, laughing at its humour, passing over the dangerous passages with sympathetic blankness, and at the curtain interrupting their applause with vain calls for the author. There was general agreement that Mr Posnet was a very mild-spoken ruffian in comparison with the reports of him; and some people questioned whether they had been victims of an Abbey hoax. 'There is no feeling in Dublin except amusement about the more or less false pretences by which a huge audience was attracted last night to the Abbey Theatre,' reported *The Times*. 'Everybody today is enjoying the story of Mr Shaw's cleverness and the Censor's folly ... The play is perfectly innocuous; it could not shock the most susceptible Irish feelings.' On this point opinion was unanimous. The Churches refused to make a protest (some clergymen actually preached sermons celebrating the play); and *The Irish Times* commented that if ridicule were as deadly in Britain as in France, the censorship would be 'blown away in the shouts of laughter that greeted *Blanco Posnet*'.

Shaw sent his congratulations. 'You and W. B. Y[eats]. handled the campaign nobly,' he wrote to Lady Gregory. 'You have made the Abbey Theatre the real centre of capacity and character in the Irish movement: let Sinn Fein and the rest look to it.' Though people agreed that the Abbey had vanquished the Castle, no one could tell what effect this Irish victory would have on the Censor in England.

It was this that Shaw at once set out to test by asking Annie Horniman (who as lessee of the Abbey had been involved in the Castle battle) to apply for a licence to produce *Blanco Posnet* at her new repertory theatre, the Gaiety, in Manchester. The play was submitted in its Irish version which, as George Redford noted, was 'practically identical' to the text sent to him by Beerbohm Tree, with all the objectionable passages still in position. Under these circumstances, Redford added, 'there is no ground on which I could ask the Lord Chamberlain to reconsider his decision'. But Shaw was able to remind him that plays could be considered more than once. The performance in Dublin, which had elicited good opinions from critics and clergymen, was ample evidence, he contended, that an error of judgement had been made. He therefore requested a re-submission to the Lord Chamberlain. This Redford was obliged to do: but the Lord Chamberlain gave the same decision. Shaw had now achieved his purpose. 'What the Censorship has actually done exceeds the utmost hopes of those who, like myself, have devoted themselves to its destruction,' he wrote in *The Times*.

There was one more move for him to make with *Blanco Posnet*. He allowed it to be performed in the centre of London by the Abbey Theatre Company under the protection of the Stage Society. The English could now see for themselves that his reputedly blasphemous piece was no more than 'a moving and strongly sentimental tract', as Desmond MacCarthy was to describe it. ' ... But, thanks to the Lord Chamberlain, it can only be performed in holes and corners. What sort of unfermented dough must serve for brains . . . those whom he relies on I cannot imagine.' The whole affair, including Shaw's publication in a newspaper of the words to which the Lord Chamberlain took offence, had dramatized the full absurdity of the system. 'Let us all dance on the prostrate body of Mr Redford as violently as we can,' exhorted Max Beerbohm in the *Saturday Review*.

All in all, Shaw concluded, 'the defeat of the Censorship was as complete as anything human can be.'

*

These escapades with *Blanco Posnet* had exasperated the authorities. 'Mr Redford has a fixed delusion that I am a dangerous and disreputable person, a blasphemer and a blackguard,' Shaw wrote to the manager of the Gaiety Theatre, Ben Iden Payne.

He used Payne for an extra skirmish that summer. Between the end of March and the beginning of May 1909, he had composed a one-act satirical farce called *Press Cuttings*. Amusingly exploiting his own fear of women and merging it with the general fear of a German war, he coupled the cause of feminism to his fight against the censorship by naming two of his characters General Mitchener and Prime Minister Balsquith (who enters dressed as a woman). On 24 June Redford returned the manuscript in order to give its author 'the opportunity of eliminating all personalities, expressed or implied'. He called attention to the rule: 'No offensive personalities, as representation of living persons to be permitted on the stage.'

This must have been what Shaw calculated would happen. It was as if he were borrowing pent-up memories, deliberately recreating all the discontents he had experienced before the Vedrenne-Barker management of the Court Theatre, and seeking to avenge them. Now, in *The Times*, the *Observer* and elsewhere, he assured the public that he had been 'careful not to express a single personality that has not done duty again and again without offence in the pages of *Punch*'; and he expressed wonderment at the Lord Chamberlain's failure to censor J. M. Barrie for representing him as Superman in his sketch *Punch and Judy*. More privately he let it be known that he had used the name Mitchener 'in order to clear him of all possible suspicion of being a caricature of Lord Roberts', its model (obviously not General Kitchener) being the Duke of Cambridge, Commander-in-Chief of the British Army and brother to Queen Victoria. As for the well-worn *Punch* figure of Balsquith, it was neither Balfour nor Asquith 'and cannot in the course of nature be both'.

Having again ridiculed the principles of the censorship, Shaw employed the energies of the Women's Suffrage movement to deflate its workings.

The Civic and Dramatic Guild was created, and two 'private receptions' of the play were given under its auspices at the Court Theatre early that July. Shaw then altered the names of Mitchener and Balsquith to Bones and Johnson (the ringmaster and clown of the Christy Minstrels) and Iden Payne re-submitted the play which was licensed for public performance on 17 August, and opened the following month at the Gaiety in Manchester. 'Imagine, then, the reaction of the capacity audience at our first performance,' wrote Iden Payne. 'In the crucial scene the Prime Minister forced his way into the War Office disguised as a militant suffragette . . . When he had removed his woman's attire, Bones exclaimed, "Great Heavens, Johnson!" When the innocuous name was heard there was a roar of laughter, followed by loud ironic applause, which was repeated when Johnson could be heard to answer "Yes, Bones".'

There were some who felt that Shaw was prostituting his talent in these forays against the censorship. Yet many playwrights now agreed that some liberalization of the law was needed. The case seemed overwhelming. But it was important that these playwrights, and other writers interviewed by the Select Committee, should speak with a reasonably unanimous voice. In various multigraphed letters to members of the Society of Authors, Shaw assigned to himself the job of voice-trainer. He coached them tirelessly, showing where one or other had gone off-key during a performance, and expounding the general effect their chorus should produce on its select audience.

' . . . witnesses must be careful not to put forward the contention that the freedom of the stage would be absolutely safe. The proper reply is that its risks would be no greater than the risks of the freedom of the press, freedom of speech, and freedom of public meeting . . . they are the price of liberty and progress . . . We must stiffen our attitude in this respect by holding on doggedly to the distinction between censorship and law. We must not give the slightest countenance to the proposal to empower a local authority to withdraw a licence on its own opinion of a play. We must stick to it that it is to act only on a conviction at law.'

These multigraphed letters to fellow-writers and interviewees were accompanied by an eleven-thousand-word statement that Shaw had prepared as his own evidence. 'I have been working like 50,000 steam navvies at this business of the Select Committee to inquire into the censorship,' he wrote on 28 July. Two days later he came before the Committee himself. His examination was to consist of eighty-six questions, many of them specifically on his written evidence which, at the Committee's invitation and his own expense, he had got distributed beforehand. However, the

Committee now informed him that it could not admit his printed statement into the record since to do so would be acting against precedent. Shaw argued that some of the distinctions he wished to make were not easy to bring out simply in replies to questions, and he cited three precedents from the 1892 Committee (one of them Henry Irving) which had accepted written evidence in favour of the censorship. At this the Committee cleared the room, discussed the matter in camera, and then, reopening its doors, repeated without explanation that 'it would not be permissible to print the statement as part of the evidence'.

Shaw was completely taken aback by this act of double censorship. He had been publicly slapped in the face. 'They treated me very inconsiderately,' he complained uncharacteristically to Lord Lytton. The Committee Chairman, Herbert Samuel, had been away the morning this decision was taken, and next day Shaw wrote to him stating his grievance, 'which is always a valuable property in an agitation like this.

'The sudden volte face when I cited precedent, the dramatic secret conclave, the point blank refusal without reason given, are too good to be thrown away . . . I shall fly to the last refuge of the oppressed: a letter to The Times.'

This transferring of the scene of action to *The Times* angered some of the Committee. Shaw's letter appeared on 2 August; and three days later, when he arrived to resume his evidence, he was told that the Committee 'have no further questions to ask you'. He was ceremoniously handed back copies of his censored plays together with the proofs of his written evidence by the members of the Committee. But the public watching this *coup de théâtre* did not know that the Committee members had privately kept extra copies with which they had asked Shaw to supply them. It was an apparent humiliation and Shaw had to call on all his acting skill to conceal his resentment. 'I need hardly say that after my dismissal this morning I wrote to The Times again,' he told Samuel who, he speculated, might be able to put him in the Clock Tower for breach of privilege. ' . . . I should like to be on again in the 2nd Act, so to speak.'

But he had gone out of control. When he was blocked sexually as in his marriage, or made impotent by the Censor, his words surged out immoderately. His Preface to *Getting Married*, recommending freedom from marital constraint through economic independence and open divorce, went on for over twenty-five thousand words – the longest before-play yet. His eleven thousand words of written evidence against the censorship, which he incorporated as a minority report into his Preface to *The Shewing-up of Blanco Posnet*, was judged by Conrad to be 'somewhat imbecile – in the classical meaning of the word'. Shaw had sought to inflict imbecility on those members of the Committee who supported the censorship: to embezzle them of their wits. He was acting the modern Don Quixote Tree had wanted him to dramatize in *Blanco Posnet*, the man who 'is always right and always apparently wrong with smaller and more practical people round him'. He had turned his plays into the accoutrements with which the Don set out to fight his battles.

In the Blakean sense, to persist in one's imbecility is to grow wise: and Shaw did persist. 'Do you think there is any chance of the decision being rescinded?' he asked Samuel. '. . . I cannot think for the life of me why you let them spoil your bluebook by cutting me out of it.' Samuel's answer was simple: Shaw's evidence was too long.

'I saw that I had to deal with a hostile majority,' Shaw excused himself, '. . . So I misconducted myself.' His words spilled out all over the place. He could not stop. The Committee had treated Redford – 'the filter that my life's work has to pass through' – most decorously. He felt aggrieved; he felt aggravated. 'No other man alive would have taken such abominably thoughtless treatment in good part,' he protested. He had considered the subject more deeply and made himself better informed on it than any member of the Committee. Then he had worked by the rules – their rules – won every round fairly and been judged the loser. 'I have sat on committees for 25 years and know pretty well what is on the cards,' he wrote, '. . . but I am bothered in this case.'

There are signs throughout this affair of Shaw struggling to gain control of himself. 'Oh, if parliaments & committees would only do just what I tell them!' He converted the hearings into a book auction and its Committee members into victims of the craze for collecting curious first editions. He apologized to the public for having treated this abject bench of men so much better than it deserved. He interpreted his defeat as a vicarious victory for his author-allies: 'the result quite justified me; for they were extraordinarily civil to all the later witnesses & let them put in what they liked.' He placed himself unofficially in charge of the Committee, as if it were a theatre company, prompting its chairman Herbert Samuel as to exactly what he must do. He must call the Bishop of St Albans ('a sportive old bird'); he must call Thomas Hardy and 'ask him whether he considers *The Dynasts* a practicable stage play and why he has not written plays instead of novels'; he must call the Chief Rabbi and the whole Sanhedrin – and, of course, he must call the King. 'Fate will drive you into my corner . . . that is where my stage instinct comes in,' he volunteered. '. . . What is the use of knowing a practical play-producer unless you get some tips from him.' Having tipped the Chairman he

235

finally retired to Ireland. The Committee would have to get on without him as best it could.

The Report was published on 8 November 1909. What comes out most strikingly is the evidence of what Shaw would call the idealists. Representatives from the theatre managers' organizations argued that since censorship had not inflicted any injury on serious drama in England, the authority of the Lord Chamberlain should be extended; representatives from actors' associations also spoke of the desirability of maintaining a censorship which protected their members from taking unpleasant parts in undesirable plays; A. B. Walkley, drama critic of *The Times* and President of the Society of Dramatic Critics, believed the censorship to be justifiable because it reflected the rough common sense of the man in the street (though the whole importance of the theatre, he added, was much overrated) and Lena Ashwell, lessee of the Great Queen Street Theatre and soon to play the Polish aviatrix in *Misalliance*, wanted the Censor as protection against the man in the street; W. S. Gilbert thought it imperative that audiences be protected against 'outrages' – the theatre was 'not the proper pulpit from which to disseminate doctrines possibly of anarchism, of socialism, and of agnosticism'; George Alexander and Bram Stoker felt the Censor had done the State some service and been beneficent to themselves also. And so on. It was a vivid example of what a valuable insurance the censorship was to managers, and even actors, against authors getting them into trouble. In any event, in a quiet way, many authors too, if they were doing well, did not really want to change the system. 'A censorship of any kind acts inevitably as a protection to the average author,' Shaw wrote afterwards. 'He is never censored; and those who are censored are not only his commercial rivals, but are generally putting up the standard on him and changing the fashion.'

A team of authors whom Shaw had been training – including Archer, Granville Barker, J. M. Barrie, Chesterton, Galsworthy, Gilbert Murray and Pinero – all gave evidence against the censorship, but they did not speak as collectivist Shavians and their counter-proposals varied. Some of these variations found their way into recommendations attached to the Report which proposed that future licensing be optional and the unlicensed plays take their chance in the courts; that music halls be treated equally at law; that the power of the veto be abolished and doubtful cases referred to a special committee of the Privy Council. This was far from sufficient for Shaw. 'What it comes to is a plan to make the censorship compulsory for the theatre and a dead letter for the music hall by bringing in the theatre lessor,' he wrote to Herbert Samuel. '. . . The Privy Council idea is a good one – a real political innovation.'

But no political innovation actually took place since no legislation was passed to implement these proposals. Instead, an advisory committee was appointed the following year to assist the Censor. It was an illustration in the art of contriving methods of reform, once an abuse becomes oppressive enough, that leaves matters exactly where they were. Although the censorship was later on applied to plays with greater leniency and intelligence, it was extended more powerfully to films where Shaw's intercession also came to nothing. He felt again a complete outsider. 'Nobody pays any attention to my solution of the censorship question,' he said over twenty years later. 'If they will not listen to reason on a comparatively simple matter such as this, how can one expect they will accept a reasoned interpretation and solution of still more vexatious problems.' Eighteen years after his death, stage censorship was abolished in Britain and a form of licensing introduced.

Where the law does not change public opinion so much as become changed by it, most reformers are tempted to exploit non-legal methods. Shaw had tried to improve things by letter and by law: this was temperamentally the most natural way for him to act. He was a scholar-revolutionary, kept sane by his humorous spirit. His paradoxical tactics for changing society had not been to break its laws, but to obey them pedantically, ingeniously, literally, until by laughing consent they were finally rendered impractical. In his fashion he used the parliamentary system to get improvement with a minimum of pain. The typewriter became his heartbeat. But for the first time it seemed as if all the thought and feeling of this work was issuing nowhere. His job of creating the mind of the country had been taken away from him. He was in his fifty-fifth year; as he grew older this sense of powerlessness was to intensify. Looking back, he came to believe that it had been this Censorship Committee that altered his views on how to obtain political results. 'It made an end for me of the claim of the majority to be taken seriously.' He was forced through his frustration into a belief in the inevitability of violence: 'the whole ridiculous transaction,' he wrote, ' . . . was a lesson to me on the futility of treating a parliamentary body with scrupulous courtesy and consideration instead of bullying them and giving them as much trouble as possible.' He had forgotten how much trouble he gave.

The philosophy of violence that makes its appearance in Shaw's later life was a product of his sexual and then his political neutering; and a reaction to having been made to feel as ineffectual as his mother had believed him to be. This was the true misery of life, the being used up for no purpose you could experience in your own existence. The means were not justified that brought no ends: he had no children and he had no

237

CHAPTER V

[1]

I am a specialist in immoral and heretical plays. My reputation has been gained by my persistent struggle to force the public to reconsider its morals. In particular, I regard much current morality as to economic and sexual relations as disastrously wrong; and I regard certain doctrines of the Christian religion as understood in England today with abhorrence. Preface to The Shewing-up of Blanco Posnet

'To me God does not yet exist; but there is a creative force constantly struggling to evolve an executive organ of godlike knowledge and power; that is, to achieve omnipotence and omniscience; and every man and woman born is a fresh attempt to achieve this object,' Shaw wrote in a letter to Tolstoy accompanying *The Shewing-up of Blanco Posnet*. 'The current theory that God already exists in perfection, involves the belief that God deliberately created something lower than Himself . . . '

'Whoever admits that anything living is evil must either believe that God is malignantly capable of creating evil, or else believe that God has made many mistakes in His attempts to make a perfect being. But if you believe, as I do, and as Blanco Posnet finally guesses, that the croup bacillus was an early attempt to create a higher being than anything achieved before that time, and that the only way to remedy the mistake was to create a still higher being, part of whose work must be the destruction of that bacillus, the existence of evil ceases to present any problem; and we come to understand that we are here to help God, to do His work, to remedy His old errors, to strive towards Godhead ourselves.'

The vast incomprehensibility of life was comforting to Tolstoy on whom Shaw's 'intelligent stupidities' jarred painfully. Why did he want to break men's faiths? Where was the gravity in all this dispiriting intellectual play that merged paradox with blasphemy by standing the divinity upside down? 'Life is a great and serious affair,' Tolstoy rebuked him. Shaw's theology sounded perverse: whatever he could not reduce within his cerebral comprehension, he expelled as a joke. 'Why should humour and laughter be excommunicated?' Shaw had asked. 'Suppose the world were only one of God's jokes, would you work any the less to make it a good joke instead of a bad one?' 'The problem about God and evil is too important to be spoken of in jest,' answered Tolstoy. ' . . . I received a very painful impression from the concluding words of your letter.' This drew a blank from Shaw who had previously told Henry James that: 'Almost all my greatest ideas have occurred to me first as jokes.'

Shaw had made a similarly painful impression on Henry James. James's god was art: the adventurous and speculative imagination of the artist that 'from the moment direction and motive play upon it from all sides, absolutely enjoys and insists on and incurably leads a life of its own.' To Shaw this seemed aesthetically wayward. He was no ' "Arts for Art's sake" man, and would not lift my finger', as he wrote to Tolstoy, 'to produce a work of art if I thought there was nothing more than that in it.' He found James's work as dispiriting as Tolstoy found Shaw's. Their confrontation had taken place following James's submission to the Stage Society of a one-act adaptation, called *The Saloon*, from his story 'Owen Wingrave'. The Reading Committee of the Stage Society had rejected it and asked Shaw to write and tell James.

'Shaw's writing – Bernard Shaw,' he began. But which Bernard Shaw was writing? Technically, of course, it was the committee man, swaggeringly opinionated, describing James's play as 'a houseful of rubbish', though granting it had been put together 'with such consummate art'. Also writing was the socialist who saw in art the most powerful of all propaganda forces and who, despite having had to 'preach the enormous power of the environment,' had 'never idolized environment as a dead destiny', believing that 'we can change it: we must change it: there is absolutely no other sense in life than the work of changing it'.

One of the new men was writing, too, who came from the same generation as Wells. Shaw wanted to use the new discoveries of science as one might a set of keys and codes to escape from the philosophical determinism closing in on them since their births. James's adapted ghost story about a young pacifist in a military family who dies from an act of self-assertion is an exploration of the irreversible forces of the past – 'one of the most "deterministic" [tales] James ever wrote', his biographer Leon Edel calls it. It was this horror of genetic inevitability that Shaw found 'sticking in my gizzard ever since'.

James seemed a man of the past and Shaw of the future – the novelty of the future. James believed that the grasping imagination of the artist reached back and, taking hold of unconscious motives, gave the artist psychological reasons with which to create beautiful things. 'It is art that *makes* life,' he instructed Wells, who had previously been instructed by Shaw that James belonged to a different camp from theirs, ambience

Freudian rather than Marxist. James recognized in art a force as mysterious and unalterable as Tolstoy's God. 'I know of no substitute whatever for the force & beauty of its process,' he wrote. It was this fatalism, breaking out at the word of Darwin in the 1860s, and purveyed too through the novels of George Eliot, that had gained new intellectual ground and, so Shaw protested, persuaded people who had lost their faith in a Tolstoyan God 'that Man is the will-less slave and victim of his environment'. Shaw wanted to replace that God with a more positive substitute. 'What is the use of writing plays?' he demanded, ' – what is the use of anything? – if there is not a Will that finally moulds chaos itself into a race of gods with heaven for an environment . . . ' In other words, there is a divinity rough-hews our ends, we shape them as we will – using art as our chief contrivance. To Tolstoy this was impious vanity. And to James, the advice that proceeded from it – that he stick on a happy ending to his play since he 'could give victory to one side just as artistically as to the other' – revealed a wholly 'shallow and misleading' conception of what art was.

Finally it seemed to be the writer of prefaces, tracts, fanfares, encyclicals rather than the dramatist writing: the didactic critic and advertiser of plays, who had laid down terms in the Preface to *Getting Married* for the contract of matrimony and was to frame in the Preface to *Misalliance* a Magna Charta for the rights of children. ('I have owed that debt to the childhood of the world since I was a child myself.')

It was this preface writer too who insisted on the moral purpose of the plays. Shaw wanted more control over his destiny than Tolstoy's rigorous God of love allowed, and more free will than was dreamed of in James's pre-existentialism, with its freedom only to die. 'You have given victory to death,' Shaw accused James. Tolstoy had given victory to the next world. But Shaw wanted to win battles for this world. He wanted power, he wanted knowledge, and by changing the environment he wanted to father a new generation of men and women. His manifesto, sounding vacantly in the minds of Tolstoy and James, filled the vacancy left by his committee politics and his marriage.

He was a political playwright. *Blanco Posnet*, no less than *Widowers' Houses* or *Mrs Warren's Profession*, had been written for contemporary use: a court scene to convince a court – even *Press Cuttings* was a farce designed to blow up a farcical situation. Yet all Shaw's works were imbued with a religious spirit as obsessive as Tolstoy's and, however topical, had been determined in form by precedents from the past.

The Bernard Shaw not writing to Henry James was a playwright who had lost his sense of pragmatic certainty (his 'Shawness') as to what his

241

plays were saying, who admitted that other people's insights might perhaps be more valid than his own, and whose unconscious processes filtered into these plays layers of suppressed autobiography. This mysterious *alter ego*, undermining the social reformer, was also a ghost that mocked the champion of free will and floated free of the scholar bent over his theatrical formulas. He seemed invisible to the writer of prefaces. For he was not obviously an executive organ of a creative force, but a dreamer of the absurd, wondering whether 'the world were only one of God's jokes', who had provisionally called one of his plays *Just Exactly Nothing*.

*

Back in April 1909 advertisements had begun to appear for a new repertory scheme opening in the West End of London. There was a gust of publicity: then a grandiose pause. Some speculated that here was a scheme that would revive the already legendary days of the Court Theatre; others believed it might fulfil the objects of a National Shakespeare Theatre.

The man behind this rumoured enterprise was a powerful Broadway impresario Charles Frohman and the man behind Frohman was J. M. Barrie. They had met a dozen years earlier in America and started a profitable friendship. Frohman was 'my kind of man', Barrie decided – someone shy, successful and of vast vitality, who had tumbled romantically in love with the stage. Barrie called Frohman 'the man who never broke his word', which was to say that Frohman trusted him. He had endorsed Barrie's wistful enthusiasm for the avant-garde by investing in some of the Court's non-profit-making productions. And now he allowed Barrie to persuade him to convert one of his chief London theatres, the Duke of York's, to experimental repertory. Productions of plays new, revived, and unwritten were placarded there, including works by Granville Barker, Henry James, John Masefield, Somerset Maugham, Gilbert Murray, Pinero, Shaw and Barrie himself – though not Galsworthy's *Justice*, with which, almost a year later, the season actually began. As a list of 'Frohmannational Theatricalities' this read well. But there seemed no policy of selection or attempt to reconcile the claims of art with those of the treasury. 'I feel that we must fix our character at once by being repertory in the second week and with a sufficient company it should be practicable,' Barrie wrote rather desperately to Barker who was to direct some of these productions. But an air of vagueness hung around. Though a number of playwrights had undertaken to co-operate with Frohman, 'we none of us (Shaw, Galsworthy, and I) have anything more definite about our plays – nothing on paper that is,' Barker reported to Gilbert Murray whose version of *Iphigenia in Taurus* was contracted for by Frohman but not put on.

Despite their doubts about running a repertory theatre with a star company, people had faith in Frohman. They believed in his American reputation. He was a man of sumptuous generosity and wonderful schemes, the controller of scores of theatres and engineer of numberless triumphs. They entrusted their capital to him in a spree of theatre backing, confident that here was a hard-headed businessman who would look at nothing that didn't pay. 'If Mr Frohman were really that sort of man, I should not waste five minutes on his project,' wrote Shaw in a dissenting opinion. 'He is the most wildly romantic and adventurous person of my acquaintance . . . a famous manager through his passion for putting himself in the way of being ruined. The repertory theatre will be one of his extravagances; and this is probably its attraction for him.'

The play Shaw wrote for Frohman between early September and early November 1909 catered extravagantly to this passion. *Misalliance* was a denial of the melodrama Frohman had hoped for after *Blanco Posnet* – a return to the disquisitory tactics of *Getting Married*, simply the minute-by-minute passing of a day at a Surrey villa. 'I have carefully cherished, repeated & exaggerated every feature that the critics denounced,' Shaw declared seven weeks before the opening. 'I have again gone back to the classic form, preserving all the unities – no division into acts, no change of scene, no silly plot, not a scrap of what the critics call action . . . I shall be sorry to see my old colleagues leaving the theatre angry, weeping, broken men . . .'

According to Barrie's biographer, Andrew Birkin, Frohman 'worshipped mothers and children'. He was (like Barrie) childless, and filled with reverence for the family. He seemed a simple man but 'I cannot do business with babies,' Shaw later told Barker with whom he wished to establish his own superior parental-business credentials. He had deliberately chosen the theme of parents and children because it was close to Frohman's heart: then treated it in a way comically antipathetic to the innocent tycoon. 'We cant all have the luck to die before our mothers, and be nursed out of the world by the hands that nursed us into it,' says one of the characters mocking Frohman's sentimentality. ' . . . No man should know his own child. No child should know its own father,' he adds, matching Shaw's doubts against Frohman's ideals. The social experiment of the family is shown throughout the play to be a failure. 'Oh home! home! parents! family! duty! how I loathe them! How I'd like to see them all blown to bits!' exclaims one of the children of a happy marriage. It was Frohman, too, whom Shaw seems partly to have had in mind when he wrote to Archibald Henderson that 'the handling of the Parents and Children theme is painfully searching, and should be studied by all Uplifters who call glibly on parents to give sexual instruction to their children. Parents . . . are just the people to whom sexual discussion with their children is impossible.'

Shaw told Henderson that *Misalliance* 'is on the plan of *The Taming of the Shrew*'. Characteristically he reverses matters. If Shakespeare's farce is the chastening of a woman whose moods tormented him, Shaw's 'debate in one sitting' is a humbling of men from the governing classes at whose homes he had felt miserably ill at ease when he came to England, and who had so recently humiliated him over the censorship.

Though he seems also to have translated incidents from *The Bacchae*, *Misalliance* is largely a re-working of Barker's play *The Madras House*. Shaw had sat grinning through Barker's first reading of the work before going off to compose his companion piece. The many cross-references between the two plays have been convincingly located by Margery Morgan. The contrapuntal style, too, of *Misalliance* is a variation of *The Madras House* whose strange atmosphere of sexual power and barrenness also fills the country house of John Tarleton where Shaw set his play. Barker used the metaphor of the drapery trade, with its *haute couture*, to represent the decadent culture of contemporary western civilization: Shaw uses Tarleton's Underwear.

Contemporary critics, to whom these derivations were not apparent, responded to *Misalliance* as an oddly isolated and disintegrating work, without proper beginning or end, forebears or likely progeny. 'The debating society of a lunatic asylum – without a motion, and without a chairman,' was *The Times* critic's description. ' . . . What they do is of little importance. They talk . . . they do not keep to the point because there is no point to keep to.' Desmond MacCarthy, too, was to feel that Shaw 'had not a clear notion where his perceptions in this case were leading him. It is inconclusive.' And Max Beerbohm, on whom it produced 'a very queer effect', objected to 'the unreality, the remoteness from human truth, that pervades the whole "debate" . . . a debate, to stand the test of the theatre, must . . . have some central point, and it must be progressive; must be about something, and lead to something. *Misalliance* is about anything and everything . . . '

Monitoring a revival of the play in 1939, *The Times* critic commented: 'Plays of discussion that lead nowhere in particular are likely to disappoint their first audiences who naturally expect to be carried to some unusual destination. With the lapse of time inconclusiveness comes to seem a positive merit.' With a further lapse of time these same qualities of unreality and madness, and the fracturing of standard plot procedures, have again altered their focus and may be seen as having their destination in the mystification and illusion of modern theatre. *Misalliance* has affinities with the drama of Pirandello, where events 'erupt on the instant, arbitrarily', as Eric Bentley described them, 'just as his characters do not approach, enter, present themselves, let alone have motivated entrances; they are suddenly there, dropped from the sky'.

'I may not have many ideas but what ideas I have are consecutive,' says the brainless Johnny Tarleton who claims to be 'a natural man . . . sane, healthy, unpretending.' The extravagantly inconsequential ideas, the air of pretence and unnaturalness, the insane incidents that cluster within the second part of this play – an abrupt descent from the skies of a Polish equilibrist demanding a Bible, music-stand and six oranges ('billiard balls will do quite as well'); the emergence from a portable Turkish Bath of a cringing homicidal clerk, pistol in hand, crying 'I am the son of Lucinda Titmus' – all help to establish Shaw's kinship with Ionesco (who was not born until late in 1912) and show him to be, in R. J. Kaufmann's words, 'the godfather, if not actually finicky paterfamilias to the theatre of the absurd.' There are also links with contemporary innovations, from Post Impressionism to Dadaism, that show G.B.S. (whom Wyndham Lewis both BLASTED and BLESSED) was familiar with the early experiments of modernists and had his own agenda for clearing away the dominance of the well-made play comparable to theirs.

Also hovering in the play, as Michael Billington has observed, is the dark spirit of Joe Orton. 'When Lord Summerhays, an ex-colonial governor, announces that "anarchism is a game at which the police can beat you", and when Summerhays's twerpy son is transformed into a man by something unspecified the aviatrix does to him in a gymnasium, we are close to the world of *Loot* and *What the Butler Saw*.'

At the time of its first production, however, the critics were able to use points of reference solely from within Shaw's earlier work. 'He repeats not merely from his previous plays,' wrote Max Beerbohm, 'but from within the play itself.' Hypatia Tarleton, chasing and being chased by her aircraft pilot through the woods, is up to the same game as Ann Whitefield with Tanner (though she also owes something to Amber Reeves and her adventure with Wells). The uncontrollable cry-baby Bentley Summerhays resembles Eugene Marchbanks: 'Only the same hand could have produced both,' noted Shaw. And that veteran of the underwear trade, John Tarleton, though he has superficial traces of Andrew Carnegie, Gordon Selfridge and the 'universal provider' William Whitely (who was shot dead by a young man claiming to be his illegitimate son), is 'a comic Undershaft', as Shaw himself informed the actor Louis Calvert.

Shaw's apparently formless technique provided him with a method for loosely stitching his own experiences into the texture of the work. Critics had complained that all his characters were himself: and in a sense this was true. The house of *Misalliance* (which owes something to his sister-in-law's home at Edstaston) is a monumental, multi-faceted self-portrait where incompatible aspects of his personality confront one another. Julius Baker, alias Gunner, arises from the Turkish Bath, prophesying revolutions despite being unable to fire a single bullet, to speak for the loveless ineffectual Sonny who had lost his mother and been imprisoned in the Dublin land agents Uniacke Townshend. 'You *were* Gunner for a few months,' Shaw's Irish friend McNulty acknowledged. 'But you grew; you expanded. You grew in all directions.'

Some of these directions are charted by the other characters. Bentley Summerhays exhibits Shaw's thin-skinned capacity when young for provoking dislike (and occasionally protectiveness) from others; Joey Percival shares with him the culturally advantageous experience of having three fathers (his natural one, a tame philosopher in the house and his Italian mother's confessor corresponding to George Carr Shaw, Uncle Walter Gurly and Lee) and this significantly controls his character: 'I'm the son of three fathers. I mistrust these wild impulses'; Lord Summerhays, the experienced man who feels 'still rather lost in England', voices some of Shaw's political convictions about government and reveals a shrinking Shavian sensitivity to sexual matters ('Can no woman understand a man's delicacy?' he asks); John Tarleton owns Shaw's moneymaking abilities, the vitality that drives him into endless public work, and a self-educated obsession with book-learning ('Have you learnt everything from books?' he is asked); and his son and daughter, Hypatia and Johnny, convey something of Shaw's contempt for these Shavian characteristics, in particular the actionless vacuum with its polished walls of 'Talk! talk! talk!'.

Into this stuffy Shavian mansion, reverberating with many discordant echoes of Shaw's upbringing, comes the heavenly invader Lina Szczepanowska (pronounced [fi]sh-ch[urch]-panovska). She comes, it seems, in answer to Shaw's prayer for positive action as much as to Hypatia's plea for 'adventures to drop out of the sky'. Like a bird she lands from above: the authentic superman-woman for whom Doña Ana has cried 'to the universe'. She is the Life Force incarnate, a goddess whose 'profession' it is 'to be wonderful' and who, arriving from the future, is to have her second coming in *St Joan*. 'Lina is the St Joan of *Misalliance*. She comes into that stuffy house as a religious force,' Shaw was to write to the actress Irene Vanbrugh. ' . . . She is devoted to difficult and dangerous exercises, and has a nun's grave disapproval of stunts that are not really either difficult or dangerous, and of acting and clowning. In fact she is very like a modern nun except that her sexual morality is not that of the Church: marriage is to her a sale of herself: she must be free. Her stage foundation is a grave and almost mystical beauty; and Tarleton has the surprise of his life when, touched by it, he finds that he can't buy it, even for love.'

Lina's appearance 'in full acrobatic trapeze dress, as dazzling as possible, to make her effect when she throws off her masculine cloak' is the most astonishing entrance to be made in a Shaw play. After this *dea-ex-machina*, the direction of *Misalliance* changes. Up to this point the audience has been at an Edwardian country house party and heard the capitalist middle class in conversation with the aristocracy. It is conventional drawing-room comedy of manners – Johnny even has the celebrated query popularly supposed to have been coined in the 1920s: 'Anybody on for a game of tennis?' The talk is chaotically lucid and fossilizes the characters in their social compartments. The old are divided from the young, the rich from the poor, men cut off from women, parents from children: almost everyone is inhibited from any kind of initiative that can destroy these fixtures. It is Shavian isolation.

Lina comes from a different world: she is a foreigner to the class system. In her the characters are confronted by the spirit of the future, from where the manners and values of their polite world look absurd. 'Wont you take off your goggles and have some tea?' enquires Mrs Tarleton after Lina has crashed into the greenhouse. The tone of the play now changes from realism into magic realism. 'These woods of yours are full of magic,' exclaims the aviator Joey Percival to John Tarleton who, rejuvenated by Lina's presence, begins to sing:

> There is magic in the night
> When the heart is young.

Is this reality or is it a dream? 'Oh, I must be dreaming,' remarks John Tarleton. 'This is stark raving nonsense.' And Mrs Tarleton agrees: 'Well, I'm beginning to think I'm doing a bit of dreaming myself,' she says. Shaw wants his audience to see that there is more truth in their dreams than in the actuality that has preceded it. The bomb he puts under the British class system is a comedy, and the fuse is his frustration. 'It should be clear by now that Shaw is a terrorist,' wrote Brecht. 'The Shavian terror is an unusual one, and he employs an unusual weapon – that of humour.'

In the first part of the play Shaw was working in a traditional genre: in the second part he attempted to do something new: 'A specially developed example of high comedy,' he called it. The two parts together make an oblique connection between words and actions – the most casual remarks in the first part being translated into happenings later on. Lina is the genius of action – in something of the same fashion as St Joan is a military genius. The play is obsessed with action, though the characters themselves are unable to change anything. In the Shavian perspective, the captain of industry and the colonial administrator have grown obsolete. John Tarleton is incensed that his human destiny should be restricted to underwear. 'I ought to have been a writer. I'm essentially the man of ideas,' he insists. 'Laugh if you feel inclined: no man sees the comic side of it more than I . . . a man like any other man. And beneath that coat and trousers a human soul. Tarleton's Underwear!' Lord Summerhays (the name deriving from Wells's Samurai) also feels increasingly redundant in the twentieth century. 'Here everything has to be done the wrong way, to suit governors who understand nothing but partridge shooting . . . and voters who dont know what theyre voting about,' he complains. 'I dont understand these democratic games; and I'm afraid I'm too old to learn . . . Democracy reads well; but it doesnt act well, like some people's plays.'

This is the expression of Shaw's own disillusionment, enlarged after years of campaigning for the Fabians and for authors, and culminating recently in his censorship defeat. His pessimism is deepened by what he sees as an inferior generation to come: Tarleton's two children representing simply sex (Hypatia) and money (Johnny); and Lord Summerhays's son (an old young man partly modelled on Bertrand Russell) representing fear – the fear of growing up. These are the poisoned fruits of capitalism.

Capitalism is threatened in *Misalliance* by two types of invader. Julius Baker, alias Gunner, comes as revolution fuelled by personal grievance and carried out by force of arms. 'I came here to kill you and then kill myself,' he tells John Tarleton, his mother's alleged seducer. 'Begin with yourself, if you dont mind,' Tarleton replies. In the behaviour of the various inhabitants of the house we see the tactics bourgeois society uses to tame potential revolutionaries – how it tricks and intoxicates them, how it torments them with assistance: 'Let me hold the gun for you,' John Tarleton politely offers. And when Mrs Tarleton hears of Julius Baker's attempt on her husband's life, she exclaims: 'Oh! and John encouraging him, I'll be bound!' In such a contrived atmosphere it is difficult for the political terrorist to take even himself seriously, since he too has been created by an absurd social system and has no occupation other than terrorism – even his threats sound ridiculous: 'Rome fell. Babylon fell. Hindhead's turn will come.'

Shaw's other invaders represent salvation, coming from the future not the past, the air and not the earth. It is Lina who disarms Julius Baker – a symbol of Shaw's preference for evolution to revolution. She brings someone and takes someone away. She brings Joey Percival who, though not particularly admirable himself, is the best mate for Hypatia who demands that her father 'buy the brute for me'. This is the biological method of serving the Life Force. The intellectual method is advanced by Lina's invitation to take Bentley Summerhays off in the aeroplane. Bentley's terrified acceptance of this is comparable to the birth of 'moral passion' in Sonny, lifting him above the fearful religious climate of Ireland. When Lina carries Bentley away 'she is devoting him to death, as she devotes herself every day', Shaw later wrote. ' . . . it is to that that Bentley responds. It is a hieratic act on her part.' Shaw also responds to the possibility of death. His optimism was growing more remote and fantastic. The next time that salvation hovers in the skies in a Shaw play, it will take the form of the Zeppelin raid at the end of *Heartbreak House*. This longing to cleanse the world through the wholesale extinction of man can already be heard in Lina's long final speech – a tirade hurled in dismissal of the other characters. 'There should be an agony of indignant shame carrying it along like a torrent,' Shaw instructed Irene Vanbrugh. This solitary spirit was his offering to feminism. 'I am an honest woman: I earn my living. I am a free woman: I live in my own house. I am a woman of the world,' Lina declares. ' . . . I am strong: I am skilful: I am brave: I am independent: I am unbought: I am all that a woman ought to be . . . '

Shaw had wanted Lillah McCarthy to deliver these lines, but she was ill and the part went instead to Lena Ashwell. She was celebrated for playing heavily emotional roles that called upon her 'to bear an illegitimate child or stab someone to death and then suffer gorgeously for her sins'. Shaw, who had a 'tremendous opinion' of her acting, looked forward to her achieving 'the real miracle of our art' in his play. But though Yeats believed she had brought to the role something 'extremely rare: *beautiful gaiety*', the public (misled by the manly clothes into expectations of 'coarse gaiety') could not see it. Barker, who called her 'hopeless', could not see it either, and nor could Lina herself. This was the first Shavian role she had taken and it did not suit her. She disliked the goggles, tunic and pants; she felt thrown off balance by the unorthodoxy of the play; and, hating Shaw's dry feminism, she later dismissed her part as 'small and hardly in my line'. Shaw's 'dissecting brain', she added, did not belong to the theatre and his 'surgery of life' could not create plays. He was an observer, a critic, a destroyer of tradition. Her imperviousness to G.B.S. was warmly approved by Charlotte and she became one of the few actresses whom Charlotte Shaw befriended.

The mismatching of Lina and Lena was not the only misalliance of the play. 'West End snobbery perishes in my presence,' Shaw wrote to Ben Iden Payne's wife, Mona Limerick, who was to play Hypatia. But it was on West

End snobbery that the success of Frohman's experiment depended. He had spent money heroically on the rehearsals and scenery, the casts and advertisements, convinced that the intellectual drama only needed handling by himself instead of highbrow cranks to make it pay.

His season opened on 21 February 1910 with Barker's production of Galsworthy's *Justice*. It was not just a play but a major contribution to the campaign for prison reform – the impact of a wordless scene in a cell was referred to by Churchill when introducing a provision into Parliament for more humane legislation. There were respectful notices, mixed with some wonder at the intrepid choice of a play dealing with the evils of solitary confinement for an evening's entertainment in the West End. Shaw's country house burlesque, opening two nights later, made a confusing contrast. The *Globe* judged it to be 'absolutely his worst play' and the *Standard*, which described it as 'arrant nonsense', doubted whether it would have ever reached the stage if written by someone else.

The enterprise crashed almost immediately. Dion Boucicault had been engaged to produce some of the plays, so Shaw and Barker had nothing like the same control over what was done as at the Court. Instead of the capacity houses of three hundred pounds he anticipated, Frohman was getting less than half. He sat there paralysed, amazed, caught between his investors who wanted quick returns and big profits, and his new colleagues in the higher drama who, explaining that repertory needed time to accumulate its audience, congratulated him on doing so well. He was panic-stricken. A triple bill of two small plays by Barrie (*Old Friends* and *The Twelve Pound Look*) and a posthumous, incomplete, unhumorous comedy, partly in verse, by Meredith, called *The Sentimentalists*, was introduced at the beginning of March, and followed nine days later by *The Madras House* which Barker had been slow in finishing. The confusion deepened and receipts did not rise though the business done by *Misalliance* and *The Madras House* would have counted as success at a small theatre. Desperately, Frohman fell back on two popular revivals, Pinero's *Trelawny of the Wells* and Barker and Laurence Housman's Court Theatre success *Prunella*, which helped to restore the confidence of his backers. Eventually King Edward VII came to the rescue. He died. And Frohman, his commercial and sentimental interests at last coinciding, joined the general shutting-down of theatres.

The season had lasted ten weeks and *Misalliance* was performed eleven times, *The Madras House* ten. But Frohman grew proud of his achievement. The feeling gathered in him that he had left 'an imperishable monument of artistic endeavour': and he was mightily relieved that he had left it. In any case, the Duke of York's had been a dramatically inappropriate site for repertory, having no storage space for scenery which, after each production, had to be left outside the building or conveyed to a warehouse across the Thames. Frohman's experience in the ordinary routine of theatrical management was contrary to the repertory principle, and he cancelled his plans to take the Barker, Galsworthy and Shaw plays to America.

'The Shaw-Frohman combination is off ... his power stops at the commercial frontier,' Shaw announced to Barker who was so disappointed that he briefly considered becoming a citizen of Germany. There was nothing for it, they decided, but to turn their failure into propaganda once more on behalf of a National Shakespeare Theatre. In a lecture called 'The Theatre: the Next Phase' delivered in London on 9 June, Barker argued that Frohman's experiment had shown that, though a repertory theatre could not be made to pay in the commercial sense, 'the practicability of modern repertory had been proved ... We are breaking new ground, enlarging the boundaries of the drama, fitting it for every sort of expression'. Nothing, of course, would do but a National Theatre. 'Ought it not be opened at the very latest the day after to-morrow?' In concert with this speech, Shaw published a self-drafted interview three days later in the *Observer*. 'The season at the Duke of York's was well worth doing,' he believed, ' ... because I shall never be able to persuade English men of business to endow the National Theatre unless I am in a position to say that I have exhausted all the resources of private enterprise.'

[2]

My life belongs to the whole community and as long as I live it is my privilege to do for it whatsoever I can. I want to be thoroughly used up when I die, for the harder I work, the more I live. I rejoice in life for its own sake. Life is no 'brief candle' to me. It is a sort of splendid torch which I have got hold of for the moment; and I want to make it burn as brightly as possible before handing it on to future generations.
'Art and Public Money' (1907)

H. G. Wells had been one of those to whom Shaw, emerging from the rough Welsh seas off the coast of the Fabian Summer School, had reported his near death from drowning. His fellow-swimmer Robert Loraine, though a young and powerful man, had experienced a worse time, being 'badly handicapped as a meat-eater'. Generously Shaw passed on the results of their swimming lesson to Wells: 'Renounce H. G.: abstain.'

'Wasted chances! You shouldn't have come out,' Wells returned. 'There you were – lacking nothing but a little decent resolution to make a distinguished end. You should have swum to Loraine, embraced him & gone to the bottom – a noble life wasted in an insane attempt to rescue an actor-manager . . . As for me I could have sailed in with one or two first class obituary articles . . . invented a series of confidential conversations & practically gutted your "serious side" . . . But fundamentally you are a weak man. You & I know it. No advice of mine will save you from a fourth act & too much.'

Shaw claimed to be 'dead against this exhibition sparring' because 'I do it so well that the sympathy goes to my opponent'. They were quite different from his platonic displays with Chesterton. But on this occasion Wells had done it better. Neither of them enjoyed these knockabouts for long – they turned too deadly. But others did, and Wells found himself positively pressed forward into the ring by a new supporters' club among the Fabian nursery. His spirits rose: he felt game enough. The two of them squared up in front of the Fabian Arts Group in April 1907. They were to debate Wells's Samurai – his intellectual élite in *A Modern Utopia*. Among those who saw themselves as Fabian Samurai the dangers of priggishness, Wells warned, and the opportunities for 'bright and brilliant personal displays' were enormous. Everyone knew whom he meant. Beatrice Webb answered that 'most of the great reformers had been consummate prigs . . . [and] her husband was, perhaps, the best prig of the lot.' Then Shaw brightly and brilliantly sketched the future of these Samurai, leading Wells's élite straight back to the starched collar class system of England.

Though many Fabians were unsure of Wells's aims, he still seemed their man of the future. Even Shaw believed in his imaginative grasp of technology. His potent spell promised a new era for Fabianism. 'He is a man of outstanding genius,' wrote Edward Pease. ' . . . his energy and attractive personality added radiance to the Society only equalled in the early days.' During 1907 the membership doubled. There was an influx of younger women and men from the universities, many of them drawn by what Rupert Brooke called 'the wee fantastic Wells'.

The Webbs recognized the value of Wells and of Shaw in this new Fabian boom; and they cradled the pleasant suspicion that 'our own constructive thought' might also be helping to attract 'considerable numbers of followers in the near future'. Part of this optimism had seeped in from the political climate of the country. After 1906, when the Liberal

Party won its large parliamentary majority, the time seemed favourable for reform. 'We do not deceive ourselves by the notion that this wave of Liberalism is wholly progressive in character,' Beatrice noted in her diary. For years the Webbs had been plotting to meet those who 'really have the power to alter things'. Yet they were cursed with what Wells called their 'knack of estranging people'. They had moved out of touch with the Labour Party (which Shaw accused of exploiting rather than abolishing capitalism), alienated their allies among the Tories and made the Liberal Government impervious to permeation.

Shaw's plays and Wells's novels had helped to create a middle class with expectations of swift social change. The failure of Campbell-Bannerman's Government to initiate any policy of reform soon led to middle-class discontent with Liberalism and a swelling support for the Labour Party. It was this turn in allegiance by progressive intellectuals that had given rise to the new Fabian boom.

It was the Society of Shaw and Wells, rather than of the Webbs, that these new members were joining. This was one of the reasons why Beatrice suspected the sudden Fabian popularity. She sensed an odour of sexual anarchy. Their new recruits 'lived the most unconventional life', she observed during the Fabian Summer School, 'stealing out on moor or sand, in stable or under hayricks, without always the requisite chaperon to make it look as wholly innocent as it really is.' Could she be certain that it was innocent? Mostly, she believed, these young people took along works of political science. Even so, their conversation was surprisingly free. And their gym costumes gave several of the elderly nondescript Fabians some bad quarters of an hour. Beatrice felt apprehensive, too, when the economics had to stop, of where their 'larky entertainments' could lead. There was danger in innocence. There was danger everywhere.

Beatrice knew the blind and undiscriminating power of sex. Blindly and without discrimination she suspected Shaw and Granville Barker, no less than Wells, of letting themselves go 'pretty considerably' with women. The future of socialism belonged to the 'practical mystics' – they were her Samurai. She could not see that Shaw also wanted to believe this. His *Misalliance* was to offer Beatrice's faith in religious thought and Wells's instinct for biological trial-and-error as concurrent ways of human progress. But Beatrice had so curbed her 'lower desires' that she seemed unaware of how controlled the erotic motive was in Shaw's play, or that the absence of love (about which everyone spoke so garrulously) was one of the factors that insulated his characters in their separate compartments. She was to describe *Misalliance* as 'disgusting', wondering whether her friend Shaw was not 'obsessed with the rabbit-warren aspect

253

of human society'. There were no men and women in his play, only males and females. Sometimes she despaired. She would rather die than live in a world conducted on such lines. 'I think probably the revelations with the H. G. W. various sexual escapades largely suggested the play,' she wrote. She seemed to have no means of telling, as could the young Fabians, the difference in such matters between Shaw and Wells.

Shaw tried to suppress sex as one might quarantine a virus, acting as if to arrest genetic lovelessness from spreading to another generation. Wells, as if to make up for early emotional loss, was hungry for sex. Among the young Fabians, Shaw behaved with the manners of a benign committee chairman, his conversation mixing instruction with unflagging public entertainment. 'He was personally the kindest, most friendly, most charming of men,' remembered Leonard Woolf.

' . . . he would come up and greet one with what seemed to be warmth and pleasure and he would start straight away with a fountain of words scintillating with wit and humour . . . but if you happened to look into that slightly fishy, ice-blue eye of his, you got a shock. It was not looking at you . . . it was looking through you or over you into a distant world or universe inhabited almost entirely by G.B.S., his thoughts and feelings, fancies and phantasies.'

Wells's eyes were of a more penetrating blue, and when they looked at you they looked at no one else. Though less commanding than Shaw in front of crowds, his personality was more seductive. He seemed vulnerable; even his uncertainties were endearing – so often they were your own. He appeared 'nearer and more sympathetic than other men', wrote Dorothy Richardson.

Shaw had invited Wells to the Fabian Summer School in Merioneth, but Wells did not go. He was happy at Sandgate where he had found new emotional energy among an alternative group of Fabians. They came from what the *Fabian News* called 'the all-pervading younger generation' and they were mostly women. There was a good-looking flirtatious writer, Violet Hunt, whom he entreated to 'be nice to a very melancholy man'. There was Hubert Bland's plump and beautiful, illegitimate daughter Rosamund, who was said to enjoy the admiration of men. 'I have a pure flame for Rosamund,' Wells enthused. There was Amber Reeves, sweet, pretty, coaxing, who loved visiting the Wellses at Spade House. 'She adores you both,' her mother confided to Jane Wells. ' . . . You are good fairies to all these young people. It must be very pleasant to realize what a lot of happiness you give them.' And it was true. Lucy Masterman remembered her holiday at Sandgate as an 'impression of perpetual sunshine, health and ease'. There was no inducement for Wells to leave this sunshine for the freezing seas of Merioneth. 'I am ready to go on working for [socialism],' he wrote, ' . . . in the meantime having just as good a time and just as many pleasant things as I can.'

Women now numbered more than a quarter of the Fabian membership, and following the defeat of Wells over revision of the Basis they threatened to create a special committee and bring in an amendment supporting votes for women. Though universal suffrage had been favoured in principle by the Fabians, their tract on *Women* had been pending for over ten years – too painstaking an exercise, it was now felt, in gradualism. All they had was Wells's lecture on 'Socialism and the Middle Classes' which advocated freer sexual relations and endowed motherhood. Shaw was appointed to discuss the matter with the Fabian spokeswoman, Amber Reeves's mother Maud Pember Reeves. There were few differences between them: Shaw supported women's suffrage and believed that women themselves should have the principal place in the suffrage campaign. He therefore returned to the executive with a recommendation that it agree to the women's wishes. As a result, 'the establishment of equal citizenship between men and women' was added to the Objects of the Society and this became the single amendment made to the Fabian Basis before the end of the First World War. A Women's Group (with Jane Wells on its executive) was formed – also a Biology Group and a Socialist Medical League – and the Fabian women arranged themselves into a useful platoon in the fight for enfranchisement.

The backbone of Shaw's feminism was financial self-respect: he spoke in particular of equal pay for actresses and the economic independence of wives. He wanted the Fabian Society to stand for political equality as the universal relation between citizens without distinction of sex, colour, occupation, age, talent or hereditary factors; and he advocated 'the explicit recognition by legally secured rights or payments of the value of their domestic partners and to the State as housekeepers, child bearers, nurses and matrons'. Declaring himself to be 'uncompromisingly on the side of giving the suffrage to women', he urged them to 'have a revolution – they should shoot, kill, maim, destroy – until they are given the vote'. As a collectivist he did not centre his arguments on the rights of individuals as Wells did, but treated women as valuable units of government that had not yet been fitted into the political machinery of the country. Women would do best for society, he reasoned, when they did best for themselves. He wanted to see them, in equal numbers with men, on all political organizations, including the House of Commons. 'The only decent government', he had said in 1906, 'is government by a body of men and women.' He dreamed of combining the minds of men and women to produce a better political animal, fighting with surprising belligerence many feminist battles on the platform, in the press, and through his prefaces; and insisting, in the interests of political equality, on the similarities between men and women.

It was this political 'discovery' that 'a woman is just like a man', that peopled Shaw's plays with beings who, if not actually androgynous, have only the minds of women without their precious bodily fluid. He had replaced the Victorian stereotype of the womanly woman with Woman the Huntress, but 'the pursuit has about as much sex appeal as a timetable', complained Frank Harris. He looked forward to a time when, in the course of evolution, ecstasy of intellect would replace sexual passion. Meanwhile, though the sexual 'syringeing' of women by men had 'compensations which, *when experienced*, overwhelm all the objections to it', he later admitted to St John Ervine, ' . . . I always feel obliged, as a gentleman, to apologise for my disgraceful behaviour.' This 'apology' infiltrated his writing, against which some women revolted even when admiring the moral elegance of his argument.

'I am a woman,' says the man in one of Shaw's plays to the girl; 'and you are a man, with a slight difference that doesnt matter except on special occasions.' Wells did not feel this difference to be slight, and the occasions were special to him in a completely non-Shavian sense – that is, not by their infrequency. If Shaw was a distant uncle to the Fabian nursery, Wells was its permissive father. Like Shaw, he publicly defended the rights of women, in particular condemning conventional sexual morality and the marriage laws founded on it. But Wells dared to do what he dared to advocate. It was because of his notoriety that several rebellious young women, oppressed by Edwardian conventionality, sought him out. He was not simply on the side of the young, he was in many ways one of them, a more dangerous and exciting figure than Shaw. 'I'm a thoroughly immoral person,' he wrote early in 1907, ' . . . discursive, experimental & fluctuating . . . '

Although no scandal about his affairs had yet broken into public view, Wells had been accused in the press of having manufactured through his books a paramour's Utopia. 'Socialistic men's wives, we gather, are no less than their goods, to be held in common,' wrote a reviewer of *In the Days of the Comet*. And the *Spectator* told its readers that Wells had made 'Free Love the dominant principle for the regulation of sexual ties in his regenerated State'. Against such charges, Shaw defended Wells on behalf of the Fabians. 'The view that domestic partnerships are simply civil contracts, and that people should be as free to form or dissolve them as if they were a business partnership,' he wrote, ' . . . has no more to do with the advocacy of "promiscuous intercourse" than Mr Wells's views on expropriating the landlords have to do with the advocacy of indiscriminate theft . . . the Fabian Society is not committed to any views on the marriage question.'

But Shaw and the Webbs feared that the cry of 'Fabian Free Love' might prove such a strong electoral slogan as to set socialism back a decade. Wells had come forward in England as a socialist leader: he was not at liberty to throw his emotional match-ends about in powder-magazines. There had almost been an explosion over his relationship with Rosamund Bland, the brown-eyed secretary of the Fabian nursery. The Society had hummed with rumours of how Hubert Bland had intercepted the pair at Paddington Station. But these rumours were confined within the Society and did not reach the public. Shaw had circled round with sallies of advice but, knowing few of the facts, he was not well employed. 'What an unmitigated moral Victorian ass you are,' Wells accused him. 'You play about with ideas like a daring garrulous maiden aunt but when it comes to an affair like the Bland affair you show the instincts of conscious gentility and the judgment of a hen . . . '

'You don't know, as I do, in blood & substance, lust, failure, shame, hate, love & creative passion. You don't understand & you can't understand the rights & wrongs of the case into which you stick your maidenly judgment any more than you can understand the aims of the Fabian Society that your vanity has wrecked. Now go on being amusing.'

And Shaw did go on. His vanity insisted that he could not be hurt by such tirades. Besides, it was Wells's vanity that had been more bruised in their collision, and it was his role as the prophet of sexual liberation that appeared more likely to wreck the Society. He wanted the Fabians expressly to repudiate bourgeois marriage and introduce a scheme for children's allowances releasing the mother from economic dependence on the father. Between the spring of 1907 and the spring of 1908 he had gone to few meetings but at the elections in 1908 he was again voted on to the executive. Suddenly in March 1908 he had submitted fresh plans for amending the Fabian Basis. It seemed the same story all over again. But this time both the Webbs and Shaw were heavily preoccupied with other matters, such as the coming campaign for reform of the Poor Law, and they replied perfunctorily. This response was typical, Wells felt, of the conspiracy between the Old Gang to block his initiatives. They only *pretended* to encourage him. 'You two men are the most intolerable egotists,' he told Webb, 'narrow, suspicious, obstructive, I've ever met.'

Shaw quickly moved in with all his artillery blazing away at the man who had dared attack his Sidney Webb. 'You annoy Webb extremely by your unruliness and by your occasionally *cold* incivilities . . . in public work we must proceed on publishable lines . . . '

'You may draw caricatures of us; but you must not copy our signatures at the foot of cheques. There is an art of public life which you have not mastered, expert as you are in the art of private life. The fine art of private life consists almost wholly in taking liberties: the art of public life consists fundamentally in respecting political rights. Intimate as I am with Webb, I should no more dream of treating him as you have treated him than of walking into the House of Lords & pulling the Lord Chancellor's nose.'

Pernickety points of etiquette like this meant nothing to Wells: far better to say what you thought openly. Wells wanted speed rather than gradualism, more propaganda than research, directness in place of permeation, and a great movement of opinion that would jump obstacles. He looked for an expansion from devious and drudging coterie politics – not into a Fabian parliamentary party, but on to a political platform that would carry his campaigning voice round the country whenever he chose to raise it on matters of national interest. The logical place to start these changes was at the *Basis*. 'If you want the present helpful expansion of Fabian influence & socialist training to go on under the most favourable conditions, you must alter the Basis,' he warned Shaw. 'You can get that done, I can't. It isn't in my line of aptitude.' Each wanted to collaborate *de haut en bas*, treating the other as his assistant. Wells would not be converted into a piece of clockwork Shavian machinery; and Shaw could not abandon the Webbs to a Wellsian hit-or-miss experiment with the future. For both of them Fabianism was a matter of socialist property. They had reached an impasse.

Only Shaw among the Fabian elders had really wished Wells to stay on the executive. Webb and Bland had plainly wanted him to leave – and Wells too was desperately eager to go: all they differed on was the manner of his going. When he did go it was offhandedly and on a matter about which they were in some agreement. At a by-election in the spring of 1908, Wells supported the Liberal candidate, Winston Churchill, whose 'rapidly developing and broadening mind . . . [was] entirely in accordance with the spirit of our movement'. His motives for this action seem to have been mixed between a natural preference for Churchill over a dull socialist candidate incapable of winning the contest, and a wish to strengthen opposition to the Tory candidate, William Joynson-Hicks, who had accused him of being 'a nasty-minded advocate of promiscuous copulation'. At the annual meeting of the Fabian Society on 22 April 1908, Wells was accused of betraying 'the glorious principles of socialism' by a number of members who did not know that Webb was then privately 'permeating' Churchill over reform of the Poor Law. Webb was obliged therefore to offer some lukewarm defence of Wells against his critics – but Wells could not let the moment slip, and using Webb's qualified remarks as his spur, he reared up and trotted off the platform. His letter of resignation did not reach Pease until the middle of September. The chance of converting the middle classes to socialism had found the Fabians 'divided and un-decided', he wrote, and 'it is to other media and other methods that we must now look for the spread and elaboration of those collectivist ideas which all of us have at heart'. He would go back to writing novels.

This resignation, which the executive gratefully accepted ten days later, was an act of mercy. During the winter of 1908-9 what Beatrice called 'a somewhat dangerous friendship' between Wells and Amber Reeves intensified. Amber graduated with a double first in moral sciences and conceived Wells's child at about the same time. What made it worse for Beatrice to contemplate was that they had enjoyed sexual intercourse, so she heard, in the girl's rooms 'within the very walls' of Newnham College. In what light would the Fabians now regard Wells's plans for endowed motherhood? To make matters blacker, the lovers then crazily decamped to France. The events, as they emerged over the year 1909, began to unsteady Beatrice. 'The perturbation caused by such intimacies' hardly left her 'any brain to think with'. First she was irritated that Wells could intermittently go on living with his wife as if nothing were wrong; she was also affronted when Amber (pushed perhaps by Wells) ran for the cover of a marriage of convenience to a chivalrous barrister with the tautological name of Blanco White, giving Wells's daughter a legitimate birth; then she felt exasperated on hearing that the arch-sensualist was persisting with the liaison even following that marriage; finally the publication of *Ann Veronica*, Wells's novel advertising the affair, drove her frantic. Was this the 'other media' by which Wells had promised to spread collectivism? 'H. G. W. has no conception how he will be hit by that story getting about,' she wrote to Sidney. 'What a fool the man was not to go away and delay publication of *Ann Veronica*!'

The situation was serious. Amber's father was Director of the London School of Economics; her mother was prominent among the Fabian Women's Group; her lover was a Fabian; her husband was a Fabian; and she herself had been treasurer of the Cambridge University Fabians. Even Jane Wells, the complaisant wife, was on the Fabian executive. Worse still, it was the Webbs who had introduced Wells to the Reeves family. 'I wish we had never known them,' Beatrice exclaimed. Something would have to be done. But what? Already it was too late. Clergymen were shaking their pulpits with denunciations of *Ann Veronica* and her creator; the *Spectator* had called it 'a poisonous book', and the National Social Purity Crusade brandished the novel at the head of its campaign for formal censorship in circulating libraries. 'From the outset,' Wells complained, 'Ann Veronica was assailed as though she was an actual living person.' Reviewers who knew something of Wells's biography took the opportunity to treat Ann as if she were Amber. The criticism overflowed from the book and cascaded into Wells's life. 'I can't stand this persecution,' he cried out. 'He will disappear,' Beatrice predicted, 'for good, from reputable society.' He did resign from the Savile Club; and Jane was asked to quit the Fabian executive.

Beatrice felt intensely involved. She insisted that Wells would be supremely and permanently wretched. 'I doubt whether he will keep his health – and he may lose his talent'; and she believed that Amber, who was alternately a 'little pagan' or 'poor little Amber', had been placed in the gutter – 'a ruined woman, doomed to sink deeper into the mire'. Once Beatrice had been anxious lest Wells, after his resignation from the executive, became a Fabian enemy like Ramsay MacDonald. 'Don't shake us off altogether,' she had appealed. 'It won't be good for either the Webbs or the Wells and will be very bad for the common cause.' She had wanted to keep him 'as an asset to the cause' – a pet asset in a kennel, Wells felt. All this stopped now that he was a danger, an abomination. 'The end of our friendship with H. G. Wells,' she noted in her diary in the summer of 1909.

Beatrice had done what she could. She had written letters to Fabians with teenage daughters; she had spoken to Blanco White and counselled Amber. She had also been in touch with Shaw. But Shaw took a different view. Now that Wells was only a subscriber to the Fabian Society, it was permissible to view the affair as part of that fine art of private life which consisted in taking liberties. Wells excelled at this kind of social experiment. So people should 'shut up' about it. The Fabians must simply calculate how best to head the matter off from crashing further into public awareness, where it did not belong. 'The situation can be saved by letting it alone,' he instructed Beatrice. ' . . . I aim at the minimum of mischief.' But Beatrice was appalled. 'He [Shaw] has even suggested to Reeves that he should entertain all three to dinner every week to show his approval!'

Shaw had already written sympathetically to Wells. 'Occasionally,' Wells responded, 'you don't simply rise to a difficult situation but soar above it & I withdraw anything you would like withdrawn from our correspondence in the last two years or so . . . ' For despite everything, there was part of Shaw that warmed to Wells's escapading. Some writers had to act foolishly in order to write well. And it was certainly true that, in respect of sex, Wells's romances were far more authentic than Victorian fiction. 'Mr Wells does not shirk facts because they are considered scandalous, especially when the conventional foundation of that view of them is becoming more and more questionable,' Shaw was to write a dozen years later; 'but I cannot find in his books a trace of that *morbidezza* which . . . is very largely produced by the fact that the writers have no real experience of what they are writing about, and are the victims of a baffled *libido* rather than a Casanovesque excess of gallantry.' The mixed vocabulary of this tribute indicates the changing culture through which these Fabians were passing. Moral absolutes were melting away and strange philosophies rising to obscure rock-like old religions. In this shifting landscape it was dangerous finding one's way alone. Wells's expedition, it appeared, had been disastrous. 'All this arises because we none of us know what exactly is the sexual code we believe in,' observed Beatrice, 'approving of many things on paper which we violently object to when they are practised by those we care about.'

The scandal of 'free-er love' might have smashed the Fabians, but Shaw also feared that Fabianism would be diluted without Wells. His mission had been to unite opposing qualities within the Society, but there seemed no combination between Wells and the Webbs that was not explosive. The future was mined with explosives.

*

Wells's place as Fabian activist was almost immediately occupied by Beatrice herself. Until recently she had not put herself forward in Fabian circles as much more than an aide to Sidney. But in the spring of 1909, wishing no longer to be 'an appendage of the Old Gang', she promised the Society 'to make a new start'. This deeper involvement arose in part from her changed attitude to the role of women in politics. Some twenty years before she had signed an anti-suffrage manifesto drafted by Mrs Humphry Ward. It 'is the spiritual function of a woman to be the passive agent bearing a man's life!' she had emphatically instructed Sidney before their marriage. But as feminism expanded into the political atmosphere, and it became clear that the Liberal Government was not going to introduce any concessionary legislation, Beatrice's mood altered. Her impatience with some of the militant pioneers of women's suffrage was overtaken by a feeling of distaste over the 'coarse-grained things' being said by 'coarse-grained men' opposed to emancipation. The old prejudice gradually evaporated in her and towards the end of 1906 she sent

Millicent Fawcett, president of the National Union of Women's Suffrage, her formal recantation. Women were 'rapidly losing their consciousness of consent in the work of government and even feeling a positive obligation to take part in directing this new activity,' she wrote in her letter which was published in *The Times*. 'This is, in my view, not a claim to rights or an abandonment of women's particular obligations, but a desire more effectually to fulfil their functions by sharing the control of State action in those directions.'

Nothing did more to alter Beatrice's views than her experiences as a member of the Royal Commission on Poor Law. She had been appointed by Arthur Balfour during the last days of his Government at the end of 1905. Before that, as she admitted, 'I have never myself suffered the disabilities assumed to arise from my sex.' This had been the root of her anti-feminism. But her three years' work on this largely man-dominated Commission left her wondering: 'Are all men quite so imbecile as that lot are? I sit and watch them and wonder ... It makes me feel intolerably superior.'

Beatrice's intrigues on the Poor Law Commission with her team of special investigators were remarkably similar to Wells's 'odd mixture of underhand manoeuvres and insolent bluster' among the Fabians. 'It will need all my self-command to keep myself from developing a foolish hostility and becoming self-conscious in my desire to get sound investigation,' she recorded in her diary. 'Certainly the work of the Commission will be an education in manners as well as in Poor Law.' She trained like an athlete for this work, cutting down all but business intercourse, rising for her cold bath and quick walk at six-thirty, feasting off bread and cheese and drawing on Sidney's 'blessed strength and capacity'. Yet her manners did deteriorate. 'From first to last she has declined whilst in the Commission to merge her individuality in it, but claims the right of unrestricted free action outside,' wrote the mild-mannered chairman. Her determination not to be overawed by 'great personages who would pooh-pooh a woman', her obsession with the virtues of the Webb plan to 'drain the morass' of poverty, and her impatience in launching this plan in a draft report lost her the chance of gaining support from other members of the Commission. 'It will be amusing to see how much "Webb" this Commission will stand,' she wrote. Her Minority Report, completed early in 1909, was signed by three other Commissioners.

Everyone had been dissatisfied with the ramshackle Poor Law of 1834. Some saw it as expensive and inefficient; others as inadequate and demoralizing. The Royal Commission's terms of reference had been to recommend changes in the administration of the law or new legislation dealing with distress. Beatrice wanted to break up the Poor Law altogether and replace it with a comprehensive scheme of welfare that allocated responsibilities for assisting those below a national minimum to a series of Government departments dealing with specific causes of poverty, such as chronic sickness, old age and unemployment. She was contemptuous of the Majority Report which sought by simple unemployment insurance to alleviate the circumstances of the destitute and necessitous only. Shaw sensed that the Minority Report was a much more important document than most people yet realized. 'It may make as great a difference in sociology and political science as Darwin's "Origin of Species" did in philosophy and natural history,' he predicted. ' . . . It is big and revolutionary and sensible and practicable at the same time, which is just what is wanted to inspire and attract the new generation.'

The Report lies somewhere between Bentham and Beveridge. Beatrice's collectivist scheme was to be a blueprint for the Welfare State, but it also retained something of the puritanism of Bentham who had believed in the utilitarian device of the workhouse to 'grind rogues into honest men'. Beatrice was haunted by this problem of the able-bodied unemployed. 'I dream of it at night,' she wrote, 'I pray for light in the early morning.' For those who lacked capacity she recommended compulsory training; and for those who lacked will, disciplinary supervision and treatment that came close to a penal labour colony. Believing that a grant from the community should be conditional on better conduct from the individual, she was later to express criticism of Beveridge's proposed extension of unconditional unemployment doles on the grounds that this would encourage malingering.

Beatrice had predicted that her Minority Report would be reviewed far more favourably than the Majority Report. In fact it was the Majority Report that got the better press. She felt utterly depressed. 'Now I am in a state of collapse,' she wrote early in 1909. Nevertheless she was determined to expend all her energies, and Sidney's, in this breaking-up of the Poor Law. From the Fabian point of view, the political situation appeared to have improved. After Campbell-Bannerman suffered a heart attack in April 1908, a new Government was formed with Asquith its Prime Minister – a man 'inclined to carry out our ideas', Beatrice thought. But Asquith left much of this work to two future Prime Ministers, Winston Churchill (President of the Board of Trade) and Lloyd George (Chancellor of the Exchequer): and neither of them was sympathetic to the Webbs. Sidney and Beatrice therefore decided to deploy the Fabian Society on a national campaign. This was the sort of enterprise Wells had been urging on the Fabians before his resignation – it was 'quite after my own heart', he told Beatrice, ' . . . [and] expresses just that deliberately Constructive Socialism which I have always advocated . . . to replace the sterile and uninspiring basis of the Fabian Society'. Here was the 'new start' Beatrice had promised the Fabians: no more wire-pulling or salon politics, but a missionary crusade of 'raging tearing propaganda' to change the mind of the country about destitution.

Again she went into training. 'As a preparation I practise voice presentation between 6.30 and 8 a.m. every morning on the beach – orating to the Waves!' she wrote after the Fabian Summer School. ' . . . It is rather funny to start on a new profession after 50!' The turmoil of a political movement gave her the thrill of feeling 'admiration and willing obedience to my will'. Yet it was a 'curiously demoralizing life', and she often felt nostalgic for her previous 'quiet life of research'. Nevertheless she spurred herself on to be an itinerant agitator. 'It is no use shirking from this life of surface agitation, from this perpetual outgiving of personality.'

Beatrice had uttered her Minority Report as a separate Fabian work in two volumes totalling 946 pages. This was one of the difficulties of their campaign. Though the Report was extraordinarily far-seeing, it proved difficult to expound to electors; and it was impossible to convince governments that an impossibly complex bureaucracy would not be needed to set it up. There was a problem also, after the last Liberal election win in 1910, in persuading anyone why such a complex administrative upheaval was to be preferred to Lloyd George's National Insurance Bill. With the passing of what Beatrice called this 'rotten' Bill in 1911, the Webbs' campaign was to collapse.

'Lloyd George and Winston Churchill have practically taken the *limelight*,' Beatrice conceded. She had needed the talents of Wells and Shaw to combat such brilliantly effective slogans as Lloyd George's 'Ninepence for fourpence' advertising contributory social insurance. But Wells, though he joined the campaign 'very much as a drop of water, when it encounters a pailful, lines up with the rest', was too busy working at his caricatures of the Webbs ('really very clever in a malicious way,' Beatrice noted) in *The New Machiavelli*. And Shaw seemed to have 'got sick of the Fabian Society' and 'lost the power of doing anything except in imperative emergencies,' he later explained, 'partly through having too many irons in the fire, partly through age, fatheadedness, & heavy preoccupation with remoter solutions than I can impose on the F[abian] S[ociety]'.

Beatrice's Minority Report had a formative influence on Shaw's political thinking, not so much through its practical recommendations as at the point where it broke from the commercial tradition of the nineteenth century and went straight to the issue of public welfare. It was not enough, the Report stated, to secure every man a minimum wage for the work he found to do. 'You must provide the wage anyhow, and enable him to find all the work that exists, and if there is no work available you must still spend the wage on him in keeping him fit for work when it does come,' Shaw wrote in a review of the Report. 'His right to live, and the right of the community to his maintenance in health and efficiency, are seen to be quite independent of his commercial profit for any private employer. He is not merely a means to the personal ends of our men of business; he is a cell of the social organism, and must be kept in health if the organism is to be kept in health.'

From the Webbs' national minimum wage, Shaw's mind moved on to an annual salary that would in effect be an equal share of the national product. Then, in or about December 1910, he came up with a new definition of socialism capable of changing human behaviour. He seems to have started writing a book on this subject, but adapted what would have been its opening chapter into a lecture which he gave the Fabians on 9 December 1910 at the Memorial Hall in Farringdon Street. This was part of a series entitled 'Some Open Questions of Socialism' and was called 'The Simple Truth about Socialism'. The simple truth about socialism was that it meant equality of income – 'a state of society in which the entire income of the country is divided between all the people in exactly equal shares, without regard to their industry, their character, or any other consideration except the consideration that they are living human beings ... that is Socialism and nothing else is Socialism'.

Though Shaw did not have much confidence in imposing this 'remoter solution' on the Fabians, he felt that Lloyd George's plans for pensioning the elderly and taxing unearned income made it imperative for socialists to regain the initiative in radical thinking about the redistribution of income. Equality was fundamental to socialism, he argued, and without it all Lloyd George's schemes to take from the rich and give to the poor would seem predatory. For without equality nothing could be done except to organize capitalism on a more stable, scientific and commercially profitable basis. The political turmoil following publication of the Minority Report provided an opportunity to introduce socialist principles into the debate of how to reorganize the country, substituting social service for private profit as a motive for human action. Shaw replaced Lloyd George's old age pension with a life pension: 'We must proceed by taxation as Mr Lloyd George does,' he told the Fabians: 'but our object should [be] ... the reduction of all excessive incomes to the normal standard.' He hoped that the task of the Fabian Society in the future would be to work out the practical path towards equality – he even threw out the suggestion, in Wellsian fashion, that the Fabian Basis be amended so as to commit all members to equality. This was to remain the touchstone of Shaw's socialism for the rest of his life.

Though he believed that the Minority Report would 'prove the most momentous political event of our time', Shaw's socialism was a theorizing romancing philosophy out of focus with Beatrice's careful considerations. He supported her campaign with various speeches and articles, but most often advanced his 'old age' or 'stardom' as reasons for not soldiering along with her. Perhaps, Beatrice reflected, the art of pleasing in literature had taken too much out of him. He might have been 'of great value', yet he seemed cocooned by his own writings. Besides 'he will orate and go off on to the sex question, which does not interest Sidney', she wrote in the spring of 1911:

'Then, Charlotte does not really like me and I do not really care for her! . . . as a matter of fact there does not seem much reason for meeting – and therefore we seldom meet . . . which is somewhat sad, as he and Sidney have always cared for one another: they are perhaps each other's most long-standing friends. Possibly if we threw ourselves into the work of the Fabian Society I might increase my intimacy with Charlotte and therefore of the two of us with Shaw.'

But it was too late. Beatrice had wanted the Fabians to gain kudos from the Minority Report and believed her revivalist campaign to be a means of also reviving the Society after the decampment of Wells. But the business of permeating the whole nation, including its non-socialists, seemed to need a political body more neutral than the Fabians; and later in 1909 she and Sidney had formed the National Committee for the Prevention of Destitution, with campaign offices in the Strand midway between the London School of Economics and the Fabian headquarters. This organization had drawn away many of the active Fabians, with the result that by 1911 the Society had reached a crisis 'not of dissent, but of indifference'. It was this indifference that had come between the Webbs and Shaw. 'You must both bear in mind that when you formed the National Committee instead of putting the Minority Report into the hands of the Fabian Society, you threw the Society aside as useless on my hands,' Shaw told the Webbs early in 1911. ' . . . It was really Wells over again: you felt, like him, that you couldnt be hampered in your work by the need for getting anything past that old Executive. And you were quite right . . . I, too, like you & Wells, have neither time nor disposition to pass my work through that clogged and muddy filter . . .'

The Webbs could hardly dispute Shaw's contention. Certainly Beatrice was planning to throw herself, and Sidney, back into Fabian work and transfer the research and publicity from their campaign to a reconstituted Society: but first they had arranged to go on a sabbatical voyage round the world. Sidney had actually toyed with the notion of resigning from the executive before they embarked, but Shaw, snatching the initiative from him, 'not only announces his intention of resigning, but persuades some half a dozen others of the Old Gang to resign also', Beatrice fulminated. 'All with the view to making room for young men who are not there!'

G.B.S. saw in the Webbs' year abroad an excellent chance for retirement and the opportunity for rearranging the executive without political controversy. He had always intended to resign himself, he reminded Edward Pease, 'when I had completed my quarter of a century service; but what with Wells and one thing and another the moment was not propitious . . . if we do not resign now, we shall never resign'.

Shaw and Webb had often spoken of resignation. Shaw had spoken of it also to Wells, but Wells had doubted him. After all, Shaw had arrived at his quarter of a century service on the executive only in 1910. 'I think Sidney *must* retire,' Shaw now urged. Neither Bland, nor he himself, nor Stewart Headlam would stand again – perhaps not even Granville Barker either. The clearing out of the Old Gang would be pretty well complete – so why not make it complete and simultaneous? Otherwise a succession of such shocks over a year or more would 'reduce the Society to the condition of a village in an earthquake district'. Far better, Shaw advised Sidney, than attempting to steal away one by one would be to make a feature of it and give the Society the unusual sensation of being alive: 'we must all go together, with the limelight on, and full band accompaniment.' To avoid any smash-up, he suggested something 'violent and fantastic' in the form of a Fabian House of Lords – a new body called the Senate and its elderly members Senators. 'They can wear togas if necessary,' he speculated, '& be accompanied by lictors.' Webb reduced this to a less colourful proposal for a class of consultative executive members, but the scheme was generally felt to be undemocratic, and dropped. At the executive elections in April 1911, Webb came top of the poll and stayed on: Shaw, Bland and three other members resigned; and their five replacements, remarkable for lack of youth and radicalism, fulfilled all Beatrice's pessimistic predictions.

The Fabians continued to busy themselves with a string of expedient small jobs that, in Shaw's vocabulary, need not have been called socialism at all. Looking back some years later, he wondered whether the Old Gang should not have left half a dozen years earlier and taken the risk of handing everything over to Wells. 'In a way he [Wells] was fundamentally right in seeing that he could do nothing unless The Society would definitely accept him and trust him, and get rid of us,' Shaw wrote. 'God only knows whether the Society had not better have done it.'

[3]

I confess I am getting old and childish and easily amused. (1904)

In the half-dozen years before the war Shaw whipped up more than half a dozen one-act trifles – skits, farces, extravaganzas for the stage – often anaesthetizing his fears of sex or death, and written mostly in a style which Virginia Woolf described as that of 'a disgustingly precocious child of 2 – a sad and improper spectacle to my thinking'. The event-plots of these pieces tell the story of Shaw's contribution to magic and absurdity, and rearrange fragments and visions of his life into revealing patterns.

The Fascinating Foundling was knocked off early in August 1909 for a charity performance at the request of Elizabeth Asquith, daughter of the Prime Minister. Shaw provided the piece with a subtitle – 'A Disgrace to the Author' – that may have been prompted by its kinship to what he had disapproved of in *The Importance of Being Earnest*.

As with *Major Barbara*, the story revolves round the destiny of orphans. A smart and beautiful young man forces his way into the ante-room of the Lord Chancellor's office, and engages his elderly clerk in a broadsword combat (fire tongs versus poker). This parody of a Shakespearian duel is interrupted by the indignant appearance of the Lord Chancellor. The young man explains that he is Horace Brabazon, a foundling, and has come to the Lord Chancellor as 'father of all the orphans in Chancery' to ask for two trifling items: one is a theatrical engagement, the other a wife – 'someone old enough to be my mother,' he explains, ' . . . Not old enough to be your mother . . . I attach some importance to that distinction . . . One mustnt overdo these notions.' After he leaves a second caller arrives (a benign profile of the Lord Chancellor in a newspaper that day appears to have attracted these visitors). She is Anastasia Vulliamy, a good-natured, rather flighty girl and a most superior foundling, having been discovered 'on the doorstep of one of the very best houses in Park Lane'. She too wants the Lord Chancellor 'to be a father to me'. Her pet dog has been stolen, her cat has behaved too indecently to be kept in the same house: she would like to try out a husband, 'someone I can bully'. Horace Brabazon returns for his symbolic walking-stick. She at once proposes to him, recommending a three-week engagement: 'You are only on approval, of course.' He protests that she is too young. But once he understands that like him she is a foundling and will bring no family to make him miserable, he grows excited and hopeful.

ANASTASIA   I havnt a relation in the world.
BRABAZON   [clasping her] Mine! Mine! Mine!

The Fascinating Foundling was published seventeen years later in *Translations and Tomfooleries*. *The Glimpse of Reality* was a more sombre tomfoolery which took Shaw nearly eighteen months to complete and eighteen years to see performed, chiefly because he kept mislaying it. He had begun this 'tragedietta' in March 1909 to exhibit Granville Barker's 'remarkable talent for acting mortal terror of death' when, on some occasion or other, he might want a playlet. It is set in the fifteenth century and takes place at an inn on the edge of an Italian lake. A devout friar aged one hundred and thirteen is hearing the confession of a young girl, Giulia. He urges her to press close to him as he is deaf. She does so, telling him that in order to win a sufficient dowry for her to marry a fisherman she is to decoy young Count Ferruccio ('a devil for women') to the inn. The Count will then be killed by her father who will claim the reward. The venerable friar flings off his gown and beard and reveals himself as the young Count. Giulia's father, the innkeeper, and her fiancé, the fisherman, appear, and all four of them sit down to supper, eating, drinking and talking. The Count negotiates for his life: he rages, he tempts, he charms, he bribes – but in a complicated tactical game he shows himself to be 'a man with no soul: one who has never done anything or been anything', and is defeated.

For the first time in his life he has come up against something real, 'something that does not care for me'. From infancy he has been fed on dreams and grown up a spoilt cub. Now he begins to have a living faith, if only in the reality of death. 'There is nothing like a good look into the face of death,' he says, ' . . . for shewing you how little you really believe and how little you really are.' With this glimpse of reality his terror of death, which is really a terror of terror, falls away. He speaks fearlessly, and his words strike the innkeeper and fisherman as so unusual that, believing him mad and therefore under the protection of God, they refuse to murder him. The scene ends with ingenious plans to benefit all four of them.

Among the other playlets of this period were 'An Interlude', 'A Thumbnail Sketch of Russian Court Life in the XVIII Century', 'A Piece of Utter Nonsense', and 'A Demonstration'. The 'Interlude', which was Shaw's subtitle for *The Dark Lady of the Sonnets*, is a miniature work of art.

It was composed between 17 and 20 June 1910, and since Shaw would not lift his finger – even for three days – to produce a work of art 'if I thought there was nothing more than that in it' he made the play, at the suggestion of Edith Lyttleton, into a *pièce d'occasion* supporting the appeal for a British National Theatre.

It is a midsummer night on the terrace of the Palace at Whitehall, overlooking the Thames, in the spacious times of Elizabeth I. A Beefeater stands on guard. He is approached by a cloaked man resembling a ghost. 'Angels and ministers of grace defend us!' he cries. The cloaked figure stops and writes, then speaks. What a good theatrical scene, he declares, the two of them in the moonlight would make. He is no ghost, but a man come to keep tryst with his Dark Lady 'whose pretty looks have been mine enemies'. The Beefeater relaxes: he knows this dark lady well enough, 'a warm bit of stuff', who is always making trysts with men – the previous night it had been with young Lord Pembroke. 'You may say of frailty that its name is woman,' he casually remarks. The man turns pale at this information, yet luxuriates in the phrase and makes a note of it – at which the 'well-languaged' warder dubs him 'a snapper-up of such unconsidered trifles': and down that goes too on the man's tablet.

The Beefeater moves discreetly off and an apparition appears. It is a sleepwalking lady wrapped in a cloak, who wanders along the terrace cursing the cosmetics that have peppered her with freckles: 'Out, damned spot . . . All the perfumes of Arabia will not whiten this Tudor hand.' The man, enchanted by this word-imagery, mistakes her for his mistress, the mysterious 'woman colour'd ill'. He takes her arm, wakes her, and only then discovers that she is a stranger fair. To introduce himself he mentions that he is 'the king of words', and rhapsodizes over her own word-skill – he has so bad a memory, he adds, he must catch them on his tablets. He puts his arms round her . . . but suddenly the two of them are knocked sideways by the Dark Lady who, 'like a morning thrush', has come stooping along the terrace and been jealously listening. During this falling-about the three characters are revealed to one another – as Granville Barker, Suzanne Sheldon and Mona Limerick. For it is they who, in the first presentation at His Majesty's Theatre on 24 November 1910, played Shakespeare, Queen Elizabeth and Mary Fitton.

Shakespeare finds courage in his inflated view of himself as a man of family; but the maid of honour, Mistress Fitton, is terrified and warns the Queen against taking any notice of this playwright – his awful power with language can flatter or abuse, and 'I am tired of being tossed up to heaven and dragged down to hell at every whim that takes him'. Only fear strikes any words out of her that Shakespeare finds worth taking down and she is eager to leave the scene of danger. But Queen Elizabeth, for all her vanity, is a *femme inspiratrice* and practically every word she utters is Shakespearian. 'I am not here to write your plays for you,' she eventually rebukes him. Indeed, Prospero-like, Shaw has called her there, together with Shakespeare, as history's two most commanding witnesses to plead the cause of endowing a National Theatre. This is the boon that Shakespeare asks of his Queen: for it is about writing plays, not making love, that he is serious. Bringing us up to date, the Queen tells him that it will be three hundred years or more before England accepts the truth of what he has said, but 'if I could speak across the ages to our descendants, I should heartily recommend them to fulfil your wish'.

To the play Shaw attached a Preface framing, in its touching picture of the Shakespearian scholar Thomas Tyler, 'specialist in pessimism', a dreadful warning against the academic habit of using the past as a refuge from the present. In this Preface, which combined a contemporary portrait of Frank Harris with a posthumous portrait of Shakespeare, he attempted to bring the past up to date by using it as an illustration of the present. Shakespeare lives on in each of us and all Shakespearian criticism, either factual or fantastical, is a form of autobiography. Harris's Shakespeare had turned out a deep-voiced sentimentalist; Shaw's Shakespeare is piteously devoid of sentiment and filled with 'an irrepressible gaiety of genius'. This Shavian Shakespeare makes impish comedy out of his own misfortunes (as Shaw had done in *The Fascinating Foundling*); he is inspired by his love of music, grows immune to the weaknesses of passion and, by virtue of this indomitable detachment, becomes superhuman. He is also master of irony. 'I am convinced,' Shaw concludes, 'that he was very like myself.'

The 'state of levity' which Shaw insists buoyed up Shakespeare's life and was even present at his death, floats through almost all Shaw's playlets whose subtitles have a similar mutinous tone to Shakespeare's popular comedies – *Much Ado About Nothing, As You Like It, What You Will*. It was not beyond Shaw to reason that his 'Piece of Utter Nonsense', otherwise called *The Music-Cure*, might have been achieved by Shakespeare had he been born in 1856 instead of 1564. In fact it was a topical skit written as a curtain-raiser for the play he had finally persuaded G. K. Chesterton to write. Chesterton's drama, which shows love miraculously conquering diabolical evil, was called *Magic*. Shaw's variety turn is a piece of magic realism suggesting that this miracle of love is an hallucination, like the concept of evil.

Lord Reginald Fitzambey cannot stand very much reality. He hates his present existence as an under-secretary in the War Office. His single talent is for music. 'I am not fit for public affairs,' he confesses. ' . . . I have a real genius for home life.' But because his father is a Duke he has been obliged to enter Parliament. Now, as the curtain goes up, he is in the hands of a doctor and suffering from a breakdown after being accused of improperly buying shares in the British Macaroni Trust. This is Shaw's reference to the recent Marconi shares scandal in which various members of the Cabinet (particularly the Attorney General, Rufus Isaacs, whose brother Godfrey was Managing Director of the Marconi Company and a director of the American Marconi Company) had been accused of using government information for profitable dealing. Their chief accuser had been Cecil Chesterton who was charged with criminal libel. In Gilbert Chesterton's view the Marconi case was the last considerable attempt to purge Parliament and would some day be seen 'as one of the turning-points in the whole history of England and the world'. To Shaw's mind it was a lot of hot air which he summed up in an article called 'Wireless Indignation'. Cabinet Ministers, he argued, were neither saints nor criminals: they were ourselves. 'I did what any fellow would have done,' Reginald Fitzambey says. 'I bought all the shares I could afford.'

The doctor gives him some opium and he 'sees' a laughing crocodile about to play the piano with its tail – which is Shaw's reference to De Quincey's alligator and his unconvincing version of evil. The doctor concludes that he should double the dose after which 'if anything comes it will be something pretty this time'. He leaves, and a lovely lady pianist appears. This is Strega Thundridge, 'the female Paderewski'. She tells Reginald that his mother has engaged her for a terrific fee to play the piano in his room for two hours. Reginald cannot escape – the staircase, corridors and grounds are crowded with people waiting to hear this music. There follows, as she plays Chopin's Polonaise in A Flat, an optimistic essay on the effects of opium upon the romantic imagination. These two perfect anti-types find themselves in perfect harmony. 'I want a strong arm to lean on,' declares Reginald, ' . . . a breadwinner on whose income I can live without the sordid horrors of having to make money for myself . . . ever since I was a child I have had only one secret longing, and that was to be mercilessly beaten by a splendid, strong, beautiful woman.' Strega Thundridge, whose natural strength has been marvellously expanded by her playing of left hand octave passages, is that splendid, muscular creature. She too has a dream: 'It is a dream of a timid little heart fluttering against mine, of a gentle voice to welcome me home . . . of someone utterly dependent on me, utterly devoted to me' whom, she promises, she would beat sometimes to a jelly, before casting herself into an ecstasy of remorse. He plays the wedding march, she plays the bass – an echo of Shaw's pre-marital duets. They embrace fiercely and confront their terrible destiny together.

The Music-Cure, Shaw revealed, 'is not a serious play'. He had finished it on 21 January 1914 and it was first presented a week later to celebrate the hundredth performance of Chesterton's *Magic*. 'There is, however, no pressing reason why the thing should be performed at all,' Shaw advised. It had taken him almost nine months to bring himself to complete it, during which time (between 29 July and 13 August 1913) he had also written *Great Catherine*.

Shaw's Catherine, he tells us in his 'Author's Apology', is the Catherine whom Byron had celebrated in *Don Juan*.

> In Catherine's reign, whom glory still adores
> As greatest of all sovereigns and w----s.

Byron may leave the impression that he said very little about Catherine, but that very little was 'all there really is to say that is worth saying', Shaw insisted. 'His Catherine is my Catherine and everybody's Catherine.' Shaw's Catherine is moreover Shaw's Elizabeth, a woman set in authority over men. Shakespeare had turned Elizabeth into Caesar; Shaw turned his female Caesars into great sentimental comedians who played their queenly roles as 'eccentric character parts, and produced scene after scene of furious harlequinade with the monarch as clown . . . ' The part of Catherine was created for the actress Gertrude Kingston who had formerly made her reputation 'as an impersonator of the most delightful feather-headed and inconsequent ingenues'. 'It will always be a joy to me that you destined her [Catherine] for me,' the actress wrote to the playwright. ' . . . you have made me famous.' But Shaw dismissed the thing as 'boyish rubbish . . . a music-hall sketch, and utter slosh at that'.

There is no real plot in *Great Catherine*. It is an eighteenth-century encounter, spread across four bravura scenes, between some extreme personalities. There is an 'outrageous ruffian', the genial and gigantic Shavian villain Prince Patiomkin; there is Catherine the Great as described by Byron; a caricature Englishman, the stiff and insular Captain Edstaston of the Light Dragoons (who is Britannus escaped from *Caesar and Cleopatra* and now named after Shaw's sister-in-law's house) and his invincibly snobbish fiancée Claire. Here were the comic stereotypes with whom Shaw felt most at ease. 'This is carrying a joke too far,' protests the Captain as the semi-drunken Patiomkin carries him into the Empress's *petite levée* and dumps him on her bed. And that is what Shaw is doing, carrying the joke as far as it will go – and further. 'This is perfectly ridiculous,' says Claire surveying the Empress's court which, after Shaw's juvenile rearrangement, has been converted into a nursery. In this nursery the pain and fear of adult life evaporate. The Captain, for example, though threatened with five thousand blows of the stick, with being skinned alive, having his tongue ripped out or his eyelids cut off, is actually trussed up and tickled by the Empress's toe – far worse, he tells her, than being roasted, basted, beheaded, hanged or quartered.

That rulers behave like children is an adult criticism and one that here received its endorsement when the Lord Chamberlain's Comptroller recommended (besides modification to the captain's uniform) that Patiomkin be made a teetotaller and Catherine a monogamist so as to avoid giving offence to Grand Duke Vladimir of Russia, a friend of the British Royal Family. Such absurdities support Shaw's point that 'the fiction has yet to be written that can exaggerate the reality of such subjects.' Yet Shaw did not so much exaggerate as overrule reality by enveloping such subjects in the dream-world he had ostracized in *The Glimpse of Reality*. Shaw's sympathy with these Caesars and Elizabeths and Catherines grew out of the emotional uncertainty he shared with them and which fills the atmosphere of these skits and sketches. There is no evil in Shaw's plays: his characters are either 'mad' or behave badly out of fear – and it is this fear of life that these playlets replace with the fun and games Shaw had credited to Shakespeare and called 'an irrepressible gaiety of genius'. But they show too, in a childlike way, the sources of his fear: physical cruelty and the dominance of death, but also infant sexuality and its bearing on the adult operation of the sex instinct. Catherine wishes she could have Captain Edstaston not as her lover but 'for my museum'; Elizabeth and Shakespeare are in earnest about their work and only play at sexual passion. But in the secret place of Shaw's fantasies, set in the never-never lands of far away and long ago, such prescriptions against sex are inoperative. 'The truth is that a man (or a woman) should never take his (or her) innocence for granted in matters of sex,' he wrote to Edith Lyttelton, 'in which ANYTHING is possible and even probable.'

It is this guilty world of ANYTHING that these playlets invade, and that sometimes disgusted Shaw. 'I cant stand the Fascinating Foundling,' he told Lillah McCarthy. *The Music-Cure* was 'abominable trash' and 'simply unbearable' in performance. *Great Catherine* was 'heartbreaking' to watch but 'I cannot go and blame the actors for the failure of a bad play'. Such disgust was partly a reaction from the plays' many autobiographical associations. The role of Strega Thundridge, for example, was written for an actress who had started her career as a talented pianist and whom Shaw had encircled with romantic dreams that became so persistent he could hardly tell where the dream ended and reality began. It was an affair that virtually began by her bedside while she was ill and which is comically retold in *Great Catherine* where the fastidious Captain Edstaston is deposited on Catherine's bed by the romantic Prince Patiomkin.

Shaw had given a 'demonstration' of this affair in another of his short plays. This was not set far away or long ago, but at any time, anywhere, to demonstrate how easily dreams might at any moment become real. Its first title, *Trespassers Will Be Prosecuted*, had been suggested by a notice posted on the gate of Edith Lyttelton's house (she being a confidante of Shaw's wonderful actress). After three weeks' work in the summer of 1912, he finished the play on a 'Gt Northern train passing Holloway', removed the warning, *Trespassers Will Be Prosecuted*, and substituted *Overruled*.

Overruled had a difficult life that did not augur well for dreams or reality. It had been extracted by Charles Frohman, with Pinero's *The Widow of Wasdale Heath* and Barrie's *Rosalind*, as part of a triple bill bringing together London's three principal dramatists on one programme. Shaw went to the opening night and passed on the audience's reactions in a letter to Pinero: 'they simply loathed us. They weren't indifferent: we didnt fall flat; they were angrily disgusted: we were trampled on, kicked and hurled downstairs and out into the street.' Since that 'poor devil' Frohman was once more involved, Shaw eagerly claimed credit for 'the most appalling failure on record: the only regular right down failure I ever had'. His play had come on first and the public hated it, laughing against its will three or four times – 'a hideous laughter as if someone had tickled a grindstone or made a face at a chained dog'. *Overruled* seemed to plummet them into hell where Pinero had mocked them with an idyll. Mercifully they had been snatched back into heaven at the end by a sentimental piece of 'Barriefication'. 'Barrie fattened on the corpses of our reputations,' Shaw told the playwright, R. C. Carton. 'When the curtain went up on his play and discovered Irene Vanbrugh, the relief, the joy, the gladness was so enormous that before a word was spoken the audience cheered madly for several solid minutes ... And yet everybody thought my play was a dead cert.'

Despite its failure, Shaw believed his little play to be 'really a work of some merit' and that it had come to such signal grief because of poor casting. Yet the audience's dislike was part of its quality – 'it is a slight, desiccated thing,' wrote St John Ervine over forty years later, ' ... full of the embarrassing skittishness which he was apt to display when sex relations were involved.' For years Shaw had been objecting to the teasing versions of adultery presented on the stage. In his own plays he had either replaced adultery with other passions or rephrased it impersonally as the workings of a biological technology. But in *Overruled* he claimed to have displayed marital infidelity and introduced the act of sexual intercourse itself (so far as this was practicable) to the theatre. It was remarkable that no one noticed.

The event-plot of the play explains some of the mystery. It is a summer night at a seaside hotel. A lady and gentleman are sitting together on a chesterfield in a corner of the lounge. He throws his arms round her and it seems might possibly do more when suddenly he finds out that she is married. She too is astonished to learn that he has a wife – particularly since they have been cruising round the world each believing the other to be single. They can neither advance nor retreat, but seem suspended on the chesterfield between making love and parting from each other. It appears that they may have tricked themselves into sexual intercourse if only because, as the lady says, 'Nothing – not life nor death nor shame nor anything can part us.' At that moment they hear the voices of a man and a woman in the corridor, and spring apart to opposite sides of the lounge. These voices belong to their respective husband and wife who enter, occupy the still-warm chesterfield and begin to enact a somewhat similar love scene. It transpires that both married couples had decided to enjoy a holiday away from each other and go round the world in opposite directions. The second flirtation is interrupted by the first couple, and there follows what Shaw calls in his Preface to the play 'a clinical study' of how polygamy actually occurs 'among quite ordinary people'.

Shaw's cast of lovers is 'ordinary' in the sense that they are types. The two wives represent two kinds of realist, the social and the emotional. The two husbands belong to different categories of moralist, the man who believes it does not matter what we do so long as we are prepared to admit it is wrong, and the man who cannot do anything unless he is convinced it is right. But these adulterous couples are not 'ordinary' in their behaviour, since *Overruled* is not a realistic play. Shaw's technique 'is as far removed from realism as eighteenth-century technique', wrote Desmond Mac-Carthy in a review. 'His characters seldom speak words they would actually utter; each says instead the things most typical of his or her point of view . . . The movement of the characters in dialogue is as symmetrical as figures in a square dance, but . . . an artificial comedy such as *Overruled* cannot be played by actors whose skill is limited to imitating the behaviour of people in a hotel lounge.' Here was one reason why Shaw's play had seemed a 'dead cert' on reading and had failed in performance. In all these playlets the actors, thinking the lines funny, spoke them for laughs instead of playing their parts hard. Before any amusement is possible, it is essential for the audience to be convinced that, however artificial and extraordinary they are, these characters take themselves seriously. Their words have to be converted into actions by the players who must 'dramatize the argumentative climaxes of exasperation, insult and apoplectic outrage', Irving Wardle commented after a revival of *Overruled*. 'They have to incarnate four disembodied points of view into four flesh and blood personages. And they have to introduce the element of sensual attraction which Shaw chose to omit.'

The play is a 'demonstration' of two opposing theses. In the world of the theatre its source was the first work to have come under Shaw's notice as drama critic of the *Saturday Review*: Sydney Grundy's *Slaves of the Ring*. Conceived as a one-act burlesque of Grundy's fashionable three-act 'tissue of artificialities' involving 'a quadrille of lovers instead of a pair', *Overruled* was also put on offer as a 'model to all future writers of farcical comedy'. Twenty years later this option was to be taken up by Noël Coward in his own version of Shaw's world-cruising quadrille, *Private Lives*, where the mixed-up couples once again meet in an hotel with each other's partners.

Shaw used his Preface to argue that, in the long tradition of theatre adultery from Restoration comedy to the Parisian school, 'nobody tells the truth'. For a reasonably healthy public opinion on sex questions we needed data as to our actual conduct and real thoughts. Since we were permitted to speak in jest of what might not be spelled out in earnest, farcical comedy was specially privileged against social taboos: so Shaw experimented with *Overruled* as that 'one outlet for the truth'.

Overruled does demonstrate certain truths outside the world of the theatre about the married man who was now entering his late fifties. The play threatens a change of life but characteristically in reverse. The two couples are shown purging their inclinations of all moral guilt, but the play is also a therapeutic device to drench, with what Desmond MacCarthy called its 'fountain of irrational gaiety' (that Shakespearian 'gaiety of genius' again) the fires of sexual frustration that had been accumulating within Shaw over fifteen unconsummated years of marriage. 'You see, it's a great many years since Ive been able to allow myself to fall in love,' explains one of the husbands. ' . . . I thought I had lost the power of letting myself fall really and wholeheartedly in love.' And the second husband confesses: 'Year after year went by: I felt my youth slipping away without ever having had a romance in my life; for marriage is all very well: but it isnt romance.' In his optimistic fantasy Shaw assigns the wives of these marriages a perfect tolerance of adultery. 'If you will be so very good, my dear, as to take my sentimental husband off my hands occasionally, I shall be more than obliged to you,' says one wife to the other who is perfectly willing to comply since, she says, 'I like to be loved. I want everyone round me to love me.'

But Shaw's wife was far from feeling this, and to that extent this farcical comedy was an outlet for his wishes rather than a clinical study of how polygamy was soon to threaten their marriage. Nor is there a resolution to the work, only the spirit of procrastination and confusion between real thoughts and actual conduct. In the play he gives priority to the thought as master of the deed; but in the Preface, where he maintains that those who profess advanced views are mostly 'the last people in the world to engage in unconventional adventures of any kind', he actually opposes the 'demonstration' of his play. Was the play to overrule the Preface, or the Preface overrule the play? The inconsistency registers Shaw's sexual tension and the uncertainty with which he now briskly accelerated into the last great romance of his life, for which *Overruled* had served as curtain-raiser.

[4]

I can't stand people who will not believe anything because it might be false nor deny anything because it might be true. (1914)

The quantity of people, objects, duties, events from which Charlotte had to remove G.B.S. was mounting. From some of them, to her relief, he positively welcomed removal. 'Anything to avoid Christmas in England!' he had called out on 23 December 1910 before sailing next morning from Bristol to Jamaica. For a fortnight Charlotte and he rolled with two Bishops very damnably on the rough seas, arriving on the evening of 6 January at Kingston, where they were met by their old Fabian friend Sydney Olivier, the Governor General. He put them up at King's House, his new post-earthquake palace and 'a masterpiece of *nouveau* art' in reinforced concrete. Next day they motored across Jamaica and Shaw, who had been pleased at how quickly he had gained his sea legs, found himself unable to regain his equilibrium on land. For forty-eight hours he was disabled by a severe headache from all talking, writing, reading. Then they returned, via Christiana, to King's House. 'I am taking photographs in 100th of a second through yellow screens & watching the lizards and dragon flies,' he wrote to Granville Barker. ' . . . Charlotte (in a padded dressing gown) is quite happy . . . The trees & mountains look pleasantly theatrical through the mosquito curtains . . . ' After six days on the island, and an interview with the *Gleaner* in which G.B.S. laid down plans for the rebuilding of Kingston, they embarked for another fortnight at sea. 'On the whole it was a good move, this,' Shaw concluded, though he'd hardly

278

had time to get used to the novelty of 'bananas and sugar canes and coloured villages and eighty in the shade in January'.

An enormous parcel of work stood waiting in London. This time he got his land legs at once. There was a talk on socialism to give at the Finsbury Park branch of the Independent Labour Party; another on clean air at the local Smoke Abatement Society; and a third at Birkbeck College on the part played by music and drama in education. There were interviews and letters to be drafted, and even an introduction to someone else's lecture – an inter-disciplinary address by Frederick Evans to members of the Camera Club on the history of the pianola. He had to superintend, too, on 21 February, Constable's publication of three plays with their Prefaces in one volume: *The Doctor's Dilemma*, *Getting Married* and *The Shewing-up of Blanco Posnet*. Two months later the first edition of *Misalliance* appeared - in Trebitsch's translation; and this was almost immediately followed by his collected *Dramatische Werke* in Berlin, to which he contributed an introduction: 'What I owe to German Culture'. At the same time, occasionally crashing into rocks of exasperation, he was endeavouring to float his credit with American culture by investing a good deal of time in Archibald Henderson, his simple loyal biographer. In hasty intervals he reviewed Aylmer Maud's biography of Tolstoy and Houston Chamberlain's *The Foundations of the Nineteenth Century* which he had read on the boat: and he found time to appear as character witness for an actor who was pleading guilty to a charge of attempting to chloroform and rob his foster-mother. In the thick of all this he involved himself in a disastrous revival of *Arms and the Man*; and produced a new play that became his first long-running success in London.

He had finished *Fanny's First Play* on 5 March 1911, after seven interrupted months. The play had been born of Shaw's interest in some of the most topical elements then fermenting in England, from the suffrage movement to the growing powers of the police. But he had worked on it anywhere but England: in the remote Gothic hotel at Parknasilla on the south-west coast of Ireland; and at sea while steaming to and from Jamaica. One consequence of writing in such far-off places about up-to-the-minute political issues seemed to be a strange unfastening of the theme from its treatment. This dislocation was to produce, in the judgement of one critic, 'the type of alienation which Brecht thought necessary to a dispassionate argument'.

The play depicts two middle-class families, the Gilbeys and the Knoxes, associated in business and by their strictly brought-up son and daughter, Bobby and Margaret, who are engaged to be married. It shows us how in such a conventional society the children are more likely than their parents to be realists providing they can gain their spiritual freedom through some independent experience of life – in this case fourteen days' imprisonment for drunk and disorderly behaviour and assaulting the police. Such unruliness is an expression of the Life Force, Shaw implies: it is the reaction against a static society. As a result of this glimpse of reality in prison Bobby Gilbey and Margaret Knox are also released from their social prison and free to acknowledge that their feelings for each other are those of brother and sister. They break off their engagement: Bobby marries a prostitute and Margaret a footman who (in characteristic Shavian reversal) reveals himself as the younger brother to a Duke. Both are marrying outside their social cells and acting in accord with the natural morality of sexual instinct rather than artificial rules of an enclosed system.

That was the complete play when Shaw and Charlotte arrived from their holiday in Jamaica at 10 Adelphi Terrace, and when Lillah McCarthy (who could spy their arrival from her rooms at 5 Adelphi Terrace) came to see Shaw. She told him that she had borrowed some money from Lord Howard de Walden; that she was setting herself up as an actress-manager at Gertrude Kingston's Little Theatre below her apartment: and she asked him for a play. *Fanny's First Play* was too short. But on the plan of *The Taming of the Shrew*, Shaw ingeniously added an Induction and an Epilogue, and early in March handed Lillah this 'Easy Play for a Little Theatre' that would last through an evening's entertainment. 'The idea of the Induction is this,' Shaw explained to Charles Ricketts who designed the costumes. 'A certain Count O'Dowda . . . loathes modern industrial England, and has spent his life in Venice, in the footsteps of Byron, Shelley, and the Brownings.'

'He has lived the perfect artistic life, with his daughter, tolerating nothing later than the XVIII century. But he has consented to send his daughter to Cambridge for two years as it is his own university, and he feels quite sure that it is still untouched by the XIX century. The young lady of course gets up to her neck in the New Machiavellyism and writes an ultra modern suffragette play – Fanny's first play – the performance of which nearly kills the unfortunate old gentleman.'

Fanny O'Dowda, who naturally belongs to the Cambridge Fabian Society, has persuaded her father to have her play anonymously performed, 'with real actors and real critics' at his country house for her nineteenth birthday. The Count expects it to be a 'work of art', of the kind that Shaw himself would not lift a finger to create. The aesthetic differences separating father from daughter reinforce the conflict of the parents and children in Fanny's play; and the sexual liberation of the young people in her play is complemented by Fanny's intellectual liberation from the rule of the theatrical critics, who are a police force of the mind and imagination.

'It turned out most unexpectedly that I had added to the list of stock comic figures – the mother-in-law, the greengrocer, the comic servant &c &c – the comic dramatic critic,' Shaw discovered. Nearly twenty years before he had tried out a dramatic critic as a figure of comedy in *The Philanderer*, but only now, it seemed, had theatrical journalism made the public sophisticated enough to enjoy the fun Shaw was making of his critics. It could, for example, recognize in Mr Trotter the anonymous critic of *The Times*, A. B. Walkley. 'We rather like Mr Trotter,' wrote Walkley in his review, 'probably for the usual reason that we are all apt to admire our opposites. He is a genuine invention . . . a pure figment of the imagination, wholly unlike any actual person. The other critics of the party have obvious originals.' The original of Mr Vaughan was the *Daily News* drama critic E. A. Baughan who had described the author of *Man and Superman* as 'an anaemic idealist', judged *John Bull's Other Island* to be 'formless' and decided after seeing *Caesar and Cleopatra* that 'Mr Shaw is not really a humorous man at all.' Mr Gunn was Shaw's pseudonym for Gilbert Cannan, novelist, playwright and theatre critic of *The Star* who two years earlier had used Shaw and Granville Barker as figures in his descriptive play *Dull Monotony*. The fourth critic is a composite figure called Flawner Bannal whose commonplace opinions are taken to echo those of the average playgoer and who represents the run-of-the-mill reviewer – with something added from Shaw's own early days in journalism.

In the Epilogue these critics debate the authorship of the play they have just seen, naming Barrie, Granville Barker and Pinero, and offering scholarly comparisons with *The Admirable Crichton*, *The Madras House* and *The Second Mrs Tanqueray*. 'I believe it's Shaw,' blurts out Flawner Bannal. 'Rubbish!' retorts Gunn. 'Rot!' exclaims Vaughan. They all agree that Shaw is incapable of feeling passion or writing a play. All he wants is to 'set us talking about him' – which to their disgust he makes them do.

With its variety of stock Shavian themes and characters (from the footman who continues the work of the waiter from *You Never Can Tell* to the religiously-inspired Mrs Knox whose sermon on inner happiness will be developed in *Too True to be Good*), *Fanny's First Play* is almost a parody of Shaw. The play's structure had evolved, in much the same way as had the full version of *Man and Superman*, and it takes to the point of caricature the Shavian practice of ending the drama in the middle of the play and letting the discussion take over – a logical development in someone who had criticized other dramatists for ending their work once it had started to get interesting.

The anonymity of Fanny's marsupial play was matched by a paraphernalia of mystery strung round the authorship of the whole piece, with Shaw insisting that this *secret de polichinelle* formed part of the work. 'I have not put my name to it,' he told Lillah McCarthy when handing her the typescript, and he urged her to reveal that the author's name began with a *B*, so encouraging the rumour that it was by Barrie.

Fanny's First Play by Xxxxxxx Xxxx opened at the Little Theatre on 19 April 1911. 'It was like old time at the Court,' Shaw told Vedrenne two days later, 'except for the void left by Vedrenne.' But this was not repertory: instead they ran the play continuously for as long as the public wanted it – the way Vedrenne had always wished to run Shaw's plays at the Court. 'It is really amusing – considering who wrote it,' Shaw admitted: and the public agreed. For the first time the Shavian drama seemed to have won through to genuine popularity – as William Archer and Max Beerbohm had for years been predicting. On 1 January 1912 it transferred to the Kingsway Theatre and later completed a run of 622 performances. 'I thought that . . . you touched your highest, often striking the human note,' wrote Herbert Beerbohm Tree.

*

The coronation celebrations of King George V and Queen Mary that summer provided another incentive for Shaw and Charlotte to get abroad. 'I had to leave London a week ago,' he wrote to his Spanish translator Julio Brouta on 26 June 1911, 'partly to avoid the coronation, but mainly because I was quite worn out by the season's work, and had to recuperate or die.' His exhaustion was so severe that the programme of recuperation needed to be extreme. Shaw's diary lists some forty towns in France, Switzerland, Austria, Germany and Italy that he and Charlotte visited over the next sixteen weeks. They travelled with the patient Kilsby and his boisterous motor car (which behaved very nicely) and spent many hours motor-mountaineering back and forwards along the most impassable tracks that Shaw could find over the Alps and Dolomites. 'In the valleys, in the towns, in the hotels, in the hideous heat, I have been wretched,' he informed Trebitsch; 'but on the mountains I revive.'

Charlotte presided over this revival with nervous satisfaction. 'I am glad to say that G.B.S. really seems much better *on the whole*,' she reported to Edward Pease. ' . . . he drives the car with no apparent difficulty now, & that makes an immense difference to his spirits . . . That is the form G.B.S.'s energy takes, & I try to think I like it!'

At various places on their itinerary Shaw would arrange to collect a budget of his letters. With this correspondence, Charlotte observed, came relapses in his health. But Shaw found himself resenting her attitude. It was not business, but being so continually out of touch with his business, that was worrying. He was suffering too from inconceivable headaches. 'Decidedly I must be breaking up,' he wrote to Granville Barker. There was cholera in Italy; France was a blast furnace of heat and their continual crossing and re-crossing of immense passes where no car had previously been eventually rendered him 'dead beat physically and, intellectually, idiotic'. They could not go on many more of these holidays together: it would end in the sanatorium.

He was back in harness, 'a heavily preoccupied & mostly exhausted genius', in the second week of October. Charlotte kept him gently on the move between Ayot and Adelphi Terrace, then boarded him up at Edstaston with her sister and brother-in-law for Christmas and the New Year. Here, on 2 January 1912, he began a new play, 'a religious harlequinade', he described it to Frances Chesterton, '...about Christian martyrs'. Playwrights had never adequately mined the fun in these historical subjects or explored the agreeably amusing veins of in-struction and edification, he told Pinero after three days' work on it. 'Do you know anyone who can play a lion well, with a practicable tail, for the Christian Martyr scene in the arena?' The last of the seventy-eight pages of shorthand manuscript was finished on 6 February and sent to his secretary Judy Gillmore for typing. He had written the principal part for Lillah McCarthy, hoping to lure her and Granville Barker away from the Shakespearian productions to which a gift of £10,000 from Lord Lucas had happily committed the new Lillah McCarthy-Granville Barker Management. And he succeeded – though not for another fifteen months. In the meantime he sent the typescript to Gilbert Murray to go over 'and correct any howlers' and read it to the Barkers, J. M. Barrie and G. K. Chesterton who, delighted by the comedy, was one of the few people to be impressed by the religious feeling of the work.

There had been religious feeling in *Fanny's First Play* which revealed what Desmond MacCarthy called Shaw's 'growing interest in the significance of religious conversions'. But few people had noticed this. 'I thought he was going to mellow into deeper thought and feeling, instead of which he wrote *Fanny's First Play*!' Beatrice Webb had protested. She wanted Lillah McCarthy to persuade him 'to do a piece of serious work'. *Fanny's First Play* was 'a brilliant,' Beatrice conceded, 'but slight and somewhat futile performance'. She could hardly have recognized it as the same play described by Desmond MacCarthy as belonging to 'that serious section of his dramatic works, his religious farces'.

Androcles and the Lion was also a religious work, being an offshoot from *Major Barbara*. Desmond MacCarthy's description of it as a 'religious pantomime' recalls Count O'Dowda's execration of this genre: 'that vulgar, ugly, silly, senseless, malicious and destructive thing the harlequinade of a nineteenth century English Christmas pantomime!' This was a view that Shaw could share, having as Corno di Bassetto written that, rather than sit out another pantomime, 'I should choose death'.

Death was the subject of Shaw's pantomime. Desmond MacCarthy believed that in *Androcles and the Lion* Shaw had invented a new form, the nearest equivalent to which were 'those old miracle plays in which buffoonery and religion were mixed pell-mell together'. Shaw himself, while subtitling the work 'A Fable Play', added to the pantomime some elements of satirical comedy and historical melodrama, and turned his Roman arena into a variety theatre with a Call Boy announcing the successive entertainments: 'Number six. Retiarius versus Secutor . . . Number eleven! Gladiators and Christians! . . . Number twelve. The Christian for the new lion.' It was a characteristic flourish of Shavian extravaganza.

The complexity of genre derives from the two plays that 'inspired' Shaw and from the peculiar nature of his inspiration. The first was J. M. Barrie's *Peter Pan*, written for idealized children and then in its first great vogue. Max Beerbohm had drawn a caricature of Barrie 'reading it to a circle of elderly people and children', Shaw remembered. 'The elderlies were beaming with enjoyment; the children were all asleep. I agreed, and wrote "Androcles" to show what a play for children should be like.' Shaw had criticized *Peter Pan* for patronizing children. 'When I was a child I could not endure stuff written down to children,' he later recalled. 'I devoured Pilgrim's Progress, Gulliver, Robinson Crusoe, Arabian Nights, Grimm's Tales, Hans Andersen and the Bible narratives, all written for adults . . . Barrie's *Peter Pan*, written throughout down to the supposed child capacity, is in that respect a failure.' *Androcles and the Lion* is written for children of all ages in the belief that children, like adults, 'do not respect a play that does not rise over their heads occasionally'.

The play was also intended as an antidote to Wilson Barrett's enormously popular religious melodrama *The Sign of the Cross*. The irony here was that Shaw was writing *Androcles and the Lion* for Lillah McCarthy who had spent eight years in Wilson Barrett's company, starting as the wicked Berenice playing next to Wilson Barrett's Marcus Superbus in the London production of *The Sign of the Cross*. Shaw had reported on this production in the *Saturday Review*. 'The whole drama lies in the spectacle of the hardy Roman prefect, a robust soldier and able general, gradually falling under the spell of a pale Christian girl, white and worn with spiritual ecstasy,' he wrote. ' . . . As she gradually throws upon him the fascination of suffering and martyrdom, he loses his taste for wine; the courtesans at his orgies disgust him; heavenly visions obsess him; undreamed-of raptures of sacrifice, agony, and escape from the world to indescribable holiness and bliss tempt him; and finally he is seen, calm and noble, but stark mad, following the girl to her frightfully voluptuous death. It is a tremendous moral lesson . . . though I am pagan enough to dislike most intensely the flogging and racking and screaming on the stage . . . '

As someone who had combined business with piety by shrewdly exploiting the average person's concept of religious art, Wilson Barrett had made himself a legitimate target for Shaw's wit. 'Depend on it,' G.B.S. alerted readers of the *Saturday Review*, 'we shall see Mr Wilson Barrett crucified yet.' Prior to crucifixion, and in a literary version of Palm Sunday, he had been festooned with praise by the most celebrated writer of the day, author of *The Sorrows of Satan*, Marie Corelli. She had been able to find in Wilson Barrett's 'choice and scholarly' language, 'the unpurchasable gift of genius' which could have led him to 'win the laurels of the poet had he not opted for those of the dramatist' – an encomium that Shaw described as unanswerable. 'I must either hold my tongue or else re-write the play to shew how it ought to be done.' Holding his tongue was never in the Shavian line: so in *Androcles and the Lion* he rewrote Wilson Barrett's work. '*Androcles* parallels *The Sign of the Cross* in persons and their relationships and in scenes and their arrangement,' the critic Martin Meisel found. 'It is in deliberate contrast with *The Sign of the Cross* in its view of early Christianity as an influence on these persons and in its view of the conflict between paganism and Christianity.'

Wilson Barrett's scripture-drama had traded on the sado-masochistic exaltations of the whip, the stake and the lions. But the audience at *Androcles* is forbidden such sensations. 'The men in that audience tomorrow will be the vilest of voluptuaries: men in whom the only passion excited by a beautiful woman is a lust to see her tortured and torn shrieking limb from limb,' the Roman Captain tells Lavinia. 'It is a crime to gratify that passion.'

Shaw renounces too the fairy tales of Christianity which had been the substance of *The Sign of the Cross* but which Lavinia, as she waits for death, finds 'fading away into nothing'. Are the Christian stories any truer than those about Jupiter and Diana, the Roman Captain presses her, and does any educated man really believe them? To which Lavinia replies that death is 'so real a thing that when it comes close, all the imaginary things – all the stories as you call them – fade into mere dreams beside the inexorable reality. I know now that I am not dying for stories or dreams'. 'Are you then going to die for nothing?' the exasperated Captain demands. And Lavinia answers that she is dying for something greater than dreams, something too big to understand or give a name to.

This is the same undefined decision to die as Dick Dudgeon made in *The Devil's Disciple*. Both of them belong to the future and instinctively wish to disentangle themselves from the present. The difference between realists such as Dick Dudgeon and Lavinia, and the philistine majority, is that they choose death rather than let it choose them; their decision to live or die is the last ditch of free will. Though the action conforms to the death-resurrection pattern familiar in seasonal myths, the fact that Shaw's spokesman and spokeswoman for the Life Force should both volunteer for death and be saved only by the improbabilities of extravagant event-plots, reflects a pessimism that needed the constant somersaulting of paradox to turn up at the surface so courageously cheerful – like the Christian prisoners in *Androcles* who are 'determined to treat their hardships as a joke'.

After leaving the Fabian executive Shaw fixed his imagination on far-off solutions to political problems. To Beatrice Webb, still active in the Fabian campaigns, his remote focus seemed fantastically impractical. But this was what Shaw meant by the term 'religious'. It was disinterested in the sense that he could not benefit from such work. He set his gaze over the horizon at a time when Christianity would have expressed itself politically as communism; when there would be no more conflict of personal or private property; when our system of atrocious punishments had been abandoned; when we had put a stop to the commercial prostitution of humanity by establishing an exactly equal income for everyone; when we could trust our future to our instinct and develop our sensibilities to the extent of recognizing our fellow feeling with all living beings on earth. This distant view of democracy and economic socialism, imbued by what Shaw understood as the essence of Christianity, was what moved him to take up Aulus Gellius' ancient legend of Androcles and set his play some sixteen hundred years off from the contemporary world.

From a modern perspective Lavinia is seen as being truly religious. 'The hand of God is upon me,' she says. But it is not exclusively the hand of a Christian god. 'Religion is such a great thing that when I meet really religious people we are friends at once,' she tells the Captain, 'no matter what name we give to the divine will that made us and moves us.' This is Shaw's own position. 'I do not profess to be a Christian,' he said in 1913 during an address on 'Christianity and Equality' at the City Temple. '. . . I have no religion whatever in the sectarian sense. In this my position is curiously like that of Jesus himself, who seems to have been regarded by all sects as a person of no religion.' In the Shavian sense Jesus was one of a number of Supermen who appear in history to show us the future of human evolution. It was a future we still had not reached and for which Shaw was to make his appeal in the sombre Preface to *Androcles*: 'Why Not Give Christianity a Trial?'. Jesus had been the first Christian, but by choosing a death that was not to be avoided by any Shavian manipulations of event-plot, he had become the last Christian too. 'Christianity was a growing thing which was finally suppressed by the crucifixion.' Since then all civilizations had been elaborate organizations for the prevention of Christianity. The entire social order of Britain remained profoundly anti-Christian. We were still choosing Barabbas. 'Our police and soldiers, all our coercive forces profess to prevent murder and theft, but they do not. They do not profess to prevent Christianity, but they do.'

Shaw's imaginary journey to the early so-called Christian era gave him the distance to comment dispassionately on the twentieth century. The Roman centurions are our own police and soldiers; the Emperor, who is 'a divine personage', is our monarchy; Lavinia and Androcles are aspects of a religious spirit that animated Shaw himself. But 'the saint is always embarrassed by finding that the dynamiter and the assassin, the thief and the libertine, make common cause with him.' The powerful and choleric Ferrovius, whose 'sensibilities are keen and violent to the verge of madness', is a human lion in the prime of life whose kingdom is very much of this world: which is to say he belongs to the present. In the hour of trial he reverts from passive Christianity to the warrior's faith that sees God in the sword. 'Mars overcame me and took back his own,' he says. 'The Christian god is not yet. He will come when Mars and I are dust; but meanwhile I must serve the gods that are, not the God that will be.' Spithio is avowedly a Christian as any respectable gentleman in Victorian or Edwardian England might claim to be; he is a moral opportunist who hopes on a technicality to slip into heaven just before closing time.

Androcles and the Lion is another of Shaw's nursery plays. As the chocolate soldier gets the better of the professional cavalry officer in *Arms and the Man*, so the 'small, thin, ridiculous little' Greek tailor Androcles triumphs over the Roman Emperor who behaves like the Mayor of Toy Town. Androcles is a Wellsian hero, recognized by Wells himself in a letter to Shaw as 'one of your greatest creations, the holy silly man . . . I could almost find it in me to try an imitation'. While Lavinia's more sophisticated faith depends upon the necessary strength to stand alone and is the basis for a political creed, the ability of Androcles to overcome fear arises from his religious sense of being at one with the creatures in the narrative of life. 'Death is the last enemy to be overcome,' Shaw said in a speech this year, 'and we have not overcome it even yet.' The dreadful monster of death is reconstituted in *Androcles* as a nursery animal called Tommy, a frisky, clever, coquettish creature which 'purrs like a motor car' and transforms the ghastly arena of death into a dance hall. 'What a pretty liony-piony situation it is, with no thought at all for the realities of Christian martyrdom,' Stevie Smith later wrote. 'And underneath there beats a heart of fear that cannot allow suffering . . . '

Many autobiographical impulses prompted *Androcles and the Lion*. There was the birth of moral passion when Sonny nerved himself to throw off Christian superstition. There was Shaw's discovery of socialism which gave him a creed and a cause to live for, switched on his intelligence, and sent his arguments bristling and glittering into the world. There was his experience five years earlier of being carried away off the coast of Wales with Robert Loraine by the current of a rough sea. The certainty that 'I was on the point of inevitable death' had destroyed 'the whole interest and importance of my imaginary world, usually the largest part of my world', he told the actress Rosina Filippi. 'The reality of death tolerated nothing near it except things equally real . . . ' By importing this real experience into his imaginary world he hoped to give Lavinia's imminent death its verisimilitude and bring people 'face to face for the first time with the grim reality of persecution and their own complicity in it, and perhaps hurt their eyes with a flash of the unbearable radiance of real religion' – everything that Stevie Smith felt the play had failed to do since he now used an actual experience to fortify his imaginary world.

In the lion that 'holds up his wounded paw and flaps it piteously before Androcles', Brigid Brophy has seen a likeness to the literary lion who once boasted to Beatrice Webb he was 'untameable' and who had then been tamed by Charlotte into marriage 'on one leg' and led off for a honeymoon on crutches.

But there is another way of seeing the paradisiacal dance that Androcles and this wonderful animal perform in the forest at the end of the Prologue. Androcles then is a long-suffering married man 'addicted to Christianity' (as his wife Megaera complains) in much the same way as Shaw was addicted to work. The journey through the forest with his wife has all the tension and bickering that were beginning to fill Shaw's holidays with Charlotte. When Androcles 'embraces the lion' and 'the two waltz rapturously round and round and finally away through the jungle', he is expressing Shaw's desire to be off on some wild escapade. When he triumphantly dances again with the lion at the end of the play in the Roman arena, his wife Megaera has gone – no one cares where. But her last words of the Prologue – 'you havnt danced with me for years; and now you go off dancing with a great brute beast that you havnt known for ten minutes . . . ' – are a comic variation of a complaint Shaw was soon to hear from Charlotte.

✳

'I have written a new play quite unlike any of the old ones,' Shaw notified Trebitsch on 7 March. 'It would make quite a good opera book for Strauss.' Even without dictionaries, it must have occurred to Trebitsch that one of the principal characters resembled a lion. Was this another joke? His friend Shaw appeared to be suggesting that Max Reinhardt should build a huge circus to accommodate the forthcoming translation.

What Shaw did not tell Trebitsch was that he had started yet another play that morning. A few words he had exchanged with George Alexander, actor-manager of the St James's Theatre, during an interval in his production of *Bella-Donna*, had fired him – and this, as Charlotte clearly saw, was on top of all his other raging commitments. He had recently been elected to the Academic Committee of the Royal Society of Literature and to the Council of the Academy of Dramatic Art, and still busied himself in all things Fabian. More than ever seemed to be going on in the spring of 1912. There had been an eruption of labour disputes among railway workers, cotton operatives and dockers. The coal miners were on strike; feminists were breaking windows; there was fresh agitation in Ireland for Home Rule and new legislation covering military emergencies. Shaw exercised himself over everything: making political speeches at Coventry and Southampton; discussing Ireland with Winston Churchill and corresponding about the functioning of democracy with Keir Hardie; writing on profit-sharing for the *Bystander*, on free speech for the *Fabian News* and, as an illustration of free speech, letting it be known in the *Saturday Review* that he would be prepared to shoot industrial malingerers. 'Perhaps just for one generation we might allow the plea of inculcation,' he relented. Malingerers, of course, were not miners or feminists, but ladies and gentlemen living the lives of social parasites on unearned incomes. Their social disadvantages of family, public schooling and vaccination had given them little chance. But this plea would lose its force after a generation of socialism.

As one of the most famous socialists in Britain, Shaw was invited this March to take on capitalism single-handed by superintending the management of a Yorkshire mill. This mill was to be placed at his disposal without rent and he was free to put as much capital into it as he pleased. Here would be a test of the socialists' claim to have their principles accepted on commercial and economic grounds. 'It might, indeed, be a pleasant relaxation from the hurry and bustle of life in London,' volunteered the Leeds manufacturer who made the proposal. Shaw at once accepted his offer, 'providing that the gentleman who makes it obtains at the same time a charter establishing Socialism in Yorkshire I shall then be happy to take over the factory, or, indeed, any other in any part of the world, on precisely the same conditions'.

The hurry and bustle so devoured G.B.S. as to leave little of his time for Charlotte. When alone they hardly spoke; when they did speak they broke out into quarrelling. To preserve contact with what she had believed in, Charlotte was making a selection of passages from Shaw's writings which she agreed with Constable to publish under a similar arrangement to her husband's. By April the work for this compilation, arranged alphabetically under a hundred and ninety-five headings, was pretty well complete, and it was obvious to her that the time had come for a resounding holiday. She proposed that they go off together to Rome – and G.B.S. said no. In the fourteen adhesive years of their marriage, though there had been a few cracks, such a parting was unprecedented. Charlotte made it clear that she was ill and needed a change; but still he would not go with her. What she needed, he believed, was what they both needed: a change from each other. How stupid, then, to change everything – air, language, meals, habits, country – except that main condition of their lives, and to intensify that condition violently by isolating themselves in a foreign place where they knew practically no one else. Their nerves would never stand it. Charlotte 'quarrelled furiously with me the moment she suspected what I was at until I wished her at the South Pole', Shaw confided to Beatrice Webb. He had suggested that she might take her sister or a friend, but eventually she decided to sail alone. 'She took leave of me,' Shaw told Beatrice, ' . . . in a way that left Charles I taking leave of his family simply nowhere.'

This was disappointing for Trebitsch who had finally decided to visit Ayot St Lawrence at Easter to find out about this lion play with its martyrs and gladiators – Charlotte would make it all clear. 'I think you had better give it up,' Shaw recommended. Charlotte sailed on 12 April with no idea of how long she might remain in Rome, and 'I shall spend part of the time motoring about the country'.

What turned out to be a six-weeks' separation was 'an enormous relief to her', Shaw insisted, 'and quite a beneficial change for me'. The benefit was more obvious than the relief. As if to punish G.B.S. Charlotte clung to her coughs and colds. But so that she might be with him retrospectively and in spirit, G.B.S. sent her every two or three days a narrative-through-letters of his motoring tour round England. 'I feel fearfully incomplete, though I rather like the novelty of being a bachelor too,' he told her the day before he set out.

The motor party consisted of co-drivers Kilsby and Shaw, and passengers Judy Gillmore (who was shortly to get married to a naval officer and give up her job as Shaw's secretary) and Granville Barker who was to catch up with them later. The weather was all sunshine: but Judy seemed to have got St Vitus's Dance and could not keep her ankles quiet; and Kilsby too was not quite himself, having been deprived of all beer and sugar in his tea by a doctor, who prescribed little but whisky – which may have contributed to the irregular rhythm of their travels. They advanced, sometimes bounding forwards at the rate of a hundred miles per day, by way of Cambridge, Peterborough and Lincoln, to York, where they stopped. While waiting for Granville Barker to join them, there was time for some adventuring. Out they went and joined a party of learned men, headed by a clerical dignitary, who were being conducted around York Minster. 'They said nothing,' Shaw reported to Charlotte, 'but seemed impressed and somewhat bewildered.'

'The shyness of the great kept them aloof from us. In the end they hurried out, shepherded by their dignitary, and did not think to tip the verger. Then said the verger to me "I could not very well tell you before them, sir; but the fire in 1828 was the work of a madman." "Why?" said I. "Who are they?" "Lunatics, sir, from the asylum." I think the bystanders were rather disappointed on finding that we – Judy and I – were sane.'

Barker turned up late one night and next day the four of them left York, making a long circuit through Ripon, and arriving at Harrogate where *How He Lied to Her Husband* was to be performed. Shaw and Barker together were like two schoolboys, endlessly and idiotically quoting Shakespeare. Possibly to be out of earshot, Judy had developed into a fast and indefatigable walker. 'She flies up hills, leaving us gasping and trudging after in our elderly manner.' There were plenty of misadventures to keep them happy. In Charlotte's absence, Shaw let a barber loose on his hair using a 'machine' that mowed him bald and reduced his beard to the aspect of a worn-out brush. 'I now look like an elderly Frenchman travelling with his daughter.' At Windermere they went by motor boat down the lake and were caught in the tempest and uproar of the hydro-aeroplanes which 'nearly blew us into the lake'.

Then, apparently on Shaw's instructions, Barker suspended himself from a nail to calculate his weight and 'fell with an appalling bang on his back on the stones'.

They pressed on as far north as Carlisle. Shaw drove until he almost fell asleep at the wheel and then collapsed with one of his periodic headaches; Judy went down with an overwhelming cold; Barker limped off home exhausted; and Kilsby was left with his 'pet bag of scrap iron' doctoring the car.

Then, the weather changing to rain and mist, Shaw was struck down by a vigorous lumbago. 'Ow-ow-ow-ow!!! Have you ever had lumbago?' Trebitsch made out. ' . . . I am really desolate at missing you and your wife . . . Ow-ow-ow-ow-ow-ah-ooh-ow!!!!!' He also sent his lumbago off to Rome to compete with Charlotte's influenza. 'Lumbago is a fearful thing. Possibly it is appendicitis. Possibly spinal paralysis . . . as to climbing stone walls across the hills with Judy – ah-oo-ow!' Lumbago was also Shaw's answer to an enterprise that Trebitsch and Charlotte had devised for luring him over to Paris to see a production of Hamon's translation of *Mrs Warren's Profession* before making a tour together of the châteaux country. 'G.B.S. is most tiresome, as you well know, about letters,' Charlotte wrote to Trebitsch. 'He writes to me – oh, yes! – but he *never* answers any of my questions, and it is quite hopeless to get him to reply about business.'

Rather than Hamon's *Mrs Warren* in Paris Shaw preferred Janet Achurch's 'ghastly' production of *Captain Brassbound* at the Liverpool Repertory Theatre – 'the effect was dismal' with several actors openly quarrelling onstage with the prompter who had interrupted their artistic pauses. But 'Janet pulled it though. She is really better than anyone else'.

The perils of road-journeying now grew extreme. Neither in Ireland nor on the Continent had Shaw experienced such narrow shaves. At one fork in the road where Kilsby found himself steering while his employer reversed, the car toppled over a bank: 'she slid down gracefully like the elephant on the chute at the Hippodrome – backwards – without the slightest shock, except one of surprise to Kilsby . . . ' But nothing deterred Shaw. 'I resolved to prolong our drive,' he continued. Producing a map, he pointed to a road which looked all that a road should be, but which soon ascended so steeply that the car again refused. Shaw and Judy, by this time expert in emergencies, jumped out and began searching for stones to arrest the monster's descent, but it rolled backwards over Judy's finger – and she fainted. 'Kilsby got his shoulders under her like a fireman; I heaped her up on him,' Shaw recounted to Charlotte, 'and he carried her up the hill to an open place where we laid her down and laid our by no means clean handkerchiefs, dipped in mountain water mud, on her forehead . . . I hope the healing of the nail will not be too painful . . . This is a shocking country for motoring.'

They rushed her back to a surgeon and, responding to Shaw's optimism ('the jaunt evidently agrees enormously with her') she said she was game to go on, though Shaw had to 'cut up her meals for her, poor infant'. Proceeding more cautiously now they came to Blackpool, which was in festivity. Princess Louise had opened a new promenade and everything was illuminated, most enchantingly the tram-cars – 'a triumph of crimson and gold fire'. This was Blackpool's first taste of royalty. Thousands of dancers moved to the tempo of band music over acres of parquet floor. 'The sentimental solemnity of the waltzing is beyond description,' Shaw exulted. 'The two-steps are more joyous; and the lancers approach, by comparison, delirium . . . Kilsby says he will bring Mrs Kilsby here for their next holiday.'

To heighten Judy's morale Shaw introduced her to a socialist hairdresser. 'Judy is all right,' he predicted. But on returning to the hairdresser he found she had again fainted. The vagabondage of their trip had been too much, and shortly afterwards she admitted that she wanted to return to London. Since her naval officer was soon to be landing there 'I did not dissuade her', Shaw wrote, and rather reluctantly put her on the train back.

So now there were two. They raced on to Edstaston where 'Mrs Chum' and her husband, the Colonel, put Shaw to work chopping down gorse, adding cramp to his other ailments. But: 'the place is looking delightful, all leaves & blossoms, and soft summer airs,' he informed Charlotte. ' . . . today from eleven to four we three chopped and hacked and piled up heaps of furze bushes for burning like three field laborers.'

Charlotte returned on 22 May and Shaw met her at Southampton. Now that they were together, what had their separation shown? Charlotte could hardly have envied Judy's predicament which might so easily have been her own. G.B.S. had endured the same headaches, cramps, accidents, lumbagos and exhaustion as ever. Nevertheless, the difference had been Judy. 'The chief fun of the tour is her enjoyment of it,' he had explained to Charlotte shortly after Judy's accident. 'I never realized how very staid she is as secretary in Adelphi Terrace until I saw her gambolling like a rabbit or a lamb in the open.'

Already he was working himself to a standstill once more, and crossing swords with Conan Doyle over the sinking of the *Titanic* as he waited for Charlotte's boat to arrive. His target was the public appetite for romance. 'Why is it that the effect of a sensational catastrophe on a modern nation is to cast it into transports, not of weeping, not of prayer, not of sympathy with the bereaved nor congratulation of the rescued, not of poetic expression of the soul purified by pity and terror, but of a wild defiance of inexorable Fate and undeniable Fact by an explosion of outrageous romantic lying?' he asked in the *Daily News and Leader*. ' . . . What is the use of all this ghastly, blasphemous, inhuman, braggartly lying?'

'Here is a calamity which might well make the proudest man humble, and the wildest joker serious. It makes us vainglorious, insolent and mendacious . . . Did the press really represent the public? I am afraid it did. Churchmen and statesmen took much the same tone. The effect on me was one of profound disgust, almost of national dishonor . . . It seems to me that when deeply moved men should speak the truth.'

He was accused by Conan Doyle of treating a tragic accident with levity and lack of good taste, of distorting this wonderful epic into a perverse thesis, of accusing everyone except himself of lying while needlessly hurting people's feelings. The argument went backwards and forwards in the newspapers for a fortnight, reminiscent of the opposing roles played by the two men in the Boer War, and foreshadowing Shaw's unpopularity in the First World War. For most readers, as one of Conan Doyle's biographers wrote, 'would rather have been wrong with Conan Doyle than right with Bernard Shaw'.

By early June two ingredients had been added to Shaw's career: a new woman and a new play. The new woman was . . . Ann M. Elder. Approved of by Charlotte, young and efficient – she put G.B.S. in mind of 'a very attractive bullfinch' – Ann took Judy's place as his secretary and was to work with him for seven years before, like Judy, deserting him for a husband.

The new play was *Pygmalion*. Shaw took it round that month to read to George Alexander. The professor of phonetics appealed to him so well that he told Shaw he could settle his own terms and name any actress he liked for the flower girl – except the actress for whom Shaw had written it, Mrs Patrick Campbell. Engage *her* for another play, after her appalling behaviour in *Bella-Donna*, Alexander would not. 'I'd rather die,' he appealed to Shaw. But Shaw had set his heart on her. He was so excited by the prospect that he restarted his correspondence with Ellen Terry. Eliza Doolittle was almost as wonderful a fit for Mrs Patrick Campbell, he confessed, as Lady Cicely had been for Ellen: 'for I am a good ladies' tailor, whatever my shortcomings may be.'

'It was a joy to get your letter,' Ellen replied. '*I'm* in love with Mrs Campbell too, or rather I'd like to be, but something tugs me back . . . The flower-girl idea is thrilling.'

[5]

I badly need some sort of humanizing.
I have loved – and have survived it.
I shall never quite get over it.
Shaw to Mrs Patrick Campbell (1913, 1914, 1912)

He had been 'violently in love' with Mrs Patrick Campbell from the start: and fearfully on his guard. Her sexual power was more compelling than Ellen Terry's charm, and when he used it as a warning to Janet Achurch, contrasting Mrs Pat's eruptions with the integrity of Duse, he had been giving a warning to himself. But despite all her deficiencies of temperament which he had faithfully reported, as a dramatic critic, to his readers, the appearance on stage of her light, wonderfully-proportioned figure thrilled him; and her vivid theatrical instinct intensified his excitement as he sat watching her.

He had seen her in many plays, never knowing what to expect. 'She creates all sort of illusions, and gives one all sorts of searching sensations,' he wrote. 'It is impossible not to feel that those haunting eyes are brooding on a momentous past, and the parted lips anticipating a thrilling imminent future ... Mrs Patrick Campbell is a wonderful woman.' She had been 'wonderful' as Juliet, though unable to act the part; and a disquietingly mad Ophelia. Shaw had been delighted by her also as the heroine of 'the celestial bed' in *Nelson's Enchantress*; and made ecstatic by her beauty of movement and tone when she played Militzia in *For the Crown*. 'You will tell me, no doubt, that Mrs Patrick Campbell cannot act,' he lectured his *Saturday Review* readers. 'Who said she could? – who wants her to act? who cares twopence whether she possesses that or any other second-rate accomplishment? On the highest plane one does not act, one *is*. Go and see her move, stand, speak, look, kneel – go and breathe the magic atmosphere that is created by the grace of all these deeds ... ' Yet sometimes she would act the dramatist clean off the stage, casting an extraordinary glamour round such plays as *The Second Mrs Tanqueray* or *The Notorious Mrs Ebbsmith*. 'Clearly there must be a great tragedy somewhere in the immediate neighbourhood,' Shaw concluded. ' ... But Mr Pinero has hardly anything to do with it.'

Shaw was envious of Pinero. He wanted Mrs Pat for his own play-world and even tried to take her daughter from Pinero's *The Thunderbolt* to act Raina in *Arms and the Man*. He had written his Cleopatra for her too, but Mrs Pat only read the copyright performance, not caring for a world where the Shavian Caesar remained so impervious to her serpent's tongue. She was better formed for the mature Cleopatra of Shakespeare's world than Shaw's marvellous child. *Caesar and Cleopatra* had been a dramatization of their relationship thus far as critic and actress. The dazzled Caesar who retains his full self-possession is G.B.S., sworn critic of the *Saturday Review*, who amusingly declares his tragic infatuation, names Mrs Pat as Circe, and states his intention of making 'the best attempt I can to be Ulysses'.

As a dramatist he had neglected Caesarion; as a dramatic critic he overlooked Telegonus. He believed that like Caesar he had the antidote to romance; that he could, like Ulysses, drink from the cup unharmed – and without harming others. He wanted to re-enact the Greek legend, with no descent to Hades before sailing on escorted by favourable winds. He wanted to annexe Circe's Island of Aeaea as part of the fantastic Shavian Empire; and to serenade his Circe, not distantly in his Saturday column, but through his acts on stage – to direct her, fill her with his words.

Before conceiving 'Mrs Pat Cat' as his kittenish Cleopatra, he had imagined her playing the showily-dressed ex-prostitute and brothel proprietress Mrs Warren; had seen her too as Julia Craven, the womanly woman founded on Jenny Patterson in *The Philanderer*; and as the Strange Lady playing opposite Johnston Forbes Robertson in place of Ellen Terry and Henry Irving in *The Man of Destiny*. He had tried to interest them in *The Devil's Disciple*, but by September 1897 everything else 'has been driven clean out of my head by a play I want to write to them in which he [Forbes Robertson] shall be a west end gentleman and she an east end dona in an apron and three orange and red ostrich feathers'.

Fifteen years later he had written this play. The liaison between Forbes Robertson and his 'rapscallionly flower girl' as Shaw had called her was long over, and Mrs Pat had returned briefly to the St James's. Sir George Alexander would have made as good a West End gentleman as Sir Johnston Forbes Robertson: but what mattered to Shaw was that Mrs Pat should become the cockney flower girl: a Galatea to his Pygmalion. But when naming his play *Pygmalion*, which audiences may have associated with Burne-Jones's Pygmalion series and W. S. Gilbert's *Pygmalion and Galatea*, he had apparently not considered that after the King of Cyprus had made his ivory statue, fallen in love with it, and prayed to Aphrodite to give it life, he married the girl and had a son by her called Paphus.

Shaw looked no further than the miracle of having Mrs Pat bring his creation to life in the theatre. But would she stand for such a vulgar role? Not daring to offer it to her directly, he formed a stratagem. This involved Mrs Pat's close friend Edith Lyttelton at whose house he arranged to read his play on 26 June 1912, when Mrs Pat was expected to be present. She came: heard Shaw's amazingly awful cries of 'Nah-ow' and even 'Ah-ah-ah-ow-ow-ow-ow!'; recognized his clever mimicry of her own voice: and realized that this part of Eliza Doolittle was meant for her. She might have interrupted. She could have left. But Shaw read with spellbinding power and she listened.

Next day she wrote to thank him for 'thinking I can be your pretty slut' and inviting him to come and discuss the business proposals for *Pygmalion*. 'I wonder if I could please you,' she wrote. ' . . . We said so little yesterday. I mustn't lose time – my days are numbered surely.'

He went at once to her house in Kensington Square. It was now her turn to put forth spells. Confident in his superiority over 'a dozen such Dalilahs', Shaw scorned the danger. But taking his hand she touched his fingers against her bosom and by this 'abandoned trick' he was undone. 'I fell head over heels in love with her,' he confessed to Granville Barker, ' – violently and exquisitely in love – before I knew that I was thinking about anything but business.' They were together for an hour, driving in a taxi, visiting a lord who might back her production of his play, and sitting on the sofa in her white-panelled drawing-room. He walked on air all afternoon and the next day 'as if my next birthday were my twentieth', he told Ellen Terry. His beard was going white, he was on the verge of fifty-six but 'I have not yet grown up'. She was forty-seven and still beautiful. 'Is there no age limit?' he wondered. There had never been 'anything so ridiculous, or so delightful, in the history of the world'. He was determined, however, that his infatuation should last no longer than a day or two, and by the end of the month declared that G.B.S. was himself again. 'I did not believe that I had that left in me,' he acknowledged in a letter to Mrs Pat – or Stella as he was to call her. 'I am all right now, down on earth again with all my cymbals and side drums and blaring vulgarities in full blast; but it would be meanly cowardly to pretend that you are not a very wonderful lady, or that the spell did not work most enchantingly on me for fully 12 hours.'

Shaw's recovery was signalled by a frightful migraine and pages of 'horrid' business practicalities about producing *Pygmalion* 'behind which my poor timid little soul hides'. Yet his feelings kept sentimentally interrupting his professional literary manner. 'I wish I could fall in love without telling everybody,' he wrote. He told Lillah and Barker; he told Barrie, Edith Lyttelton, Ellen Terry, Lady Gregory . . . and he told Charlotte. 'I must now go and read this to Charlotte,' he concluded one of his letters to Mrs Pat. 'My love affairs are her unfailing amusement: all their tenderness recoils finally on herself.'

But Charlotte had already experienced quite enough recoil over the business of Erica Cotterill. To help with *Getting Married* perhaps, G.B.S. had encouraged that young girl disgracefully, she sometimes thought. It had gone so far that they had actually been forced to threaten her with the police. But Shaw felt Charlotte's accusations were unjust. Was it his fault that, having received his advice to 'join some Socialist Society', Erica had become a Fabian and followed him devotedly back from his lectures to Adelphi Terrace? Could he seriously be blamed for not having foreseen that, after accepting tickets to his plays, she would write a play herself in which the heroine declares her passion to have 'some gorgeous thing to live for and love with every atom of my whole soul', and that she would point to G.B.S. as this 'gorgeous thing' and hand the play to Charlotte? Had he acted wrongly by informing Erica that her letters (which he scrupulously showed his wife) were illegible, simply because she was to go off, employ a printer, and begin publishing her correspondence to him as a series of 'accounts' totalling a quarter of a million words, dedicated to Shaw 'whom I love'? And where was the harm in inviting her to lunch and introducing her to some friends – unless it had lain in her decision to camp in the woods nearby and come racing up to Ayot on her motor-bicycle under the trance-like conviction that he was dying and that Charlotte's house belonged to her? No: he had done no wrong.

Yet her exasperating naïveté touched him at times with its loneliness and oddity so that, after almost seven agonizing years, he was still locked in correspondence with her in the summer of 1912. 'You stalk like a baleful ghost in strange and unearthly ways at strange and unearthly hours, appalling, oppressing, obsessing, troubling, spreading panic,' he accused her. ' . . . You are an extraordinary creature, and always on the verge of rousing my intense hatred of mad people.' He had already predicted she would 'either die a lunatic before you are 33 or be the greatest English woman writer – indeed one of the greatest of English writers – before you are 40'. Her hypnotic style, undivided, ecstatic, insistent, was as unstoppable as his own. She wrote along a single rhythmic sentence and in one key identified by Shaw as E flat minor. This was a letter missing from the Alpha and Omega of his own prose. Her pages were emotional orgasms: she felt, thought, lived upon the page as if it were her body. Reluctantly he counselled her to adopt literature as a profession. Anyone else in the world would have paid a guinea subscription to the Society of Authors and got guidance from its secretary. As it was, Shaw would have to guide her and take care of the more personal matters her parents had neglected. She must not grow up into another Jenny Patterson.

He sent for her: bullied her with his high-speed opinions 'like things that come out of machines when you pull them'. But: 'I didnt want to be scolded,' she wrote, 'I wanted to be loved, and perhaps I nearly cried.' Then something happened. He pulled away, and laughed. 'What would have come if you had not held me back and I had knelt down to you?' she wanted to know. 'Would you have laughed then? . . . would you have felt nothing of what was in me flooding round you – and what would have come if you had felt it? . . . were you hidden deep from your conscious mind *afraid* of feeling it?'

He sent her away: and started his correspondence course. 'Now listen to me.' She was an adult not a baby; strong not weak; and exquisite. But everything was made impossible by her nymphomania. He tutored her on what she was and what she was not and what she ought to be and ought not to be and what she must do about it all. He reminded her about her mother and father and herself like 'three clocks always arguing about the correct time'. He pointed out things too about himself (his spectacles and teeth and other matters to do with his hair and feet). And so that she should make no mistake, he pointed to his wife, and the iron laws of domestic honour, and the covenant of bread and salt. Then he explained about life and the Life Force, about seducers and socialist orators; and then about divine sparks and ultimate goals, and things to do with prima donnas and athletes, saints, poets. And after the explanations poured forth the advice. She should marry; she should marry as quickly as possible. Marriage was an acquired taste, like eating periwinkles with a pin. If she chose someone by the same rule as (for example) she might choose a horse, someone of the right size, shape, complexion and (in the horsedealer's sense) without vices, she could with surprising certainty become fond of him – after which, her anxieties would drift away and she could put her energy into work. There was no sense in hiding things, so she had better inform her husband that she loved Shaw . . . on second thoughts, it might be a good plan to marry someone with a fist who could knock her down when she began to talk too much. Then after the advice came the education. 'When an adult woman and an adult man caress one another, the result is entirely different from the result of your kissing your mother.' The person to whom she behaved in that perfectly happy way would lose all power of doing anything but the thing that would result in her having a baby. 'It is entirely natural for a hungry man to take a loaf of bread & eat it. It is entirely natural for an adult woman to kiss a man she likes. People who do these natural things are socially impossible . . . '

But Erica *was* socially impossible and the woman least fitted in the world to be Eliza Doolittle to his Henry Higgins. 'You hardly yet know how to behave yourself at all,' he complained, 'being the very worst brought-up young woman I have ever met . . . ' There was more than the obvious vanity that Charlotte witnessed to keep him on this 'case'. He identified Erica with Sonny. He had been 'just as shy & sensitive as you are'. So now he tried to give this 'terrified child' all the parental help he had missed himself. 'Nothing is more difficult than to realize a superiority which the world has always treated as an inferiority,' he wrote to her, unravelling the nature of paradox. 'But it must be done. People in a false position are always extraordinarily disagreeable . . . ' He remembered how disagreeable he had been when first he came to London, and thought he saw a reflection of this in Erica. But no amount of Shavian coaching could change her. For she had her own insights and saw that he too was still immature: 'youre a child all the while acting that youre a man,' she countered. '*Why* do you act – what *use* is it – it deceives no deep parts – and if it did how would it help in the end . . . '

'in all the whole stream of people that have come out of you theres not one that moves me first and last for itself – you watch and study and get behind and master things in them . . . and then you suddenly do a thing – you suddenly *use them* . . . you *force* them . . . *consciously* youre using them to expose some evil or falsehood or whatever its chosen to be called . . . you are your own what can be called dupe first and last and through and through and right down to your deepest places – cant you feel that everything of any kind that comes from you, work speeches plays letters . . . comes *at its root* from a pose or attitude of some kind . . . not deliberate conscious deceptions . . . a thing which appears both to yourself and to other people to be the thing which is absorbing your whole attention yet is *not* the thing . . . but only a cover for it.

All Shaw's goading and scolding and ordering about had made no difference. Erica would not smarten up her writing, or learn her biology, or master the simplest legal obligations of society. She was insupportable. She wanted the creative force of the universe to leap into activity within their bodies, and to this end she had abused his friendship frightfully. The strain was too much. 'I would not stand it from Cleopatra herself.'

But, in Stella Campbell, he had become involved with a modern Cleopatra, and to Charlotte's mind there was no telling what he would not stand. Over the Erica Cotterill affair, Charlotte had interceded by sending her a terminal letter (drafted by G.B.S.), forbidding the girl her house and her husband. To separate him from Mrs Pat she reintroduced their motoring holidays on the Continent – six weeks' furious touring through France and Germany, with G.B.S. and Kilsby up front and Mrs Cholmondeley sitting grimly next to Charlotte in the back. They started on 27 July.

*

'All I ask is to have my own way in everything,' Shaw had reasoned with Stella, 'and to see my Liza as often as possible.' Charlotte's tactics in removing G.B.S. from Mrs Pat were never subtle, and had in any case been accidentally nullified when Stella's taxi had 'a blinding bang' with another vehicle near the Albert Hall, quite seriously injuring her. Unable to carry on in *Bella-Donna* with black eyes, bruises, aches and swellings, she decided to go away first to Aix-les-Bains and then Chamonix, and left three days after the Shaws. For part of August she was tantalizingly close. 'I have only to push on to Tresenda,' Shaw wrote from Bad Kissingen, 'turn to the right, skirt Lake Como, hurry through Milan, dash through the Little St Bernard (being myself the Great St Bernard), make through Albertville to Chambery, and then be in your arms in an hour. But back I must turn for all that, leaving your arms empty . . . '

No one had their way that summer. The waters at Aix and the air of Chamonix were of little benefit to Stella who arrived back in London feeling less well than when she set out. Meanwhile, the tonics in Bad Kissingen proved poisonous to G.B.S. – one mouthful ('which will suffice for the rest of my life') and he made a dash for the Alps, and at fall of evening on 6 August, ruptured the car. This appeared a more dramatic accident than Stella's (it 'nearly cost the life of myself and the three people I was driving') and largely her fault since, instead of minding the road Shaw had filled his head with the music of a thousand letters he was writing her, with 'millions of additional verses'.

The rest of the holiday was an automobile saga. After ten night hours on a hillside 'keeping up the spirits of my chauffeur and warding off ghosts and foreign devils from him while he took the whole transmission to pieces and put it together again', they returned to Bad Kissingen and deposited the two women for three further weeks of voluptuous cures. Charlotte 'gasps in rarefied air whilst her sister wallows in mud', Shaw notified Stella. ' . . . Neither of them, by the way, is in the least ill; but Charlotte wants to get thin; and her sister wants to get plump; so they have both agreed to be asthmatic and have treatments.'

Kilsby and G.B.S. then launched themselves across Europe dragging the broken car over frontiers and through customs houses, in blizzards and

301

on omnibus trains, to the factory at Luneville. Every day G.B.S. sent Charlotte a commentary on their misadventures.

'In one of the villages a tyre burst with such a report that it almost blew the street down ... Sixty miles of rain, mud, lime, slime, deafening wind ... with the car violently skidding and screwing into the ditch at every turn of the wheels ... ploughing through unheard-of ruts of slippery limestone mud, finally seemed to get its teeth full of paving stones. It banged and smashed and gritted and finally reduced us ... to admit that our journey was over ... and we got her into a monstrous outhouse which serves to shelter the carts and poultry ... I doubt if we shall ever meet again ... Tomorrow we shall attach a couple of brewery horses to her and have her hauled to the railway station.'

While the car was being put to rights at Luneville, Shaw and Kilsby headquartered themselves twenty-seven kilometres off at Nancy. 'Imprisonment in Nancy is rapidly driving me mad,' G.B.S. complained. His escape was work. He corrected the proofs of a new Prologue to *Caesar and Cleopatra*; and he made final revisions to *Overruled*, the study of marital infidelity which he had come up with the previous month. 'It has an air of being outrageous,' he advised Charlotte; 'but it really does drive in its moral, which is that four reasonably amiable people in a matrimonial difficulty find themselves with nothing to guide them but a morality which will not work ... '

His letters to Charlotte were regular, amusing, friendly, informative – he even asks her to send a rough proof of *Pygmalion* to Mrs Pat who 'now says that her notion of bliss is to travel for a year and have a letter from me every week'. Shaw's letters to Stella were performances of a kind that Charlotte had never received. 'Stella, do not ever bully me: you don't know how easily frightened I am,' he wrote from Nancy. ' ... let me write; and do you pray for us both; for there is always danger when that devilment is at work. Let us take life as it comes, and love and hate and work without dramatizing it more than we can help.' But it was impossible for Shaw not to dramatize it. He had been born with the instinct to show off which his mother, feeling no pride in his tricks, had stifled. His hunger for love fed on his imagination and found romantic consummation in his dreams. 'If you knew all the adventures we have had already in the imaginary world which is my real world,' he told Stella, 'you would blush to the remotest contours of your enchanting person.' Stella fulfilled an important adolescent need in Shaw untended by the years of his marriage. 'You are a figure from the dreams of my boyhood,' he told her. Their relationship became an intoxicant, a magic formula that took him back to what he described as 'the indescribable heartbreak of Ireland'. She reminded him of that 'bewitching Calypso' with the beautiful 'black tresses' with whom he had fallen in love shortly before leaving Dublin. 'Once, in my calfish teens,' he told Stella, 'I fell in love with a lady of your complexion; and she, good woman, having a sister to provide for, set to work to marry me to the sister. Whereupon I shot back into the skies from which I had descended, and never saw her again.'

The Calypso whom he originally loved was married and, being taken care of in reality, able to inhabit his imagination freely. His retreat from the sister was in effect a flight from reality, with which his emotions could not cope. But Stella, alias Mrs Pat, seemed to represent both sisters and threatened to bring the real and his imaginary worlds into collision. 'Do you think I can live by imagination alone,' he chided her after insisting a little earlier that he was 'a man of imagination with no heart'. From this crisis of heart there arose a steam of emotional histrionics and bubbling hyperbole. These letters have none of the artistry of the Ellen Terry correspondence: Shaw's relationship with Ellen had been on paper. But to Stella 'I dont know why: I cant write. Writing is no use . . . It is past letter writing with me. There are things one cannot put on paper . . . All that paper love is nothing: the real thing is in the marrow of my bones and the roots of my nerves.' The spoken not the written word was Stella's art ('I have always been an odious letter writer') and she used her body to interpret words. Their love affair therefore 'was acted, not written' and the correspondence incidental. But everything got out of control. 'I am trying not to act,' he wrote. ' . . . I must break myself of this.'

Stella 'was the beauty of the moonlight', wrote Rebecca West, 'as Ellen Terry was the beauty of the sunlight'. She shone like a star through his dreams. Her fascination seemed more than could be accounted for by exotic looks – the lustrous coils of dark hair, ghostlike pallor, blazing eyes, mesmerizing voice. Her whole adoration, like his, had been for her mother from whom she inherited the musical gifts that G.B.S. tried to accommodate in *The Music-Cure*. Like him, she was reckless yet fundamentally respectable. He was attracted by strong women, she to weak men. Her maiden name was Tanner, which Shaw had chosen for his self-portrait in *Man and Superman*. She had married Patrick Campbell when she was twenty and pregnant. It seemed romantic, but however handsome he looked Patrick Campbell was not a creature of romance. He worked modestly in an insurance office until deciding to seek his fortune in Australia. He left his wife in the suburbs of London, with two small children, giving piano lessons; and returned eight years later, without a fortune, to find her the toast of London as a celebrated actress. He escaped again and finally achieved a romantic end, being shot dead in the front rank of a charge with fixed bayonets against Boer rifles. She had not remarried, but recently, unknown to Shaw, involved herself with a good-looking, well-connected, insolvent officer, 'a bit short on brains', called George Cornwallis-West, who was unhappily married to the famous American beauty Jennie Jerome, widow of Lord Randolph Churchill.

Mrs Pat wanted to be loved and she wanted to act great roles; but she was impossible to live with and almost impossible to act with. 'If she *absolutely* fitted in a part, she can wear it,' judged Pinero, 'but she can't wear anyone else's.' In the part of the neurotic Paula Tanqueray, who marries a respectable man in order to live down a sordid past and then kills herself to be rid of him and his virtuous daughter, she appeared to fit so perfectly that many people believed her own life to be a version of Mrs Tanqueray's. The late Victorian and Edwardian theatre had very few good roles for actresses. She needed a playwright who believed in the equality of women and men in the theatre to write for her. She could see, as Shaw could, that *Pygmalion* was a most fruitful product of their relationship. But though his child-play made her laugh, so that she nicknamed him Joey after Grimaldi the clown; and though she was attentive to the commercial undertones of what he wrote to her, she underrated the emotional fires she had lit up in him, knowing he had 'a foot firmly caught in the kitchen door'. His 'carnival of words' looked to her like a verbal smoke-screen that might have been blown over the pages by Eugene Marchbanks. 'God bless you for the smiles you make us smile,' she answered him, 'and forgive you for your literary lack-of-taste misdemeanours that make us squirm.'

But it was a delightful game and Stella played it beautifully. As for Shaw, he was feeling his part so deeply he sometimes forgot they were on stage. 'Playing Romeo has given me an ill-divining soul,' he told Edith Lyttelton: 'I cannot foresee the happy ending.'

*

By the time G.B.S. and Charlotte scrambled back to England, Shaw had made up his mind to sell the car. It was four years old, had covered seventy thousand miles, and gave him lumbago. But being fond of it, he postponed the sale for another eleven years and added to his stable a brisk little motor-bicycle in green enamel with which to amaze the good people of Ayot.

This machine (which he rode 'like a thunderbolt') suited his new spirit of recklessness which seemed to gain in response to everyone else's illness. Stella was confined to bed: Charlotte had fallen down; neither seemed able to recover from their continental cures. More serious still was his mother's illness. While at Nancy he had heard from his sister Lucy that 'the Mar' had suffered a stroke. He had sometimes commented that his mother was 'quite likely to survive me; and I am rather selfishly inclined to hope that she may bury me instead of me burying her' – meaning that her death was on his mind. Over the next six months, she had two more strokes before dying. She had continued into her seventies as a peppery music teacher at the North London Collegiate School for Girls; and she had continued living at 29 Fitzroy Square until the lease gave out, when Shaw bought for her the lease of 8 Park Village West, near Regent's Park. In her retirement she became economically more dependent on G.B.S., as did Lucy. 'I have now stock enough of my own to secure my mother & sister against all contingencies,' Shaw told Beatrice Webb that summer. Since meeting Stella, he had wanted to revoke the marriage settlement which, should he die first (in a car or motor-bicycle accident perhaps) made his family dependent on his wife. It was inappropriate, especially since they disliked Charlotte. Not that Bessie and Lucy seemed troubled: they spared George their gratitude. However hard he worked he was still 'a dreadful procrastinator' to his mother and a 'smug and prosperous idler' to his sister.

Yet Lucy could not help associating herself with her brother's success. She liked to claim that she typed his plays and that he stole his best witticisms from her. She boasted that they were both 'thorough blackguards', but Fate ('with her usual inscrutable workings and apparent lack of discrimination as to deserts') had raised up the brother and 'dealt her blows' to the sister. It was difficult not to feel bitter. 'I have a most uncomfortable intuition that the good things of this world which have poured into George's lap in the last three or four years are rubbing the sharp edges and crisp individuality off his intellect,' she cautioned a friend. ' . . . My worst dread about him is that he may become commonplace – I could stand anything but that. I still wish for his own sake that he had not married.' Such 'intuitions' over George's 'luxurious life' and 'comfortable marriage' derived from her own ill-sorted career and the sense of insult she carried after the break-up of her marriage. In her early forties she had caught a cold, neglected it, got pneumonia, then pleurisy 'and the result is tuberculosis'. She had spent her convalescence in Jenny Patterson's house, and when the doctor broke the news to her that she might be going to die, her reaction had been 'absolute relief, rest and even exaltation'. The doctors, however, acting promptly and emphatically, had apparently cured her. 'When it was quite certain I was going to get better (for the time being anyway),' she wrote to a friend, 'I couldnt express to you the sinking and weary disappointment . . .'

There seemed little to live for. Her lungs were still vulnerable and she had lost her voice. For almost a decade she exiled herself in Germany while her husband, Charles Butterfield, carried on in London. Then, one October evening in 1908 shortly after returning to England, she had been stopped in the foyer of the Coronet Theatre, Notting Hill, and told by the manager, Eade Montefiore, that her singing husband and his actress wife had been living together during all Lucy's years abroad. 'Although I had taxed him with almost every failing a man could have, I never for one moment suspected him of infidelity,' she admitted.

Shaw advised divorce and paid the costs – £91 13s. 8d. – needed to prevent Charles Butterfield from contesting the action. 'The case was absolutely straightforward . . . and it went through quickly,' Lucy wrote, 'but the nervous strain waiting for it to come on for two months was very trying, and how people go through with defended and complicated cases and come out alive, goodness alone knows.' After a convalescence at Baden Baden she returned in time for the decree absolute on 19 July 1909. 'I can find money for you as soon as you want it,' Shaw had told her early the following year. She needed some money to pursue good health from place to place. She contemplated Switzerland, but the glaciers terrified her; she thought of America, but the place she'd heard was riddled with hypnotism. She spent time by the sea and kept coming back for short periods to her mother's Park Village house.

Mother and daughter had a patchy but strong relationship. Bessie was 'a great old war horse' and could never see what Lucy was making such a fuss about. A disappointing career, a broken marriage, chronic ill health, almost no money – these were hardly things to complain of. As for herself, Bessie kept her powder dry (three hundred pounds in the bank) and put her trust in spiritualism. She seemed to prefer her friends when dead and would spend an hour each day chatting to them at the Ouija board. They liked to tell her of the death of other friends: and she would hurry out for the wreaths. They told her, too, what she suspected: that the sort of success which had come to George 'doesn't count for anything up here'. Lucy too experimented with the planchette and received some extraordinary communications from Rajah Mahattan, Knight Oliphant, Master Bariole and other unknown exotics on the subject of the planet Mars which she sent, with disappointing results, to the Astronomer Royal. Bessie when 'influenced' filled the house with drawings though she could hardly hold a pencil at other times. At the end of her life she had also become involved with a mediumistic photographer in the hope of obtaining a spirit-likeness of her dead daughter 'Yuppy', but her spirit faces seemed unrecognizable to Lucy and George. 'I do wish you would attend the spirit photo conference & really see for both me and yourself,' she had appealed to George. ' . . . that there are spirit photos just as sharp as those on earth there is not the slightest doubt.' Shaw didn't trouble her with his scepticism: 'one cannot shatter a consolation and a hope as one could criticize a scientific experiment.' But he had been somewhat useless to Bessie, as men were. No wonder she had kept no 'photo of my son as a boy or child', as she informed Archibald Henderson. ' . . . Nor have I a single letter.'

Now as she lay dying she shocked everyone, getting 'ridiculously cured . . . by a Christian Scientist who broke into the house and meditated on her whilst she slept', Shaw reported. This cure did not prevent her death. Lucy was with her most of the time, and George (who came and went) provided two nurses. 'She is now very near the end,' Lucy wrote. 'I have been watching her trying to die for five weeks since the last seizure. Her body and all her organs are so sound that she seems unable to get away . . . the strain has been terrible.' Shaw too, in his fashion, felt the strain: 'my mother is dying, they say, but *wont* die – makes nothing of strokes – throws them off as other women throw off sneezing fits,' he wrote to Lady Gregory. Lucy had reported on 6 December that 'it is a question of days or even hours now,' but Bessie held on for over ten weeks more. Her attitude to her own death appeared the same as her attitude to life: she ignored it. Lucy had described her pursuing her way 'victoriously over any obstacle in her path, which she flouts with beautiful scorn'. Her illness was arduous for her family, but she did not appear to suffer. 'She was unconscious for 16 weeks,' Lucy recorded, 'and passed out in her sleep so quietly and imperceptibly that I could not believe it when they said she was gone.' On 19 February 1913 she telegraphed George, who was in Oxford, with the news: 'All over.'

To Lucy it seemed as if all was over for her too. 'My mother's exit has made an astonishing abyss in our little kingdom,' she told a friend. 'I never realized how completely she was the Alpha and Omega of all my hopes and fears and acts. Both consciously and subconsciously she guided and influenced everything I ever did. I feel as if the rock had vanished from under my house and I was tumbling about in the sand.'

When her mother's body was taken from the house Lucy 'completely broke to pieces'. George put her in the care of a 'chest specialist' who had cured himself of consumption, and he insisted that she stay in bed. 'A halt had to be called if I did not want to follow Mama,' Lucy wrote, 'which I certainly did.'

She was not well enough to go to the funeral service and cremation at Golders Green on 22 February. Four people turned up: the chaplain, the undertaker, Shaw and Barker – whose presence revived the rumour that he was Shaw's natural son. The question had arisen as to whether there should be a religious service for a spiritualist who had not attended a place of worship for more than thirty years. Shaw chose the Church of England service partly because he did not want to deprive the chaplain of his optional fee, and partly because he was curious to see 'how the ceremony would affect me'. Years later he was reported as saying it was unaccountably morbid and should be scrapped; but he felt at the time that despite passages which 'were deader than anyone it has ever been read over . . . it is the most beautiful thing that can be read as yet'. As for the parson, Barker and he could have made him technically perfect with a couple of rehearsals.

The only person to whom Shaw could write about this day was Stella 'who understands about one's mother, and other things'. The words of the burial service had been altered a little for a cremation. 'A door opened in the wall; and the violet coffin mysteriously passed out through it and vanished as it closed,' he told Stella. ' . . . I went behind the scenes at the end of the service and saw the real thing . . . it is wonderful.'

'I found there the violet coffin opposite another door, a real unmistakeable furnace door. When it lifted there was a plain chamber of cement and firebrick. No heat, no noise, no roaring draught. No flame. No fuel. It looked cool, clean, sunny, though no sun could get there. You would have walked in or put your hand in without misgiving. Then the violet coffin moved again and went in, feet first, And behold! The feet burst miraculously into streaming ribbons of garnet colored lovely flame, smokeless and eager, like pentecostal tongues, and as the whole coffin passed in it sprang into flame all over; and my mother became that beautiful fire.'

They were told that if they wanted to see it all through they should return in thirty minutes, and they went off and wandered round Hampstead Garden Suburb. 'When we returned we looked down through an opening in the floor to a lower floor close below,' Shaw wrote that night to Stella. 'There we saw a roomy kitchen, with a big cement table and two cooks busy at it.'

'They had little tongs in their hands, and they were deftly and busily picking nails and scraps of coffin handles out of Mamma's dainty little heap of ashes and samples of bone. Mamma herself being at the moment leaning over beside me, shaking with laughter. They swept her up into a sieve, and shook her out; so that there was a heap of dust and a heap of calcined bone scraps. And Mamma said in my ear, "Which of the two heaps is me, I wonder!"'

For the first time she was behaving as her son commanded. The relief was enormous. He realized how little he had known about her. They made dust of the bone scraps; he remembered the wonderful face and wasted little figure; then scattered the remains of his mother over a flower bed. The day had had some 'wildly funny' moments and been 'a complete success'. The aesthetic effects also had been remarkable: and he made a note to buy some shares in the cremation business. That afternoon he drove back to Oxford and at Notting Hill Gate (the car being in 'a merry mood') 'accomplished a most amazing skid, swivelling right round across the road one way and then back the other, but fortunately not hitting anything . . . '

*

'My mother cut a wisdom tooth when she was 80,' Shaw wrote to Stella that February. 'I ask myself sometimes am I cutting a folly tooth at 56? Still, one has to become as a little child again – in that kingdom by the sea.' His mother's death seemed to promise him emergence from the long shadow of his Dublin childhood, as his sea holidays at Dalkey had once done. Two years earlier he had cautioned Archibald Henderson that 'there are certain things that I do not want said during my mother's lifetime'. Three years later he was encouraging a still more improbable biographer named Demetrius O'Bolger 'to reconstruct my childhood' about which, he promised, 'I can tell you freely now that my mother is dead'.

This freedom intensified his love for Stella to whom 'I opened the grave of my childhood' and from whom he expected a miraculous resurrection. 'I do not believe in mortality,' he told her. In his imagination she was transfigured, so that she became everything he had once looked for in Lucinda Elizabeth Shaw and tried to replace with Alice Lockett, Jenny Patterson, Florence Farr, Janet Achurch and Charlotte too. She was his Virgin Mother and his Dark Lady, his playmate and working-partner, his magical friend. He had become a mass of wants that now rushed out towards her. He wanted to 'have a woman's love on the same terms as a child's', he implored, ' . . . to hear tones in a human voice that I have never heard before, to have it taken for granted that I am a child and want to be happy . . . and suddenly find myself in the arms of a mother – a young mother, and with a child in my own arms who is yet a woman: all this plunges me into the coldest terror as if I were suddenly in the air thousands of feet above the rocks or the sea . . . in an ecstasy which must be delirious and presently end in my falling headlong to destruction . . . And yet I am happy, as madmen are . . . I no longer regret anything.'

Stella's mysterious illness heightened their affair. At first she liked using it to tempt him, writing to say that the doctor had forbidden her to see absolutely anyone – except himself. And so, as her daughter-in-law Helen Campbell noted, 'Mr Bernard Shaw came into the picture – and came, and came, and came.' Stella could always 'whistle for me when you want me', and he would go galloping up the stairs, three at a time, with beard flying, to 'my most agitating heart's darling'. He was, he told her, 'most frightfully in love with you'. At these *levées*, sitting by the bed, he was allowed to put his arms round her waist, and they would kiss. But he did not make love to her, Stella confided to Edith Lyttelton, he made advances.

As her health deteriorated a more sombre note entered their relationship. 'I have been very ill,' she informed him. Sometimes, on account of this illness, she begged him to 'be patient with me', then in other moods she urged him on: 'I think if you don't come and see me rather soon there won't be me to see.' He went backwards and forwards. 'I love you for ever and ever and ever, Stella,' he wrote. Her setback had made him desperately anxious. 'I had set my heart on your getting well with a rush this time,' he told her. 'Oh you must, you must, you shall. You shall be torn out of bed and shaken into rude health. Or else I will get into the bed myself and we shall perish together scandalously.' But she did not get well. 'Four doctors have just left – 3 knights – and they tell Helen she must search at once for the man I love and bring him to me, and he must be told that he is to obey me entirely . . . any hesitancy might kill.'

Early in 1913 she had entered a nursing home in Hinde Street for an exploratory operation. Shaw continued to visit her whenever possible. At his most sympathetic, he charmed and flattered her, made her smile, made her forget the illness and the operation. 'Himself living in dreams,' she testified, 'he made a dream-world for me.' In return she let him play 'in the nursery of my heart' where he felt happy beyond reason – 'I shall never be unhappy again.' Had she been well perhaps she might not have let their fantasy-attachment proceed so far, but it was now too late, she acknowledged, 'to do anything but *accept* you and *love* you'. He basked in this acceptance of love. 'I have slipped out of the real world,' he told her; and from the nursing home she responded, 'I want to sit in a hayfield with you in the sun shining . . . '

But Stella never lost sight, as Shaw seemed to, of the traps in their relationship. There were traps everywhere: for example Charlotte. 'Your wife will never like me,' she stated. Shaw wished to remain loyal to

25A Shaw rehearsing a scene from *Androcles and the Lion* with Lillah McCarthy and
Harley Granville-Barker, St James's Theatre, London, 1913;
B Winter Garden Theatre, London, 1934

26 Mrs Patrick Campbell

27 Shaw, after Rodin's 'Thinker', photographed by Alvin Langdon Coburn, 1906

28 Shaw playing the piano in the hall at Ayot St Lawrence

29 Shaw at Lady Gregory's house, Coole Park, 1915

30　Lucinda Elizabeth Shaw, shortly before her death in 1913

31 Lucinda Frances ('Lucy') Shaw

HIS MAJESTY'S THEATRE
HERBERT TREE
PYGMALION

MILES·LITHO·Cº

32 Poster, 1914

Charlotte while loving Stella. 'I throw my desperate hands to heaven and ask why one cannot make one beloved woman happy without sacrificing another,' he cried out. 'We are all slaves of what is best within us & worst without us.' He recognized that Charlotte, with her sensitiveness, her susceptibility to worry, needed protection; and he had tried to explain this to Stella. Charlotte was proud; she was vulnerable to other women; and her own health had not been good – 'I had an anxious moment'. Charlotte's own anxious moments seemed strung continuously together. Only that February she had said that she never knew where George spent his afternoons. Once she had given no thought to such things. Now she was full of doubts. So he told her what the rest of London already seemed to know: that he had not been at committees or in the theatre on those afternoons but at Stella's bedside.

Charlotte was devastated. For the first time in their marriage G.B.S. had been keeping something important from her. Despite Shaw's ostensible belief that his love affairs were Charlotte's unfailing amusement, he had not continued reading to her his correspondence with Stella. His wish to protect her seemed no more to Charlotte, however, than the keeping of a guilty secret. No wonder she had felt so anxious, and lain gasping in bed with asthma and bronchitis. She refused ever to meet this 'middleaged minx' or leave calling cards on her – and this offended Mrs Pat's sense of propriety. She began to grow hostile to what she called the 'suffragette' figure of Shaw's wife. Realizing that Shaw could never be prised away from Charlotte, she started on the nerve-racking game of making him late for lunch or supper with her, scoring little victories and stirring up Charlotte's anxieties.

Early in March Stella left the nursing home and went to convalesce in Brighton. No malignancy had been found, but as she began to recover so her romance with Shaw clouded. She resented this marriage-attachment of 'Mr and Mrs Mouse' and chided Shaw on his timidity. What a *blind blind* man' he had been – let him 'look into my eyes for two minutes without speaking if you dare!' His advances could have led to love-making if – 'if only you'd eat red steaks and drink beer your spirit would be meet, I mean meet to mate – no I dont mean that . . . ' But she did mean it, even if she might not have wanted it. Since Shaw's 'Mother is dead & Charlotte is your wife I'll be your grandmother', she mocked him. 'You are all right for Charlotte. You'll do for Barker . . . but the Italian peasant must have a blue sky and a scent to worship . . . the emerald must keep its colour.'

'Dearest Liar,' Shaw addressed Stella, not wishing to believe some of the things she was saying to him. A curious counterpoint was developing between what she had called his 'coquetries, and my iron will'. There was no need for him to warn her against falling in love with him as he had warned other women. He sensed that she could beat him at his own game 'and revenge his earlier victims'. He knew the unhappiness he risked. For safety, he should 'live in a lighthouse and work, work, work; for I am a slave by nature'. But 'I am still in love with Stella . . . Cannot help it', he found himself writing. ' . . . You have beaten me,' he wrote to her in Brighton, ' – my first defeat, and my first success.'

Late in March Shaw and Charlotte left for two weeks in Ireland. It seemed a safe move: except that on the way to Holyhead G.B.S. suddenly charged the car into a range of hummocks and a telegraph pole ('It was a first class accident'); and except too that in this country of his childhood, 'all the old longing for beauty and blessing get stirred up in me' so that he switched his emotional focus back to 'my girl, my beauty, my darling, barefooted, dusty petticoated, or my mother of angels, or a dozen lovely wild things . . . '

They were staying not far from Dublin with Horace Plunkett, an unspeakable private bore and admirable public servant who founded the agricultural co-operative movement in Ireland. Plunkett was a puzzle to the Shaws. 'He devoted his life to the service of his fellow-creatures collectively; and personally he disliked them all,' G.B.S. later recalled. 'He kept open house in Foxrock for all visitors of any note, rich or poor, to Ireland; and he hated all his guests. He remained a bachelor for the sake of Lady Fingal, and was unquestionably in love with her; yet I never felt convinced that he quite liked her.'

There seemed nothing for G.B.S. to do in the atmosphere of this house but 'work, work, work, hurling off articles and despatching arrears of business, and writing volleys of letters'. In one of his letters he explained to Stella how these circumstances pleased Charlotte. She had suddenly got well 'and changed from a fiend into a green-eyed mermaid, smiling & fascinating & dressing in diamonds & generally dispensing charm and childish happiness . . . She realizes her superiority now. Quite right too . . . Dont grudge her . . . '

But Stella had not been pleased by Shaw's efforts to strike some balance between the two women 'I was born to love'. That April, after they had all returned to London, she began to exploit what she saw as the limitation of Charlotte's marriage to G.B.S.: its childlessness. 'Am I going to learn something?' Shaw had asked. 'I wonder – no; you have done your duty and suffered your suffering in that way. But I havnt. I must bring forth something. A sister for Eliza.' Stella knew that Shaw felt a reverence and sense of humility before the fact of childbirth. 'A sort of pang goes through me from the base of my heart down to my very entrails,' he had written to

Sylvia Brooke, Ranee of Sarawak, when she was pregnant with her first child. ' . . . you are going to be torn to pieces and come to life again with a terrible contempt for fragile male things that would be broken by such creative miracles . . . '

'I am a sentimental elderly person with a frightful sensitiveness to the Life Force, which, as it springs at you and forces you to make this tremendous effort for it, at the same time stirs up every tenderness for you to the point of positive heartbreak . . . If I could go in with you, and we could rush through cheering and charging together, and sharing the wounds and howling and writhing in company, then I should not fail you; but, as it is . . . I must watch The Times for the announcement of the colossal relief, the victory, the triumph . . . '

Shaw had denied himself a share in this miracle, and been joined by Charlotte in a conspiracy of denial they called their marriage. Stella, who had 'suffered her suffering' and given birth to a son and daughter while her husband was alive, now reported to Shaw that 'I could have 6 more children'. She had been examined by Shaw's own doctor who, she told him, confirmed her claim. She was still young enough. But all Shaw apparently wanted to create with her was a new play. 'Has earth or heaven anything better to offer me,' he had asked, 'than reading my plays to you (except living them with you?).' Sometimes Stella could be merciless over his failure to live his plays. 'Whats the difference between being addicted to drink and overlaying your baby,' she demanded that April, '– and being addicted to work and neglecting your hearts love?'

Shaw had warned her that only on paper was he brave. Sometimes she felt pinned to his sheets of paper like a Painted Lady. Though he had assured her that 'you are now an important part of my property', she seemed to exist only in the make-believe of his mind. 'I think I have fallen into a hornet's nest,' she told him. 'I think you are mad. I think I am pretending to be what it amuses you to think I am.' He had been generous with offers of money, but she had no status in his life – all that belonged to Charlotte; and she had no future.

In the second week of June, Stella summoned Shaw to her house and told him that she was thinking of marrying George Cornwallis-West. He was a simple man where Shaw had been too 'brain-proud'; he was quiet while Shaw talked so incessantly he gave her headaches; George had touched her too with his helplessness and dependence ('Live, Stella,' he had pleaded during her illness, 'live and help me') when Shaw had merely been amusing: besides he was prepared to divorce his wife and Shaw was not.

In the train travelling back to Ayot that night Shaw wrote that Stella's marriage to 'the other George' would cut him off for ever from what was common and young in his humanity. 'I say he is young and I am old; so let him wait until I am tired of you,' he wrote. ' . . . And about you I am a mass of illusions. It is impossible that I should not tire soon: nothing so wonderful could last . . . I will hurry through my dream as fast as I can; only let me have my dream out.'

It was something of a relief to Shaw to leave the country at the end of the month and spend a few days in Germany with Granville Barker. Though there were still delightful moments with Stella – making up verses for her (though he was sometimes lost for any rhyme to her name except umbrella), or going with her to Richmond Park where he taught her to jump from the ground on to a bench as part of her convalescence, the strain had got much worse. He had felt 'all torn to bits' behaving so artificially with Charlotte. Of course she guessed what he was up to much of the time and was hurt by his evasions. She had accidentally come upon a list of meetings mischievously entered by Stella in Shaw's pocket diary. There had been dreadful scenes. 'And I,' he had ended one of his notes to Stella, ' - ha! steps on the stair! Now for it!' Another time Charlotte had caught him speaking to her on the newfangled telephone and flared up into an appalling rage. Seeing someone suffer like this gave Shaw 'a sort of angina pectoris', he told Stella. ' . . . it hurts me miserably . . . I must, it seems, murder myself or else murder her.'

To help her resist these lacerating and destructive impulses Charlotte had taken up with a spiritual healer whom she met at Lena Ashwell's house. James Porter Mills was a bad-tempered old man from America who had travelled the world with his eccentric wife (known as 'the Healer') perfecting an eclectic system of conduct and belief which he called the 'Teaching'. The incoherence of his thought combined with the undenia-ble power of his personality and lecturing performances had a profound effect on Charlotte. She felt a compulsion to apply these principles, whatever they might be, to the painful upheaval of her emotions. The result was that, in the middle of some terrible scenes with G.B.S. that appeared likely to culminate in violence, she would convulsively recover her balance, smile dizzily, and be changed back into 'the happy consort of an easygoing man'. But damage had been done, and in the priority she gave to Dr Mills's 'Teaching' over Fabianism and the Life Force, Charlotte was being unfaithful to G.B.S. in the only way open to her.

'This is a terrific romance,' remarked J. M. Barrie, 'and at last Shaw can blush.' Living opposite G.B.S. in Adelphi Terrace, Barrie witnessed Mrs Pat courting them both for plays. 'He [Shaw] and I live in the weather house with two doors,' he teased her, 'and you are the figure that smiles on us and turns up its nose at us alternatively.' That summer Stella decided to appear in Barrie's *The Adored One* which was to open in September – and Shaw was grateful. To go into rehearsals now with Stella in *Pygmalion* would 'probably kill me' he had calculated. 'Barrie's play is the surest and most lucrative,' he urged her. It was as much as he could do to go round to her house on his return from Germany. He found her grieving over the death of Edith Lyttelton's husband and in no mood to be humoured. She actually shut the door in his face with an exclamation of relief. He had thought that he could only experience the suffering of others, never his own. But now he felt it, and he was shocked. A little later that July, in the middle of reading a letter from Edith Lyttelton, he found to his astonishment that he was crying, and concluded that he must have become horribly over-worked. 'You may ask why I shouldnt cry; but it is not in my line: bad taste is what I am good at,' he wrote to her. 'Bad taste dries tears . . . that is, when I can control myself; but when my inside all turns into hot water & wells up into my eyes . . . then it is time to go off to Devon and come back a man of iron . . . '

He arrived in Devon and put up for a week with Granville Barker at the Torcross Hotel near Kingsbridge, feeling 'all in rags'. Everything except his adoration of Stella seemed tedious and insipid. He knew that she had only to give him a particular look for all the iron to turn to water. 'This clown misses Joey,' she relented. But she must be alone to study the Barrie play. 'I will hide in the sands somewhere . . . '

'When I am solitary you are always with me,' he answered. 'When you are solitary by the sea, where shall I be?'

She did not want him with her. 'Its getting difficult not to love you more than I ought to love you,' she reassured him. ' . . . But by the sea I must be alone – you know.'

He did not want to know: 'nothing is lost or forgotten,' he told her. He returned to Adelphi Terrace and on the afternoon of 8 August took Charlotte to Liverpool Street Station to catch the boat train for Marseilles. He intended to join her at the end of the month for a six-week tour of France. On leaving the station he went straight down to the Kent coast where he knew Stella had borrowed the theatrical producer Nigel Playfair's cottage at Ramsgate. But she was not there. Answering the door late that night, the Playfairs' housekeeper informed him that Mrs Campbell, her maid, her chauffeur, and her dog, had transferred to the Guildford Hotel on Sandwich Bay. Shaw walked off into the dark, an exhausted figure in his Norfolk jacket, making his way back across the sands.

Stella was not pleased to see him next morning. For two days he struggled to entertain her and make her sympathetic to him, so that they might go to bed together. But he had made his entrance in the wrong scene. The Guildford Hotel was far from being the private tomb of love they had created in her London bedroom. She felt embarrassed by him. She was intending to marry George Cornwallis-West and Shaw's presence with her in this fashionable place could be deeply compromising. 'Please will you go back to London today,' she wrote to him, ' - or go wherever you like but dont stay here – If you wont go I must – I am very very tired and I oughtn't to go another journey. Please dont make me despise you.'

But Shaw would not go. He had come so far and there would never be another opportunity like this, with Charlotte out of the country – an opportunity to spend one week with Stella with perhaps one or two nights. He was not greedy: he had not hurried her. After reading the note he searched the hotel and went looking for her in the darkness along the sands. Eventually he found her and they ordered a nightcap. Tired herself, Stella noticed with irritation how sleepy he was. Why hadn't he understood? They arranged to meet next morning before breakfast for a bathe in the sea – though not before eight o'clock, she insisted. But by half-past seven she was speeding along the coast, with her chauffeur and maid and dog and luggage towards Littlestone-on-Sea. At eight o'clock punctually Shaw knocked at her bedroom door. 'Come & bathe,' he called. A cheerful chambermaid answered, telling him that they had gone – and he pretended to have muddled the dates. She had left him a note: 'Goodbye. I am still tired – you were more fit for a journey than I - .'

He returned to his room and tried to write out his distress. 'I am deeply, deeply, deeply wounded . . . I cannot bring you peace, or rest, or even fun.' He made attempts to minimize the loss: 'the loss of a woman is not the end of the world. The sun shines: it is pleasant to swim: it is good to work: my soul can stand alone . . . I have treated you far too well, idolized, thrown my heart and mind to you . . . Go then: the Shavian oxygen burns up your little lungs.' But whatever 'wild nonsense' he came up with, daggers of pain continued to thrust into him. He felt cut to pieces. How could she have done it – and not even known what she was doing? The world was horribly changed. He looked up at her room where he had imagined happiness, and there was nothing. Everything had been a mirage, and 'I shall die of thirst after all'. For the truth was inescapable. Of his 57 years 'I have suffered 20 and worked 37', he declared. 'Then I had a moment's happiness: I almost condescended to romance. I risked the breaking of deep roots and sanctified ties . . . ' and now, on that desolate strand, 'what have I shrunk into?'

He completed *Great Catherine*, to which he would later add his 'Author's Apology', and he kept mailing letters to Stella wherever she was: again that night ('Sandwich. Darkness') then next morning ('Another day that might have been a day!') and after he had returned to London ('back from the land of broken promise'). It seemed to him that she had been more gratuitously cruel than a child, and he turned all the blame on her. She was a 'one-part actress'. She used her sex appeal irresponsibly, furtively, without discrimination, blundering about after life then huddling up and screaming when it opened its arms to her. She was a man's disgrace and infatuation. He felt the need of some monstrous retribution. 'I have not said enough vile things to you.'

'Come round me all the good friends whom I have neglected for her. Even her slanderers shall be welcome ... give me anything that is false, malicious, spiteful, little, mean, poisonous or villainous, and I will say it if only it hurts you. I want to hurt you because you hurt me.'

But Shaw's rhetoric was not hurtful for, as Stella understood, 'you have no claws'. Nevertheless, because she had been driven to inflict real pain, she needed to defend her action, and her retaliation against him was more piercing than anything he had written about her. 'No daughters to relieve your cravings – no babies to stop your satirical chatterings, why should I pay for all your shortcomings,' she demanded. ' . . . You lost me because you never found me – I who have nothing but my little lamp and flame – you would blow it out with your bellows of self.' Yet the depth of his feelings startled her, and she felt his suffering as he had felt Charlotte's. 'You are trying to break my heart with your letters,' she appealed. ' . . . What other thing was there for me to do? I had to behave like a man . . . '

Because they were 'useless, these letters; the wound will not heal', she agreed to see him once they were both back in London and applied some words of kindness. He occupied himself as best he could, swimming at the Royal Automobile Club, reading *Great Catherine* to Gertrude Kingston, visiting the zoo and stroking a lion as part of the preparation for Granville Barker's production of *Androcles*, and writing to his 'ever dearest love' Charlotte about his business life. He was to join her in France in the second week of September and he welcomed the paraphernalia of travel as a distraction from the ache he felt each morning when he woke. For the romance, if not the relationship, with Stella was at an end, and the experience had confirmed all his beliefs about love. One could not help at moments valuing someone so irrationally above others. But it was a hideous business: 'the quantity of Love that an ordinary person can stand without serious damage,' he measured, 'is about 10 minutes in 50 years.'

CHAPTER VI

[I]

*I am a Mr Jorkins on the New Statesman; Clifford Sharp
is Mr Spenlow.* (1912)

Beatrice Webb was one of those who had viewed the emotional frothing
between G.B.S. and his 'somewhat elderly witch' with distaste. It was such
a cruel and trivial business. Beatrice warmed to Charlotte in her trouble.
Lying on the sofa, speaking 'in a singularly gentle and dignified way',
Charlotte had told her all about it: and the two women shook their heads.
Surely it was time, Beatrice sighed, for her old friend to have outgrown
these flirtations with odd females. The reaction of such vanity on a
declining vigour could only lead to intellectual deterioration.

Beatrice felt caught up in the egotistical wreckage of this affair. In the
summer of 1912, she had begun appealing to G.B.S. to help her and
Sidney launch a new Fabian weekly journal. But he had displayed little
faith in their scheme. To make a socialist paper successful, he told them,
would prove the most difficult of all their economic achievements. It
needed more than principles and enthusiasms; it needed the habit of
readability that came from professional excellence and could not be gained
without high rates for contributors. Unless they established in the mind of
the railway traveller a certainty that he would be amused and interested by
their paper for the next hour of his journey they would never capture the
sixpenny public.

It was as bait for this public that Beatrice wanted Shaw's name as a
regular contributor. Yet he was reluctant to give up the time and energy he
had hoped to reserve for more permanent work. He would hand over some
money, but 'I wont write'. Why disturb the sleep of second childhood? 'My
fear in the matter is that we are too old,' he answered Beatrice.
' . . . Unless you can find a team of young lions . . . and give them their
heads, the job cannot be done . . . My bolt is shot: I should not serve you
by attempting to lag superfluous on the stage I once adorned.'

But Beatrice persisted. 'We are too old to make a failure of this
business,' she countered, ' - now we have undertaken it we must see it
through to a big success.' The *New Statesman*, as it came to be called, was
to be a platform for the reformist middle class, and her and Sidney's last

venture before their retirement: a truly Fabian enterprise. Without such an organ of serious political criticism, establishing their collectivist doctrine by constant iteration and illustration, the Fabian movement might as well not exist. It had little place in H. W. Massingham's brilliantly edited, non-ideological weekly, the *Nation*; while A. R. Orage's the *New Age*, after becoming a forum for general controversy, had settled for Guild Socialism, the English variant of syndicalism that aimed to transfer control of industry not to the State but to the workers represented by their trade unions. There was need for a well-informed pugnacious journal voicing Fabianism in the contemporary political debate – one that featured G.B.S., instead of leaving him to write for their opponents.

So Shaw was persuaded. He became one of the *New Statesman*'s original proprietors and directors, put up (with a cheque for a thousand pounds) one fifth of its capital, purchased approximately two thousand four hundred shares and sent out a series of letters soliciting subscribers. And Beatrice was pleased. 'I think that as you will get both the wit of G.B.S. and the wisdom of the Webbs every week for one guinea post free,' she wrote to one subscriber early in 1913, '. . . I am offering you a good bargain.'

Almost everything, Shaw told Beatrice, would depend on the tact and dash of their editor. The Webbs had chosen Clifford Sharp whom Sidney thought a 'weak, timid and slow' man, but Beatrice believed him to be 'a good man of business', and moreover a 'safe' writer. Sharp turned out an able, though disagreeable, editor of the *New Statesman*. His credentials were faultless. He had remained a steadfast member of the Fabian executive during one of its least potent phases, had married H. G. Wells's ex-love Rosamund Bland, and had helped the Webbs' anti-Poor Law campaign as editor of the *Crusade*. But no one really liked him. He was a 'chilly and saturnine' man about whom hung 'an atmosphere of intellectual Jeyes' Fluid, moral carbolic soap, spiritual detergents', wrote Leonard Woolf, whom he put in mind of 'an old, mangy, surly, slightly dangerous dog'. Imperialist by temperament, Sharp did not share many of the radical preoccupations of socialism such as abolition of capital punishment, removal of the House of Lords, and proportional represen- tation; he was not pro-birth-control or anti-vivisection. But he was a thoroughgoing collectivist: and that was what mattered most to the Webbs.

'The first number has been a huge success,' Shaw reported following its publication on 12 April 1913. But already there were signs of a collectivist crisis. Not wishing to find himself presiding over a raucous weekly symposium, Sharp relied on the anonymity of his contributions to help him achieve a single tone and unity of style throughout the paper. 'It is not usual for a journal to communicate to the public the names of those of its staff who contribute unsigned articles,' he wrote in the first number.

'We feel, however, that, in view of the promises which have been made, and which have possibly induced many persons to subscribe to *The New Statesman*, we owe it to our readers to explain that Mr Bernard Shaw and Mr Sidney Webb will as a rule write editorially in our columns, and that the present issue includes, in fact, more than one contribution from each of these gentlemen.'

Shaw's unsigned contributions on feminism and income tax, the performance of motor cars, the ethics of prize fighting and the duties of the poet laureate were too variously surreal or futuristic to blend into the mood of brisk, didactic, common sense that Sharp wanted to establish. Many of Shaw's interventions struck him as oddly flippant. The two of them, it was said, saw eye to eye on nothing except Ireland, Municipal Trading and Death Duties – 'we did not even agree about the Income Tax,' Sharp added. He therefore proposed that G.B.S. should be treated as an exception to the rule of anonymity and be allowed to sign his contributions. But Shaw refused. 'I have had enough of being the funny man and the privileged lunatic of a weekly paper.' He knew that the Webbs, with many other Fabians and socialists, now regarded his views as eccentric, and he may have resented Beatrice's notion ('I know very well what you think of me') that only his name was of value to the paper: 'The *New Statesman* is in fact the one weekly in which Shaw's name never appears,' she complained in her diary that summer, 'and it is Shaw's name that draws, not his mind . . . He will not cooperate on terms of equality.'

To Shaw's mind here was true paradox. He had willingly agreed to co-operate on terms of equal anonymity so as to permeate the editorial voice in traditional Fabian style with authentic Shavian dissonances. Collectivism did not mean to him a regimentation of tone, but the release of differing individual talents for a generally harmonious purpose. There was no good reason he could see why these Shavian ripples and involutions should not appear next to Sharp's polished surfaces which, he liked to point out, were in their grain essentially Tory. Sharp was exercised by current stupidities and abuses, but not by those matters of long-term principle that interested G.B.S. – without which he could deal with political affairs, Shaw believed, only by 'contriving a political crisis every week to make the paper interesting'.

Sharp reminded G.B.S. somewhat of his father. He was a moral teetotaller who drank: a man also of late hours and cloudy scandals over money and women. Though it was psychologically impossible for Shaw to trust him, he behaved at some levels with remarkable generosity. 'He has always been extraordinarily nice to me personally,' Sharp told Beatrice, ' – so much so that I never felt inclined to resent in the least the good-humoured contempt which he never concealed. I think he is much the most generous and sweetest-tempered person I ever came across.' Watching the widening difference between the two men, Beatrice noted in her diary that G.B.S. was 'estranged from the *New Statesman* and Sharp, but he is not at all hostile. "It is not my organ, but it may be none the worse for that."'

Nevertheless he proved a troublesome contributor, refusing to let Sharp know 'whether or not he was going to write, and what he was going to write about, until, on the day the paper goes to press, there appears on Sharp's table two or three columns – sometimes twice that amount – on any subject that he (Shaw) happens to fancy.' Sharp met such difficulties with courage and ingenuity. 'I am very favorably impressed by his standing up to me,' Shaw admitted. After correcting one article on the trial of Cecil Chesterton over the Marconi affair to bring it in line with the law and the facts, he was to be accused by G.B.S. of inserting 'nots' into his sentences. On another occasion when Shaw made use of the Belgian General Strike to argue against the use of such strikes on the grounds that they hit the poor rather than the rich, Sharp printed his article as an unsigned letter in refutation of which he commissioned an unsigned letter from Sidney Webb.

The differences between the two men were to be exacerbated by the war, during which, Sharp wrote, the *New Statesman* represented Shaw's views 'in scarcely a single particular'. Sharp needed consistent fortitude against Shaw's magnanimous and subversive tactics. Their battle was for authority. Sharp believed that authority automatically belonged to him as editor: but Shaw needed this authority for his iconoclastic opinions and believed himself to be morally justified in usurping it. 'The time has come for me to be old and savage,' he asserted. He used everything except his money and his position as proprietor in their struggle. His weapons were words. 'His practical generosity has always been accompanied by the most utter and discouraging intolerance in other directions,' Sharp protested to Beatrice in 1916.

Sharp's view was that such ecstatic irresponsibilities as Shaw's had no place in his paper; and Beatrice, though she and Sidney were themselves to sever their relationship with Sharp later on ('your turn will come,' Shaw predicted), tended to support the editor, partly because she felt out of sorts with G.B.S. 'The New Statesman enjoys the distinction of being the only paper in the world that refuses to print anything by me,' Shaw was to write in the autumn of 1916, '... and I am compelled, as I have been more or less all my life, to depend for publicity on the more extreme Conservative organs of opinion.'

*

One advantage of starting the *New Statesman*, Beatrice had promised Shaw, 'is that you and we are apparently going to exchange our thoughts much more than we have done for the past 15 years'. But she remained unhappy about him. His 'big brain', which should have worked so elastically in time with her own thinking, and Sidney's, had been 'spoilt by intense vanity and intellectual egotism'. It was clear to her that this corruption of his character had spread from Mrs Patrick Campbell, who actually described the *New Statesman* without G.B.S. as 'a dull affair'. 'The relationship is one of gross mutual flattery, each pandering to the other's morbid craving for the recognition of unique genius,' Beatrice had erupted. '... he is the fly and the lady the spider.'

Shaw had been more than usually subdued in the autumn of 1913, trying to regain his old habit of holding back hopes, as he flew round France on what Stella called his 'honeymoon' with Charlotte. 'I am horribly unhappy every morning,' he wrote to her, '... you have wakened the latent tragedy in me ... I am as lonely as God.' On his return he tried to keep hidden from their friends these hideous vicissitudes of mood and the memory of Stella that 'tears me all to pieces'. Now that the affair had ended, Beatrice began to feel more sympathetic towards him. Instead of hanging around Mrs Pat's bedroom he was making a positive effort to keep in with the Fabians. 'He has attended every one of our six public lectures, and taken the chair twice,' she approved. '... Apparently he keeps away from Mrs Pat, and he and Charlotte are outwardly on the best of terms.' It was not wholly displeasing to Beatrice that Shaw's recent plays, of which she did not think much, had been unsuccessful. *The Music-Cure* was presented for just seven performances at the Little Theatre; *Great Catherine*, 'foredoomed to failure', ran for thirty performances at the Vaudeville and had not been very well reviewed – 'perhaps one expected a little more,' wrote A. B. Walkley in *The Times*. More surprisingly, Barker's production of *Androcles and the Lion*, with shimmering post-impressionist designs by Albert Rothenstein, had come off after fifty-two performances at the St James's Theatre. The play had puzzled people. 'But what's the point to the whole thing?' Desmond MacCarthy heard one man say to another as they left the theatre. Several dramatic critics shared this bewilderment. The *Morning Post* felt it would 'give offence to not a few'. What offended people was the quality Clifford Sharp

322

and Beatrice Webb disliked in Shaw's writings for the *New Statesman*, and what E. A. Baughan in the *Daily News* described as 'very heavy fooling mixed with serious ideas'. It was Desmond MacCarthy, in the *New Statesman*, who retaliated on behalf of Shaw's contrapuntal tone. 'An English audience has not as a rule sufficient emotional mobility to follow a method which alternates laughter with pathos, philosophy with fun, in such rapid succession.'

Everyone had loved the lion, a delicious beast with the most alluring howls and pussycat antics, and 'the one character in the whole range of Shavian drama,' commented A. B. Walkley warmly, 'who never talks.' But it was the lion's evening rather than the playwright's. The *Manchester Guardian*'s critic reported that the words 'vulgarity', 'blasphemy', 'childish' were to be heard at the end of the performance, and predicted that 'Mr Shaw's new play will scandalise . . . the most characteristic part of the English public [which] . . . cannot understand being passionately in earnest about a thing and in the same breath making fun of it.' And so it proved. 'Religious people write me wild letters about it,' Shaw complained 'washing my feet with their tears and drying them with their hair.' Those who did not write to him posted their complaints to the popular press:

'This blasphemous work of that prince of hypocritical egoists is a disgrace to the author, the Censors and all concerned. How long will the British public be content to let this man Shaw make use of the Christian religion as the medium for the display of his blasphemous, egotistical, selfish philosophy, which never can be witty in the true sense of the word, and of which any healthy-minded heathen nigger would probably be thoroughly ashamed?'

As these denunciations grew so Shaw for once seemed to lose his patience. He felt angry and upset. 'People who have no religion will doubtless be shocked at my play,' he responded. 'Others will not. I have nothing to do with these people who are shocked . . . ' For Christmas and the New Year he went to Devon and Cornwall for a fortnight's tour with Kilsby and the car, the Webbs and the young syndicalist secretary of the Fabian Research Committee, William Mellor. The scenery had 'an almost Irish charm'. Each day they would set off walking over ten or thirteen miles of researched country, with the car panting in attendance to take them, when exhausted, to the most luxurious hotel in the neighbourhood. 'Our old friend and brilliant comrade is a benevolent and entertaining companion,' Beatrice allowed. But he was 'getting rapidly old physically, and somewhat dictatorial and impatient intellectually, and he suffers from restlessness', she observed. 'We talked more intimately than we have done

323

for many years. He is interested in the newer developments of Fabianism, not at all impressed with militancy or syndicalism, a good deal less anxious to conciliate the newcomers than we are.'

Shaw's life was changing – everything was changing – from comedy to tragedy. The change seemed to be shifting part of his political and theatrical terrain, leaving him fragmented. From Cornwall he wrote to Charlotte: 'I miss you, as you would be happy here, and I like to be with you when you are happy.' From Devon he wrote to Stella, reminding her of their love a year ago: 'I believe we were both well then, and have been ill ever since.' He could not conceal these divisions from the sharp eyes of Beatrice. 'He is still fond of Charlotte and grateful to her,' she noted, 'but he quite obviously finds his new friend, with her professional genius and more intimate personal appeal, better company.'

Stella had taken little notice of Joey's letters this winter. 'I ought to have written,' she acknowledged. ' . . . But there has been much to do and to think over, and letter writing to you – seemed irrelevant – thats all.' *The Adored One* had not been a success, and Barrie's attempts at rescue by rewriting parts of it had failed. 'The reality of life closes in upon one,' Stella wrote. She began to look differently at Shaw. 'Be quite serious in your friendship for me,' she appealed. ' - I am so troubled just now, and must put aside trimmings and prettiness.' Though still uncertain as to whether Shaw wanted her to play Eliza 'for the joy of making a fool of me', she had recently approached Beerbohm Tree about *Pygmalion*. Having already heard from George Alexander that this play was 'a winner' Tree asked Shaw to come to His Majesty's and read it to him. The reading took place high up in the dome of the theatre, and before the end of the third act Tree had made up his mind to stage it. Rehearsals were to begin in February 1914. Tree's 'admiration for you and the play is ENORMOUS', Stella wrote enthusiastically to Shaw. 'I'll be tame as a mouse and oh so obedient – and I wonder if you'll get what you want out of me . . . '

Ibsen was compelled to acquiesce in a happy ending for A Doll's House in Berlin, because he could not help himself, just as I have never been able to stop the silly and vulgar gag with which Eliza in Pygmalion, both here and abroad, gets the last word and implies that she is going to marry Pygmalion. Shaw to Archer (19 April 1919)

Pygmalion marks the climax of Shaw's career as a writer of comedies. Fifteen years in gestation, and a return in feeling and form to the period of his *Plays Pleasant*, it emerged as an ingeniously constructed work of art, integrating Faustian legend with Cinderella fairy tale, a comedy of manners with a parable of socialism. Written in his mid-fifties, so near to his mother's death and to the flowering of his romance with Stella Campbell, the play weaves together a variety of Shavian themes, sources and obsessions, imaginatively rephrasing the relationship between his mother and Vandeleur Lee, and casting Mrs Pat as the emotional replacement for Mrs Shaw. Its vitality and charm endeared *Pygmalion* to audiences, with whom it has remained Shaw's most popular 'romance'. 'There must be something radically wrong with the play if it pleases everybody,' he protested, 'but at the moment I cannot find what it is.'

He enjoyed describing *Pygmalion* as a dry didactic experiment to demonstrate how the science of phonetics could pull apart an antiquated British class system now tied together by little more than a string of impressions and appearances. 'The reformer we need most today is an energetic phonetic enthusiast,' he was to write in his Preface. Such a laboratory method of cutting down social barriers was Shaw's gesture towards removing the power for change from fighting men who were threatening to alter the world by indiscriminate warfare, and handing it to men of words whom he promoted as 'among the most important people in England at present'. In this context, the character of Henry Higgins (who appears as a comic version of Sherlock Holmes in Act I) takes his life from the revolutionary phonetician and philologist Henry Sweet, who had died while the play was being written. Shaw (later to be appointed chairman of the British Broadcasting Corporation's Advisory Committee on Spoken English) had been introduced to Sweet in the early 1880s by his friend James Lecky. In any other country in the world, he declared, Sweet would have been 'better known than I am myself'. Writing to Robert Bridges in 1910 about the need for a phonetic institute, he had described Sweet as the man 'I had most hopes of'. It was Bridges who, the following year, retained Shaw to speak at the Phonetic Conference on spelling reform at University College, London, where he had loudly blown Sweet's trumpet. After the debate he sent a letter to Sweet explaining what he had said. 'There is no such thing as a standard pronunciation. There is no such thing as an ideal pronunciation,' he wrote.

'Nevertheless . . . it is perfectly easy to find a speaker whose speech will be accepted in every part of the English speaking world as valid 18-carat oral currency . . . all you have to do is to write down the best practicable phonetic representation of the part of Hamlet as spoken by Forbes Robertson, and publish it with a certificate signed by half a dozen persons of satisfactory social standing, NOT that the pronunciation represented is the standard pronunciation or ideal pronunciation, or correct pronunci- ation, or in any way binding on any human being or morally superior to Hackney cockney or Idaho american, but solely that if a man pronounces in that way he will be eligible as far as speech is concerned for the post of Lord Chief Justice, Chancellor at Oxford, Archbishop of Canterbury, Emperor, President, or Toast Master at the Mansion House.'

It was this experiment, in a more sophisticated format, that Shaw transferred to Higgins's laboratory in Wimpole Street, with its phono- graph, laryngoscope, tuning-forks, wax cylinders and organ pipes – 'I have long given up the idea of inducing you to do anything,' he told Sweet. This is a live experiment we are shown on stage, and as with all such laboratory work it is necessary for the Frankenstein doctor to behave as if his creation were insentient. 'She's incapable of understanding anything,' Higgins assures his fellow-scientist Colonel Pickering. 'Besides, do any of us understand what we are doing? If we did, would we ever do it?' When Pickering asks: 'Does it occur to you, Higgins, that the girl has some feelings?', Higgins cheerily replies: 'Oh no, I dont think so. Not any feelings that we need bother about. Have you, Eliza?'

Shaw conducts a second social experiment through Eliza's father, Alfred Doolittle, an elderly dustman of Dickensian vitality who partly owes his existence to Boffin, the character who in *Our Mutual Friend* inherits a fortune out of dust. Doolittle is any one of us. When asked by Higgins whether he is an honest man or rogue, he answers: 'A little of both, Henry, like the rest of us.' But he is more rogue than honest man in the dusty moral climate of pre-war London. Being his name, he does as little as possible – some bribery here or there, a little blackmail, more drinking, an occasional change of mistress: and he provides positively no education at all for his illegitimate daughter 'except to give her a lick of the strap now and again'. Yet he has all the quick wits and superficial charm of the capitalist entrepreneur. He is society's free man – free of responsibilities and conscience. 'Have you no morals, man?' demands Pickering. 'Cant afford them, Governor,' Doolittle answers. Undeserving poverty is his line: 'and I mean to go on being undeserving. I like it,' he adds. His disquisition on middle-class morality is intended by Shaw to have the same subversive effect as Falstaff's discourse on honour.

Yet this is the man whom Shaw chooses as the first recipient of what he calculates to be a reasonable income-for-all. As the result of Higgins's joking reference to Doolittle as the most original moralist in England in a letter to an American philanthropist, the undeserving dustman is left £3,000 a year on behalf of the Wannafeller Moral Reform World League. In Act II he had made his entrance with 'a professional flavour of dust about him'. In Act V when his name is announced and Pickering queries, 'Do you mean the dustman?', the parlourmaid answers: 'Dustman! Oh no, sir: a gentleman.' He is splendidly dressed as if for a fashionable wedding, with dazzling silk hat, patent leather shoes and buttonhole. Shaw's point is not that a gentleman is merely a dustman with money in the same way as a flower girl with phonetic training can be passed off as a duchess: it is that moral reformation depends upon the reform of our economic system. As Eric Bentley writes: 'He was giving the idea of the gentleman an economic basis.' At a speech to the National Liberal Club in 1913, Shaw called for a constructive social scheme for the creation of gentlemen – not the sham gentlemen of hereditary qualifications who lived in idleness, but a new breed of moral gentlemen who claimed a handsome dignified existence and subsistence from their country, who gave in return the best service of which they were capable and whose ideal was to give their country more than they received from it. It is this that Doolittle dreaded and derided, and now finds himself dragged into. 'It's making a gentleman of me that I object to,' he protests. 'Who asked him to make a gentleman of me? . . . I have to live for others and not for myself: thats middle class morality.'

Shaw is at the same time conducting an experiment with the Pygmalion legend by making Higgins create a petrified social statue of Eliza. Under his tutelage she becomes a doll of 'remarkable distinction and beauty . . . speaking with pedantic correctness of pronunciation and great beauty of tone', which Mrs Higgins tells her son is 'a triumph of your art and of her dressmaker's'. This dummy figure replaces the 'draggle tailed guttersnipe . . . more brute than being' whose life Higgins acknowledges to have been real, warm and violent – 'you can feel it through the thickest skin: you can taste it and smell it without any training or any work'. The classical Pygmalion, believing all women to be prostitutes, had prayed to Aphrodite to make his ideal statue come alive so that he could marry her –

which may mean, as Arnold Silver has argued, that he 'would be committing incest in marrying the woman he had fathered partheno-genetically'. Shaw's flower girl, whom Higgins has manufactured into a replica duchess by the beginning of Act IV, is then transformed by the action of the Life Force into an independent living woman – whom Higgins refuses to marry. However, the transformation scheme, in which Higgins lays his hands on Eliza like a sculptor's creative act, is a struggle the implications of which are sexual.

'Eliza tries to control herself . . . she is on the point of screaming . . . He comes to her . . . He pulls her up . . . LIZA *[breathless] . . . She crisps her fingers frantically.* HIGGINS *[looking at her in cool wonder] . . .* LIZA *[gives a suffocated scream of fury, and instinctively darts her nails at his face]* !! HIGGINS *[catching her wrists . . . He throws her roughly into the easy chair]* LIZA *[crushed by superior strength and weight].* HIGGINS *[thundering]* Those slippers LIZA *[with bitter submission]* Those slippers'

This sexual sub-text provided by the stage directions contains many sado-masochistic undertones, and is voiced as a suspicion by the other characters in the play. Pickering puts the question to Higgins simply: 'Are you a man of good character where women are concerned?' and adds 'I hope it's understood that no advantage is to be taken of her position.' Eliza herself who repeatedly insists that she's 'a good girl' is prudishly shocked by the mirror in Higgins's bathroom and tells him 'I've heard of girls being drugged by the likes of you.' Doolittle arriving to rescue his daughter from 'worse than death', then selling her to Higgins for five pounds, assures him that she will 'soon pick up your free and easy ways' and advises him to 'marry Eliza while she's young and dont know no better'. Higgins's housekeeper, Mrs Pearce, seeing him tempt Eliza with chocolates and promises of taxi-rides, bursts out: 'Stop, Mr Higgins. I wont allow it. It's you that are wicked. Go home to your parents, girl; and tell them to take better care of you.' The police inspector too, whom Higgins and Pickering call in when Eliza disappears, 'suspected us of some improper purpose', Pickering reveals. Even Higgins's mother believes that her son 'must be perfectly cracked' about his flower girl. But Higgins himself resists every innuendo.

This was important to Shaw. When he had been coaching Florence Farr he suggested that she 'should learn the science of phonetics for dramatic purposes' and be appointed Beerbohm Tree's resident professor of phonetics at His Majesty's Theatre. Sweet, of course, had been the man to teach her. 'He will probably say that two years residence at Oxford is indispensable, as he has a genius for making everything impossible both for himself and everybody else,' he had written to Florence. 'He is the most savagely Oxonian and donnish animal that ever devoted his life to abusing all the other dons . . . See him and try what you can make out of him.'

Nothing had come of Shaw's phonetic plan for Florence, and when he tried to revive it in *Pygmalion* Sweet's genius for 'making everything impossible' again seemed to obstruct him, and he turned his mind to another 'genius' as a model for Higgins, the author of *The Voice*, Vandeleur Lee. Higgins's asexual association with Eliza is consequently authorized by Shaw's faith in his mother's 'innocence', and written as an endorsement of his own legitimacy. The platonic arrangement depends not only on Higgins's statement that he is 'a confirmed old bachelor, and likely to remain so', as Lee had done (though not Sweet who was married), but more importantly on the professional circumstances of their relationship. 'You see, she'll be a pupil,' Higgins explains to Pickering, 'and teaching would be impossible unless pupils were sacred.' Higgins's voice tuition of Eliza takes the place of the singing lessons Lee had given Bessie (Lucinda Elizabeth Shaw) and to reinforce this substitution Shaw provides Higgins's pupil with the same name as Lee's pupil.

HIGGINS   Whats your name?
THE FLOWER GIRL   Liza Doolittle
HIGGINS   [*declaiming gravely*] Eliza, Elizabeth, Betsy and Bess,
They went to the wood to get a bird's nes':

Near the beginning of Act II Eliza complains to Higgins, 'One would think you were my father', and he replies: 'If I decide to teach you, I'll be worse than two fathers to you.' Near the end of the play he suggests to her, 'I'll adopt you as my daughter and settle money on you if you like. Or would you rather marry Pickering?' What seems clear is that Higgins can assume almost any family relationship with Eliza except that of husband. 'I've never been able to feel really grown-up and tremendous, like other chaps,' he tells Pickering. He explains the reason to his mother who has regretted his inability to fall in love with any woman under forty-five. 'My idea of a lovable woman is somebody as like you as possible,' he tells her. 'I shall never get into the way of seriously liking young women: some habits lie too deep to be changed.'

While she lives in Higgins's house, Eliza remains a bought woman and simply his creation, as Galatea had been Pygmalion's. But the transformation scene, which is a deflowering of Eliza, leads to her rebirth and, with the handing over of her necklace, a severing of the umbilical cord. The scene ends with the same implicit sexuality as it began. Higgins eats

329

his Adam-and-Eve apple, and the divorce of his previous partnership with Eliza, dramatized by the throwing-away of the ring, is complete. In the middle of this scene Higgins tells Eliza: 'Now you are free and can do what you like.' What she does is to escape to his mother's house where, the stage directions inform us, 'she is very much at home'. Finding her there in the last act, Higgins exclaims: 'Five minutes ago you were like a millstone round my neck. Now youre a tower of strength: a consort battleship.' What has apparently impressed Higgins is Eliza's statement that she will teach others 'what you taught me. I'll teach phonetics' – in much the same way as Bessie had taught 'the Method' in London independently of Lee.

In this final act, Shaw was rewriting the legend of Svengali and his pupil Trilby. When Svengali dies of a heart attack, Trilby's voice is silenced, she cannot sing at her concert, and she follows Svengali into death. In Shaw's version Eliza's voice speaks truly once she emerges from Higgins's bullying presence and walks out to a separate life. But other forces were at work in the final act obliging Higgins himself to speak increasingly with the voice of G.B.S., the public figure that had developed from Vandeleur Lee; while Eliza comes to represent the emotions that Stella Campbell was introducing into his life. Higgins's description of Eliza as a 'consort battleship' has something of the armoured impregnability Shaw attributed to his mother ('one of those women who could act as matron of a cavalry barracks from eighteen to forty and emerge without a stain on her character'). But no one else in the play regards Eliza in this light. Mrs Higgins calls her 'naturally rather affectionate'; Doolittle admits she is 'very tender-hearted'; and Eliza herself demands: 'Every girl has a right to be loved.' She also tells Higgins that she had 'come to care for you', and though she adds that she does not 'want you to make love to me', this is clearly a tactical statement added so as not to alarm Higgins at the start of their new relationship: for love is what she does want. She wants to be valued.

What Higgins wants is less clear. He claims he has created an ideal wife – 'a consort for a king' – yet, since she represents his mother, he must resist her emotional appeal with supermaniac brutality: 'I wont stop for you ... I can do without anybody. I have ... my own spark of divine fire ... I care for life, for humanity; and you are a part of it that has come my way and been built into my house. What more can you or anyone ask? ... If you cant stand the coldness of my sort of life, and the strain of it, go back to the gutter.'

The purpose of Higgins's experiment has been 'filling up the deepest gulf that separates class from class and soul from soul'. It is half successful, half a failure. The class gulf is filled at the garden party, dinner party and reception: the gulf between Eliza and Higgins remains. Eliza has changed, but Higgins admits 'I cant change my nature.' He is, as Eliza says, 'a born preacher' and that seems to be the only role he can sustain. Lacking the intimate voice, he seems 'cold, unfeeling, selfish' to Eliza. 'I only want to be natural,' she says. But can Higgins be natural? There seems a chance when, with '*sudden humility*', he confesses to her that 'I have learnt something from your idiotic notions: I confess that humbly and gratefully. And I have grown accustomed to your voice and appearance. I like them, rather.' Where will these feelings lead to if she accepts his invitation to go back to him 'for the fun of it'? There is no mention of sex: but Higgins is enticing her into the beginnings of a Shavian open marriage. The original ending of the play is carefully ambiguous, reflecting Shaw's uncertainties over his romance with Stella. He could not marry her: she could not remain for ever his pupil as an actress learning from his theatrical direction. But might they become lovers? The question is left open to our imagination:

MRS HIGGINS   I'm afraid youve spoilt that girl, Henry. But never mind, dear: I'll buy you the tie and gloves.

HIGGINS   [*sunnily*] Oh, dont bother. She'll buy em all right enough. Good-bye. *They kiss. Mrs Higgins runs out. Higgins, left alone, rattles his cash in his pocket; chuckles; and disports himself in a highly self-satisfied manner.*

Critics of the play have agreed with Eric Bentley that 'this is the true naturalistic ending' and that Shaw's subsequent series of attempts to clear up its ambiguity, stimulated by the actors' and public's response to the sub-text, have blurred the outline of its elegant structure. The faint poignancy of the ending lies in the half-emergent realization that there is to be no satisfactory marriage for this Cinderella; while a feminist reading tells us that Higgins cannot be approved of as a husband. Popular opinion wanted Shaw not to shatter the fairy tale – which he would do by going further. 'I call it a romance,' he told a reporter, 'because it is the story of a poor girl who meets a gentleman at a church door and is transformed by him into a beautiful lady. That is what I call romance. It is also what everybody else calls a romance, so for once we are all agreed.' But the public wanted his Miltonic bachelor to be transformed into the beautiful lady's lover. 'This is unbearable,' Shaw cried out. Once his love affair with Stella had ended, he could not bear to speculate on what might have happened that time when 'I almost condescended to romance'. He instructed his translators, therefore, that there was to be 'no sentimental nonsense' about Higgins and Eliza being lovers. 'Eliza married Freddy [Eynsford-Hill]' he told Trebitsch; 'and the notion of her marrying Higgins is disgusting.' In other words Eliza married a double-barrelled nonentity like George Cornwallis-West, and Higgins's agonizing boredom with the Eynsford-Hill family reflects Shaw's own impatience with the smart visitors who sometimes crowded him out of Stella's house.

The history of *Pygmalion* was to develop into a struggle over this ending. For the play's first publication in book form in 1916, Shaw added a sequel, like the last chapter in a novel, recounting 'what Eliza did'. Her decision not to marry Higgins, he explained, was well-considered and guided by instinct. The differences between them of age and income, when added to Higgins's mother-fixation and exclusive passion for phonetics, was too wide a gulf to bridge. He told the story of Eliza and Freddy, Mr and Mrs Eynsford-Hill, as invitingly as he could: but the public went on preferring its own version. By the 1920s he had begun advising his translators to add lines in their own languages for Higgins to end the play on. 'It is important that the actor who plays Higgins should thoroughly understand that he is not Eliza's lover,' he instructed Julio Brouta, his Spanish translator. ' . . . When he is left alone on the stage at the end he should just go out on the balcony and look down making it clear that he is watching Eliza's departure in the carriage. He then comes back into the room, excited and triumphant & exclaims "Finished, and come to life! Bravo, Pygmalion!"'

After much tampering Shaw made his final version of the end on 19 August 1939.

MRS HIGGINS   I'm afraid youve spoilt that girl, Henry. I should be uneasy about you and her if she were less fond of Colonel Pickering.

HIGGINS   Pickering! Nonsense: she's going to marry Freddy. Ha ha! Freddy! Freddy!! Ha ha ha ha ha!!!!! [*He roars with laughter as the play ends*]

But by now this laughter sounded as hollow as Higgins's prediction – and even Shaw's printers had begun to query his intentions. 'I assure you that Liza *did* marry Freddy,' he again insisted, 'and that Higgins never married anybody . . . their marriage would have been a revolting tragedy.'

The English-language film of *Pygmalion*, written and made between 1936 and 1938, gave Shaw an extra opportunity to remove 'virtually every suggestion of Higgins's possible romantic interest in Liza'. He was particularly anxious to achieve this having loathed the sentimental German and Dutch film adaptations. His screenplay even omits the word 'consort' and leaves Higgins calling Eliza a 'battleship'. But the producer of the film hired other screenwriters who added a 'sugar-sweet ending' which Shaw found out for the first time at a press show two days before its première. 'Nothing of the kind was emphasised in my scenario,' he wrote. Nevertheless it was widely reported that G.B.S. had approved the romantic reconciliation.

But one battle he apparently did win. 'Hamon, my French translator, says that it is announced that Lehar is making an operetta of Pygmalion,' he notified Trebitsch in the summer of 1921. ' . . . Can you warn him that he cannot touch Pygmalion without infringing my copyright, and that I have no intention of allowing the history of The Chocolate Soldier to be repeated.' For almost thirty more years he made the same reply to all composers and resisted every pressure to 'degrade' his play into a musical. 'I absolutely forbid any such outrage,' he wrote when in his ninety-second year. *Pygmalion* was good enough 'with its own verbal music'.

*

A number of Shaw's plays had first been presented abroad. Richard Mansfield made *The Devil's Disciple* popular in America before its production in England; Arnold Daly put on *How He Lied to Her Husband* in New York before it was taken up by Barker and Vedrenne at the Court Theatre, and had also achieved 'a sort of snivelling success' with *Candida*; *Caesar and Cleopatra* was played in front of both German and American audiences over a year before English theatregoers had their chance of seeing it; and *The Shewing-up of Blanco Posnet* enjoyed its controversial run in Dublin a full twelve years before the Lord Chamberlain permitted its first public presentation in London.

Much of this had been either accidental or forced on Shaw by circumstances. But after 1906, as a mark of what he owed to German culture, he arranged for Trebitsch's translations of many of his plays to appear in book form before they were published in Britain. Following Frohman's disastrous London production of *Misalliance*, 'the pressure which has been put on me for some years past in Germany to produce my plays there in the first instance, and so avoid the reports of disastrous failure which invariably follow my London productions, was redoubled', he wrote. 'It seemed for the moment impossible to expect any newspaper reader to go to a play so furiously denounced as intolerable.'

Pygmalion, which was first published in book form in Germany, Hungary and Sweden (plus an unauthorized edition in America), received its theatrical début at the Hofburg Theater in Vienna on 16 October 1913, and was played a fortnight later at the Lessingtheater in Berlin. 'There is no legal difficulty about performing an English play in Germany before it is performed in England,' Shaw had written soothingly to Trebitsch. '. . . I should rather like the English production of one of my plays to be anticipated abroad. But it is very important that a foreign production of this kind should not be a failure.' *The Times* on 17 October 1913 reported that the opening night in Vienna, 'before a crowded house', had 'met with an excellent reception from the audience, which among a number of distinguished personages included the Archduke Francis Ferdinand'.

In an interview for the *Observer* Shaw described this première as a compliment paid to him by German and Austrian culture 'which I value very much'. *Pygmalion* had been performed with the assistance of the Emperor and the Imperial city in a beautiful theatre splendidly subsidized and free of rent. 'I am handsomely paid for my work,' he reported. 'In London, with an equally popular play, the ground landlord leaves less than nothing for me and for the management . . . Meanwhile, huge endowments are proposed for football, pedestrian races, and throwing the hammer.'

However, there were two small clouds floating over these foreign productions of *Pygmalion*.

The central situation of the play also appears in Shaw's novel *Love Among the Artists* where the Welsh Beethoven, Owen Jack, gives elocution lessons to Madge Brailsford, a middle-class girl whom he helps by this training to become a successful actress. But an alert German critic pointed out the extraordinary resemblance of Shaw's story to the adventures of Smollett's hero with a sixteen-year-old beggar girl in Chapter 87 of his novel *Peregrine Pickle* – and the British press immediately took this up as the real reason why Shaw had produced his play out of the country. It showed 'an amusing ignorance of English culture', Shaw countered. 'The one place where I should have been absolutely safe from detection is London.' He had never read *Peregrine Pickle* – or rather he had read it only in his youth and not cared for it – and he did not realize that 'Smollett had got hold of my plot', he admitted to the *Observer*. 'He is quite welcome to it.' Later he was to speculate on the likelihood of this incident from the novel having 'got lodged in my memory without my being conscious of it and stayed there until I needed it'. None of this affected the morality of his position. 'If I find in a book anything I can make use of, I take it gratefully,' he stated. 'My plays are full of pillage of this kind . . . In short, my literary morals are those of Molière and Handel.' To the end of his life Shaw maintained this indifference towards critics who fussed over plagiarism, describing them as 'mostly foolish amateur detectives'. Shakespeare had taken his goods where he could find them; Shaw himself had once invented a scene in a play which he intended to use until he found it expressed with similar words in Jerome K. Jerome's *The Passing of the Third Floor Back*. 'Do not scorn to be derivative,' he urged his friends. ' . . . the great thing is to be able to derive – to see your chance and be able to take it . . . Read Goldsmith on originality.'

The other cloud was a rumour that the actor playing Higgins in Berlin had introduced a 'horrible gag' into the play suggesting that he and Eliza shared the same bedroom. At least in London, where Shaw was producing the play himself, such travesties would not be permitted. Though Stella's reputation among actor-managers was alarmingly unstable, she had promised to be obedient, while Tree could not recall that 'there is much ill feeling'. Nevertheless, when Shaw turned up for rehearsals in the second week of February he found His Majesty's a madhouse.

Famous for his testing absent-mindedness, Tree was the despair of playwrights. He greeted Shaw warmly, but with obvious surprise. It was as if he believed himself to be the author of *Pygmalion*. His head hummed with plans for the play, including a sumptuous ball scene. For he had experience of collaborating with other dramatists – for example, Shakespeare into whose *Richard II* he introduced a very effective pet dog, and whose *Twelfth Night* he had improved by the addition of four miniature copycat Malvolios. His performances were histrionic and hugely entertaining to his fans, but they relied on a good deal of improvisation especially when he was not quick enough to reach the stage furniture in time and pluck from its niches the pieces of paper on which he had written out his more troublesome lines. His style of acting, in such diverse roles as Beethoven, Svengali, Julius Caesar or Colonel Newcombe, was unchangeable; but he loved to disguise himself with beards, uniforms, vine leaves and ear-trumpets. In this respect, Professor Higgins was a disappointment. It seemed he was required to do little more than dress and speak normally: and this bewildered him. In vain did he plead with Shaw to let him take large quantities of snuff, to use a Scots accent, to vault on to the piano from time to time, to indicate an addiction to port by walking with a limp and a stick.

'I daresay the play will get produced somehow before Christmas,' Shaw wrote to Edmund Gurney who was playing Doolittle. Delays were most often caused by Tree's absences as he wandered off somewhere in the middle of a scene, and by his reappearances with brainwaves of how to take over other roles (such as Doolittle) or fill the theatre with philosophical dustmen and flower girls. To Shaw's businesslike mind it seemed miraculous that any production ever took place at His Majesty's. Tree had with dignity assured him that 'I will not place myself in the position of receiving a rebuff,' and was taken aback when Mrs Campbell hurled a slipper bang in his face. His morale shattered, he collapsed into a chair while the cast tried to get him to understand that this was part of the play. The worst of it was, Shaw wrote, that 'it was quite evident that he would be just as surprised and wounded next time'.

Shaw was strangely convinced that Tree was a tragedian and Stella a comedian. He treated them both as delinquents. 'I am sending a letter to Tree which will pull him together if it does not kill him,' he informed Stella. But Tree reflected in his notebook: 'I will not go so far as to say that all people who write letters of more than eight pages are mad, but it is a curious fact that all madmen write letters of more than eight pages.' In Stella's view it was splendid of Tree to accept 'with gentle indifference letters that would have made a frenchman "call you out"'. As for herself, she could 'always find a good use for a little piece of paper'.

In her fashion, Stella worked hard at Eliza Doolittle. 'It needs a giants strength and great calmness,' she wrote to Shaw, 'but you will pull us through with success I know. I will help all I can for I realise what you want.' Her prompt copy of *Pygmalion* was pencilled with encouraging scribbles: 'My hand is held out Joey . . . I'll do my level best . . . Your delicious play needs real greatness . . . gentle Joey.'

But Shaw was not always so gentle. Though often maddened by Tree, 'I could never bring myself to hit him hard enough,' he regretted. But on Stella he believed that 'no poker was thick enough nor heavy enough to leave a solitary bruise'. He had been partly persuaded of this by her treatment of him outside the theatre and by the knowledge that she thrived on conflict; and partly driven to it by her insistence on extravagant inessentials, such as her dressing-room raised to stage level, converted into a tent, and erected round a piano. 'You are wonderful at rehearsal,' Stella had written to him early on, 'and we'll all shed our blood for you.' A little later, however, he was 'AWFUL' and she felt like shedding everyone else's blood. She would make faces, put out her tongue, turn her back on Tree ('But it's a very nice back, isn't it?') and finally drive him screaming from his own stage. For days they communicated only through an intermediary, leaving Shaw to continue rehearsals with their understudies.

Stella's tantrums masked a lack of confidence. She had never played in comedy before; she had no knowledge of Covent Garden flower girls; and she was thirty years too old for the part. 'Dreadfully middle-aged moments,' Shaw observed in his rehearsal notebook. Occasionally he did not keep such observations to himself. 'If you must say – things,' Stella wrote to him, 'I'll try and take them lying down . . . because none of us can spare the time to take that side of you that *hurts* seriously!' But Shaw treated her as inconsiderately as Higgins treated Eliza. At least twice she refused to continue rehearsing while he remained in the theatre. He gathered his papers together, announced that he would leave town, but got no further than Covent Garden (where he recuperated at a performance of Wagner's *Meistersinger*) and Adelphi Terrace. Frantic appeals from other members of the cast, and by Tree himself, recalled him: 'I think your flight is a cowardly evasion of your responsibilities and thus to leave me to the tender mercies of Mrs Patrick Campbell seems to me almost unbrotherly,' Tree generously chided him. ' . . . I do hope you will come back to us very soon, for I greatly value your suggestions and your helpfulness. It is obvious that your own play needs your own spirit brooding over it.'

So Shaw came back, was greeted by Tree as some friend who had dropped in, and enjoyed an orgy of interference into everything from the scene-painting and wig-making to costume-designing and programme-printing. Then all the teasing and tantrums started up again. At one moment, as he knelt before Stella imploring her to speak the lines as he directed, she told the actors: 'That's where I like to see my authors, on their knees at my feet.' But as he went on talking, advising, correcting, she grew irritated – 'Oh Joey, what a fool you are!' – and walked away. She was frightened of over-preparation. 'Shaw had a horrible time,' remembered Margaret Bussé who was playing Clara Eynsford-Hill. As if to illustrate this he had some photographs taken that 'had to be destroyed because they resembled an old dog after a fight', – but not before he had sent one to Stella enquiring 'Aren't you ashamed?' and another to Tree inscribed 'This is your work.'

Opening night was set for 11 April 1914. The week before was marked by two spectacular disappearances. Stella had written to Shaw of the 'many worries in my heart'. She was 'full of anxiety'. The nature of her anxiety became clear when, instead of going to the theatre on Monday 6 April, she took off for the Kensington Registry Office where she married George Cornwallis-West two hours after his decree absolute came through. From there they went on a three-day honeymoon to a golfing resort near Tunbridge Wells, returning in time for Stella to take part in the dress rehearsal at His Majesty's on Friday evening. 'Of *course* I knew about the marriage,' Tree lied to the press assembled in the dress circle bar, 'and I'm very happy for both of them, but naturally I was sworn to secrecy . . . contrary to popular rumour there have been no quarrels between us, in fact rehearsals have progressed with the most delightful smoothness & harmony.'

In Shaw's estimate the other George had been 'a braver man than I was'. He could reflect now on the consequences of his own timidity. The day before the news of Stella's marriage appeared in the papers, Charlotte had sailed for America. She had not been well that winter. She did not know that her husband's affair with Mrs Pat was over – how could you ever tell such things? The long rehearsals of *Pygmalion* had been agony for her, and she did not want to witness their first night climax. So on 8 April she left England with her friend Lena Ashwell and joined their guru James Porter Mills and his wife. These last months, while G.B.S. occupied himself at His Majesty's, Charlotte had been preparing an abstract of Mills's 'Teaching' which he persuaded her to publish as a business prospectus entitled *Knowledge is the Door: A Forerunner*. It was a comfort to her that Dr Mills was not brilliant or literary. She felt calmed by his healthful hints and transcendental eavesdropping. From his communications with the Silent Partner, she had learnt that *'there is no need to give way to human feeling . . .* we can gradually quiet the waves of emotion'.

Tree had employed his gift for publicity, heaping interview on interview, to create a great swell of excitement round the first night. 'A good deal will depend on whether you are inspired at the last moment,' Shaw wrote to Stella that morning. ' . . . You leave everything to chance.' But Stella reassured him: 'I'll obey orders faithfully, I am so thankful you carried through your giant's work to the finish.'

Shaw sat by himself in the teeming theatre: not far off was the other George, Stella's 'GOLDEN man'. The curtain lifted on the first act with 'real' rain falling round the portico of St Paul's Church, Covent Garden. All went smoothly and well. In the second act Edmund Gurney, who had been listening to Lloyd George's speeches in the House of Commons to pick up the right tone of contempt for the aristocracy, scored a colossal success as Doolittle. Stella 'played superbly and ravished the house almost to delirium' throughout the third act, and 'Tree's farcical acting was very funny here'. But Eliza's sensational exit line, 'Not bloody likely,' purple rumours of which had been staining the newspapers, nearly wrecked the play. The audience gave a gasp, there was a crash of laughter while Mrs Pat perambulated the stage, and then a second burst of laughing. The pandemonium lasted well over a minute. 'They laughed themselves into such utter abandonment and disorder,' Shaw wrote to Charlotte in America, 'that it was really doubtful for some time whether they could recover themselves and let the play go on.'

Tree had been in a pitiful state of nerves, begging Shaw to substitute 'blooming' or 'ruddy' for his dreadful word. Now he felt frightfully pleased and excited. He relaxed. He expanded. 'He was like nothing human; and he wallowed ecstatically in his own impossibility, convinced that he was having the success of his life,' Shaw wrote. Much of the dialogue between Higgins and Eliza held special meanings for Shaw – echoes from the controlling influence of his mother ('I cant change my nature') and overtones of his unhappy romance with Stella ('I hadnt quite realised that you were going away . . . I shall miss you Eliza.') It was a duet scored with melancholy pathos – and Tree made it all absurd; 'For the last two acts I writhed in hell,' Shaw wrote to Charlotte. ' . . . The last thing I saw as I left the house was Higgins shoving his mother rudely out of his way and wooing Eliza with appeals to buy ham for his lonely home like a bereaved Romeo. I went straight home to bed and read Shakespear for an hour before going to sleep to settle myself down.'

What consolation there was for Shaw lay in Stella's performance. He almost cheered when, in the fourth act, her second slipper shot practically knocked off Tree's head. 'She could not carry off the fifth act in the same way,' he admitted; 'but she let him rave and fired broadside after broadside with such effect that the scene did not hang fire . . .'

Stella had followed his directions as if she were Eliza imitating Higgins. To thank her, and because he could not endure going backstage after the performance, Shaw invited her and her new husband down to Ayot next day. 'You *must* consent to receive Cornwallis-West in the country,' he wrote winningly to Charlotte that night. 'He has a dog Beppo, a huge black retriever, who plays hide & seek, distinguishes between right & left when he is given instructions, takes people's hats off when ordered, and is withal a grave & reverend signor. I believe you would ask them both to stay for a month on condition that Beppo came too. They were very nice, & are very happy. They treat me as a beloved uncle.'

Because of Tree's irresistible 'genius for bad acting and erroneousness', Shaw doubted if *Pygmalion* could succeed. Once its success became apparent, Tree chivvied him to come back and see it – he had 'only one ambition in the world,' Stella reported, 'that you should be pleased with his Higgins'. But Shaw was adamant: 'no mortal consideration would induce me to sit it out again.' Instead he went up to Yorkshire for a week's walking and motoring holiday with the Webbs, then retired down to Ayot for some motor-bicycling and photography. From various letters and bundles of press cuttings he learnt that the play 'wallows in big houses' but was suffering from more dismal Tree-fooleries. 'Come soon – or you'll not recognize your play,' Stella appealed. But he would not. 'I resist all entreaties to revisit it. Never no more.' Tree had written complaining that the play was too long now that Mrs Pat's changes of dress took up more time than the changes of scene and her delightful dressing-room *levées* had extended the intervals. Stella had written also complaining that the play was too long now that Tree had decided to take five minutes between each word and each bite of his apple, and that she was suffering from facial paralysis from trying to express, during these interminable periods, some sort of intelligent feeling. 'You are no shepherd,' she remonstrated, ' - or you would have taken more care of your fold.' Shaw did not shorten the play since 'cutting it would only make it seem longer', but he relented to the extent of attending the hundredth performance on 15 July.

It was awful. It was appalling. It was worse than anything he had imagined. His directions had been wonderfully circumvented. Instead of flinging the ring down on the dessert stand at the end of Act IV, Eliza on her knees clutched and gazed on it feelingly – there were no words because the emotion was obviously too deep. In the brief interval between the end of the play and fall of the curtain, the amorous Higgins threw flowers at Eliza (and with them Shaw's instructions far out of sight) – a theatrically effective gesture, as Nicholas Grene has observed, 'reversing the image at the end of Act I where Eliza threw her flowers at Higgins'. And there were other embellishments so shocking that Shaw felt it was hopeless to get the play back on its proper plane. 'But I very strongly resented the breach of faith, and never entered the theatre again during its run,' he later wrote to Tree's daughter Viola. 'I should have resented it more, but that your father was so utterly innocent of the meaning of the play, and so pleased with himself as Eliza's lover, that he had no idea of the outrage to me . . . '

Tree claimed that his improvements delighted the audience: and it was this public that Shaw really blamed. What had happened to its taste and serious instincts, its sense of proportion? During these hot summer months there had been turmoil in Ulster over Asquith's Home Rule Bill, and hunger strikes among the militant suffragettes in London. Then on 28 June, the Archduke Franz Ferdinand, who had been at the première of *Pygmalion* in Vienna, was shot: and Europe moved to the edge of war. But for much of this time 'all political and social questions have been swept from the public mind by Eliza's expletive', Shaw reported. The Bishop of Woolwich cried out for it to be banned; Bishop Weldon felt saddened that such a vulgar word had to be uttered by a married lady with children; the playwright Sydney Grundy judged that 'although there is no harm in Shaw's uncarnadined adverb when informed by genius, from Shaw's pen it is poison,' and concluded that 'public opinion is gathering storm over this deeply resented outrage'. Scholars and intellectuals duelled in the columns of *The Times*, *Westminster Gazette* and *Cambridge Review* over the origin of 'bloody'. The Oxford Union met and voted in favour of a motion declaring 'a certain sanguinary expletive' to be 'a liberating influence on the English language', but the Debating Society at Eton deplored 'the debasement and vulgarization of the commercial theatre'. The *Daily*

Express got hold of an authentic Covent Garden flower girl called Eliza, took her to the play and reported her as being shocked. 'No self-respecting flower girl would say such a word ... it sounded simply horrible.' At 10 Downing Street the Prime Minister received a letter of protest from the Women's Purity League; and at His Majesty's, Tree was reprimanded by the Theatre Managers' Association. 'The Word was passed by the Lord Chamberlain and there my responsibility ends,' he told the press. ' ... Besides, I would like to add that a Word which is generally applied to Queen Mary Tudor should not be censored in a flower-girl.' Nevertheless Tree had been shaken by the chorus of abuse, and instructed Margaret Bussé to omit the repetition of bloody later in Act III – a repetition Shaw had put there to predict and satirize its fashionably affected use in London society that season.

The summer days persisted hot and sunny; the public continued to come to *Pygmalion*: but Tree was bored. He wanted to go on holiday and had announced that the play would come off late that July. 'It is quite absurd that the notice should go up at the end of a £2,000 week!' protested Stella. But by the last week of July they had all dispersed – Stella and George with dogs and fishing rods to Ireland; Tree for a visit to Marienbad; and Shaw to spend his fifty-eighth birthday addressing a mutinous Fabian Summer School near Keswick. Tree had attributed the bloody rumpus over *Pygmalion* to 'the flatness of the political situation'. 'Triviality', Shaw wrote, 'can go no further.'

[3]

As for going mad, dont you wish you could? The trying thing is to be sane with everyone else (except the rogues who are taking advantage of it) as mad as hatters. Ugh! What's the use of talking about it? (1916)

Nations are like bees: they cannot kill except at the cost of their own lives. Common Sense about the War

The Fabians were unprepared for war. To Shaw's eyes their general commitment to disarmament was political and psychological naïveté. Most of them believed that outbreaks of modern international war were caused by the capitalist struggle for markets and, pending the collapse of capitalism, could be dealt with by means of the General Strike. Even at the Fabian Summer School that July when the Research Department, chaired by Shaw, undertook to keep its ideas 'under continuous reconsideration',

341

Sidney Webb had still discounted the probability of a European war for the very reason that 'it would be too insane'.

Shaw also thought it insane – and all the more likely for that. What was the Balance of Power diplomacy that had been shuttling back and forwards through the early years of the century but 'paranoic insanity'? Militarism in all countries had developed, he argued, 'not from the needs of human society, but because at a certain stage of social integration the institution of standing armies gave monarchs the power to play at soldiers with living men instead of leaden figures'. German culture in particular had got stuck in this obsolete *Roi Soleil* system. A sensible foreign policy therefore was one that headed her back into the main human road 'with such violence as may be necessary'. This was why Shaw did not favour unilateral disarmament. 'It is no discredit to be prepared for war,' he was to write. 'All nations should be prepared for war. All houses should be protected by lightning conductors.' Until there existed a European police force, Britain must be prepared (unilaterally if need be) 'to make war on war' if she wanted to exercise an effective foreign policy. Sidney Webb's pacifism was that of the sane man. But at a time of war fever 'everyone is more or less mad, and sanity is positively dangerous'.

He had started to become involved in international politics shortly after the Russo-Japanese War. Disturbed by the rising tension between Britain and Germany, he responded to an appeal from Count Harry Kessler to humanists, artists and intellectuals in both countries for an *entente cordiale* and agreed to draft the English side of an exchange of testimonials expressing mutual esteem. Wishing to test whether this was to be anything more than an occasion for graceful phrase-making and suspecting that Britain, which ruled the waves, would like to sink the German navy, he inserted in his friendly letter a statement to the effect that England regarded a strong German fleet as an additional guarantee of civilization. Kessler welcomed this letter as 'quite admirable, and most amusing and interesting besides', but a number of eminent Edwardians refused to sign. The controversial passages were then deleted, Shaw withdrew his signature, and the two letters were printed in *The Times* signed by forty Germans (including Richard Strauss and Siegfried Wagner) and forty-one Britons (including Thomas Hardy and Edward Elgar). The result, in Shaw's opinion, was dangerous 'twaddle'. He was now convinced that they were all sleeping under a powder magazine. Kessler and others had acted in good faith but been exploited by German and British militarists who had signed letters that would not embarrass them if they went to war the following day. Writers should not permit language to be used so misleadingly. Their function was to be awkward and truthful: and to alert their readers to what was really happening.

What was really happening was that Germany and Britain were preparing for war. Europe was ready for an explosion, as if surfeited with the material gains of the previous hundred years. Germany's chronic pride in militarism was apparent. Thomas Mann was to speak of the hearts of poets standing in flame 'for now it is war! ... Nothing better, more beautiful, happier could befall them in the whole world'. In England, where Rupert Brooke was to thank God for matching us with His hour, romantic militarism was dressed up in all sorts of custom-made moral tailoring made to fit the righteous Christian, the hard-headed businessman, travelling adventurer, puritan character-builder. The influential figure of Lord Roberts, for example, in a letter to *The Times* in 1911 about imperial unity, had refashioned his ancient jingoism into the clothing of 'social reform' and recommended its introduction into the primary school system as a sort of uniform. '"My country right or wrong",' he wrote; '"and right or wrong my country" is the sentiment most treasured in the breast of any one worthy of the name of man' – which Shaw paraphrased as 'teaching a Christian to disobey Christ at the commands of a non-commissioned officer'. When he came to write his Preface to *Androcles and the Lion* late in 1915, his reappraisal of the Gospels amounted to a denunciation of war as a method of solving international disputes and a proposal for adopting non-Pauline Christian principles as an alternative political policy.

Shaw put himself in the business of prediction. He used the hypothetical future to dislodge popular contemporary ideas. He set war in the context of peace, and peace in the context of war. The ethics of peace were crucial because, once war started, countries surrendered every other consideration except victory. 'It is one of the horrors of war,' he warned Carl Heath, secretary of the National Peace Council, in 1911, 'that both parties abandon the ground of right and wrong, and take that of kill or be killed. That is a reason for making an end of war, and in the meantime keeping political power out of the hands of bellicose persons.'

Increasingly, as the long-plotted war came nearer, Shaw felt the urge to ridicule English moral pretensions – like the gentleman in *Love's Labour's Lost* who enters crying: 'Now step I forth to whip hypocrisy.' It seemed impossible for him to touch on foreign policy without, at each stroke of his pen, shocking some moral section of the community. He hated the silence of diplomacy which placed him in a vacuum where nothing he said could be heard. Laughter was one of his devices for shattering this vacuum – laughter to disperse the mystique that such subjects were unsafe for public discussions and the least indiscretion might precipitate a catastrophe. Preparation for war necessitated so much secrecy and lying on the part of belligerent Governments as to develop an unthinking habit: 'if anyone remarks at noon that it is twelve o'clock, some minister automatically articulates a solemn public assurance that there is no ground for any such suspicion,' Shaw later wrote, 'and gives private orders that references to the time of day are to be censored in future.'

'We can do nothing but clamor for an entente with Germany,' he had advised his fellow Fabian Robert Phillimore early in 1912. ' . . . Foreign policy, I may add, is not my subject. I do not know enough about it to meddle effectively.' Fifteen months later he had divined that the great secret of Britain's foreign policy was that it had no foreign policy. In an article for the *Daily Chronicle* on 18 March 1913 he proposed one: a triple alliance against war by England, France and Germany, the terms being that 'if France attack Germany we combine with Germany to crush France, and if Germany attack France, we combine with France to crush Germany'. From that starting point, he continued, the combination might be added to from Holland and the Scandinavian kingdoms 'and finally achieve the next step in civilization, the policing of Europe against war and the barbarians'. He repeated this formula, which was another magical trinity for achieving self-integration, in a Hegemony of Peace speech at King's Hall, Covent Garden on 11 November, and again in an article on the comity of nations entitled 'The Peace of Europe and How to Attain It' in the *Daily News* on New Year's Day 1914. 'I want international peace,' he stated. Those barbarians within our frontiers, who advocated war as a tonic, should not be let loose on foreigners but rather sent for annual war sports to Salisbury Plain, he suggested, to 'blaze away at one another' until the survivors (if any) felt 'purified by artillery fire'. Thanks to his age, he added gaily, and the general feeling that his character was past praying for, 'militarism does not affect me personally'.

According to *The Times*, Shaw's speech produced much laughter; and according to himself his articles produced no effect. 'Nobody took the smallest public notice of me,' while in private it was said that such a declaration 'might provoke war'. His sense of exclusion was reinforced when, lunching with the German ambassador Prince Lichnowsky, he asked him what he thought of this peace initiative and was told that such problems were better left to the Foreign Secretary Sir Edward Grey and other professional politicians and diplomats – which might have been a better answer if politicians and diplomats were required to do the fighting. 'Can anybody suggest an alternative policy?' Shaw had asked. But there seemed no alternative. 'Complete failure of my campaign,' he noted. This failure, together with his feeling of isolation from other Fabians and rejection by the Government, contributed to the somewhat aggrieved tone and massive outpouring of Shaw's writings on the war. A war symposium published by the *Daily Citizen* on 1 August he described as 'about as timely and sensible as a symposium on the danger of damp sheets would be if London were on fire'. But, he added: 'it is important that our statesmen and diplomatists should understand that there is a strong and growing body of public opinion to which all war is abhorrent, and which will suffer it now only as a hideous necessity arising out of past political bargains in which the people have had no part and the country no interest ... We muddled our way in and we may have to fight our way out.'

*

He had planned to go with Charlotte to the International Socialist Congress in Vienna that summer, but gave it up because of the war news. The two of them were at a hotel at Salcombe in Devonshire on 4 August. Shaw first heard of the declaration of war on coming down to breakfast. A very typical middle-aged Englishman 'after a fairly successful attempt to say unconcernedly "I suppose we shall have to fight them" suddenly became spitefully hysterical and changed "them" into "those swine" twice in every sentence'. Here was an early symptom of an epidemic that soon covered the country: 'the ordinary war-conscious civilian went mad.' In this general craziness people rejoiced at the prospect of a first-rate fight, as if it were a liberation. The excitement, the dread of being thought unpatriotic even by fools with white feathers for brains, was to leave the country at the mercy of anyone in authority. 'This is the greatest fight ever made for the Christian religion,' the Bishop of London declared, ' ... a choice between the nailed hand and the mailed fist.' Kitchener's finger was to point at everyone. The upper and the upper-middle classes were exhorted to sacrifice their butlers, chauffeurs, gamekeepers and grooms for service at the front. Old men postdated their births, dyed their hair, and lined up at the recruiting offices; old women lamented that their ineligibility to serve as nurses would prevent their killing the German wounded; mothers hustled their sons into uniforms and off to the trenches; a fifteen-year-old cadet at the Royal Naval College was publicly flogged when he tried to go home.

In the heat and scare of these early months, people needed enormous doses of self-righteousness and sanctimonious indignation to endure the shock of war. A chauvinistic industry, manufacturing foreign monsters, quickly expanded. A general in France, writing to one of the many journalists who were compiling succulent menus of German atrocities,

345

apologized that 'there has been only one atrocity lately and that was not a good one'. Not everyone was so meticulous. Newspapers competed for hellish horrors to answer the clamour of their readers – 'like the clamor', Shaw reported, 'of an agonizingly wounded combatant for morphia.' The whole country buzzed with stories of revolting obscenities – Germans tossing babies on the points of their bayonets; Germans burning field hospitals full of British wounded; Germans going into battle driving crowds of women before them; Germans making collections of fingers. Shaw searched for some practical line of reasoning to set against this hell. Would such spectatorial enjoyment, he queried, really encourage recruitment? Surely it was kinder to those who had sons and husbands at the front *not* to insist that they must be horribly mutilated if they fell into enemy hands? 'Since you expect to go out soon, I really refuse to leave you troubled in spirit by that man with his eyes gouged out,' he reassured George Cornwallis-West. It was amazing how this totally blinded refugee careered around – he was far too quick for anyone to have seen, though all had heard of him. Elsewhere, a number of Belgian nurses whose hands everyone knew to have been scissored off by the Huns had, he was glad to see, 'grown new ones and were in prime condition'. 'As you know, the truth about war is always bad enough,' he concluded, 'but there really isn't a solitary scrap of evidence that the Germans . . . are behaving worse than we should behave in the same circumstances.'

Among the most loudly baying patriots were the British disciples of Dr Mills. They could not tolerate Charlotte's pacifism, her refusal to assist this righteous war in any capacity 'except that of a reluctant taxpayer'. Worst of all in their eyes were her anxieties over poor Trebitsch. She felt a spring of joy on hearing that he had failed his medical examination. What a merciful escape from glory! 'You will die prematurely,' G.B.S. assured him, 'at the age of 98 in a hotel lift, from ascending too rapidly.' His doctor was quite right. 'If you attempted to do military service, you would fall from your horse in the first charge,' Trebitsch learnt; 'the horse would stumble over you, all the other horses would stumble over it, and the whole squadron would be disgracefully annihilated.'

Shaw felt this concern for all his translators – those other selves shredded in conflict. 'WHAT A HIDEOUS SITUATION CIVILIZATION TEARING ITSELF TO PIECES,' he had wired to Trebitsch on 4 August. '. . . YOU AND I AT WAR CAN ABSURDITY GO FURTHER MY FRIEND-LIEST WISHES GO WITH YOU UNDER ALL CIRCUMSTANCES.' Next day he and Charlotte went on to Torquay where they were to stay for a couple of months at the Hydro Hotel. 'Charlotte is quite comfortable here, as there is no housekeeping, plenty of bathing, taxicabs to get about in, shops galore, and every sort of urban amenity,' Shaw wrote to Beatrice Webb. 'This suits me pretty well too, as I have a lot of work in hand.'

They were to return more than once to the Hydro Hotel. For G.B.S. it became like a study centre, and he a postgraduate there. Everything was taken care of so that he could concentrate on work which, over the next three months, yielded more than fifty thousand words about the war: 'I do not hold my tongue easily.' In his first statement, drafted on 6 August, he set out the predicament as he continued to see it. Britain had placed herself in such a position that she had to enter the war on the side of France. But France, Germany and Britain were committing a crime against civilization for the political benefit of Russia and 'to ask me or any other sane man to create an illusion of nobility and purity and patriotism round such a crime is to ask honest people to do the work of dupes and fools,' he wrote.

'We shall have to fight and die and pay and suffer with the grim knowledge that we are sacrificing ourselves in an insane cause, and that only by putting up a particularly good fight can we bring ourselves out of it with credit. For my part I can only hope that all the western powers involved will quit themselves so heroically that they will be forced to divide the honors of war and shake hands for ever . . . For the present time there is only one thing to be done besides fighting . . . And that one thing is to set to work immediately to draft the inevitable Treaty of Peace which we must all sign when we have had our bellyful of murder and destruction.'

This was to be the focus of almost all Shaw's propaganda. While others were concentrating on warfare, he was contemplating the peace. He accused the generals and politicians of being unable to think further ahead than the length of a bayonet, and he urged Beatrice Webb and other Fabians to cultivate 'long range firing more than you do, or you will leave forts unreduced in your rear which will undo half your work later on'. The real enemy was not Germany, he maintained, but jingoists, junkers and militarists in all countries. Therefore, in moments of optimism, he would represent the war as an opportunity of victory for the Suffragettes, the Irish volunteers and socialists everywhere.

Shaw used the press to try and gain an authoritative platform. Disgusted by the militancy of the clergy (who like Anthony Anderson, the Presbyterian minister in *The Devil's Disciple,* had been transfigured into choleric men of war) he recommended through the *New Statesman* that churches all over Europe should close their doors until the war ended. In an article for the *Daily News* he judged the responsibility for war as lying almost evenly between the squalid British commercial adventurers and

347

Germany's overweening militarists. And in the *Saturday Review* he went on to deny that violation of Belgian neutrality was a *casus belli*. 'If we go into battle as superior persons,' he warned, 'we shall be licked.' He believed that our irritating high-minded airs might drive America into the war on Germany's side, especially if we persisted with our assumption that America should feel proud to have her ships plundered for copper and contraband by the British. As a counter-stroke of Shavian foreign policy, and using his new American literary agent Paul Reynolds, he placed an 'Open Letter to the President of the United States of America' in the *Nation* and the *New York Times*, appealing to him as 'the spokesman of Western Democracy' to rally the neutral powers for the purpose of demanding both sides to withdraw from Belgium ('the effect of our shells on Belgium is precisely the same as that of the German shells') and fight out their quarrel on their own territories. Behind this invitation lay the stick-and-carrot prediction that history would judge Germany to have been the wrong side on which to intervene, and that Washington ('still privileged to talk common humanity to the nations') would inevitably chair the world conference that settled the peace.

The British press had been immediately eager for Shaw's war contributions. But after three months, when he had vented his disgust on England and Germany as 'a couple of extremely quarrelsome dogs' and advised the soldiers in both armies to 'SHOOT THEIR OFFICERS AND GO HOME', many newspapers had blacklisted him. 'In any ordinary time I should have been delighted to publish your letter with every word of which I agree,' wrote the editor of the *Manchester Guardian*, C. P. Scott, 'but at this horrible time one has to consider so many things which one would like to ignore . . . your letter would be highly disturbing to many minds. That of course is the object of it and a very excellent object. But I suppose one's duty now is to encourage and unite people and not to exercise and divide.'

Shaw recognized the power of this call for suspending controversy in the face of national danger, but countered it with the argument that able-bodied soldiers in the trenches depended on able-minded civilians at home to guard the popular liberties and constitutional safeguards of their country. Soldiers must be protected while their backs were turned from those abuses of power – such as the suspension of by-elections – not necessary for the defeat of the enemy.

People at home might be tempted to do such things because they were like invalids who, having been injected with official legends, were going through shrieking nightmares of vituperation. 'I have sat at England's bedside during her delirium,' Shaw was to write. He saw himself as a doctor who reluctantly admits that his horror-struck patient may need chauvinistic drugs, but believes that the quality of his recovery depends upon their withdrawal as soon as possible. 'I do not grudge a mother the shelter of a lie any more than I grudge a soldier the shelter of a clump of briars,' he wrote; 'but the more thoroughly we realize that war is war, and death death, the sooner we shall get rid of it.' In the autumn of 1914 he still had confidence that ordinary people 'will come right again when the war is over'. Once the spasms wore off, after the monthly casualty figures began to arrive affecting almost every family in the country (already in November there were 89,954 British casualties), then these people, who were essentially nerve cases, would need some antidote to the hyper-patriotic rage produced by governmental mendacity and administered daily by the press. His *Common Sense about the War* was a complicated prescription prepared as a remedy against defeatism for those emerging from these bloody fantasies. On 14 November it appeared as a monumental supplement to the *New Statesman*. 'I have told the truth about the war,' Shaw claimed; 'and stated the democratic case for it.'

*

Until noon each day Shaw worked in the roof garden of the Hydro Hotel. Before lunch he would swim and after lunch continue working in his suite. Sometimes he went for joy rides in the car around the coast; sometimes he went and listened to Basil Cameron's concerts at the pavilion. After dinner he read.

It was impossible to think of anything except the war. 'It has so occupied me that everything else has gone by the board,' he told his sister Lucy. The notion of rehearsing an American production of *Pygmalion* was 'an almost unbearable horror under existing circumstances'. Official documents hastily put together by the foreign offices of each country – the *White* and *Blue*, *Yellow* and *Green*, *Red* and *Orange* books – arrived at the hotel to be examined as by a literary critic comparing texts. Never can there have been a war in which the belligerents had such correct cases. Austria had the assassination of an Archduke; Germany the mobilization of Russia and the threatening articles of the Franco-Russian alliance; Britain the impeccable Treaty of 1839. All the provocations were valid according to the most accredited precedents. Academically, on all sides, the war was perfectly in order. 'I had to slave for months getting the evidence,' Shaw wrote to Alfred Sutro, 'and I had to revise and revise . . . It makes me sick to recollect the drudgery of it all.'

He also read all the newspapers, sensing behind the governmental official voice the mood of the country which was beginning in small measures to infiltrate Torquay. When a depressed Granville Barker came down for a few days, he and Shaw were threatened with shooting by a panicky coastguard as they walked along the beach. The hotel porter, a German who had registered as an enemy alien, was suddenly handcuffed and 'deported to the innermost centre of Britain – to Exeter, in fact' – so that he could not signal to German submarines. A little later wounded Belgians began to crowd the hospitals and commandeer the hotels as convalescent homes. They told lively stories of how they had slaughtered German prisoners at Liège, speaking in French so as not to confuse the idealistic welcome they were receiving.

Shaw needed to feel up to his chin in what was going on. He could not sit quietly at home and continue with his peaceful work as he advised others to do – he would rather actively represent such peace-desirous people. He saw them as an army that had given him his commission to address the American President or censure the British Prime Minister or Foreign Secretary. Neither Asquith nor Grey, he believed, were the real spokesmen of their times. 'You and I and Arnold Bennett will have to save this war,' he wrote to Hall Caine. He hated Grey – 'a Junker from his topmost hair to the tips of his toes . . . [with] a personal taste for mendacity' – for his part in the sensational horror at the Egyptian village of Denshawai in 1906, when the British colonial power administered floggings, hangings and penal servitude for life after a rumpus arising from some pigeon shooting. Shaw also disliked Asquith who, with unintended irony, had dismissed him as a ladies' man. This governing class, with its circle of ignorant plutocrats and titled snobs, was above listening to him. But it needed a simple paradox of the pen to place himself above them. 'The Government does not represent the nation,' he stated. ' . . . England has no respectable spokesman with modern ideas.' He wanted his own class of men, Chesterton and Wells, Bennett and Bertrand Russell, to rise at the head of a popular movement and replace Asquith with someone such as Winston Churchill whose unsuccessful Gallipoli campaign he was to support. 'The British Public', he wrote in *Common Sense about the War*, 'had all along been behind Mr Winston Churchill.' Shaw felt rather attracted to the bumptious jolly figure of Churchill, describing him as 'an odd and not disagreeable compound of Junker and Yankee'. He recognized that Churchill's frank, anti-German pugnacity was enormously more popular in the country than the moral babble of Asquith and Grey. As a bit of a writer, too, Churchill should understand that war, being an affair of human nature and a matter of instinct over reason, was the province of novelists, playwrights and even philosophers. So Shaw kept his eye on Churchill as someone who might emerge in Europe as a Shavian-permeated superman. But while the Asquith-Grey administration lasted, he went on using shock tactics to force his way into contention and turn public opinion around. 'Our job is to make people serious about the war,' he wrote to Bertrand Russell. 'It is the monstrous triviality of the damned thing, and the vulgar frivolity of what we imagine to be patriotism, that gets at my temper.'

Here was his occupation: to bring an avalanche down on the heads of England's political diehards and give the war the character of a democratic crusade. Nevertheless, he risked offending his friends and fellow-writers, fifty-three of whom (including Archer, Barker, Barrie, Chesterton, Gilbert Murray and H. G. Wells) had signed an official declaration supporting the 'free and law-abiding ideals of Western Europe' over 'the iron military bureaucracy of Prussia'. 'Nobody else seems to have any power of seeing what is really going on,' Shaw complained. ' . . . I begin to despair of the intellectuals.'

Shaw's position in *Common Sense about the War* was that of the Irishman who, when asked for directions, replies that he wouldn't start from here. It was given the Shavian dimension by the fact that England had not asked for directions. He was therefore obliged to step out dangerously into the traffic unfurling his flag of Irish immunity from English sentimentalism and transmit unsolicited signals. He was full of quixotic anomalies. He attacked the Government for its superior airs then claimed superiority himself over it: 'I made a better case against Germany than the Government case.' He described the political leaders of Europe as immature, but in language of shocking juvenile levity – 'in this military business one has to pretend that everything is a joke,' he later confided to Hesketh Pearson. He accused Grey of pedantry over the pseudo-legal justification of war provided by a seventy-five-year-old treaty ('nobody cared twopence about treaties'), then flourished his own pedantic scrap of paper. He struggled to establish himself as a representative of the people, while owning that had his triple alliance averted war the British public would have been 'greatly disappointed'. Finally, he took over political word-of-command and waged his own battle up and down the columns of the *New Statesman* until, as Robert Lynd commented, the war was spoken of as if it were between the Allies on the one hand and, on the other, Germany, Austria, Turkey and Bernard Shaw.

The manifesto is an autobiographical document. The scattering of European socialists and of his own translators – Trebitsch in Germany, Hamon in France, Vallentin from Sweden and others throughout Europe with whom he attempted to keep up friendly contacts – felt like the splitting of his very selves and gave his advocacy its special intensity. 'I believe the mass of the nation feels about the war very much as you and I do,' he reassured Trebitsch: 'that is, they feel it to be a frightful failure of civilization that there should be a war at all between civilized western powers.' And to Hugo Vallentin, he wrote: 'What dreadful things! But keep Sweden quiet if you can . . . ' The inadequacy of such appeals reinforced his sense of powerlessness. 'I could do very little,' he confessed. From this futility as a man of letters arose his prayer for a strong man of action who would establish peace by international force of arms.

Shaw attempted to answer the question: what is the war about? The explosive combination had erupted from a prodigious evil: that of mounting wealth throughout Europe untapped by any corresponding equitable distribution of this wealth. The war was borne on the soils and sighs of monstrous inequality as a crude method of advancing social organization. Politicians still believed it was a question of Union Jacks and tricolours and Imperial Eagles – but these were merely toys to keep them smiling: 'there are only two real flags in the world henceforth,' Shaw wrote: 'the red flag of Democratic Socialism and the black flag of Capitalism.' The militarists of Europe had used this energy of dissatisfaction for their sport of war, and all the excitable dupes and adventurous young men joined in. Shaw reasoned that historically the militaristic case was valueless because it led to the establishment of what the militarists themselves most dreaded – a dramatic example in this war was to be the collapse of tsardom and the rise of communism in Russia. 'The Democratic case, the Socialist one, the International case is worth all it threatens to cost,' he predicted. This is one of many overwhelming reasons for building the state on equality of income. 'Democracy without equality is a delusion more dangerous than frank oligarchy and autocracy. And with Democracy there is not hope of peace.'

Beatrice Webb paid tribute to Shaw for having 'kept the crucial purpose of socialism before us'. He had reminded *New Statesman* readers of her Minority Report which, if introduced in 1909, would have provided the machinery for dealing with destitute Belgian refugees – whom he classed as being in the same economic category as unemployed Britons. They had been honourably received by British families; but their support could not be left to individual hospitality (which in the nature of things would diminish) or to the prodigious begging of private charities. Until the unemployed were properly organized on socialist lines, he suggested that Britain would have to treat these refugees, though unguarded and unfenced, as well-fed German prisoners of war ('whose friendly hat wavings to me and my fellow passengers as I rush through Newbury Racecourse Station in the Great Western Express I hereby acknowledge publicly and with all possible good feeling').

Shaw's long-term aim was straight. He foresaw that the enormous demand for coal, cloth, boots, army rations, weapons, ammunition, transport vehicles, ships and all other accessories of war, would arrest the huge exports of capital and transform them into wages – besides doubling taxation on unearned incomes. He pointed out how the Government had already taken control of railways, bought up all the raw sugar, regulated prices, guaranteed the banks, suspended the operation of private contracts and achieved many of 'the things it had been declaring utterly and eternally Utopian and impossible when Socialists advocated them'.

He also attempted to provide socialists with something like a foreign policy. For years they had repeated the old shibboleth of the International: 'Proletarians of all lands, unite' and assumed that they were above militaristic passions. But now they found themselves just as helplessly entangled and identified with their respective warring nations as anyone else. Like anyone else, and under the plainest reasonable necessities of social solidarity, they had to go to the trenches and fight. But Shaw insisted that they had the additional duty of questioning their own belligerent Governments as to what they were fighting about, so that this question would be brought to a conference table when the map of Europe was redrawn and its political constitutions so reformed that 'this abominable and atrocious nuisance, a European war, shall not easily occur again'.

During war we live in a political truce; in peacetime the political war begins again. Shaw wanted socialists to prepare for this struggle by ensuring that on enlistment labourers found themselves better fed, paid, clothed than before. 'They are trying to frighten the men into enlisting,' he had written to Stella Campbell on 6 October. 'I am telling them not to enlist until their wives are properly provided for. At present they get sixteen shillings a week until the man is shot, when they get five.' Churchill had called for a widows' subsistence of seven-and-sixpence, but been overruled by Lloyd George's five shillings – which gave the German bullet, Shaw declared, a double effect. He recommended the appointment of working-class representatives to the War Office, and the reform of the 'tyrannical slave code called military law' so that the soldier could serve as a citizen with all his rights intact. 'We must free our soldiers,' he appealed, 'and give them homes worth fighting for.'

This was Shaw's case for open diplomacy, full civil rights, a fair livelihood for the soldier and his dependants, and genuine working-class democracy in place of 'Asquith's pseudo-democracy, which uses Mutiny Acts in time of peace to imprison Labour leaders and muzzle the Labour Press'. In his thirty years of public work Shaw had seen 'man after man in the Labour movement sell out because he could not trust his future to the loyalty of the workers', he wrote, 'and I should perhaps have had to sell out

353

myself long ago if I had not possessed certain powers as a writer which made me a little more independent than others'. Armed with this independence, 'I have put my best brains and skill at the service of the Labour cause'.

*

'Every Englishman is against you,' warned Henry Arthur Jones. Shaw had modelled his *Common Sense about the War* on Tom Paine's *The Rights of Man*, and it blew up a similar dust-storm of abuse. Libraries and bookshops removed his works from their shelves; newspapers instructed their readers to boycott his plays. The editor of *The Clarion*, Robert Blatchford, described his manifesto as 'the meanest act of treachery ever perpetrated by an alien enemy residing in generous and long-suffering England', and described its author as the sort of man who 'would tell an old friend that his dog is not full bred, that its muzzle is turning grey, and that it has blunt teeth', never understanding that his friend 'saw best and loved most the love-light in the dear old doggie's eye'. In the House of Commons the Member of Parliament for Shropshire, Ludlow, was cheered when he challenged the Solicitor-General: 'Are we to understand those for whom Mr Shaw writes can publish anything they like, however detrimental to this country?' A cartoon appeared in the press showing G.B.S. wearing an Iron Cross. At the Royal Naval Division the Prime Minister's son, 'Beb' Asquith, announced that he 'ought to be shot'. And in America former President Theodore Roosevelt called him a 'blue rumped ape' and lumped him with 'the unhung traitor Keir Hardie' among a 'venomous' herd of socialists, all 'physically timid creatures'. 'You are not so loved here as you were,' Granville Barker reported from New York where he was producing *Androcles and the Lion*. 'The "Common Sense about the War" raised you up many enemies and turned some of your friends very sour.'

Feeling themselves implicated, some writers reacted dramatically. The best-selling novelist W. J. Locke suddenly sprang up and screamed: 'I will not sit in the same room with Bernard Shaw!' J. C. Squire put it to his readers that G.B.S. should be tarred and feathered. Elsewhere, Christabel Pankhurst wrote of the 'freakish mental processes' that had made Shaw 'jester to the British public' but that had gone 'beyond a joke' when he began campaigning from his armchair as Englishmen were 'dying on the battlefield'. In a private letter, Henry Arthur Jones enquired if Shaw realized that he was regarded as 'a man who, for the sake of showing his agility, kicked and defamed his mother when she was on a sick-bed?' And in an open letter, subtitled 'A Manual for the Haters

354

of England', he later blasted him with an enormous vituperative sentence:

'The hag Sedition was your mother, and Perversity begot you. Mischief was your midwife and Misrule your nurse, and Unreason brought you up at her feet – no other ancestry and rearing had you, you freakish homunculus, germinated outside of lawful procreation . . . '

More painful to Shaw was the response of those he loved. Archer's son, whom from childhood Shaw had called 'Tomarcher', sailed home from New York on the first available steamer to rejoin his volunteer corps and was sent to Flanders. 'I did not realize that Tom was in the London Scottish,' Shaw wrote to Archer. 'It is a sickening business this sending lambs to the slaughter because we are governed by bloody fools wirepulled by damned thieves.' But Archer, fiercely patriotic, felt differently. After lunching with Shaw in London, he came away reflecting on his friend's passions for 'seeing, and believing, the opposite of what other people saw and believed'.

Shaw had also hoped to get support from G. K. Chesterton. 'He must help me over this war job,' he wrote to Chesterton's wife, Frances. But Chesterton, who had been seriously ill during late 1914 and early 1915, was 'hungry for hostilities'. The war excited the dark side of his nature. 'I have always thought there was in Prussia an evil will,' he wrote to Shaw. This geographical psychology seemed absurd to G.B.S. 'Of course there is an evil will in Prussia,' he agreed. 'Prussia isn't Paradise. I have been fighting that evil will, in myself and others, all my life.' Chesterton's hatred seemed to Shaw the amiable weakness of a mind in which the war had lodged as mediaeval fantasy. And to Chesterton, Shaw appeared equally unreal. 'You are wrestling with something too romantic for you to realize. It is the real thing . . . ' he wrote. 'I think you are a great man; and I think your first great misfortune was that you were born in a small epoch. But I think it is your last and worst misfortune that now at last the epoch is growing greater: but you are not.'

Chesterton neither sent this letter to Shaw nor published it. But Wells chimed in with the public outcry, making much the same point when recognizing G.B.S. as 'one of those perpetual children who live in a dream of make-believe . . . that he is a person of incredible wisdom and subtlety running the world. He is an elderly adolescent still at play,' Wells continued in the *Daily Chronicle*.

' . . . It is almost as if there was nothing happening in Flanders. It is almost as if there was no pain in all the world. It is under the inspiration of such delightful dreams that Mr Shaw now flings himself upon his typewriter and rattles out his broadsides. And nothing will stop him. All through the war we shall have this Shavian accompaniment going on, like an idiot child screaming in a hospital . . . He is at present . . . an almost unendurable nuisance.'

Shaw calculated that it was 'precisely because *Common Sense* made people so angry that they attended to it'. But the attention he got was a form of 'seeing red' that coloured people's vision of what he really wrote about the war. 'I hate this war; and, as you know, I have criticized the English Government very severely for not taking the steps which, as I believe, would have prevented it,' he wrote to Trebitsch. 'But if I were a German, I should criticize the Berlin Government with equal fierceness for having made the war.' In fact he did write 'The German Case Against Germany' in May 1916, but by that time he was widely regarded as a German sympathizer. 'I am not what is called pro-German,' he wrote, ' . . . neither am I an anti-German.' He was an international socialist who insisted that the real gentleman put away his spites and vanities and refused to hate his enemy in wartime. But this attitude had no comfortable place in a country exulting in the announcement that all German music was to be banned at concerts and where two Rothensteins out of three were changing their name to Rutherston. People reminded one another how Shaw had snubbed England and amused Germany over the première of *Pygmalion*; how he had championed Wagner and more recently in a newspaper controversy with Ernest Newman supported Richard Strauss; and how for many years he had set himself to be the interpreter of representative German philosophers such as Nietzsche and Schopenhauer. They were informed too of a favourable review he had given to a darkly suspect book for fair-haired Aryans, *The Foundations of the Nineteenth Century* by Houston Chamberlain, that was later described by the Kaiser as God-given to the German people. No wonder G.B.S. had fashioned himself after Goethe's Mephistopheles: he had always found his spiritual home in Germany. Even 'his Fabian ideas of social reconstruction', claimed the *Daily Chronicle*, 'are inspired by Berlinese notions of symmetry'.

In such conditions it was difficult for Shaw to gain a hearing. His reasoning was impeccable; his offence emotional. 'In the right key one can say anything,' he wrote to Bertrand Russell, 'in the wrong key, nothing: the only delicate part of the job is the establishment of the key.' But many writers felt he had gone off-key. Henry James, who was soon to become a British citizen, claimed that he had not been able to read Shaw's *Common Sense* at all because 'his horrible flippancy revolts me'. Arnold Bennett, too, had described as a 'disastrous pity' Shaw's percentage of 'perverseness, waywardness, and harlequinading'. Others resented his apparent lack of change; the key was still the same – a combination of immaturity and sophistication, brilliance and prolixity. He was attempting to do everything: chastise the Government, belabour the public at large, provide an historical examination of diplomatic events, satirize the whole continent of war-struck lunatics. His view shifts from a sharp to blurred focus and back as he moves from passages of subjective certainty to unsure areas where he tries to confine himself to valid public evidence. It is as if he is searching for a refuge from terror in this lengthy analysis of what has already happened beyond repair.

Shaw's jokes, such as his suggestion to those who wanted unconditionally to smash Germany that they should leave the men alone and go about killing all her women, were his natural method of expression. He could not really believe in the atrocities. 'If we did not die of laughter at the humours of war we should of horror,' he admitted to Robert Loraine; and to his sister Lucy he confessed: 'one has to learn to laugh at such things in war or else go mad.' He asked those (like Arnold Bennett) who objected that his jokes did not fit the hour to ignore the 'imbecilities and brutalities' of his style and fix on the content. But this was impossible. The style gave him perspective – that of an adult carrying on his shoulders a child (who is himself) from the scene of the crime. The Shavian wit was like an instinctive snap of detachment that appeared to cut him off from the natural chaos so that he could regard what was going on all round him as already some way past. 'Shaw is often ten minutes ahead of the truth,' wrote Woodrow Wilson's brother-in-law Stockton Axson, 'which is almost as fatal as being behind the time.'

Shaw claimed that his *Common Sense* was as nearly just under the circumstances 'as human nature can bear'. He had known that some of his writings during the first year of war would make readers 'howl like a dog at a ballad concert'. But he was surprised by the volume and intensity of this howling as it ascended and turned from protest to attack. He felt his isolation. 'Thanks for your friendly hail,' he wrote acknowledging a letter from Bertrand Russell. 'It really is necessary for people who can keep their heads to pass the time of day occasionally lest they should begin to fear that they, and not the others, are the madmen.'

Hostility flared up all over the place. At the urging of Hall Caine, he had written 'a fierce piece of rhetoric about Belgium' for *King Albert's Book*, an anthology published by the *Daily Telegraph* for the benefit of Belgian refugees. Hall Caine described Shaw's contribution as 'gorgeous . . . one of the most brilliant things I had in the book'. But no one had agreed with him. 'The battle began in my own household,' he reported, 'extended to the staff of the Daily Telegraph, thence to my own editorial staff, thence to

357

the printer . . . ' It culminated with a declaration from the *Daily Telegraph* proprietors that if Hall Caine insisted as editor on retaining Shaw's item '*the book would not go out of their office*'. Chivalrously he offered to resign his editorship, but Shaw withdrew his piece. 'You are an angel,' Hall Caine wrote. 'It is a marvel to me how well you stand it.' A couple of weeks later the *Daily Telegraph* proprietors were bewildered to learn that the Commission for Relief in Belgium had asked Shaw, in the name of the Belgian minister in London, to help the refugees 'by means of your powerful pen' – which he answered with a pamphlet *The Case of Belgium*. 'Splendid! You've certainly got the "laugh on us",' Hall Caine responded. ' . . . I am almost inclined to throw up my cap.'

There were few such neat and happy endings. When James F. Muirhead, editor of *Baedeker*, resigned from the Society of Authors, claiming that 'I cannot consent that any part of my affairs should be in any way under the control of a man of whom I think as I do of you,' Shaw tried to reason him into staying, and eventually stepped down himself from the two committees at the Society of Authors where for the past ten years he had been the chief source of energy and initiative. Muirhead was an admirer of Shaw's, counting the shocks he had given Britain over the past thirty years 'among the most salutary influences brought to bear on that country'. But by 1915 he had been driven to a belief in something he called the 'myopia of genius'. With all his extraordinary microscopic and telescopic powers G.B.S. seemed 'unable to see clearly the simple contours visible to every man of merely normal vision,' he wrote. ' . . . you really do not understand why you are at present a cause of offence to 99 out of every 100 people that I meet.'

Shaw's retreat from the Society of Authors had finally been forced on him by members of the Dramatists' Club, most of whom signified their unwillingness to meet him at their lunches. 'I am wiping the slate, and getting clear of the whole thing,' he wrote. For both these dramatic exits he gave the same ostensible reason: that of preventing a professional association from turning into a political group.

It had needed courage to go on writing as he did. 'It was not easy,' he admitted. He endured the long campaign of hatred against him with remarkable good humour and lack of bitterness. 'I know of no other literary man of anything like his eminence who would have taken such treatment so good-naturedly,' wrote Desmond MacCarthy. Almost he seemed unperturbed. 'I am not afraid of unpopularity,' he told Beatrice Webb. After all, he could easily recover everyone's good opinion by inserting an exclamation even more shocking than 'Not bloody likely' into his next play. 'The time has come for me to be old and savage,' he had written. But he could not get angry with people he met – 'it breaks my back completely,' he explained in a letter begging not to be introduced to Lloyd George. 'That's the worst of Shaw,' Hugh Massingham remarked to Frank Swinnerton: 'he can't get angry.' But he was long-lastingly affected. There seemed no standard, or principle, by which to measure conduct. Much that he had tried to reform was slipping back. 'In the course of thirty years' activity in the Press, in the theatre, and on the platform, Mr Shaw has probably done more than any other living man to influence and to create opinion on an immense variety of subjects,' the *New Statesman* had proclaimed in November 1914. Two years later, the *New Statesman* having refused to publish his articles, he resigned his directorship 'because after spending thirty years in keeping Englishmen from quarrelling,' he wrote to Beatrice Webb, 'I find that they remain invincibly persuaded that I am a mischief maker, a liar and a wrecker.'

Below the surface of his forbearance, layers of disillusion were forming. He would take imaginative revenge against this society by threatening it with his Zeppelin raid at the end of *Heartbreak House*, and by scoring victories over the 'Goddams' in the person of St Joan. He would recharge his optimism, too, by prophetically gazing through heartbreaking facts into the haze of Shavian hypotheses. 'I don't expect anybody but myself to see as far as I do,' he told the Webbs – an expectation amply to be justified by the public's blindness over *Back to Methuselah*. Meanwhile, he kept his spirits whirring with colossal swanking. 'The longer I live the more I see that I am never wrong about anything,' he admitted to Wells. He overcame his opponents with marvellous flights of exaggeration, rising *au dessus de la mêlée* and out of earshot of the tumult: '*NOBODY* can differ with me about the war,' he informed G. K. Chesterton; 'you might as well differ from the Almighty about the orbit of the sun.'

He protected himself too with brighter paradoxes. He had a special postcard printed acknowledging the responses to his *Common Sense* that were not unpublishably obscene, and declared himself 'astonished that a mere pamphlet has been able to do so much'. The war, he complained, 'has made me excessively popular.' He was ferociously busy minding his own business – which was, of course, influencing everyone else and altering opinion in the country. Whether by ecstatically reviewing Henry Arthur Jones's anti-Shavian diatribe or putting himself in charge of his own expulsion from the Dramatists' Club ('I suppose I shall have to teach them how to do it'), he became expert at converting every rebuff into another victory. 'All the forts opened fire on me,' he had reported to Stella Campbell who was touring *Pygmalion* in America; 'and they have capitulated one after the other . . . my enemies are my footstool.'

About those matters that might have stirred approval – his cheque for £200 to the Belgian refugees; his £20,000 contribution to the British War Loan; even his prophetic message to the Moors, rising through the combined prose styles of the Old Testament and Burton's *Arabian Nights* and exhorting them not to revolt against the French – about all this he kept uncharacteristically quiet. Partly it was a matter of self-respect, and partly that of outmanoeuvring those who wished to surround him with obloquy. 'Unless you make a reputation at once for being utterly impossible, implacable, inexorable, you are lost,' he was to advise his French translator, Augustin Hamon. Shaw had made such a reputation, and was becoming a lost man in politics. 'I intended to be effective,' he wrote. But before the war was over he admitted to Hamon that 'I have no effective influence with the Labor party,' and subsequently told Lady Gregory that 'I have the whole English press against me whenever I move; and the politicians will not do anything for anyone who has not a press backing.' He lost, too, a working combination with most of his colleagues, even Sidney Webb. He had hoped that 'when Junkers fall out common men may come by their own' and thought to represent the future of these common men. But when Junkers fall out another lot fall in. 'I have not had my way, because I wanted the Asquith-Grey regime to be overthrown by us for the right reasons,' he wrote to Sidney Webb at the end of 1916; 'and it has been overthrown by the Northcliffe press for the wrong ones ... and Lloyd George is Prime Minister, God help him.'

*

'When war comes the time for arguing is passed.' But Shaw could not keep from arguing. He persisted in occupying that vacant moral lot he had once said would be abandoned for the killing fields of war. He even invented new arguments in favour of war-arguing. Not until the English nation clamoured daily for the impeachment of its ministers, dismissal of its generals, the superannuation of its officials and rejuvenation of its Government by more public-spirited and less party-minded men would England find its true bearings and put forth its strength. Therefore Shaw argued as other people in another war were to dig: for victory. He could not comprehend the primitive and irrational nature of war – it seemed beyond the reach of his sophisticated reason. He broke the patriotic pact suspending controversy, which he regarded as a political conspiracy, as though ministers and functionaries of all sorts, civil and military, would buckle-to in consternation under the lash of such insistent criticism.

In this spirit, he had set about a terrific sequel, *More Common Sense about the War*, continuing the business of disentangling the history and issues of the war from the official Government excuses that had been put about to encourage recruitment. But 'I am so addled by it that it has lost all meaning for me, and I must be guided by the impression it makes on you,' he appealed to Beatrice Webb. It impressed Beatrice as being muddle-headed and irascible, and so Shaw left it 'mouldering on my desk' unpublished.

But much of what he had written in *More Common Sense about the War* was filtered into other writings and war speeches. From these he emerged congratulating himself on having found his way through the cannon smoke in which so many others had become lost. 'I have nothing to withdraw,' he wrote. He was the operatic realist; other writers a chorus of chanting idealists; and then there were the formations of philistine hordes. He would appear before a number of this wandering majority, smiling, back-slapping, urging them over to his own clear-sighted ground. Whenever he was criticized, he counter-attacked. When accused of giving propaganda ammunition to Germany he retorted that it was his accusers themselves who had done that, Germany having attacked him bitterly until it noticed similar attacks in England. 'I offered England the most powerful literary weapon yet forged to employ against Germany. She let the Germans take it out of her hand and rap her knuckles with it.'

He had an answer for everything: often a wonderfully exasperating answer, formed in the conviction that it was as much his duty to face criticism as it was the soldiers' to face bullets – if not actually to attract them. Full of the appalling slaughter at Neuve Chapelle and at the Gallipoli landing, he mocked the outcry that arose in the spring of 1915 over the sinking of a popular Atlantic liner, the *Lusitania*. Here at last was something small enough – the killing of saloon passengers – for the public imagination to grasp. He heartily welcomed it, and the execution of Nurse Edith Cavell, for the effect it would produce on America, the moral centre of the neutral world. 'I even found a grim satisfaction,' he afterwards wrote, 'very intelligible to all soldiers, in the fact that the civilians who found the war such splendid British sport should get a sharp taste of what it was to the actual combatants.' During the first Zeppelin raids he advocated that movable metal arches should immediately be placed in school playgrounds so that children might know where to run when the Zeppelins came, but before this suggestion was implemented people considered it so defeatist (only Massingham would publish Shaw's proposal) that he felt goaded into recommending a judicious bombard-ment of London. 'In fact if we had any sense we would bombard London ourselves, and demolish the Houses of Parliament and all the new government offices for aesthetic reasons just as we should demolish the slums for sanitary reasons.' Early in 1917 he went so far as to draft a Fabian manifesto declaring for a republican solution of the territorial problems raised by the war. In domestic politics, he imagined the establishment of a socialist party pledged to reform the constitution and make the British Empire a federal republic. This would bring Britain into line with friends and allies such as the United States, Portugal and France – all opposed to monarchism as an obsolete idolatry – and swing the balance of power away from what he derogatorily called German royalism. 'Battles won for kings are not won for the people,' he wrote. 'Socialism has always and necessarily been federalist and republican ... until it has brought federal republicanism into being as the standard political form of modern civilization, it will find itself helplessly entangled in dynastic wars ...'

The most difficult long-term problem for Shaw was recruitment. There could be no denying that the government's painting of the war as a simple and heroic scene of knight errantry, with England as Lancelot-Galahad, Germany as the wicked giant and Belgium as the beautiful maiden, had been wonderfully popular. Shaw acknowledged that any state of public opinion – however visionary or deluded – which made for recruitment was not to be lightly disturbed. German patriotism, he noted, had been a paraphrase of our own. But after three months of war fever, recruitment had begun to fall off, Shaw claimed, and with it the justification for keeping the nation in its fool's paradise disappeared. 'Official cases and disputed points of international law,' he declared, 'are poor fare to recruit on.' After *Common Sense* 'the recruiting got on its feet again,' he wrote, once the War Office 'withdrew the silliest of its placards, and faced the necessity for higher pay and better treatment of recruits'. The tales of knight errantry then faded, by Shaw's account, and the establishment of Britain's position on the basis of diplomatic facts put her on much better terms with the neutral nations.

This optimistic gloss on events, outshining governmental propaganda, recruited his own energies into the fight. He wanted to bring the same people up to the same guns equipped with a far better arsenal of attitudes, motives, opinions; to place them in the same trenches looking forward without detestation toward the gentlemen-soldiers opposite, and looking back with prescient scepticism at the politicians who had arranged this grotesque firing line. Lytton Strachey, eager for a pacifist oration, went to one of his lectures and reported 'poor dear Mr Shaw talking about "England" with trembling lips and gleaming eyes, and declaring that his one wish was that we should first beat the Germans, and then fight them again, and then beat them again, and again, and again! He was more like a nice old-fashioned Admiral on a quarter-deck than anything else. And the newspapers are so stupid that, simply because he's Mr Shaw, they won't report him – instead of running him as our leading patriot.'

The newspapers did send their reporters to his speeches, but only to see him hissed and mobbed. He had posed an unsolvable problem – for himself no less than the Press Bureau. He had declared the usefulness of making his audiences angry, but came to realize that English anger would be exploited by the German press which had already described him as being persecuted in London, fearful of assassination, and living under house arrest with sentries at his doors. The failure of his speeches to evoke hissing and mobbing – 'reporters who were sent to see me torn limb from limb withdrew copyless' – was partly due to the nature of his audiences which mingled 'smart persons of the soulful type – Lady Diana [Manners] for example' with clusters of prominent Fabians. They were, in short, very like theatre audiences – full of young people in bright clothes – for whom he gave excellent performances without benefit of reviews. Most people did not know by now whether he was a pacifist or a conscriptionist – or if neither, whether this was because, as *Punch* put it,

> We find you faithful to your ancient plan
> Of disagreeing with the average man,
> And all because you think yourself undone
> Unless in a minority of one.

But it was true: he *was* neither pacifist nor conscriptionist. 'It seems to me that all Socialists should advocate compulsory national service, both civil and military,' he wrote. 'But compulsory soldiering is another matter.' It was agonizing to see, for example, the short, red-faced, Bunterish Cecil Chesterton got up in Khaki as a C-class private and looking as if he could camouflage himself 'as a beetroot on a sack of potatoes by simply standing stock still'. Shaw himself would have cut a far sharper figure in uniform. In the first days of the war he had seen a company of volunteers come swinging along Gower Street and 'to my utter scandal I was seized with a boyish impulse to join them'. As a 'superannuated person' he felt the inappropriateness of urging young people to take up arms. He criticized the Derby Scheme, which was bullying and cajoling men into voluntary service, for its 'appalling bad stage management' as well as the perverted economic and emotional basis on which it was founded. When the first Conscription Act was announced early in 1916, Shaw accused the government of having been driven into surrendering the nation to financially ruinous military slavery by the French, who had objected to Britain profiteering from the war. 'If the decision is to be Conscription, let it be faced, not as a temporary expedient,' he wrote in the *Daily News*, 'but as an advance in social organization.' The second Conscription Act became effective on 25 May 1916, a week before the Battle of Jutland. It was an emergency measure, with little considered legal character. Every military authority now became a press gang. The superstition that all Britons were free was kept up by a clause in the Act which reserved the liberty of people to refuse service on conscientious grounds, but neither the qualifications nor the treatment of this category of exempt person were defined. The result was that conscientious objectors, though nominally privileged to refuse service, were in practice rancorously persecuted: 'as far as the question was one solely of courage the Conshy was the hero of the war,' Shaw was to write, 'and the man who would not enlist until he was forced was the coward.'

All over the country there were cases of ill usage and vindictive sentences: and Shaw, though he advised no one to seek exemption as a conscientious objector and 'should not have objected myself if I had been liable to serve', was greatly exercised by this widespread maltreatment. He intervened in the case of an employee in the Education Department of the London County Council who was sent for miscellaneous duties to a military barracks, because such a decision meant that 'public education is of no service to the country'. How could the Government reasonably claim that 'to take an educated man of special literary talent and aptitude from the work of national education, and to set him to sweep barracks, dig latrines, or wait at table on an officers' mess is to effect a stroke of national economy which will materially help to win the war'? He objected to the composer Rutland Boughton's work being described as 'not of the least national importance'. Despite all the musical entertainments for the troops it was as if military tribunals believed that fine art was frivolous and out of place in wartime, 'and that all a man needs to be a complete Englishman is football in peace, fighting in war, and a formula about his duty to King and Country to save himself the trouble of thinking'. He appeared as a character witness at a court martial on behalf of Clarence Norman, a journalist whom he had employed to make verbatim reports of his speeches in shorthand and who was imprisoned for two and a half years for ignoring his call-up papers. And he used the cases of two other conscientious objectors of recognized integrity, Stephen Hobhouse and Clifford Allen, to demonstrate the common misuse of the Government's opportunist legislation by military tribunals with an understandable contempt for politicians. 'If Mr Hobhouse is imprisoned for a single hour,' he wrote in Massingham's *Nation*, 'the law is broken and the good faith of the Government discredited.'

Shaw studied the evidence, took trouble to be legally exact, and chose each case with care. He knew that conscientious objectors were 'a very mixed lot'; also that his own reputation could damage their chances at tribunals. 'They will not accept letters; and the mention of my name would bring all the prejudice against me on your back in addition to that against the Conscientious Objector,' he warned Clive Bell who was to change from art critic into fruit farmer. ' . . . I am afraid the tribunal will not recognize art criticism, as work of national importance; and the plea may do more harm than good.'

'After all, a shoeblack's work is of national importance, and a baker's, and a farmer's; but they dont exempt shoeblacks and bakers and farmers . . . Unless the doctor can rescue you, I advise you to yield to the conscience of the community and see the military business through from the inside.'

Spiteful persecutions made imprisonment virtually perpetual by repeated sentences for the same offence – which with hard labour could become sentences of death. A new crime had been created, but instead of enacting a penalty for its breach, the legislators transferred the criminal to the army so that he could be physically coerced into compliance. 'It is worth noticing that Quakers have been persecuted with the utmost ferocity,' Shaw wrote, 'whilst pugnacious objectors who simply objected to this particular war and openly declared that they would fight in a class war have been treated with comparative indulgence.'

He also gave sympathetic advice to one or two deserters, destroying the letters for their protection and writing confidentially so as not to undermine his own publicity as 'an old advocate of compulsory service'. This advocacy, which was calculated to strengthen his arguments for a fairer law and better treatment of individuals, baffled some of his audiences who were further disorientated by his satirical analogies: 'no sophistry can exalt the public utility of killing a foreigner above that of creating an Englishman,' he challenged. ' . . . All the same, if a nun conscientiously objected to compulsory maternity, I should recognize that I was up against something that had to be respected, and should star her for celibate service in her own vocation, or provide some other means of evasion.'

According to Rebecca West, it was Shaw's spirit of mockery that inspired him to these controversial flights. He was like Swift rather than Shelley, and whatever he said, the effect of his words was to question rather than inspire the prosecution of the war. Fascinated by his imaginative power, the public now came to consult him concerning the saving of its soul. Watching him as he walked on to the platform and began speaking, Rebecca West perceived that Shaw's virtue was getting thin with dilution. 'The passing of middle age has wiped the aggressive strangeness from his face, by mitigating with silver the redness of his hair and the pirate twist of his eyebrows, and has revealed a predominant quality of noble and unhysteric sensitiveness,' she wrote. 'In public life there is not time for such sensitiveness . . . when he began to speak, and the Irish accent shivered over his musical voice like the wind over a lake, one perceived another reason why he should not enter into politics.'

H. G. Wells had reasoned similarly from a different standpoint. Shaw's mind, he reckoned, had been 'early corrupted by public speaking & later almost entirely destroyed by the committee habit'. But Shaw always worked against the grain of his natural sensitivity. 'We want chamber opera: music is an *intimate* thing,' he wrote to Ernest Newman. But he had trained himself as a witness of grand opera and cultivated what he called a 'weakness for five-point-nine fortissimos'. His plays were built in this world of opera and politics, with a private voice stilled or sounding far off in fantasy. 'The theatre is passing away from me as a sort of wild oats: I go back to politics, religion & philosophy,' he wrote to Stella Campbell. 'They give me frightful headaches, but satisfy my soul.' But after two or three years of mud and blood at the front, intellectual and spiritual looting at home, he felt that 'one knows why Shakespeare and Swift were so bitter' after the wars against Philip II and Louis XIV. To overcome early bitterness he had removed himself from the intimate thing and forced his way into politics – but now felt pessimistically uncertain of his place in public life: 'I no longer have any confidence in my notions of what this generation needs to have said to it,' he told Wells.

It seemed impossible to go on writing plays, if only because 'the most important thing for an artist is to avoid unnecessary friction.' In these days of clashing events, art could 'only be carried by the deaf', Rebecca West acknowledged. 'And the artist who, like Mr Shaw, abandons it, at least shows that he has good hearing and is listening to the world.'

But he wanted a world that listened to him. As part of the process of 'continuous reconsideration', the Fabian Research Department had commissioned Leonard Woolf to investigate the causes of the war. Against a background of Bloomburgian scepticism, Woolf records, 'I did an immense amount of work on this'. His conclusions were produced as a two-part report; the first section, appearing like Shaw's *Common Sense* as a supplement to the *New Statesman*, in 1915. Leonard Woolf then added a second part, and the whole work was published in 1916 as a book, *International Government*, to which Shaw supplied an American Preface.

Leonard Woolf had argued that the first step towards the prevention of war must be the creation, as part of international government, of a supranational authority. His examination of the minimum requirements for such a body and his description of its probable structure comprised the first detailed study for the League of Nations. There was much in this analysis to appeal to Shaw. He wanted to use his fame to amplify this Fabian project. 'I am not the man to lose an opportunity of preaching at the utmost admissible length when I find myself installed as a great prophet,' he pointed out.

But he was a prophet without disciples, disestablished, needing affirmations. Shaw's League of Nations floats with its dreaming spires like an academy for supermen and superwomen with supranational tribunals to try for murder all statesmen who were accessories to declarations of war. It is a sublime factory, too, where Undershaft's weapons are manufactured by a professor of Greek and his wife, charged with defending democracy from those who, seeking mob popularity, sacrifice the morrow to the day, the eternal to the temporal. It is also a Palace of Revolution, shimmering across the wilderness where Shaw preached, in which international matters are taken away from those whose outlook, and interests, and type of character, are formed by official habits disabling them from all wide human purposes and deep human concerns – and given to a world concert of people addressing itself wholeheartedly to the welfare of us all. Finally, this visionary League stands as a temple for Shaw's paradoxes, his Abbey of Theleme, where all is conducted in a style magnificently opposed to the ordinary world.

[4]

To a man who has produced a modern comedy,
a campaign is child's play.
'Joy Riding at the Front'

The ordinary world, over which crawled a population of tanks, V-Boats and Zeppelins, appeared scarcely less fantastical than Shaw's *phalanstère*. At the end of 1916 Lloyd George's new War Cabinet had rejected Germany's peace proposals: but after two and a half years of continuous warfare, the moral imperatives of the conflict were flaking away and public opinion veering more sympathetically to 'Dearest G.B.S. (who is splendid about the war)' as Ellen Terry called him.

He had always found some supporters. Keir Hardie had 'felt the thrill' of his writings and predicted that when *Common Sense*

367

'. . . gets circulated in popular form and is read, as it will be, by hundreds of thousands of our best people of all classes, it will produce an elevation of tone in the National life which will be felt for generations to come.'

There had been the suggestion that a popular edition should be prepared by Arnold Bennett. When purged of the satirical absurdities readers accepted so literally, Bennett believed that Shaw's writing, which contained 'the most magnificent, brilliant, and convincing common sense that could possibly be uttered', would inaugurate a healthier period of discussion. Nothing came of this plan, though Shaw himself endorsed it. 'You, and I and Wells and Webb should be working together,' he urged Bennett late in 1916. '. . . However, it can't be helped – we must do the best we can ploughing our lonely back gardens.' Shaw had looked for a coalition of the intelligentsia to heighten faith and courage in the community. He believed it was the duty of representatives of art and literature in all countries to keep moral considerations above the nationalistic level of the war. But though these writers gained no authority beyond what each could separately extort by the persuasiveness of his pen, at least the atmosphere had eased, and more people were now walking out and waving to one another over their back fences. Both J. C. Squire and W. J. Locke had come up and shaken Shaw's hand. Wells, too, having made a long detour round international diplomacy had gone through 'disillusionment about the beneficence of our war-making'. Finding no justifying purpose, he later admitted 'how gravely I had compromised myself by my much too forward belligerence and my rash and eager confidence in the liberalism, intelligence and good faith of our Foreign Office and War Office . . . ' But he did not replace pro-war with anti-war zeal. His conclusions coincided with Shaw's. 'Peace will have to be kept – forcibly,' he wrote. 'For ages.'

Adelphi Terrace had been damaged in an air raid; an anti-aircraft station, with searchlights and soldiers' sheds, was put up in Ayot St Lawrence. Shaw continued, as in peacetime, to divide his weeks between the two places. The villagers at Ayot suspected him of being a German spy because he kept a light perpetually burning in a window at the top of the house. 'We thought they wanted to show the German planes the way,' explained Mrs Edith Reeves. So when Shaw offered his neighbours the use of his cellar as a shelter during raids, they felt unable to accept. After all, he had been there less than a dozen years. They knew his car and motor-bicycle well enough; they knew his dog Kim, 'the village terror': but they did not know himself or what to make of his remarks about this 'most *maddening* war'. Their suspicions began to blow away after the famous Hertfordshire Blizzard of 1915. 'He came out and worked hard with the other menfolk for days on end, sawing up trees which had been torn up by their roots and lay blocking the road,' one of them remembered. Another noted approvingly that he got 'pally' with the 'poorest people in the village as well as with the "top ten"'.

It was the Zeppelin raids above all else that gave everyone a shared subject of conversation. One Zeppelin, after voyaging majestically over the Shaws' house on its way to London, was shot down near Ayot St Lawrence on 1 October 1916. Next morning Shaw rode off through the rain to see the wreckage. It presented itself as two lumps of twisted metal framework in a watery field splashed over all day by huge and happy crowds. 'The police were in great feather,' he reported, 'as there is a strict cordon, which means you cant get in without paying.' But admission was cheap and well worth the price. 'I didnt half cheer, I tell you,' Shaw heard one girl remark. Nineteen bodies lay in a barn at the edge of the field. 'May I go in?' asked one woman. 'I would like to see a dead German.' But the police did not admit ladies. 'Corpses are extra, no doubt,' Shaw wrote; 'but I did not intrude on the last sleep of the brave.'

He had admired the audacity of the pilot, and been so enchanted by the sky-spectacle against the stars, so impressed by the magnificent orchestration of the engines, that 'I positively caught myself hoping next night that there would be another raid'. Apparently he was unaffected by the deaths. Having seen the Zeppelin fall like a burning newspaper, 'with its human contents roasting for some minutes (it was frightfully slow)', he had gone back to bed and was asleep in ten minutes. Reflecting on this, and wishing to convey his private mind, he confided to the Webbs: 'One is so pleased at having seen the show that the destruction of a dozen people or so in hideous terror and torment does not count . . . Pretty lot of animals we are!'

Charlotte appeared more profoundly unaffected. She no longer met Shaw's theatrical friends, had withdrawn from the Fabian Society, and wrapped herself round with remoter preoccupations. She felt proud of her husband's fame, but shared few of his interests; was wreathed in smiles, but seemed out of it all. To Augustus John, painting Shaw's portraits at Coole in 1915, Charlotte looked a 'fat party with green eyes who says "Ye-hes" in an intellectual way ending with a hiss'; to Virginia Woolf she appeared like a very stupid 'fat white Persian cat', which had rolled itself up on a cushion of Indian mysticism and gone to sleep. 'When she got me alone she tried to convert me,' Virginia wrote after a weekend together in the summer of 1916, 'and lent me little books about the Sentras, which she had to hide from Mrs Webb'. Unluckily for Charlotte, Beatrice Webb spied these little books beside her bed and nosed out their contents. Each was about three thousand words long – the size of a good Shavian monologue – and covered such topics as wisdom, holiness and faith. 'The thesis is that by continuous meditation, or self-hypnotism, you will rise above the self-conscious self and realize the "God Power" within you,' Beatrice noted sceptically. Charlotte confided to Virginia Woolf that Beatrice, though a wonderful person, 'had no idea of religion'. But the truth was that Charlotte's sentimental quietism mocked the 'spiritual muddle' in which Beatrice found herself. As a religious agnostic she reacted with irritation to Charlotte's easy answers and (according to Virginia) 'jeered at poor old Mrs Shaw'. But it was the spectacle of *rich* old Mrs Shaw that had aggravated Beatrice – this woman whose decent restlessness had been stilled by a religious placidity removing her from 'all efforts to make things better for those who are suffering from their heredity or environment'. Beatrice had felt sympathetic to Charlotte when she was suffering over her husband's intrigue with Mrs Pat: what antagonized her over this indulgence in American and Indian mysticisms was the lack of suffering. Sometimes she suspected herself of unfairness to Charlotte – but it was exasperating to see her beaming with such overflowing contentedness in the middle of this appalling war: she appeared so little *inconvenienced* by it all. She had quelled her anxieties over G.B.S., erased all her rheumatic aches by occult meditation and banished the agony of warfare from her mind.

At the beginning of 1917 Shaw began a new diary. 'I am going to try to keep it for a year,' he noted, 'as a sample slice of my life.' Altogether he kept it for ten days, and the sample slice it cut from his Ayot routine shows why he did not prolong it. There was no time. Even during the most uneventful days he was hectically occupied. All morning he poured out his 'intolerable opinions' which, when not targeted on the war, covered income tax, 'young age pensions', typhoid fever, theatre rents, the condition of Irish roads – and could be picked up by readers of the *Woman's Dreadnought, Somerset County Gazette*, and much of the American press. At half past one there was the brief interval of lunch with Charlotte, both reading books; the two of them would go into the garden where Charlotte sawed logs and G.B.S. split them with a beetle and wedges. Sometimes, to warm his feet, he would hurry through the village with his West Highland terrier ('the first dog I ever had who was an untameable growler . . . Yet we spoil him'); when he needed to go further he would set off for a spin and a spill on his motor-bike, and come rushing back to tighten the nuts on the front wheel (a 'worrying job'). At half past four he allowed himself a cup of chocolate, while Charlotte drank tea. Then he would press on with his writing again, often dealing with more letters that

Ann Elder had sent down from London. 'It is one of my troubles that I have so much business to do in connection with my former work that I have less and less time to work seriously in the present,' he wrote. 'As I grow old, I find for some reason that I attend to business the first thing in the morning, whereas formerly I always devoted the morning to my creative work, and attended to my business at long intervals, and sometimes not at all.' The second interval of the day – called dinner – began at half past seven: after which he would read and end the evening singing and playing the pianola – his repertoire ranging from Strauss's *Elektra* and Liszt's transcription of Beethoven's Ninth Symphony to MacDowell's sonatas, Gounod's songs, arias from the operas of Mozart and Wagner, and a good deal of miscellaneous Berlioz, Elgar and Schumann. Finally he would go up to Charlotte's room to say good-night, and retire to his own bed with the *Economic Journal* or one of the other journals 'which one has to look through more or less thoroughly'.

Early that month he received an invitation from Douglas Haig, Commander-In-Chief of the British army, to visit the Front. 'Charlotte said I must go, as I ought to see this terrible thing for myself,' he noted. 'I grumbled that I should see nothing except a conventional round on which all the journalists are sent; but . . . my interest increased as the day went on.' By the following week he had come to feel that he 'was not free to refuse'. He wrote to Massingham and to Wells, both of whom had been to the Front, and on their advice arrayed himself in khaki tunic and breeches, and a pair of trench boots for the yellow Flanders mud: but all his camouflage was defeated, and his visibility intensified, by a mantle of brilliant snow covering the battlefield.

In this blunted landscape, with its splintered and scarred trees, its signposts without villages, Shaw found some devastating material from which to replenish his paradoxes. Privately he confided to Lady Gregory that his week at the Front had been 'a most demoralizing experience'. Publicly in the *Daily Chronicle* he reported: 'I enjoyed myself enormously and continuously.' Both statements contained truth, and were a repeated shorthand for his translation of demoralizing early life into a career of sustained and serious comedy. He set out to console those who had husbands, brothers, sons, friends in the trenches, or who were themselves in training for that ordeal, with a beam of black entertainment. He confidently assured everyone that there was no inevitability at the Front of being killed. On the contrary, death was very uncertain: the gas was crazily blown in the wrong direction, the high explosives and other infernal engines of destruction were so appallingly imprecise that the 'Somme battlefield was very much safer than the Thames Embankment with its race of motors and trams'. Of course the devastation was terrific – and yet not wholly to be deplored. As the member of a sanitary authority, he knew that many of the old towns had been badly in need of demolition. Even the aesthetic aspect of some places had been enhanced – the cathedral at Arras, for example, looked finer as a ruin than when he had last seen it intact; the Little Square, too, had been most 'handsomely knocked about' and many old buildings, such as the Cloth Hall at Ypres, would gain a more beautiful existence in the memory than they had ever achieved in actuality. And there were other consolations readers could look forward to. Once artillery shells had been improved so as to provide more lateral than vertical energy, they could be employed in the general reshaping of civilian life, not only for easy clearance of slum areas, but as a method of ploughing farmers' fields and releasing labourers from unendurable drudgery.

Drudgery was one of the hardships of war: but the military love of display provided many colourful diversions. Whenever an aeroplane sailed across the blue, delightful white puff-balls blossomed in the sky around it. Every night was Guy Fawkes Night. The guns hurled their fiery shells joyously into the air and set up a bombardment that must have been especially appealing to those who enjoyed plenty of percussion in the orchestra – it was finer than Tchaikovsky's *1812*. He had difficulty believing that the man lying by the roadside was not a tramp taking a siesta during the booming and whizzing of this band music, but a gentleman who had lost his head. Behind the lines bayonet practice was conducted without the least blood lost, and imparted a bank holiday air to the place which really looked magnificent in the snow and sunshine. The trenches were crammed with pacifists, socialists and internationalists, all freed from theoretical illusions, all damning the party politicians with the greatest heartiness, and despite uncomfortable outdoor conditions, 'no more hopelessly wretched than I'. Fighting men, Shaw explained, escaped the perpetual money worries of their civilian counterparts and the debasing egotism of their continual preoccupation with commerce. Added to this there was human nature's curious fascination with peril: at the Front something exciting was always happening that satisfied man's heroic instincts. Looking round, it was possible to hope that war would socialize men, that 'there will be ennobled men to set against maimed ones, and saved souls against dead bodies.'

'This is an argument, not for the perpetuation of war but for the purification of peace, but as long as peace remains unpurified, and war remains in some respects nobler, let us give it its due, and not deliver ourselves to the oppression of an unrelieved horror.'

This horror is forced invisibly between the lines of Shaw's writing. It was as unacceptable as his mother's abandonment of him, and he rubs it over with a similar glaze of paradoxes to polish off the pain and reflect it as something economically unacceptable. It was impossible, Shaw lamented, to fight cheaply: British taxpayers had to be reminded of how inconceivably wasteful this business was: 'it burns the house to roast the pig.' War could do many things, he argued, but it could not end war. 'A victory for anybody is a victory for war.' He predicted that economic rather than military forces would eventually end it all, and that the only benefits of this vast calamity would lie in the employment of military virtues for a decently organized civilian life. For in the army, instead of your hand being against every man's and every man's hand against you, 'you are continually trying to get things done in the best possible way for the benefit of your comrades in arms, of your country, of the whole of which you are a part ... whereas commerce is normally competitive and places your individual pocket before all the higher objects of ambition'.

Shaw's ten-thousand-word report of his experiences as a war tourist revived questions of his loyalty. One Member of Parliament reminded the House of Commons that G.B.S. had advised British soldiers to shoot their officers and go home, and demanded if this were the sort of man who should be officially invited to the British front line. 'I have always found that when any gentleman visits the front in France,' replied the Government spokesman, 'he comes back with an added desire to help the British Army and is proud of it.' The House of Commons filled with cheers – this time on Shaw's behalf. Many who had accused him of German sympathies now wondered whether he was actually in the service of the British Government to advertise the country's celebrated freedom of speech. Others thought his head was turned after being treated as *persona grata* by the Foreign Office and entertained to lunch by the Commander-in-Chief. Observing him to be 'an interesting man of original views', Haig had changed his plans and taken G.B.S. to a demonstration of experimental weapons. But though he relished this outing and later voted Haig 'the most interesting new writer of the past twelve months', Shaw privately judged him to be an academician of war, stiff in manners and with a depressingly mechanical mind – 'a first rate specimen of the British gentleman and conscientiously studious soldier, trained socially and professionally to behave and work in a groove from which nothing could move him, disconcerted and distressed by novelties and incredulous as to their military value, but always steadied by a well-closed mind and unquestioned code', Shaw wrote a couple of years after Haig's death. ' ... He made me feel that the war would last thirty years, and that he would carry it on irreproachably until he was superannuated.'

Though he greeted the news of the first revolution in Russia that March as 'a gain to humanity', and described the entry of America into the war on 6 April as a 'first class moral asset to the common cause against junkerism', Shaw felt politically gloomy. He had been welcomed by the Commander-in-Chief and then, a few days later, rebuffed by the Prime Minister who struck out his name from the 'list of persons with ideas' proposed for the Reconstruction Committee to advise on post-war social problems. G.B.S. no longer spoke with such a lonely voice, but he was still an outsider. In a speech at King's Hall, Covent Garden, that March, his disappointment seeped into his political attitude. All great reforms, he said, had at their back some calamity. But the calamity of this war had been too horrible and the reforms, which were slowly coming, had been won at too great a price. The mass of people who stood to benefit most from change were hesitant. 'The great purpose of democracy,' he concluded, 'is to prevent you from being governed better than you want to be governed.'

That July he was sixty-one. 'Any fool can be 60,' he explained to Trebitsch, 'if he lives long enough.' Sixty of course was nothing for a man of his age. Charlotte had taken off for Ireland that summer for the sake of her lumbago, leaving G.B.S. to revert somewhat to his bachelor ways. He was seeing much of Kathleen Scott, formidable widow of the Antarctic explorer Robert Falcon Scott – 'a wonderful woman' he called her and a model Shavian heroine: 'first rate at her job, adventurously ready to go to the ends of the earth at half an hour's notice with no luggage but a comb with three teeth in it, and always successful.' Her job was sculpting – she made a bust and full-length statuette of G.B.S. in bronze. She forcefully smoothed down Charlotte's nerves and during periods of grass-widowhood G.B.S. was sometimes allowed to stay with Kathleen, especially after her marriage in 1922 to Hilton Young. 'We got on together to perfection,' he recorded. Though she had been widowed in 1912 after only four years of marriage, she never played the grief-stricken widow. When in his company, Shaw was pleased to observe, 'she did not seem to feel her loss at all'.

After Stella had gone off to marry Cornwallis-West 'I really thought I was a dead man,' Shaw admitted, 'until I recovered my sanity by going right back to my economics and politics, and put in a hard stint of work on this abominable war.' But by 1917 he had come to feel that 'my bolt is shot as to writing about the war'. In so far as it could do any good, the war was already over, though that August it had dragged on into its fourth year.

Shaw spent the month sitting as a Fabian delegate to the Allied Socialist Conference at Westminster, and appearing as 'a sort of bishop' at a girls' school in Surrey which the Fabians had commandeered for their 1917 Summer School. The conference, which voted in favour of another conference in Stockholm to define the Allies' relationship with Kerensky's new Russian Government, wrangled for two indecisive days over a statement of war aims: it was, Shaw declared to Charlotte, 'an absurd but intentional fiasco'. The Summer School, with its continuous racket of lecturing, dancing and flirting, was more jolly. Realizing that he would be classed a social failure unless he could respond to repeated applications for the pleasure of a waltz, 'I boldly faced the situation, and took twelve lessons,' he told Henry Salt. 'The funniest part of it was that I was found to possess a senile and lumbering *diable au corps* which made my King David-like gambols amusing to myself and not so utterly unbearable for my unfortunate partners as might have been expected.' Photographs of this event testify to his exaggerated success. The Ethical Body was on the move. 'If I am to keep up my dancing we must buy a gramophone,' he suggested to Charlotte.

He turned down the chance of an amusing holiday at the Italian Front partly because 'I am so horribly ignorant of Italian politics'. He had also expected to visit Stockholm: but Lloyd George refused to issue British socialists with passports for 'a fraternizing conference with the enemy'. Shaw believed it would have been 'dishonest to go to Stockholm and pretend that we, any more than the German Socialists, had political power or influence enough to prevent the fullest advantage being taken of a victory'. Nevertheless, the deviousness over passports had been 'one of the silliest mistakes yet made by our Government in its dealings with Labor', and he judged Lloyd George to be 'an atrocious P.M.'. In any case, war was not a socialist game. 'I must get away for a moment from Fabians & politics or I shall go mad.' He decided to make for Ireland and enjoy the open skies of Parknasilla where Charlotte had been staying with her sister. 'I shall be all the better for a few weeks of the sea before I go back to the winter routine,' he wrote to her. 'Also it is some time since we have met.'

He arrived on 10 September and early the following month reported that he had been 'boating and bathing and making butter in a dairy ever since'. Work was impossible. 'In the Atlantic air one grows big and rank and Irish,' he wrote to Beatrice Webb. ' . . . this is the Land of the Free compared to England. The submarine campaign is conferring untold benefits on the coast population; and petrol can generally be obtained from information supplied by the parish priest.'

The art of the dramatic poet knows no patriotism.
Preface to *Heartbreak House.*

'I feel rather disgusted with the theatre,' Shaw wrote to Lillah McCarthy in the summer of 1917. Earlier in the war his box office appeal had plummeted. 'The moment is not happily chosen for resuming the old Shavian capers, which were among the strangest by-products of the long peace,' decided A. B. Walkley in a *Times* review of *Fanny's First Play* which had been unsuccessfully revived in 1915. The world of Shaw's plays, with their 'fund of travestied facts and lopsided judgments', seemed to be passing away. There were many who felt that war had reversed the whole current of life: that theatres, museums, picture galleries and schools should be converted into hospitals and barracks. To the surprise of these people the stage grew incomparably popular between 1914 and 1918. Initially it was occupied by recruiting plays with patriotic songs, such as *England Expects* which was produced at the London Opera House and featured a harangue in the interval by the fire-eating chauvinist and fraudulent financier Horatio Bottomley. Shaw, who went to see one of Bottomley's Union Jack perorations, reported: 'It's exactly what I expected: the man gets his popularity by telling people with sufficient bombast just what they think themselves and therefore want to hear.' For a specialist in the unexpected there was suddenly no audience. Each night the auditoriums were crowded to the doors with thousands of men in khaki on leave from the Front who had never been to a theatre before and did not know what to expect. 'At one of our great variety theatres I sat beside a young officer, not at all a rough specimen, who, even when the curtain rose and enlightened him as to the place where he had to look for his entertainment, found the dramatic part of it utterly incomprehensible,' Shaw wrote. 'He did not know how to play his part of the game.'

'He could understand the people on the stage singing and dancing and performing gymnastic feats. He not only understood but intensely enjoyed an artist who imitated cocks crowing and pigs squeaking. But the people who pretended that they were somebody else, and that the painted picture behind them was real, bewildered him.'

Producers and actor-managers ransacked their memories for out-of-date musicals and revues to exploit the bliss of soldiers who were happy to be no longer under fire and ready to be delighted by every young girl they saw and old joke they heard. The theatrical values of London suddenly reverted to antique farces played in bedrooms with four doors and a window, identical to the bedrooms of flats above and below them, and all occupied by jealous husbands and wives mistaking one bedroom for another.

Shaw's contribution to this wartime theatre was four playlets that caricature, in juvenile fashion, the economic and social changes brought about in Germany, England and Russia by the Great War: and the lack of any change in Ireland. His characters are preposterously named – Archdeacon Daffodil Donkin, Ermyntrude Roosenhonkers-Pipstein – and preposterously re-cast. Wives of fashionable architects take jobs as tea ladies; eminent medical men become waiters in hotels; daughters of archdeacons, who in peacetime marry millionaires, are widowed and obliged to seek posts as ladies-in-waiting to princesses who themselves have grown meek and impoverished. Through the lens of war distinguished members of the governing class are revealed as imbeciles; private soldiers with medals are raised above high-born generals who formerly were their landlords; victorious Emperors declare themselves hopelessly bankrupt and great empresses are transformed into revolutionary spirits. Shaw made the plots of these playlets more ludicrous and their action more knock-about than any bedroom farce – then having appealed to the popular nonsensical mood (what he called a 'national disaffection to intellect'), he tried to introduce a few moments of serious reflection. At the end of *The Inca of Perusalem*, for example, which he rattled off in a few days early in August 1915, the absurd Inca, whose athletic moustache 'is so watched and studied', we are told, 'that it has made his face the political barometer of the whole continent', ceases to be a lampoon on the Kaiser, and speaks in the tones of the Devil from *Don Juan in Hell*. Shaw wanted to remind his audiences that war had long been a favourite food of their imagination – when men had no battles to fight they played at war in their films and magazine stories. Since all of us were partly infected by the same passion, we could not simply blame one man, the Kaiser, for making us fight. 'You talk of death as an unpopular thing,' the Inca replies when accused of having caused the war. 'You are wrong: for years I gave them art, literature, science, prosperity, that they might live more abundantly; and they hated me, ridiculed me, caricatured me. Now that I give them death in its frightfullest forms, they are devoted to me . . . They grudged a few hundreds for their salvation: they now pay millions a day for their own destruction and damnation. And this they call my doing!'

Shaw had written *The Inca of Perusalem* for Gertrude Kingston to play in America. 'But it's rather dangerous,' he warned Vedrenne; 'and I dont seriously recommend it.' The Lord Chamberlain's office had passed it for performance only on condition that 'the make-up of the Inca does not too closely resemble the German Emperor' and references to his grand-mother, uncle and cousin (which could be taken to be Queen Victoria, King Edward VII and King George V) were muted. 'Apparently we are on the eve of concluding peace, Gertrude Kingston commented to Shaw on 15 November 1915, 'since we are not allowed to parody the German Emperor!' This was not the danger Shaw had foreseen. By using the ancient privilege of comedy to chasten Caesar's foibles he feared that he might seem to be trifling with a deadly peril. 'Why does everybody make fun of me?' demands the doomed Inca. 'Is it fair?' And the merry widow Ermyntrude, speaking as the Inca's equal, puts Shaw's answer before they drive off for a cup of tea at the zoo. 'Yes: it is fair. What other defence have we poor common people against your shining armour, your mailed fist, your pomp and parade, your terrible power over us? Are these things fair?'

Though no one 'dared dream of [it] at first', *The Inca of Perusalem* was presented in Birmingham late in 1916 where the audience 'has swallowed it tamely enough', and a few months afterwards in Dublin where the Irish Nationalists, taking it for a satire on British belligerence (and the Inca as a misunderstood humanist), greeted it with political cheering.

Shaw's satire against wartime England was an exaggerated stunt, *Augustus Does His Bit*, which he threw off in August 1916 for Madame Vandervelde, wife of the Belgian socialist minister, to be performed at a matinée in aid of the Belgians. It had been prompted by a Government appeal to dramatists and theatre managers for didactic pieces inculcating war saving. Shaw's 'Unofficial Dramatic Tract', which he subtitled 'A True-to-Life Farce', was 'my patriotic response to that appeal', he informed the drama editor of the *Evening Standard*. In fact, as he privately wrote to Vedrenne, 'it isn't patriotic. Augustus does his bit energetically; but the consequences are of the most ruinous kind – Molière's L'Etourdi up to date'. This skit on high-born officialdom and crass bureaucracy at home (Lord Augustus Highcastle produces a bullet which had been flattened by contact with his skull) was well recognized at the Front where it opened the hearts of all military personnel: but it did not gain much recognition in London. 'War seems unpropitious to Shavian wit,' noted *The Times*. '. . . He has simply evolved an idiot out of his own consciousness and ascribed to him the follies of his own imagination.'

Also brimful of Shavian idiots, according to Shaw, was Russia – though these were mostly of the officer class against whom he calculated the Revolution to have been directed. *Annajanska*, his 'revolutionary romancelet', is a half-hour bravura piece. Written during three December days in 1917 – a month, that was, after the Bolshevik Revolution and a week before Russia signed an armistice with Germany – Shaw hands the derelict power created by the fall of tsardom not to two Dictators of the Proletariat or elaborately educated middle-class idealists, but back to a 'wild grand duchess'. He did not mean to convey by this reversion that *plus ça change . . .* but to exploit the apparent paradox of the most radical event in his lifetime having erupted in the most politically backward country. In Britain there was popular indignation over the desertion by an ally: but Shaw sensed that, though it had all begun as an incident in the war, the revolutionary measures being taken in Russia over dealing with land, industry, education and religion were to be of a magnitude and significance that nobody could yet apprehend. 'Suddenly came the cataclysm. It was the crash of an epoch,' he wrote. 'The mountainous dyke within which western Capitalism had been working for centuries cracked and left a gap the whole width of Europe from the Baltic to the Black Sea. Mere writing cannot describe it: it makes metaphor silly.'

Annajanska is mere writing and may best be regarded as a present to Lillah McCarthy. 'Not a penny of royalty would he take,' she recorded. ' . . . It was to be, to the world, a translation from the Russian by Gregory Piessipoff, but ostriches with their heads in the sand are invisible compared with Shaw's anonymity.' The extravaganza, which took her mind off other worries, enabled Lillah to make an athletic entrance dragging in two exhausted soldiers, fire off several fusillades, give vent to Shaw's republican enthusiasm and democratic doubts, and dominate the Coliseum stage in a magnificent green and black Russian fur coat designed by Charles Ricketts. 'I went home very tired,' she wrote happily.

Shaw had wanted to populate his stage Ireland with more of these Shavian farceurs, but 'when it came to business, I had to give up all the farcical equivoque I described to you,' he wrote to Lady Gregory, 'and go ahead quite straightforwardly without any ingenuities or misunderstandings.' *O'Flaherty, V.C.*, Shaw's other Irish play, had been conceived in the summer of 1915 while staying with Lady Gregory at Coole ('the scene is quite simply before the porch in your house') and was written at the Hydro Hotel at Torquay in early September. It had two purposes, both unfulfilled: to help the resources of the Irish Players at the Abbey Theatre and to serve as an Irish recruiting poster in disguise. He had intended a four-handed light comedy (with small but important additional roles for a thrush and a jay) that would appeal strongly to what he called 'the Irishman's spirit of freedom and love of adventure'. But as he wrote, a portrait emerged of the Irish character that 'will make the Playboy seem a patriotic rhapsody by comparison', he apologized to Lady Gregory.

'. . . *C'était plus fort que moi*. At worst, it will be a barricade for the theatre to die gloriously on.'

'I long to see him,' Lady Gregory replied but, by the time Shaw had passed *O'Flaherty V.C.* for the press, she had left for America. Shaw instructed his printer to send half a dozen rehearsal copies to W. B. Yeats. 'It is by no means certain that it will be licensed in England,' he wrote tentatively to Yeats; 'and a few preliminary trials in Dublin might do no harm . . .' Having been asked by Sir Matthew Nathan, Under-Secretary for Ireland, for help over Dublin Castle's disappointing recruitment campaign, he had taken a famous recent Irish exploit – the killing of eight German soldiers and capture of fifteen others singlehanded by Private Michael O'Leary – and Shavianized it for the stage. This was an obvious subject for a recruiting play and may additionally have appealed to Shaw because he had successfully campaigned nearly twenty years earlier for pensions to be paid to holders of the Victoria Cross. War issues for Irishmen, he argued, were different from those of Englishmen: 'incomprehensible as it seems to an Englishman, Irish patriotism does not take the form of devotion to England and England's kind.' More effective, he reckoned, was an appeal to the Irishman's boredom at home by advertising the war as an opportunity to travel abroad at the British Government's expense. 'Is your uprooting from the bank desk a calamity which you would undo if you could, or is it an enlargement of your experience & an intensification of your life which you would not have missed for anything, & which is worth the risks you have had to run?' he asked a lance corporal at the Front.

In *O'Flaherty V.C.* Shaw attempted to answer this question by exploiting a magical optimism focused increasingly in his later years beyond the limits of humanity. But the reality of Ireland was so timelessly implanted in him that his pessimism shines through and colours the play, the ending of which 'is cynical to the last degree', he revealed to Lady Gregory. The enlargement of O'Flaherty's experience at the Front, and the intensification of his life abroad, induces in him an unbearable realism. 'Knowledge and wisdom has come over me with pain and fear and trouble,' he says. 'I've been made a fool of and imposed upon all my life.' He sees everything for what it is: Irish patriotism is mindless ignorance; Irish eyes are tightly closed; Irish family life grows more terrible than life in the trenches; an Irish general is 'no more fit to command an army than an old hen'; his Irish sweetheart, no longer the angelic colleen, is ruthless and mercenary; and his mother herself becomes an appalling termagant ('a Volumnia of the potato patch') whose 'batings' at home have proved wonderful training for O'Flaherty's acts of bravery in the army. 'Some likes war's alarums; and some likes home life,' O'Flaherty concludes. 'Ive tried both, sir; and I'm all for war's alarums now. I always was a quiet lad by natural disposition.'

The war has been well worth while for O'Flaherty because it has opened up the possibility of a new life. If he gets through unscathed he will leave Ireland, leave his mother and covetous girlfriend, and 'have a French wife'. But Shaw's happy ending was hardly adequate compensation for a recruiting play that has its hero exclaiming: 'Dont talk to me or any other soldier of the war being right. No war is right.' And: 'Youll never have a quiet world til you knock the patriotism out of the human race.' This was not what Sir Matthew Nathan had been expecting. He consulted General Sir John French, Commander-in-Chief of Home Forces and soon to be made Lord Lieutenant of Ireland, and, having brooded on it with him, wrote to say that they both believed the production should be postponed. It was a tactful letter. 'This war does give to the most thinking of all peasantries the chance of contact with the wider world which will enable them to rise above the hopelessness derived from their old recollections and surroundings,' agreed Nathan. But any performance, he insisted, would lead to 'demonstrations' smothering the 'fine lessons' of the play and giving prominence to other passages that taken out of context would be used for propaganda by the Central Powers. Horace Plunkett, to whom Shaw also sent a copy, agreed: 'I am afraid that in the present state of feeling in Dublin its presentation might be made the occasion for a riot in the theatre.'

So Shaw's picture of Ireland as unmitigated hell was not played at the Abbey, but received its first presentation on 17 February 1917 at Treizennes in Belgium where Shaw attended a dress rehearsal. Robert Loraine was O'Flaherty and the other parts were played by officers of the Royal Flying Corps, while the men put on a performance of *The Inca of Perusalem*. Later that year Shaw himself read *O'Flaherty V.C.* to a hospital full of wounded soldiers near Ayot. 'They gave me three cheers, and laughed a good deal,' he told Lady Gregory; 'but the best bits were when they sat very tight and said nothing.'

Though *O'Flaherty V.C.* was not performed by the Irish Players until it had softened into 'A Reminiscence of 1915' at the end of 1920 – and then only in London – Shaw's reputation seemed suddenly to have come alive in Ireland. After seven years without a Shaw production, the Abbey Theatre staged what amounted to an extraordinary festival – seven Shaw plays between the autumn of 1916 and the summer of 1917. And what was happening in Ireland appeared to be happening in other parts of the world. He had received official permission to export manuscripts and printed plays. The American manager William Brady had presented *Major Barbara* in New York; the British-born actor William Faversham successfully introduced *Misalliance* to American audiences and had broken the box office records set by *Pygmalion* with his American tour of *Getting Married*. Throughout Europe, in neutral countries as well as lands held by the Allied and the Central Powers, all manner of Shavian productions were appearing – among them *Androcles* in Stockholm, *Candida* in Budapest, *Pygmalion* in Warsaw, *Mrs Warren's Profession* in Helsinki, *Widowers' Houses* in Prague and *The Devil's Disciple* pretty well simultaneously in Copenhagen and Vienna. In Britain too there was a recovery of interest in his work – *Man and Superman* had been performed in its entirety in Edinburgh, and half a dozen other plays were touring the country from Plymouth to Birmingham. The London theatre stood ready at last for a new comedy from G.B.S. But he felt oddly undecided. He had begun a shorthand draft of a new play – first referred to as 'Lena's Father', then provisionally called *The Studio in the Clouds* – on 4 March 1916. The rhythm of his composition had been uniquely tentative. 'I, who once wrote whole plays *d'un seul trait*, am creeping through a new one (to prevent myself crying) at odd moments, two or three speeches at a time,' he wrote to Stella over thirteen weeks later. 'I dont know what its about.' By the end of that year he had written enough for a first act, 'filling the stage with the most delightful characters under the pleasantest circumstances,' he let William Archer know; 'but whether it is preoccupation with the war and with business, and with all sorts of interest more urgent than the theatre, I have left them there for months and months, hopelessly stuck. This has never happened before.' Nine months on, after his return from Ireland in October 1917, he still felt 'perplexed' and wondered if this perplexity was a symptom of his age. 'I am beginning to write quantities of stuff without being able to make up my mind to regard them as finished and publish them,' he confided to Hugo Vallentin. He was generally confident of finishing it some day, and perhaps not badly, but still felt extraordinarily reluctant to let it out of his hands and into the theatre. The title had now been changed to *Heartbreak House*. 'We must be content to dream about it,' he advised Lillah McCarthy the following summer. 'Let it lie there to shew that the old dog can still bark a bit.'

[6]

... the government of one nation against its will by another nation raises no question of whether such government is good or bad: it is itself misgovernment, and would be bad even if it produced perfect order and mutual material prosperity ... the worst tyranny is that which imposes a higher standard of conduct than is natural ... I object to being governed by a superior race even more than by an inferior one, so that the Englishman may take it as he likes, as superior, inferior or equal: I object to his governing me. (1917)*

'If you want to bore an Irishman, play him an Irish melody, or introduce him to another Irishman,' Shaw had written. ' . . . Abroad, however, it is a distinction to be an Irishman; and accordingly the Irish in England flaunt their nationality.' His own Irish nationality, emphasized by the clear vowels and correct terminals of his Dublin accent, was a financial asset, he contended: for his original motive for leaving Ireland, like his mother's, had been economic. 'I do not regret my emigration to London, which was not, of course, merely an emigration from an Irish city to an English one, but a necessary transfer of my business to a European metropolis.' Since he left, the Irish Renaissance had changed the literary business potential of Dublin, but when Yeats later approached him, hoping to persuade eminent Irish writers to move back to Dublin so as to make the capital city of their own country 'famous in Letters', Shaw was horrified. 'I could never do that,' he answered. 'They would find me out in a week.'

They would have found a seething revulsion that bellowed out whenever he was forcibly reminded of this city of his discontent. It had not changed. Returning there after more than thirty years, he saw that 'the houses had never been painted since and the little shops had eggs in the windows, with mice and rats running over them, and rubbish that looked as if on its way to the dust heap'. Later, after reading parts of *Ulysses*, he was to congratulate Joyce on having rubbed the Irish people's noses in this filth. 'It is a revolting record of a disgusting phase of civilization; but it is a truthful one,' he asserted in a letter to the book's publisher Sylvia Beach; 'and I should like to put a cordon round Dublin; round up every male person in it between the ages of 15 and 30; force them to read it ... all that foul mouthed, foul minded derision and obscenity ... I have walked those streets and know those shops and have heard and taken part in those conversations. I escaped from them to England ... '

Joyce had used his genius to recreate Dublin: Shaw turned away. 'I drove into Dublin today and cursed every separate house as I passed,' he had written to Stella Campbell. Then he drove out again. He wanted to dissolve this squalid past into a radiant future: and he advised Ireland to lift her eyes from the iniquitous Treaty of Limerick (1691), cease puffing her sails with the rhetoric of stale grievances, and replace her preoccupation over national divisions with an overall political emancipation.

Shaw separated Dublin from Ireland and overlaid biography with history. 'I have given up the Dublin people as hopeless,' he told Lady Gregory. But he could not give up Ireland: 'I am an Irishman and I have not forgotten.' He addressed himself to almost every major social and political problem that arose in Ireland, gaining renown as a fabulous Irish Sea-St George's Channel creature made legendary by its extravagant tricks. What other person could have demanded, but be refused, membership of the Irish Convention; be offered, but decline, nomination to the Irish Senate; accept the first presidency of the Irish Academy of Letters, but turn down the first presidency of Eire (which he was never offered) while granting that he 'had better play his [President de Valera's] hand for him'? He showed his characteristic perversity by recommending that Ireland be established as a sanatorium where the English should be sent to gain flexibility of mind: and by advising Britain to sell Ireland to America in order to pay off her national debt. He was to leave the country to 'stew in her own juice' by not returning there after 1923: then registered as a citizen of the Irish Free State twelve years later.

His career was studded with illuminating acts of generosity to Ireland. He campaigned with Lady Gregory to recapture Hugh Lane's pictures according to the wishes expressed in an unwitnessed codicil to Lane's will; and he promised the Lord Mayor of Dublin a donation of one hundred guineas as his contribution towards a good municipal gallery to house them. He presented the Assembly Rooms at Carlow, which he had inherited from his uncle Walter Gurly, to the Catholic Bishop of Kildare and Leighlin for conversion into a technical school and was largely responsible for the fine Technical College which later developed on that site; he attempted to set up an Irish film industry to which he offered to donate *Saint Joan*, being 'desirous that his plays shall employ and develop the dramatic genius of his fellow-countrymen and make Ireland's scenic beauties known in all lands'; he persuaded the Irish Government to introduce the Voluntary Civic Improvement Fund to facilitate the municipalization of property by which he transferred the remainder of Walter Gurly's land and buildings to the Carlow Urban Council. Later he would hand the manuscripts of his novels to the National Library of

Ireland and finally leave the National Gallery of Ireland one third of his residuary estate.

But Shaw's words spoke louder than his actions. He pronounced Ireland's political debates to be 'baby talk', her papers 'comics', her history mere 'police news', and her education a hellish training that prolonged the 'separation of the Irish people into two hostile camps' – 'monastically and inhumanly puritanical' Irish Catholicism versus 'snobbish and violently political' Irish Protestantism. 'I quite expect before long to see the beginning of a movement to establish an Irish sun and moon on the grounds that the present articles are English.' He described Irish houses as disease-ridden slums: 'Let us grieve, not over the fragment of Dublin city that is knocked down, but over at least three-quarters of what has been preserved,' he declared after the Easter Rising of 1916. 'How I wish I had been in command of the British artillery on that fatal field! How I should have improved my native city!' With the introduction of the Censorship of Publications Act in 1925 he condemned this 'amazing exhibition of Irish moral panic', complained of Ireland's 'amateur Inquisition', and castigated her lack of birth control and sex education as a monstrous folly 'perpetuated by way of purifying Ireland'. He also ridiculed the Gaelic League for loosening the country's hold on a vital twentieth-century acquisition, the English language. 'Why not write your name in genuine vernacular Irish as O'Dogherty?' he demanded of Bearnard O'Dubhthaigh from the Department of Education. 'I dont spell my name Shaigh'. And he commiserated with those children whose parents put them through an artificial exercise 'comparable to fifth-century Latin and having as much to do with vernacular Irish as fifth-century Latin had to do with vernacular Italian of that period'. If left to its crew of romantics Ireland would slip back into the Atlantic 'as a little green patch' about which nobody outside the country cared twopence. He therefore counselled all patriots 'to go to bed and stay there until the Irish question is settled'.

He could not accept this advice himself. The superbly controlled impartial style with which he dived into Irish politics concealed interests that were passionately autobiographical. The fact that he was an Irishman 'has always filled me with a wild and inextinguishable pride': the fact that he had been brought up in Protestant circles had given him a preference for being 'burnt at the stake by Irish Catholics than protected by Englishmen'. These Protestant circles had included many Catholics from Lee's musical society which became Shaw's harmonizing model for Irish society – a single unified nation full of the turbulence that was natural in a progressive democratic country. Finally, as a metaphor blessing the separation of his parents, he prescribed a cure for the bad blood flowing from the unhappy historical marriage of England and Ireland – a parting by consent rather than absolute divorce, together with a legal wand of oblivion moved over all past warring. To nurture malice, Shaw warned, 'is to poison our blood and weaken our institutions with unintelligent rancor'.

Shaw used 'every device of invective and irony and dialectic at my command' to assuage Ireland's longing for freedom. The impulse was as intense as any that had filled his mother, longing to be rid of her husband. He had merged the two subjects – divorce legislation and the constitutional independence of nations – when covering the Parnell scandal of 1890. Home Rule had suddenly come within reach when a majority of Irish Members of Parliament pledged to the issue had been returned to Westminster. But at the height of his leadership of the Irish Party, Charles Parnell had been cited as co-respondent in a divorce case involving the wife of another Irish Member of Parliament and his political future seemed ruined. In letters to *The Star*, Shaw had argued that 'the whole mischief in the matter lay in the law that tied the husband and wife together and forced Mr Parnell to play the part of clandestine intriguer, instead of enabling them to dissolve the marriage by mutual consent, without disgrace to either party'. He therefore advised Parnell to 'sit tight' and urged the Irish Party to unite behind him – otherwise the Liberal Government would exploit the disunity and abandon its commitment to Home Rule. The verdicts of antiquated laws, he added, 'can produce no genuine conviction of its victims' unfitness for public life'. Similarly repugnant was the legally enforced tie between England and Ireland, he implied, where under the Coercion Act 'constitutional reformers are driven to employ all the devices of criminals'.

After the failure of Gladstone's first Home Bill in 1886, Shaw provided 'A crib for Home Rulers' in the *Pall Mall Gazette* where he presented a historical agenda for Ireland's social growth. 'First, the individual will have his personal liberty, in pursuit of which he will at last weary out and destroy feudal systems, mighty churches, medieval order, slave-holding oligarchies,' he wrote. ' . . . Then he will enlarge his social consciousness from his individual self to the nation of which he is a unit; and he will have his national liberty as he had his personal liberty, nor will all the excellent reasons in the world avail finally against him . . . '

'The third step is the federation of nationalities; but you cannot induce him to forgo the achievement of national independence on the ground that international federation is a step higher . . . there is no federating nationalities without first realizing them . . . the conquered subject races will destroy great empires when their time comes, if the empires persist in opposing them.'

Shaw carried this campaign for Irish federated Home Rule through the failure of Gladstone's second Bill in 1893 and the eventual academic success of Asquith's third Bill in 1914. He turned to England: Providence had not uniquely exempted the British Empire from the inevitable readjustments of social development, he warned, and to delay legislation for the sake of a quiet life would throw up more trouble than it saved – English leadership 'consists for the most part in marking time ostentatiously until they are violently shoved, and then stumbling blindly forward (or backward) wherever the shove sends them'. He turned to Ireland: her population must not lose its sense of humour in the conceit of imagining itself a Chosen People, he advised, or in those chivalrous ideals that led to such an agonizing desire to die for Ireland: the country had borne no more than her share in the growing pains of human society most of which had been inflicted not by the English but by fellow Irishmen – 'it is, on the whole, a mistake to suppose that we are a nation of angels'. Then, having irritated one and exasperated the other, he turned to both countries and, like Shakespeare's expiring Edward IV, implored them to 'take each other's hand' and 'swear your love'. But Shaw united England and Ireland only in their determination to ignore everything he recommended.

In the 'Preface for Politicians' which he attached to *John Bull's Other Island* in 1906, Shaw had predicted that 'we can do nothing with an English Government unless we frighten it . . . under such circumstances reforms are produced only by catastrophes followed by panics in which "something must be done"'. Ireland's catastrophe was the 'ghastly' Easter Rising of 1916. Shaw made clear his support for 'any Irishman taken in a fight for Irish independence against the British Government, which was a fair fight in everything except the enormous odds my countrymen had to face'. He felt anxiety lest relations between the two countries be fatally poisoned by acts of reprisal from the frightened English Government. 'The men who were shot in cold blood after their capture or surrender were prisoners of war,' he objected, after twelve of the insurgents had been executed. If the English had had the imaginative courage to take this advice and stop treating their captives as traitors 'it seems possible that the IRA might not exist today,' wrote E. R. Dodds over sixty years later, 'and Southern Ireland might be part of the British Commonwealth'.

Shaw's most quixotic intervention was on behalf of Roger Casement. Casement had taken advantage of the war to seek help from Germany for the cause of Irish independence, but on the eve of the Easter Rising he was captured by the British as he stepped ashore in Ireland from a German submarine. Feeling in England ran high against Casement who, as a British subject, would inevitably be found guilty of high treason. People were bitterly at odds over this treason. Much of the money for his defence was raised in America. In England writers as various as Conan Doyle and Arnold Bennett appealed for clemency on grounds that ranged from Casement's mental health to Britain's political expediency. Much poetical support came from Ireland. Beatrice Webb noticed that, when Charlotte spoke in support of him, her 'eyes flashed with defiance'. So Beatrice took Casement's old friend, Alice Green, who was helping organize his defence, to see the Shaws. It was a painful meeting. Alice Green desperately needed money to engage a first-rate defence lawyer: Shaw insisted that, since no credible denial of the facts was possible, paying lawyers to come up with technical ingenuities, to exchange legal compliments or simply make the usual pickpocket's claim, 'Please gentlemen, I didn't do it', would be throwing money down the drain. Instead he proposed 'an extreme and daring frontal attack on the position of the Crown'. Casement was to conduct his own case, admit the facts, plead Not Guilty and apply as an Irish Nationalist to be held as a prisoner-of-war. To this proposal Alice Green tearfully objected that Casement was extremely ill and incapable of handling a court full of lawyers: in which case, Shaw retorted, 'we had better get our suit of mourning'. So the meeting broke up: Alice Green retiring in dismay; Beatrice feeling a fool for having intervened; and G.B.S. striding into his study to compose a speech for Casement which would 'thunder down the ages'.

'Almost all the disasters and difficulties that have made the relations of Ireland with England so mischievous to both countries have arisen from the failure of England to understand that Ireland is not a province of England but a nation, and to negotiate with her on that assumption . . . I am neither an Englishman nor a traitor: I am an Irishman, captured in a fair attempt to achieve the independence of my country; and you can [not] . . . deprive me of the honors of that position . . . My neck is at your mercy if it amuses you to break it: my honor and my reputation are beyond your reach . . . Gentlemen, I have done my duty: now it is your turn.'

Magnificent theatre: but was such a speech legally sensible? Offended by the pain he had unnecessarily caused Alice Green, Beatrice accused Shaw of conceitedly playing word games with a tragedy-laden crisis and attempting to stage the life-or-death defence of this poor man as if it were a 'national dramatic event'. But to Casement himself, Shaw's instinct appeared sound. He felt delight at the speech. 'I shall be so grateful if you will convey to Bernard Shaw my warmest thanks,' he told the Sinn Fein sympathizer Gavan Duffy; 'his view is mine, with this exception – that I should never suggest to an English court or jury that they should let me off as a prisoner of war, but tell them "You may hang me, and be damned to you".'

Such a man was beyond saving either by orthodox legal methods – which Charlotte could have financed – or by an unconventional Shavian production, which possibly did have some chance of appealing to one or two members of the jury. But Shaw had eliminated from his mind Casement's physical debility and crowded his speech with historical analogies confusing to a jury. Casement later regretted not using what he called 'the only defence possible, viz., my own plan and that of G.B.S.' There had been nothing to lose: but he was dissuaded by Alice Green and other friends, found guilty, and sentenced to be hanged. Only then did 'the virtually dead man' rise to make his own lengthy speech from the dock, using a portion of what G.B.S. had written for him. In the fortnight between the Court's verdict and the date of sentence, Shaw tried hard to win Casement a reprieve on the grounds of political expediency. 'I cannot make matters any worse than they are,' he told H. W. Nevinson, 'and there is just an off chance that I might make them better.' He wrote to *The Times* which rejected his letter, published letters in the *Manchester Guardian* and the *Daily News*, and anonymously drafted a petition to Asquith warning him that hanging would make Casement a national hero. 'His trial and sentence have already raised his status in Nationalist Ireland; but it lacks the final consecration of death. We urge you very strongly not to effect that consecration.' Casement was hanged on 3 August 1916.

It had been a meeting between two knights errant. Shaw had failed to gain Casement a reprieve in England or himself a reputation in Ireland because he thought it bad tactics to accuse the British Government of exploiting the notorious Black Diaries. His motives were simple: he wanted to stem any superfluous addition to the bad blood between neighbouring countries. But his methods were disingenuous and evasive. Like the constitutional reformers he had described under the Coercion Act, he was 'driven to employ all the devices of criminals'. Both sides looked at him as a good-natured busybody 'assuring the one that the other is really a very decent fellow and at the same time suggesting how what he calls "a misunderstanding" can be cleared up', wrote Francis Stuart in 1937. ' . . . Of his good intentions we have no doubt, but, like all such mediators, he merely adds fuel to the flames. To neither party can he appear as anything but in the way.'

To those claiming that the unification of Ireland would result in Protestants and Catholics cutting one another's throats, Shaw had replied that 'civil war is one of the privileges of a nation'. Such extermination was 'too much to hope for,' he added darkly, though mankind 'still longs for that consummation'. If 'hatred, calumny, and terror have so possessed men that they cannot live in peace as other nations do, they had better fight it out and get rid of their bad blood that way'. Blood reasons seem to have inhibited him from taking a similar attitude over England and Ireland. Here were two long-trained pugilists, ambitious to fight it out, being continually refereed apart by G.B.S. on obscure technical points. The only blows seemed to fall on his own head.

The biggest blow was his failure to get nominated as one of the fifteen eminent Irishmen on the Convention Lloyd George set up in the summer of 1917 to work out a solution to Home Rule. 'It is perfectly clear that I ought to be in the business,' he explained to R. B. Haldane, 'not only by pre-eminent celebrity but because I am the only public person who has committed himself to the only possible solution: to wit, federation of the four home kingdoms.' He also appealed to Lloyd George and to his colleague Horace Plunkett (who was chairman of the Convention), but could not elbow himself into the business: 'unanimity (negative) on that subject was achieved at once,' he wrote to Henry Salt. On the chance of being admitted as a late appointment, he made a tactical advance in the second week of September to Parknasilla from where he continued to press advice on Plunkett. A month later, when the Convention was in session, he moved up to stay with Plunkett outside Dublin, manipulating proceedings behind the scenes. At their first meeting almost ten years before Plunkett had noted that Shaw was 'hopeless about Ireland', but added: 'I could make him a little hopeful if I saw more of him.' They had seen more of each other and Plunkett's co-operative movement did revive Shaw's hopes. But he felt anxious. 'What I have dreaded all along,' he told Plunkett, 'is the usual political expedient of a settlement that is no settlement.' He believed that Plunkett's team of politicians would be brought round to the federal solution only if sufficient discussion could be mounted beyond the Convention to make them feel there was a body of public opinion for it. On his return to London therefore he accepted an invitation from the editor of the *Daily Express*, a newspaper specially hostile to him during the war, to tell its readers how to unravel the Irish problem. 'I have said that if I write two or three articles on the Irish settlement they must be syndicated so as to appear simultaneously in Dublin, Cork and Belfast as well as in London,' he informed Plunkett. ' . . . Until some sort of agreement is arrived at I can do no good in Ireland except through my pen . . . I can avail myself of my liberty to make people think by a liberal use of the pickaxe.'

Shaw's series of articles, which were later issued in Dublin and London as a pamphlet, *How to Settle the Irish Question*, assembled a brilliant array of arguments for the inevitability of federation. This conclusion, which he described as 'Home Rule for England', possessed similar magical properties for reconciling opposites to the triple alliance in *Common Sense about the War*, and he frequently edged Wales out of the equation to achieve his mystical three-in-one – 'the federation of the three nations (four if you count the Welsh)'. He then reinforced this combination by building three parliaments – National, Federal and Imperial – in his imagination for 'the three kingdoms alike'.

After eight deliberating months Plunkett's Convention voted for an Irish Parliament with authority over the whole country. 'The story becomes more thrilling as it draws to an end,' Shaw wrote to Plunkett in March 1918 after reading the proof sheets of his secret report to the King. '. . . I await the report with some nervousness'. The moment came: the report made no sound. The Government had 'funked it'. After the futility of all his manoeuvres, Shaw was left feeling that it had been another instance of the unreality in Dublin politics.

But the frontiers of political reality were shifting, removing G.B.S. further into the shadows. The extreme nationalist party Sinn Fein, which had refused to participate in Plunkett's Convention, had rapidly evolved into a political power, winning seventy-three seats at the December 1918 election. Parnell's old Irish Party, which won seven seats, had passed away. Those members of Sinn Fein who were not in prison refused to attend Westminster and formed their own assembly (Dáil Éireann) in Dublin, representing a completely independent Republic of Ireland – which was immediately declared illegal by the British Government.

Shaw had advocated federation as early as 1888 and he was still advocating it more than thirty years later. The flaw in his logic, as he had once expressed it himself, lay in the problem not being 'one of logic at all, but of natural right'. England's extreme procrastination had produced Ireland's extreme reaction. With the heightening of circumstances the focus of Ireland's natural right had moved, leaving Shaw's consistency as a remnant of historical academicism – and Ireland, he knew, was 'deaf to academic discussion'. The arguments he had marshalled to promote federation could now be used with equal point to support the separatism he opposed. He hated Sinn Fein's glorification of nationalism: yet thirty years before he had written of nationalism being 'an incident of organic growth [which] . . . we shall have to accept'. The young Shaw had looked backwards and reasoned that all abstract utilitarian discussion, when the historical method is excluded, is beside the point because 'like Democracy, national self-government is not for the good of the people: it is for the satisfaction of the people'. The older Shaw was utilitarian in his view of the present, held an abstract vision of the future and, impatiently excluding the historical method, attacked the hollowness of national independencies and neutralities which were set up 'not by the internal strength of a nation's position, but by the interested guarantees of foreign Powers'.

In his 'Preface for Politicians' he had diagnosed the condition of Ireland as being like that of 'a man with cancer: he can think of nothing else . . . A healthy nation is as unconscious of its nationality as a healthy man of his bones. But if you break a nation's nationality it will think of nothing else but getting it set again. It will listen to no reformer, to no philosopher, to no preacher, until the demand of the Nationalist is granted . . . That is why everything is in abeyance in Ireland pending the achievement of Home Rule'.

But it was Shaw's political thinking rather than Irish politics that was lately in abeyance. Ireland's cancer had worsened and now demanded the fiercer remedies of separatism. Shaw regarded the policies of Sinn Fein as symptoms of the disease and not parts of a homoeopathic medicine. 'Sinn Fein means We Ourselves: a disgraceful and obsolete sentiment, horribly anti-Catholic,' he wrote in *How to Settle the Irish Question*. ' . . . Ireland is the Malvolio of the nations, "sick of self-love", and . . . Sinn Fein's delight is to propagate this morose malady.'

Ireland eventually placed its future in the hands of the insufferable quacks and windbags of the two rival religions, and in tearing itself away from England tore itself apart. Watching this process was to be intensely painful for Shaw. He had been pushed aside. He had become the reformer, philosopher and preacher to whom no one listened. 'Plunkett's failure to get me nominated to the Irish Convention shews how sure they [British politicians] are that I am safely negligible,' he had written to Lady Gregory, 'but dangerous if they gave me a chance.' By the end of the war his chance had finally gone.

'As to devoting myself to Ireland,' he had earlier surmised in a letter to Mabel Fitzgerald, 'I doubt whether Ireland would at all appreciate my services.' In his fashion he was devoted to Ireland, but except for its landscape – Keegan's 'holy ground' – he thought of it as he thought of himself: unlovable. He wanted to shed the identity attached to his birthplace and inhabit an anonymous place. 'Your inscription is a blazing lie,' he wrote at the end of his life to repudiate a plaque proclaiming his Irish virtues which a Dublin workman proposed to erect in Synge Street. 'All my political services have been given to the British Labor movement and to International Socialism.'

[7]

Literature should never be at war.
Shaw to Henry Newbolt
(25 July 1920)

The Shaws did not enter the pandemonium of revelry on Armistice Day. They stayed at Ayot. 'The dozen unfortunates in khaki whose contribution to the great victory has been a year of idleness and boredom in this village assembled when the news came,' G.B.S. wrote to Lady Gregory, 'and cheered as if they had been over the top daily for four years; but that was all.'

But Shaw did not rejoice. These years of helplessness seemed to have made a cavity within him. He might devote himself to the salvation of humanity in the abstract, but after the routine absorption of death, day after day, one bereavement more or less seemed hardly worth noticing. He appeared to have lost the power of feeling and begun seeking refuge in callousness. 'Every promising young man I know has been blown to bits lately,' he told Lady Mary Murray; 'and I have had to write to his mother.' He had written to Stella Campbell at the beginning of 1918 when her son Alan Campbell was killed by the last shell from a German battery. 'My beloved Beo is killed,' she had scribbled to him – but he could not find words of polite consolation. 'It is no use; I cant be sympathetic: these things simply make me furious,' he burst out. ' . . . Oh, damn, damn, damn, damn, damn, damn, damn, damn, DAMN DAMN! And oh, dear, dear, dear, dear, dear, dearest!'

A month later the news reached him that Robert Gregory had been shot down in his plane and was dead. In a letter prefiguring Yeats's two poems 'An Irish Airman Foresees His Death' and 'In Memory of Major Robert Gregory', he wrote consoling Lady Gregory: 'To a man with his power of standing up to danger – which must mean enjoying it – war must have intensified his life as nothing else could; he got a grip of it that he could not through art or love. I suppose that is what makes the soldier.' His rage and swearing over Alan Campbell's death had quietened and he used that tragedy – used Stella's reaction – to bring Augusta Gregory comfort. 'Like Robert he seemed to find himself in doing dangerous things. His mother thinks he got all the life he wanted out of the war and nothing else could have given it to him.'

'I was hoping for a letter from you,' Lady Gregory replied. 'I knew it would be helpful.'

Most griefs were beyond help. 'I know you will be very sorry for us,' J. M. Barrie had written after his much-loved godson George Llewelyn Davies had been shot dead near Ypres. Barrie was losing all sense of war being glorious. Though also living in Adelphi Terrace, he could not bear to give the news in person, but pushed his note through the door of the Shaws' apartment. When he read it, Shaw wept.

William Archer was another who suffered bereavement. His son 'Tomarcher' had been invalided home, accepted a commission, and in February 1918 married and passed a deliriously happy honeymoon in Ireland. Then, the war still dragging on, he volunteered afresh for the firing line, was wounded at Mount Kearnel, and died in a German hospital not long before the Armistice. 'He left his young widow to take his place in his parents' affection, the newly beloved daughter succeeding to the newly lost beloved son,' Shaw recorded. 'Yet Archer was loth to let the son go. He renewed an old interest in super-rational research; investigated dreams and the new psycho-analysis; and even experimented unsuccessfully in those posthumous conversations in which so many of the bereaved found comfort. And so, between daughter and son, the adventure of parentage never ended for Archer.'

The sons of Shaw's printer William Maxwell and the actor Richard Mansfield had also been slaughtered. And there were others, such as the hopelessly unsoldier-like Cecil Chesterton who had visited Shaw before leaving for the Front and whose death soon afterwards from trench fever was another of those events 'which so often brought home with a personal stab the fundamental waste and folly of the whole miserable business', he wrote in the late 1920s. ' . . . It is impossible to describe what I used to feel on such occasions.'

On other occasions Shaw used his comic energy to suspend a tent of miraculous cheerfulness over the wounded. He lectured Robert Loraine who had been shot in the small of his back ('the bullet coming out of his collar bone after going up through his lung and knocking his heart into his left elbow') on the importance of being kept 'in the lowest spirits, as laughing cannot be good for shrapnel in the lung'. Shaw counted himself a medical expert on this condition, one of his uncles having lost a lung and 'though he recovered all his previous robustness of habit, yet he died of it after lingering in this state for forty-seven years'. He felt a particular fondness for Loraine (who named him and Charlotte his next of kin) and had dispatched precious lavatory paper to him at the Front, offered him money and advice on how to turn his experiences into a book during his convalescence, and did not demur when Loraine boasted of having dropped monster bombs on German market places. In the summer of

1918 Loraine was again wounded, and his left kneecap being shattered, advised that his leg might have to be amputated. 'If the worst comes to the worst, I suppose one can play Hamlet with a property leg,' Shaw calculated. ' . . . an artificial leg of the best sort will carry you to victory as Henry V. If you . . . are lame, it means a lifetime of Richard III, unless I write a play entitled *Byron*.' He recommended Loraine to size up his leg from a business point of view: consider the pension – lameness couldn't be a fraction so valuable as amputation. As for flying, 'when it comes to aerial combat, the more of you that is artificial the better'.

Loraine's leg was saved. But to St John Ervine, who did lose a leg that summer, Shaw sent hasty congratulations on his being 'in a stronger position'. Having two available legs, when had Shaw himself ever groused because he did not have three? So why should any man, especially a writer, be wretched because he hasn't two? 'You will have all the energy you have hitherto spent on it to invest in the rest of your frame. For a man of your profession two legs are an extravagance,' G.B.S. assured him. ' . . . You are an exceptionally happy and fortunate man, relieved of a limb to which you owed none of your fame, and which indeed was the cause of your conscription; for without it you would not have been accepted for service.'

Such black parodies of the Shavian dialectic were 'the cheering remarks one makes now to the sacrifice of this horrible war'. There were other kinds of casualties too. Kathleen Scott had collapsed from nervous strain and overwork, and given up her job at the Ministry of Pensions. Janet Achurch, Shaw's Candida from a pre-war age whom he still sometimes believed capable of acting better than anyone else, had died. 'So that adventure is over,' he responded to Charles Charrington. ' . . . Now Janet is again the Janet of 1889, and immortal. Better that than half dead, like me.'

✳

The war also finished off the marriage between Granville Barker and Lillah McCarthy. Shaw had been dismayed by their marriage, which they had rehearsed together in his *Man and Superman* at the Court Theatre: and he was to be long-lastingly deprived as a consequence of their divorce. Early in the war they had gone to America where the volcano in Barker 'had erupted unexpectedly and amazingly', Shaw later narrated. 'He fell madly in love – really madly in the Italian manner.' The Helen who had enchanted him was an unspectacular figure in her late forties, an occasional poet and minor novelist, withdrawn in manner, though secretly ambitious. She was also the wife of Archer Milton Huntington, heir of a railroad fortune and one of the American millionaires who had provided a

395

guarantee against loss for Barker's theatrical season in New York. 'I hear Lillah and Barker are doing splendidly . . . they ought to have a brilliant season,' Stella Campbell had reported from Chicago. Six months later she wrote again wondering why they had departed. 'I thought Lillah and Barker seemed disappointed with their American Season. They should not be. They made a fine impression – and it's a pity they went back.'

Barker's attachment to Helen Huntington had stopped any theatrical developments that might have become possible in America and deepened his disenchantment with the stage. He had returned to England in June 1915 promising Lillah that his affair with Helen was over, but also warning her that 'there is nothing for you or for me, not even our salaries' from their American trip. He was some five thousand pounds in debt, but two thousand of this was owed in royalties to G.B.S. who immediately wrote it off and was able to help in other ways. 'Barker has chucked the theatre,' he announced that July to Gilbert Murray. After joining a Red Cross unit, Barker drove over to France – then in September headed off back to America, this time to give a series of lectures paying off his debts. He had made what Shaw called a sudden resolution to devote himself to poverty and playwriting. 'I cannot very well remonstrate, as I have been for years urging him to stick to his own proper job of writing plays and leave production and management to people who cant do anything else,' Shaw explained to Pinero that October. 'He selected the most disastrous possible moment to take me at my word . . . However, it cant be helped; and it's a good job anyhow. He is doing a lecturing tour in the States, and will be back, probably, towards the end of next month. Meanwhile Lillah is at a loose end . . .'

On his way to the States, Barker had written to Lillah: 'my dear wife – I love you very much if you please – and I'm not very far from you. Distance doesn't mainly count.' But he was also corresponding with Helen, and instead of returning to England at the end of the lecture tour he sent Lillah a letter asking for a divorce. She went, 'all frozen on a cold January night', to Shaw's flat in Adelphi Terrace.

'Shaw greeted me very tenderly and made me sit by the fire. I was shivering . . . How long we sat there I do not know, but presently I found myself walking with dragging steps with Shaw beside me . . . up and down Adelphi Terrace. The weight upon me grew a little lighter and released the tears which would never come before . . . he let me cry. Presently I heard a voice in which all the gentleness and tenderness of the world was speaking. It said: "Look up, dear, look up to the heavens. There is more in life than this. There is much more."'

Avoiding England, Barker made straight for the Red Cross in France, informing Shaw of his movements and engaging him to act as his agent to procure the divorce. Since Lillah had already made him her confidant, he was now placed in one of those awkward and unrewarding positions for which nature seemed to have intended him. He went to work at once instructing Barker to write Lillah a letter her lawyers could use, advising Lillah what he had done, what Barker was doing, and what she should do – which was to get someone to counsel her as he was counselling Barker. Accordingly she chose the other playwright-resident of Adelphi Terrace, J. M. Barrie. He, like Shaw, believed that the domestic crockery had been too badly broken to be worth mending, but his advice was swamped by Lillah's emotionalism. Was it likely, she demanded, that Barker knew his mind better than his own wife did? What friend could deny that she, and not this false Helen, was the true love of Barker's life? Once this transitory-Atlantic affair was over, like a dizzy spell of seasickness, he would be coming back to her. This put Barrie's and Shaw's arguments into perpetual check, for it was impossible to recommend anything without offering Lillah an insult – 'a monstrous, incredible, unbearable, unpardonable, vulgar insult', Shaw defined it. With an ingeniously flattering paradox, he tried to hand her the initiative. 'Quite seriously, I have come to the conclusion that you had better get rid of Harley,' he agreed. '. . . the sooner you set yourself free the better for you, and the more creditable for him, as you are now at the height of your powers, and . . . I gravely doubt whether Harley is fit for married life at all . . . It is in your power to demand your release; he cannot refuse it.'

Barker had expected everything to be cleared up by the spring. He sailed back to America and continued fuming there impatiently. 'Can we reach no milestone in this business?' he demanded. '. . . What in heaven's name she is waiting for I don't know. I really believe she has some idea in her head that no divorce is complete without a scandal.' His own requirements were simple: 'pen, ink and paper, please God, will always be the only *necessity* of life for me'. But he also owned a modest British pride in 'caring to show American gentle-people that in England we are not all either barbarians or cads in such matters'. This delicate patriotism forbade him obliging Lillah with a scandal. 'If anger at the futility of it all left one any room for sorrow,' he lamented, 'I could and would be sorry.'

Poised between Lillah's obduracy and Barker's exasperation, 'I had a difficult time of it,' Shaw afterwards admitted. He was losing the confidence of both parties. Lillah had complained to Barrie that G.B.S. was taking the matter with disgraceful lightness, while Barker wrote chiding him: 'I wish I could get a little assistance in the effort.' Shaw attempted to ease away the pain by making the whole business a product of anachronistic divorce laws and by reminding himself that since there had never been a marriage of true minds, Barker and Lillah could not be expected to show remorse or tenderness or any point of contact which he could use to bring them to reason. 'Everything has gone to the devil,' he wrote despairingly to Stella.

Once conscription was brought in, Barrie had written to Barker advising him to come back and join the army as a private soldier. He reasoned that Barker himself must stand a better chance than his friends of persuading Lillah that he did not love her. 'I don't object to conscription in theory,' Barker had notified Shaw. ' . . . what socialist would?' Again he was ferried over to Europe, enlisted in the Royal Horse Artillery, then swiftly transferred to an officer cadet school in Wiltshire. Many of these summer and autumn weekends he spent at Ayot nervily plotting divorce tactics with G.B.S. and Charlotte or with Barrie in London. Driven mad by the delay he implored Shaw to offer Lillah a settlement of five or six hundred pounds a year for life. Since Barker had no money, Lillah immediately realized that he must be in collusion with Helen – and sent this information on to the unsuspecting Archer Huntington in America. 'There was an almighty explosion at the other end,' Shaw later reported, 'and Helen never forgave me for being, as she thought, solely responsible for Lillah's letter.'

By the end of the year Lillah at last felt driven to start proceedings for the restitution of conjugal rights, and the decree was made absolute in the late spring of 1917. Barker waited in America, armed with a commission on the General List for 'special duties' in the Intelligence Corps. It was not until the summer of 1918 that Helen received her final decree in Paris, for which Barker waited in England, going 'weekly every Saturday during the winter' of early 1918 to Ayot. On 21 June that year G.B.S. and Helen met for the first time: and detested each other. 'The guilty pair are not yet married,' Shaw reported to Lillah. ' . . . When it happens I will let you know as soon as I know myself.' They were married on 31 July, but let Shaw know nothing. 'I surmise that you are married; but it is only a surmise,' he wrote to Barker on 26 August. 'It is desirable that your friends should be in a position to make a positive affirmation on the subject. An affectation of ecstasy so continuous as to make you forget all such worldly considerations is ridiculous at your age.'

Shaw was not to know that they had both altered their ages, Helen reducing hers by almost eight years, on the marriage certificate. They wanted to free their lives from the sort of considerations he was emphasizing, and start again. He recognized that Barker was in a difficult

398

position between being loyal to him and considerate to his wife, but came to feel that he was offered only one chance of getting over this difficulty with a weekend invitation towards the end of 1918. This visit was not a success. Charlotte had disapproved of Barker's divorce as setting a precedent for G.B.S., and she blamed Helen for introducing such dangerous unpleasantness into all their lives. Shaw tried to take the long term view and for the present entertain them all by reading out part of his new play *Back to Methuselah*. But 'I was, I suppose, tired out when I read it; for it has never seemed quite so tedious before', he apologized afterwards to Barker. 'I did not pity you, as it is all in your day's work; but it was rather hard on Helen to have such a depressing beginning of my playreading.'

But it was the end rather than a beginning. 'Virtually we never met again,' Shaw wrote. He did his Panglossian best to be optimistic. The very unreality of Barker's and Lillah's marriage 'that made the tempest over its dissolution so merciless also cleared the sky very suddenly and completely when it was over,' he concluded. 'The end was quite happy.' For a couple of years Lillah continued acting mechanically, but after her marriage in 1920 to the Oxford botanist Frederick Keeble, she pretty well left the stage. 'You must begin a new career as a new woman,' Shaw was to tell her. And she responded: 'Life begins again. I find new delights every day & am re-born.'

But it seemed to Shaw that Barker was buried alive rather than reborn. He could accept Lillah's settling down in the dignity of her maturity far more easily than Barker's seclusion and silence. His loss to the theatre was far greater: and then there was the personal loss. 'I could not intrude when I was not welcome.' Certain that 'our old sympathy remained unaltered and unalterable' even if Barker could not show it, he carefully made no advances in Helen's direction. He was prepared to keep out of their way 'for six months or six years' if necessary. But after six years, 'the devil entered into me'. Though he had not seen them during this time, he had picked up various reports. They had bought a grand Jacobean mansion in Devon called Netherton Hall (renamed by Shaw Nethermost Hell). Here, his name newly-hyphenated, his socialism cast off, and attended by fifteen servants (including a liveried footman) Granville-Barker completed a perfectionist work on the sociology of the stage, *The Exemplary Theatre*, and one unperformed play – 'the fruit of a sybaritic and uxorious Henry-jamesism', Shaw judged – called *The Secret Life*. 'We shall have to keep on insulting him for his sterility,' Shaw commanded St John Ervine, 'or he will be dead before he gets another play on to the stage.' He tried to stir him up by likening him to Swinburne at Putney; by spurring William Archer on to 'tell him to do something thoroughly vulgar: he needs contact with earth'; and by inventing a Barker Relief Expedition consisting of mutual friends: Lawrence of Arabia, Thomas Hardy and J. M. Barrie whom, Florence Hardy had told him, Helen looked upon 'as an almost divine being, & absolutely devoted to herself'.

A dramatic opportunity to intercede arrived in May 1925 when he was asked to give a vote of thanks after Granville-Barker's address on the theatre at King's College in the Strand. 'I praised Barker's speech to the skies and said that his retirement from the stage to become a professor was inexcusable,' Shaw told Hesketh Pearson. This eulogy of his past work, followed by the denunciation of his present retirement, brought the house down. 'Barker was now placed in a very ticklish position, and I was not wholly unconscious of what his wife would be thinking of me,' Shaw conceded. Lord Balfour, who was in the chair, rose to the rescue with a clever closing speech during which Shaw suddenly began to feel in great pain – 'as if my backbone had turned into a red-hot poker' was how he described the sensation to Lady Rhondda. Fearful of being seen ill in public, he was determined to sit it out – after which, the pain from the top to the base of his spine became so frightful that he could not even bend down to get into a taxi. Somehow he reached home on foot. 'I really thought I was done for.' Charlotte removed him to Ayot where he lay flat and helpless on his bed for a fortnight until one day, a month later, with a great effort of will he decided to walk down the road – and instantly the pain vanished. Later on he related this extraordinary event to Lady Colefax who was at the meeting and who revealed that Helen Granville-Barker had been sitting exactly behind him, not three feet away, leaning forward with her eyes glued to his backbone. 'I have never seen such hate in any eyes before.'

This story enabled Shaw to cast Helen as a witch who had placed her spell on Granville-Barker so that 'he ceased to be the independent human being we had all known'. This was less disconcerting to him than the belief that they were both perfectly happy and therefore, since Granville-Barker was not bound to sacrifice his happiness for the glory of English Literature, there was nothing more to be done. In his position 'I should regard myself as a damned soul', Shaw fulminated to Archer. But Granville-Barker had been retreating from this Shavian position into his 'natural Henry Jamesism' before he met Helen. His second marriage exchanged one unreality for another. Helen recreated him as a fairy castle Prince, her dream world companion. Every syllable Shaw uttered recalled an unamicable past and threatened to dissolve this fantasy. All communication with him was therefore shut down until early in the 1930s when Lillah McCarthy invited Shaw to contribute a Preface to her memoirs. He agreed and arranged for the publisher to send Granville-Barker this Preface (which contained a celebration of Lillah's historic stage collaboration with Barker, as well as biographical sidelights on their marriage and divorce). As a result Granville-Barker suddenly turned up at Ayot demanding that the book be withdrawn. Instead, and rather to his dismay, Granville-Barker's name was withdrawn and the book appeared without any reference to him: his past had been obliterated. Twenty minutes after leaving Ayot he returned to take an effusive farewell of Charlotte: and this was the last time they saw him.

From the moment their divorce had been agreed, Barker wished to forget Lillah. 'Let it alone,' he had written to Shaw advising him against renewed incursions into the affair. But resenting his blackmailing go-between role, Shaw had sought to improve matters retrospectively. He asked Granville-Barker to find Lillah work – the acrobat perhaps in an American production of *Misalliance*. But Granville-Barker would have nothing to do with his ex-wife whose very name disturbed Helen. 'I am invited to hit you half a dozen times with a sledge hammer,' Shaw wrote to Lillah; 'and because in doing so I crumpled one of the leaves in the other lady's bed of roses she will never forgive me, though you have at least schooled yourself to tolerate me.' He could not quench his pleasure on learning of Helen's fury when, Frederick Keeble being knighted, Lillah became Lady Keeble. Helen had wanted a glittering knighthood for her husband – and had she not cut him off from all commerce with the theatre he might have been given one: he would certainly have been given a peerage by Ramsay MacDonald, had he not thrown up socialism. This reflection 'must have been gall and wormwood to her', Shaw imagined. He could not believe that Granville-Barker had chosen this idyll for himself. 'Cannot you persuade Mr Granville Barker to stay here and produce Shakespeare,' Raymond Mortimer was to ask Helen years later during one of her last visits to London. To his horrified embarrassment the old lady burst into tears. 'Everyone blames me,' she answered, 'but it is not my fault: it is Harley's.'

Shaw blamed Helen. That was what people were like. When Barker died in 1946 the shock 'made me realize how I had still cherished a hope that our old intimate relation might revive'. In a letter to the *Times Literary Supplement* enclosing an old photograph of his friend he had taken in the days of their intimacy, he was to quote Swinburne:

> Marriage and death and division
> Make Barren our lives

This was the epitaph for a war whose survivors would always be avenging their wounds. It had been a frightful experience. 'A good many people have died in simple horror, mercifully without quite knowing it,' Shaw wrote to Henry Salt whose wife Kate died early in 1919. Another casualty was Shaw's sister Lucy. She had never wholly recovered from the death of her mother. Suffering from a 'nervous irritation' that was aggravated by the crackle and thud of a rifle range in Albany Street Barracks, she moved from her mother's house at the beginning of the war, and was looked after by Eva Schneider, the daughter of the German family she had lodged with in Gotha. Shaw was generous to Eva and, with Lucy's doctor, helped to arrange her exemption from deportation through repeated applications to the Home Office establishing Eva as his sister's permanent nurse-companion. Financially he was also conscientious over Lucy's needs, though otherwise 'I am forced to neglect her as I am forced to neglect everything else'. He had seen most of her when he was seeing most of Stella. They had used Lucy's home as one of their meeting places, enabling Lucy to boast that 'among my most frequent visitors is Mrs Patrick Campbell'. One time Stella had brought Sara Allgood, a leading Irish player, with her. G.B.S. also turned up and the three of them gave 'quite a good concert', Stella playing the piano, Sara singing plaintive Irish airs in a tearful contralto while 'George sang all sort of things in a throaty baritone, whilst Mrs Pat made fun of him. They ended up by dancing a Scotch reel in the hall to the tune of *Wee Macgregor* on the gramophone: such a party of lunatics they looked'. Shaw complimented Stella on having 'brought out the nice side of Lucy that I haven't seen since she was a girl'. But Lucy's brief happiness glowed more brightly in the knowledge that she had joined a conspiracy against 'Carlotta', as she still called Charlotte, who had never received her at Ayot or Adelphi Terrace, and whose heart was 'still apparently unsoftened towards me even by New Thought'.

During the war G.B.S. visited Lucy at intervals of months, sometimes many months. 'I saw Lucy the other day and was told that it was my first visit for six months,' he wrote to Stella at the end of 1915, 'though it seemed to me to be six weeks . . . She always asks for news of you; and I supply as much as I happen to possess.' The tuberculosis was no longer active but her apprehension over the Zeppelin raids – worse often than the raids themselves – seemed to be killing her. 'She is in bed, fearfully ill,' Shaw notified Stella. ' . . . [Her] address for the moment is 2 Grove Park, Camberwell Grove . . . Later, the Crematorium, Golders Green.' Kept alive by the devotion of Eva, she somehow pulled through and in the Easter of 1917 the two of them moved with difficulty to Sussex Lodge, a pretty house with a wilderness of a small garden on Champion Hill in south-east London – a few minutes' walk from her previous address. Lucy had reckoned that, being close to an anti-aircraft battery (she could actually hear the officer giving orders), 'we shall always know when the Zepps are on the way' and that this would be a comfort. She had not realized that they were also near a bombing exercise ground and within sound of the gun testing at Woolwich Arsenal. Amid the continuous din, 'we didn't know whether a raid was on or not'. And when it was on, the booming of the big defence gun in the next field 'which seemed to blow the house away every time it went off', the noise of exploding bombs and the terrifying sight of a Zeppelin descending through the sky in flames was altogether too much for her. 'My nerves seemed to have collapsed,' she wrote to a friend. ' . . . I could not stand the strain.'

Shaw then rented a house at Okehampton in Devon where Lucy and Eva travelled in the summer of 1917. 'I have run away from the air raids which threatened to "do for me" altogether,' she wrote. ' . . . The journey was a great trial, but terror lent energy to my weakness.' Despite eating almost nothing and going nowhere she had become 'a very expensive person' she remarked wryly – '*my brother indulges me in any extravagance I express the least wish for*'. Shaw kept on Sussex Lodge with a caretaker and, a few weeks after the Armistice, Lucy returned on a stretcher and in an ambulance to London. Her condition was gradually deteriorating. The doctor told Eva that she did not want to live and was slowly starving herself to death. Eva did all she could to persuade her, spoonful by spoonful, to keep alive; and Mrs Pat sent all sorts of delicacies from Fortnum & Mason. 'My heart aches for her,' Stella wrote to Shaw. She liked Lucy. She liked accepting her admiration, exchanging old theatre stories, deflecting her ironies to G.B.S. In the early weeks of 1920 she hired a car and went several times to see her. 'Eva seemed to think it would give her joy to see you for a minute,' she wrote to G.B.S. After Lillah's wedding on Saturday 27 March he went round in the late afternoon and sat by Lucy's bed. 'I am dying,' she told him. 'Oh no,' he replied conventionally: 'you will be all right presently.' He took her hand and they were silent then. 'There was no sound except from somebody playing the piano in the nearest house (it was a fine evening and all the windows were open),' he remembered, 'until there was a faint flutter in her throat. She was still holding my hand. Then her thumb straightened. She was dead.'

The doctor officially informed him that after suffering from shell-shock, she had become anorexic, and starved herself to death. 'My body to

ACKNOWLEDGEMENTS

The same team which helped me to prepare *The Search for Love* has worked on *The Pursuit of Power*: that is, Sarah Johnson who did the typing; Richard Bates who transferred her typescript on to disc; Vivian Elliot who checked quotations and supplied illustrations; and Margery Morgan who passed a critical eye over every chapter. At Chatto & Windus my editor has again been Hilary Laurie whose valuable suggestions have been complemented by some sympathetic 'nitpicking' (as he calls it) from Joe Fox at Random House. I renew my thanks to them all with the hope that they will be able to last the course to the end of *The Lure of Fantasy*. With that volume I propose bringing up to date the names, works and institutions listed in the Bibliographical Note and Acknowledgements which appeared in *The Search for Love*.

ILLUSTRATIONS

Back endpaper, 15B, 26 Courtesy of the BBC Hulton Picture Library. 9, 11A, 30 Courtesy of the British Library. 3, 10B, 11B, 13, 31 Courtesy of the British Library of Political and Economic Science. 14B Courtesy of Allan Chappelow *Shaw the Villager and Human Being*, Charles Skilton, London, 1961. 16 Courtesy of Allan Chappelow *Shaw 'The Chucker-Out'*, George Allen and Unwin, London, 1969. 18A Courtesy of St John Ervine *Bernard Shaw, His Life, Work and Friends*, Constable, London, 1956. 5, 23 Courtesy of Archibald Henderson *Playboy and Prophet*, Appleton, New York, 1932. Front endpaper, 14A Courtesy of Archibald Henderson *Life and Works*, Hurst and Blackett, London, 1911. 20 Courtesy of Dan H. Lawrence *Collected Letters Vol III*, Max Reinhardt Ltd, London, 1979. 25A Courtesy of F. E. Lowenstein *Bernard Shaw Through the Camera*, B. & H. White Publications Ltd, 1948. 10A Courtesy of Norman and Jeanne MacKenzie *The First Fabians*, Weidenfeld & Nicolson, London, 1977. 6, 7, 25B, 32 Courtesy of Mander and Mitchenson Theatre Collection. 12 Courtesy of The National Portrait Gallery. 2A, 2B, 28, 29 Courtesy of The National Trust. 18B *100 Years of Fabian Socialism 1884–1894*, Fabian Society, 1984. 1 Courtesy of Margot Peters *Bernard Shaw and the Actresses*, Doubleday, New York, 1980. 17 Courtesy of P.A.-Reuter Photos Ltd. 19 Courtesy of Patricia Pugh *Educate, Agitate, Organise. 100 Years of Fabian Socialism*, Methuen, London, 1984. 8 Courtesy of Margaret Shenfield *Bernard Shaw, a Pictorial Biography*, Thames and Hudson, London, 1962. 4 Courtesy of Sotheby's, London. 24 Theatre Museum, London. By courtesy of the trustees of The Victoria and Albert Museum. 21, 27 Courtesy of Stephen Winsten *Jesting Apostle*, Hutchinson, London, 1956. 15A Courtesy of Stephen Winsten *GBS 90*, Hutchinson, London, 1946.

INDEX

her father's house in Ireland, 103, 107; asks Wells to lecture to Fabian Society, 133; seconded by Wells to his Special Committee, 139, 140, 141; translates Brieux's plays, 180; encourages Shaw to sit to Lytton, 180–1; invites Rodin and arranges sitting for Shaw, 181–2; uses photographs of bust for *Selected Passages from the Works of Bernard Shaw*, 184; caught up in French May Day 'revolution', 184–5; receives sketches from Rodin, 185; dislikes Epstein's bust of Shaw, 186–7; rents Rectory at Ayot St Lawrence, 188, 189; takes Shaw to France, 189–90, and Wales, 192; approves of Fabian Summer Schools, 192; takes Shaw to the continent and Ireland, 194–5; injured in motoring accident, 195; brief career as motorist, 206; tours Algeria and Tunisia, 207–8; in Ireland, 208, 209; in France, 209; 'positively loathes' Shaw, 209; fondness of children, 210; on sixteen-week tour of continent with Shaw, 282–3; quarrels with Shaw, 288, 290; completes selection of Shaw's writings, 290; leaves for Rome alone, 290–1; tries to lure Shaw to Paris, 292; returns to England, 293; intercedes in Erica Cotterill affair, 300; with Shaw on tour in France and Germany, 301; remains in Bad Kissingen, 301; and Shaw's affair with Mrs Patrick Campbell, 310–11, 314, 318; with Shaw in Ireland, 312; influenced by James Porter Mills, 314; leaves for Marseilles, 315; with Shaw in France, 322; joins Mills and wife in America, 337–8; publishes *Knowledge is the Door*, 338; with Shaw in Devon, 345; anxieties over Trebitsch, 346; at Hydro Hotel, Torquay, 346–7; effects of religious conversion on, 369–70; with Shaw at Ayot, 370–1; supports Roger Casement, 388; disapproves of Granville-Barker's divorce, 399

Shaw, George Bernard: convalesces at Pitfold, 3; sets to work on *The Perfect Wagnerite*, 3 (*see Works*); breaks arm, 3; has operation on foot, 4; Charlotte (q.v.) as sentinel over, 4, 5; falls off bicycle and sprains ankle, 4; financially dependent on Charlotte, 5–6; separates his work from the experience of his life, 6; Beatrice Webb on, 6, 10, 117, 322, 323–4, 352; foot worsens, but improves, 6, 7, 9–10; Charlotte moves him to Blen-Cathra, 7; completes *Caesar and Cleopatra*, 7 (*see Works*); his health improves, 7; completes *Captain*

Brassbound's Conversion, 7 (*see Works*); in Cornwall, 7–8; on six-week cruise on *Lusitania*, 8, 36; returns to London, 9; revises political philosophy under influence of Wagner, 11–14; attempts at persuading Ellen Terry to play in *Captain Brassbound's Conversion*, 21–3, 25–7, 29, 31–2; meets briefly with Ellen Terry, 30; publishes *Three Plays for Puritans*, 33–4 (*see Works*); angry at inability to get plays performed, 35–6; alarmed at news of Boer War, 36; differs with Conan Doyle over war, 37; attempts to unite Fabians over South African issue, 39–41; drafts *Fabianism and the Empire*, 40 (*see Works*); re-examines political thinking, 41–2; supports Lord Rosebery, 45, 118; fails to win St Pancras and leaves local politics, 46–7; publishes *Man and Superman*, 48 (*see Works*); meets and subsequent friendship with Trebitsch (q.v.), 48–54; invites Hamon (q.v.) to be his French translator, 55–6; caricatured by Beerbohm, 59–60; taken by Charlotte on holidays in England and abroad, 60–2; completes *The Admirable Bashville*, 63 (*see Works*); assists Granville-Barker in directing *The Admirable Bashville* 64–5; publishes *Man and Superman* as a book, 67–8; wants to import Hegelianism into English politics, 72–3; invited by Yeats to write play for the opening of Abbey Theatre, 82–3; completes *John Bull's Other Island*, 83 (*see Works*); writes *How He Lied to Her Husband*, 83 (*see Works*); contrasted with Yeats, 90; angry at the Abbey's rejection of O'Casey's *The Silver Tassie*, 90–1; impressed by Granville-Barker as actor, 91, 92; dissatisfied with Stage Society, 92; finds Barker's plays 'fascinating', 93–4; friendship with Barker, 94–5; joins management of Stage Society, 95; produces *Mrs Warren's Profession*, 96; produces *John Bull's Other Island* at Court Theatre, 97–100; impressed by Eleanor Robson, 100, and writes *Major Barbara* (*see Works*) for her, 101; 'overwhelmed' with work, 102; completes *Passion, Poison, and Petrification*, 102–3; with Charlotte in Ireland, 103, 106–7; has better relationship with Mary Cholmondeley, 107; reads *Major Barbara* to Gilbert Murray, 107, 108; enjoys working with Murray, 111–12; produces *Major Barbara* at Court Theatre, 115–16; and

118, 122; on Wells, 146; on resigning from the Fabian Society, 267

Robert Phillimore, on Britain's entente with Germany, 344

Arthur Pinero, on Gilbert Murray, 111–12; on the Society of Authors, 223; on *Overruled*, 275; on *Androcles and the Lion*, 283; on Granville-Barker, 396

Ada Rehan, on *John Bull's Other Island*, 98

Eleanor Robson, on *Major Barbara*, 100, 101, 103, 106, 114, 115

William Rothenstein, on his activities, 9

Annie Russell, on playing Barbara, 115

Bertrand Russell, on the War, 351; on finding the 'right key', 356; on his support, 357

Henry Salt, on this 'triumph over the (medical) profession', 4; on the Boer War, 43; on Charlotte, 59; on learning to waltz, 375; on his failure to get nominated to Irish Convention, 390; on the casualties of war, 402

George Samuel, on the Boer War, 42

Herbert Samuel, on censorship, 236

Arthur Schopenhauer, on the Will, 18–19

J. L. Shine, on Larry Doyle in *John Bull's Other Island*, 98

Alfred Sutro, on the War, 349

Ellen Terry, on his childhood, 6; on Cornish holiday, 7; on the opposition between male and female principles, 21; on Lady Cicely in *Captain Brassbound's Conversion*, 21–2, 25–6, 29; on the 'sordid side of business', 33; on his impotence as a playwright, 36; on Maybury Knoll, 61–2; on Mrs Patrick Campbell in *Pygmalion*, 294

Tolstoy, on existence of God, 239; on Art for Art's sake, 240

Siegfried Trebitsch, on translating his plays, 50, 54; on his own work, 52, 53; on Shaw's financial help to the Hamons, 57; on public speaking, 60; on house in Scotland, 61; on *The Admirable Bashville*, 62–3, 65; on *Man and Superman*, 67; on *John Bull's Other Island*, 83; on Granville-Barker's *The Marrying of Ann Leete*, 93–4; on *The Doctor's Dilemma*, 169; on May Day in France, 185; on fighting against censorship, 228; on motor-mountaineering, 282; on *Androcles and the Lion*, 289; on his lumbago, 292; on *Pygmalion*, 332, 333, 334; on his doing military service, 346; on the War, 351–2, 356; on being sixty, 374

Viola Tree, on her father's production of *Pygmalion*, 340

Charles Trevelyan, on a religion of evolution, 72–3

Hugo Vallentin, on the War, 352; on his inability to finish *Heartbreak House*, 382

Irene Vanbrugh, on Lina in *Misalliance*, 246–7, 249

J. E. Vedrenne, on Salvation Army band playing, 108; on the press, 172, 174; on *The Inca of Perusalem*, 377–8

A. B. Walkley, on the Cabinet and the Fabian Society, 121; on *The Doctor's Dilemma*, 158

Graham Wallas, on his 'contempt for the status quo', 27

Ensor Walters, on going to Bruges, 61

Beatrice Webb, on arriving at Hindhead, 3; on Lord Rosebery, 45; on staying in Dorset, 61; on staying with the Cholmondeleys, 107; on *Fabianism and the Fiscal Question*, 124; on Wells, 131; on railway journeys, 207; on quarrelling with Charlotte, 290; on his finances, 305; on writing for the *New Statesman*, 318; on staying in Torquay, 346–7; on his unpopularity, 358; on resigning from the *New Statesman*, 359; on *More Common Sense about the War*, 361; on staying in Ireland, 375

Sidney Webb, on Charlotte, 5; on the Fabian Society, 129; on the defeat of Asquith and Grey, 360

H. G. Wells, on finding a house, 180; on almost drowning, 193; on Chesterton, 219; on art and Henry James, 240–1; on never being wrong, 359; on his place in public life, 366

W. B. Yeats, on *John Bull's Other Island*, 83; on *O'Flaherty, V. C.*, 380

Works:

The Admirable Bashville or Constancy Unrewarded, 49, 62–6, 92, 96

'Aerial Football', 191

Androcles and the Lion, 283, 284–9, 317, 322, 323, 343, 354, 382

Annajanska, 378–9

Arms and the Man, 49, 51, 52, 92, 177, 279, 287, 295

'Art and Public Money', 251

Augustus Does His Bit, 378

Back to Methuselah, 75, 115, 188, 215, 359, 399

Caesar and Cleopatra, 7, 10–11, 14–18, 19–20, 23, 25, 27, 28, 32, 41, 49, 76, 90, 92, 96, 102, 177, 273, 281, 295–6, 302, 333

Candida, 27, 48, 49–50, 51, 52, 81, 91, 92, 96, 97, 102, 149, 333, 382

Captain Brassbound's Conversion, 7, 8, 10, 11, 20–3, 25, 26–30, 31–2, 92, 102, 292

Also available now,
the first volume of Michael Holroyd's masterly biography

Volume I · 1856–1898
The Search for Love

'It is instantly recognisable as a brilliant commedia from the elegant master-hand that cast the spell of Lytton Strachey and Augustus John. Buoyed up with a mass of hidden documentation, it sails along with the swift, complex life of a major novel of manners.'

Richard Holmes *The Times*

'Here is the most comprehensive account ever made of Shaw's activities as a child fantasist, teenage rent collector, unpublished novelist, street-corner socialist, philanderer, pugilist, critic, playwright and bicycling enthusiast.'

Irving Wardle *Vogue*

'It is a masterful exercise in biographical magic, like a conjuring performance, demonstrated dexterously and unassumingly to a serious purpose, some Orson Welles presentation of word and wizardry.'

John Osborne *The Spectator*

'We regard Mr Holroyd with awe, as a prodigy among biographers. He has done his work calmly, in an admirably clear and concise style that is all his own . . . the quality of the work makes us eager for the two volumes that are to come.'

Robertson Davies *New York Times Book Review*

Volume III · 1919–1950
The Lure of Fantasy
to be published in 1991

Michael Holroyd was born in 1935 and is half-Swedish and partly Irish. In 1968 his *Lytton Strachey* was acclaimed as a landmark in contemporary biography and, six years later, his *Augustus John* confirmed his place as one of the most influential modern biographers. He has worked for fifteen years on the research and writing of *Bernard Shaw*. The first volume, published in 1988, was hailed by George Painter as 'one of the finest literary biographies of our half-century . . . It may well turn out to be the greatest of them all.'

Michael Holroyd lives in London and is married to Margaret Drabble. He was appointed a CBE in January 1989.

The title on page iii is set in
Caslon Old Face,
the design favoured by Bernard Shaw
when he was directing the manufacture
of his books at R. & R. Clark, Edinburgh.
The text is set in Linotron Ehrhardt,
a typeface derived from similar seventeenth-century
Dutch sources as Caslon Old Face.